# THE COMPLETE
# CROCK POT
# COOKBOOK

DELICIOUS 1001 RECIPES FOR
BEGINNERS AND ADVANCED USERS

**Amelia Mason**

ISBN-13 : 979-8693006256

Copyright © 2020 by Amelia Mason

All rights reserved. No part of this book may be reproduced in any form without permission in writing from the author

## Disclaimer

No part of this works may be reproduced, distributed or transmitted in any form or by means, electronic or mechanical, including photocopying, recording or by any information storage and retrieval system express without written permissions from the author. This book is for motivating yourself. The views expressed are those of the author alone and should not be taken as expert instructions of commands. The reader is responsible for his or her own actions and decisions.

# INTRODUCTION

# Hello! Welcome to my book of recipes for the Crock Pot.

My recipes are simply too delicious to keep to myself. And it's the only cookbook you'll need to make the most delicious Crock Pot recipes you've ever tasted!

If there's one kitchen appliance I can't live without, it's my Crock Pot. This gadget has changed my life completely in the kitchen! Gone are the days when I spent hours each week, prepping and then cooking meals. And so many times those meals were tasteless, with leftovers that no one wanted to eat.

Then along came my Crock Pot Pressure Cooker... and now I make delectable meals every day. Quick cooking, tasty recipes - and I have leftovers my family fights and squabbles over! Like the juiciest pork shoulders and spicy rice dishes. In my book, you'll find a collection of mouthwatering and flavorsome recipes from every cuisine.

One of the biggest appealing features of the Crock Pot is that it makes fresh and fast homey meals in no time. Whether you're vegetarian or love your meat and chicken, my book has the best recipes for making amazing, healthy meals. And make sure you make an extravagant cheat recipe on those days when you're not counting calories and fat! Those are the best recipes of all. In this book, I share my favorite recipes with you, and I'll help you get familiar with the Crock Pot, so you know exactly how to use one. Breakfasts, appetizers, Sunday dinners, and delightfully sweet desserts! I have just the recipe for you.

**So now, let's learn all about the Crock Pot so you can start cooking!**

## My Crock Pot Recipes

Ready to use your Crock Pot? I've created some great recipes for my Crock Pot, and now I'm

sharing them with you. These recipes are easy to follow... and the result is delicious!

Before you start cooking, let's take a look at some of the basics for using my recipes for the Crock Pot, basics that will make it easier for you to jump right in and make some great meals.

## What can you cook in your Crock Pot?

Any foods that you usually cook in liquid can be cooked in the Crock Pot, such as beans, rice, risotto, soups, and stews. Chicken and meats are great cooked in an electric pressure cooker, so long as you don't want them to be crispy. And don't forget your vegetables. Steam broccoli, green beans, and cauliflower. Harder vegetables such as carrots, onions, and potatoes cook nicely in the pressure cooker.

# Contents

INTRODUCTION .................................................................................................... 3
    WHAT CAN YOU COOK IN YOUR CROCK POT? ................................................. 3
WHAT IS A CROCK POT? ..................................................................................... 18
HOW DOES A CROCK POT WORK? ..................................................................... 18
UNDERSTANDING YOUR CROCKPOT .................................................................. 18
BENEFITS OF USING A CROCKPOT ...................................................................... 18
HOW TO USE THE CROCKPOT ............................................................................ 19
TIPS AND TRICKS FOR USING THE CROCKPOT ................................................... 19
SLOW COOKER OR CROCK-POT? ....................................................................... 19
WHAT'S THE DIFFERENCE BETWEEN A CROCK POT AND A SLOW COOKER? .... 20
WHAT EACH FUNCTION MEANS ........................................................................ 20
**MEASUREMENT CONVERSION CHART** ............................................................ 21
    BREAKFAST RECIPES ..................................................................................... 24

| # | Recipe | Page | # | Recipe | Page |
|---|---|---|---|---|---|
| 1. | Crustless Three-Meat Quiche | 24 | 22. | Onion and Tomato Eggs | 28 |
| 2. | Cheesy Eggs in Hollandaise Sauce | 24 | 23. | Egg and Beef Green Casserole | 28 |
| 3. | Almond & Gala Apple Porridge | 24 | 24. | Bell Pepper & Onion Frittata | 28 |
| 4. | Chorizo and Kale Egg Casserole | 24 | 25. | Deliciuos Coconut Pancake | 28 |
| 5. | Eggs & Smoked Salmon | 24 | 26. | Sweet Potato Tomato Frittata | 29 |
| 6. | Sweet Potato & Carrot Egg Casserole | 25 | 27. | Cherry and Dark Chocolate Oatmeal | 29 |
| 7. | Vanilla Quinoa Bowl | 25 | 28. | Lemon and Chocolate Bread Pudding | 29 |
| 8. | Crispy Bacon and Egg Burger | 25 | 29. | Pear-Coconut Porridge with Walnuts | 29 |
| 9. | Zesty and Citrusy French Toast | 25 | 30. | Crock Pot Egg Bake | 29 |
| 10. | Cheddar and Eggs Hash Bake | 25 | 31. | Delicious Banana Bread | 30 |
| 11. | Classic Sunday Big Pancakes | 26 | 32. | Drinkable Vanilla Yogurt | 30 |
| 12. | Apricot and Raisin Oatmeal | 26 | 33. | Chocolate Banana Bread | 30 |
| 13. | Banana and Cinnamon French Toast | 26 | 34. | Banana Bread with Granola | 30 |
| 14. | Bacon and Colby Cheese Grits | 26 | 35. | Treacle Sponge with Honey | 31 |
| 15. | Poached Eggs with Feta and Tomatoes | 26 | 36. | Sticky Pecan Buns with Maple | 31 |
| 16. | Carrot & Pecan Muffins | 27 | 37. | Village Pie | 31 |
| 17. | Kale, Tomato & Carrot Quiche | 27 | 38. | Crunchy Toast with Cinnamon | 31 |
| 18. | Easy Softboiled Eggs | 27 | 39. | Pumpkin Creamy Muffins | 32 |
| 19. | Cheese and Thyme Cremini Oats | 27 | 40. | Egg Souffle with Cheese | 32 |
| 20. | Herby Pork Breakfast Biscuits | 27 | 41. | Onion Tart | 32 |
| 21. | Whole Hog Omelet | 28 | 42. | Crunchy Cake with Coffee | 32 |

43. Eggplant Parmesan in Slow Cooker ..................... 33
44. Golden Veggie Pie ................................. 33
45. Muscovado Cheesecake for Slow Cooker ............... 33
46. Veggie Breakfast Casserole ......................... 33
47. Nutella French Toast ............................... 34
48. Soufflé with Scallions and Dill ..................... 34
49. Cranberry Apple Oatmeal ............................ 34
50. Chicken Casserole .................................. 34
51. Blueberry and Corn Muffins ......................... 35
52. Twisted Roll with Caramel and Pecan ................ 35
53. Ginger and Pineapple Oatmeal ....................... 35
54. Country French Toast with Ham ...................... 35
55. Candid Orange Granola .............................. 36
56. Chocolate Rolls with Cherries ...................... 36
57. Tunisian Flavored Eggs ............................. 36
58. Charlotte with Herbs ............................... 36
59. Tortilla with Cheese and Green olives .............. 37
60. Currant and Raspberry Pudding ...................... 37
61. Broccoli Strata with Tomatoes and Cheddar .......... 37
62. Slow Cooker Cake with Honey ........................ 37
63. Slow Cooker Quiche ................................. 38
64. Mashed Potatoes with Ricotta ....................... 38
65. Ricotta Cheesecake with Lemon ...................... 38
66. Fritata with Goat Cheese and Ham ................... 38
67. Crumbled Gooseberry Flapjack ....................... 39
68. Cheesy Tater Tot ................................... 39
69. Egg Casserole in Slow Cooker ....................... 39
70. Corn Pudding with Cheese ........................... 39
71. Spiced pears in chocolate sauce .................... 39
72. Apple crumble cake ................................. 40
73. Banana French Toast with Milk ...................... 40
74. Cheese Grits in Slow Cooker ........................ 40
75. Pineapple Cake with Pecans ......................... 41
76. Potato Casserole for Breakfast ..................... 41
77. Delicious cinnamon rolls ........................... 41
78. Quinoa Pie in Slow Cooker .......................... 41
79. Quinoa Muffins with Peanut Butter .................. 42
80. Veggie Omelette in Slow Cooker ..................... 42
81. Apple pie with oatmeal ............................. 42
82. Vanilla French Toast ............................... 42
83. Pumpkin Spiced Oatmeal ............................. 43
84. Greek Eggs Casserole ............................... 43
85. French Toast with Chocolate Chip ................... 43
86. Egg and Ham Casserole for Slow Cooker .............. 43
87. Vegetarian Pot Pie ................................. 44
88. Baked Beans for Slow Cooker ........................ 44
89. Quinoa Energy Bars ................................. 44
90. Overnight Apple Oatmeal ............................ 44
91. Basic Overnight Quinoa and Oats .................... 44
92. Blueberry Porridge ................................. 45

## LUNCH RECIPES .................................................. 45

93. French Onion Soup for Slow Cooker .................. 45
94. Maple Bacon and White Bean Soup .................... 45
95. Chicken Minestrone in Slow Cooker .................. 46
96. Tomato Soup with Rigatoni .......................... 46
97. Chicken and Burrito Bowls .......................... 46
98. Mac and Cheese pasta in Slow Cooker ................ 46
99. Pumpkin couscous with lamb ......................... 46
100. Pappardelle ragout with duck ...................... 47
101. Oxtail and Chorizo Stew ........................... 47
102. Slow Cooker Soup with Ham ......................... 47
103. Slow Cooker Soup with Celery and Bacon ............ 48
104. Lamb Shank in Slow Cooker ......................... 48
105. Spicy chicken with fennel stew .................... 48
106. French Farmhouse Chicken Soup ..................... 48
107. Bean soup served with toasts ...................... 49
108. Chicken ragout with red wine ...................... 49
109. Egg noodles with Red Beef ......................... 49
110. Autumn Pumpkin Soup ............................... 50
111. Bone Broth in Slow Cooker ......................... 50
112. Creamy vegetable curry with chickpea .............. 50
113. Lamb Chunks with Honey ............................ 50
114. Chickpea curry with vegetables .................... 51
115. Soup with lentils and goat cheese ................. 51
116. Ragout with Beef and Carrot ....................... 51
117. Ham and pea soup foe Slow Cooker .................. 51
118. Summer Curry in Slow Cooker ....................... 52
119. Slow Cooker meatballs with rigatoni ............... 52

# SIDE DISHES RECIPES .................................................................................. 53

120. Indian Spiced Lentils ............................................ 53
121. Quinoa Risotto with Asparagus ........................... 53
122. Rice noodles with Coconut Beef ......................... 53
123. Chicken with rice and sesame ............................ 53
124. Steak with Onions and Pepper ........................... 54
125. Caesar sandwiches with Chicken ....................... 54
126. Thai Chicken in Slow Cooker .............................. 54
127. Pork Tacos with Cabbage ................................... 54
128. Simple Salsa Chicken .......................................... 55
129. Summer Risotto with mushrooms and peas ...... 55
130. Spring Minestrone in Slow Cooker ..................... 55
131. Frittata with Red Pepper and Feta ..................... 55
132. Chicken Taquitos in Slow Cooker ....................... 56
133. Korean Beef Tacos in Slow Cooker .................... 56
134. Quinoa Chicken in Slow Cooker ......................... 56
135. Slow Cooker Squash ........................................... 56
136. Hot Beans with Pork ........................................... 57
137. Beans with Bacon and Cranberry Sauce ........... 57
138. Stuffing with Cranberries and Apple .................. 57
139. Barbeque Beans in Slow Cooker ........................ 57
140. Ratatouille in Slow Cooker ................................. 58
141. Hot German Salad with Potatoes ...................... 58
142. Chicken and Cole Slaw ....................................... 58
143. Slow Cooker Carrots with Herbs ........................ 59
144. Tricolor potatoes with Garlic and Rosemary ..... 59
145. Spinach and Artichoke in Slow Cooker .............. 59
146. Creamy Corn with Cheese .................................. 59
147. Brussels sprouts for Slow Cooker ...................... 59
148. Herbed Fingerling Potatoes in Slow Cooker ...... 60
149. Buttered Corn in Slow Cooker ............................ 60
150. Slow Cooker ham and pea soup ........................ 60
151. Baked beans in Slow Cooker .............................. 60
152. White Chicken Chili in Slow Cooker ................... 61
153. Thai Red Curry in Slow Cooker .......................... 61
154. Slow cooker peas with asparagus ..................... 61
155. Tacos and Sriracha Mayo ................................... 61
156. Apple Cider Chicken in Slow Cooker ................. 62
157. Sweet Potatoes with Apples .............................. 62
158. Spinach Lasagna in Slow Cooker ....................... 62
159. Broccoli and Cauliflower with Cheese topping ....... 62
160. Summer Vegetables with Chickpeas ................. 63
161. Sweet Potatoes with Bacon ............................... 63
162. Mashed Potatoes with Garlic ............................. 63
163. Sweet and Spice beetroots ................................ 63
164. Macaroni with American Cheese ....................... 64
165. Squash Summer Gratin ...................................... 64
166. Squash in Cranberry Sauce ................................ 64
167. Brussels sprouts and Maple Syrup .................... 64
168. Wild Rice with Cherries ...................................... 65
169. Vegetable Curry with Garbanzo ........................ 65
170. Kale and Eggplant Panzanella ............................ 65
171. Sweet Potato Lentils in Slow Cooker ................. 65
172. Butternut Squash with Chili ............................... 66
173. Tikka Masala with Chicken in Slow Cooker ....... 66
174. Enchilada Soup with Chicken ............................. 66
175. Spicy Black Eyed Peas in Slow Cooker .............. 66
176. Tender Taters in Slow Cooker ............................ 67
177. Parmesan Rice with Chicken .............................. 67
178. Collard Greens in Slow Cooker .......................... 67
179. Mexican Pinto Beans with Cactus ...................... 67
180. Pizza Potatoes in Slow Cooker ........................... 68
181. Carrots with Chinese species ............................. 68
182. Baked Beans in Slow Cooker .............................. 68
183. Sweet Sauerkraut In Slow Cooker ..................... 68
184. Collard Greens in Slow Cooker .......................... 69
185. Creamed Corn in Slow Cooker ........................... 69
186. Casserole with Spinach Noodles ........................ 69

## VEGETARIAN AND VEGAN ................................................................................ 69

187. One-Pot Mushroom and Brown Rice ................. 69
188. Asian-Style Tofu Noddle Soup ........................... 70
189. Hearty Colorful Vegetable Soup ........................ 70
190. Kale and Spinach Cream Soup ........................... 70
191. Fake Mushroom Risotto the Paleo Way ............ 70
192. Pressure Cooked Ratatouille .............................. 70
193. Veggie Burger Patties ......................................... 71
194. Potato Chili .......................................................... 71

| # | Recipe | Page |
|---|---|---|
| 195. | Bean and Rice Casserole | 71 |
| 196. | Harissa Turnip Stew | 71 |
| 197. | Meatless Shepherd's Pie | 71 |
| 198. | Vegetarian Spaghetti Bolognese | 72 |
| 199. | Spicy Moong Beans | 72 |
| 200. | Sweet Potato and Baby Carrot Medley | 72 |
| 201. | Pickled Pepperoncini and Parmesan Dip | 72 |
| 202. | Vegetables and Beef Brisket Stew | 72 |
| 203. | Creamy Potato Slices with Chives | 73 |
| 204. | Stuffed Red Peppers with Quinoa and Zucchini | 73 |
| 205. | Spiced Bok Choy Soup with Spiralized Zucchini | 73 |
| 206. | Easy Spaghetti Squash with Spinach Dip | 74 |
| 207. | Mediterranean Steamed Asparagus with Pine Nuts | 74 |
| 208. | Eggplant and Goat Cheese Homemade Lasagna | 74 |
| 209. | Sautéed Leafy Greens | 74 |
| 210. | Celery-Pumpkin Autumn Soup | 74 |
| 211. | Mashed Broccoli with Mascarpone | 75 |
| 212. | Easy Buttery Corn on the Cob | 75 |
| 213. | Delicious Eggs de Provence | 75 |
| 214. | Spicy Tomato Dip | 75 |
| 215. | Hummus Under Pressure | 75 |
| 216. | Herby Steamed Potatoes | 76 |
| 217. | Sicilian-Style Deviled Eggs | 76 |
| 218. | Vegan Sausage and Pepper Casserole | 76 |
| 219. | Spanish Baked Eggs | 76 |
| 220. | Tamari Tofu with Sweet Potatoes and Broccoli | 76 |
| 221. | Collard Greens Hummus | 77 |
| 222. | Potatoes and Peas Bowl | 77 |
| 223. | Saucy BBQ Veggie Meal | 77 |
| 224. | Lemony and Garlicky Potato and Turnip Dip | 77 |
| 225. | Vegan Swiss Chard Dip | 77 |
| 226. | Cheesy Asparagus and Spinach Dip | 78 |
| 227. | Classic Italian Peperonata | 78 |
| 228. | Spicy Tomato Sauce | 78 |
| 229. | Zesty Carrots with Pecans | 78 |
| 230. | Pressure Cooked Devilled Eggs | 78 |
| 231. | Tomato Zoodles | 79 |
| 232. | Easy Street Sweet Corn | 79 |
| 233. | Candied Holiday Yams | 79 |
| 234. | Chipotle Pumpkin Soup | 79 |
| 235. | Navy Beans with Parsley and Garlic | 79 |
| 236. | Walnut & Cinnamon Coconut Potatoes | 80 |
| 237. | Cheesy Acorn Squash Relish | 80 |
| 238. | Potato and Spinach Bowl | 80 |
| 239. | Savory Vegetarian Sandwiches | 80 |
| 240. | Effortless Cannellini and Black Bean Chili | 80 |
| 241. | Thyme-Flavored Fries | 81 |
| 242. | Tomato and Kale "Rice" | 81 |
| 243. | Minty Cauliflower Tabbouleh | 81 |
| 244. | Spicy Cannellini Bean Salad with Dates | 81 |
| 245. | Flavorful Tofu Bowl | 81 |
| 246. | Tofu and Veggie 'Stir Fry' | 82 |
| 247. | Spicy Tofu Vegan Stew | 82 |
| 248. | Cheesy Sour Veggie Casserole | 82 |
| 249. | Garlicky and Chili Pomodoro Zoodles | 82 |
| 250. | Buttery Parsley Corn | 82 |
| 251. | Eggplant Escalivada Toast | 83 |
| 252. | Mushroom and Veggie Baguette | 83 |
| 253. | Root Veggie Casserole | 83 |
| 254. | Coconut Zucchini Soup | 83 |
| 255. | Potato Chili | 83 |
| 256. | Red Lentil Dhal with Butternut Squash | 84 |
| 257. | Leafy Green Risotto | 84 |
| 258. | Mini Mac and Cheese | 84 |
| 259. | Tempeh Sandwiches | 84 |
| 260. | Veggie Flax Burgers | 84 |
| 261. | Beet Borscht | 85 |
| 262. | Asparagus Dressed in Cheese | 85 |
| 263. | Spicy Pinto Bean Chili | 85 |
| 264. | Tropical Salsa Mash | 85 |
| 265. | Apple and Red Cabbage Vegetarian Dinner | 85 |
| 266. | Squash and Sweet Potato Lunch Soup | 86 |
| 267. | Green Minestrone Stew with Parmesan | 86 |
| 268. | Broccoli and Chickpea Stew | 86 |
| 269. | Pearl Barley and Butternut Winter Soup | 86 |
| 270. | Smoked Tofu Bowl | 87 |
| 271. | Basil and Tomato "Pasta" | 87 |
| 272. | Kale Chips with Garlic and Lime Juice | 87 |
| 273. | Pears in Cranberry Sauce | 87 |
| 274. | Zucchini Coconut Burgers | 87 |
| 275. | Roasted Potatoes with Gorgonzola | 87 |
| 276. | Chickpea Bell Pepper Soup | 88 |

277. Potato & Leek Patties ............................................. 88
278. Lime & Mint Zoodles ............................................. 88
279. Cabbage, Beet & Apple Stew................................ 88
280. Blueberry Oatmeal with Walnuts........................ 88
281. Quick Coconut Moong Dhal ................................ 88
282. Squash in Cheesy Cream ..................................... 89
283. Veggie Cassoulet with navy beans ..................... 89
284. Marinated Mushrooms in Slow Cooker ................. 89
285. Vegan Corn Chowder in Slow Cooker .................... 89
286. Green Collard Beans in Slow Cooker ..................... 90
287. Loaded Potato Soup in Slow Cooker ..................... 90
288. Hot Smashed Potato Soup..................................... 90
289. Onion, Pepper and Sausage Mix........................... 90
290. Taco Chili in Slow Cooker..................................... 91

## POULTRY RECIPES ................................................................................................. 91

291. Delicious BBQ Pulled Turkey ............................... 91
292. Balsamic Chicken Thighs with Pears.................. 91
293. Cheesy Drumsticks in Marinara Sauce............... 91
294. Turkey Thighs with Fig Sauce ............................. 92
295. Creamy Chicken with Mushrooms and Carrots ..... 92
296. Turkey with Tomatoes and Red Beans................ 92
297. Orange and Cranberry Turkey Wings ................ 92
298. Chicken Drumettes in Creamy Tomato Sauce........ 92
299. Delicious Turkey Meatloaf .................................. 93
300. Spicy Rosemary Chicken ..................................... 93
301. Creamy Chicken in Beer Sauce ........................... 93
302. Barbecue Wings ................................................... 93
303. Lemon-Garlic Chicken Thighs ............................. 93
304. Italian-Style Chicken Breasts with Kale Pesto........ 94
305. Jasmine Rice and Chicken Taco Bowls ............... 94
306. Honey-Ginger Shredded Chicken......................... 94
307. Coconut-Lime Chicken Curry .............................. 94
308. Hungarian Chicken Thighs in Cherry Tomato Sauce
 ...................................................................................... 95
309. Black Currant and Lemon Chicken ..................... 95
310. Buffalo Chicken Chili ........................................... 95
311. Tuscany-Style Sund-Dried Tomato Chicken .......... 96
312. Gorgeous Chicken Fajitas with Guacamole............ 96
313. Mediterranean Chicken Meatballs ...................... 96
314. Sweet and Gingery Whole Chicken ..................... 96
315. Feta and Spinach Stuffed Chicken Breasts........... 97
316. Lemon-Garlic Chicken with Herby Stuffed ............ 97
317. Fennel Chicken Breast......................................... 97
318. BBQ Sticky Drumettes......................................... 97
319. Herby Balsamic Chicken ..................................... 98
320. Effortless Coq Au Vin.......................................... 98
321. Cajun Chicken and Green Beans ........................ 98
322. Turkey Breasts in Maple and Habanero Sauce ...... 98
323. Greek-Style Chicken Legs with Herbs..................... 98
324. Chicken Stew with Shallots and Carrots................ 99
325. Thyme and Lemon Drumsticks with Red Sauce..... 99
326. Easy and Flavorful Chicken Legs........................... 99
327. Creamy and Garlicky Chicken ............................... 99
328. Asian-style Sweet Chicken Drumsticks................ 100
329. Mexican Cheesy Turkey Breasts.......................... 100
330. Sweet Potato & Chicken Curry ............................ 100
331. Chicken with Water Chestnuts............................ 100
332. Chicken with Red Potatoes & Green Beans.......... 100
333. Creamy Southern Chicken ................................... 100
334. Easy Chicken Soup .............................................. 101
335. Pear and Onion Goose......................................... 101
336. Chicken Piccata ................................................... 101
337. Stewed Chicken with Kale ................................... 101
338. Turkey with Fennel and Celery............................ 102
339. Mexican Chicken................................................. 102
340. Chicken in Roasted Red Pepper Sauce................. 102
341. Turkey and Potatoes with Buffalo Sauce............. 102
342. Fall-Off-Bone Chicken Drumsticks...................... 102
343. Coconut Chicken with Tomatoes ......................... 103
344. Cherry Tomato and Basil Chicken Casserole ....... 103
345. Sweet and Smoked Slow Cooked Turkey............. 103
346. Chicken and Beans Casserole with Chorizo ......... 103
347. Creamy Turkey Breasts with Mushrooms ............ 103
348. Sweet Gingery and Garlicky Chicken Thighs ....... 104
349. Simple Pressure Cooked Whole Chicken.............. 104
350. Chicken Bites Snacks with Chili Sauce ............... 104
351. Hot and Buttery Chicken Wings .......................... 104
352. Tasty Turkey with Campanelle and Tomato Sauce
 ...................................................................................... 105
353. Chicken with Mushrooms and Leeks ................... 105
354. Hearty and Hot Turkey Soup............................... 105

355. Green BBQ Chicken Wings .................................. 105
356. Hot and Spicy Shredded Chicken........................ 105
357. Homemade Cajun Chicken Jambalaya................. 106
358. Salsa and Lime Chicken with Rice ...................... 106
359. Homemade Whole Chicken ................................. 106
360. Herbed and Garlicky Chicken Wings................... 106
361. Duck and Green Pea Soup .................................. 106
362. Teriyaki Chicken Under Pressure......................... 107
363. Young Goose for Slow Cooker ............................ 107
364. Homemade Chicken with Dumplings ................. 107
365. Mexican-styled Slow Cooker Chicken ................. 107
366. Yellow Rice with Turkey wings ........................... 107
367. Slow Cooker Turkey Wings ................................. 108
368. Chicken Alfredo in Slow Cooker ......................... 108
369. Quick-to-Cook Chicken ....................................... 108
370. Slow Cooker Turkey with Dumplings ................. 108
371. Flavored Chicken in Rustic Italian Style.............. 108
372. Hot Turkey Meatballs .......................................... 109
373. Shredded Turkey in Barbeque Sauce .................. 109
374. Lemon-Fragrant Chicken .................................... 109
375. Turkey with Indian Spice .................................... 109
376. Gluten-free Chicken Soup................................... 109
377. Hawaiian Spice Slow Cooker Chicken ................. 110
378. Chicken Soup with Rice ...................................... 110
379. Tunisian-Styled Turkey ....................................... 110
380. Hot Buffalo Chicken Lettuce Envelopes............... 110
381. Chicken with Pear and Asparagus ...................... 111
382. Sweet Chicken with Parmesan ........................... 111
383. Cornish Hens with Olives.................................... 111
384. Slow Cooker Chicken in Thai Sauce .................... 111
385. Leftovers Soup with Turkey Meat ....................... 112
386. Chicken Livers Mix .............................................. 112
387. Slow Cooker Chicken with Italian dressing.......... 112
388. Barbeque Chicken Sliders................................... 112

389. Slow Cooker Turkey in Beer Marinade ................ 113
390. French Onion and Chicken Soup......................... 113
391. Turkey Bacon Cassoulet ...................................... 113
392. Tagine Chicken in Slow Cooker........................... 113
393. Slow Cooker Turkey with Potatoes ..................... 114
394. Chicken Breast with Bacon and Feta .................. 114
395. Chicken with Quinoa and Mustard ..................... 114
396. Creamy Chicken with Pasta ................................ 114
397. Summer Burrito with Turkey .............................. 115
398. Bloody Mary Chicken.......................................... 115
399. Super Easy Cornish Hens .................................... 115
400. Balsamic Chicken in Slow Cooker....................... 115
401. Hot Turkey in Italian Style .................................. 116
402. Slow Cooker Baked Chicken with Paprika........... 116
403. Sour and Sweet Chicken..................................... 116
404. Turkey breast with herbs.................................... 116
405. Spicy Buffalo Wings in Slow Cooker ................... 116
406. Slow Cooker Jambalaya...................................... 117
407. Italian-styled creamy chicken ............................ 117
408. Tortilla Soup with Duck...................................... 117
409. Chicken Fajitas in Slow Cooker .......................... 117
410. Spice Chicken legs.............................................. 118
411. Latin Chicken in Slow Cooker ............................. 118
412. Turkey for Thanksgiving ..................................... 118
413. Whole Baked Chicken......................................... 118
414. Boneless Turkey with Garlic and Herbs .............. 119
415. Chicken Corn with Chili ...................................... 119
416. Barbeque Goose for Sandwich ........................... 119
417. Turkey Soup with Split Peas ............................... 119
418. Classic Pheasants for Slow Cooker...................... 119
419. Cornish Hens in Plum Glazing............................. 120
420. Shredded Chicken in Barbeque Sauce ................ 120
421. Whole Lemon Chicken in Slow Cooker ............... 120
422. Buffalo Soup with Chicken Wings ...................... 120

## BEANS & GRAINS RECIPES ..................................................................................... 121

423. Prawns in Moong Dal......................................... 121
424. Herby White Bean and Corn Dip ........................ 121
425. Delicious Yellow Split Lentil Beef Stew ............... 121
426. Celery and Cheese Chickpea Stew ...................... 121
427. Meatless Lasagna ............................................... 121
428. Banana and Fig Millet ........................................ 122

429. Parsley Pureed Navy Beans................................. 122
430. Mexican-Style Black Bean and Avocado Salad ..... 122
431. Rosemary Goat Cheese Barley ............................ 122
432. African Lentil Dip ................................................ 123
433. Quinoa Pilaf with Cherries.................................. 123
434. Bean and Bacon Dip............................................ 123

435. Cinnamon Bulgur with Pecans ............................ 123
436. Peach Quinoa Pudding ...................................... 123
437. Mushroom and Farro Beans ............................... 123
438. Pear and Almond Oatmeal ................................. 124
439. Kidney Beans with Bacon and Tomatoes ........... 124
440. Navy Beans with Ground Beef ........................... 124
441. Curried Chickpeas ............................................. 124
442. Mixed Bean Italian Sausage Chili ...................... 124
443. Navy Bean Dip ................................................... 124
444. Cannellini Beans Chili ....................................... 125
445. Ham and Parmesan Grits ................................... 125
446. Black Bean and Mushroom Spread ................... 125
447. Farmer's Meal .................................................... 125
448. Butter Bean and Kale Stew ................................ 125
449. Mushroom and Parmesan Barley ....................... 126
450. Tasty Three-Bean Stew ...................................... 126
451. Simple Cornbread .............................................. 126
452. Lemony Oats with Chia Seeds ........................... 126
453. Cheesy Chicken Quinoa .................................... 126
454. Mouth-Watering Lima Beans ............................ 127
455. Pearl Barley with Mushrooms ........................... 127
456. Cheesy Sausage and Egg Bundt Cake ................ 127

## SOUPS AND STEWS ........................................................................................................ 127

457. Irish Lamb Stew ................................................. 127
458. Spicy Beef and Potato Soup ............................... 128
459. Creamy Curried Cauliflower Soup .................... 128
460. Pressure Cooked Chili ....................................... 128
461. Pumpkin, Corn, and Chicken Chowder ............. 128
462. Cheesy Swiss Chard Relish ................................ 128
463. Spanish-Style Chorizo and Broccoli Soup ......... 129
464. Chicken Enchilada Soup .................................... 129
465. Spicy Beef Chili with Worcestershire Sauce ..... 129
466. Cream of Broccoli Soup ..................................... 129
467. Chicken & Pancetta Noodle Soup ...................... 130
468. Fall Pumplin and Cauliflower Soup ................... 130
469. Pork Roast Green Chili ...................................... 130
470. Pepperoni and Vegetable Stew ........................... 130
471. Smoked Sausage and Seafood Stew ................... 131
472. White Wine Red Peppers ................................... 131
473. Ham and Pea Soup ............................................. 131
474. Pomodoro Soup .................................................. 131
475. Skim and Fast Miso and Tofu Soup ................... 131
476. Navy Bean and Ham Shank Soup ...................... 132
477. Lentil Soup ........................................................ 132
478. Beef Soup with Tacos Topping .......................... 132
479. Creamy Chicken Stew with Mushrooms & Spinach ................................................................. 132
480. White Beans and Easy Chicken Chili ................ 133
481. Mushroom and Beef Stew .................................. 133
482. Tortellini Minestrone Soup ................................ 133
483. Chipotle Chile sin Carne .................................... 133
484. Fresh Tagliatelle Pasta Bolognese ..................... 133
485. Spicy Sweet Potato Cubes .................................. 134
486. Noodles with Tuna ............................................. 134
487. Cabbage-Onion Side with Pears ........................ 134
488. Classic Mashed Potatoes .................................... 134
489. Creamy Potato and Scallion Salad ..................... 134
490. Chili and Cheesy Beef Pasta .............................. 135
491. Garlic & Herb Potatoes ...................................... 135
492. Potatoes and Green Beans .................................. 135
493. Paprika Hash Browns ........................................ 135
494. Cauliflower and Pea Bowl ................................. 136

## DESSERTS RECIPES .......................................................................................................... 136

495. Pressure Cooked Cherry Pie .............................. 136
496. Impossible Oatmeal Chocolate Cookies ............ 136
497. Honeyed Butternut Squash Pie .......................... 136
498. Homemade Chocolate Pudding ......................... 136
499. Almond Pear Wedges ......................................... 137
500. Vanilla and Yogurt Light Cheesecake ................ 137
501. Chocolate Molten Lava Cake ............................. 137
502. Peaches with Chocolate Biscuits ....................... 137
503. Peanut Butter Bars ............................................. 137
504. Apricots with Blueberry Sauce .......................... 138
505. Cinnamon and Lemon Apples ........................... 138
506. Milk Dumplings in Sweet Cardamom Sauce ..... 138
507. Delicious Stuffed Apples .................................... 138
508. Coconut Crème Caramel .................................... 138

| # | Title | Page |
|---|---|---|
| 509. | Juicy Apricots with Walnuts and Goat Cheese | 139 |
| 510. | Almond Butter Bananas | 139 |
| 511. | Crema Catalana | 139 |
| 512. | Tutty Fruity Sauce | 139 |
| 513. | Homemade Egg Custard | 139 |
| 514. | Hazelnut Chocolate Spread | 139 |
| 515. | Tiramisu Cheesecake | 140 |
| 516. | Citrus Cheesecake | 140 |
| 517. | Chocolate and Banana Squares | 140 |
| 518. | Compote with Blueberries and Lemon | 140 |
| 519. | Full Coconut Cake | 141 |
| 520. | Restaurant-Style Crème Brulee | 141 |
| 521. | Bonfire Lava Cake | 141 |
| 522. | Buttery Banana Bread | 141 |
| 523. | Strawberry Cottage Cheesecake | 141 |
| 524. | Berry-Vanilla Pudding Temptation | 142 |
| 525. | Fruity Cheesecake | 142 |
| 526. | Black Currant Poached Peaches | 142 |
| 527. | Easiest Pressure Cooked Raspberry Curd | 142 |
| 528. | Apple and Peach Compote | 143 |
| 529. | Very Berry Cream | 143 |
| 530. | Creamy Almond and Apple Delight | 143 |
| 531. | Coconut Pear Delight | 143 |
| 532. | Hot Milk Chocolate Fondue | 143 |
| 533. | Poached Pears with Orange and Cinnamon | 143 |
| 534. | Crispy and Sweet Holiday Treats | 144 |
| 535. | Caramel-Pear Pudding Cake | 144 |
| 536. | Double-Berry Cobbler | 144 |
| 537. | Dark Chocolate Fondue with Fruit Kabobs | 144 |
| 538. | Raspberry Fudge Brownies | 145 |
| 539. | Walnut Apple Crisp | 145 |
| 540. | Peppermint Pretzel Candies | 145 |
| 541. | Pumpkin Spiced and Pomegranate Cheesecake | 145 |
| 542. | Coconut-Mocha Poached Pears | 146 |
| 543. | Ginger-Orange Cheesecake | 146 |
| 544. | Candy Bar Fondue | 146 |
| 545. | Dutch Apple Sweet Pudding Cake | 146 |
| 546. | Chocolate Fondue | 147 |
| 547. | Crustless Lemony Cheesecake | 147 |
| 548. | Gingerbread Pudding Cake | 147 |
| 549. | Chocolate Bread Pudding with Mocha | 147 |
| 550. | Orange-Caramel Pudding Cake | 147 |
| 551. | Fruit Compote with Spicy Ginger | 148 |
| 552. | Old-Fashioned Rice Pudding | 148 |
| 553. | White Chocolate with Apricot Bread Pudding | 148 |
| 554. | Strawberry Mojito Shortcakes | 149 |
| 555. | Peach Graham Cracker Summer Cake | 149 |
| 556. | Slow Cooker Berry Crisp | 149 |
| 557. | Ginger Chicken in Lettuce Cups | 149 |
| 558. | Peach Upside Down Cake | 150 |
| 559. | Apple-Cherry Cobbler | 150 |
| 560. | Chocolate Cherry Slow Cooker Cake | 150 |
| 561. | Slow Cooker Apple Crisp | 150 |
| 562. | Rice Pudding in a Slow Cooker | 151 |
| 563. | Caramel Apples in Sweet Dip | 151 |
| 564. | Autumn Pumpkin Sweet Pie | 151 |
| 565. | Sweet Scones with Chocolate Drops | 151 |
| 566. | Pumpkin and Coffee Sweet Cake | 152 |
| 567. | Peach Cobbler in Slow Cooker | 152 |
| 568. | Cinnamon Roll for Slow Cooker | 152 |
| 569. | Pineapple and Coconut Cake | 152 |
| 570. | Chocolate Chip Slow Cooker Cookie | 152 |
| 571. | Pumpkin and Bread Pecan Pudding | 153 |
| 572. | Carrot Cake with Creamy Topping | 153 |
| 573. | Dump Cake with Chocolate | 153 |
| 574. | Fudged Brownies in Slow Cooker | 153 |
| 575. | Dump Cherry Cake | 154 |
| 576. | Fudgy Brownies with Strawberries | 154 |
| 577. | Butterscotch Fondue | 154 |
| 578. | Chocolate and Peanut Butter Cake | 154 |
| 579. | Triple-Berry Cobbler | 155 |
| 580. | Chocolate Pudding Cake | 155 |
| 581. | Vanilla Tapioca Pudding | 155 |
| 582. | Apples with Cinnamon and Dark Brown Sugar | 155 |
| 583. | Bananas Foster in Slow Cooker | 156 |
| 584. | Slow Cooker Reindeer Poop | 156 |
| 585. | Warm Berry Slow Cooker Compote | 156 |
| 586. | Triple Coconut Cake | 156 |
| 587. | Slow Cooker Black Forest Cake | 157 |
| 588. | Apple Bread Pudding with Cinnamon | 157 |
| 589. | Peanut Butter Cake in Slow Cooker | 157 |
| 590. | Bread Pudding in the Slow Cooker | 157 |

591. Stuffed Apples.................................................. 158
592. Hazelnut Pudding Cake...................................... 158
593. Cherry-Chocolate Cluster Bits with Salted Almonds ........................................................................ 158
594. Nutty Pumpkin-Pie Pudding ............................... 158

## MAIN DISHES RECIPES .................................................................................................................. 159

595. Summer Cabbage Rolls for Slow Cooker .............. 159
596. Risotto with Bacon and Mushroom...................... 159
597. Tangy Roast in Slow Cooker ................................ 159
598. Chicken Stroganoff for Slow Cooker .................... 159
599. Zesty Chicken Barbeque ...................................... 160
600. Chicken with Dumplings in Slow Cooker ............. 160
601. Beef Roast for Slow Cooker.................................. 160
602. Seasoned Beef with cream ................................... 160
603. Slow Cooker Kalua Pig ........................................ 161
604. Slow Cooker Spicy Pulled Pork ............................ 161
605. Soup with Italian sausage .................................... 161
606. Chicken with Lemon Juice and Oregano.............. 161
607. Lasagna with Beef for Slow Cooker ..................... 161
608. Mexican Meat in Slow Cooker.............................. 162
609. Summer Pot Roast for Slow Cooker ..................... 162
610. Pork Chops in Sour Cream................................... 162
611. Corned Beef with Cabbage ................................. 162
612. Beef Stroganoff in Slow Cooker........................... 163
613. Carnitas in Slow Cooker...................................... 163
614. Hot Potatoes with Pork........................................ 163
615. Pizza for Slow Cooker ......................................... 163
616. Autumn Mushroom and Beef Delight ................. 163
617. Sausages with Sauce............................................ 164
618. Beef and Broccoli in Slow Cooker ....................... 164
619. Chicken with Pineapples in Slow Cooker ............ 164
620. Western Omelette in Slow Cooker....................... 164
621. Western Omelette in Slow Cooker....................... 165
622. Cheesy Macaroni for Slow Cooker....................... 165
623. Stuffed Cabbage with Meat and Tomatoes .......... 165
624. Chicken Thighs with Peaches .............................. 165
625. Potato Casserole with Cheddar............................ 166
626. Baked Potatoes Stuffed with Ham ....................... 166
627. Spaghetti Squash in Slow Cooker........................ 166
628. Hash Brown Casserole with Cheese..................... 166
629. Chicken Chili Recipe........................................... 166
630. Steak with Beans and Crumbs ............................ 167
631. Turkey and Summer Vegetables in Slow Cooker .. 167
632. Chicken Spaghetti in Slow Cooker...................... 167
633. Slow Cooker Chicken with Carrots ..................... 167
634. Summer Risotto in Slow Cooker ......................... 168
635. Tropical Chicken with Pineapple ........................ 168
636. Sauerkraut with Sausage in Slow Cooker ............ 168
637. Slow Cooker Vegetarian Mash ............................ 168
638. Simple Slow Cooker Enchiladas .......................... 168
639. Stuffed Peppers for Slow Cooker......................... 169
640. Slow Cooker Chicken with Vegetables ................ 169
641. Baby Carrots Roast in Slow Cooker .................... 169
642. Slow Cooker Creamy Oatmeal ............................ 169
643. Mac in Cheese for Slow Cooker........................... 170
644. Spicy Pasta with Mushrooms and Chicken .......... 170
645. Pepperoni Pizza in Slow Cooker ......................... 170
646. Venison Stew in Slow Cooker ............................. 170
647. Chile Verde in Slow Cooker ................................ 171
648. Slow Cooker Chicken with Pasta and Cream ....... 171
649. Mussaman Potato Curry in Slow Cooker ............. 171
650. Mexican Roast in Slow Cooker ............................ 171
651. Chili Chicken with Beans ................................... 172
652. Chicken with Bread Cubes .................................. 172
653. Broccoli Beef in Slow Cooker .............................. 172
654. Slow Cooker Pizza with Ravioli .......................... 172

## PASTA & SIDE DISHES .................................................................................................................... 173

655. Turmeric Carrot Mash......................................... 173
656. Kale and Carrots Side ......................................... 173
657. Balsamic Capers Beets........................................ 173
658. Mushroom and Zucchini Platter ......................... 173
659. Frascati and Sage Broccoli.................................. 173
660. Cabbage and Pepper Side................................... 174
661. Lemony Buckwheat Salad .................................. 174
662. Sweet and Mustardy Carrots .............................. 174
663. Pizza Pasta.......................................................... 174
664. Stewed Yams with Zucchini................................ 174

| | |
|---|---|
| 665. Lemony Rutabaga and Onion Salad ..................... 175 | 687. Miso Sweet Potato Mash ....................................... 179 |
| 666. Creamy Goat Cheese Cauliflower ......................... 175 | 688. Spaghetti with Meatballs ....................................... 179 |
| 667. Garlicky Sweet Potato Mash .................................. 175 | 689. Creamy Tomato and Basil Soup ........................... 180 |
| 668. Lime Cabbage with Coconut ................................. 175 | 690. Sicilian Eggplant Delight ....................................... 180 |
| 669. Gnocchi with Butternut Squash and Tomatoes .... 175 | 691. Creamy Coconut Squash Soup ............................ 180 |
| 670. Ricotta Cheese Lasagna with Mushrooms ............ 176 | 692. Sicilian Eggplant Delight ....................................... 180 |
| 671. Basil Eggplant Delight ........................................... 176 | 693. Creamy Coconut Squash Soup ............................ 180 |
| 672. Orange Potatoes with Walnuts .............................. 176 | 694. Vegetable and Cannellini Beans Pottage .............. 181 |
| 673. Red Cabbage with Apple ...................................... 176 | 695. Garlicky Zucchini and Carrot Noodles .................. 181 |
| 674. Cheese Tortellini with Broccoli and Turkey .......... 176 | 696. Rosemary and Garlic Potatoes ............................. 181 |
| 675. Spinach and Tomato Side ..................................... 177 | 697. Simple Mediterranean Asparagus ........................ 181 |
| 676. Smoky Asian-Style Tomato Chutney ..................... 177 | 698. Warm Chili Soup ................................................... 181 |
| 677. Vegetable Soup ..................................................... 177 | 699. Spicy Cauliflower with Peas ................................. 182 |
| 678. Savoy Cabbage and Beetroot Borscht Soup .......... 177 | 700. Flavorful Bell Peppers ........................................... 182 |
| 679. Hearty Artichokes and Garlic Green Beans .......... 177 | 701. Spinach with Cottage Cheese ............................... 182 |
| 680. Silky Cheese and Cauli Soup ................................ 178 | 702. Sausage Penne ..................................................... 182 |
| 681. Easy Mushroom Pâté ............................................. 178 | 703. Zucchini and Cherry Tomato Delight .................... 182 |
| 682. Cheesy Soup with Tortillas ................................... 178 | 704. Cauliflower Side with Pomegranate and Walnuts .. 183 |
| 683. Power Kale and Chickpea Soup ............................ 178 | 705. Simple Steamed Potatoes .................................... 183 |
| 684. Sour Cream Veggies .............................................. 179 | 706. Pea and Sweet Potato Bowl .................................. 183 |
| 685. Cajun Potatoes with Brussel Sprouts ................... 179 | 707. Orange Broccoli Parmesan ................................... 183 |
| 686. Turmeric Kale with Shallots .................................. 179 | |

## SNACKS & APPETIZERS RECIPES .................................................................................. 183

| | |
|---|---|
| 708. Christmas Egg Custard ........................................ 183 | 726. Cheese and Prosciutto Eggs ................................. 187 |
| 709. Chicken Enchilada Pasta ..................................... 184 | 727. Porcini and Sesame Dip ....................................... 187 |
| 710. Paprika Potato Slices ........................................... 184 | 728. Pico de Gallo with Carrots .................................... 187 |
| 711. Cheesy Fingerling Potato Rounds ........................ 184 | 729. Buttery Beets ........................................................ 187 |
| 712. Tahini, Carrot, and Spinach "Hummus" ............... 184 | 730. Ricotta and Cheddar Veggie Appetizer ................. 187 |
| 713. Balsamic Carrots ................................................. 184 | 731. Southern Chicken Dip .......................................... 188 |
| 714. Colby Cheese and Pancetta Frittata .................... 184 | 732. Appetizer Meatballs ............................................. 188 |
| 715. Eggs de Provence ................................................ 185 | 733. Potato and Bacon Snack ...................................... 188 |
| 716. Kale Hummus ...................................................... 185 | 734. Chili Sriracha Eggs ............................................... 188 |
| 717. Pea and Avocado Dip ........................................... 185 | 735. Bacon and Cheese Pasta ..................................... 188 |
| 718. Pressure Cooked Eggplant Dip ............................ 185 | 736. Mini Beefy Cabbage Rolls .................................... 189 |
| 719. Garlicky Pepper and Tomato Appetizer ............... 185 | 737. Salmon Bites ........................................................ 189 |
| 720. Turnip and Sultana Dip with Pecans ................... 185 | 738. Salty and Peppery Potato Snack .......................... 189 |
| 721. Spicy Homemade Peanuts ................................... 186 | 739. Blue Cheese and Bacon Polenta Squares ............ 189 |
| 722. Lemony Cippolini Onions .................................... 186 | 740. Turmeric Potato Sticks ......................................... 189 |
| 723. Party Duck Bites .................................................. 186 | 741. Jalapeno and Pineapple Salsa .............................. 190 |
| 724. Ziti Pork Meatballs ............................................... 186 | 742. Three-Cheese Small Macaroni Cups .................... 190 |
| 725. Chili Hash Browns ............................................... 186 | 743. Agave Carrot Sticks .............................................. 190 |

744. Nutty Carrot Sticks ............................................. 190
745. Buttery Potato Sticks ......................................... 190
746. Chicken Dip with Black Beans ......................... 190
747. Taco Bean for Tortilla or Chips ....................... 191
748. Little Smokie Sausages ..................................... 191
749. Mushrooms in Marinade .................................. 191
750. Seafood Dip with Cheese ................................. 191
751. Jalapeno Peppers with Chicken ...................... 192
752. Pumpkin Granola with Nutella ....................... 192
753. Slow Cooker Sauerkraut Dip ........................... 192
754. Meatballs Appetizer ........................................... 192
755. Barbeque Kielbasa in Slow Cooker ................. 192
756. Cheese and Beef Carne ..................................... 193
757. Superheated Peanuts in Syrup ......................... 193
758. Spicy Beef Balls .................................................. 193
759. Buffalo Chicken Dip .......................................... 193
760. Meatballs with Bacon in Slow Cooker ............ 193
761. Chutney and Spiced Chips ............................... 194
762. Broccoli Dip with Cheese .................................. 194
763. Cocktail Sausages in Glaze ............................... 194
764. Slow Cooker Snacks with Lemon Zest ........... 194
765. Pork Wraps in Slow Cooker ............................. 195
766. Italian Mix in Slow Cooker ............................... 195
767. Hoisin mushrooms with garlic ......................... 195
768. Chicken with Peanut Sauce .............................. 195
769. Asian Tacos with Cabbage ................................ 195
770. Crab Dip in Slow Cooker .................................. 196
771. Greek Meatballs with Cheese Stuffing ............ 196
772. Crabmeat Dip Recipe ........................................ 196
773. Queso Dip for Slow Cooker .............................. 196
774. Tamale Dish with Chips .................................... 197
775. Asian Spicy Wings ............................................. 197
776. Lettuce Cups with Chicken .............................. 197
777. Chocolate oatmeal bars ..................................... 197
778. Chocolate Fudge for Slow Cooker ................... 198
779. Balsamic Pork with Honey ................................ 198
780. Jalapeno Peppers stuffed with Sausage ........... 198
781. Spinach Dip with Artichokes ............................ 198
782. Stuffed Potato Skins ........................................... 199
783. Jalapeno Taquitos in Slow Cooker ................... 199
784. Barbeque Bites in Slow Cooker ........................ 199
785. Chicken Bites in Moroccan Style ..................... 199
786. Jalapeno Bites with Cheese and Bacon ........... 200
787. Spicy Cajun Pecans ............................................ 200
788. Seafood Dip Appetizer ...................................... 200
789. Wrapped Bacon Hot Dogs ................................ 200
790. Swiss Fondue in Slow Cooker .......................... 200
791. Bean Queso with Cheese ................................... 201
792. Spicy Champignons ........................................... 201
793. Sugared and Spicy Nuts .................................... 201
794. Small Beef Nachos ............................................. 201
795. Cereal Mix for Slow Cooker ............................. 202
796. Baked Tater Tots ................................................. 202
797. Spice Nachos with Chicken .............................. 202
798. Fajitas with Chicken and Beef .......................... 202
799. Marsala Mushrooms in Slow Cooker .............. 202
800. Hot Dogs with Chili and Cheese ..................... 203
801. Beer chicken buns .............................................. 203
802. Sandwiches with Pulled Beef ........................... 203
803. Sweet Bacon Pigs ................................................ 203
804. Cheese and Beer Dip ......................................... 203
805. Buffalo Wings for Slow Cooker ....................... 204

# MEAT RECIPES ............................................................................................................. 204

806. Pork Meatballs with Apple Sauce .................... 204
807. Pork Steaks with Apple and Prunes ................ 204
808. Pork Sausage with Bell Peppers and Sweet Onions ............................................................................................. 205
809. Pork with Rutabaga and Granny Smith Apples .... 205
810. Gourmet Bacon, Potato, and Endive Casserole .... 205
811. Pork Chops in Merlot ........................................ 205
812. Braised Red Cabbage and Bacon ..................... 206
813. Orange & Cinnamon Pork ................................ 206
814. Pork Roast with Mushrooms in Beer Sauce ......... 206
815. BBQ Pork Butt .................................................... 206
816. Apple and Cherry Pork Tenderloin ................. 206
817. Pork Chops with Brussel Sprouts .................... 206
818. Spicy Ground Pork ............................................ 207
819. Beans and Pancetta Kale and Chickpeas ........ 207
820. Rutabaga & Apple Pork .................................... 207
821. Brussel Sprout Pork Chops with Onions ........ 207
822. Sunday Night Pork Meatloaf ............................ 208

| | | |
|---|---|---|
| 823. Holiday Sweet Spare Ribs | 208 | |
| 824. Shredded Pork in Sweet BBQ Sauce | 208 | |
| 825. Pork & Cabbage Soup with Veggies | 208 | |
| 826. Pineapple Pork Loin | 209 | |
| 827. Pork Cutlets with Baby Carrots | 209 | |
| 828. Ground Pork and Sauerkraut | 209 | |
| 829. Chili Pork Meatloaf | 209 | |
| 830. Pork and Green Onion Frittata | 209 | |
| 831. Herby Pork Butt and Yams | 210 | |
| 832. Tangy Pork in Tomato Sour Cream Sauce | 210 | |
| 833. Ground Pork with Cabbage and Veggies | 210 | |
| 834. Dinner Pork Roast | 210 | |
| 835. Short Ribs with Mango Sauce | 210 | |
| 836. Pork Sausage with Cauliflower and Tater Tots | 211 | |
| 837. Tamari Sauce Pork Belly with Garlic | 211 | |
| 838. Pork Fillets with Worcestershire Sauce | 211 | |
| 839. Italian Sausage over Muffins | 211 | |
| 840. Rosemary Dijon-Apple Pork | 212 | |
| 841. Short Ribs with Red Wine Gravy | 212 | |
| 842. Fast Onion-Flavoured Pork Ribs | 212 | |
| 843. Apple Pork Ribs | 212 | |
| 844. BBQ Pork Rib Chops with Root Vegetables | 212 | |
| 845. Pork Chops with Apple Cider | 213 | |
| 846. Savory Fettuccine with Beef Sausage | 213 | |
| 847. Sloppy Joes and Coleslaw | 213 | |
| 848. Tomato Meatballs | 213 | |
| 849. Mexican Brisket | 214 | |
| 850. Beef Stew with Quinoa | 214 | |
| 851. Mustard Rump Roast with Potatoes | 214 | |
| 852. Traditional Beef Ragu | 214 | |
| 853. Spicy Shredded Beef | 214 | |
| 854. Bourbon and Apricot Meatloaf | 215 | |
| 855. Beef Hot Pot | 215 | |
| 856. Beef Sausage and Spinach Stew | 215 | |
| 857. Simple Cheesy Meatballs | 215 | |
| 858. No-Fuss Beef Chuck Roast | 216 | |
| 859. Chuck Roast with Root Vegetables and Herbs | 216 | |
| 860. Beef Coconut Curry | 216 | |
| 861. Sweet Balsamic Beef | 216 | |
| 862. Beef & Russet Potatoes Soup | 216 | |
| 863. Spicy Beef and Pinto Bean Chili | 217 | |
| 864. Russet Potatoes Flank Steak | 217 | |
| 865. Beef and Cabbage with Tomato Sauce | 217 | |
| 866. Sticky Baby Back Ribs | 217 | |
| 867. Saucy Beef and Rice | 217 | |
| 868. Beef & Tomato Soup | 218 | |
| 869. Ginger-Flavored and Sweet Pork Belly | 218 | |
| 870. Shredded Beef the Caribbean Way | 218 | |
| 871. Port Wine Garlicky Lamb | 218 | |
| 872. Pork Loin Chops with Sauerkraut | 218 | |
| 873. Pork with Tangy Tomato Sauce | 219 | |
| 874. Cheesy Rigatoni with Pancetta | 219 | |
| 875. Delicious Pork Shoulder with White Cabbage | 219 | |
| 876. Braised Chili Pork Chops | 219 | |
| 877. Pork Butt with Mushrooms and Celery | 220 | |
| 878. Pork Ribs in Walnut Sauce | 220 | |
| 879. Pork Chops and Mushrooms in Tomato Sauce | 220 | |
| 880. Citrusy Beef | 220 | |
| 881. Chuck Roast with Potatoes | 220 | |
| 882. Beef Medley with Blue Cheese | 221 | |
| 883. Steak and Veggies with Ale Sauce | 221 | |
| 884. Beef Cabbage Rolls | 221 | |
| 885. Beer-Dijon Braised Steak | 221 | |
| 886. Beef with Creamy Sour Sauce | 221 | |
| 887. Smothered Cinnamon BBQ Ribs | 222 | |
| 888. Onion Steaks in Gravy | 222 | |
| 889. Ground Beef and Sauerkraut | 222 | |
| 890. Beef Ribs with Button Mushrooms | 222 | |
| 891. Veal Shoulder and Mushrooms | 222 | |
| 892. Potted Rump Steak | 223 | |
| 893. Pot Roast in Gravy | 223 | |
| 894. Herbed Lamb Roast with Potatoes | 223 | |
| 895. Lamb Habanero Chili | 223 | |
| 896. Lamb Stew with Apricots | 224 | |
| 897. Marinated Flank Steak | 224 | |
| 898. Corned Beef with Celery Sauce | 224 | |
| 899. Tender Onion Beef Roast | 224 | |
| 900. Herbed Beef & Yams | 224 | |
| 901. London Broil in Slow Cooker | 225 | |
| 902. Three Packs roast mix | 225 | |
| 903. Mongolian Beef in Slow Cooker | 225 | |
| 904. Sweet Pork in Slow Cooker | 225 | |

905. Shoyu Pork Recipe for Slow Cooker ..................... 226
906. Ham and Pineapple in Slow Cooker ..................... 226
907. Pork Spare Ribs in Slow Cooker ......................... 226
908. Puerto Rican styled Pork ..................................... 226
909. Juicy Turkey Breast in Slow Cooker ..................... 226
910. Black Beans with Pork Tenderloin ....................... 227
911. Slow Cooker Chuck and Potato Roast.................. 227
912. Beef Barbacoa with Tomato Sauce...................... 227
913. Cranberry Pork in Slow Cooker .......................... 227
914. Slow Cooker Beef Lasagna.................................. 228
915. Pork Chops for Slow Cooker ............................... 228
916. Slow Cooker Beef Chops..................................... 228
917. Leg of Lamb with Herbs...................................... 228
918. Apple-Cider Marinated Pork ............................... 229
919. Pepperoncini Beef in Slow Cooker ...................... 229
920. Chili Beef Soup .................................................. 229
921. Juicy Kalua Pig in Slow Cooker .......................... 229
922. Slow Cooker Braciole in Slow Cooker.................. 230
923. Greek Pulled Pork in Slow Cooker ...................... 230
924. Pork with Sauerkraut in Slow Cooker.................. 230
925. Texas-styled pulled pork .................................... 230
926. Barbacoa Beef in Slow Cooker............................ 230
927. Brisket with Yellow Onions................................. 231
928. Slow-Cooker Shredded Orange Pork ................... 231
929. Tater Tot and Beef Casserole ............................. 231
930. Whole Meat Loaf in Slow Cooker........................ 231
931. Bulgari Beef in Slow Cooker ............................... 232
932. Squirrel and Liver Dish ...................................... 232
933. Slow Cooker Burrito Beef Pie.............................. 232
934. Small Meatloaves in Slow Cooker ....................... 232
935. Island Spiced Kielbasa ....................................... 233
936. Stout Stew for your Slow Cooker ....................... 233
937. Philippine Sandwich Meat .................................. 233
938. Stuffed Peppers in Slow Cooker.......................... 233
939. Slow Cooker Brats in Wisconsin Style ................. 234
940. Shepherd's Homemade Pie ................................ 234

## FISH & SEAFOOD RECIPES ..................................................................... 234

941. Lobster and Gruyere Pasta ................................. 234
942. Prawns and Fish Kabobs .................................... 234
943. Glazed Orange Salmon....................................... 235
944. Clams in White Wine .......................................... 235
945. Almond-Crusted Tilapia ..................................... 235
946. Wrapped Fish and Potatoes................................ 235
947. Fancy Shrimp Scampi with Soy Sauce................. 235
948. Tuna and Pea Cheesy Noodles ........................... 236
949. Lemon Sauce Salmon ......................................... 236
950. Creamy Crabmeat .............................................. 236
951. Mediterranean Salmon ....................................... 236
952. Scallops and Mussels Cauliflower Paella.............. 236
953. Buttery and Lemony Dill Clams........................... 236
954. Shrimp and Egg Risotto ..................................... 237
955. Garlicky Mackerel and Vegetables Parcels ........... 237
956. Salmon with Broccoli and Potatoes..................... 237
957. Veggie Noodle Salmon ....................................... 237
958. Crab Cakes ........................................................ 238
959. Steamed Salmon Filets with Paprika-Lemon Sauce
................................................................................ 238
960. Deliciously Sweet and Spicy Mahi Mahi.............. 238
961. Power Greens with Lemony Monf Fish ................ 238
962. Alaskan Cod with Fennel and Beans ................... 239
963. Sea Bass Stew.................................................... 239
964. Tilapia Chowder ................................................. 239
965. White Wine Steamed Mussels............................. 239
966. Cod in a Tomato Sauce ...................................... 239
967. Party Crab Legs.................................................. 240
968. Squid and Peas .................................................. 240
969. Sweet and Sour Slow Cooker Shrimp ................. 240
970. Crawfish and Shrimp Duo................................... 240
971. Shrimp Marinara for Slow Cooker ....................... 240
972. Asian-styled salmon with diced vegetables .......... 241
973. Creamy spaghetti with shrimp and cheese .......... 241
974. Poached Salmon in Slow Cooker ......................... 241
975. Clam Casserole with Green Peppers ................... 241
976. Tuna and Celery Meat Casserole ........................ 242
977. Halibut with Lemon and Dill ............................... 242
978. Slow Cooker Chowder with Shrimp and Bacon .... 242
979. Crabmeat dip in Slow Cooker ............................. 242
980. Salmon with Lemon and Dijon sauce................... 243
981. New England Clam Dip in Slow Cooker ............... 243
982. Tuna and Noodle casserole................................. 243
983. Shrimp casserole with white............................... 243

984. Pineapple Milkfish in Slow Cooker ........................ 244
985. Lobster Bisque in Slow Cooked ............................ 244
986. Clam and Vegetable Soup .................................... 244
987. Quick and easy Tuna Casserole ........................... 244
988. Classical Clam Soup in Slow Cooker ................... 245
989. Maple Syrup Salmon in Slow Cooker .................. 245
990. Tilapia seasoned with Citrus ................................ 245
991. Seafood with rice soup ......................................... 245
992. Classical Asian Miso Soup .................................. 245
993. Summer Soup with Lemon Salmon ..................... 246
994. Easy Seafood Pie .................................................. 246
995. Jambalaya in Slow Cooker ................................... 246
996. Summer Seafood Casserole .................................. 246
997. Hearty fish soup with corn ................................... 247
998. Asian Seafood mix ................................................ 247
999. Coconut Rice with Mango Shrimp ....................... 247
1000. Jamaican Spicy Salmon ...................................... 247
1001. Crab Soup with Dry Sherry ................................ 248
1002. Crabmeat and Cream Corn Soup ........................ 248
1003. Spice Chowder with Seafood ............................. 248

# What is a Crock pot?

**Crock-Pot is the original designer and manufacturer of the slow cooker** – offering three types of slow cooker, each boasting their own unique features and benefits. Discover your skills and talents in the kitchen with our exceptional products at your side, and produce restaurant-quality meals for your friends and family with ease. Enhance the taste and texture of simple, low-cost ingredients with slow cooking, letting the flavors marry together over a matter of hours, without the need for stirring.

In today's world, time is of the essence. Emphasis is on things being done instantly and this includes our food. But crock pot takes the opposite approach. Instead of zapping the food like a microwave or squishing it together like a pressure cooker, the crock pot lets the food simmer for 4- 14 times longer than it would normally take. In short, a crock pot is the reverse of a pressure cooker.

Crock pot has a long and colorful history. Originally made out of clay and stone in prehistoric times and heated on the hearth, the crock pot was an invaluable tool for women who had to juggle a dozen domestic responsibilities at any given moment. It allowed food to be cooked with very low chance of burning. We use almost identical shapes and sizes as those crock pots of the old, except with modern materials and using electricity.

# How does a Crock pot work?

After putting the food in, you pour some liquid (stock, wine, water) into the crock pot and turn it on. The crock pot will heat up to 80-90 °C, heating the liquid so it becomes steam, but not the super- heated kind like in pressure cookers. The steam will circulate inside the crock pot, evenly spreading heat over the food. After cooking for several hours (possibly longer if you used lower settings), the food is ready. Crock pots generally have a temperature probe inside, which determines when the food is cooked and automatically lowers the temperature to keep the food warm.

# Understanding Your Crockpot

Also called a slow cooker, a crockpot is a countertop kitchen appliance that allows you to cook food at temperatures lower than the boiling point. As a result, the food is cooked longer so you can prepare food a few hours before you are ready to eat your meals.

Crockpots are not only used to make soups and stews but literally all types of foods including your favorite desserts. The crockpot has a heavy bottom made from a thick material with a heating element that cooks food at a temperature that ranges between 710C and 740C.

# Benefits of Using a Crockpot

Crockpots are becoming very popular as more and more people want to take charge of their health and still eat healthy meals. But aside from convenience, there are so many benefits why you ought to use a crockpot when cooking food. Below are the benefits of why you ought to use a crockpot.

## Cooks cheaper cuts of meat better than ordinary pots:

Meats that are cheaper cuts come with hard connective tissues. Although they create tastier dishes, they are tough to cook on the stovetop. But if you have a crockpot, cheaper meat cuts are cooked longer thus this method of cooking can bring out the best flavor of tougher meat cuts.

### CONSUME LESS ELECTRICITY:

A crockpot consumes less energy than stovetop cookers, so you can save more on your utility bills for a longer period of time.

### FOOD DOES NOT BURN:

The low-temperature setting that the food is cooked makes it safer to cook your food without the fear of burning it.

## HOW TO USE THE CROCKPOT

- Using a crockpot does not involve rocket science. In fact, it is so easy to use it that you can't go wrong with this kitchen device. Below are nifty tips on how to use the crockpot.
- Fill the crockpot with ½ liquid. Using too much liquid requires a longer time to heat up the food thus you may need another hour or two to cook your food.
- Place meat and root vegetable at the bottom of the pot as the food is submerged in the hot liquid. This will also allow the meat to soak up on the juices thus making it more delicious.
- Trim off excess skin when cooking as this will cook the food quickly and might create smoke especially if the liquid used is too littles
- The lid of the crockpot is made of glass so there is no need to lift the lid to check the food constantly. The thing is that whenever you lift the lid, you lose heat to cook your food and you may need to extend the cooking time to another half an hour.

## TIPS AND TRICKS FOR USING THE CROCKPOT

The thing is that you can cook different types of food in a crockpot. But if you want to make delicious meals using your crockpot just like the pro, there are some tips and tricks that you need to take note of. Below are the things that you need to know when using a crockpot.

- As much as possible, cook the meat in the skillet first to add that smoky flavor to it. But make sure that you drain some of the fats before cooking.
- Add tender vegetables during the last minutes of the cooking time so that they do not get overcooked.
- If the cooking time is long, add the dairy products like milk and cream last. Overcooking them often results in curdling.
- When cooking seafood such as shrimps or squid, add them last because they might take on a rubbery texture.

## SLOW COOKER OR CROCK-POT?

The term slow cooker is the generic name for an appliance that uses heating elements all around the insert, which bring food up to safe temperatures. Crock-Pot is the Rival corporation's registered trademark for its slow cookers. All Crock-Pots are slow cookers, but not all slow cookers are Crock-Pots. Other popular slow cooker brands include All-Clad, Cuisinart, and Hamilton Beach.

When you're shopping for a slow cooker, please keep in mind that there are appliances on the market referred to as slow cookers that have their heating element only on the bottom. Don't buy one of these to use for the recipes in this book. Appliances with heating elements only on the bottom heat food more slowly than those with heating elements all around the insert. Experts do not recommend cooking large cuts of meat in this type of slow cooker (although it works for soups and stews). So when purchasing your slow cooker, please make sure it is a true one with heating elements all around the insert.

## What's the difference between a Crock Pot and a Slow Cooker?

Crock pot is a subtype of slow cooker. On the outside, both crock pot and slow cookers look the same: heating segment, lid and pot. Crock pot was initially specialized for cooking beans, but over time it evolved into crock pot of today that can handle plenty of recipes. Originally being a brand name, crock pot eventually became a generic name for any kind of slow cooker. To be exact, crock pot today refers to any kind of slow cooker that has a ceramic pot inside the heating unit.

Both crock pot and slow cooker share a lot of similarities in design, such as being able to hold food in an airtight fashion inside the pot.

## WHAT EACH FUNCTION MEANS

Crock Pot Express Pressure Cooker comes with a very comprehensive front that has display and functions you need to select before the cooker starts cooking your meal. Before you continue reading the recipes in this cookbook, it would be quite useful to learn what each function means.

- **Brown/Sauté** If you select this function, you will be able to cook your meal without the protective lid on the cooker. By pressing this function twice you have set the browning function; by pressing sauté and function and adjusting the button twice your cooker is ready for simmering.
- Keep the food **Warm/Cancel** – If you select this function you can cancel the previously selected function or simply turn off your Crock Pot Express.
- **Meat/Stew** – As the name says, this function is for cooking meat and stew. Adjusting the cooking time will set the cooker to cook the meat to the desired texture.
- **Poultry** – This is the function suitable for cooking chicken and turkey meat or any MEAT/STEW dish. You can set your desired pressure level as well as cooking time depending on your preferences or based on the requirements in the recipe you follow.
- **Rice/Risotto** – If you are cooking rice (any type of rice) set this function. The cooker will automatically cook your rice under low pressure; the time needed for the cooking will depend on the level of water you poured into the pot.
- **Steam** – Suitable for steaming vegetables or seafood, this function works better if you use it with the quick pressure releasing in order to avoid overcooking (which can happen if you let your Crock Pot Express release its pressure naturally).

↑ **Soup** – This is the function you need when cooking soups and broths. You can manually adjust the cooking time by clicking the 'Adjust' button (it all depends on how you want your soups, or based on your recipe).

↑ **Beans/Chili** - Crock Pot Express Pressure Cooker comes with this function that helps you prepare the best chili or beans. You can manually adjust the cooker from thirty to forty minutes, depending on how you prefer your chili or beans.

# MEASUREMENT CONVERSION CHART

The charts below will help you to convert between different units of volume in US customary units.

Please note that US volume is not the same as in the UK and other countries, and many of the measurements are different depending on which country you are in.

It is very easy to get confused when dealing with US and UK units! The only good thing is that the metric units never change!

Every effort has been made to ensure that the Measurement Charts on this page are accurate.

## VOLUME EQUIVALENTS (LIQUID)

| US Standard | US Standard (ounces) | Metric (approximate) |
|---|---|---|
| 2 tablespoons | 1 fl. oz. | 30 mL |
| ¼ cup | 2 fl. oz. | 60 mL |
| ½ cup | 4 fl. oz. | 120 mL |
| 1 cup | 8 fl. oz. | 240 mL |
| 1½ cups | 12 fl. oz. | 355 mL |
| 2 cups or 1 pint | 16 fl. oz. | 475 mL |
| 4 cups or 1 quart | 32 fl. oz. | 1 L |
| 1 gallon | 128 fl. oz. | 4 L |

## VOLUME EQUIVALENTS (DRY)

| US Standard | Metric (approximate) |
| --- | --- |
| ⅛ teaspoon | 0.5 mL |
| ¼ teaspoon | 1 mL |
| ½ teaspoon | 2 mL |
| ¾ teaspoon | 4 mL |
| 1 teaspoon | 5 mL |
| 1 tablespoon | 15 mL |
| ¼ cup | 59 mL |
| ⅓ cup | 79 mL |
| ½ cup | 118 mL |
| ⅔ cup | 156 mL |
| ¾ cup | 177 mL |
| 1 cup | 235 mL |
| 2 cups or 1 pint | 475 mL |
| 3 cups | 700 mL |
| 4 cups or 1 quart | 1 L |

## OVEN TEMPERATURES

| Fahrenheit (F) | Celsius (C) (approximate) |
| --- | --- |
| 250°F | 120°C |
| 300°F | 150°C |
| 325°F | 165°C |
| 350°F | 180°C |
| 375°F | 190°C |
| 400°F | 200°C |

| | |
|---|---|
| **425°F** | 220°C |
| **450°F** | 230°C |

# WEIGHT EQUIVALENTS

| US Standard | Metric (approximate) |
|---|---|
| ½ ounce | 15 g |
| 1 ounce | 30 g |
| 2 ounces | 60 g |
| 4 ounces | 115 g |
| 8 ounces | 225 g |
| 12 ounces | 340 g |
| 16 ounces or 1 pound | 455 g |

# BREAKFAST RECIPES

### Crustless Three-Meat Quiche

Ready in about: **50 minutes** | Serves: **4** | Per Serving: Calories 523; Carbs 6g; Fat 40g; Protein 32g

INGREDIENTS
6 Eggs, beaten
1 cup Ground Sausage, cooked
4 Bacon slices, cooked and crumbled
2 Green Onions, chopped
½ cup Milk
4 Ham Slices, diced
1 ½ cups Water
1 cup Cheddar Cheese, grated
A pinch of Salt and Black Pepper

DIRECTIONS
- Lower a trivet and pour in the water. Make a sling with foil to remove the dish. In a bowl, combine the eggs, milk, salt, and pepper. Set aside.
- Mix the sausage, cheese, bacon, ham, and onions in a baking dish and pour the egg mixture over. Place the baking dish inside the cooker.
- Cover with aluminum foil, and close the lid. Turn clockwise to seal and cook on MEAT/STEW mode for 30 minutes. When it goes off, do a quick pressure release. Let cool before slicing it, and serve.

### Cheesy Eggs in Hollandaise Sauce

Ready in about: **12 minutes** | Serves: **4** | Per Serving: Calories 231; Carbs 9g; Fat 13g; Protein 15g

INGREDIENTS
4 Bread Slices, roughly chopped
4 Eggs
½ cup Arugula, chopped
4 slices Mozzarella Cheese
1 cup Water
1 ½ Ounces Hollandaise Sauce

DIRECTIONS
- Place the steamer basket in the cooker and pour water. Divide the bread pieces in between 4 ramekins.
- In a bowl, whisk the eggs and mix with arugula. Divide this mixture among the ramekins. Cover them with aluminum foil and place them in the steamer basket. Select BEANS/CHILI mode, and adjust the time to 8 minutes. Lock the lid and turn the valve to close. It will take a few minutes before pressure is built inside the cooker.
- When cooking is over, do a quick pressure release. Remove the ramekins from the cooker and discard the foil. Top with a slice of mozzarella and some hollandaise sauce.

### Almond & Gala Apple Porridge

Ready in about: **8 minutes** | Serve: **1** | Per serving: Calories 445; Carbs 40g; Fat 18g; Protein 4g

INGREDIENTS
½ cup Almond Milk
3 tbsp ground Almonds
1 Gala Apple, grated
1 tbsp Almond Butter
2 tbsp Flaxseed
A pinch of Cinnamon
¼ tsp Vanilla Extract

DIRECTIONS
- Place all ingredients in your pressure cooker. Give the mixture a good stir to combine the ingredients well.
- Seal the lid, and cook on BEANS/CHILI at High pressure for 5 minutes. When ready, release the pressure quickly. Stir well and transfer the mixture to a serving bowl.

### Chorizo and Kale Egg Casserole

Ready in about: **30 minutes** | Serves: **4** | Per serving: Calories 426; Carbs 13g; Fat 30g; Protein 24g

INGREDIENTS
8 ounces Chorizo, cooked
1 tbsp Coconut Oil
6 Eggs
¾ cup Leeks, sliced
1 ½ cups Water
1 cup Kale, chopped
1 Sweet Potato, shredded
1 tsp Garlic, minced
1 tsp roughly chopped Parsley

DIRECTIONS
- Place the veggies in a greased baking dish and set aside. Set to SAUTÉ at High and melt the coconut oil. Sauté garlic, kale, and leeks for 2 minutes, until fragrant. Beat eggs in a small bowl, and pour them over the veggies.
- Stir in chorizo and potato. Pour the water in the pressure cooker and set a wire rack. Lower the baking dish on the rack. Cook on BEANS/CHILI for 25 minutes at High. Do a quick pressure release. Sprinkle with chopped parsley.

### Eggs & Smoked Salmon

Ready in about: **8 minutes** | Serve: **1** | Per serving: Calories 240; Carbs 2g; Fat 17g; Protein 19g

INGREDIENTS
4 slices Smoked Salmon
4 Eggs

1 tsp Cilantro, chopped
A pinch of Paprika
A pinch of Pepper
1 cup Water

DIRECTIONS

- Pour the water into the pressure cooker and lower the trivet. Grease 4 ramekins with cooking spray or olive oil. If using silicone ramekins, skip this step. Place a slice of smoked salmon at the bottom of each ramekin. Crack an egg on top of the salmon. Season with pepper and paprika and sprinkle with the cilantro.
- Arrange the ramekins on top of the trivet and seal the lid. Set BEANS/CHILI at High pressure for 5 minutes. When the timer goes off, release the pressure quickly.

## Sweet Potato & Carrot Egg Casserole

Ready in about: **15 minutes** | Serves: **4** | Per serving: **Calories 220; Carbs 17g; Fat 7g; Protein 6g**

INGREDIENTS

8 Eggs
½ cup Milk
2 cups Sweet Potatoes, shredded
1 cup Carrots, shredded
½ tbsp Olive Oil
½ tsp dried Parsley
¼ tsp Pepper
¼ tsp Paprika
¼ tsp Garlic Powder

DIRECTIONS

- Heat the olive oil on SAUTÉ mode at High. When hot and sizzling, add the carrots and sweet potatoes. Add the herbs and spices, stir well to combine, and cook the veggies for about 2-3 minutes.
- Meanwhile, beat together the eggs and almond milk in a bowl. Pour the mixture over the carrots and stir to incorporate well. Seal the lid, hit BEANS/CHILI for 7 minutes at High.
- When ready, do a quick pressure release and open the lid carefully. Serve and enjoy!

## Vanilla Quinoa Bowl

Ready in about: **13-15 minutes** | Serves: **4** | Per Serving: **Calories 186; Carbs 3g; Fat 3g; Protein 6g**

INGREDIENTS

1 cup Quinoa
2 tbsp Maple Syrup
1 tsp Vanilla Extract
1 ½ cups Water
A pinch of Sea Salt
A bunch of fresh mint leaves, for garnish

DIRECTIONS

- Put all ingredients in your pressure cooker. Stir to combine well. Seal the lid and turn clockwise to seal. Set to BEANS/CHILI mode and adjust the time to 12 minutes.
- When ready, do a quick pressure release. Open the lid and fluff with a fork. Ladle to serving bowls and top with mint leaves for fresh taste optionally.

## Crispy Bacon and Egg Burger

Ready in about: **15 minutes** | Serves: **1** | Per Serving: **Calories 368; Carbs 31g; Fat 13g; Protein 20g**

INGREDIENTS

1 Bun
1 Egg
2 slices Bacon
1 tsp Olive Oil
1 tbsp Gouda Cheese, grated
1 cup Water

DIRECTIONS

- Het oil on SAUTÉ at High, and cook the bacon until crispy, about 2-3 minutes per side. Remove to a paper towel and wipe out excess grease. Put a trivet and pour water in the cooker. Crumble the bacon in a ramekin, and crack the egg on top.
- Sprinkle with Gouda cheese, cover with aluminum foil and place the ramekin on top of the trivet. Seal the lid. Cook for 15 minutes at High on BEANS/CHILI. When ready, do a quick pressure release.
- Assemble the burger by cutting the bun in half and placing the mixture in the middle. Tip: You can assemble in between 2 slices of bread and heat in a pan for a few minutes.

## Zesty and Citrusy French Toast

Ready in about: **35 minutes** | Serves: **4** | Per serving: **Calories 455; Carbs 64 g; Fat 16 g; Protein 15 g**

INGREDIENTS

Zest of 1 Orange
1 cup Water
¼ cup Sugar
2 Large Eggs
3 tbsp Butter, melted
1 ¼ cups Milk
½ tsp Vanilla Extract
½ loaf of Challah Bread, cut into pieces
A pinch of Sea Salt

DIRECTIONS

- Whisk together all ingredients, except for the water and bread, in a large bowl. Dip the bread in the bowl and coat with the mixture. Arrange coated bread pieces in a baking pan that fits inside the cooker.
- Add the trivet and pour the water in. Lower the baking pan onto the trivet. Close the lid and turn clockwise to seal. Adjust the time to 25 minutes on BEANS/CHILI mode at High pressure.
- When ready, press CANCEL, and do a quick pressure release by turning the valve to "open" position.

## Cheddar and Eggs Hash Bake

Ready in about: **10 minutes** | Serves: **4** | Per serving: **Calories 459; Carbs 42g; Fat 20g; Protein 27g**

INGREDIENTS

6 small Potatoes, shredded
6 Large Eggs, beaten
½ cup Water
1 cup Cheddar Cheese, shredded
1 cup Ham, diced

Cooking spray, to grease

DIRECTIONS

- Grease with some cooking spray the inner pot of your pressure cooker and set to SAUTÉ mode at High. Add the shredded potatoes and cook until lightly browned, for 5-6 minutes. Pour in the water.
- Meanwhile, in a bowl, mix the ham, cheese, and eggs, and add to the pressure cooker. Stir to combine well.
- Seal the lid and set to BEANS/CHILI for 10 minutes.
- It will take a few minutes before pressure is built inside the cooker. Do a quick pressure release.

## Classic Sunday Big Pancakes

**Ready in about: 30 minutes | Serves: 6 | Per serving: Calories 432; Carbs 58g; Fat 16g; Protein 11g**

INGREDIENTS

3 cups All-purpose Flour
¾ cup Sugar
5 Eggs
¼ cup Olive Oil
¼ cup Sparkling Water
¼ tsp Salt
1 ½ tsp Baking Soda

**To Serve:**

2 tbsp Maple Syrup
A dollop of Whipped Cream

DIRECTIONS

- Start by pouring the flour, sugar, eggs, olive oil, sparkling water, salt, and baking soda into the food processor and blend them until smooth.
- Pour the batter in the pressure cooker, and let it sit in there for 15 minutes. Seal the lid, and select BEANS/CHILI mode at Low pressure for 15 minutes.
- Once the timer goes off, quick-release the pressure. Stick in a toothpick, and once it comes out clean, the pancake is done.
- Gently run a spatula around the pancake to let loose any sticking.
- Then, slide the pancakes into a serving plate. Top with the whipped cream and drizzle the maple syrup over it to serve.

## Apricot and Raisin Oatmeal

**Ready in about: 15 minutes | Serves: 4 | Per serving: Calories 325; Carbs 78g; Fat 4g; Protein 8g**

INGREDIENTS

2 ¼ cups Water
1 ½ cups Steel Cut Oats
1 ½ cups Almond Milk
A handful of Raisins
8 Apricots, chopped
1 tsp Vanilla Paste
¾ cup Brown Sugar

DIRECTIONS

- Combine all ingredients in your pressure cooker. Set it to RICE/RISOTTO mode, seal the lid, and cook for 8 minutes, at High pressure. Once cooking is over, do a quick pressure release.

## Banana and Cinnamon French Toast

**Ready in about: 50 minutes | Serves: 6 | Per serving: Calories 313; Carbs 39g; Fat 15g; Protein 8g**

INGREDIENTS

1 ½ tsp Cinnamon
¼ tsp Vanilla Extract
6 Bread Slices, cubed
4 Bananas, sliced
2 tbsp Brown Sugar
1 tbsp White Sugar
½ cup Milk
¼ cup Pecans, chopped
3 Eggs
¼ cup Cream Cheese, softened
2 tbsp cold and sliced Butter
¾ cup Water

DIRECTIONS

- Grease a baking dish and arrange half of the bread cubes. Top with half of the banana slices. Sprinkle with half of the brown sugar. Spread cream cheese over the bananas.
- Arrange the rest of the bread cubes and banana slices on top. Sprinkle with brown sugar and top with pecans. Top with butter slices. In a bowl, whisk together eggs, white sugar, milk, cinnamon, and vanilla.
- Pour the mixture into the baking dish. Place the trivet inside the cooker and pour the water. Lower the baking dish onto the trivet. Cook on MEAT/STEW for 30 minutes at High. Do a quick pressure release.

## Bacon and Colby Cheese Grits

**Ready in about: 20 minutes | Serves: 4 | Per serving: Calories 280; Carbs 8g; Fat 21g; Protein 14g**

INGREDIENTS

3 slices smoked Bacon, diced
1 ½ cups grated Gruyères Cheese
1 cup ground Grits
2 tsp Butter
Salt and Black Pepper
½ cup Water
½ cup Milk

DIRECTIONS

- Select SAUTÉ at High and fry the bacon until crispy, for about 5 minutes. Set aside. Add grits, butter, milk, water, salt, and pepper to the pot and stir using a spoon. Seal the lid and select STEAM at High for 10 minutes.
- Once the timer has ended, do a quick pressure release again. Immediately add the cheddar cheese and give the pudding a good stir. Dish the cheesy grits into serving bowls and spoon over the crisped bacon.

## Poached Eggs with Feta and Tomatoes

**Ready in about: 10 minutes | Serves: 4 | Per serving: Calories 125; Carbs 8g; Fat 7g; Protein 6g**

INGREDIENTS

4 large Eggs
2 cups Water
2 large Cherry Tomatoes, halved crosswise
Salt and Black Pepper to taste
1 tsp chopped Fresh Herbs, of your choice
½ cup Feta cheese, crumbled
4 slices toasted Bread
DIRECTIONS
- Pour the water in and fit a trivet at the center of the pot. Grease the ramekins with the cooking spray and crack each egg into them. Place the ramekins on the trivet. Seal the lid, and select STEAM for 3 minutes at High.
- Do a quick pressure release. Remove ramekins onto a flat surface. In serving plates, toss the eggs in the ramekin over on each bread slice, top with the feta cheese and cherry tomatoes, and garnish with chopped herbs.

## Carrot & Pecan Muffins

*Ready in about:* **30 minutes | Serves: 8 | Per serving: Calories 265; Carbs 6g; Fat 25g; Protein 6g**

INGREDIENTS
¼ cup Coconut Oil
½ cup Milk
½ cup Pecans, chopped
1 tsp Apple Pie Spice
1 cup Carrots, shredded
3 Eggs
½ cup Pure & Organic Applesauce
1 cup ground Almonds
1 ½ cups Water
DIRECTIONS
- Pour the water into the Pressure cooker and lower the trivet. Place the coconut oil, milk, eggs, applesauce, almonds, and apple pie spice, in a large mixing bowl.
- Beat the mixture well with an electric mixer, until it becomes fluffy. Fold in the carrots and pecans. Pour the batter into 8 silicone muffin cups and arrange them on top of the trivet.
- Seal the lid, and cook on BEANS/CHILI mode at High pressure for 15 minutes. When it goes off, do a quick pressure release. Remove the muffins, and wait for a few minutes before serving.

## Kale, Tomato & Carrot Quiche

*Ready in about:* **30 minutes | Serves: 4 | Per serving: Calories 170; Carbs 7g; Fat 10g; Protein 13g**

INGREDIENTS
1 Carrot, shredded
1 Tomato, chopped
½ cup Kale, chopped
¼ cup Milk
¼ Onion, diced
½ Bell Pepper, diced
1 tsp Basil
A pinch of Pepper
¼ tsp Paprika
8 Eggs
1 ½ cups Water
DIRECTIONS
- Pour the water into your pressure cooker and lower the trivet. Place the eggs, milk, pepper, basil, and paprika, in a large bowl. Whisk until well combined and smooth.
- Add the veggies to the mixture and stir well to combine.
- Grease a baking dish with some cooking spray and pour in the egg and veggie into it. Place the baking dish on top of the trivet. Seal the lid, and cook on BEANS/CHILI at High pressure for 20 minutes.
- Do a natural pressure release, for about 10 minutes. Remove quiche from the cooker, and serve!

## Easy Softboiled Eggs

*Ready in about:* **10 minutes | Serves: 8 | Per serving: Calories 130; Carbs 1g; Fat 9g; Protein 9g**

INGREDIENTS
8 Eggs
1 cup of Water
DIRECTIONS
- Pour the water into the pressure cooker and add in the eggs. Seal the lid, and cook on BEANS/CHILI mode for 5 minutes at High pressure.
- When ready, do a quick pressure release by moving the handle from Prepare an ice bath and drop the eggs in, to ease the peeling.

## Cheese and Thyme Cremini Oats

*Ready in about:* **20 minutes | Serves: 4 | Per Serving: Calories 266; Carbs 31g; Fat 12g; Protein 9g**

INGREDIENTS
8 ounces Cremini Mushrooms, sliced
2 cups Chicken Broth
½ Onion, diced
2 tbsp Butter
1 cup Steel-Cut Oats
½ cup Cheddar Cheese, grated
2 sprigs Thyme
½ cup Water
1 Garlic Clove, minced
Salt and Pepper to taste
DIRECTIONS
- On SAUTÉ mode at High, melt the butter and stir-fry onion and mushrooms for 3 minutes, until soft. Add garlic and cook for 1 minute. Stir in oats and cook for another minute.
- Pour in water, broth, oats, and mix in thyme sprigs. Season with salt and pepper. Seal the lid, and set on BEANS/CHILI for 20 minutes. Quick release the pressure. Remove to serving bowls and sprinkle with grated cheddar.

## Herby Pork Breakfast Biscuits

*Ready in about:* **30 minutes | Serves: 8 | Per serving: Calories 445; Carbs 31g; Fat 22g; Protein 26g**

INGREDIENTS
1 ½ pounds Ground Pork
8 Biscuits
¾ cup Apple Cider
1 ½ cups Milk

½ cup Flour
3 tsp Butter
½ cup Onions, chopped
1 tsp Garlic, minced
1 tsp Thyme
1 tsp Rosemary
Salt and Pepper, to taste

DIRECTIONS
- Melt butter SAUTÉ mode at High, add the pork and cook until browned. Add onions and garlic and cook for another 1-2 minutes, until soft. Stir in the cider, thyme, and rosemary. Seal the lid and cook for 20 minutes on BEANS/CHILI mode at High.
- When ready, release the pressure quickly. Whisk together the flour and milk, and pour in over the pork. Seal the lid. Cook on BEANS/CHILI at High pressure for 5 minutes. Release the pressure quickly, and serve over biscuits.

## Whole Hog Omelet

Ready in about: **40 minutes** | Serves: **6** | Per serving: **Calories 489; Carbs 38g; Fat 2g; Protein 32g**

INGREDIENTS
6 Eggs, beaten
1 cup Cheddar Cheese, shredded
½ cup Ham, diced
1 cup ground Sausage
4 Bacon Slices, cooked and crumbled
½ cup Milk
2 Green Onions, chopped
Salt and Pepper, to taste
1 ½ cups Water

DIRECTIONS
- Whisk all the ingredients together, in a bowl. Transfer to a baking dish. Pour 1 ½ cups water in your pressure cooker and lower the trivet. Place the dish on top of the trivet.
- Seal the lid and cook for 20 minutes on BEANS/CHILI at High. When done, do a quick release.

## Onion and Tomato Eggs

Ready in about: **20 minutes** | Serves: **2** | Per serving: **Calories 380; Carbs 13g; Fat 16g; Protein 15g**

INGREDIENTS
4 Eggs
1 Tomato, chopped
1 Red Onion, diced
¼ tsp Garlic Powder
A pinch of Cayenne Pepper
A pinch of Black Pepper
1 ½ cups Water

DIRECTIONS
- Pour the water into the pressure cooker and lower the trivet. Grease a baking dish with some cooking spray. Beat the eggs along with the garlic powder, cayenne, and black pepper.
- Add tomatoes and onions; stir to combine. Pour the mixture into the greased baking dish. Place the baking dish on top of the trivet and seal the lid.
- Cook BEANS/CHILI at High pressure for 8 minutes. After the beep, do a quick pressure release. Remove the baking dish from the pot, and serve.

## Egg and Beef Green Casserole

Ready in about: **40 minutes** | Serves: **4** | Per serving: **Calories 422; Carbs 13g; Fat 30g; Protein 24g**

INGREDIENTS
8 ounces Ground Beef
6 Eggs, beaten
¾ cup Leeks, Sliced
¾ cup Kale, chopped
1 Sweet Potato, peeled and shredded
1 Garlic Clove, minced
1 tbsp Olive Oil
A pinch of Pepper
1 ½ cups Water
Cooking spray, to grease

DIRECTIONS
- Grease a baking dish with cooking spray and set aside. Melt the oil on SAUTÉ at High. Add the leeks and cook for about 2 minutes.
- Add the garlic and cook for about 30 seconds. Add the beef and cook for a few more minutes, until browned. Transfer to a bowl. Add the remaining ingredients and stir well to combine. Pour the water and lower the trivet.
- Pour the egg and beef mixture into the greased baking dish and place on top of the trivet. Seal the lid, select BEANS/CHILI mode for 25 minutes at High. Release the pressure quickly. Serve and enjoy!

## Bell Pepper & Onion Frittata

Ready in about: **15 minutes** | Serves: **2** | Per serving: **Calories 241; Carbs 6g; Fat 16g; Protein 15g**

INGREDIENTS
3 Eggs
¼ cup Bell Pepper, diced
¼ cup Onion, diced
2 tbsp Milk
¼ tsp Garlic Powder
A pinch of Turmeric Powder
1 ½ cups Water

DIRECTIONS
- Pour water into the pressure cooker and lower the trivet. Grease a small baking dish with cooking spry. In a bowl, beat eggs along with milk, turmeric, and garlic powder.
- Add onions and bell peppers and stir well to combine. Pour the mixture into the greased baking dish and place it on top of the trivet. Seal the lid, select BEANS/CHILI and cook for 8 minutes at High. After the timer goes off, release the pressure quickly. Serve and enjoy!

## Deliciuos Coconut Pancake

Ready in about: **55 minutes** | Serves: **4** | Per serving: **Calories 358; Carbs 39g; Fat 15g; Protein 16g**

INGREDIENTS
1 cup Coconut Flour
1 tsp Coconut Extract
2 tbsp Honey
2 Eggs

1 ½ cups Coconut Milk
1 cup ground Almonds
½ tsp Baking Soda
Cooking spray, for greasing

DIRECTIONS
- Whisk together eggs and milk, in a bowl. Stir the other ingredients gradually, while constantly whisking. Spray the inner pot of the pressure cooker with some cooking spray and pour the batter inside.
- Cook on BEANS/CHILI for 20 minutes at High. Do a quick pressure release. Serve with castor sugar.

## Sweet Potato Tomato Frittata

Ready in about: **28 minutes** | Serves: **4** | Per serving: **Calories 189; Carbs 11g; Fat 11g; Protein 10g**

INGREDIENTS
6 Large Eggs, beaten
1 Tomato, chopped
¼ cup Almond Milk
1 tbsp Tomato Paste
1 tbsp Olive Oil
2 tbsp Coconut Flour
1 ½ cups Water
5 tbsp Onion, chopped
1 tsp Garlic Clove, minced
4 ounces Sweet Potatoes, shredded

DIRECTIONS
- Beat eggs, tomato, milk, and oil in a bowl until mixed. Add flour, onion, garlic, and potatoes and stir. Pour the egg mixture into a greased baking dish.
- Add a trivet in the Pressure cooker and pour the water in. Lay the baking dish onto the trivet and select BEANS/CHILI mode. Adjust the time to 18 minutes at High pressure.
- When ready, do a quick pressure release by turning the valve to "open" position.

## Cherry and Dark Chocolate Oatmeal

Ready in about: **15 minutes** | Serves: **4** | Per serving: **Calories 283; Carbs 54g; Fat 6g; Protein 5g**

INGREDIENTS
3 ½ cups Water
cup Cane Sugar
1 cup Steel-Cut Oats
3 tbsp Dark Chocolate Chips
1 cup Frozen Cherries, pitted
A pinch of Sea Salt

DIRECTIONS
- Put all ingredients, except the chocolate, in your pressure cooker. Stir well to combine, seal the lid, and set to BEANS/CHILI for 12 minutes at High.
- Do a quick pressure release, stir in chocolate chips, and serve.

## Lemon and Chocolate Bread Pudding

Ready in about: **45 minutes** | Serves: **4** | Per serving: **Calories 467; Carbs 51g; Fat 14g; Protein 12g**

INGREDIENTS

3 ½ cups Bread, cubed
¾ cup Heavy Cream
1 tsp Butter, melted
2 tbsp Lemon Juice
Zest of 1 Lemon
3 Eggs
3 ounces Chocolate, chopped
½ cup Milk
¼ cup plus 1 tbsp Sugar
2 cups Water
1 tsp Almond Extract
A pinch of Salt

DIRECTIONS
- Beat the eggs along with ¼ cup sugar, in a bowl. Stir in cream, lemon juice, zest, extract, milk, and salt. Soak the bread for 5 minutes. Stir in the chocolate.
- Pour the water in your pressure cooker and add a trivet. Lightly grease a baking dish with melted butter. Pour in the batter. Sprinkle the remaining sugar on top. Lower the baking dish on the trivet.
- Seal the lid and cook on BEANS/CHILI at High pressure for 18 minutes. Do a quick pressure release.

## Pear-Coconut Porridge with Walnuts

Ready in about: **8 minutes** | Serve: **1** | Per serving: **Calories 568; Carbs 38g; Fat 48g; Protein 9g**

INGREDIENTS
½ cup ground Walnuts
1 ounce Coconut Flakes
1 Pear, diced
½ cup Coconut Milk

DIRECTIONS
- Place all ingredients in your pressure cooker and stir well to combine. Seal the lid, and cook on BEANS/CHILI for 3 minutes at High. Do a quick pressure release, and serve in a bowl.

## Crock Pot Egg Bake

Unusual taste with simple products! You'll be happy with this receipt!

Prep time: **15 minutes** Cooking time: **8 hours** Servings: **8**

INGREDIENTS:
One pack tater tots
Diced Canadian bacon
2 small onions
Cheddar cheese
12 chicken eggs
Parmesan
1 cup milk
4 tbsp simple flour
1 tsp salt
Pepper

DIRECTIONS:
- Cover the bottom of the crockpot with cooking spray or just oil. Preheat Slow Cooker to 120-130 degrees.
- Divide all the dry ingredients into three parts. Place the tots, sliced bacon, onion and cheeses. Repeat all the layers for three times.

- In a separate mixing bowl, combine the eggs, milk, pepper and salt. Pour the egg mixture over the other ingredients.
- Place the dish into your Slow Cooker for nine hours on LOW mode.

**Nutrition: Calories: 164 Fat: 9g Carbohydrates: 9g Protein: 19g**

## Delicious Banana Bread

So healthy and light! This banana bread will fill you with energy and good mood!

**Prep time: 15 minutes Cooking time: 4 hours**
**Servings: 3**

INGREDIENTS:
Two chicken eggs
Half cup softened butter
One cup sugar
Two cups plain flour
Half teaspoon baking soda
Salt
Three medium bananas

DIRECTIONS:
- First, cover with cooking spray and preheat your Slow Cooker. Combine eggs with sugar and butter. Stir well.
- Mix in baking soda and baking powder.
- Peel and mash bananas, mix them with flour and combine with eggs. Pour the dough into cooking dish and place it into Slow Cooker.
- Cook on LOW temperature regimes for 3-4 hours.
- When ready, remove the bread with a knife and enjoy your breakfast! To serve use fresh bananas, apples or berries to your taste.

**Nutrition: Calories: 130 Fat: 8g Carbohydrates: 5g Protein: 7g**

## Drinkable Vanilla Yogurt

Yes, this is long enough to cook, but it is cheaper and healthier than store-bought! Moreover, it is totally worth it!

**Prep time: 5 minutes Cooking time: 18 hours**
**Servings: 8**

INGREDIENTS:
Half gallon organic milk
Half cup organic yogurt (NOTE: with live cultures)
Maple syrup
Pure vanilla extract
Bananas or berries (optional)

DIRECTIONS:
- Pour the milk into your Slow Cooker and leave to cook for three hours on LOW setting.
- When the mixture reaches 150-170 degrees, take it out and allow to rest for three hours (until it is 110 degrees).
- Ladle milk from the Slow Cooker to another mixing bowl and add in the yogurt. Place it back to Slow Cooker and stir well.
- Do not turn it on, just cover with a large blanket and leave for 10-12 hours.
- You can remove a little part of yogurt and save it as a starter for your next batch. Add the vanilla extract or maple syrup.
- Serve with your favorite fruits or berries.

**Nutrition: Calories: 150 Fat: 7g Carbohydrates: 3g Protein: 8g**

## Chocolate Banana Bread

Healthy and delicious – all in one!

**Prep time: 15 minutes Cooking time: 5 hours**
**Servings: 8**

INGREDIENTS:
Four medium bananas
One cup brown sugar
Two chicken eggs
Melted butter
Half cup Greek yogurt
Vanilla extract
Two cup plain flour
One tsp. baking powder
Salt
Cinnamon
One chocolate chunk

DIRECTIONS:
- Preheat Slow Cooker to 180 degrees. Peel and mash bananas well.
- Add in sugar, yogurt, butter, eggs and vanilla.
- Mix up flour with baking powder, soda, salt and cinnamon. Sift flour mix into banana mixture. Stir gently.
- Fold in the chocolate.
- Coat the Slow Cooker dish with olive oil and pour the dough in.
- Cook for 4-5 hours on LOW temperature mode, until the bread is ruddy.

**Nutrition: Calories: 210 Fat: 4g Carbohydrates: 5g Protein: 8g**

## Banana Bread with Granola

Easy and fast enough to make! You will like this delicious banana bread!

**Prep time: 15 minutes Cooking time: 3 hours**
**Servings: 5**

INGREDIENTS:
Three cup granola
One cup banana chips
One cup salted peanuts
Half cup quinoa (uncooked)
Brown sugar
Cinnamon
Salt
6 tbsp. butter
Half cup peanut butter
2 tbsp. honey
One ripe banana
2 tbsp. vanilla extract

DIRECTIONS:
- Preheat the Slow Cooker to 200 degrees. Cover the Slow Cooker dish with baking sheets.
- In a big bowl, combine banana oats, granola, peanuts, quinoa, sugar and salt. In a pan, heat butter and peanut butter, add honey. Melt for 4 minutes.
- After butter and honey melted, stir in vanilla and banana.

- Pour the granola mixture in the baking dish and place it into the Slow Cooker. Cook for 4-5 hours on HIGH mode.

**Nutrition: Calories: 180 Fat: 4g Carbohydrates: 5g Protein: 6g**

## Treacle Sponge with Honey

Taste the perfect duo and it could be your favorite receipt!

**Prep time: 30 minutes Cooking time: 3 hours Servings: 4**

INGREDIENTS:
One cup unsalted butter
3 tbsp. honey
1 tbsp. white breadcrumbs (fresh)
One cup sugar
One lemon zest
3 large chicken eggs
Two cup flour
2 tbsp. milk
Clotted cream (to serve)
Little brandy splash (optional)

DIRECTIONS:
- Grease your Slow Cooker dish heavily and preheat it. In a medium bowl, mix the breadcrumbs with the honey.
- Melt butter and beat it with lemon zest and sugar, until fluffy and light. Sift in the flour slowly.
- Add the milk and stir well.
- Spoon the mixture into the Slow Cooker dish. Cook for several hours on LOW mode. Serve with honey or clotted cream.

**Nutrition: Calories: 200 Fat: 10g Carbohydrates: 20g Protein: 10g**

## Sticky Pecan Buns with Maple

Easy and tasty to make!

**Prep time: 15 minutes Cooking time: 5 hours Servings: 12**

INGREDIENTS:
6 tbsp. milk (nonfat)
4 tbsp. maple syrup
Half tbsp. melted butter
1 tsp. vanilla extract
Salt
2 tbsp. yeast
Two cup flour (whole wheat)
Chopped pecans
Ground cinnamon

DIRECTIONS:
- Lightly coat the inside of your Slow Cooker with non-stick cooking spray. For dough, combine milk, vanilla butter and maple syrup. Mix well.
- Microwave the mixture until warm and add the yeast. Let sit for 15 minutes. Sift in the flour and mix in until the dough is no more sticky.
- For filling, mix together the maple syrup and cinnamon.
- Roll out the dough and brush it with the maple filling. Roll up into a log and slice into 10-12 parts. Place the small rolls into the Slow Cooker.

- Prepare the caramel sauce: combine milk, butter and syrup. Pour the sauce into the Slow Cooker. Bake for 2 hours on HIGH mode.

**Nutrition: Calories: 230 Fat: 5g Carbohydrates: 29g Protein: 42g**

## Village Pie

Homemade pie tastes like in childhood and brings health and happiness!

**Prep time: 30 minutes Cooking time: 2 hours Servings: 10**

INGREDIENTS:
Three tbsp. olive oil
Beef mince
Two small onions
Three carrots
Three celery sticks
Two garlic gloves
Three tbsp. flour
Thyme
Five big potatoes
One tbsp. butter
Cheddar
Nutmeg

DIRECTIONS:
- In a large saucepan, fry the beef mince until browned.
- Finely chop all the vegetables and add to the mince. Cook on a gentle temperature until soft. Add the garlic, tomatoes and flour. Cook for several minutes.
- For the mash, boil potatoes until tender and mash with the milk and three quarters of the cheese. Prepare the Slow Cooker6 spray the inside with the cooking spray.
- Place the meat into the dish and cover with the mash.
- Sprinkle over the remaining cheese and cook on HIGH for 2-3 hours.

**Nutrition: Calories: 500 Fat: 25g Carbohydrates: 29g Protein: 19g**

## Crunchy Toast with Cinnamon

Cinnamon toast – great choice for cold mornings and hot tea!

**Prep time: 15 minutes Cooking time: 5 hours Servings: 8**

INGREDIENTS:
3chicken eggs
Half cup milk
2 tsp cinnamon
Nutmeg
Salt
2 cups cornflakes
Sliced almonds
2 tbsp butter
8 bread slices

DIRECTIONS:
- Cover your cooking form with olive oil. Preheat your Slow Cooker to 200 degrees.
- In a large bowl, whisk together the eggs, milk, nutmeg, cinnamon, salt. Set aside. Melt the butter in a small bowl.
- Dip each bread slice into butter and egg mixture.

- Layer the bread slices in the Slow Cooker and cook for 2-3 hours on LOW temperatures.

**Nutrition: Calories: 345 Fat: 3g Carbohydrates: 7g Protein: 9g**

## Pumpkin Creamy Muffins

Pumpkin is favorite for every meal – check it out in your breakfast!

**Prep time: 15 minutes Cooking time: 6 hours Servings: 24**

INGREDIENTS:
Cream cheese
Three chicken eggs
Two cups sugar
Two cups flour
2tbsp pecans
3tbsp butter
Cinnamon
Salt
2tsp baking powder
1 small pumpkin
3tbsp vegetable oil
Vanilla extract

DIRECTIONS:
- Prepare for cooking: heat your slow cooker and coat muffin forms with olive oil or melted butter. In a separate bowl, mix one egg, cream cheese, three tablespoons sugar, half cup flour, butter, cinnamon and pecans. Set this bowl aside.
- Take another large bowl and combine the remaining sugar, salt, flour, soda, baking powder in a large bowl.
- Beat the remaining eggs with eggs, vanilla and oil.
- Combine both mixtures together and divide the batter on two parts.
- Divide the first part of the batter between forms evenly, place the cream in the center of each one, then fill with a second part of the batter.
- Place into the Slow Cooker and cook for 6 hours on LOW temperatures.

**Nutrition: Calories: 380 Fat: 4g Carbohydrates: 14g Protein: 12g**

## Egg Souffle with Cheese

Make your morning a little bit French with this amazing meal!

**Prep time: 15 minutes Cooking time: 4 hours Servings: 10**

INGREDIENTS:
Six chicken eggs
1 tsp dry mustard
Salt
Half tsp ground pepper
Four cups milk
12 slice sandwich bread
One large red bell pepper
Cheddar cheese

DIRECTIONS:
- Beat eggs and mix them with mustard, pepper, salt and milk.
- Cover the Slow Cooker dish with anti-sticking cooking spray and preheat to 180 degrees. Cut red pepper into small pieces.
- Stir the pepper with bread mixture and add cheese.
- Pour the bread mixture into the Slow Cooker and cook on HIGH temperatures for 4 hours. Before cutting and serving leave to cool for 10 minutes.

**Nutrition: Calories: 234 Fat: 4g Carbohydrates: 5g Protein: 8g**

## Onion Tart

Unusual, but very tasty and healthy start to your morning!

**Prep time: 15 minutes Cooking time: 4 hours Servings: 8**

INGREDIENTS:
Green onions
2 tbsp lemon juice
Half cup red wine
Salt
Black pepper (fresh-ground)
2 tbsp olive oil
1tsp thyme (fresh leaves)
Manchego cheese
2clove garlic
Lemon zest to taste

DIRECTIONS:
- Heat your Slow Cooker to 200 degrees.
- Pour the water into the Slow Cooker dish, add one tablespoon to boil. Take green onions and add them to the water, boil for 2-3 minutes.
- Remove the onions from the Slow Cooker and cut.
- In a large pan, combine the onions, lemon juice, olive oil, pepper and red wine. Cook until caramelized.
- Combine the Manchego cheese, garlic and lemon zest. Spread on the bottom of the Slow Cooker. Add the onions as a top and cook on LOW temperatures for 4 hours.

**Nutrition: Calories: 330 Fat: 5g Carbohydrates: 22g Protein: 9g**

## Crunchy Cake with Coffee

Try this one with a cup of hot coffee and wake up for a new day!

**Prep time: 15 minutes Cooking time: 5 hours Servings: 8**

INGREDIENTS:
Two cup plain flour
Half cup milk (whole)
One teaspoon baking powder
Salt
Half cup unsalted butter
Salt
Sugar
Two chicken eggs
Half teaspoon vanilla extract
Half teaspoon lemon extract

DIRECTIONS:
- Heat the Slow Cooker to 200 degrees. Coat the Slow Cooker dish with butter and dust with flour. In a large baking bowl, mix the sifted cake flour, salt, baking powder and cinnamon.
- Bat in utter, the sugar and the eggs.

- Add vanilla, lemon extract, and beat with milk on medium speed until it is very blended. Pour the batter into prepared Slow Cooker and bake for 5 hours on MEDIUM temperatures.

**Nutrition: Calories: 380 Fat: 4g Carbohydrates: 12g Protein: 8g**

## Eggplant Parmesan in Slow Cooker

Perfect receipt for the spring season – try and you will love this!

⏱ **Prep time: 20 minutes Cooking time: 8 hours Servings: 12**

INGREDIENTS:
Three eggplants
Salt
3 large chicken eggs
Half cup milk
One cup breadcrumbs (gluten-free)
Parmesan cheese
Four cups marinara sauce
Mozzarella cheese

DIRECTIONS:
- Prepare the eggplant, peel and cut into thin rounds. Rinse the eggplant rounds, add salt and pat dry.
- Preheat Slow Cooker before using.
- Pour the marinara sauce in the bottom of Slow Cooker. In a shallow bowl, whisk together milk and the eggs.
- In another bowl, stir together the breadcrumbs and Parmesan cheese.
- Dip the eggplant rounds firstly in the egg mixture and secondly in the breadcrumbs. Layer the eggplant slices in the Slow Cooker.
- Pour with the sauce and cook on LOW temperature for 8 hours.

**Nutrition: Calories: 158 Fat: 10g Carbohydrates: 20g Protein: 26g**

## Golden Veggie Pie

Another vegetarian pie – and another healthy receipt for your daily start!

⏱ **Prep time: 15 minutes Cooking time: 5 hours Servings: 8**

INGREDIENTS:
Butter
Two onions
Four carrots
Celery (1 head)
Four garlic gloves
Chestnut mushrooms
Thyme
Dried green lentil
Half cup milk
Cheddar cheese
Cup red wine (optional)
3 tbsp. tomato puree

DIRECTIONS:
- Clean and dice the vegetables.
- For the sauce: melt the butter on a pan and fry carrots, onions, celery and garlic until mild. Add the mushrooms and cook for another 5 minutes.
- Add herbs and lentils.
- Pour over the wine and simmer for around 50 minutes. Take off heat and mix in the tomato puree.
- Preheat your Slow Cooker and add the diced potatoes. Cover with water and cook for one hour. Remove water and combine the potatoes with the pan mix.
- Place back to the Slow Cooker and cook for 2-3 hours on HIGH temperatures.

**Nutrition: Calories: 168 Fat: 4g Carbohydrates: 6g Protein: 8g**

## Muscovado Cheesecake for Slow Cooker

Unusual cheesecake with muscavado will amuse you with its perfect taste!

⏱ **Prep time: 30 minutes Cooking time: 2 hours Servings: 10**

INGREDIENTS:
Melted butter
3-4 oat biscuits
6 tbsp. hazelnuts (blanched)
One cup muscovado sugar
4 tbsp milk (full-fat)
Cream cheese
2tbsp flour (plain)
1 tsp vanilla extract
3large chicken eggs
1tbsp Frangelico (optional)
2 tsp corn flour
2tbsp golden sugar
One cup blackberries

DIRECTIONS:
- Prepare the Slow Cooker: grease the inside with a foil or parchment.
- Roll the foil in circle and place it on the bottom of the dish (as a trivet for the future cheesecake). Put the biscuits into a food processor and make fine crumbs.
- Add the butter and blend well. Tip the mix into the tin and chill for 10-20 minutes. In a pan, combine the muscovado and milk, then leave to cool.
- In another bowl, beat the cream cheese, vanilla, eggs and flour and stir until smooth. Pour everything into the tin and place it inti Slow Cooker.
- Cook for 2 hours on HIGH. Cool before serving.

**Nutrition: Calories: 613 Fat: 29g Carbohydrates: 47g Protein: 10g**

## Veggie Breakfast Casserole

Simple casserole for breakfast – and one of the favorite Slow Cooker meals.

⏱ **Prep time: 15 minutes Cooking time: 5 hours Servings: 8**

INGREDIENTS:
6 big potatoes
Bacon
1 small onion (diced)
Cheddar Cheese (Shredded)

Red Bell pepper (diced)
10-12 chicken eggs
One cup milk

DIRECTIONS:
- Start preheating the Slow Cooker.
- Spray the bottom of the Slow Cooker with special cooking spray to avoid sticking.
- Cut bacon into small stripes and cook (or buy already dried bacon to fasten the process). Place three potatoes on the bottom of the Slow Cooker.
- Layer your bacon and the other INGREDIENTSpeppers, cheese, onions, and remaining potatoes. In another medium bowl, mix eggs with mil. Pour this mixture over the layered ingredients.
- Salt and pepper.
- Cook on LOW temperature for 4 hours.

**Nutrition: Calories: 198 Fat: 5g Carbohydrates: 8g Protein: 12g**

## Nutella French Toast

Nutella and bananas – what a perfect duo for your daily start!

Prep time: 15 minutes Cooking time: 2 hours
Servings: 8

INGREDIENTS:
One loaf bread
6 large eggs
Two cups vanilla almond milk
Cinnamon
Vanilla extract
2 tbsp. Nutella
Salt
1 tbsp butter
Four bananas
1tbsp brown sugar

DIRECTIONS:
- Cover the bottom of Slow Cooker with olive oil or baking spray. Cut the bread into cubes and place it into the Slow Cooker.
- Combine the eggs with milk.
- Add vanilla extract, cinnamon, salt and Nutella. Pour the mixture over the bread and mix well. Cook on HIGH temperature for 2 hours.
- When it is almost ready, slice the bananas and add to a bowl.

**Nutrition: Calories: 124 Fat: 6g Carbohydrates: 8g Protein: 9g**

## Soufflé with Scallions and Dill

Light and healthy breakfast!

Prep time: 15 minutes Cooking time: 4 hours
Servings: 6

INGREDIENTS:
One red bell pepper
Half cup milk
Six table spoons flour
Three tablespoons crumbs
Five tablespoons butter
Salt
Five egg yolks
Seven egg whites
Two large scallions
Two tablespoons dill (chopped)
Half tablespoon pepper (freshly ground)

DIRECTIONS:
- Roast the pepper directly over an open flame. Turn it until blistered on all sides. Preheat your Slow Cooker to 100-130 degrees.
- Put the peppers into the Slow Cooker dish and leave for 20-30 minutes to steam. When ready, remove skin, stem and seeds. Chop the pepper.
- Coat your Slow Cooker dish with a cooking spray and whisk milk and butter with flour. In another medium bowl mix the egg yolks and add them to flour mixture.
- Then, mix the egg whites just a little and mix with other products. Bake for 2-3 hours on LOW and garnish with dill.

**Nutrition: Calories: 210 Fat: 4g Carbohydrates: 5g Protein: 8g**

## Cranberry Apple Oatmeal

Cranberries and apple – the real way to make the oatmeal very delicious!

Prep time: 15 minutes Cooking time: 5 hours
Servings: 8

INGREDIENTS:
Four cups water
2 cups oats
Half cup dried cranberries
Two big apples
Half cup brown sugar
Fresh cranberries
2tbsp butter
Cinnamon
Salt

DIRECTIONS:
- Grease your Slow Cooker with a cooking spray. Preheat. Peel and core the apples. Dice into small cubes.
- Add the apples in the Slow Cooker and cover with the water. Add other ingredients into the dish.
- Cook on HIGH temperature for 8 hours (or on LOW for 3). Serve with milk and fresh cranberries.

**Nutrition: Calories: 190 Fat: 4g Carbohydrates: 9g Protein: 9g**

## Chicken Casserole

Chicken casserole will give you energy to star your day!

Prep time: 10 minutes Cooking time: 4-7 hours
Servings: 4

INGREDIENTS:
Butter
Half tbsp olive oil
One large onion
Two chicken thigh fillets
Three garlic gloves
Six baby potatoes
Two carrots
Mushrooms (any)
Chicken broth
2 tsp Dijon mustard

DIRECTIONS:

- In a frying pan, combine butter and olive oil. Heat.
- Dice onions and add to pan for 10 minutes to caramelize. Toss the chicken in the mix of flour, salt and pepper.
- Add the chicken and garlic to pen and fry for 5 minutes.
- Transfer the pan mixture to the Slow Cooker and add the remaining ingredients. Stir well and cook on LOW temperature for 7 hours.
- Serve with Dijon mustard.

**Nutrition: Calories: 382 Fat: 9g Carbohydrates: 30g Protein: 4g**

## Blueberry and Corn Muffins

Blueberry muffins – perfect for tea with your family!

⏱ **Prep time: 15 minutes Cooking time: 5 hours Servings: 12**

INGREDIENTS:
One cup cornmeal
One cup flour
2tsp baking powder
Granulated sugar
One chicken egg
One cup buttermilk
6 tbsp butter
One cup blueberries
One cup corn kernels (fresh)

DIRECTIONS:
- Preheat your Slow Cooker to approximately 200 degrees. Grease the muffin forms with olive oil.
- Mix flour, cornmeal, sugar, salt and baking powder.
- In another large bowl mix egg, butter, buttermilk, and stir until combined well. Fold in corn and blueberries.
- Combine egg-mixture with flour mixture.
- Pour the dough into muffin forms and cook on HIGH for 5 hours.

**Nutrition: Calories: 315 Fat: 5g Carbohydrates: 12g Protein: 8g**

## Twisted Roll with Caramel and Pecan

Caramel and pecan will give you strengths to start your working day!

⏱ **Prep time: 15 minutes Cooking time: 4 hours Servings: 8**

INGREDIENTS:
Two tbsp. softened butter
Half cup brown sugar (dark)
Softened Cream Cheese
Toasted pecans
Ground cinnamon
Prepared pizza dough

DIRECTIONS:
- Butter the bottom and sides of your Slow Cooker. Sprinkle the bottom with 2-3 tablespoons sugar. In a separate bowl mix together butter and cream cheese until smooth.
- In another bowl, stir pecans, salt, remaining sugar and cinnamon.
- Roll the dough, spread it with the cream cheese and sprinkle with sugar.

- Cut the dough into 5-6 even strips. Twist each strip into a spiral. The ends of each strip pinch together. Complete making big twisted roll.
- Place the roll into the Slow Cooker and cook on LOW for 4 hours.
- Before serving, cover with caramel glaze. Mix up the brown sugar (three tablespoons), butter and three tablespoons cream and boil in a small pan.

**Nutrition: Calories: 349 Fat: 7g Carbohydrates: 32g Protein: 9g**

## Ginger and Pineapple Oatmeal

A little spicy, but very energetic meal for your morning tea!

⏱ **Prep time: 15 minutes Cooking time: 4-5 hours Servings: 4**

INGREDIENTS:
Two cups rolled oats
Two cups chopped pineapple (or one half)
Ginger
One cup chopped walnuts
Salt
Two cups milk (whole)
Maple syrup (to taste)
2 chicken eggs
2 tsp vanilla extract

DIRECTIONS:
- Preheat the Slow Cooker to 200 degrees.
- Meanwhile, stir pineapple, oats, ginger, walnuts, and salt in a large bowl. Divide the oat mixture among four ramekins.
- In another bowl, whisk all another ingredients.
- Pour the milk and syrup mixture among the ramekins.
- Place the ramekins into the Slow Cooker and bake on HIGH temperatures for 4-5 hours. To serve, add the extra maple syrup on the side.

**Nutrition: Calories: 440 Fat: 4g Carbohydrates: 13g Protein: 10g**

## Country French Toast with Ham

Toast with ham and maple syrup – unusual taste for an unusual morning!

⏱ **Prep time: 15 minutes Cooking time: 5 hours Servings: 6-8**

INGREDIENTS:
4 large chicken eggs
2 tsp vanilla extract (pure)
Half teaspoon nutmeg (ground)
Pure maple syrup
Salt
Butter (for griddle)
One cup milk
One cup cream
8 slices ham
8 slices toast bread

DIRECTIONS:
- Start with preheating your Slow Cooker over medium temperatures.. Mix up milk, eggs, cream, and maple syrup.
- Stir until combined well. Add nutmeg and vanilla to the eggs mixture, and some salt to taste.

- Cover the Slow Cooker bottom with some butter or special baking spray. Place the ham slices on the bottom and cover with the bread.
- Cook for 2 hours on LOW temperatures.
- To serve slice the French toast into medium portions and add maple syrup alongside.

**Nutrition: Calories: 500 Fat: 7g Carbohydrates: 5g Protein: 22g**

## Candid Orange Granola

The delicious granola with oranges will wake you up!

⌀ Prep time: 15 minutes Cooking time: 2 hours
Servings: 4

INGREDIENTS:
Four big oranges
Three cup sugar
Two cups granola
Yogurt (plain)
Dark chopped chocolate

DIRECTIONS:
- Take off the peel from the oranges and cut half of it into small strips.
- Preheat your Slow Cooker and fill with water. Simmer the orange strips for 30 minutes. Add sugar and boil until it dissolved. Then take the orange strips off.
- Chop remaining orange strips and mix them with almond granola. Boil for 2-3 hours on HIGH temperatures until ready.
- Serve with finely chopped chocolate and plain yogurt. You can also add clementine segments, if you like.

**Nutrition: Calories: 223 Fat: 4g Carbohydrates: 9g Protein: 7g**

## Chocolate Rolls with Cherries

Chocolate with cherries – yes, you can eat this on your breakfast!

⌀ Prep time: 15 minutes Cooking time: 5 hours
Servings: 12

INGREDIENTS:
Butter (room temperature)
Active dry yeast
Half cup granulated sugar
3 chicken eggs
4 cups plain flour
Cinnamon
Two cup fresh cherries
5 tbsp. cherry preserves
One bar bittersweet chocolate

DIRECTIONS:
- Butter your Slow Cooker and start preheating it.
- In another bowl, stir together granulated sugar with milk. Add the yeast to your milk mixture and wait until foamy.
- Sift one cop flour into your milk and combine with electric mixer or kitchen combiner. Add egg, salt, butter and remaining flour and beat until combined.
- Place the dough in a warm place and wait until begins to rise. In a separate bowl, mix together cinnamon and brown sugar.
- Cut the dough into 12 pieces, form of each one a strip and roll it.

- Cover with cinnamon mixture and bake in Slow Cooker for 5-6 hours on LOW.

**Nutrition: Calories: 335 Fat: 8g Carbohydrates: 12g Protein: 12g**

## Tunisian Flavored Eggs

Egg with Tunisian flavors – add to your breakfast another spice taste!

⌀ Prep time: 15 minutes Cooking time: 5 hours
Servings: 4

INGREDIENTS:
2 tbsp butter
1 tsp harissa
Half cup Merguez sausage (chopped)
8 chicken eggs
Salt
8 tbsp milk yogurt (whole)
Fresh mint leaves
Black pepper (ground)

DIRECTIONS:
- Brush four cooking forms with butter or spray with cooking spray. Heat the sausage in a pan for 3-4 minutes to cook thoroughly.
- In a small bowl, whisk half teaspoon water, four teaspoons olive oil and harissa. Add 2 eggs into each bowl, spice with salt and pepper.
- Combine both mixtures together.
- Preheat your Slow Cooker and place the jars in it. Cook for 3 hours on LOW temperatures or 5 hours on HIGH.

**Nutrition: Calories: 450 Fat: 5g Carbohydrates: 22g Protein: 7g**

## Charlotte with Herbs

You can taste this with some herbal tea as well!

⌀ Prep time: 15 minutes Cooking time: 5 hours
Servings: 8-10

INGREDIENTS:
White bread
Salt
6 tbsp butter
One cup onion (chopped)
2 clove garlic
1 cup artichoke hearts (chopped)
1 cup fontina cheese
8 chicken eggs
Milk cream
5 tbsp. ricotta cheese
Half cup chopped parsley
Fresh parsley
Ground black pepper
3 tbsp. grated cheese

DIRECTIONS:
- Heat Slow Cooker to 200 degrees. Brush the cooking dish with butter.
- Place the bread slices over the bottom. Slightly overlap each slice.
- In a pan, heat the remaining butter; add the chopped onions and salt. Fry until lighty golden (around 10 minutes).

- Add the garlic for one more minute.
- Add Fontina and remove the pan from heat.
- In large bowl, whisk milk cream, ricotta eggs, herbs, salt and pepper. Pour this mixture over the bread.
- Place the cooking dish into Slow Cooker and cook for 4-6 hour on HIGH.

**Nutrition: Calories: 313 Fat: 6g Carbohydrates: 19g Protein:12**

## Tortilla with Cheese and Green olives

Love olives! This receipt is created for you!

⌓ Prep time: 15 minutes Cooking time: 5 hours
Servings: 8

INGREDIENTS:
Olive oil
One yellow onion
Salt
6-7 red potatoes
Half teaspoon ground pepper
8 chicken eggs
Half cup green olives (chopped)
Manchego cheese
DIRECTIONS:
- Preheat your Slow Cooker to 200 degrees.
- In a pan, heat 2 tablespoons oil, add chopped onion and salt. Cook until translucent and set aside. Into the same pan, add 2 tablespoons oil and half of potatoes. Cook for 10 minutes or until potatoes begins to soften.
- When ready, mix with onions, eggs and olives.
- Pour the mixture into the baking dish and top with cheese.
- Transfer the baking dish to Slow Cooker and bake on LOW until eggs are set.

**Nutrition: Calories: 423 Fat: 4g Carbohydrates: 23g Protein: 33g**

## Currant and Raspberry Pudding

Summer season is for berry puddings. This one – a must have to try!

⌓ Prep time: 15 minutes Cooking time: 5 hours
Servings: 12

INGREDIENTS:
One loaf bread
Unsalted butter
Red currants (fresh)
Raspberries (fresh)
3 chicken egg
2 egg yolks
Half cup sugar
Salt
1 tsp vanilla extract
One cup milk (whole)
DIRECTIONS:
- Preheat your Slow Cooker well.
- Cut the bread into slices and brush each one with butter.
- Place the bread slices in a baking dish. Overlap each slice slightly. Cover the bread with half of raspberries and currants.
- In another bowl, whisk the eggs, egg yolks, salt, vanilla, sugar and milk. Pour this mixture over the bread.

- Place the dish into Slow Cooker and bake for 2 hours on HIGH temperatures or 4-5 hours on LOW.

**Nutrition: Calories: 334 Fat: 6g Carbohydrates: 34g Protein: 9g**

## Broccoli Strata with Tomatoes and Cheddar

Love eggs with cheese? Add some broccoli for a delicious taste!

⌓ Prep time: 15 minutes Cooking time: 5 hours
Servings: 8

INGREDIENTS:
Butter
Four cups bread cubes
1-2 cups shredded Cheddar cheese
1 cup tomatoes
8 chicken eggs
1 cup broccoli florets (frozen)
1 tbsp parsley (fresh and chopped)
3 cups milk
Salt
Ground pepper
Ricotta cheese
1 tsp herbs de Provence
DIRECTIONS:
- Butter your baking dish and place the bread in it.
- Cover the bread with one cup Cheddar, diced tomatoes, broccoli and parsley. In a separate bowl, mix together milk, eggs, pepper and salt.
- Pour the egg mixture over the bread cubes, press gently.
- Cover with Ricotta cheese, remaining Cheddar and herbs de Provence sprinkles. Preheat Slow Cooker to 200 degrees.
- Place the cooking dish with bread inside and bake on LOW for 5-6 hours. Serve warm with fresh vegetables.

**Nutrition: Calories: 311 Fat: 4g Carbohydrates: 18g Protein: 14g**

## Slow Cooker Cake with Honey

Honey and vanilla – delicious and healthy way to start your day!

⌓ Prep time: 15 minutes Cooking time: 4 hours
Servings: 10

INGREDIENTS:
One cup butter
One cup sugar
Honey
5 large chicken eggs
2 tsp vanilla extract
One cup flour
1tsp baking powder
DIRECTIONS:
- Preheat the Slow Cooker to 200 degrees.
- Spray the baking dish with cooking spray or cover with butter.
- In a large bowl, beat the butter, honey and sugar with a mixer until fluffy and light. Beat in the eggs and vanilla extract.
- Sift the flour, add baking powder, and salt. Stir until smooth.

- Transfer the dough into the baking dish and prepare on HIGH temperatures for 4 hours. Cool for 15 minutes before serving.

Nutrition: Calories: 311 Fat: 4g Carbohydrates: 19g Protein: 43g

## Slow Cooker Quiche

Creamy, delicious and tasty.

*Prep time: 15 minutes Cooking time: 3-5 hours*
*Servings: 10*

INGREDIENTS:
2 roll-out pie crusts
9 large chicken eggs
One cup heavy milk cream
Mozzarella cheese (shredded and smoked)
One cup smoked ham (shredded) half teaspoon ground mustard
Half cup onion (diced)
One garlic clove
Broccoli florets

DIRECTIONS:
- Chop all the vegetables and ham.
- Place bell peppers, onions, and garlic into a skillet for 5 minutes to soften.
- Place out the pie crusts on the parchment. Overlap in the center, and you will get one piece of crust.
- Gently place your crust in the Slow Cooker, pressing the bottom and sides.
- In a separate bowl, whisk the eggs, ground mustard, cream and salt until frothy.
- Add the vegetables, cheese and ham to the eggs and pour this mixture over the crust. Cook on HIGH for 4 hours
- Cool for 10 minutes before cutting and serving.

Nutrition: Calories: 346 Fat: 13g Carbohydrates: 33g Protein: 45g

## Mashed Potatoes with Ricotta

Tasty and milky, full of energy for your daily start!

*Prep time: 15 minutes Cooking time: 5 hours*
*Servings: 8*

INGREDIENTS:
6-7 large yellow potatoes
2 tsp salt
Half cup milk (whole)
Ground black pepper
One cup Ricotta (fresh)

DIRECTIONS:
- Preheat the Slow Cooker.
- Peel the potatoes and cut them into one-inch cubes.
- Place the potatoes into the baking dish, add salt and cover with water.
- Transfer the cooking dish to Slow Cooker and cook on LOW for 4-5 hours until softened. When ready, mash the potatoes and stir in milk, ricotta, butter and pepper.
- Blend until all the ingredients are fully combined. Serve only hot.

Nutrition: Calories: 455 Fat: 6g Carbohydrates: 23g Protein: 9g

## Ricotta Cheesecake with Lemon

Cheesecake with lemon – sweet and unforgettable breakfast!

*Prep time: 15 minutes Cooking time: 3-4 hours*
*Servings: 10*

INGREDIENTS:
One cup cracker crumbs
4 tbsp butter
4 lemons
One cup sugar
4 tbsp cornstarch
Reduced-fat cream cheese
4 chicken eggs
Ricotta cheese (part-skim)
2 cups light cream
2 tsp vanilla extract

DIRECTIONS:
- Preheat your Slow Cooker to 150 degrees.
- In a baking form, combine cracker crumbs and butter. Firmly press to the bottom and bake for 1 hour on HIGH temperatures.
- Meanwhile, grate the peel from lemons and squeeze the juice. In a separate bowl, blend cornstarch and sugar.
- In a large bowl beat ricotta with cream cheese until smooth (use a kitchen mixer). Beat in the sugar mixture, eggs, light cream, vanilla and lemon juice and peel.
- Pour dough onto crust and bake for 2 more hours.
- To serve, use the center slices of lemon as a garnish.

Nutrition: Calories: 290 Fat: 4g Carbohydrates: 17g Protein: 9g

## Fritata with Goat Cheese and Ham

Cheese and ham – a perfect couple for your breakfast idea!

*Prep time: 15 minutes Cooking time: 5 hours*
*Servings: 8*

INGREDIENTS:
8 large chicken eggs
Half cup heavy cream
Chopped ham
Salt
Black pepper (freshly ground)
Asparagus (cut into two-inch pieces)
1 garlic clove
6 radishes
Goat cheese (crumbled)

DIRECTIONS:
- Preheat your Slow Cooker to 200 degrees.
- In a separate bowl, whisk the eggs, cream, ham with pepper and salt.
- In a skillet, melt butter and add asparagus. Simmer for 4 minutes (until crisp-tender) Add scallions, radishes, garlic and cook for another 4 minutes.
- Transfer the pan mixture into buttered baking dish and cover with eff mixture. Cover with goat cheese and cook in the Slow Cooker for 3-4 hours on HIGH. Serve as soon as ready.

Nutrition: Calories: 400 Fat: 18g Carbohydrates: 22g Protein: 33g

## Crumbled Gooseberry Flapjack

Another summer receipt for your good mood and healthy body!

**Prep time: 20 minutes Cooking time: 5 hours**
**Servings: 8**

INGREDIENTS:
5 large apples
Zest 1 lemon
Juice 1 lemon
Half cup golden caster sugar
1 cup gooseberry
2 tsp cornflour
Vanilla ice-cream or custard (to serve)

DIRECTIONS:
- Preheat the Slow Cooker to 140 degrees. In separate pan, melt the butter and syrup.
- Mix the dry ingredients and stir them into the butter mixture. Peel, core and dice apple to small cubes.
- Place the apples into a pan and add lemon juice. Stir in corn flour with the sugar. Stir in the gooseberries and lemon zest.
- Heat the Slow Cooker again and butter it.
- Place the dough in it and cook for 5 on LOW temperatures.

**Nutrition: Calories: 500 Fat: 17g Carbohydrates: 40g Protein: 8g**

## Cheesy Tater Tot

Try this delicious one – and it will be your favorite!

**Prep time: 15 minutes Cooking time: 5 hours**
**Servings: 8**

INGREDIENTS:
4 slices bacon (cooked)
5 breakfast sausages
2cups cheddar cheese
2 cups milk (whole)
3large chicken eggs
Half teaspoon onion powder
Half teaspoon black pepper
Pinch of salt
Pack tater tots (frozen)
Parsley (for garnish)

DIRECTIONS:
- In a large skillet, cook sausage over medium heat.
- Drain the sausages and layer them onto the buttered bottom of Slow Cooker dish. Cover the sausages with two cups of the cheese.
- In separate bowl, hand-whisk eggs with milk, onion powder, salt and pepper. Then pour gently over the cheese.
- Cover the upper layer with the frozen tater tots.
- Set your Slow Cooker to 200 degrees and bake on LOW for 4-5 hours.

**Nutrition: Calories: 435 Fat: 19g Carbohydrates: 33g Protein: 35g**

## Egg Casserole in Slow Cooker

Casserole for morning tea – energetic start for your day!

**Prep time: 15 minutes Cooking time: 5 hours**
**Servings: 8**

INGREDIENTS:
Butter
2 tbsp olive oil (extra virgin)
One cup cremini mushrooms (sliced)
12 croissants (mini)
Baby spinach
Half cup Gruyere cheese (grated)
8 large chicken eggs
Salt
Pepper
2cups whole milk

DIRECTIONS:
- Butter your baking dish.
- Cook the mushrooms on a buttered pan, until golden brown.
- Stuff the croissants with spinach and half-cup cheese. Transfer the croissants to the baking dish. Place the mushrooms into the baking dish among the croissants.
- In separate bowl, combine egg with milk and add pepper and salt. Pour this mixture over the croissants.
- Sprinkle with the remaining cheese and bake for 2 hours at LOW temperatures.

**Nutrition: Calories: 551 Fat: 33g Carbohydrates: 40g Protein: 7g**

## Corn Pudding with Cheese

Light pudding is perfect for any season and good for your health!

**Prep time: 15 minutes Cooking time: 5 hours**
**Servings: 8**

INGREDIENTS:
One cup milk (whole)
Pepper (freshly ground)
4 tbsp grits
Cheddar
3large chicken eggs
Half can creamed
corn Salt

DIRECTIONS:
- Preheat Slow Cooker to 200 degrees.
- Bring milk to a simmer in a small saucepan. Add grits and salt. Cook for 5-30 minutes until grits thicken.
- Meanwhile, using the food processor, combine the corn to puree. Mix the corn, 2 egg yolks, Cheddar into grits, add salt and pepper.
- In a separate bowl beat egg whites to stiff peaks with a mixer. Gently fold into egg mixture. Divide the dough among 8 ramekins and bake on HIGH in the Slow Cooker for 2-3 hours.

**Nutrition: Calories: 500 Fat: 19g Carbohydrates: 45g Protein: 40g**

## Spiced pears in chocolate sauce

You will definitely love cooking and tasting the delicious and ripe fruit in chocolate sauce

**Prep time: 10 minutes Cooking time: 50 minutes**
**Servings: 4**

INGREDIENTS:
Two cups brown sugar
One vanilla pod
One cinnamon stick
Anise star
Lemon (for strips)
4 cloves
Fresh root ginger
4 peers
One dark chocolate bar
Cup of milk
Vanilla ice cream (optionally) to serve

DIRECTIONS:
- Firstly, prepare the INGREDIENT Speel the pears, cut 2-3 strips of the lemon zest (you can use a potato peeler), peel and slice the ginger.
- Preheat your Slow Cooker.
- Put all the ingredients (except lemon zest and the ice cream) in a pan and fill it with water. Simmer in Slow Cooker on HIGH for 10 minutes to infuse.
- Drop the pears, put the pan back into Slow Cooker and stew for 30 minutes until soft.
- For the chocolate sauce, put the chocolate into a medium bowl, add milk and cinnamon, and stir until melted.
- To serve, take out the pears, dip them in sauce to cover with the chocolate. Serve each fruit with scoop of ice cream and a stripe of lemon zest.

**Nutrition: Calories: 500 Fat: 35g Carbohydrates: 45g Protein: 6g**

## Apple crumble cake

Tasty apple pie will be a perfect start for your perfect day! Taste it with your favorite juice or tea, you surelyl will like it!

**Prep time: 15 minutes Cooking time: 30 minutes Servings: 6**

INGREDIENTS:
6 big sweet apples
4-5 tbsp apricot or apple jam
One orange juice
One cup oats (porridge)
Half cup flour
1 tsp cinnamon
1 tbsp butter
Half cup muscovado sugar
1 tbsp honey

DIRECTIONS:
- Preheat Slow Cooker to 185 degrees.
- Peel and core the apples, slice them into small half-moons.
- Mix the apple slices with the apricot or apple jam and orange juice. Butter the Slow Cooker dish and spread the apples over its bottom.
- Mix the oat porridge, cinnamon and flour in another bowl. Add the small butter chunks, stir gently, mix in the sugar and the honey, mix until clumps.
- Cover the apple pieces with the crumbles, leave in the Slow Cooker for 30 minutes. To serve cool the dish for 10 minutes, add ice cream or custard.

**Nutrition: Calories: 400 Fat: 10g Carbohydrates: 30g Protein: 6g**

## Banana French Toast with Milk

Delicious breakfast with ingredients you probably will find in your refrigerator. Simple and easy!

**Prep time: 10 minutes Cooking time: 2 hours Servings: 4**

INGREDIENTS:
1 stale French baguette (or a day old bread)
4 ripe bananas
Half cup cream cheese
3 chicken eggs
2 tbsp brown sugar
Half cup chopped pecans or walnuts
5 tbsp skim milk
2 great tbsp honey
Cinnamon, nutmeg, vanilla extract
2 tbsp butter

DIRECTIONS:
- Cut the baguette or bread into small slices; cover it with cheese on both sides. Arrange the bread slices in one row on the bottom of your Slow Cooker dish.
- Slice bananas into rounds and layer them over the bread, cover with small butter slices. Mix sugar and nuts, sprinkle the bananas with it.
- In another bowl, beat and slightly mix the eggs with a whisk. Add milk, nutmeg, cinnamon, honey and vanilla extract. Stir until fully combined. Pour this mixture over the bananas.
- Preheat Slow Cooker to 200 degrees and cook the dessert on HIGH for 2 hours. Serve warm, with honey and milk.

**Nutrition: Calories: 180 Fat: 3g Carbohydrates: 30g Protein: 6g**

## Cheese Grits in Slow Cooker

Nourishing but light cheese grits will be a source of your energy from the beginning of the day!

**Prep time: 5 minutes Cooking time: 5-7 hours Servings: 8**

INGREDIENTS:
Half cup stone ground grits
5-6 cups water
2 tsp salt
Half cup Cheddar cheese (shredded)
6 tbsp butter
Black pepper (optionally)

DIRECTIONS:
- Preheat Slow Cooker, spray the dish with cooking spray or cover with butter. In a wide bowl, mix together grits and water, add salt.
- Cook on LOW temperatures for 5-7 hours (you can leave it overnight)
- Remove the dish from Slow Cooker, cover butter on top. Stir with the whisk to an even consistency and fully melted butter.
- To serve, sprinkle more cheese on top and black pepper to your taste. You can also add some chopped parsley or basil.
- Serve warm.

**Nutrition: Calories: 173 Fat: 7g Carbohydrates: 4g Protein: 6g**

## Pineapple Cake with Pecans

Delicious pineapple cake is perfect both for breakfast and as a dessert! You will love cooking and eating this!

⌛ Prep time: 20 minutes Cooking time: 3-4 hours
Servings: 10

INGREDIENTS:
Two cups sugar
Two cups plain flour
2 eggs
4 tbsp vegetable oil
Can pineapple with juice (crushed)
1 tsp baking soda
1 tsp vanilla extract
Salt

### For icing:

1 cup sugar
Hal cup butter
6 tbsp evaporated milk
3tbsp shredded coconut
Half cup chopped pecans (toasted)
DIRECTIONS:
- Preheat your Slow Cooker to 180-200 degrees.
- Take a medium bowl and combine all cake ingredients.
- Mix a dough until evenly combined and then pour into Slow Cooker dish. Bake for 3 hours on HIGH; check if it is ready with a wooden toothpick.
- When the cake is ready, make the icing: in a medium saucepan, combine sugar, evaporated milk, butter, and salt. Bring to boil, and then simmer with a lower heat for 10 minutes.
- Add the coconut (to the icing).
- Pour the icing over hot cake and sprinkle with nuts.
- To serve, let cake cool, then cut it and serve with your favorite drinks.

**Nutrition: Calories: 291 Fat: 7g Carbohydrates: 6g Protein: 5g**

## Potato Casserole for Breakfast

Perfect gluten-free breakfast to feed a really big family! Tasty and healthy!

⌛ Prep time: 5 minutes Cooking time: 4 hours
Servings: 10

INGREDIENTS:
4big potatoes
5-6 sausages
Half cup cheddar cheese (shredded)
Half cup mozzarella cheese
5-6 green onions
10 chicken eggs
Half cup milk
Salt
Black pepper
DIRECTIONS:
- Preheat Slow Cooker; spray its dish with non-stick cooking spray. Rub the potatoes into small pieces and put them into the dish.
- Cover the potatoes with rubbed sausages. Add both cheeses and the green onions.
- Continue the layers until all space in the dish is full.
- In a medium bowl, mix together wet ingredients (milk, eggs). Pour it into the main dish. Add salt and pepper.
- Leave to cook on LOW during 5 hours (or until the eggs are set). Serve with guacamole or green onions.

**Nutrition: Calories: 190 Fat: 10g Carbohydrates: 5g Protein: 10g**

## Delicious cinnamon rolls

Easy to make, great flavor, perfect for fast breakfast! You will definitely enjoy it!

Prep time: 30 minutes Cooking time: 2 hours Servings: 10

INGREDIENTS:
Two cups warm water
1 tbsp active yeast (dry)
2 tbsp wild honey
3cups plain flour
1 tsp salt
4tbsp butter
4 tbsp brown sugar
1 tsp cinnamon
DIRECTIONS:
- In a bowl, mix up water, yeast and honey. Stir with a mixer and after the dough is homogenous, let it rest for several minutes (mixture will rise).
- Sift flour and add salt. Mix on low to let the ingredients come together, then increase the mixing speed to medium.
- Remove dough and allow to rise on a floured table.
- Roll dough into medium rectangles. You can use a pizza cutter to make the sides even. Spread butter over the dough. Sprinkle it with sugar and cinnamon.
- Roll the dough rectangles into long log, and then cut it into 10-12 pieces.
- Cover the bottom of your Slow Cooker with foil, place the rolls over it and cook on HIGH for 2-3 hours.
- To serve use fresh berries or mint leaves.

**Nutrition: Calories: 190 Fat: 5g Carbohydrates: 7g Protein: 8g**

## Quinoa Pie in Slow Cooker

Healthy and juicy homemade pie. Incredible way to amaze your guests with delicious breakfast!

⌛ Prep time: 10 minutes Cooking time: 4 hours
Servings: 8

INGREDIENTS:
2 tbsp almond butter
2 tbsp maple syrup
Cup vanilla almond milk
1 tsp salt
Half cup quinoa
2 chicken eggs
Cinnamon
Half cup raisins
5 tbsp roasted almonds (chopped)
Half cup dried apples
DIRECTIONS:

- Spray the Slow Cooker dish with no-stick spray or cover it with foil (or parchment paper).
- In another bowl, mix the almond butter and maple syrup. Melt in in a microwave until creamy (about a minute).
- Add almond milk, salt and cinnamon. Whisk the mass until it is completely even. Add the eggs and remaining products, Mix well.
- Preheat your Slow Cooker to 100-110 degrees.
- Pour the dough into the dish and place it into Slow Cooker. Cook for 3-4 hours on HIGH mode. To serve, remove the pie out of the dish with a knife. Cool in the refrigerator.

**Nutrition: Calories: 174 Fat: 8g Carbohydrates: 20g Protein: 6g**

# Quinoa Muffins with Peanut Butter

The perfect breakfast for summertime!

Prep time: 10 minutes Cooking time: 4 hours Servings: 8

INGREDIENTS:
One cup strawberries
Half up almond vanilla milk
1 tsp salt
5-6 tbsp raw quinoa
2 tbsp peanut butter (better natural)
3 tbsp honey
4 egg whites
2 tbsp peanuts (roasted)

DIRECTIONS:
- Preheat your Slow Cooker to 190 degrees.
- Line the cooking dish bottom with parchment paper; additionally spray it with cooking spray. Dice the strawberries and place them over the dish.
- Sprinkle with honey and place the dish into the Slow Cooker for 10-15 minutes (for releasing juices).
- In another pot, mix up the almond milk and salt. Boil with quinoa until ready.
- In a separate bowl, combine egg whites and almond butter. Join with the quinoa and wait until milk is absorbed.
- Fill the muffin forms with quinoa mixture; place the strawberries on the top. Bake in Slow Cooker on LOW until quinoa is set (about 4 hours).
- To serve, cool the muffins and decorate them with whole strawberries.

**Nutrition: Calories: 190 Fat: 6g Carbohydrates: 8g Protein: 6g**

# Veggie Omelette in Slow Cooker

Tasty and healthy vegetable omelette. Super easy to make!

Prep time: 5 minutes Cooking time: 2 hours Servings: 4

INGREDIENTS:
6 chicken eggs
Half cup milk
Salt
Garlic powder
White pepper
Red pepper
Small onion
Garlic clove
Parsley
5 small tomatoes

DIRECTIONS:
- Grease the Slow Cooker dish with butter or special cooking spray.
- In separated bowl, mix up eggs and milk. Add pepper and garlic. Whisk the mixture well and salt. Add to the mixture broccoli florets, onions, pepper and garlic. Stir in the eggs.
- Place the mixture into the Slow Cooker dish. Cook on HIGH temperatures (180-200 degrees) for 2 hours.
- Cover with cheese and let it melt.
- To serve, cut the omelette into 8 pieces and garnish the plates with parsley and tomatoes.

**Nutrition: Calories: 210 Fat: 7g Carbohydrates: 5g Protein: 8g**

# Apple pie with oatmeal

Healthy and beneficial breakfast for you and your home mates! You will find the source of happiness and energy while tasting this!

Prep time: 10 minutes Cooking time: 4-6 hours Servings: 4

INGREDIENTS:
1cup oats
2large apples
2 cups almond milk
2 cups warm water
2 tsp cinnamon
Pinch nutmeg
Salt
2 tbsp coconut oil
1 tsp vanilla extract
2 tbsp flaxseeds
2 tbsp maple syrup
Raisins

DIRECTIONS:
- Grease your Slow Cooker. Rub a couple spoons of coconut (or olive) oil. Peel the apples. Core and chop them into medium size pieces.
- Starting with the apples, add all the ingredients into Slow Cooker. Stir (not too intensively) and leave to bake for 6 hours on LOW. When ready, stir the oatmeal well.
- Serve the oatmeal into small cups. You can also garnish it with any berries or toppings you like.

**Nutrition: Calories: 159 Fat: 12g Carbohydrates: 9g Protein: 28g**

# Vanilla French Toast

You will be pleased with this receipt and the excellent taste!

Prep time: 15 minutes Cooking time: 8 hours (overnight) Servings: 6

INGREDIENTS:
One loaf bread (better day-old)
2 cups cream
2 cups milk (whole)
8 chicken eggs
Almond extract

One vanilla bean
5 tsp sugar
Cinnamon
Salt

DIRECTIONS:
- Coat the Slow Cooker dish with the cooking spray.
- Slice bread into small pieces (1-2 inches). Place them into the dish overlapping each other. In another dish, combine the remaining ingredients until perfectly blended.
- Pour the wet mixture over the bread to cover it completely.
- Place the dish into Slow Cooker and cook on very LOW temperatures (100-120 degrees) for 7-8 hours. You can leave it overnight so the next morning it will be ready).
- To serve, slightly cool and cut the French Toast.

**Nutrition: Calories: 200 Fat: 6g Carbohydrates: 4g Protein: 8g**

## Pumpkin Spiced Oatmeal

Low in sugar and fats, this will be a perfect choice for your daily start.

**Prep time: 5 minutes Cooking time: 3 minutes Servings: 4**

INGREDIENTS:
One cup dry oats
Four cups water
Half cup milk (fat free)
Half pumpkin
2 tbsp light brown sugar
Salt
Cinnamon
Gloves
Ginger
Nutmeg

DIRECTIONS:
- Spray the inside of the Slow Cooker dish with cooking spray or coat it with oil. Preheat your Slow Cooker to 120 degrees.
- Mix-up oats with milk and water. Wait until soft. Peel the pumpkin and cut it into small pieces.
- Combine the pumpkin with oats in the dish and place it into the Slow Cooker for an hour.
- Take it off and smash the pumpkins. Place the dish back to Slow Cooker and leave for 8 hours (overnight) on LOW.
- In the morning, serve the oatmeal into small bowls.

**Nutrition: Calories: 190 Fat: 8g Carbohydrates: 4g Protein: 6g**

## Greek Eggs Casserole

Easy to cook and healthy to eat. This receipt will amaze your home mates and guests!

**Prep time: 15 minutes Cooking time: 6 hours Servings: 8**

INGREDIENTS:
10 chicken eggs
Half cup milk
Salt
1tsp black pepper
1 tbsp red onion
Half cup dried tomatoes
1 cup champignons
2cups spinach
Half cup feta

DIRECTIONS:
- Set the temperature of your Slow Cooker to 120-150 degrees.
- In a separate wide bowl combine and whisk the eggs. Add salt and pepper. Mix in garlic and red onion. Whisk again.
- Wash and dice the mushrooms. Put them into wet mixture. At last, and add dried tomatoes.
- Pour the mixture into the Slow Cooker crockpot.
- Top the meal with the feta cheese and cook on LOW into the Slow Cooker for 5-6 hours. Serve with milk or vegetables.

**Nutrition: Calories: 180 Fat: 8g Carbohydrates: 4g Protein: 8g**

## French Toast with Chocolate Chip

Love chocolate but want to stay healthy? So this receipt is for you!

**Prep time: 5 minutes Cooking time: 3 minutes Servings: 3**

INGREDIENTS:
One loaf French bread
4 chicken eggs
2 cups milk
brown sugar
vanilla extract
1 tsp cinnamon
4 tbsp chocolate chips

DIRECTIONS:
- Cut the bread into small cubes.
- Coat the bottom and side of the Slow Cook crockpot with special cooking spray or olive oil. Place the bread cubes into the dish.
- Take another medium bowl and mix the eggs, sugar, and milk. Whisk with cinnamon and vanilla until all the ingredients well mixed. Pour the mixture over the bread cubes. Toss slightly to coat.
- Cover the dish and place it in your refrigerator overnight. Cover with the chocolate chips, and cook on LOW for 4 hours.

**Nutrition: Calories: 200 Fat: 8g Carbohydrates: 2g Protein: 7g**

## Egg and Ham Casserole for Slow Cooker

Tired of eggs with bacon? Try this one and fall in love with the receipt.

**Prep time: 10 minutes Cooking time: 2 hours Servings: 6**

INGREDIENTS:
6 chicken eggs
Half teaspoon salt
Black pepper
Half cup milk
Half cup Greek yogurt
Thyme
Half teaspoon onion powder
Half teaspoon garlic powder

43

Champignons
Spinach
Cup pepper jack cheese
Cup hum (diced)

DIRECTIONS:
- In a wide bowl, whisk the eggs with pepper, salt, milk and yogurt. Add garlic powder and onion powder.
- When smooth, dice and stir in the champignons, cheese, spinach and ham. Spray your Slow Cooker with a cooking spray.
- Pour your egg-and-mushroom mixture into the Slow Cooker. Cook on HIGH temperature for 2 hours.

**Nutrition: Calories: 250 Fat: 4g Carbohydrates: 9g Protein: 10g**

## Vegetarian Pot Pie

Even vegetarians can taste this one!

**Prep time: 15 minutes Cooking time: 5 hours Servings: 6**

INGREDIENTS:
6 cups chopped vegetables (peas, potatoes, tomatoes, carrots, brussels sprouts)
1-2 cups diced mushrooms
Two onions
Half cup flour
4 gloves garlic
2 tbsp. garlic
Thyme (fresh)
Cornstarch
2 cups chicken broth

DIRECTIONS:
- Wash and chop vegetables (or by frozen packed). Toss with flour to cover vegetables well.
- Mix with the broth slowly, when well combined with flour. Preheat the Slow Cooker and place the vegetables into it.
- Cook on LOW temperatures for 8-9 hours, or on HIGH – for 6-7 hours. Mix up cornstarch with the water and pour into the vegetable mix.
- Place it back to the Slow Cooker for 15 minutes. Serve hot with fresh vegetables.

**Nutrition: Calories: 267 Fat: 7g Carbohydrates: 29g Protein: 7g**

## Baked Beans for Slow Cooker

Healthy and delicious beans for your energy breakfast!

**Prep time: 10 minutes Cooking time: 8 hours Servings: 8**

INGREDIENTS:
1 cup dried beans
1 medium onion
Half cup brown sugar
Molasses
Tomato sauce or plain ketchup
1 tbsp. Worcestershire sauce
1 tbsp. balsamic vinegar
Salt
Pepper

DIRECTIONS:
- Start with preheating your Slow Cooker.
- Rinse dried beans and place them in Slow Cooker overnight. Cover beans with the water. Drain the beans in the morning and place them back into Slow Cooker.
- Dice all the other vegetables and add them in Slow Cooler too. Pour two cups of water and molasses.
- Add salt and pepper.
- Cook on LOW temperature for 8-9 hours (or 4 hours on HIGH). Serve warm with preferred vegetables.

**Nutrition: Calories: 210 Fat: 4g Carbohydrates: 5g Protein: 8g**

## Quinoa Energy Bars

**Serves: 4 Preparation Time: 10 minutes Cooking Time: 8 hours**

INGREDIENTS
2 cups quinoa flakes, rinsed
½ cup nuts of your choice
½ cup dried fruits of your choice
¼ cup butter, melted
1/3 cup maple syrup

INSTRUCTIONS
- In a mixing bowl, combine all ingredients.
- Compress the ingredients in a parchment-lined crockpot. Close the lid and cook on low for 8 hours.

**Nutrition information: Calories per serving: 306; Carbohydrates: 39.9g; Protein: 7.3g; Fat: 13.9g; Fiber: 3.7g**

## Overnight Apple Oatmeal

**Serves: 4 Preparation Time: 5 minutes Cooking Time: 6 hours**

INGREDIENTS
4 apples, peeled and diced
¾ cup brown sugar
2 cups old-fashioned oats
4 cups evaporated milk
1 tablespoon cinnamon

INSTRUCTIONS
- Stir in all ingredients in the crockpot.
- Close the lid and cook on low for 8 hours. Add in butter if desired.

**Nutrition information: Calories per serving: 521; Carbohydrates:109.5 g; Protein: 16.4g; Fat: 11.6g; Fiber: 12.6g**

## Basic Overnight Quinoa and Oats

**Serves:8 Preparation Time: 5 minutes Cooking Time: 5 hours**

INGREDIENTS
1 ½ cups steel-cut oats
½ cup quinoa
4 ½ cups evaporated milk
4 tablespoons maple syrup
1 teaspoon vanilla extract

INSTRUCTIONS
- Stir in all ingredients in the crockpot.
- Close the lid and cook on low for 7 hours. Top with your favorite topping.

**Nutrition information: Calories per serving:194; Carbohydrates: 31.8g; Protein:8.9 g; Fat: 6.9g; Fiber: 3.5g**

## Blueberry Porridge

Perfect for berry-lovers – healthy and tasty!

- **Prep time: 5 minutes  Cooking time: 5-6 hours**
  **Servings: 4**

INGREDIENTS:
One cup jumbo oats
Four cups milk
Half cup dried fruits
Brown sugar or honey
Cinnamon
Blueberries

DIRECTIONS:
- Heat the Slow Cooker before the start.
- Put the oats into The Slow Cooker dish, add some salt/
- Pour over the milk (or the mixture of milk and water for less creamy).
- Place the dish into the Slow Cooker and cook on LOW temperature for 7-8 hours (overnight). Stir the porridge in the morning.
- To serve, ladle into the serving bowls and decorate with your favorite yogurt or syrup. Add blueberries (or any other berries or fruits you like).

**Nutrition: Calories: 210 Fat: 4g Carbohydrates: 5g Protein: 8g**

# LUNCH RECIPES

## French Onion Soup for Slow Cooker

Perfect choice for French cuisine fans!

- **Prep time: 30 minutes  Cooking time: 12 hours**
  **Servings: 6**

INGREDIENTS:
3 yellow onions
2 tbsp. olive oil
2 tbsp. melted butter (unsalted)
Black pepper (freshly ground)
Pinch salt
10 cups beef broth
2 tbsp. balsamic vinegar
3 tbsp. brandy (optional)
6 baguette slices (to serve)
2 cups Gruyere cheese (to serve)
Chopped shallot or onion

DIRECTIONS:
- Chop the onion and place it into large Slow Cooker. Mix in the butter, salt, olive oil and black pepper. Cook on low overnight.
- In the morning, add to onion the broth and balsamic vinegar.
- Cover with the lid and cook for another 6-8 hours on LOW (the longer you cook, the more intensively flavors you will get).
- Pour the soup into small bowls and place them into preheated oven. Top each bowl with the toast and cheese and bake for 30 minutes.
- To serve, place the chopped onions on a side of each bowl.

**Nutrition: Calories: 455 Fat: 33g Carbohydrates: 61g Protein: 54g**

## Maple Bacon and White Bean Soup

Try this soup with bacon – and it will be your favorite!

- **Prep time: 25 minutes  Cooking time: 12 hours**
  **Servings: 8**

INGREDIENTS:
Two cups white beans (dried)
One red pepper
1 ham bone
8 cups chicken broth
5 slices maple bacon
2 carrots
1 red pepper
1 onion
Half cup diced ham
2 celery stalks
Thyme
4 cloves garlic
Zest and juice of half lemon
Salt and pepper to taste
Chopped parsley (fresh)

DIRECTIONS:
- In a deep bowl, cover the beans with cold water and leave to soak overnight.
- In the morning drain the beans and place them into Slow Cooker, cover with broth and add ham. Cook on high for 3-4 hours.
- In a small frying pan, cook the bacon slices until crispy. Add the red pepper, onion, celery, garlic and carrots. Add salt and cook for ten minutes
- Add the aromatic mixture into Slow Cooker and stir well with beans.
- Let cook on HIGH for an hour or two. In the end, add the chopped parsley and lemon zest. You can serve it hot or cold – it is tasty both ways.

**Nutrition: Calories: 443 Fat: 32g Carbohydrates: 65g Protein: 33g**

## Chicken Minestrone in Slow Cooker

Easy to make and very delicious!

**Prep time: 5 minutes Cooking time: 3 hours
Servings: 3**

INGREDIENTS:
2 chicken thighs
1 bay leaf
One medium leek
1 can tomatoes
Three cloves garlic
3 medium carrots
One teaspoon salt
2 celery stalks
4 cups chicken broth
2 cups water
4 cups shredded cabbage
1 can beans
One medium zucchini
DIRECTIONS:
- To make the broth, preheat Slow Cooker and place in it the chicken, leek, tomatoes with juice, celery, bay leaf, carrots, garlic. Add some pepper and salt to taste.
- Cover with water and chicken broth and cook for 6 hours on low mode. Cut the chard leaves into one-inch pieces and place in separate bowl.
- Add the sliced cabbage, halved zucchini and refrigerate until the broth is prepared.
- When the broth is ready, add in the vegetable and combine well. Turn the Slow Cooker on HIGH and leave for 30 minutes.
- To serve, add the pasta into your soup.

**Nutrition: Calories: 551 Fat: 37g Carbohydrates: 42g Protein: 53g**

## Tomato Soup with Rigatoni

You should try this Italian receipt!

**Prep time: 25 minutes Cooking time: 3 hours
Servings: 8**

INGREDIENTS:
6 cups tomato sauce
2 tbsp. olive oil
Salt
Half tsp sugar
One package rigatoni
4 cloves garlic
2cups whole-milk
Half cup Parmesan Cheese
Red pepper to taste
DIRECTIONS:
- Coat the inside dish of your Slow Cooker with a cooking spray Rinse the rigatoni in cold water and drain carefully.
- Right in the bowl of your Slow Cooker mix the noodles, cottage cheese, tomato sauce, one cup shredded mozzarella, olive oil, spinach, garlic, sugar, red pepper and salt. Stir well.
- Turn on the Slow Cooker and set the LOW temperature mode. Prepare the rigatoni for 3-4 hours. In ten minutes before ready cover with Parmesan and cook until the cheese is melted.

**Nutrition: Calories: 469 Fat: 43g Carbohydrates: 55g Protein: 63g**

## Chicken and Burrito Bowls

Small bowl and plenty of energy!

**Prep time: 5 minutes Cooking time: 3 hours
Servings: 3**

INGREDIENTS:
One or two chicken breasts (boneless)
2 tsp chili powder
One cup brown rice
2 tsp salt
One cup chicken stock
One can diced tomatoes
One teaspoon cumin
One cup frozen corn
One can black beans
DIRECTIONS:
- Cover the chicken breasts with diced tomatoes, mix well and add half-cup chicken stock, cumin, chili powder and salt.
- Place in a wide Slow Cooker dish. Ingredients should cover chicken evenly. Cover the lid and leave the chicken to cook on HIGH for 3-4 hours.
- When it is time, add the rice, frozen corn, black beans and chicken corn. Continue to cook under the lid for another 4 hours.
- When the rice is ready, use two forks and shred the chicken into small pieces (bite-size). Serve the burrito in small bowls garnished with cheese or diced green onions.

**Nutrition: Calories: 551 Fat: 30g Carbohydrates: 146g Protein: 51g**

## Mac and Cheese pasta in Slow Cooker

Amazing pasta for your healthy lunch!

**Prep time: 26 minutes Cooking time: 2-3 hours
Servings: 8**

INGREDIENTS:
3 cups shredded Cheddar
Half teaspoon salt
Two cups whole milk
One cap elbow macaroni
Half teaspoon dry mustard
Two cups whole milk
DIRECTIONS:
- Combine the ingredients (except cheese) in Slow Cooker. Stir well to combine everything evenly. Cover with the lid and cook on HIGH from 2 to 4 hours.
- In 2 hours after you started the cooking process, check if the pasta is soft and there is no liquid. When it is 10 minutes remaining to finish, sprinkle the cheese over the pasta and cook until the cheese is melted.
- Serve this pasta straight from the cooking dish.

**Nutrition: Calories: 566 Fat: 36g Carbohydrates: 48g Protein: 61g**

## Pumpkin couscous with lamb

Perfect for autumn!

**Prep time: 10 minutes Cooking time: 2-3 hours
Servings: 6**

INGREDIENTS:
2 tbsp. olive oil
Two red onions (halved and sliced)
2 cinnamon sticks
6 lamb shanks
3 garlic cloves
3tsp cumin (ground)
2 tsp paprika
4cups Massel beef stock
Cherry tomatoes (canned)
Half cup chopped coriander (fresh)
2 tbsp. brown sugar
Butternut pumpkin
2 cups couscous
Half cup fresh mint (chopped)

DIRECTIONS:
- Heat your Slow Cooker to 180 degrees.
- Cover the frying skillet with 1-tablespoon olive oil and cook the lamb for 5-7 minutes (until brown). Transfer to the Slow Cooker dish.
- Using the remaining oil, fry the onion until soft. Add cumin, crushed garlic, cinnamon, paprika and coriander. Leave for a minute until aromatic.
- Add sugar, tomato, half the mint and half the fresh coriander. Stir in the beef stock. Pour the mixture into Slow Cooker.
- Cook for 3-4 hours on HIGH temperature mode.
- To serve, divide among bowls and garnish with remaining mint and coriander.

**Nutrition: Calories: 480 Fat: 14g Carbohydrates: 31g Protein: 32g**

## Pappardelle ragout with duck

Hot ragout for lunch – what else do you need for a beautiful day?

⏲ **Prep time: 30 minutes Cooking time: 4-5 hours**
**Servings: 6**

INGREDIENTS:
One small onion (brown and chopped)
Frozen duck
Half cup pancetta
One celery stick
Two garlic cloves
One carrot (small)
2 bay leaves (dried)
Three rosemary sprigs
One cup chicken stock
One cup pinot noir
Half cup green olives
Pappardelle pasta (to serve)
Parmesan (finely grated, to serve)
Chopped parsley (to serve)

DIRECTIONS:
- Prepare the duck: discard backbone and take off all exec fat. Quarter the duck and cover with salt. Cook the duck in a deep buttered skillet over high heat until it gets brown (for 5-6 minutes).
- Preheat your Slow Cooker to 110 degrees. Cover the dish with reserved chicken fat.
- In a separate pan, cook the onion, pancetta, carrot, celery, bay leaves and garlic. Stir time after time.
- Place duck and vegetable mixture into Slow Cooker. Cover with wine, tomato and stock. Add rosemary.
- Cover the lid and cook on high mode for 4 hours. Serve with parmesan, pasta and parsley.

**Nutrition: Calories: 504 Fat: 23g Carbohydrates: 7g Protein: 51g**

## Oxtail and Chorizo Stew

This is easier than you think! Just let it try and cook this!

⏲ **Prep time: 25 minutes Cooking time: 4 hours**
**Servings: 4**

INGREDIENTS:
Oxtail pieces
4 tbsp olive oil (extra virgin)
1 garlic cloves
1 onion (chopped)
1 tsp paprika
1 primo chorizo
1carrot (chopped)
Half orange zest
2rosemary sprigs
2 cans tomatoes (whole peeled)
2 cups red wine
14-16 cherry tomatoes
Flat-leaf parsley (to garnish)
3 cups beef stock

DIRECTIONS:
- Preheat your Slow Cooker to 170 degrees and butter the dish.
- Place oxtail to a large saucepan and cover with cold water. Slowly bring to the boil and prepare for 15-20 minutes. Rinse and set aside.
- Preheat olive oil in a large saucepan. Add onion, carrot, chorizo and garlic. Stir and cook for 4 minutes.
- Add paprika, 1 rosemary sprig and orange zest. Salt and pepper.
- Place oxtails in the Slow Cooker dish, cover with vegetables and tomato. Pour in wine and stock. Cook for 3-4 hours on high.
- Serve with mash potatoes or any other side dish you like.

**Nutrition: Calories: 544 Fat: 39g Carbohydrates: 49g Protein: 33g**

## Slow Cooker Soup with Ham

Delicious and healthy soup for your middle day!

⏲ **Prep time: 23 minutes Cooking time: 8 hours**
**Servings: 8**

INGREDIENTS:
2 cups navy beans
2 large carrots
6 large potatoes
2 medium shallots
2 large celery stalks
1 ham bone
Salt
8 cups water
Thyme leaves
Minced sage
1 loaf crusty bread

DIRECTIONS:

- In a large plate, stir the potatoes, celery, beans, carrots, shallots sage and thyme. You can do it right in Slow Cooker, but then do not forget to butter it.
- Place the vegetable mix into Slow Cooker and nestle the ham bone in the middle. Pour in the water to cover evenly all the ingredients.
- Cover with the lid and cook on LOW regime for 8 hours.
- Remove ham bone, cool and shred it, then combine again with the soup. Serve hot with crusty baguette.

**Nutrition: Calories: 467 Fat: 28g Carbohydrates: 43g Protein: 52g**

## Slow Cooker Soup with Celery and Bacon

Try to cook it overnight – and you will get a perfect dish the next day!

**Prep time: 27 minutes Cooking time: 7 hours Servings: 4-6**

INGREDIENTS:
One yellow onion (large)
10-12 small white potatoes
One bunch celery
3 garlic cloves
4 cups chicken broth
6-4 slices bacon (thick-cut)
Salt
Half teaspoon white pepper
4 tbsp heavy cream or milk
DIRECTIONS:
- Preheat your Slow Cooker for 100-110 degrees and butter the cooking dish.
- Chop the celery, potatoes and onion into medium and equally sized cubes. Mince the garlic. Place the prepared vegetables in your Slow Cooker and cover with chicken broth.
- Season with pepper and salt to taste. Cook on LOW mode for 5-7 hours.
- Before serving, puree the soup with a stick blender (can do iy right in Slow Cooker) and serve in small bowls with bacon over top.

**Nutrition: Calories: 577 Fat: 43g Carbohydrates: 46g Protein: 33g**

## Lamb Shank in Slow Cooker

Try this lamb – and you will not forget it!

**Prep time: 15 minutes Cooking time: 3 hours Servings: 6**

INGREDIENTS:
2 tbsp. plain flour
2 tbsp. olive oil
Six lamb shanks
One brown onion
Half cup red wine
2 cups tomato pasta
2 garlic cloves
2 cups chicken broth or stock
3 sprigs rosemary (fresh)
5 small potatoes
One peeled turnip
chopped fresh parsley
DIRECTIONS:
- Mix the flour with salt and pepper. Place the lamb shanks into the mixture and toss to cover well. Cover a large frying pan with olive oil and fry lamb shanks until browned from both sides.
- Add the garlic and chopped onion to the pan and cook until lightly softened.
- Place the lamb into Slow Cooker; add wine, stock, rosemary, pasta and bay leaves. Add carrots and peas to the dish.
- Cover the dish and cook for 3-4 hours on HIGH temperature.
- Before the serving stir in minced parsley and season with salt and pepper.

**Nutrition: Calories: 602 Fat: 9g Carbohydrates: 21g Protein: 60g**

## Spicy chicken with fennel stew

The long time infuses the chicken flavor and makes your lunch delicious and spicy!

**Prep time: 15 minutes Cooking time: 5 hours Servings: 4**

INGREDIENTS:
Olive oil
Two fennel bulbs
Two chicken thighs
Two tablespoons flour (plain)
Four anchovies (chopped finely)
Three garlic cloves
One red chili (chopped)
Can diced tomatoes
Half cup white wine
Italian bread (to serve)
Fennel fronds (to garnish)
DIRECTIONS:
- Heat a skillet over medium temperature and add one tablespoon of olive oil. Add fennel and cook stirring until golden (for 6-8 minutes)
- Transfer kennel to the Slow Cooker and heat the remaining olive oil in the same skillet.
- Cut the chicken and toss in flour, so it will coat evenly. Fry for 6-7 minutes (until browned well). Add anchovy, garlic and chili to chicken and cook for another 2-3 minutes.
- Add wine, wait until boil and then simmer for a couple minutes. Add tomatoes and transfer chicken to Slow Cooker.
- Cover and cook on LOW for 5 hours.
- To serve, cut the bread and garnish with fennels.

**Nutrition: Calories: 1536 Fat: 25g Carbohydrates: 18g Protein: 48g**

## French Farmhouse Chicken Soup

Perfect for a winter or fall day, when you need to warm with a bowl of hot soup.

**Prep time: 10 minutes Cooking time: 6 hours Servings: 4**

INGREDIENTS:
2 tsp olive oil (extra virgin)
6 chicken eggs
2 carrots (diced)

2 celery stalks (trimmed and sliced)
One leek (thinly sliced)
1 fennel bulb (diced)
Chicken stock (salt-reduced)
3 thyme sprigs (fresh)
Half cup frozen peas
Four slices crusty bread (to serve)

DIRECTIONS:
- Heat the olive oil in a non-stick skillet over medium heat.
- Add chicken and fry for 5-7 minutes until browned from all sides. Transfer to the Slow Cooker. Cover the chicken with carrot, celery, fennel, leek, thyme and stock. Add salt and pepper to taste. Cover the lid of the Slow Cooker and cook for around 5 hours on LOW temperature.
- When cooking time is almost over, add the peas (in the last 10-15 minutes).
- Take the chicken off the soup and remove all the bones. Shred roughly and place back to soup. Sprinkle with fennel fronds and serve the soup with crusty bread.

**Nutrition: Calories: 850 Fat: 12g Carbohydrates: 64g Protein: 50g**

## Bean soup served with toasts

Warm and satisfying soup with beans and toasts to maintain your day!

⌚ **Prep time: 12 minutes Cooking time: 7 hours**
**Servings: 4**

INGREDIENTS:
One cup borlotti beans (dried)
One large brown onion (finely chopped)
1 tsp olive oil (extra virgin)
4 celery sticks
1 large carrot
Finely chopped pancetta
3 garlic cloves
2 tsp fresh rosemary (chopped)
1 red chili
2 cups chicken stock
2 cups water
Tuscan cabbage
4 slices grilled bread
1 tbsp. fresh basil

DIRECTIONS:
- Place the beans in a large bowl and cover with cold water. Leave overnight to soak then drain. Put the beans in a saucepan and cover with cold water. Set the medium heat and wait until boil. Cook for around 10 minutes.
- Preheat the olive oil in a non-stick skillet over medium heat.
- Chop the onion, carrot, celery and pancetta and cook until soft (for 4-5 minutes). Add the garlic, chili and rosemary. Cook until aromatic.
- Preheat the Slow Cooker and place in the onion mixture, stock, beans and water. Cover and boil on LOW for 6-7 hours.
- Serve in small bowls with toast.

**Nutrition: Calories: 540 Fat: 9g Carbohydrates: 35g Protein: 20g**

## Chicken ragout with red wine

Just try and taste this! Perfect meal to get warm on a cold winter day!

⌚ **Prep time: 25 minutes Cooking time: 7 hours**
**Servings: 6**

INGREDIENTS:
1 tbsp olive oil (extra virgin)
1 chicken fillet
1 red onion
2 celery stalks
2 garlic cloves
1 carrot
Finely chopped pancetta
One cup red wine
One cup chicken stock
Barilla Fettuccine
Half cup pecorino
3 sprigs rosemary (fresh)
Steamed green beans
Chopped parsley (to serve)

DIRECTIONS:
- Dice all the vegetables finely.
- Heat a frying pan with olive oil, set over medium heat.
- Cook chicken for 5 minutes until it is browned. You can work in batches.
- Add celery, onion, pancetta and carrot. Stir and cook for 8-9 minutes until the vegetables start to soften.
- Add garlic and simmer for a minute to fragrant. Add wine, wait until boil and cook for 1-2 minutes.
- Transfer the pan mixture to Slow Cooker and combine with rosemary, stock and tomato paste. Cook for 6 hours on LOW.
- Shred chicken in Slow Cooker with two forks and cook for another 30 minutes. Add pasta to the chicken and combine well.
- To serve sprinkle with pecorino, add parsley and beans.

**Nutrition: Calories: 745 Fat: 15g Carbohydrates: 43g Protein: 334g**

## Egg noodles with Red Beef

Fast, healthy and delicious lunch for you and your family!

⌚ **Prep time: 15 minutes Cooking time: 4-5 hours**
**Servings: 4**

INGREDIENTS:
2 tbsp. plain flour
Beef steak
1-2 tbsp. peanut oil
One cup chicken stock
Half cup dry sherry
4 tbsp. soy sauce
6 crushed cardamom pods
Sliced ginger (fresh)
1 cinnamon stick
Half teaspoon fennel seeds
Egg noodles (to serve)
Coriander sprigs, to serve)

DIRECTIONS:
- In a large bowl, toss the beef with the flour to fully coat.

- Take a large non-stick skillet and heat 2 teaspoons olive oil (over medium heat).
- Separate the beef into three parts and cook in batches each one for 3-4 minutes. After ready, transfer the beef to slow cooker.
- Cover the beef with sherry, stock, cardamom, ginger, anise star and fennel seeds. Sprinkle with soy sauce.
- Cook on HIGH temperatures until tender beef (for 4-5 hours). Before serving top with coriander.

**Nutrition: Calories: 930 Fat: 19g Carbohydrates: 7g Protein: 45g**

## Autumn Pumpkin Soup

Get warm and eat a tasty autumn soup!

Prep time: 30 minutes Cooking time: 4 hours
Servings: 4-6

INGREDIENTS:
Half medium-sized butternut pumpkin
2-3 medium potatoes
Salt
Black pepper (cracked)
1-2 tsp mild curry powder
1 onion
One cup cream (full)
Chili powder to taste (optional)
2 cups vegetable stock

DIRECTIONS:
- Cut and peel the pumpkin, remove skin and seeds. Chop the potatoes and fine dice the onion.
- Place the vegetables in the Slow Cooker. Add salt and pepper.
- Cook for 4-6 hours on LOW temperatures until the pumpkin and potatoes are tender. When ready, wait until cool and stir with a food processor until smooth consistence. Stir in the chili powder and cream.
- To serve, warm again a little bit.

**Nutrition: Calories: 355 Fat: 9g Carbohydrates: 5g Protein: 21g**

## Bone Broth in Slow Cooker

The perfect choice for a cold winter day!

Prep time: 15 minutes Cooking time: 24 hours
Servings: 6

INGREDIENTS:
Beef bones (you can gather a mix of knuckle, marrow and meat bones)
6 sprigs thyme
2tbsp apple cider vinegar
1 browned onion (halved)
2 quartered carrots
4 garlic cloves
One bay leaf
2 chopped stalks celery

DIRECTIONS:
- Preheat your oven 200 degrees (or 180, if your oven is fan-forced). Place your bone mix on a roasting tray and cook for 30-40 minutes. Place all the bones and fat in Slow Cooker.
- Add the quartered carrots, garlic, halved onion and chopped celery. Pour the water to cover the ingredients.
- Close the lid and simmer for 24 hours on LOW (you can add more water if some vaporize during the cooking time).
- Take off and strain into a separate large bowl. Chill before serving.

**Nutrition: Calories: 293 Fat: 1g Carbohydrates: 5g Protein: 13g**

## Creamy vegetable curry with chickpea

Try to cook this during summer season!

Prep time: 20 minutes Cooking time: 4 hours
Servings: 6

INGREDIENTS:
2 tsp vegetable oil
2 tbsp. Madras curry paste
One can light coconut cream
1 red capsicum
1 small cauliflower (cut into florets)
One medium pumpkin (cut into small cubes)
3 chopped tomatoes
One cup green beans
Two cups chickpeas
1Lebanese cucumber
One cup plain Greek yogurt
4 bread slices

DIRECTIONS:
- Cut the capsicum, pumpkin and cucumber into small cubes, Chop the tomatoes, halve the beans, drain and rinse chickpeas.
- Heat olive oil in a large saucepan over medium heat.
- Add curry paste and stock. Wait until simmer and transfer to Slow Cooker. Add the pumpkin, capsicum and coconut cream to the Slow Cooker.
- Cook on LOW temperature for 3 hours.
- Add tomato and cauliflower. Cook for another 15 minutes. Cover with chickpeas and beans, prepare for 30 minutes.
- To serve, combine coriander, cucumber and yogurt in a separate bowl. Serve with the bread and yogurt.

**Nutrition: Calories: 773 Fat: 20g Carbohydrates: 51g Protein: 20g**

## Lamb Chunks with Honey

Make your lunch warm and sweet!

Prep time: 20 minutes Cooking time: 4 hours
Servings: 4

INGREDIENTS:
Half cup soy sauce
3 tbsp honey
2garlic cloves
Black pepper
1 star anise
Fresh ginger
1 brown inion
1 tbsp vegetable oil
1 sliced orange
4 lamb shanks
1 red chili
1 tsp sesame oil
1 green onion
4 cups rice (steamed)

Halved baby pak choy

DIRECTIONS:
- In separate bowl, combine honey, soy sauce, garlic, ginger, black pepper and star anise. Put diced brown onion and carrots in Slow Cooker.
- Add the sliced orange over the onion and carrot.
- In a large frying pan heat the vegetable oil and cook lamb for 4-5 minutes on medium heat (or until browned all sides). Place to Slow Cooker.
- Cover with the lid and prepare on HIGH temperatures for 4 hours).
- Transfer lamb to a baking tray and cook in the oven for 14 minutes on 180 degrees. Meanwhile, add sesame oil, star anise to Slow Cooker. Cook for 15 minutes.
- Serve lamb with pac choy and rice.

**Nutrition: Calories: 549 Fat: 10g Carbohydrates: 37g Protein: 30g**

## Chickpea curry with vegetables

So delicious and spicy – your lunch will bring you new powers for your day!

Prep time: 15 minutes Cooking time: 4 hours
Servings: 4

INGREDIENTS:
1 tbsp vegetable oil
One brown onion (large)
2 garlic cloves
3 tsp ground cumin
2 tbsp curry powder
Half juiced lemon
One can diced tomatoes
One cup chickpeas
One large carrot
1 red capsicum
One cup cauliflower
Half cup mushrooms
4 small yellow squash
1,5 cup broccoli florets
To serve, jasmine rice, salt, natural yogurt

DIRECTIONS:
- Preheat vegetable oil in a large skillet (over medium heat). Add chopped onion, stir and cook for 3 minutes until soft. Add garlic, cumin and curry powder and cook until aromatic. Stir in mashed potatoes and simmer for 3-5 minutes.
- Pour half-cup water, vegetables, chickpeas and 2 tablespoons lemon juice. Bring to boil. Spoon to the Slow Cooker and prepare on HIGH for 4-6 hours.
- Serve with the rice and yogurt.

**Nutrition: Calories: 938 Fat: 7g Carbohydrates: 19g Protein: 15g**

## Soup with lentils and goat cheese

Set the work on pause for a bowl of hot soup!

Prep time: 25 minutes Cooking time: 3 hours
Servings: 4

INGREDIENTS:
One brown onion
2 celery sticks
1 swede
1 carrot
1 garlic clove
Half cup red lentils
One can diced tomatoes
2 cups vegetable stock
2 tbsp fresh chives
1baguette (sliced diagonally)
3 teaspoons ground cumin
Half cup goat cheese

DIRECTIONS:
- Finely chop the onion, carrot, celery, swede, fresh chimes. Crush the garlic clove.
- Place the vegetables along with lentils, stock, tomatoes and cumin in your Slow Cooker. Cover with the lid and cook until thick soup and tender vegetables (for 3 hours on HIGH temperature).
- Preheat your grill and place the bread on the baking tray. Cook until golden for 2-3 minutes each side.
- In a small bowl, combine the cheese with chimes and spread over the toasted bread. Serve the soup in a bowls with toast and cheese.

**Nutrition: Calories: 957 Fat: 9g Carbohydrates: 16g Protein: 27g**

## Ragout with Beef and Carrot

Healthy and satisfying dish for any occasion!

Prep time: 15 minutes Cooking time: 4 hours
Servings: 4

INGREDIENTS:
2tbsp plain flour
Gravy beef
3tbsp olive oil
2large onions (brown)
Half cup tomato paste
2 crushed garlic cloves
Half cup red wine
3large carrots
1cup Massel beef stock

DIRECTIONS:
- Cut beef into small cubes and place it into a wide dish with flour, salt and pepper. Coat the beef with flour mixture and remove the excess.
- Heat one tablespoon olive oil in a large skillet and fry the beef cubes over medium heat. Place the beef into Slow Cooker.
- Add onion to skillet, stir and cook for 4-6 minutes until soft. Add tomato paste and garlic. Simmer for one more minute.
- Pour in wine and bring to boil slowly. Simmer until wine reduced or for 5 minutes. Pour sauce over beef and combine softly.
- Cook on HIGH for 4 hours. Serve with the pasta.

**Nutrition: Calories: 731 Fat: 22g Carbohydrates: 10g Protein: 33g**

## Ham and pea soup foe Slow Cooker

Easy to make and very tasty – you should try this!

Prep time: 15 minutes Cooking time: 7 hours
Servings: 4

INGREDIENTS:
One tablespoon olive oil
One brown onion (small)
2 sticks celery
2 garlic cloves
One cup ham hock
5 large potatoes
One cup green peas (split)
3 cups chicken stock-salt-reduced
Fresh parsley (to serve)

DIRECTIONS:
- Chop small brown onion, rush garlic cloves and dice celery.
- In large frying pan, heat the oil over medium-high temperature. Add onion and prepare, stirring, around three minutes.
- Wait until the onion is soft, add celery, garlic, and diced potatoes. Stir and cook for three minutes, then transfer to Slow Cooker.
- Add ham hock, stock and peas. Pour with 4-5 cups cold water. Cover the lid and cook on LOW mode for six hours.
- Shred ham and return the dish in Slow Cooker for an hour. To serve, sprinkle with chopped parsley.

**Nutrition: Calories: 458 Fat: 16g Carbohydrates: 50g Protein: 32g**

## Summer Curry in Slow Cooker

Hot and spicy – just like the summer!

**Prep time: 10 minutes Cooking time: 8-9 hours Servings: 4**

INGREDIENTS:
1 tbsp peanut oil
Beef steak
4 tbsp massamam curry paste
6 cardamom pods
1 medium brown onion (halved)
2 garlic cloves
1 cinnamon stick
2 large carrots
Steamed rice
1-2 cup coconut milk
6 large potatoes
2 tbsp. fish sauce
1 tbsp. palm sugar
1 tbsp. lime juice
Coriander leaves and peanuts (to serve)

DIRECTIONS:
- Trim the beef steak, chop into small cubes.
- Place the beef cubes into the preheated large skillet with peanut oil. Cook until browned (for 5-6 minutes).
- Transfer the meat to buttered Slow Cooker.
- Heat the same pan again and add onion. Fry until softened, then add curry paste and garlic. Prepare until aromatic, and then transfer to Slow Cooker.
- Cover with cinnamon, cardamom, potatoes, carrots, sugar and wish sauce. Pour in the coconut milk.
- Cover the lid and leave to cook for 8 hours on LOW mode. Serve with rice and sprinkled peanuts.

**Nutrition: Calories: 534 Fat: 33g Carbohydrates: 45g Protein: 52g**

## Slow Cooker meatballs with rigatoni

Delicious and healthy lunch for busy people!

**Prep time: 20 minutes Cooking time: 7 hours Servings: 4**

INGREDIENTS:
Pork and veal mince
1 tbsp. olive oil
Pecorino cheese (finely grated)
3 garlic gloves
1 medium onion (brown)
2 tbsp. parsley (fresh leaves)
2 celery stalks
One jar tomato paste
2 tbsp. sherry (dry)
2 tsp sugar
Rigatoni pasta
Pecorino cheese and baby rocket to serve

DIRECTIONS:
- Take a large bowl and combine cheese, parsley, mince, breadcrumbs and garlic in it. Using a tablespoon, roll small parts of the mixture and form into balls.
- Heat the olive oil in a large skillet and add chopped onion and celery. Stir and cook for 3-5 minutes until softened.
- Add sherry and cook for another 2 minutes (until reduced by half). Add tomato paste and sugar. Cover with six cups of cold water.
- Place the meatballs into the Slow Cooker and pour in tomato mixture. Cook on LOW mode for 6 hours, and then add pasta. Stir well to combine. Cook for 45 minutes and season with pepper and salt.
- Serve warm with rocket and cheese.

**Nutrition: Calories: 495 Fat: 19g Carbohydrates: 64g Protein: 51g**

# SIDE DISHES RECIPES

## Indian Spiced Lentils

Indian cuisine is perfect for your lunchtime!

⏱ **Prep time: 10-15 minutes Cooking time: 3 hours Servings: 3-5**

INGREDIENTS:
Two cup cooked lentils
1 medium onion (finely diced)
1 yellow pepper
1 large sweet potato
Half tsp ground ginger
1 can tomato sauce
3 cloves diced garlic
2 tsp cumin
Cayenne pepper
2 tsp paprika
1tsp turmeric (ground)
1 tsp coriander
Half cup vegetable broth
Juice of 1 lemon
Pepper and salt to taste

DIRECTIONS:
- Chop all the vegetables to small cubes. To make the process a way faster, use a food processor or kitchen blender.
- Place all your vegetables in the Slow Cooker and cover with species. Pour over the organic vegetable broth.
- Cook on HIGH temperature mode for 3 hours (until the potatoes are soft). To serve, prepare the brown rice or just cut the naan bread.

**Nutrition: Calories: 576 Fat: 44g Carbohydrates: 76g Protein: 51g**

## Quinoa Risotto with Asparagus

Make your lunch tastier with asparagus!

⏱ **Prep time: 15 minutes Cooking time: 4 hours Servings: 6**

INGREDIENTS:
One cup rinsed quinoa
Chicken breasts
Salt
2cups chicken broth
One bunch asparagus
Black pepper (freshly ground)
2 cup peas (canned or frozen)
Three large carrots
2 cloves garlic

DIRECTIONS:
- Spray your slow cooker with a special cooking spray.
- Right in a cooking dish, combine chicken, one cup chicken broth, rinsed quinoa, carrots and garlic. Season with pepper and salt as you like.
- Cover with the lid and cook on HIGH for 3-4 hours (until the chicken is easy to shred). Shred the chicken, add the peas and asparagus and cook for 30-40 minutes more.
- Add the remaining cup of chicken broth and continue stirring until creamy.

**Nutrition: Calories: 668 Fat: 54g Carbohydrates: 83g Protein: 67g**

## Rice noodles with Coconut Beef

This will satisfy you until the dinner!

⏱ **Prep time: 15 minutes Cooking time: 7 hours Servings: 4**

INGREDIENTS:
2 tbsp. red curry paste
5 tbsp. light coconut milk
2 clove garlic
Salt
2 tsp ginger (grated)
Rice noodles
Half red onion
Snap peas
2 tbsp. fresh lime juice
Beef stew meat
Half cup basil leaves (fresh)
Chopped peanuts (optional)

DIRECTIONS:
- Right in your Slow Cooker whisk the coconut milk with minced garlic, curry paste, salt and ginger. Cut the beef and add it inti coconut milk mixture. Toss well to cover the meat fully.
- Turn on your Slow Cooker and cook under the lid for 6-7 hours on LOW mode or 4-5 hours on HIGH (check when the meat easily falls apart).
- Cook the rice noodles according to directions on the package.
- 15 minutes before the end of cooking time fold in the peas, lime juice and onion. Cook for 3 more minutes.
- Serve with sprinkled peanuts.

**Nutrition: Calories: 767 Fat: 43g Carbohydrates: 68g Protein: 54g**

## Chicken with rice and sesame

Asian dish for a lunch? Give it a chance!

⏱ **Prep time: 15 minutes Cooking time: 5-6 hours Servings: 6**

INGREDIENTS:
3 tbsp soy sauce
3-4 tbsp rice wine

1 tbsp brown sugar
8 clove garlic
3 tbsp toasted sesame oil
2 boneless chicken breasts without skin
1 fresh ginger
Half cup broccoli florets
4 cup white rice (can use frozen cooked)
2 green onions (sliced)
DIRECTIONS:
- Take a small bowl and whisk the rice wine, toasted sesame oil, soy sauce and brown sugar in it. Spray the Slow Cooker with anti-sticking spray.
- Place the chicken into the cooking dish, cover with soy mixture, fresh chopped ginger and garlic. Cover the cooking dish and turn the Slow Cooker on LOW mode. Cook for 5-6 hours.
- Shred the chicken when ready.
- Serve with warmed rice and broccoli florets. Garnish the meal with sliced green onions.

**Nutrition: Calories: 812 Fat: 54g Carbohydrates: 78g Protein: 69g**

## Steak with Onions and Pepper

Meat and vegetables – a perfect lunchtime couple!

Prep time: 11 minutes Cooking time: 8 hours
Servings: 4-5

INGREDIENTS:
One red pepper (diced)
One onion
Salt/pepper to taste
One tsp chili powder
One flank steak
Half mango
Cinnamon
One cup rice (long-grain)
3 tbsp fresh cilantro
DIRECTIONS:
- Cover the bottom and sides of your Slow Cooker with cooking spray or butter.
- Dice the onion and bell pepper, mix in tomatoes, cinnamon. Chili powder, add salt and pepper to taste.
- Place the beef parts among the vegetable mixture.
- Cover with the cooking dish lid and prepare for 4-5 hours (on HIGH temperature) or 6-7 (on LOW). In the end, check if the meat is tender and easy falls apart.
- 25-30 minutes before serving cook the rice (follow the package directions). To serve, shred the meat with two forks and garnish the mango pieces.

**Nutrition:**

**Calories: 677 Fat: 43g Carbohydrates: 66g Protein: 32g**

## Caesar sandwiches with Chicken

Don't have much time? Try this one!

Prep time: 20 minutes Cooking time: 3-4 hours
Servings: 4-7

INGREDIENTS:
4 chicken breasts (skinless and boneless)
Half cup shredded parmesan
Half cup Caesar dressing
1 tbsp parsley
Romaine leaves
2 tsp pepper
Hamburger buns
DIRECTIONS:
- Place the chicken breasts into the Slow Cooker dish ansd pour in half cup water.
- Turn on the Slow Cooker and prepare the chicken for 3-4 hours on LOW temperature mode. Take out the chicken and shred the meat with the forks.
- Return the meat back to Slow Cooker and stir well.
- Add the Caesar dressing, parmesan, pepper, parsley and combine well. Cook on low mode for another 30 minutes, the remove.
- Serve as sandwiches on the buns with romaine leaves.

**Nutrition: Calories: 674 Fat: 39g Carbohydrates: 78g Protein: 98g**

## Thai Chicken in Slow Cooker

Another amazing Asian dish!

Prep time: 17 minutes Cooking time: 4 hours
Servings: 6

INGREDIENTS:
Half coconut milk (light)
1 tbsp red curry paste
2 tbsp natural peanut butter (fat0reduced)
1 tsp grated ginger
1 large onion
1cup frozen peas
2 red bell pepper
Fresh cilantro leaves
2 chicken thighs (boneless)
Lime wedges (to serve)
1 cup rice noodles
DIRECTIONS:
- In the Slow Cooker dish mix together the coconut milk, curry paste, peanut butter and ginger. Mix in the diced onion, peppers and whole chicken.
- Cover with the dish lid and cook on LOW (for 5-6 hours) or HIGH (3-4 hours) temperatures. 12-15 minutes before serving cook the noodles (follow the package directions).
- Add the peas into the chicken mixture, cook for another 3 minutes. Serve together, garnishing with lime wedges.

**Nutrition: Calories: 469 Fat: 39g Carbohydrates: 65g Protein: 57g**

## Pork Tacos with Cabbage

Small and delicious tacos for the fast lunch!

Prep time: 15-17 minutes Cooking time: 5 hours
Servings: 4

INGREDIENTS:
One large orange
Two clove garlic
1 medium carrot
Salt
1 pork shoulder

Pepper
Pinch red pepper flakes
2 tbsp soy sauce
3 tbsp brown sugar
2 tbsp olive oil
8 small flour tortillas
1 tbsp grated fresh ginger
Half red cabbage

DIRECTIONS:
- Cut for strips of zest from orange (you can use a vegetable peeler).
- Right in the Slow Cooker dish, mix the vinegar, soy sauce, sugar, red pepper, ginger, orange zest and garlic.
- Add pork and toss well to cover.
- Turn the Slow Cooker on and cook until tender – 7-8 hours on LOW or 3-5 hours on HIGH modes. Prepare the slaw: take a large bowl and squeeze the orange juice into it. Add the oil, pepper and salt. Add the carrot and other vegetables.
- Warm the tortillas and fill them with the slaw and shredded pork.

**Nutrition: Calories: 601 Fat: 42g Carbohydrates: 53g Protein: 78g**

## Simple Salsa Chicken

Easy to make and very satisfying!

**Prep time: 5-11 minutes Cooking time: 6-8 hours Servings: 6**

INGREDIENTS:
4 chicken breasts (skinless and boneless)
Salt
2 cups salsa (take your favorite)
Pepper
Fresh lime wedges (optional for serving)

DIRECTIONS:
- Cover the bottom of your Slow Cooker with butter or anti-sticking spray. Place whole chicken breasts into the cooking dish and cover with salsa.
- Cover the lid, turn on the Slow Cooker and prepare for 4 hours on HIGH or up to 6-8 hours on LOW.
- When the chicken is soft, shred with two forks, toss well with salsa.
- You can serve in with bread or any dish immediately or refrigerate up to 5-6 days.

**Nutrition: Calories: 433 Fat: 55g Carbohydrates: 65g Protein: 38g**

## Summer Risotto with mushrooms and peas

So delicious risotto will make your day brighter!

**Prep time: 20 minutes Cooking time: 3-4 hours Servings: 8**

INGREDIENTS:
3 tbsp olive oil
4 cups vegetable broth
Half cut dry white wine
Half cup sliced shallots
Parmesan cheese (grated)
Half teaspoon black pepper
1 cup uncooked rice
1 cloves garlic
3 cups mushrooms (sliced)

DIRECTIONS:
- Warm olive oil in a large skillet (over medium heat).
- Add the shallots, garlic and mushrooms. Stirring, sauté for several minutes (5-7), until lightly browned. The mushrooms are ready when all the liquid is evaporated.
- Stir the rice into the mushroom mixture and cook for another 1-2 minutes. Place the saucepan mixture into the Slow Cooker.
- Add the wine, broth, and pepper.
- Cover the lid and leave cooking for 2-3 hours on HIGH. In the end stir in peas and cover with cheese.
- Serve while hot.

**Nutrition: Calories: 552 Fat: 64g Carbohydrates: 78g Protein: 87g**

## Spring Minestrone in Slow Cooker

Perfect for springtime and fresh vegetables!

**Prep time: 15 minutes Cooking time: 4-6 hours Servings: 4-7**

INGREDIENTS:
One sweet onion
Three cups water
3 cups vegetable stock
3 carrots
3 garlic cloves
One can diced tomatoes
2 cans beans
Fresh spinach
Uncooked pasta
12 asparagus spears
One cup frozen peas (sweet)
Half cup cheese (freshly grated)

DIRECTIONS:
- Start with dicing the vegetables, cut the onions, carrots, mince garlic. Add the can of diced tomatoes and beans.
- Place these ingredients into Slow Cooker and pour over with the stock. Leave cooking on LOW temperature modes for 4-6 hours.
- When it is 15-17 minutes left before serving, add asparagus. If you want, season with salt and any pepper you like.
- Serve hot and covered with some cheese.

**Nutrition: Calories: 752 Fat: 45g Carbohydrates: 63g Protein: 76g**

## Frittata with Red Pepper and Feta

So heathy and delicious, you will not forget it!

**Prep time: 5 minutes Cooking time: 2-3 hours Servings: 3-5**

INGREDIENTS:
1-2 tsp olive oil
3 tbsp sliced green onion
Half cup crumbled Feta
Baby kale
Roasted red pepper
8 chicken eggs

Fresh ground black pepper

DIRECTIONS:
- Tale a large saucepan. Cover the bottom with olive oil and add kale. sauté the kale for 3-5 minutes until it is softened.
- Spray the bottom of your Slow Cooker with anti-sticking spray and place the kale inside of it. Turn the Slow Cooker and set on LOW mode.
- Chop the red peppers into small pieces. Crumble the peppers with feta, sliced onions, and add to the kale in Slow Cooker.
- Pour in the beaten egg and stir well until fully combined. Continue cooking on LOW temperature for another 2-3 hours. Serve hot.

**Nutrition: Calories: 577 Fat: 43g Carbohydrates: 69g Protein: 44g**

## Chicken Taquitos in Slow Cooker

Small and fast - just try and prepare it!

Prep time: 5 minutes Cooking time: 10 hours
Servings: 3-6

INGREDIENTS:
2 chicken breasts
Half cup sour cream
Half cup chicken broth
1 tsp chipotle chili powder
Cream cheese
2 diced chipotles
1 tsp cumin
Ground black pepper
1 tsp onion powder
1 tsp garlic powder
Half teaspoon salt
8-12 tortilla rounds
1 cup cheddar cheese
Avocado, sour cream, red onion (for topping)

DIRECTIONS:
- Place the chicken breasts in your Slow Cooker, cover with chicken broth, sour cream, chipotles, cream cheese, chipotle chili powder garlic, cumin, salt, onion and black pepper.
- Turn the Slow Cooker on and prepare for 4-6 hours (using LOW temperature mode) or up to 10 hours (on HIGH mode).
- Preheat your oven to 180-200 degrees and spray the baking tray with cooking spray.
- Place the couple of tablespoons of shredded chicken into each tortilla and cover with cheese. Roll in and bake in oven for 10-13 minutes.
- Serve hot with your favorite topping.

**Nutrition: Calories: 533 Fat: 23g Carbohydrates: 29g Protein: 61g**

## Korean Beef Tacos in Slow Cooker

A little spicy Korean dish for your lunch!

Prep time: 5 minutes Cooking time: 9-10 hours
Servings: 4

INGREDIENTS:
One beef steak
3 tbsp soy sauce
1\4 white wine (dry)
One red onion
4 tbsp brown sugar
4 garlic cloves
Half tsp freshly ground pepper
2 limes
1 cup cilantro
Salt
Halg cup seedless cucumbers
3 chopped scallions
5 medium tomatoes
8 corn tortillas

DIRECTIONS:
- Right in the cooking dish of Slow Cooker mix soy sauce, brown sugar, white wine, smashed garlic cloves and black pepper.
- Place the steak into the spice mixture and add halved onion. Cook on LOW for 9 hours. On a sheet pan, broil the peeled and halved tomatoes (until brown on both sides).
- With a food processor, mix the tomatoes, cilantro, garlic, half red onion, juice of two limes, salt and scallions.
- To serve, shred the beef and place it in part along with other ingredients over corn tortillas. Roll in and enjoy!

**Nutrition: Calories: 376 Fat: 42g Carbohydrates: 21g Protein: 34g**

## Quinoa Chicken in Slow Cooker

Fast and easy! Just try this healthy one!

Prep time: 10-13 minutes Cooking time: 3-4 hours
Servings: 8

INGREDIENTS:
One and half cups quinoa
1-2 chicken breasts (boneless and skinless)
4-7 cloves garlic
4-7 cups chicken broth
Salt and other spices (to your taste)
1 tbsp olive oil
Oe lemon juice
1 bunch asparagus
2 cups peas (frozen)
Parmesan (for topping)

DIRECTIONS:
- Wash and rinse the quinoa.
- Cut the chicken into small pieces (it will be ready much faster).
- Place the chicken, quinoa, garlic, seasonings in your Slow Cooker, Cover with chicken broth. Cover with the lid and leave to cook on LOW temperature for 3-4 hours.
- When ready, add the lemon juice, pesto and peas, stir well.
- Meanwhile heat the pan and sauté asparagus until tender-crisp. Add to Slow Cooker. Top each tortilla with shredded cheese and fresh herbs.

**Nutrition: Calories: 235 Fat: 31g Carbohydrates: 23g Protein: 43g**

## Slow Cooker Squash

An amazing autumn meal with summer squash!

Prep time: 10 minutes Cooking time: 1 hour
Servings: 6

INGREDIENTS:
Large summer squash
4 tbsp butter

One small onion
Half cup cubed cheese

DIRECTIONS:
- Peel and slice the yellow summer squash. Chop one small onion. Place the vegetables into a small pot and cover with cold water.
- Bring the squash to boil, and then just simmer for 10 minutes to get the squash tender. Drain the onion with squash with colander (do not stir!)
- Gentle place the vegetables with all other ingredients into Slow Cooker. Turn it on and set on LOW mode. Cook for one hour.

**Nutrition: Calories: 183 Fat: 13g Carbohydrates: 12g Protein: 7g**

## Hot Beans with Pork

Pork notes can make this more than just a side dish!

Prep time: 20 minutes Cooking time: 7 hours
Servings: 8

INGREDIENTS:
Dried pinto beans
5 tbsp chopped pork (better salted)
4 tbsp chopped celery
2-3 tbsp bacon grease
Half cup green bell pepper
1-2 cups yellow onion
Half tsp black pepper
Chipotle chile powder
3 bay leaves
Smoked sausage
2 tbsp fresh parsley (chopped)
Fresh thyme
Water (as needed)
3 tbsp chopped garlic

DIRECTIONS:
- Soak beans for 15-20 minutes. Rinse and drain.
- Place a large pot over medium high heat and heat the bacon grease.
- Add celery, chopped onion, black pepper, chipotle powder, black pepper to the pot. Cook for about 4-5 minutes.
- Add smoked sausage, garlic, parsley, thyme and bay leaves. Prepare to get the sausage browned.
- Transfer the bean and sausage mixture into Slow Cooker and cook on high for about an hour. Then, reduce to LOW and leave for 6 hours (you can add water during the process, if needed). To serve, remove the bay leaves and mash slightly.

**Nutrition: Calories: 460 Fat: 20g Carbohydrates: 41g Protein: 19g**

## Beans with Bacon and Cranberry Sauce

Hot cranberry sauce makes this one sweet and spicy!

Prep time: 5 minutes Cooking time:
Servings:

INGREDIENTS:
One poblano pepper
One onion
One shallot
Dried cranberry beans
1 tsp salt
1 tbsp. barbeque sauce
5 cups chicken stock
5 cloves garlic
Diced bacon
Half tsp hot sauce (chipotle flavored)

DIRECTIONS:
- Cut poblano, remove the seeds and place it all over buttered baking sheet.
- Cook until the skin of pepper a little blackened and blistered (about 5-8 minutes). Leave to cool, remove the skin.
- Dice the poblano pepper and combine it with bacon, beans, shallot, salt, onion, beans, garlic and black pepper.
- Mix the ingredients and transfer to greased Slow Cooker. Pour in the chicken stock over the vegetables.
- Cook on HIGH mode for about three hours (until the beans are softened). In the end, stir in hot sauce and barbeque sauce.

**Nutrition: Calories: 271 Fat: 5g Carbohydrates: 40g Protein: 17g**

## Stuffing with Cranberries and Apple

Amazing duo or berries and apples!

Prep time: 20 minutes Cooking time: 3 hours
Servings: 10-15

INGREDIENTS:
2 cups celery (chopped)
3 tbsp butter
1 cup dried cranberries
1 tsp garlic salt
Parsley
Rubbed sage
2 cups chicken stock
1 cup chopped onion
Black pepper
8 cups cubed bread
2 cups chopped celery
2 medium apples

DIRECTIONS:
- In a wide skillet, melt the butter over medium heat.
- Add chopped onion and celery. Cook, stirring, for 5 minutes (just to get soft). Stir in the mixture cranberries and cubed apples.
- Cover the inside of your Slow Cooker with some cooking spray.
- Add stock and seasonings, place in the vegetable mixture and bread cubes. Cover and cook for three hours on LOW temperature mode.

**Nutrition: Calories: 122 Fat: 3g Carbohydrates: 20g Protein: 2g**

## Barbeque Beans in Slow Cooker

Just bbq sauce and beans – and you can prepare an amazing meal!

Prep time: 30 minutes Cooking time: 8-10 hours
Servings: 12-14

INGREDIENTS:
One package dry beans

Ground beef
1 bay leaf
2 tbsp maple syrup
2/3 bourbon whiskey
1 green bell pepper
One chopped onion
Sliced kielbasa sausage
2 tbsp honey
2 cans chicken broth
3 tbsp coarse-grain mustard
1 red bell pepper
Bacon
1-2 Worcestershire sauce
DIRECTIONS:
- Place the rinsed beans in a large and wide pot. Cover with water and add bay leaf. Bring to boil, and then simmer until the liquid is absorbed. Take off the bay leaf.
- Cook the bacon in a large skillet until evenly browned (around 5 minutes). Drain with paper towels. Mix all the ingredients in the Slow Cooker and stir well to get a smooth mixture.
- Turn on the cooking device and choose the LOW mode. Cook for 8-10 hours.

**Nutrition: Calories: 466 Fat: 19g Carbohydrates: 44g Protein: 21g**

## Ratatouille in Slow Cooker

Now you can do your favorite meal in Slow Cooker!

Prep time: 25 minutes Cooking time: 5 hours
Servings: 8

INGREDIENTS:
1 medium onion
1 red bell pepper (medium)
1 diced zucchini
1 tsp dried basil
Olive oil
2 garlic cloves
1 medium green bell pepper
1 medium eggplant
1 yellow squash
Half tsp dried thyme
2 tbsp. chopped parsley
Black pepper and salt (to taste)
1 can crushed tomatoes
1 can tomato paste
DIRECTIONS:
- Preheat the large skillet with a drizzle of olive oil.
- Add chopped onions and garlic and then cook for around two minutes.0 Stir with tomato paste and transfer to buttered Slow Cooker.
- Heat the skillet again and prepare green and red bell peppers, eggplant, summer squash and zucchini. Cook till tender for 10-15 minute, then place to Slow Cooker.
- Add crushed tomatoes and season with thyme and basil.
- Cook about 5 hours on LOW mode and serve sprinkled with chopped parsley.

**Nutrition: Calories: 164 Fat: 7g Carbohydrates: 21g Protein: 4g**

## Hot German Salad with Potatoes

Hot salad in Slow Cooker – just try this one!

Prep time: 25 minutes Cooking time: 5 hours
Servings: 4

INGREDIENTS:
8-10 small red potatoes
Half tsp celery seed
1 tsp salt
Half cup water
1 small onion
2 tbsp flour
2 tbsp sugar
5-6 tbsp apple cider vinegar
4 slices bacon
Chives (to serve)
DIRECTIONS:
- Scrub the potatoes and slice into thin pieces. Layer the potatoes and halved onions into the buttered Slow Cooker.
- Add water and cook on LOW temperature regime for 5-6 hours.
- Slice the bacon and slightly fry it until brown. Drain with a paper towel.
- In a separate bowl combine sugar, vinegar, flour, salt and celery seed. Mix to avoid any lumps. Add to Slow Cooker with fried bacon. Cook for additional 30 minutes.
- To serve, garnish with chives.

**Nutrition: Calories: 155 Fat: 8g Carbohydrates: 1g Protein: 7g**

## Chicken and Cole Slaw

Chicken with slaw – perfect both for lunch and dinner!

Prep time: 30 minutes Cooking time: 6-8 hours
Servings: 6-8

INGREDIENTS:
1 medium onion
One cup barbeque sauce
1 chicken breast
2 tbsp vinegar
2 tbsp olive oil
Half head cabbage
Avocado
3 medium carrots
1 tbsp pickle juice
2 tbsp mayonnaise
3 tbsp Greek yogurt
DIRECTIONS:
- Butter your Slow Cooker and layer its bottom with a part of diced onions.
- Place the salted and peppered chicken on the onions. Pour with bbq sauce and leave to cook for 6-8 hours on LOW mode.
- Shred the carrots and remaining onions with a food processor. Transfer the vegetables to a wide bowl. Add thinly sliced cabbage.
- In a separate bowl, combine the ingredients for dressing: Greek yogurt, avocado, pickle juice, mayonnaise, vinegar, sauce and pepper with salt.
- When the chicken is ready, drain it and toss with two forks. Combine with the cabbage mix and top with the dressing.

Nutrition: Calories: 344 Fat: 5g Carbohydrates: 42g Protein: 7g

## Slow Cooker Carrots with Herbs

Try this one and you will cook it very often!

⌀ Prep time: 15 minutes Cooking time: 4-6 hours
Servings: 4

INGREDIENTS:
6-7 long carrots
1 tsp dried dill
Salt to taste
3 tbsp butter
1 tbsp honey

DIRECTIONS:
- Wash and peel the carrots, cut them into one-inch size coins.
- In a separate saucepan, melt the butter and stir it with salt, honey and dill. You can also take a separate bowl and mix the species with already melted butter.
- Grease the bottom of your Slow Cooker and cover it with carrot coins. Pour the honey and butter mixture over the slices.
- Cook, covered with the lid, for 2-3 hours (if you use HIGH temperature mode), or for 4-6 hours (for LOW temp mode).
- To serve, transfer the carrots to a wide dish. Serve while hot.

Nutrition: Calories: 171 Fat: 4g Carbohydrates: 31g Protein: 21g

## Tricolor potatoes with Garlic and Rosemary

Spiced potatoes for any occasion!

⌀ Prep time: 13 minutes Cooking time: 4 hours
Servings: 5-6

INGREDIENTS:
One bag tricolor potatoes
1 tsp salt
4 cloves garlic
Black pepper
1 tsp oregano
2 tbsp. Parmesan (grated)
2-3 sprigs thyme (fresh)
4-5 tbsp. olive oil

DIRECTIONS:
- Wash and dry the potatoes with a towel. Do not peel – just cut in quarters or halves (depending on the size of each potato).
- Cover the bottom of your cooking dish with a cooking spray or, even better, line it with a foil. Place the potatoes and sprinkle over with olive oil.
- In a small dish, mix oregano, minced garlic, rosemary and thyme. Sprinkle the potatoes with this mixture. Add some pepper and salt to your taste.
- Cover the lid and prepare for 2-3 hours (HIGH mode) or 5-6 hours (LOW mode). Serve immediately with the sprinkles of Parmesan.

Nutrition: Calories: 232 Fat: 8g Carbohydrates: 21g Protein: 81g

## Spinach and Artichoke in Slow Cooker

Simple and healthy receipt!

⌀ Prep time: 25 minutes Cooking time: 2 hours
Servings: 8

INGREDIENTS:
2 cans artichoke hearts
Sour cream
5-6 tbsp. milk
1 small onion
Half cup feta cheese (crumbled)
2 cloves garlic
1 pack spinach (frozen)
Half cup parmesan cheese
4 tbsp. mayonnaise
Cubed cream cheese
1 tbsp. red wine vinegar
Black pepper (freshly ground)

DIRECTIONS:
- Chop the artichoke hearts well, dice the onion and crush the garlic. Butter a bottom of your Slow Cooker.
- Right in the cooking dish, combine artichoke hearts, milk, cheese, sour cream, spinach, mayonnaise, sour cream, onion, garlic, pepper and vinegar.
- Cover the lid and cook for the next 2 hours on LOW temperature mode.
- When it is about 15 minutes left, stir the ingredients and let to cook another 15 minutes. Serve hot.

Nutrition: Calories: 355 Fat: 26g Carbohydrates: 19g Protein: 14g

## Creamy Corn with Cheese

Creamy and hot meal for everyone!

⌀ Prep time: 5 minutes Cooking time: 4-6 Servings: 4-5

INGREDIENTS:

One bag corn kernels (frozen)
2 tbsp butter
Cream cheese
Half tsp sugar (if needed)

DIRECTIONS:
- Cover the inside of your Slow Cooker with cooking spray or butter.
- Right in a dish of Slow Cooker, combine the corn with butter and cream cheese.
- Cover with a special lid and prepare for 4-6 hours (if you prefer the LOW temperature modes) or for 2-3 (for HIGH mode).
- Taste the meal and add (if needed) the sugar to taste. It depends on the sweetness of the corn). Serve stirred and hot.

Nutrition: Calories: 344 Fat: 24g Carbohydrates: 19g Protein: 61g

## Brussels sprouts for Slow Cooker

Perfect for spring and summer seasons!

⌀ Prep time: 10 minutes Cooking time: 4 hours
Servings: 6

INGREDIENTS:
Half cup balsamic vinegar
Fresh Brussels sprouts
2 tbsp. olive oil
Salt

2 tbsp. brown sugar
4 tbsp. Parmesan cheese (freshly grated)
2 tbsp. unsalted butter
Ground black pepper

DIRECTIONS:
- To prepare the balsamic reduction, take a small saucepan and preheat balsamic vinegar and brown sugar in it. Bring to boil, and then simmer for 6-8 minutes.
- Right in the Slow Cooker, combine Brussels sprouts and olive oil. Season with pepper/salt and cover with butter.
- Cover on LOW temperature mode for 3-4 hours.
- To serve, drizzle with balsamic reduction and Parmesan

**Nutrition: Calories: 193 Fat: 10g Carbohydrates: 21g Protein: 7g**

## Herbed Fingerling Potatoes in Slow Cooker

Your family definitely will love this!

⌛ **Prep time: 5 minutes Cooking time: 5-8 hours Servings: 4**

INGREDIENTS:
2 tbsp butter (melted)
One bag fingerling potatoes
Crushed rosemary
Pepper
Dried dill
Dried parsley
Dried thyme
1 tsp salt
Half cup cheese (white cheddar or white cheese)
Half cup heavy cream

DIRECTIONS:
- Wash the potatoes and cut in half. Better, cut lengthwise, if there are big ones – quarter them). Cover the inside of Slow Cooker with butter or cooking spray.
- Place the potatoes in the Slow Cooker dish and toss them with remaining butter. Add all the herbs, season with salt and pepper.
- Cover the Slow Cooker with the lid and let to cook for 2-4 hours on HIGH or for 5-8 hours on LOW. In the end, stir in the cheese and cream.
- Cook for another 16-30 minutes to get the cheese melted and then serve.

**Nutrition: Calories: 455 Fat: 8g Carbohydrates: 27g Protein: 18g**

## Buttered Corn in Slow Cooker

Sweet and tasty for your friends and family!

⌛ **Prep time: 5 minutes Cooking time: 2-4 hours Servings: 4**

INGREDIENTS:
4 fresh corn cobs
Lime juice
Black pepper
Salt
4 tbsp butter (room temperature)
1 tbsp cilantro (fresh and chopped)

DIRECTIONS:
- Prepare four pieces of aluminum foil. Place each cob on the foil.
- In a small bowl, combine lime juice, spices and butter. Spread the mixture evenly over each corncob.
- Wrap each corncob with a foil.
- Spray the Slow Cooker with a cooking spray and place the corncobs over the bottom. Cook on HIGH for 2 hours or on LOW – for 3-4 hours.
- To serve, sprinkle the corn with chopped cilantro.

**Nutrition: Calories: 349 Fat: 12g Carbohydrates: 73g Protein: 8g**

## Slow Cooker ham and pea soup

Easy-to-make soup! Perfect for springtime!

⌛ **Prep time: 10 minutes Cooking time: 8 hours Servings: 9**

INGREDIENTS:
5 medium carrots
Chopped ham
4 stalks celery
4 cups chicken broth
1 chopped onion
2 cups water
1 bag split peas
Smoked paprika (optional)
Fresh chopped parsley

DIRECTIONS:
- Peel and cut all the vegetables into small pieces.
- Combine the onion, carrots, ham, celery, peas with broth and water. You can do it right in your Slow Cooker.
- Turn the Slow Cooker and on set to LOW mode. Cook for 7-10 hours. The peas should be broken. Add one more cup of water if needed.
- Serve into small bowl. Use chopped parsley as a garnish.

**Nutrition: Calories: 538 Fat: 29g Carbohydrates: 52g Protein: 33g**

## Baked beans in Slow Cooker

It takes a lot of cooking time, but it totally worth it!

⌛ **Prep time: 5 minutes Cooking time: 12-16 hours Servings: 6**

INGREDIENTS:
1 cup bourbon
Dried navy beans
1 cup barbecue sauce
3 tbsp. olive oil
1 cup water
1 cup maple syrup
2 tbsp. Worcestershire sauce
1 cup brown sugar
Mustard molasses
2 tbsp. apple vinegar

DIRECTIONS:
- Sort dry beans and rinse them over sink.
- In a large pot, cover the beans with some water and leave to soak overnight.

- Place the beans with 6 cups of water into separate bowl pot and simmer for 45 minutes. Meanwhile, combine all the remaining ingredients in the Slow Cooker and mix well.
- Add the beans in your Slow Cooker and cook on LOW mode for 12 hours (but start to check the readiness at about 7-8 hours).
- Serve while hot.

**Nutrition: Calories: 612 Fat: 34g Carbohydrates: 29g Protein: 45g**

## White Chicken Chili in Slow Cooker

Chicken with beans – a perfect lunchtime match!

**Prep time: 5 minutes Cooking time: 4 hours**
**Servings: 6-8**

INGREDIENTS:
One yellow onion (large)
3 cloves garlic
Two boneless chicken thighs
1 bay leaf
Half tsp dried oregano
1 cup frozen corn
2 stalks celery
2 tsp cumin
1 can chili pepper (green)
Salt
4cups chicken stock
1 can navy beans
Monterey jack cheese to serve

DIRECTIONS:
- Prepare you Slow Cooker and place into it the chicken, celery, garlic, onions, green chili peppers, salt, coriander, cumin, bay leaf and oregano. Stir to cover the meat with spices.
- Pour in the chicken broth to cover the ingredients.
- Place the Slow Cooker lid and prepare for 6 hours on HIGH modes (or 4 on low). In 30 minutes before the end, add the beans and corn.
- Shred the chicken well and stir with another ingredients.
- Serve with lime wedges, shredded cheese or chopped cilantro.

**Nutrition: Calories: 434 Fat: 34g Carbohydrates: 46g Protein: 28g**

## Thai Red Curry in Slow Cooker

A little spicy, but healthy and delicious!

**Prep time: 30 minutes Cooking time: 8-9 hours**
**Servings: 4**

INGREDIENTS:
Salt
Half cup brown sugar
1 cup coconut milk
Black pepper
Pork shoulder
2 tbsp curry paste
1 quartered onion
Ginger
16 corn tortillas
4 crushed garlic cloves
Vegetable oil
Chopped jalapenos
2 tbsp radishes (chopped)
2 tbsp green onions (chopped)

DIRECTIONS:
- Right in Slow Cooker, toss pork pieces with salt and pepper.
- In separate bowl, combine coconut milk, curry paste and brown sugar. Pour the mixture to the Slow Cooker dish.
- Add ginger, garlic, chicken broth and onion, mix and cook on LOW temperature mode for 8-9 hours.
- Drain and finely shred the pork.
- Warm corn tortillas on nonstick skillet. Fill them with the shredded pork. To serve, sprinkle with sour cream or add radishes or green onions.

**Nutrition: Calories: 563 Fat: 54g Carbohydrates: 32g Protein: 28g**

## Slow cooker peas with asparagus

Another dish with asparagus – overnight and healthy!

**Prep time: 15 minutes Cooking time: 9 hours**
**Servings: 4**

INGREDIENTS:
2 tbsp olive oil
Salt
Boneless beef
2 cup red wine (dry)
2 bay leaves
Black pepper (freshly ground)
1 tbsp tomato paste
2 large onions
Frozen peas
Trimmed asparagus
1 cup chicken broth
2 cloves garlic

DIRECTIONS:
- Take a large skillet and heat it with olive oil. Place the meat and fry well from all sides.
- In the Slow Cooker bowl, mix salt, bay leaves, tomato paste, pepper, garlic and crushed tomatoes. Pour over with the broth, stir well and cook on LOW temperature mode for 6-9 hours.
- In a large skilled, half-filled with water, bring to boil asparagus. Then cook for 4-5 minutes. Add frozen peas and leave cooking for another 2 minutes.
- Slice the meat into small pieces.
- Serve with veggies and topped with braising liquid.

**Nutrition: Calories: 672 Fat: 62g Carbohydrates: 27g Protein: 34g**

## Tacos and Sriracha Mayo

Fast answer to your lunchtime question!

**Prep time: 10 minutes Cooking time: 8 hours**
**Servings: 4**

INGREDIENTS:
Half cup whole milk
One halved orange
One small onion
Olive oil
Half cup mayonnaise
5 garlic cloves
2 limes
1 tbsp sriracha

1 tsp oregano
Red onion
Cilantro
Radishes
Salt
Pork shoulder

DIRECTIONS:
- In the Slow Cooker bowl, mix the orange juice, 1-cup water, oil, milk, orange rinds, oregano, onion, pork shoulder and garlic.
- Mix well and cook on LOW temperature modes for 8 hours.
- In another small bowl, combine Sriracha, mayonnaise, lime juice and salt.
- Take out the pork and reserve the excess fat and liquid. Cut meat into small slices. Warm tortillas in nonstick frying pan.
- Serve the pork wrapped in tortillas.

**Nutrition: Calories: 439 Fat: 35g Carbohydrates: 65g Protein: 43g**

## Apple Cider Chicken in Slow Cooker

Fast and healthy dish for a family dinner!

**Prep time: 5 minutes Cooking time: 3 hours Servings: 10-12**

INGREDIENTS:
1-2 tablespoon olive oil
2 bay leaves
2 tsp chopped thyme
4 celery stalks
1 tbsp chopped fresh sage
Two small chickens
4 garlic cloves
1 medium yellow onion
3 cups chicken stock
1 tbsp cornstarch
Cayenne, paprika, black pepper
Salt
One tsp chili powder
Sliced apples for garnish

DIRECTIONS:
- Preheat a large saucepan with olive oil. Add celery, bay leaves, garlic, and onion. Cook for 3-6 minutes until soften.
- Add thyme, sage and cornstarch and cook, stirring, for one more minute. Add beans and chicken; pour over with the chicken stock.
- Season with cayenne, salt, chili powder, paprika and cider.
- Transfer the saucepan ingredients to preheated Slow Cooker and leave for 12 hours on LOW mode.
- To serve, garnish with apple slices.

**Nutrition: Calories: 349 Fat: 6g Carbohydrates: 45g Protein: 54g**

## Sweet Potatoes with Apples

Sweety apple recipe tastes awesome with meat or vegetables.

**Prep time: 5 minutes Cooking time: 6-7 hours Servings: 10**

INGREDIENTS:
6-7 not big sweet potatoes
One cup whipping cream
1-2 tsp pumpkin spice
2 medium red apples
Half cup cranberries (dried)

DIRECTIONS:
- Peel and cut the potatoes into small pieces (approximately one-inch cubes) Core and cut the apples into thin wedges
- Spray your Slow Cooker with a cooking spray or cover with butter. Right in a cooking bowl combine the apples, potatoes and dried berries.
- In a separate bowl, join the cream, pumpkin spice and apple butter. Pour the mixture over the apples.
- Cover with the lid and cook for 6-7 hours on LOW-heat regimes or 3 hours on HIGH.

**Nutrition: Calories: 351 Fat: 9g Carbohydrates: 65g Protein: 2g**

## Spinach Lasagna in Slow Cooker

Love Italian? Cook this easy-to-make lasagna!

**Prep time: 30 minutes Cooking time: 3 hours Servings: 8**

INGREDIENTS:
Frozen spinach
Half cup water
1 tsp dried parsley
One chicken egg
1 tbsp Italian seasoning
4 cups shredded mozzarella
3 tbsp tomato paste
12 lasagna noodles (uncooked)
Pinch red pepper
Half teaspoon garlic powder
2 jars tomato paste
1 cup grated parmesan

DIRECTIONS:
- Take a large bowl and combine the ricotta, spinach, parmesan cheese, parsley and one egg.
- In another bowl, whisk together water, pasta sauce, seasoning, garlic powder, and tomato paste and garlic powder.
- Butter your Slow Cooker and spread the tomato paste over the bottom.
- Place the lasagna noodles and ricotta mixture over the bottom. Cover with one cup Mozzarella. Repeat in 2-3 layers.
- Cover the lid of Slow Cooker and prepare on LOW modes for 4-3 hours. To serve, leave lasagna for 30 minutes to cool.

**Nutrition: Calories: 570 Fat: 31g Carbohydrates: 41g Protein: 33g**

## Broccoli and Cauliflower with Cheese topping

Amazing vegetable receipt for you and your family!

**Prep time: 25 minutes Cooking time: 7 hours Servings: 10**

INGREDIENTS:
1 large onion
Ground black pepper (to taste)
Four cups cauliflower florets
Four cups broccoli florets

Half cup almonds
1-2 cups Swiss cheese
One jar pasta sauce
Dried thyme
Crushed basil
DIRECTIONS:
- Butter the bottom of your Slow Cooker or cover it with the anti-sticking cooking spray.
- In a separate jar, combine chopped onion, broccoli, pasta sauce, cauliflower, Swiss cheese, thyme and pepper to taste.
- Transfer the mixture into the Slow Cooker dish.
- Cover with the lid and leave to cook for 6-7 hours (on LOW temperature modes) or for around 3 hours (on HIGH).
- Serve while hot, sprinkled with almonds.

**Nutrition: Calories: 177 Fat: 12g Carbohydrates: 10g Protein: 8g**

## Summer Vegetables with Chickpeas

Healthy and delicious choice for the summer!

**Prep time: 25 minutes Cooking time: 8 Servings: 6**

INGREDIENTS:

One can Garbanzo beans
2 tbsp olive oil
2 tbsp rosemary (fresh)
4 cups baby spinach
2 cups grape tomatoes
2 cloves garlic
Half teaspoon black pepper (ground)
10 baby carrots
2 fresh sweet corn
7-8 small potatoes
2 cups chopped chicken
1 medium onion
2 cups chicken broth
Zucchini
DIRECTIONS:
- Combine garbanzo beans, oil, garlic, rosemary and pepper. You can do it in a plastic bowl with a lid or in a resalable plastic bag.
- Place the bowl into the refrigerator and leave for 12-48 hours. Put the marinated (undrained) chickpeas into Slow Cooker.
- Add corn, carrots, onion, tomatoes and potatoes.
- Pour in the broth and cook on LOW-heat for 8-10 hours.
- To serve, add zucchini, spinach and chicken (if desired). Stir until spinach wilts and serve immediately.

**Nutrition: Calories: 273 Fat: 8g Carbohydrates: 42g Protein: 12g**

## Sweet Potatoes with Bacon

Try this one with bacon for your lunch or dinner!

**Prep time: 17 minutes Cooking time: 5-6 hours Servings: 10**

INGREDIENTS:
Half spoon dried thyme
8 large sweet potatoes
4 bacon slices
2 tbsp butter
Half tsp sage (dried)

Half cup orange juice
1 tsp salt
3 tbsp brown sugar
DIRECTIONS:
- Peel and cut the potatoes into two-inch pieces.
- To avoid sticking, cover the bottom of your Slow Cooker with some butter or special cooking spray.
- Place the potatoes into Slow Cooker.
- In a separate cooking bowl, combine the INGREDIENTS: juice, thyme, brown sugar, sage and salt. Add some butter.
- Cover your Slow Cooker with the lid and cook on LOW heat temperature for 5-6 hours (or HIGH for 2-3 hours).
- When serving, sprinkle slightly over with crumbled bacon.

**Nutrition: Calories: 189 Fat: 4g Carbohydrates: 36g Protein: 4g**

## Mashed Potatoes with Garlic

Simple and healthy dish for your healthy lifestyle!

**Prep time: 27 minutes Cooking time: 6-8 hours Servings: 12**

INGREDIENTS:
5-6 large potatoes
1 leaf of bay
6 garlic cloves
One cup whole milk
3 tbsp butter
Black pepper (freshly ground)
1 tsp salt
2-3 cups chicken broth
DIRECTIONS:
- Peel and cut potatoes into thin one-inch slices.
- Place the potatoes into your Slow Cooker dish along with bay leaf and garlic. Mix in the chicken broth.
- Cook covered on LOW temperature mode for 6-8 hours, or on HIGH temperature – for 3-4 hours. When ready, drain the potato using a colander (save the liquid) and remove the bay leaf.
- Place the potatoes back to Slow Cooker and then mash with a potato masher.
- In a small sauce pan, heat the milk with butter and add stir the mixture into the mash. Serve sprinkled with freshly ground pepper.

**Nutrition: Calories: 135 Fat: 5g Carbohydrates: 21g Protein: 3g**

## Sweet and Spice beetroots

Sweet and unusual part of your diet!

**Prep time: 15 minutes Cooking time: 6-7 hours Servings: 8**

INGREDIENTS:
Half cup pomegranate juice
3 tbsp sugar
Salt to taste
1 tbsp cornstarch
2 tsp fresh ginger (grated)
5-6 golden or red beets
12 small carrots
DIRECTIONS:

- Peel the carrots and beetroots with a vegetable peeler and cut into small three-inch pieces. Take a medium saucepan and mix in it pomegranate juice with salt and cornstarch. Stir in sugar and whisk until cornstarch is dissolved.
- Stir in grated ginger and mix until smooth.
- Right in a Slow Cooker dish, combine the pomegranate juice with the carrots and beetroots. Cover the Slow Cooker lid and prepare for 6 to 7 hours on HIGH heat –temperature setting (or 4-5 on LOW).
- You can serve this meal warm (as a side dish) or cold (as a salad).

**Nutrition: Calories: 126 Fat: 1g Carbohydrates: 29g Protein: 3g**

## Macaroni with American Cheese

Perfect for big cheese fans!

**Prep time: 15 minutes Cooking time: 2 hours Servings: 8**

INGREDIENTS:
One cup cayenne pepper sauce
2-3 medium carrots
Milk (optional)
Celery
Multigrain rotini pasta (can be packaged)
Dry salad dressing mix
American cheese
DIRECTIONS:
- Peel and shred the carrots and thinly slice the celery. Torn the American cheese into bite-size pieces.
- Cover the inside of your Slow Cooker with the butter. Add multigrain rotini pasta, carrots, celery and one cup cayenne pepper sauce.
- Cover with four cups of water and stir well to combine completely.
- Cover your Slow Cooker with the lid and cook on HIGH for a couple hours (until the pasta absorbs all the liquid).
- Five minutes before the end add cheese and do not stir. To serve, add some milk for creamy taste.

**Nutrition: Calories: 307 Fat: 11g Carbohydrates: 39g Protein: 14g**

## Squash Summer Gratin

Easy, healthy and delicious meal for any summer night!

**Prep time: 13 minutes Cooking time: 7 hours Servings: 6**

INGREDIENTS:
Three cloves garlic
Small butternut squash (or half big one)
Ground black pepper
One medium onion
Half cup water
Salt
One package frozen spinach
2 cups vegetarian broth
One cup plain barley
Half cup Parmesan
DIRECTIONS:

- Pell, seed and cut butternut squash into small cubes (about 5-6 full cups). Cut the onion into small wedges.
- In a Slow Cooker, mix the squash cubes, onion, barley, spinach, salt, garlic and pepper. Cover with the broth.
- Turn on the Slow Cooker and cover with the lid. Cook for 6-7 hours at LOW temperature (or for 3 at HIGH).
- Turn off the cooker and sprinkle with Parmesan. Let stand for 10 minutes and then serve.

**Nutrition: Calories: 196 Fat: 3g Carbohydrates: 36g Protein: 9g**

## Squash in Cranberry Sauce

Try this one with cranberry sauce! So tasty and healthy, you will not regret!

**Prep time: 19 minutes Cooking time: 7 hours Servings: 4**

INGREDIENTS:
3-4 tbsp raisins
One can cranberry sauce (jellied)
4 tbsp orange marmalade
4 acorn squash
Ground cinnamon
Black pepper and salt
DIRECTIONS:
- Wash each squash and cut in length; remove seeds and dice into one-inch wedges. Butter the bottom and sides of your Slow Cooker.
- Place the squash wedges into Slow Cooker.
- Heat the small saucepan with marmalade, cranberry sauce, cinnamon and raisins. Pour into the Slow Cooker and stir all the ingredients until smooth.
- Set your Slow Cooker to LOW-temperature mode and leave the squash cooking for 6-7 hours (you can use HIGH temp as well and cook for 3 hours).
- Before serving, add some salt and pepper to taste.

**Nutrition: Calories: 328 Fat: 5g Carbohydrates: 71g Protein: 2g**

## Brussels sprouts and Maple Syrup

Unusual syrup will make the dish more delicious! Try this with your friends!

**Prep time: 23 minutes Cooking time: 4 hours Servings: 12**

INGREDIENTS:
Red onion (one cup)
Maple syrup
Half tsp salt
3 tbsp butter
Brussels sprouts
1 tbsp fresh thyme (snipped)
2-3 tbsp apple cider
Black pepper
DIRECTIONS:
- Halve the Brussels sprouts; chop red onion and fresh thyme.
- Combine the sprouts with onion right in your Slow Cooker dish, season a little with salt/pepper. Pour in the apple cider to cover slightly the vegetables.

- Cover the lid and set the Slow Cooker on LOW-heat temperature regime for 3 hours (if want faster, cook on HIGH for 1-2 hours).
- Meanwhile, mix together maple syrup, thyme and melted butter. Stir with the sprouts. To serve, garnish with fresh thyme leaves.

**Nutrition: Calories: 90 Fat: 4g Carbohydrates: 13g Protein: 3g**

## Wild Rice with Cherries

Taste this combination of rice and berries!

**Prep time: 20 minutes Cooking time: 5-6 hours Servings: 15**

INGREDIENTS:
2-3 cups wild rice
2 cups chicken broth
2 tsps marjoram (dried and crushed)
2 tbsp melted butter
2 medium carrots
Half cup dried cherries
2 green onions
Salt to taste
Half cup chopped pecans
One cup sliced and drained mushrooms

DIRECTIONS:
- Peel and coarsely shred the carrots and green onions.
- Butter your Slow Cooker and fill it with uncooked wild rice, mushrooms, carrot, marjoram, salt, melted butter and pepper.
- Pour in the broth to cover all the ingredients. Stir slightly.
- Cover the Slow Cooker lid and prepare on LOW-temperature mode for 5 or 6 hours. Then turn off Slow Cooker.
- Add dried cherries, pecans, green onions, and stir to combine the ingredients. To serve, use chopped green onions.

**Nutrition: Calories: 169 Fat: 5g Carbohydrates: 27g Protein: 5g**

## Vegetable Curry with Garbanzo

Try to cook this vegetable dish with basil and beans!

**Prep time: 25 minutes Cooking time: 5 or 6 hours Servings: 4**

INGREDIENTS:
Three cups cauliflower florets
2-3 medium carrots
One cup green bean (frozen)
One can vegetable broth
One can coconut milk
2 tbsp fresh basil (shredded)
One can garbanzo beans
3-4 tsp curry powder

DIRECTIONS:
- Cut the carrots and onions into small pieces.
- In a separate bowl, gather cauliflower, green and garbanzo beans, onion and carrots. Season with curry powder.
- Transfer the vegetable mix into the buttered Slow Cooker and pour in the broth.
- Cover with the Slow Cooker lid and do not open until ready. Cook on LOW temperature for 5 or 6 hours or on HIGH – for 2 or 3.
- In the end of cooking time add some basil and coconut milk and stir well to combine all the ingredients.

**Nutrition: Calories: 219 Fat: 7g Carbohydrates: 32g Protein: 8g**

## Kale and Eggplant Panzanella

Healthy and spicy, it may become your favorite!

**Prep time: 24 minutes Cooking time: 2 or 4 hours Servings: 6**

INGREDIENTS:
Two medium eggplants
One medium pepper (sweet and yellow)
One can roasted tomatoes
3 tbsp red wine vinegar
2 tbsp olive oil
Half cup shredded Parmesan
One clove garlic
1 tsp Dijon mustard
Half cup basil (fresh leaves)
4 cups cubed French bread
One red onion
4 cups chopped kale leaves

DIRECTIONS:
- Butter the inside of your Slow Cooker and put into it chopped eggplant, wedged onion and red pepper.
- Cover Slow Cooker and set low temperature for 4 hours or HIGH temperature for 2 hours. In 2-3 hours stir in kale and cook for another 15 minutes.
- Prepare the dressing: in a separate bowl, combine oil, mustard, vinegar, garlic and black pepper. Whisk all together well.
- Serve the vegetables in a large bowl, sprinkled with the cheese and basil leaves.

**Nutrition: Calories: 243 Fat: 9g Carbohydrates: 34g Protein: 9g**

## Sweet Potato Lentils in Slow Cooker

Sweet, fast and healthy potatoes!

**Prep time: 23 minutes Cooking time: 3 hours Servings: 6-8**

INGREDIENTS:
Three sweet potatoes
One minced onion
Three cups vegetable broth
One cup water
Four cloves garlic
Half teaspoon salt
One can coconut milk
Chili powder
Coriander
Garam masala
1-2 cups red lentils (uncooked)

DIRECTIONS:
- Peel and dice the potatoes, mince the onion.
- Preheat the Slow Cooker and fill it with sweet potatoes, minced onion, vegetable broth, garlic and spices.
- Cover with vegetable broth and cook on high mode for 2-3 hours (or until the vegetables are soft). Add the lentils and cook on HIGH for one more 1-2 hours until ready.

- Pour in the coconut milk and water (as you need to get the right consistency) Serve with fresh bread or toasts.

**Nutrition: Calories: 326 Fat: 11g Carbohydrates: 44g Protein: 13g**

## Butternut Squash with Chili

Delicious squash can be healthy – try it!

⏱ **Prep time: 10 minutes Cooking time: 6 hours Servings: 8**

INGREDIENTS:
One small onion
2 carrots
2 stalks celery
1 medium butternut squash
2 medium apples
4 cloves garlic
2 tsp chili powder
2 cups vegetable broth
One can black beans
1 can coconut oil (low-fat)
1 can chickpeas (medium)
2 tsp oregano (dried)
1tbsp ground cumin
Basmati rice (optional)
Pepper/salt to taste
2tbsp tomato paste Fresh parsley
Shredded coconut (to garnish)
DIRECTIONS:
- Place all the ingredients (except the garnish and rice) into Slow Cooker.
- Cook on HIGH temperature mode for 3 to 6 hours. If you want, you can leave it overnight for 8 hours (then cook on low mode).
- On the last hour of cooking taste and add some salt and pepper.
- If you like it spicy, you can also add some chili powder or a pinch of cayenne pepper. In the last 30-40 minutes remove the lid and let the chili to thicken.
- To serve, pour the chili over basmati rice and garnish shredded coconut and parsley.

**Nutrition: Calories: 544 Fat: 28g Carbohydrates: 65g Protein: 50g**

## Tikka Masala with Chicken in Slow Cooker

Try this delicious chicken soup as your lunch!

⏱ **Prep time: 5 minutes Cooking time: 4-8 hours Servings: 8**

INGREDIENTS:
2-3chicken thighs (without bones)
2 cloves garlic
2 tbsp tomato paste
2 tsp paprika
2 tbsp garam masala
1 can diced tomatoes
Small ginger
1 large onion
Salt
Fresh cilantro
3 tbsp coconut milk
2 cups cooked rice
DIRECTIONS:
- Cut the chicken into bite-sized pieces. Place the chicken into Slow Cooker.
- Dice the onion and place it over the chicken, add minced ginger and garlic, garam masala, salt, paprika. Cover with tomato paste and stir everything well to fully cover the chicken.
- Cover the Slow Cooker and set HIGH temperature for 4 hours or LOW for 8 hours.
- 15 minutes before the end of cooking time mix in the cream and add more species if needed. Serve with the rice and fresh cilantro.

**Nutrition: Calories: 477 Fat: 34g Carbohydrates: 61g Protein: 55g**

## Enchilada Soup with Chicken

Unusual, but healthy and amazing receipt!

⏱ **Prep time: 27 minutes Cooking time: 6-7 hours Servings: 6**

INGREDIENTS:
Cooking oil
1 tbsp sugar
2 tbsp chili powder
1 medium onion
2 garlic cloves
One can tomato sauce
Two medium tomatoes
2 cups chicken stock or broth
1 tbsp ground cumin
1 large jalapeno
1 can yellow corn
1can black beans
2-3 chicken thighs
Salt and black pepper to taste
DIRECTIONS:
- Heat two tablespoons of oil in a large frying pan (medium heat).
- Place the jalapeno and diced onions and cook until soft (5-7 minutes).
- Add chili powder, garlic, sugar, cumin, and cook until fragrant. Add the tomatoes, the stock and tomato sauce. After a little boil transfer to Slow Cooker.
- Add the chicken, beans, corn, and cook covered for 6-7 hours on LOW temperature mode. Before serving shred the chicken with two forks and stir in the heavy cream (optional).
- Serve with a bit of Cheddar cheese, cilantro or tortilla chips as a garnish.

**Nutrition: Calories: 501 Fat: 41g Carbohydrates: 55g Protein: 61g**

## Spicy Black Eyed Peas in Slow Cooker

Spicy beans will perfectly fit with meat!

⏱ **Prep time: 30 minutes Cooking time: 6 hours Servings: 6-8**

INGREDIENTS:
One medium onion
6 cups water
2 cloves garlic

One cube bouillon
One red bell pepper
4 slices bacon
Diced ham
One jalapeno chili
1 tsp cumin
Ground black pepper and salt to taste
DIRECTIONS:
- Start preheating your Slow Cooker.
- Pour in the water and add one cube of chicken bouillon, stir slowly to dissolve.
- In a separate bowl, combine the INGREDIENTS: chopped onion, bell pepper, black-eyed-peas, jalapeno pepper, garlic, ham and bacon.
- Season the mixture with cayenne pepper, salt, cumin and black pepper, Stir everything well. Transfer the mixture to your Slow Cooker and cook under the lid for 6-8 hours (using LOW temperature mode).
- Serve until the beans are ready and tender.

**Nutrition: Calories: 199 Fat: 3g Carbohydrates: 30g Protein: 14g**

## Tender Taters in Slow Cooker

Easy to make and very tasty to eat!

⌚ **Prep time: 19 minutes Cooking time: 4 hours Servings: 6**

INGREDIENTS:
Half cup butter
Water
One pinch black pepper (freshly ground)
6-8 large Yukon potatoes
One can skim milk (evaporated)
1 package gravy mix
DIRECTIONS:
- Peel the potatoes and dice them into 2-inch slices.
- Spray your Slow Cooker with cooking spray (to avoid sticking).
- Place the potato pieces in your Cooker and sprinkle just a little with a freshly grounded black pepper.
- In another bowl, whisk together water and the country gravy mix. Stir until ingredients are well blended. Pour into Slow Cooker.
- Add the evaporated milk and cook, covered, for 4 hours on LOW temperature level. To serve. Drain all excess liquid and mash with butter.

**Nutrition: Calories: 367 Fat: 16g Carbohydrates: 48g Protein: 9g**

## Parmesan Rice with Chicken

Soft chicken meat tastes amazing with melted Parmesan!

⌚ **Prep time: 32 minutes Cooking time: 4 hours Servings: 6**

INGREDIENTS:
1-2 cups white rise (take long0grain)
1/3 cup water
Half cup green peas (frozen)
Half tsp basil (can use dry)
2 cans chicken broth
2 cloves garlic
2 medium onions
Grated Parmesan
2 tbsp pine nuts
Italian seasoning
DIRECTIONS:
- Dice the onion and mince the garlic before the start.
- Butter your Slow Cooker and fill it with rinsed rise, garlic and onion.
- Take a medium saucepan and bring the water and chicken broth to boil (use high heat). Pour the liquid into rice. Add the basil and Italian seasoning. Stir finely.
- Cook under the lid for 2-3 hours on LOW temperature settings (check the readiness when all liquid is absorbed).
- Add peas and cook for another hour.
- To serve, stir in Parmesan and cover with pine nuts.

**Nutrition: Calories: 271 Fat: 4g Carbohydrates: 46g Protein: 9g**

## Collard Greens in Slow Cooker

Fast and easy dish – cook it when you are busy or do not have much time!

⌚ **Prep time: 25 minutes Cooking time: 3-4 hours Servings: 8**

INGREDIENTS:
Two cans beef stock
1 tsp white sugar
1 bay leaf
2-3 small onions
2 tsp red wine vinegar
Half tsp red pepper flakes
2 bunches collard greens
Salt
2 bunches mustard greens
1 tsp garlic powder
2 bunches turnip greens
1 can diced tomatoes
DIRECTIONS:
- Chop the onions; thinly slice collard and mustard greens. Prepare your Slow Cooker and cover it thinly with melted butter.
- Right in the Slow Cooker dish, combine green chilies, diced tomatoes and chopped onions. Add beef stock, vinegar, sugar, ham, salt, garlic powder, red pepper flakes and one bay leaf.
- Stir in the collard greens, mustard greens and turnip greens into Slow Cooker (follow this order). Cover and cook on LOW temperature regime until the greens are tender enough.

**Nutrition: Calories: 131 Fat: 4g Carbohydrates: 16g Protein: 9g**

## Mexican Pinto Beans with Cactus

Spicy beans with an unusual accent!

⌚ **Prep time: 10 minutes Cooking time: 4 hours Servings: 10**

INGREDIENTS:
Two cups pinto beans
3 slices bacon
One small onion
2 cactus leaves (no pales and large)

One jalapeno pepper
2 tbsp salt

DIRECTIONS:
- Rinse the beans and place it into your Slow Cooker. Pour in the hot water to fill the dish to the top. Add the onion, seeded and chopped jalapeno pepper and the bacon.
- Season with salt to taste and cook on HIGH regime for 3-4 hours.
- After removing all the thorns from the cactus leaves, slice them into small pieces.
- In a saucepan filled with water, bring cactus to boil and wait 15 minutes. Drain and rinse with cold water.
- Add the cactus to the beans and leave cooking for another 15-20 minutes.

**Nutrition: Calories: 153 Fat: 1g Carbohydrates: 25g Protein: 9g**

## Pizza Potatoes in Slow Cooker

Love pizza and potatoes? Just combine them in one meal!

**Prep time: 25 minutes Cooking time: 6 hours**
**Servings: 6**

INGREDIENTS:
1 tbsp olive oil
A can pizza sauce
Mozzarella cheese (grated)
1 large onion
6 medium potatoes
Pepperoni (sliced)

DIRECTIONS:
- Start with greasing and preheating your Slow Cooker.
- Take a large skillet and heat the oil over medium high heat.
- Thinly slice the onion and place it into skillet. Add potatoes and fry until the onion is mild and translucent (about 7-10 minutes).
- Drain the potatoes and place into Slow Cooker.
- Add pepperoni and Mozzarella cheese. Pour with pizza sauce. Cook under the lid on LOW temperatures about 6-9 hours.

**Nutrition: Calories: 248 Fat: 7g Carbohydrates: 36g Protein: 9g**

## Carrots with Chinese species

Healthy vegetables with spicy seasoning!

**Prep time: 10 minutes Cooking time: 8-9 hours**
**Servings: 6**

INGREDIENTS:
10-15 baby carrots
4 tbsp tamari sauce
Half cup orange juice (better use concentrate)
2 cloves garlic
1 tsp orange zest (grated)
1 tbsp honey
1 tbsp Asian sesame oil
1 tsp fresh ginger (minced)

DIRECTIONS:
- Peel and cut baby carrots, mince ginger and garlic.
- In Slow Cooker dish, mix the baby carrots, tamari juice concentrate, orange zest, toasted sesame oil on honey. Add minced garlic and ginger.
- Pour in the orange juice concentrate and mix everything well.
- Place the dish into Slow Cooker and turn on the LOW temperature mode.
- Cook for 8 hours, then turn your Slow Cooker to high temperature and continue cooking for another 30 minutes.

**Nutrition: Calories: 140 Fat: 2g Carbohydrates: 27g Protein: 3g**

## Baked Beans in Slow Cooker

Try these unusual beans for your dinner!

**Prep time: 11 minutes Cooking time: 9 hours**
**Servings: 8**

INGREDIENTS:
Four cups water
Brown sugar
1 pack navy beans (dried)
1 tsp salt
Half cup molasses
One medium onion
Dry mustard to taste
4-5 slices salt pork
Ground pepper

DIRECTIONS:
- Cover the beans with cold water and let stand overnight. Drain and transfer to pot.
- Cover with water again and bring to boil. Then simmer about 1 hour to make the beans tender. In a separate bowl, mix 4 cup water, mustard, salt, molasses, pepper and brown sugar.
- Place all the ingredients into Slow Cooker and mix everything well until smooth.
- If needed, add more water and cook covered for 8 to 10 hours on LOW temperature regime.

**Nutrition: Calories: 374 Fat: 12g Carbohydrates: 54g Protein: 13g**

## Sweet Sauerkraut In Slow Cooker

Sweet and unusual dish!

**Prep time: 20 minutes Cooking time: 8 hours**
**Servings: 8**

INGREDIENTS:
1-2 cups water
2 cups sauerkraut
One medium apple
3 tbsp brown sugar
One medium carrot
Half sweet onion
1 tsp caraway seeds
Kielbasa (fully cooked)
Ground black pepper and salt to taste

DIRECTIONS:
- Drain and rinse well the sauerkraut. Core and dice apple, mince carrot and onion.
- Butter your Slow Cooker and fill it with sauerkraut, apple, carrot, brown sugar, caraway seeds, sweet onion and salt/pepper.
- Turn on the Slow Cooker and set the low temperature mode. Cook for 7 hours on LOW mode, stirring occasionally.
- In the end of the process add kielbasa and stir one more time. Cook for another hour.

Nutrition: Calories: 264 Fat: 15g Carbohydrates: 23g Protein: 8g

## Collard Greens in Slow Cooker

Fits for any family gathering!

⏱ **Prep time: 30 minutes Cooking time: 7-8 hours**
**Servings: 4**

INGREDIENTS:
Three slices bacon
One bunch collard greens
2 cups chicken stock
Salt to taste
2 tbsp jalapeno pepper slices
Ground black pepper

DIRECTIONS:
- Cover the collard greens with salted water and bring to boil. Then, reduce the heat and simmer for 10-15 minutes.
- Transfer the drained collard greens to your Slow Cooker.
- Fry the bacon pieces in a deep skillet over medium heat. Turn occasionally until it is evenly browned.
- Combine all the ingredients in Slow Cooker, add the jalapeno slices and cover with chicken stock. Add some seasoning with black pepper and salt.
- Cook covered on LOW temperatures for 8 hours (tip: you can leave it cooking overnight).

**Nutrition: Calories: 124 Fat: 10g Carbohydrates: 5g Protein: 4g**

## Creamed Corn in Slow Cooker

Creamy and healthy corn for summertime!

⏱ **Prep time: 15 minutes Cooking time: 4 hours**
**Servings: 8**

INGREDIENTS:
One cup heavy whipping cream
Half tsp salt
5 cups sweet corn (can be frozen)
2 tbsp white sugar
1 pack cream cheese (softened)
Half tsp black pepper (freshly ground)
3 tbsp unsalted butter

DIRECTIONS:
- Prepare your Slow Cooker: grease it with some butter or olive oil.
- In a separate bowl, stir together cream cheese, whipping cream, salt, sugar and pepper. Transfer the cream mixture into Slow Cooker.
- Cook covered with the lid for 10 minutes. Then add the corn. Continue cooking on LOW temperatures regimes for 4-5 hours.

**Nutrition: Calories: 354 Fat: 27g Carbohydrates: 26g Protein: 9g**

## Casserole with Spinach Noodles

Unusual Spinach noodles for any meat or fish!

⏱ **Prep time: 19 minutes Cooking time: 3-4 hours**
**Servings: 8**

INGREDIENTS:
Dry spinach noodles
Cps cottage cheese
1-2 cups sour cream
Vegetable oil
Green onion
Garlic salt
Worcestershire sauce
All-purpose flour
Hot pepper sauce

DIRECTIONS:
- In a large pot, cook the noodles in salted water. Drain well and combine, tossing, with vegetable oil.
- Meanwhile, take a large bowl and combine flour and sour cream.
- Add cottage cheese, Worcestershire sauce, garlic salt, green onions, and hot pepper sauce. Stir everything well.
- Combine the cheese mixture with the noodles.
- Grease your Slow Cooker and place the noodle mixture into it. Cook, covered, on HIGH temperature mode for 1-2 hours.

**Nutrition: Calories: 226 Fat: 14g Carbohydrates: 14g Protein: 8g**

# VEGETARIAN AND VEGAN

## One-Pot Mushroom and Brown Rice

⏱ **Ready in about: 30 minutes | Serves: 4 | Per serving: Calories 417; Carbs 72g; Fat 7g; Protein 12g**

INGREDIENTS
2 cups Brown Rice, rinsed
4 cups Vegetable Broth
3 teaspoons Olive oil
1 cup Portobello Mushrooms, thinly sliced
Salt to taste
2 sprigs Parsley, chopped to garnish

DIRECTIONS
- Heat oil on SAUTÉ mode and cook the mushrooms for 3 minutes until golden. Season with salt and add rice and broth. Seal the lid and select BEANS/CHILI mode at High pressure for 20 minutes.
- Once the timer has ended, do a quick pressure release. Plate the pilaf, fluff with a fork and top with parsley.

## Asian-Style Tofu Noddle Soup

Ready in about: **25 minutes** | Serves: **4** | Per serving: Calories 343; Carbs 42g; Fat 21g; Protein 14g

INGREDIENTS
16 oz firm Tofu, water- packed
7 cloves Garlic, minced
2 tbsp Korean red pepper flakes (gochugaru)
1 tbsp Sugar
1 tbsp Olive Oil
2 tbsp Ginger Paste
¼ cup Soy Sauce
3 cup sliced Bok Choy
6 ounces dry Egg Noodles
4 cups Vegetable Broth
1 cup sliced Shitake Mushrooms
½ cup chopped Cilantro

DIRECTIONS
- Drain liquid out of the tofu, pat the tofu dry with paper towels, and cut into 1-inch cubes. Select SAUTÉ at High.
- Heat oil, add garlic and ginger, and sauté them for 1 minute. Add sugar, broth, and soy sauce. Stir the mixture and cook for 30 seconds. Add tofu and bok choy, seal the lid, and select STEAM at High for 10 minutes.
- Do a quick pressure release. Add the zucchini noodles, give it a good stir using a spoon, and close the lid. Let the soup sit for 4 minutes. Add the cilantro and stir with the spoon. Fetch the soup into soup bowls to serve.

## Hearty Colorful Vegetable Soup

Ready in about: **20 minutes** | Serves: **4** | Per serving: Calories 198; Carbs 28g; Fat 4g; Protein 4g

INGREDIENTS
1 (15.5 oz) can Cannellini Beans
1 Potato, peeled and diced
1 Carrot, peeled and chopped
1 cup chopped Butternut Squash
2 small Red Onions, cut in wedges
1 cup chopped Celery
1 tbsp chopped Fresh Rosemary
8 Sage Leaves, chopped finely
1 Bay Leaf
4 cups Vegetable Broth
Salt and Pepper, to taste
2 tsp Olive Oil
2 tbsp chopped Parsley

DIRECTIONS
- Add in the beans, potato, carrot, squash, onion, celery, rosemary, sage leaves, bay leaf, vegetable broth, salt, pepper, and olive oil. Seal the lid and select STEAM mode at High pressure for 5 minutes.
- Do a quick pressure release. Stir in parsley and fetch the soup into bowls. Serve with a side of crusted bread.

## Kale and Spinach Cream Soup

Ready in about: **15 minutes** | Serves: **4** | Per serving: Calories 269; Carbs 14g; Fat 14g; Protein 12g

INGREDIENTS
½ lb Kale Leaves, chopped
½ lb Spinach Leaves, chopped
½ lb Swiss Chard Leaves, chopped
1 tbsp Olive Oil
1 Onion, chopped
4 cloves Garlic, minced
4 cups Vegetable Broth
1 ¼ cup Heavy Cream
Salt and Pepper, to taste
1 ½ tbsp. White Wine Vinegar
Chopped Peanuts to garnish

DIRECTIONS
- Select SAUTÉ mode at High. Warm the olive oil, and sauté the onion and garlic, for 1 minute. Add greens and vegetable broth. Seal the lid, and select STEAM mode at High for 5 minutes. Do a quick pressure release.
- Add the white wine vinegar, salt, and pepper. Use a stick blender to puree the ingredients in the pot. Stir in the heavy cream. Spoon the soup into bowls, sprinkle with peanuts, and serve.

## Fake Mushroom Risotto the Paleo Way

Ready in about: **15 minutes** | Serves: **4** | Per serving: Calories 123; Carbs 13g; Fat 11g; Protein 3g

INGREDIENTS
1 ½ head Cauliflower
2 cups Mushrooms, sliced
1 Garlic Clove, minced
1 tsp dried Basil
1 Carrot, grated
1 cup Veggie Broth
1 tbsp Olive Oil
½ Onion, diced

DIRECTIONS
- Cut the cauliflower into pieces and place them in your food processor. Process until ground, rice- like. You should have about 6 cups of cauliflower rice.
- Heat the oil and sauté the carrots, and onions for 3 minutes, on SAUTÉ mode at High. Add the garlic and cook for one more minute.
- Stir in all of the remaining ingredients. Seal the lid, set to BEANS/CHILI for 10 minutes at High. It may take a few minutes before pressure is built inside the cooker. Do a quick pressure release.

## Pressure Cooked Ratatouille

Ready in about: **20 minutes** | Serves: **4** | Per serving: Calories 104; Carbs 11g; Fat 7g; Protein 2g

INGREDIENTS
1 Zucchini, sliced
2 Tomatoes, sliced
1 tbsp Balsamic Vinegar
1 Eggplant, sliced
1 Onion, sliced
1 tbsp dried Thyme
2 tbsp Olive Oil

2 Garlic Cloves, minced
1 cup Water
DIRECTIONS
- Add the garlic to a springform pan. Arrange the veggies in a circle. Sprinkle them with thyme and drizzle with olive oil. Pour water in your pressure cooker. Place the pan inside on a trivet. Seal the lid.
- Cook for 6 minutes on BEANS/CHILI at High. Release the pressure naturally, for 10 minutes.

## Veggie Burger Patties

Ready in about: **30 minutes** | Serves: **4** | Per serving: Calories 221; Carbs 34g; Fat 7g; Protein 4g

INGREDIENTS
1 Zucchini, peeled and grated
3 cups Cauliflower Florets
1 Carrot, grated
1 cup Veggie Broth
2 cups Broccoli Florets
½ Onion, diced
½ tsp Turmeric Powder
2 tbsp Olive Oil
2 cups Sweet Potato cubes
¼ tsp Black Pepper
DIRECTIONS
- Heat 1 tbsp oil and sauté the onions for about 3 minutes, on SAUTÉ mode at High. Add the carrots and cook for an additional minute. Pour the broth and add the potatoes.
- Seal the lid, set on BEANS/CHILI for 13 minutes at High pressure. Do a quick release. Stir in the remaining veggies. Seal the lid, and cook for 3 minutes at High. Do a quick pressure release.
- Mash veggies with a potato masher and stir in the seasonings. Let cool for a few minutes and make burger patties out of the mixture. On SAUTÉ, heat remaining oil. Cook patties for a minute on each side.

## Potato Chili

Ready in about: **30 minutes** | Serves: **4** | Per serving: Calories 297; Carbs 53g; Fat 4g; Protein 16g

INGREDIENTS
15 ounces canned Black Beans, rinsed and drained
2 cups Vegetable Broth
28 ounces canned diced Tomatoes
15 ounces canned Kidney Beans, rinsed and drained
1 Sweet Potato, chopped
1 Red Onion, chopped
1 Red Bell Pepper, chopped
1 Green Bell Pepper, chopped
1 tbsp Olive Oil
1 tbsp Chili Powder
¼ tsp Cinnamon
1 tsp Cumin
1 tsp Cayenne
Pepper Salt, to taste
DIRECTIONS

- Heat olive oil in and sauté onions, peppers, and potatoes until the onions become translucent, about 3-4 minutes, on SAUTÉ mode at High. Stir in the rest of the ingredients.
- Seal the lid, cook for 16 minutes on BEANS/CHILI at High pressure. Once ready, do a quick pressure release.

## Bean and Rice Casserole

Ready in about: **40 minutes** | Serves: **4** | Per serving: Calories 322; Carbs 63g; Fat 2g; Protein 6g

INGREDIENTS
1 cup Black Beans, soaked
5 cups Water
2 tsp Onion Powder
2 tsp Chili Powder, optional
2 cups Brown Rice
6 ounces Tomato Paste
1 tsp Garlic, minced
1 tsp Salt
DIRECTIONS
- Add all ingredients in your pressure cooker. Seal the lid, select BEANS/CHILI and adjust the time to 30 minutes at High pressure.
- When over, do a quick pressure release.

## Harissa Turnip Stew

Ready in about: **15 minutes** | Serves: **4** | Per serving: Calories 145; Carbs 16g; Fat 8g; Protein 4g

INGREDIENTS
6 Turnip, cut into halves lengthwise
¼ tsp Smoked Paprika
2 tbsp Harissa Paste
1 cup Vegetable Broth
2 tbsp Olive Oil
2 tin Tomatoes, chopped
1 tsp Garlic powder
Kosher Salt and ground Black Pepper, to taste
DIRECTIONS
- Stir in all ingredients in the pressure cooker.
- Seal the lid. Set to BEANS/CHILI and cook for 12 minutes at High. Once ready, do a quick pressure release. Serve warm.

## Meatless Shepherd's Pie

Ready in about: **17 minutes** | Serves: **4** | Per serving: Calories 224; Carbs 6g; Fat 15g; Protein 16g

INGREDIENTS
½ cup diced Celery
1 cup diced Onion
2 cups Cauliflower, steamed and mashed
1 tbsp Olive Oil
½ cup diced Turnips
1 ¾ cup Veggie Broth
1 cup diced Tomatoes
1 cup grated Potatoes
½ cup diced Carrot
½ cup Water
DIRECTIONS

- Heat olive oil and cook onions, carrots, celery, for 3 minutes, on SAUTÉ mode at High. Stir in turnips, potatoes, and veggie broth.
- Seal the lid, set to BEANS/CHILI for 25 minutes at LOW. After 10 minutes, press CANCEL and do a quick release. Stir in tomatoes. Transfer the mixture to 4 ramekins. Top each ramekin with ½ cup of mashed cauliflower.
- Pour the water into your pressure cooker and place a trivet at the bottom. Seal the lid, and continue cooking. Do a quick pressure release.

## Vegetarian Spaghetti Bolognese

Ready in about: **25 minutes** | Serves: **8** | Per serving: Calories 360; Carbs 63g; Fat 3g; Protein 15g

INGREDIENTS
8 cups cooked Spaghetti
1 cup Cauliflower Florets
2 cups Shredded Carrots
6 Garlic Cloves, minced
2 tbsp Tomato Paste
2 tbsp Agave Nectar
1 ½ tbsp dried Oregano
56 ounces canned crushed Tomatoes, undrained
2 tbsp Balsamic Vinegar
1 tbsp dried Basil
10 ounces Mushrooms
2 cups chopped Eggplant
2 cups Water
1 ½ tsp dried Rosemary
Salt and Black Pepper, to taste

DIRECTIONS
- Add cauliflower, mushrooms, eggplant, and carrots to a food processor and process until finely ground. Transfer to the pressure cooker. Stir in the rest of the ingredients. Seal the lid and cook for 10 minutes on BEANS/CHILI mode at High pressure.
- When ready, release the pressure naturally for 10 minutes. Serve the sauce over spaghetti.

## Spicy Moong Beans

Ready in about: **30 minutes** | Serves: **8** | Per serving: Calories 328; Carbs 62g; Fat 5g; Protein 10g

INGREDIENTS
1 tsp Paprika
2 tsp Curry Powder
4 cups Moong Beans, soaked and drained
1 Onion, diced
1 tsp Turmeric
Juice of 1 Lime
1 Jalapeno Pepper, chopped
1 Sprig Curry Leaves
4 Garlic Cloves, minced
2 tbsp Olive Oil
1 ½ tsp Cumin Seeds
2 Tomatoes, chopped
Salt, to taste
1-inch piece of Ginger, grated

DIRECTIONS
- Heat the oil and cook cumin seeds for minute, on SAUTÉ at High. Add onion and garlic along with curry, turmeric, ginger, and some salt. Cook for 3-4 minutes.
- Stir in jalapeno, and tomatoes and cook for 5 minutes, or until soft. Add the beans and pour water to cover the ingredients, by at least 2 inches.
- Sprinkle with lime juice and curry leaves. Seal the lid, set on BEANS/CHILI for 25 minutes at High. Do a quick pressure release. Serve hot.

## Sweet Potato and Baby Carrot Medley

Ready in about: **30 minutes** | Serves: **4** | Per serving: Calories 415; Carbs 78g; Fat 8g; Protein 7g

INGREDIENTS
1 tsp dried Oregano
2 tbsp Olive Oil
½ cup Veggie Broth
1 Onion, finely chopped
2 pounds Sweet Potatoes, cubed
2 pounds Baby Carrots, halved

DIRECTIONS
- Heat olive oil and cook onions for 3 minutes, on SAUTÉ mode at High. Stir in the carrots and cook for 3 more minutes.
- Add potatoes, carrots, broth, and oregano. Seal the lid, set on BEANS/CHILI for 15 minutes at High. Once the cooking is over, do a quick pressure release.

## Pickled Pepperoncini and Parmesan Dip

Ready in about: **15 minutes** | Serves: **10** | Per serving: Calories 146; Carbs 5g; Fat 11g; Protein 8g

INGREDIENTS
1 tbsp minced pickled Pepperoncini Peppers
12 ounces Parmesan cheese, shredded
1 ½ tbsp Flour
1 cup Tomato paste
2 tsp Olive Oil
1 cup Milk
½ tsp Cayenne Pepper
½ tsp basil
Salt and Black Pepper, to taste

DIRECTIONS
- Heat oil on SAUTÉ at High. Slowly stir in flour and keep stirring until you obtain a paste. Pour the milk and stir until the mixture thickens, then bring to a boil.
- Add the cheese and stir until melted. Add the remaining ingredients. Seal the lid, press BEANS/CHILI and cook for 5 minutes at High Pressure. Do a quick release the pressure.

## Vegetables and Beef Brisket Stew

Ready in about: **70 minutes** | Serves: **4** | Per serving: Calories 487; Carbs 41g; Fat 16g; Protein 47g

INGREDIENTS
2 lb Brisket, cut into 2-inch pieces

4 cups Beef Broth
Salt and Black Pepper to taste
1 tbsp Dijon Mustard
1 tbsp Olive Oil
1 lb small Potato, quartered
¼ lb Carrots, cut in 2-inch pieces
1 large Red Onion, quartered
3 cloves Garlic, minced
1 Bay Leaf
2 fresh Thyme sprigs
2 tbsp Cornstarch
3 tbsp chopped Cilantro to garnish

DIRECTIONS
- Pour the beef broth, cornstarch, mustard, ½ teaspoon salt, and ½ teaspoon pepper in a bowl. Whisk them and set aside. Season the beef strips with salt and pepper. Select SAUTÉ mode at High.
- Add olive oil, once heated include the beef strips and cook until brown, for about 8 minutes.
- Flip the strips halfway through cooking. Add potato, carrots, onion, garlic, thyme, mustard mixture, and bay leaf. Stir once more. Seal the lid, select MEAT/STEW at High for 45 minutes.
- Do a quick pressure release. Stir the stew and remove the bay leaf. Season with salt and pepper.

## Creamy Potato Slices with Chives

Ready in about: **10 minutes | Serves: 6 | Per serving:** Calories 168; Carbs 31g; Fat 3g; Protein 4g

INGREDIENTS
6 Potatoes
½ cup Sour Cream
2 tbsp Potato Starch
1 tbsp chopped Chives
½ cup Milk
1 cup Chicken Broth
1 tsp Salt
A pinch of Pepper

DIRECTIONS
- Peel and slice the potatoes. Coat them with salt, chives, and pepper. Add broth and potatoes in your Pressure cooker. Seal the lid, and cook for 3 minutes on STEAM mode at High pressure. Do a quick pressure release.
- Remove potatoes to a bowl, and reserve the liquid. Whisk in the remaining ingredients into the cooking juices in the pressure cooker.
- Select SAUTÉ at High, and cook for one minute, stirring constantly, until you obtain sauce texture. Pour the sauce over the potatoes and serve immediately.

## Stuffed Red Peppers with Quinoa and Zucchini

Ready in about: **40 minutes | Serves: 4 | Per serving:** Calories 409; Carbs 42g; Fat 17g; Protein 20g

INGREDIENTS
4 Red Bell Peppers
2 large Tomatoes, chopped
1 small Onion, chopped
2 cloves Garlic, minced
1 tbsp Olive Oil
1 cup Quinoa, rinsed
2 cups Chicken Broth
1 small Zucchini, chopped
1 ½ cup Water
½ tsp Smoked Paprika
½ cup chopped Mushrooms
Salt and Black Pepper to taste
1 cup grated Gouda Cheese

DIRECTIONS
- Select SAUTÉ mode at High. Warm the olive oil and sauté the onion and garlic, for 3 minutes until soft, stirring occasionally. Add the tomatoes, cook them for 3 minutes, and then add quinoa, zucchinis, and mushrooms.
- Season with paprika, salt, and black pepper and stir well. Cook them for 5 to 7 minutes, then, turn the cooker off. Use a knife to cut the bell peppers in halves (lengthwise) and remove their seeds and stems.
- Spoon the quinoa mixture into the bell peppers leaving about a quarter space at the top of the peppers for the cheese. Sprinkle them with the gouda cheese. Put the peppers in a greased baking dish and pour the broth over.
- Wipe the pot clean with some paper towels, and pour in the water. Fit the steamer rack at the bottom of the pot. Place the baking dish on top of the steamer rack, seal the li and select BEANS/CHILI at High for 15 minutes.
- Do a quick pressure release. Serve right away or as a side to a meat dish.

## Spiced Bok Choy Soup with Spiralized Zucchini

Ready in about: **35 minutes | Serves: 6 | Per serving:** Calories 115; Carbs 15g; Fat 6g; Protein 2g

INGREDIENTS
1 lb Baby Bok Choy, stems removed
6 oz Shitake Mushrooms, stems removed and sliced to a 2-inch thickness
3 Carrots, peeled and sliced diagonally
2 Zucchinis, spiralized
2 Sweet Onion, chopped
2-inch Ginger, chopped
2 cloves Garlic, peeled
2 tbsp Sesame Oil
2 tbsp Soy Sauce
2 tbsp Chili Paste
6 cups Water
Salt to taste
Chopped Green Onion to garnish
Sesame Seeds to garnish

DIRECTIONS
- In a food processor, add the chili paste, ginger, onion, and garlic; and process until pureed. Set the pressure cooker on SAUTÉ at High. Warm the oil, and cook the puree for 4 minutes, stirring constantly to prevent burning.
- Pour in the water, mushrooms, soy sauce, and carrots. Stir, seal the lid and select STEAM mode at High pressure for 3 minutes. Do a quick pressure release. Stir in the zoodles and bok choy.
- Make sure that they are well submerged in the liquid. Season with salt, cover, and let the veggies sit for 10 minutes. Dish the

soup with veggies into soup bowls. Sprinkle with green onions and sesame seeds.

## Easy Spaghetti Squash with Spinach Dip

**Ready in about:** 15 minutes | **Serves:** 4 | **Per serving:** Calories 275; Carbs 46g; Fat 9g; Protein 5g

INGREDIENTS
4 lb Spaghetti Squash
1 cup Water
For the Dip
½ cup spinach, chopped
2 tbsp Walnuts
2 Garlic Cloves, minced
Zest and juice from 1/2 lemon
Salt and ground pepper, to taste
¼ cup extra virgin olive oil

DIRECTIONS
- In a food processor put all pesto ingredients and blend until well incorporated. Season to taste and set aside.
- Put the squash on a flat surface and use a knife to slice in half lengthwise. Use a spoon to scoop out all seeds and discard them. Next, pour the water in the pressure cooker, and fit the trivet at the bottom.
- Place the squash halves on the trivet, seal the lid, and select STEAM at High for 6 minutes. Do a quick pressure release.
- Remove the squash halves onto a cutting board and use a fork to separate the pulp strands into spaghetti-like pieces. Scoop the spaghetti squash into serving plates and drizzle over the spinach pesto.

## Mediterranean Steamed Asparagus with Pine Nuts

**Ready in about:** 10 minutes | **Serves:** 4 | **Per serving:** Calories 182; Carbs 13g; Fat 15g; Protein 7g

INGREDIENTS
1 ½ lb Asparagus, ends trimmed
Salt and Pepper, to taste
1 cup Water
¼ cup Pomegranate seeds
½ cup chopped Pine Nuts
1 tbsp Olive Oil to garnish

DIRECTIONS
- Pour the water in the pressure cooker, and fit the steamer rack at the bottom. Place the asparagus on the steamer rack, seal the lid and select STEAM mode on Low pressure for 3 minutes.
- Once the timer is done, do a quick pressure release. Remove asparagus with tongs onto a plate and sprinkle with salt and pepper. Scatter over the pomegranate seeds and pine nuts, and drizzle olive oil.

## Eggplant and Goat Cheese Homemade Lasagna

**Ready in about:** 20 minutes | **Serves:** 4 | **Per serving:** Calories 288; Carbs 38g; Fat 5g; Protein 19g

INGREDIENTS
3 large Eggplants, sliced in uniform ¼ inches
4 ¼ cups Marinara Sauce
1 ½ cups crumbled Goat Cheese
Cooking Spray
Chopped Fresh Basil to garnish

DIRECTIONS
- Grease the pot with cooking spray. Arrange the eggplant slices in a single layer at the bottom of the pot and sprinkle some cheese all over. Arrange another layer of eggplant slices on top, layer with cheese again.
- Repeat the layering until you run out of ingredients. Lightly spray the eggplant with cooking spray and pour the marinara sauce all over it. Seal the lid and select BEANS/CHILI mode at High pressure for 8 minutes.
- Do a quick pressure release. With two napkins, gently remove the inner pot. Then, place a plate to cover this pot and turn the eggplant over on the plate. Garnish the eggplant and cheese with basil and serve as a side dish.

## Sautéed Leafy Greens

**Ready in about:** 10 minutes | **Serves:** 4 | **Per serving:** Calories 130; Carbs 15g; Fat 4g; Protein 13g

INGREDIENTS
2 lb Baby Spinach
1 lb Kale Leaves
½ lb Swiss Chard
1 tbsp dried Basil
Salt and Black Pepper to season
½ tbsp Butter
½ cup Water

DIRECTIONS
- Pour water in the pressure cooker and fit the trivet at the bottom. Put the spinach, swiss chard, and kale on the trivet. Seal the lid, and select STEAM mode at Low pressure for 3 minutes. Do a quick pressure release.
- Remove the trivet with the wilted greens onto a plate and discard the water in the pot. Select SAUTÉ mode and add the butter. Once it melts, add the spinachkale back to the pot, and add dried basil.
- Season with salt and pepper and stir it. Dish the sautéed greens into serving plates and serve as a side dish.

## Celery-Pumpkin Autumn Soup

**Ready in about:** 30 minutes | **Serves:** 4 | **Per serving:** Calories 98; Carbs 15g; Fat 2g; Protein 6g

INGREDIENTS
1 Celeriac, peeled and cubed
16 oz Pumpkin Puree
5 stalks Celery, chopped
1 White Onion, chopped
1 lb Green Beans, cut in 5 to 6 strips each
2 cups Vegetable Broth
3 cups Spinach Leaves
1 tbsp chopped Basil Leaves
¼ tsp dried Thyme
¼ tsp rubbed Sage
Salt to taste

DIRECTIONS
- Pour in the celeriac, pumpkin puree, celery, onion, green beans, vegetable broth, basil leaves, thyme, sage, and a little bit of salt. Seal the lid, and select STEAM on High pressure for 3 minutes. Do a quick pressure release.
- Add the spinach and stir it in using a spoon. Cover the pot and let the spinach sit in for 3 minutes or until it wilts. Use a soup spoon to fetch the soup into serving bowls.

## Mashed Broccoli with Mascarpone

Ready in about: **10 minutes | Serves: 4 | Per serving: Calories 166; Carbs 6g; Fat 13g; Protein 7g**

INGREDIENTS
3 heads Broccoli, chopped
6 oz Mascarpone
2 cloves Garlic, crushed
2 tbsp Butter, unsalted
Salt and Black Pepper to taste
1 cup Water

DIRECTIONS
- Select SAUTÉ mode at High. Melt the butter, and add the garlic. Cook it for 30 seconds, stirring frequently to prevent the garlic from burning. Then, add the broccoli, mascarpone, water, salt, and pepper.
- Seal the lid, and select STEAM at High for 3 minutes. Do a quick pressure release and use a stick blender to mash the ingredients until smooth. Adjust the taste, and serve as a side dish to a sauce of your choice.

## Easy Buttery Corn on the Cob

Ready in about: **15 minutes | Serves: 4 | Per serving: Calories 168; Carbs 11g; Fat 14g; Protein 2g**

INGREDIENTS
4 corn on the cob, husked
½ cup Butter, softened
1 ½ cups Water
Salt and white Pepper, to taste
2 tbsp finely chopped fresh cut Parsley

DIRECTIONS
- Place a trivet into your pressure cooker. Pour the water and lower the corn on the trivet. Seal the lid Set on STEAM mode and cook for 2 minutes at High Pressure.
- Once the cooking process has completed, quick release the pressure. Remove the corn to a platter, sprinkle with allspice and salt, then serve with a generous spoonful of parsley butter.

## Delicious Eggs de Provence

Ready in about: **20 minutes | Serves: 4 | Per serving: Calories 455; Carbs 18g; Fat 29g; Protein 29g**

INGREDIENTS
8 Eggs
½ cup Goat Cheese, crumbled
1 cup Cream
1 ½ cups Kale, torn into pieces
2 Shallots, chopped
½ tsp dried Oregano
½ tsp dried Thyme
1 tsp Salt
½ tsp ground Black Pepper
4 tbsp Water + 2 cups

DIRECTIONS
- In a deep bowl, whisk the eggs, water, and cream. Stir in the remaining ingredients until well mixed. Transfer the mixture into a heat-proof dish and cover with aluminium foil.
- Add about 2 cups of water to the bottom of your pressure cooker, and pace the trivet inside.
- Lower the dish onto the trivet. Select BEANS/CHILI mode, seal the lid and cook for 15 minutes at High. Once the cooking is complete, do a quick pressure release and serve immediately.

## Spicy Tomato Dip

Ready in about: **20 minutes | Serves: 10 | Per serving: Calories 84; Carbs 9g; Fat 5g; Protein 1g**

INGREDIENTS
1 cup Carrot, chopped
½ tsp Sea Salt
1 pound plum Tomatoes, peeled, cored, sliced
2 tbsp Sugar
1 tsp Jalapeno Peppers, seeded and chopped
½ cup shallot, diced
1 cup Bell Pepper, seeded and chopped
black Pepper, to taste
3 tbsp Olive Oil
1 sprig dried Rosemary
½ tsp dried basil
1 cup Waters

DIRECTIONS
- Heat oil on SAUTÉ at High, and add the bell pepper, Jalapeño peppers, carrot, shallots. Cook for about 4 minutes, until soft. Stir in the tomatoes, brown sugar, water salt, black pepper, rosemary, and basil.
- Seal the lid, press BEANS/CHILI mode and cook for 10 minutes at High Pressure. Do a quick release the pressure. Pour in the olive oil and blend with a blender, until the mixture is smooth.

## Hummus Under Pressure

Ready in about: **minutes | Serves: 8 | Per serving: Calories 161; Carbs 20g; Fat 6g; Protein 8g**

INGREDIENTS
1 Onion, quartered
1 Bay Leaf
2 tbsp Soy Sauce
¼ cup Tahini
¾ cup Garbanzo Beans
¼ cup dried Soybeans
¼ cup chopped Parsley
1 cup Vegetable Broth
Juice of 1 Lemon
2 Garlic Cloves, minced

DIRECTIONS
- Add garbanzo beans, soybeans, and broth in your pressure cooker. Pour some water over to cover them by one inch. Seal the lid, press SOUP, for 20 minutes at High pressure.

- When ready, release the pressure naturally for 10 minutes. Drain the beans and save the cooking liquid. Place the beans along with the remaining ingredients into a food processor.
- Process until smooth. Add some of the cooking liquid to make hummus thinner, if desired.

## Herby Steamed Potatoes

**Ready in about:** 15 minutes | **Serves:** 8 | **Per serving:** Calories 117; Carbs 27g; Fat 0g; Protein 3g

INGREDIENTS
1 cup Water
2 pounds Potatoes, peeled and quartered
1 tsp Salt
1 tbsp Olive Oil
½ tsp ground Black Pepper
1 tsp Cayenne Pepper
¼ tsp Rosemary
¼ tsp dried basil
¼ tsp dried Oregano
¼ tsp dried Sage

DIRECTIONS
- Place a trivet into the pressure cooker and pour the water. Lay the potatoes on the trivet, seal the lid and select STEAM mode. Cook for 10 minutes at High Pressure. Do a quick release.
- Remove the potatoes to a bowl. Add the remaining ingredients and lightly toss to coat.

## Sicilian-Style Deviled Eggs

**Ready in about:** 15 minutes | **Serves:** 6 | **Per serving:** Calories 175; Carbs 5g; Fat 8g; Protein 12g

INGREDIENTS
9 large Eggs
¼ cup Ricotta Cheese
¼ cup Mayonnaise
¼ tsp Garlic powder
1 tsp Shallot powder
Salt and freshly ground Black Pepper, to taste

DIRECTIONS
- Pour 1 ½ cups of water and add a trivet to the pressure cooker. Align the eggs in steamer basket, and lower the basket onto the trivet. Seal the lid, set to BEANS/CHILI mode for 5 minutes at High.
- Once the cooking is over, do a quick pressure release. Transfer the eggs to cold water to cool.
- Slice the egg in half and remove the yolk. Mash with a fork, and add the remaining ingredients. Split the mixture of the yolks on the egg whites and lay on a serving plate.

## Vegan Sausage and Pepper Casserole

**Ready in about:** 15 minutes | **Serves:** 4 | **Per serving:** Calories 293; Carbs 42g; Fat 8g; Protein 14g

INGREDIENTS
2 Vegan Sausage Links, sliced
2 Large Potatoes, diced
3 Bell Peppers, chopped
1 Onion, chopped
1 Zucchini, grated
1 Carrot, grated
½ cup Milk
1 cup Veggie Stock
½ tsp Cumin
¼ tsp Pepper
¼ tsp Salt
¼ tsp Turmeric Powder
1 tbsp Olive Oil

DIRECTIONS
- Heat oil on SAUTÉ mode at High, and cook the onions for 1 minute, until translucent. Stir in peppers and cook for 4 more minutes, until soft. Add sausage and cook until browned.
- Stir in the spices, stock, and potatoes. Seal the lid and cook for 5 minutes on BEANS/CHILI, at High pressure. When ready, do a quick pressure release.
- Stir in the remaining ingredients. Cook for 3 more minutes on SAUTÉ, lid off. Drain and serve.

## Spanish Baked Eggs

**Ready in about:** 10 minutes | **Serves:** 4 | **Per serving:** Calories 425; Carbs 4g; Fat 27g; Protein 37g

INGREDIENTS
8 medium-sized Eggs
8 slices Queso Manchego, Spanish cheese
4 thick slices Swiss Cheese
2 tbsp Butter, softened at room temperature
4 tbsp Spring Onions, chopped
2 tbsp fresh coriander, coarsely chopped

DIRECTIONS
- Pour 1 ½ cups of water inside your pressure cooker. Place the trivet on the bottom. Coat the bottom and sides of 4 ramekins with butter. Place the queso manchego at the bottom and crack two eggs into each ramekin.
- Add the onions and top with cheese. Lower the ramekins onto the steamer basket and cover with aluminium foil. Seal the lid, select BEANS/CHILI and cook for 5 minutes at High.
- Once done, do a quick pressure release and open the lid. Serve with fresh coriander.

## Tamari Tofu with Sweet Potatoes and Broccoli

**Ready in about:** 10 minutes | **Serves:** 4 | **Per serving:** Calories 250; Carbs 22g; Fat 12g; Protein 17g

INGREDIENTS
1 pound Tofu, cubed
3 Garlic Cloves, minced
2 tbsp Tamari
2 tbsp Sesame Seeds
2 tsp Sesame Oil
2 tbsp Tahini
1 tbsp Rice Vinegar
1 cup Vegetable Stock
2 cups Onion slices
2 cups Broccoli Florets
1 cup diced Sweet Potato
2 tbsp Sriracha

DIRECTIONS

- Heat oil and cook onion and sweet potatoes for 2 minutes, on SAUTÉ mode at High. Add garlic and half of the sesame seeds, and cook for a minute. Stir in tamari, broth, tofu, and vinegar.
- Seal the lid, select BEANS/CHILI for 8 minutes at High pressure. Do a quick pressure release. Open the lid and add in broccoli, and cook for 2 minutes, lid off. Stir in sriracha and tahini before serving.

## Collard Greens Hummus

**Ready in about: 25 minutes | Serves: 12 | Per serving: Calories 169; Carbs 22g; Fat 6g; Protein 7g**

INGREDIENTS
3 tbsp Tahini
¼ tsp ground Black Pepper
½ tsp Sea Salt
2 cups Chickpeas
1 cup Green Garlic, minced
4 ½ cups Water
2 tbsp Olive Oil
2 cups packed Collard Greens, chopped

DIRECTIONS
- Select BEANS/CHILI mode. Pour water in the pressure cooker and add the chickpeas. Seal the lid and adjust the cooking time to 20 minutes. Do a quick release, and drain the chickpeas.
- Transfer to a food processor with the greens, garlic, salt, pepper, and tahini. Pulse until you obtain a creamy mixture. Pour gradually the oil while machine is running, until everything is well incorporated.

## Potatoes and Peas Bowl

**Ready in about: 20 minutes | Serves: 2 | Per serving: Calories 185; Carbs 24g; Fat 8g; Protein 8g**

INGREDIENTS
3 Sweet Potatoes, diced
1 Onion, chopped
1 cup Green Peas, fresh
2 cups Spinach, chopped
2 tsp Garlic
1 tbsp Tomato Paste
1 tbsp Oil
½ tsp Coriander
1 tsp Cumin
1 ½ cups Water

DIRECTIONS
- Heat oil on SAUTÉ mode at High. Cook the onions and garlic for 2 minutes, until soft and fragrant. Stir in the tomato paste and spices. Pour in the water and tomato paste. Stir to combine.
- Add sweet potatoes and seal the lid. Cook for 14 minutes on BEANS/CHILI at High. When done, do a quick pressure release. Stir in spinach and cook until wilted, for a few minutes, on SAUTÉ, lid off.

## Saucy BBQ Veggie Meal

**Ready in about: 20 minutes | Serves: 4 | Per serving: Calories 244; Carbs 29g; Fat 9g; Protein 15g**

INGREDIENTS
2 Tomatoes, chopped
2 Carrots, chopped
1 cup Peas
2 Onions, chopped
1 cup Parsnips, chopped
2 Bell Peppers, diced
2 Sweet Potatoes, diced
½ cup BBQ Sauce
1 tbsp Oil
1 tbsp Ketchup
¼ tsp Cayenne Pepper
½ tsp Salt
¼ tsp Pepper
1 cup Veggie Stock

DIRECTIONS
- Heat oil on SAUTÉ mode at High. Add onions and cook for 2 minutes, until translucent. Add parsnips and carrots and cook for 3 more minutes, until soft. Stir in the remaining ingredients.
- Seal the lid and cook for 10 minutes on BEANS/CHILI mode at High pressure. When ready, and do a quick pressure release. Discard the excess cooking liquid, before serving.

## Lemony and Garlicky Potato and Turnip Dip

**Ready in: 15 minutes + chilling time | Serves: 4 | Per serving: Calories 143; Carbs 12g; Fat 10g; Protein 1g**

INGREDIENTS
3 tbsp Olive Oil
6 Whole Garlic Cloves, peeled
2 tbsp Lemon Juice
1 Turnip, cut lengthwise
1 Sweet Potato, cut lengthwise
1 cup Water
2 tbsp Coconut Milk

DIRECTIONS
- Pour in water. Place the potato, turnip, and garlic on the rack. Seal the lid, and cook on BEANS/CHILI at High pressure for 10 minutes. When done, do a quick pressure release.
- Transfer the veggies to a food processor. Add the remaining ingredients and process until smooth. Transfer to a container with a lid. Refrigerate for about 2 hours before serving.

## Vegan Swiss Chard Dip

**Ready in about: 15 minutes | Serves: 12 | Per serving: Calories 88; Carbs 3g; Fat 7g; Protein 3g**

INGREDIENTS
1 ½ cups Tofu
2 cups Swiss Chard, chopped
1 tsp dried Dill weed
2 tsp fresh Lemon Juice
½ tsp ground Black Pepper
1 tsp Salt
1 ¼ cups Vegan Mayonnaise
1 tsp Lemon Zest, grated for garnish
1 cup Water

DIRECTIONS

- Pour 1 cup water. In a baking dish, mix all ingredients, except lemon zest, and stir to combine. Cover the dish with aluminium foil. Then, make a foil sling and lower the dish on the rack.
- Seal the lid, switch the pressure release valve to close and cook for 10 minutes on BEANS/CHILI at High Pressure. When it goes off, quick release the pressure. Sprinkle with lemon zest and serve.

## Cheesy Asparagus and Spinach Dip

**Ready in about: 15 minutes | Serves: 16 | Per serving: Calories 118; Carbs 8g; Fat 8g; Protein 4g**

INGREDIENTS
18 oz Asparagus Spears, ends trimmed, chopped
12 ounces Spinach, thawed, drained and chopped
1 ½ cups Mozzarella Cheese, shredded
½ tsp ground Black Pepper
1 tsp Sea Salt
½ cup Mayonnaise
1 cup Heavy Cream

DIRECTIONS
- Select BEANS/CHILI mode and insert a trivet in the Pressure Cooker. Pour half cup of water.
- In a baking dish, add all ingredients and stir to combine. Cover with aluminium foil and lower on top of the trivet. Seal the lid and cook for 12 minutes at High. Do a quick release, and serve with crackers.

## Classic Italian Peperonata

**Ready in about: 10 minutes | Serves: 4 | Per serving: Calories 152; Carbs 17g; Fat 8g; Protein 6g**

INGREDIENTS
1 Green Bell Pepper, sliced
2 Yellow Bell Peppers, sliced
2 Red Bell Peppers, sliced
3 Tomatoes, chopped
1 Red Onions, chopped
2 Garlic Cloves, minced
2 cups Veggie Stock
2 tbsp Olive Oil
Salt and Pepper, to taste
4 cup Egg Noodles, cooked optional, to serve

DIRECTIONS
- Heat oil on SAUTÉ mode at High, and cook the onion for 2 minutes, until translucent. Stir in peppers and stir-fry for 2 more minutes. Add garlic and cook for 1 minute, until soft.
- Stir in the tomatoes and cook for 2 minutes before pouring in the stock. Seal the lid and cook for 6 minutes on STEAM mode at High. When done, do a quick pressure release.
- Check the veggies whether they are soft and cooked through. If not, cook for a few more minutes, lid off, on SAUTÉ mode at High. Drain and serve over noodles.

## Spicy Tomato Sauce

**Ready in about: 20 minutes | Serves: 16 | Per serving: Calories 50; Carbs 5g; Fat 3g; Protein 1g**

INGREDIENTS
3 pounds Tomatoes, peeled and diced
1 cup Red Onions, chopped
¼ cup Olive Oil
2 tsp Brown Sugar
½ tsp dried basil
1 Red Chilli, chopped
½ tsp dried Oregano
2 Cloves Garlic, minced
½ tsp dried Sage
Salt and ground Black Pepper, to taste
½ cup Water

DIRECTIONS
- Select SAUTÉ mode at High and heat the oil; cook the green onions and garlic until tender, for about 3 minutes. Add the remaining ingredients and seal the lid. Select BEANS/CHILI mode.
- Cook for 10 minutes at High Pressure. Do a quick pressure release. Cool before serving.

## Zesty Carrots with Pecans

**Ready in about: 10 minutes | Serves: 4 | Per serving: Calories 276; Carbs 45g; Fat 10g; Protein 5g**

INGREDIENTS
2 pounds Carrots, peeled and cut into rounds
½ cup Pecans, toasted and chopped
1 tbsp Butter
¼ cup Raisins
1 cup Water
½ Sea Salt
1 tbsp Vinegar
Freshly ground Black Pepper, to taste

DIRECTIONS
- Select SAUTÉ at High and melt the butter. Add in the carrots and cook for 5 minutes until tender. Add the raisins, water, and salt. Seal the lid, press STEAM and cook for 3 minutes at High.
- When it goes off, do a quick pressure release. Pour in the vinegar, and black pepper, and give it a good stir. Scatter the pecans over the top, to serve.

## Pressure Cooked Devilled Eggs

**Ready in about: 20 minutes | Serves: 4 | Per serving: Calories 100; Carbs 1g; Fat 8g; Protein 6g**

INGREDIENTS
4 Eggs
1 tsp Paprika
1 tbsp Light Mayonnaise
1 tsp Dijon Mustard
1 cup Water

DIRECTIONS
- Place the eggs and water in your pressure cooker. Seal the lid and cook on BEANS/CHILI for 5 minutes at High. Once cooking is over, do a quick pressure release.
- Transfer the veggies to a food processor. Place the eggs in an ice bath and let cool for 5 minutes. Peel and cut them in half. Remove yolks to a mixing dish and mash with a fork; add the remaining ingredients excluding the paprika and stir.
- Fill the egg halves with the yolk mixture. Sprinkle with paprika to serve.

## Tomato Zoodles

⏲ **Ready in about: 20 minutes | Serves: 4 | Per serving:**
**Calories 102; Carbs 10g; Fat 4g; Protein 2g**

INGREDIENTS
4 cups Zoodles
2 Garlic Cloves, minced
8 cups Boiling Water
1 tbsp Olive Oil
½ cup Tomato Paste
2 cups canned Tomatoes, diced
2 tbsp chopped Basil

DIRECTIONS
- Place the zoodles in a bowl filled with boiling water. After one minute, drain them and set aside. Heat oil and cook garlic for about a minute, until fragrant, on SAUTÉ mode at High.
- Add tomato paste, and 1 cup water and basil. Stir in the zoodles, coating them well with the sauce. Seal the lid, cook for 8 minutes on BEANS/CHILI at High. Do a quick pressure release.

## Easy Street Sweet Corn

⏲ **Ready in about: 10 minutes | Serves: 6 | Per serving:**
**Calories 130; Carbs 16g; Fat 5g; Protein 9g**

INGREDIENTS
Juice of 2 Limes
1 cup Parmesan Cheese, grated
6 Ears Sweet Corn
2 cups Water
6 tbsp Yogurt
½ tsp Garlic Powder
1 tsp Chili Powder, optional

DIRECTIONS
- Pour in water. Put the corn in a steamer basket. Place into the pressure cooker. Seal the lid, and cook on STEAM mode for 3 minutes at High. Combine the remaining ingredients, except the cheese, in a bowl.
- Once cooking is over, do a quick pressure release. Let cool for a couple of minutes. Remove husks from the corn and brush them with the mixture. Sprinkle parmesan on top and serve.

## Candied Holiday Yams

⏲ **Ready in about: 10 minutes | Serves: 4 | Per serving:**
**Calories 466; Carbs 78g; Fat 16g; Protein 4g**

INGREDIENTS
3 Yams, peeled and cubed
4 tbsp Butter
¼ cup Maple Syrup
1 cup Water
½ cup Brown Sugar
1 tsp Cinnamon
2 ½ tbsp Cornstarch
½ cup Pecans, chopped
A pinch of Salt

DIRECTIONS
- Combine all ingredients in the pressure cooker. Seal the lid and cook on BEANS/CHILI at High pressure, for 5 minutes. When ready, release the pressure quickly, and serve.

## Chipotle Pumpkin Soup

⏲ **Ready in about: 25 minutes | Serves: 6 | Per serving:**
**Calories 137; Carbs 11g; Fat 3g; Protein 6g**

INGREDIENTS
2 Chipotle Peppers, seeded and finely minced
4 cups Vegetable Broth
1 tbsp Olive Oil
1 cup Onions, peeled and chopped
2 cups Water
3 tbsp fresh Cilantro, chopped
½ tsp Cayenne Pepper
¼ tsp Black Pepper
½ tsp Salt
28 ounces canned Pumpkin Puree
1 tsp Garlic, smashed
½ tsp ground Allspice
2 tbsp Pumpkin Seeds, toasted for garnish
1 cup Heavy Cream

DIRECTIONS
- Warm oil in the cooker on SAUTÉ at High, and cook the garlic and onion until brown, for about 3-4 minutes. Add chipotle peppers, allspice, salt, cayenne pepper, and black pepper, and cook for another 2 minutes.
- Then, stir in the pumpkin, broth, and water. Seal the lid, press BEANS/CHILI and cook for 10 minutes at High Pressure. Once ready, do a quick pressure release. Transfer the soup to a food processor.
- Blend until smooth and creamy, working in batches if necessary, then pour in the heavy cream. Sprinkle with toasted pumpkin seeds and fresh cilantro to serve.

## Navy Beans with Parsley and Garlic

⏲ **Ready in about: 30 minutes | Serves: 6 | Per serving:**
**Calories 112; Carbs 19g; Fat 1g; Protein 9g**

INGREDIENTS
1 Tomato, chopped
2 tbsp Olive Oil
1 Bell Pepper, sliced
1 tsp Garlic, minced
1 cup Celery stalk, chopped
1 tbsp Tomato Puree
½ tsp Cayenne Pepper
1 tsp Salt
3 cups Water
2 cups dried Navy Beans, drained and soaked
4 Garlic Cloves, sliced
1 handful Parsley, roughly chopped, to serve
1 cup Carrots, chopped into sticks
2 small Onions, chopped

DIRECTIONS
- Sauté onions, celery, and garlic for about 3 minutes on SAUTÉ mode at High. Then, add the remaining ingredients, except for the parsley. Seal the lid, set onon BEANS/CHILI for 20 minutes at High.
- When ready, do a quick pressure release. Transfer to a serving bowl, sprinkle with parsley and serve.

## Walnut & Cinnamon Coconut Potatoes

⏱ **Ready in about: 20 minutes | Serves: 4 | Per serving:**
**Calories 387; Carbs 67g; Fat 15g; Protein 5g**

INGREDIENTS
4 Potatoes, boiled and mashed
2 tbsp Coconut Flour
¼ tsp Cinnamon
2 tbsp Coconut Milk
½ cup chopped Walnuts
1 tbsp Coconut Oil
2 tbsp Fresh Orange Juice
1 cup Water

DIRECTIONS
- Add the mashed potatoes, coconut milk, cinnamon, orange juice, and coconut oil, to a large bowl. Mix well until the mixture is fully incorporated. Grease a baking dish with cooking spray.
- Press well the potato mixture at the bottom. Top with walnuts and sprinkle with coconut flour. Pour the water into the pressure cooker and lower the trivet. Place baking dish on top of the trivet.
- Seal the lid, and cook on BEANS/CHILI at High for 7 minutes. Do a natural pressure release, for 10 minutes.

## Cheesy Acorn Squash Relish

⏱ **Ready in about: 15 minutes | Serves: 6 | Per serving:**
**Calories 167; Carbs 8g; Fat 15g; Protein 1g**

INGREDIENTS
1 cup Water
1 tsp baking soda
1 cup Parmesan cheese, grated
¼ cup Milk
1 tsp Sesame Seeds, toasted
½ tsp Sea Salt
¼ tsp Black Pepper
½ cup Butter, melted
1 pound Acorn Squash, halved
2 tbsp Apple Cider Vinegar

DIRECTIONS
- Select STEAM mode, and add water and acorn squash. Drizzle with apple cider and stir in the remaining ingredients. Seal the lid, switch the pressure release valve to close and cook for 10 minutes.
- When it goes off, quick release the pressure. Put the squash in a food processor along with parmesan cheese, and blend until smooth, then add in the milk while the machine is running. Spoon the dip into a serving bowl and sprinkle with sesame seeds to serve.

## Potato and Spinach Bowl

⏱ **Ready in about: 15 minutes | Serves: 4 | Per serving:**
**Calories 153; Carbs 15g; Fat 5g; Protein 4g**

INGREDIENTS
1 Potato, peeled and cubed
1 Onion, chopped
2 cups Spinach
2 Garlic Cloves, minced
½ cup Veggie Broth
1 tsp Lemon Juice
1 tsp ground Ginger
½ tsp Cayenne Pepper
½ tbsp Olive Oil
¼ tsp Pepper

DIRECTIONS
- Warm oil on SAUTÉ mode at High. When hot and sizzling, add the onion and cook for 2 minutes. Add the garlic, ginger, cayenne, and pepper, and cook for one more minute.
- Add the sweet potatoes and cook for another minute. Pour the broth over and stir in the spinach. Seal the lid, select STEAM for 4 minutes at High pressure. Release the pressure quickly.

## Savory Vegetarian Sandwiches

⏱ **Ready in about: 35 minutes | Serves: 4 | Per serving:**
**Calories 488; Carbs 62g; Fat 19g; Protein 28g**

INGREDIENTS
1 tbsp Vegetable Oil
4 Vegetarian Sausages, sliced
1 Garlic Cloves, crushed
½ cup Tamari Sauce
2 Shallots, chopped
2 cups roasted Vegetable Stock
2 Bell Peppers, deveined and sliced
4 Burger Buns
1 cup freshly grated Cheddar Cheese
Salt and ground Black Pepper, to taste
2 ½ cups Water

DIRECTIONS
- Heat oil on SAUTÉ at High and cook the garlic and shallots, until tender, for about 3 minutes. Stir in the sausages and cook for another 5 minutes. Add in the remaining ingredients, except for the buns and cheese.
- Select BEANS/CHILI and cook for 15 minutes at High. Once ready, do a quick pressure release. Preheat oven to 460 degrees F.
- Divide prepared mixture among 4 burger buns and top with grated cheese. Bake the sandwiches in the oven for 6-7 minutes, or until the cheese melts. Serve immediately!

## Effortless Cannellini and Black Bean Chili

⏱ **Ready in about: 30 minutes | Serves: 8 | Per serving:**
**Calories 136; Carbs 19g; Fat 7g; Protein 4g**

INGREDIENTS
2 cups Vegetable Stock
1 tsp Chili Pepper, minced
½ cup Red Bell Pepper, seeded and thinly sliced
1 cup Leeks, thinly sliced
1 tsp Garlic, minced
2 tbsp Vegetable Oil
1 cup Carrots, chopped into sticks
1 ½ cup dried Black Beans, soaked, drained and rinsed
1 ½ cup dried cannellini Beans, soaked, drained and rinsed

¼ tsp Sea Salt, to taste
½ tsp Celery seeds
5-6 Black Peppercorns
½ tsp Red Pepper flakes, crushed
24 ounces canned diced Tomatoes
½ cup Green Onion, chopped

DIRECTIONS
- Heat oil on SAUTÉ at High, and cook the garlic and leeks for 3-4 minutes. Stir in the remaining ingredients, except the tomatoes. Seal the lid, hit BEANS/CHILI and cook for 20 minutes at High.
- Once the cooking is complete, perform a quick pressure release. Add in the tomatoes, and stir occasionally for about 5 minutes. Serve garnished with green onion.

## Thyme-Flavored Fries

**Ready in about: 13 minutes | Serves: 4 | Per serving: Calories 116; Carbs 24g; Fat 1g; Protein 2g**

INGREDIENTS
1 pound Potatoes, cut into strips
1 tbsp dried Thyme
½ tsp Garlic Powder
1 tsp Olive Oil
1 cup Water

DIRECTIONS
- Place the potatoes in a large bowl. Add thyme, olive oil, and garlic, and mix to coat them well. Pour water into the pressure cooker.
- Arrange fries in a veggie steamer in a single layer. Seal the lid and cook for 3 minutes on STEAM at High pressure. Do a quick release and serve.

## Tomato and Kale "Rice"

**Ready in about: 15 minutes | Serves: 4 | Per serving: Calories 68; Carbs 8g; Fat 4g; Protein 3g**

INGREDIENTS
1 tbsp Oil
1 cup Veggie Broth
4 cups Cauliflower Rice, processed in a food processor
1 Large Tomato, chopped
½ cup Kale, chopped
1 tsp Cilantro, chopped
¼ tsp Pepper
¼ tsp Garlic Powder

DIRECTIONS
- Heat the oil on SAUTÉ. Add the tomato, cauliflower, pepper, and garlic powder. Stir well to combine and cook for a minute or two. Pour the broth over and stir in the spinach.
- Seal the lid, select STEAM for 3 minutes, at High pressure. After you hear the beep, release the pressure quickly. Open the lid carefully, serve and enjoy!

## Minty Cauliflower Tabbouleh

**Ready in about: 10 minutes | Serves: 3 | Per serving: Calories 232; Carbs 15g; Fat 18g; Protein 3g**

INGREDIENTS
2 cups Cauliflower Rice (made in a food processor)
4 tbsp Olive Oil
½ cup Spring Onions, chopped
½ Cucumber, diced
3 tbsp Lime Juice
½ cup Parsley
½ cup Mint
1 tsp Garlic, minced
1 cup diced Tomatoes

DIRECTIONS
- Heat a tablespoon of olive oil to the pressure cooker on SAUTÉ at High. Add the garlic and cook for a minute. Add the tomatoes and cauliflower, and saute them for about 2-3 minutes.
- Transfer to a bowl. Add the remaining ingredients to the bowl and give the mixture a good stir to combine well. Divide among 3 serving bowls.

## Spicy Cannellini Bean Salad with Dates

**Ready in: 35 minutes + chilling time | Serves: 12 | Per serving: Calories 195; Carbs 29g; Fat 3g; Protein 9g**

INGREDIENTS
1 cup dry Cannellini Beans, soaked
1 cup fresh Dates, halved, pitted
2 ½ cups frozen Green peas, thawed
1 cup Scallions, chopped
1 cup Tomatoes, thinly sliced
3 Cloves Garlic, minced
1 tbsp Olive Oil
¼ cup White Wine Vinegar
¼ cup Tamari Sauce
2 tsp Chili Paste
Salt and Black Pepper, to taste
½ tsp Red Pepper flakes, for garnish

DIRECTIONS
- To prepare the dressing, whisk tamari sauce, oil, vinegar, chili paste and garlic. Refrigerate overnight.
- Place the beans in your pressure cooker and pour water to cover them. Seal the lid and switch the pressure release valve to close. Select BEANS/CHILI mode and cook for 25 minutes at High Pressure.
- Once the cooking is complete, do a quick pressure release. Drain the beans and transfer to a serving bowl. Add in the rest of the ingredients, and toss with the dressing until well coated.

## Flavorful Tofu Bowl

**Ready in about: 10 minutes | Serves: 6 | Per serving: Calories 275; Carbs 10g; Fat 16g; Protein 26g**

INGREDIENTS
20 ounces Firm Tofu, cubed
2 tsp Garlic, minced
1 Onion, chopped
2 tbsp Chives, chopped
1 tsp Ginger, minced
2 cups Veggie Broth
2 tbsp Tamari
2 tbsp White Wine
3 tsp Vegetable Oil
2 cups cooked Rice to serve

DIRECTIONS
- Heat oil on SAUTÉ mode at High. Add tofu and cook until browned, for a few minutes. Meanwhile, place the remaining ingredients, except the rice, in a food processor and pulse until smooth.
- Pour this mixture over the tofu. Seal the lid and cook on STEAM for 3 minutes at High. When ready, release the pressure quickly. Stir in the rice and serve.

## Tofu and Veggie 'Stir Fry'

Ready in about: **20 minutes** | Serves: **4** | Per serving: **Calories 410; Carbs 18g; Fat 28g; Protein 25g**

INGREDIENTS
12 ounces Tofu, mashed
2 Shallots, diced
1 Tomato, diced
1 cup Parsnips, chopped
2 tbsp Olive Oil
2 tsp Sherry
¼ cup Parsley, chopped
1 tsp Garlic, minced
3 cups Water
Salt and Pepper, to taste

DIRECTIONS
- Heat oil on SAUTÉ mode at High. Add shallots, parsnips, garlic, and tomatoes; cook for 3 minutes, stirring occasionally. Stir in tofu, sherry, and season with salt and pepper.
- Seal the lid, set on STEAM, and cook for 4 minutes at High. Once done, do a quick release.

## Spicy Tofu Vegan Stew

Ready in about: **20 minutes** | Serves: **4** | Per serving: **Calories 355; Carbs 69g; Fat 3g; Protein 11g**

INGREDIENTS
1 tsp Habanero Pepper, minced
2 cups Tofu, shredded or cubed
2 Bell Peppers, diced
2 ripe Tomatoes, finely chopped
2 White Onions, chopped
1 cup Parsnips, chopped
1 cup Green peas
½ cup Barbecue Sauce
2 Carrots, chopped
4 Sweet Potatoes, peeled and diced
1 tbsp Vegetable Oil
2 tbsp Ketchup
tsp Korean Gochugaru Chile Flakes
½ tsp Salt
½ tsp Black Pepper
1 cup Water

DIRECTIONS
- Heat the oil on SAUTÉ mode at High, and cook the onions, carrots, parsnip, and peppers until soft, for about 5 minutes. Add the rest of the ingredients, and pour the water to cover the ingredients.
- Seal the lid, and cook for 10 minutes on BEANS/CHILI at High. Do a quick pressure release.

## Cheesy Sour Veggie Casserole

Ready in about: **35 minutes** | Serves: **8** | Per serving: **Calories 379; Carbs 54g; Fat 14g; Protein 11g**

INGREDIENTS
6 Potatoes, chopped
½ cup Onion, chopped
1 cup Carrots, chopped
1 cup Bell Peppers, chopped
1 cup Panko Breadcrumbs
½ cup Sour Cream
1 cup Cheddar Cheese, shredded
3 tbsp Butter, melted
2 tbsp Olive Oil
Water, as needed

DIRECTIONS
- Heat oil on SAUTÉ mode at High, and cook the onions for 2 minutes, until translucent. Add the veggies and stir-fry for 2 more minutes. Pour enough water to cover.
- Seal the lid and cook for 7 minutes on BEANS/CHILI at High. Do a quick pressure release. Transfer the veggies to a baking pan, that fits in the pressure cooker. Leave the liquid in the cooker.
- Place a trivet at the bottom. In the baking pan, stir in the remaining ingredients. Place the pan atop of the trivet, inside the cooker and seal the lid. Cook for 5 more minutes on STEAM at High. Do a quick release.

## Garlicky and Chili Pomodoro Zoodles

Ready in about: **15 minutes** | Serves: **4** | Per serving: **Calories 121; Carbs 16g; Fat 4g; Protein 3g**

INGREDIENTS
2 Large Zucchini, spiralized
½ Onion, diced
3 tsp Garlic, minced
1 tbsp Olive Oil
1 cup Tomatoes, diced
¾ cup Tomato Sauce
½ cup Water
1 tbsp freshly Basi, chopped l
2 tsp Chili Powder
Salt and Pepper, to taste

DIRECTIONS
- Heat oil on SAUTÉ at High. Cook the onions for 3 minutes, until translucent. Add garlic and cook for 1 more minute, until fragrant and crispy. Stir in the tomatoes, water and tomato sauce.
- Seal the lid and cook for 3 minutes on STEAM at High. Release the pressure quickly. Stir in the zoodles, and season with salt and pepper. Cook for 3 minutes, lid off, and stir in chili powder. Top with basil.

## Buttery Parsley Corn

Ready in about: **10 minutes** | Serves: **4** | Per serving: **Calories 310; Carbs 32g; Fat 21g; Protein 5g**

INGREDIENTS
4 ears shucked Corn
6 tbsp Butter, melted

½ tsp Salt
1 ¼ cups Water
½ tsp Chili Powder, optional
¼ tsp Sugar
2 tbsp Parsley, minced

DIRECTIONS
- Pour the water in your pressure cooker and insert a trivet. Place corn on top of the trivet. Seal the lid and select STEAM mode for 3 minutes at High. Do a quick pressure release.
- In a bowl, combine butter, salt, parsley, and chili powder, and pour over the corn, to serve.

## Eggplant Escalivada Toast

Ready in about: **30 minutes | Serves: 6 | Per serving: Calories 164; Carbs 23g; Fat 7g; Protein 5g**

INGREDIENTS
6 Bread Sliced, toasted
2 Eggplants, peeled and sliced
1 Red Bell Pepper, peeled and sliced
2 Garlic Cloves
A handful of Black Olives
2 tbsp Olive Oil
1 tbsp Tahini
Juice from 1 Lemon
A pinch of Red Pepper flakes
½ tsp Salt
¼ tsp Black Pepper
1 ½ cups Water

DIRECTIONS
- Combine the water, bell pepper and eggplant in the pressure cooker. Seal the lid and cook on BEANS/CHILI at High for 6 minutes. When ready, do a quick pressure release.
- Drain and place the eggplants in a food processor. Add lemon juice, olive oil, olives, garlic, salt, pepper, and pepper flakes. Pulse until smooth. Spread the mixture over the toasted bread and serve warm.

## Mushroom and Veggie Baguette

Ready in about: **20 minutes | Serves: 4 | Per serving: Calories 227; Carbs 20g; Fat 9g; Protein 17g**

INGREDIENTS
1 Baguette, cut into 4 equal pieces
1 ½ cups Mushrooms, chopped
1 Shallot, chopped
1 Carrot, chopped
2 Bell Peppers, chopped
1 Parsnip, chopped
2 Tomatoes, chopped
1 Garlic Clove
1 tbsp Olive Oil
1 ½ cups Vegetable Stock
Salt and Pepper, to taste

DIRECTIONS
- Melt oil on SAUTÉ at High, add shallots and garlic and cook for 2 minutes, until soft and fragrant. Stir in the rest of the veggies and cook for 5 minutes, stirring occasionally.
- Stir in the remaining ingredients. Seal the lid and cook for 6 minutes on RICE/RISOTTO at High. Release the pressure quickly. Remove to a food processor and pulse until smooth. Spread mixture over baguette.

## Root Veggie Casserole

Ready in about: **25 minutes | Serves: 4 | Per serving: Calories 378; Carbs 73g; Fat 7g; Protein 13g**

INGREDIENTS
1 Onion, diced
4 pounds Baby Potatoes, halved
2 pounds Baby Carrots
1 tsp Garlic, minced
1 tsp Thyme
1 tsp dried Parsley
2 tbsp Olive Oil
½ cup Veggie Broth

DIRECTIONS
- Heat the oil on SAUTÉ at High. When hot and sizzling, add the onions and cook for 2-3 minutes. When the onions become translucent, add the garlic and cook for another minute.
- Add the carrots and cook for another 3 minutes. Stir in the rest of the ingredients and seal the lid.
- Press BEANS/CHILI, and set the cooking time to 10 minutes at High. Release the pressure quickly.

## Coconut Zucchini Soup

Ready in about: **20 minutes | Serves: 2 | Per serving: Calories 296; Carbs 12g; Fat 25g; Protein 8g**

INGREDIENTS
16 ounces Veggie Broth
10 cups Zucchini, chopped
13 ounces Coconut Milk
1 tbsp Curry Paste
½ tsp Garlic Powder
½ tsp Onion Powder
Freshly ground Black Pepper
1/4 cup Butter, at room temperature
Crème fraîche for garnish

DIRECTIONS
- Place all ingredients, except for the coconut milk in the pressure cooker. Give the mixture a good stir to combine, and then seal the lid, select BEANS/CHILI for 10 minutes at High.
- When the timer goes off, do a quick pressure release. Remove the ingredients to a deep bowl, add coconut milk and blend with an immersion blender until smooth.
- Serve right away garnished with crème fraîche and ground black pepper, to enjoy.

## Potato Chili

Ready in about: **22 minutes | Serves: 4 | Per serving: Calories 285; Carbs 50g; Fat 5g; Protein 6g**

INGREDIENTS
4 cups Vegetable Broth
3 large Russet Potatoes, peeled and diced
2 Jalapeno Peppers, seeded and diced
1 Garlic Clove, minced
½ tsp Cumin

1 tsp Chili Powder
¼ tsp Cayenne Pepper
½ Red Onion, diced
1 tbsp Olive Oil
DIRECTIONS
- Warm oil on SAUTÉ at High. Once hot and sizzling, add onions and cook for 2-3 minutes. When translucent, add the garlic and cook for another minute. Add the remaining ingredients.
- Stir well to combine, seal the lid, and cook on BEANS/CHILI at High pressure for 8 minutes. After the beep, let the pressure release naturally, by allowing the valve to drop on its own, for about 10 minutes.

## Red Lentil Dhal with Butternut Squash

**Ready in about: 25 minutes | Serves: 6 | Per serving: Calories 325; Carbs 45g; Fat 10g; Protein 12g**

INGREDIENTS
4 ½ cups Vegetable Broth
1 ½ cups Tomatoes, diced
1 ½ cups Red Lentils, rinsed
1 heaping tsp Garlic, minced
1 cup Onions, diced
3 tbsp Olive Oil
¼ tsp Black Pepper
½ tsp Cayenne Pepper
1 tsp ground Turmeric
Juice from 1 lemon
1 tsp Salt
2 pounds Butternut squash, roughly chopped
2 tsp Garam Masala
½ cup fresh Cilantro, chopped for garnish
½ cup Natural Yogurt, for garnish
DIRECTIONS
- Warm the oil on SAUTÉ mode at High. Cook the garlic and onions for 2-3 minutes, until soft. Add the squash, Garam masala, cayenne pepper, turmeric, salt, and black pepper. Cook for 3 more minutes.
- Then, stir in the broth, lentils, and tomatoes. Lock the lid and switch the pressure release valve to close. Select BEANS/CHILI and cook for 10 minutes at High pressure. Do a quick pressure release.
- Stir in lemon juice. Ladle dhal into bowls and garnish with fresh cilantro and yogurt and serve.

## Leafy Green Risotto

**Ready in about: 20 minutes | Serves: 6 | Per serving: Calories 272; Carbs 40g; Fat 11g; Protein 6g**

INGREDIENTS
3 ½ cups Veggie Broth
1 cup Spinach Leaves, packed
1 cup Kale Leaves, packed
¼ cup Parmesan Cheese, grated
¼ cup diced Onion
3 tbsp Butter
2 tsp Olive Oil
1 ½ cups Arborio Rice
4 Sun-dried Tomatoes, chopped

A pinch of Nutmeg
Salt and Pepper, to taste
DIRECTIONS
- Heat oil and cook onions until soft, about 3 minutes. Add rice and cook for 3-5 minutes, on SAUTÉ at High. Pour in broth. Seal the lid, and cook for 9 minutes on BEANS/CHILI at High.
- Do a quick pressure release. Stir in the remaining ingredients. Leave for a 1-2 minutes, or until greens wilt.

## Mini Mac and Cheese

**Ready in about: 17 minutes | Serves: 4 | Per serving: Calories 132; Carbs 15g; Fat 5g; Protein 7g**

INGREDIENTS
8 ounces Whole-Wheat Macaroni
¾ cup Monterey Jack Cheese, shredded
2 cups Water
DIRECTIONS
- Place the macaroni and water in your pressure cooker. Seal the lid and cook on RICE/RISOTTO mode for 8 minutes at High. Do a quick pressure release, and drain the macaroni. Return to the pressure cooker.
- Stir in cheese, and cook on SAUTÉ at High, for 30 seconds until melted. Spoon between bowls, to serve.

## Tempeh Sandwiches

**Ready in about: 30 minutes | Serves: 6 | Per serving: Calories 428; Carbs 41g; Fat 23g; Protein 15g**

INGREDIENTS
12 ounces Tempeh, sliced
6 Brioche Buns
1 tsp Ginger, minced
2 tbsp Brown Mustard
2 tsp Agave Nectar
1 tsp Garlic, minced
½ tsp Smoked Paprika
½ cup Apple Cider Vinegar
½ cup Veggie Stock
2 tbsp Tamari
Salt and Black Pepper, to taste
Cooking spray, to grease
DIRECTIONS
- Coat with cooking spray and sauté the tempeh on SAUTÉ at High for a few minutes. Stir in the remaining ingredients, except the buns, and seal the lid. Cook for 2 minutes on STEAM at High.
- When ready, release the pressure quickly. Divide the mixture between the buns and serve.

## Veggie Flax Burgers

**Ready in about: 30 minutes | Serves: 4 | Per serving: Calories 123; Carbs 8g; Fat 8g; Protein 2g**

INGREDIENTS
2 tbsp Olive Oil
1 bag of Frozen Mixed Veggies Broccoli, Carrots, peas
1 cup Cauliflower Florets
1 cup Flax Meal

1 ½ cups Water

DIRECTIONS
- Pour the water into your pressure cooker. Combine the mixed veggies and cauliflower florets in the steaming basket and then lower the basket into the pot. Seal the lid.
- Select BEANS/CHILI for 5 minutes at High pressure. After the timer goes off, do a quick pressure release. Transfer the veggies to a bowl and discard the water.
- Mash the veggies with a potato masher and allow them to cool a bit, about 10 minutes. When safe to handle, stir in the flax meal and shape the mixture into 4 equal patties.
- Wipe the pressure cooker clean, and add olive oil. Set to SAUTÉ at High and wait until oil heats. When sizzling, add veggie burgers. Cook for 3 minutes then flip over and cook for 3 more minutes. Serve and enjoy!

## Beet Borscht

Ready in about: **60 minutes** | Serves: **8** | Per serving: Calories 186; Carbs 42g; Fat 1g; Protein 5g

INGREDIENTS
3 cups Cabbage, shredded
8 cups Beets, diced
3 Celery Stalks, diced
1 Onion, diced
1 Garlic Clove, diced
3 cups Veggie Stock
2 Carrots, diced
1 tsp Thyme
¼ tsp Pepper
1 ½ cups Water

DIRECTIONS
- Pour the water in the pressure cooker and lower the steamer basket. Place the beets inside the basket and seal the lid. Select BEANS/CHILI, set to 7 minutes at High pressure.
- After the beeping sound, release the pressure quickly. Remove the steamer basket and discard the water. Return the cooked beets to the pot and add the rest of the ingredients.
- Stir well to combine and then seal the lid again. Select on SOUP, and cook for 40 minutes, at High. When the timer goes off, do a natural pressure release, for about 10 minutes.

## Asparagus Dressed in Cheese

Ready in about: **17 minutes** | Serves: **4** | Per serving: Calories 224; Carbs 6g; Fat 15g; Protein 16g

INGREDIENTS
1 pound Asparagus
8 ounces Cheddar cheese
1 cup Water

DIRECTIONS
- Pour water into your cooker. Cut off the asparagus' ends. Slice the cheese in enough strips to wrap around each asparagus spear. Arrange the wrapped asparagus on a steamer basket.
- Place the basket inside the pressure cooker. Seal the lid, cook on STEAM at High for 4 minutes. When cooking is complete, press CANCEL and release the pressure quickly. Serve hot.

## Spicy Pinto Bean Chili

Ready in about: **30 minutes** | Serves: **8** | Per serving: Calories 132; Carbs 23g; Fat 3g; Protein 11g

INGREDIENTS
5 cups Vegetable Stock
1 tsp Red Pepper flakes, crushed
20 ounces canned Tomatoes, diced
1 cup Carrots, chopped into sticks
1 Green Bell Pepper, thinly sliced
3 Cloves Garlic, minced
1 cup Red Onion, chopped
½ tsp Cilantro, to garnish
Sea Salt and Black Pepper, to taste
2 ½ cups dried Pinto Beans, rinsed
1 cup Parsnip, chopped

DIRECTIONS
- Sauté garlic and onion for 3 minutes on SAUTÉ at High, with a splash of vegetable stock. Stir in the remaining ingredients, except for the cilantro. Seal the lid, press BEANS/CHILI for 20 minutes at High.
- Once the cooking is complete, do a quick pressure release. Garnish with fresh cilantro to serve.

## Tropical Salsa Mash

Ready in about: **10 minutes** | Serves: **4** | Per serving: Calories 122; Carbs 24g; Fat 4g; Protein 2g

INGREDIENTS
¼ cup Red Onions, chopped
1 cup Mango, chopped
1 cup Apples, chopped
1 cup Tomatoes, chopped
1 cup Pineapples, diced
2 tbsp chopped Mint
2 Jalapenos, minced
1 Garlic Clove, minced
2 tbsp Cilantro, chopped
¼ cup Lime Juice
1 tbsp Olive Oil
¼ tsp Sea Salt
¼ tsp Pepper

DIRECTIONS
- Heat oil on SAUTÉ at High, add the onions and cook for 2 minutes, until translucent. Add apples, pineapples, tomatoes, and mangos, and cook for 3 more minutes.
- Stir in the garlic, salt, and pepper, and cook for another minute. Transfer the mixture to a bowl. Stir in the remaining ingredients. Remove the mixture to a food processor.
- Pulse for two seconds. The mixture should not be smooth, but chunky. Serve and enjoy!

## Apple and Red Cabbage Vegetarian Dinner

Ready in about: **30 minutes** | Serves: **4** | Per serving: Calories 139; Carbs 22g; Fat 4g; Protein 4g

INGREDIENTS

1 pound Red Cabbage, shredded
½ cup Red Wine
1 cup Apples, diced
1 cup Onions, diced
1 tsp Thyme
1 ½ cups Vegetable Stock
1 tbsp Coconut Oil
1 ½ tbsp Cornstarch Slurry
1 ½ tbsp Flour
Salt and Pepper, to taste
½ tsp Brown Sugar

DIRECTIONS
- Melt oil on SAUTÉ mode at High, add onions and apples and cook for 5 minutes, until lightly browned.
- Stir in the remaining ingredients, except the slurry. Cook for 20 minutes, and bring the mixture to a boil. Stir in the slurry and cook uncovered until thickened. Serve and enjoy!

## Squash and Sweet Potato Lunch Soup

Ready in about: **30 minutes** | Serves: **4** | Per serving: Calories 243; Carbs 33g; Fat 9g; Protein 7g

INGREDIENTS
2 cups Squash, cubed
2 cups Sweet Potatoes, cubed
2 tbsp Olive Oil
1 Onion, diced
1 tbsp Heavy Cream
3 cups Veggie Broth
A pinch of Thyme

DIRECTIONS
- On SAUTÉ at High, warm the oil, and add the onions. Cook until soft, about 3 minutes. Stir in the potatoes and squash and cook for an additional minute, or until they begin to 'sweat'.
- Pour the broth over and stir in the thyme. Seal the lid, choose BEANS/CHILI for 10 minutes at High. When done, do a natural pressure release, for about 10 minutes. Stir in the cream, and serve.

## Green Minestrone Stew with Parmesan

Ready in about: **25 minutes** | Serves: **4** | Per serving: Calories 313; Carbs 25g; Fat 21g; Protein 9g

INGREDIENTS
1 head Broccoli, chopped into small florets
2 Green Bell Peppers, thinly sliced
2 Celery stalks, chopped
1 tsp Garlic, minced
1 tsp Olive Oil
4 spring Onions, chopped
4 cups Vegetable Broth
1 bunch Kale, roughly chopped
2 tsp fresh Lime Juice
Freshly grated Parmesan cheese, to serve

DIRECTIONS
- Heat the oil on SAUTÉ mode at High. Cook the spring onions and garlic until tender, for about 2 minutes.
- Add the remaining ingredients, except for kale and Parmesan cheese. Seal the lid and switch the pressure release valve to close. Press BEANS/CHILI and cook for 10 minutes at High pressure.
- Once the cooking is over, do a quick release. Add in the kale. Place the lid and cook for 12-15 minutes until tender, on SAUTÉ mode at High. Divide between 4 bowls and serve sprinkled with Parmesan cheese.

## Broccoli and Chickpea Stew

Ready in about: **35 minutes** | Serves: **4** | Per serving: Calories 415; Carbs 74g; Fat 8g; Protein 25g;

INGREDIENTS
12 ounces Chickpeas Beans, drained and soaked
1 bunch Broccoli rabe, chopped
½ head Red Cabbage, shredded
1 pound Zucchini, diced
2 Carrots, diced
2 Potatoes, diced
2 tbsp fresh Parsley, roughly chopped
2 Tomatoes, chopped
5 cups Vegetable Stock
1 tsp Fennel Seeds
½ tsp Salt
½ tsp ground Black Pepper
½ tsp Celery seeds

DIRECTIONS
- Add all ingredients in the pressure cooker. Seal the lid, select MEAT/STEW and cook for 25 minutes at High Pressure.
- When ready, do a quick pressure release. Ladle in serving bowls to serve.

## Pearl Barley and Butternut Winter Soup

Ready in about: **30 minutes** | Serves: **6** | Per serving: Calories 335; Carbs 56g; Fat 6g; Protein 9g

INGREDIENTS
1 cup Pearl Barley, rinsed and drained
1 pound Buttenut Squash, cubed
1 tbsp Chili Pepper, V
½ cup Carrots, chopped
½ cup Parsnip, chopped
2 sticks Celery, diced
1 Turnip, chopped
3 tsp Olive Oil
1 ½ tsp Salt
6 cups Water
Salt and ground Black Pepper, to taste
½ tsp Cayenne Pepper

DIRECTIONS
- Mix together barley, water, squash, celery, carrots, parsnip, turnip, and olive oil in your pressure cooker. Season with salt. Seal the lid, press SOUP and cook for 25 minutes at High Pressure.
- Once cooking is over, do a quick pressure release. Stir in cayenne pepper and ladle into bowls to serve.

## Smoked Tofu Bowl

⏱ Ready in about: **10 minutes** | Serves: **6** | Per serving:
Calories 387; Carbs 59g; Fat 9g; Protein 23g

INGREDIENTS
20 ounces Smoked Tofu, sliced
2 ½ tbsp Oyster Sauce
2 tbsp Mirin Wine
3 Garlic Cloves, minced
2 tsp Olive Oil
2 cups Vegetable Broth
1 Onion, chopped
3 cups cooked Wild Rice
2 tbsp fresh Chives, roughly chopped
Salt and Black Pepper, to taste
1-inch piece of fresh Ginger, grated

DIRECTIONS
- Select SAUTÉ mode at High. Heat the oil and stir-fry the tofu cubes until lightly browned. In a blender, add in the remaining ingredients, except the rice.
- Blend until you obtain a smooth paste. Transfer the mixture to the pressure cooker. Select STEAM and cook for 2 minutes at High pressure. Do a quick pressure release. Serve on top of cooked rice to enjoy.

## Basil and Tomato "Pasta"

⏱ Ready in about: **12 minutes** | Serves: **4** | Per serving:
Calories 64; Carbs 12g; Fat 1g; Protein 4g

INGREDIENTS
½ cup Tomato Paste
4 cups Zoodles
¼ cup Water
2 Garlic Cloves, minced
¼ cup Veggie Broth
2 cups canned Tomatoes, diced
2 tbsp fresh Basil, chopped
1 tsp fresh Parsley, chopped

DIRECTIONS
- Place all ingredients in your pressure cooker. Stir well to combine everything. Seal the lid, select STEAM for 2 minutes, at High.
- Do a quick pressure release. Open the lid carefully, serve and enjoy!

## Kale Chips with Garlic and Lime Juice

⏱ Ready in about: **15 minutes** | Serves: **4** | Per serving:
Calories 85; Carbs 8g; Fat 4g; Protein 2g

INGREDIENTS
1 pound Kale
½ cup Water
3 Garlic Cloves, minced
1 tbsp Olive Oil
2 tbsp Lime Juice

DIRECTIONS
- Wash the kale and remove the stems. Heat the oil and cook garlic for a minute, or until fragrant, on SAUTÉ mode at High. Pack the kale well inside the cooker. Seal the lid.
- Cook on STEAM mode for 6 minutes at High. Do a quick release, and drizzle with lime juice.

## Pears in Cranberry Sauce

⏱ Ready in about: **20 minutes** | Serves: **4** | Per serving:
Calories 133; Carbs 29g; Fat 0g; Protein 1g

INGREDIENTS
1 pound Pears, peeled, cored, and halved
2 ½ cups Cranberries
1 tsp Vanilla Paste
½ cup granulated Sugar
2 tsp Cornstarch
¼ tsp grated Nutmeg
½ tsp ground Cardamom
1 ½ cups Water

DIRECTIONS
- Throw all ingredients, except for sugar and cornstarch, into your pressure cooker. Select BEANS/CHILI and cook for 10 minutes at High.
- Do a quick pressure release. Remove the pears with a spoon that has long narrow holes. Then, mash the berries with a heavy spoon. Combine the sugar and cornstarch with 2 tbsp of water.
- Let simmer for 5 minutes on SAUTÉ, until it thickens. Serve the pears topped with cranberry sauce.

## Zucchini Coconut Burgers

⏱ Ready in about: **15 minutes** | Serves: **4** | Per serving:
Calories 235; Carbs 27g; Fat 7g; Protein 11g

INGREDIENTS
¼ cup Coconut Flakes, unsweetened
¼ cup Coconut Flour
½ cup Potatoes, mashed
1 large Zucchini, shredded
2 tbsp Olive Oil

DIRECTIONS
- Heat the oil on SAUTÉ at High. Meanwhile, place all of the remaining ingredients in a bowl. Mix with your hands until fully incorporated and then shape the mixture into 4 equal patties.
- When the oil becomes sizzling, add the patties and cook them for 3 minutes per side. For softer patties, add a few tbsp of water.
- Seal the lid, and cook for 2 minute on STEAM at High pressure. Once ready, let the pressure release naturally, for 5 minutes. Serve immediately.

## Roasted Potatoes with Gorgonzola

⏱ Ready in about: **20 minutes** | Serves: **4** | Per serving:
Calories 377; Carbs 28g; Fat 12g; Protein 11g

INGREDIENTS
1 ½ pounds Fingerling Potatoes,
1 cup Gorgonzola Cheese, grated
½ cup Vegetable Broth
4 tbsp Butter, melted
½ tsp Kosher Salt
½ tsp Thyme
½ tsp Cayenne Pepper

DIRECTIONS
- In your pressure cooker, add the butter, potatoes and broth. Seal the lid and switch the pressure release valve to close. Set on BEANS/CHILI mode and cook for 15 minutes at High pressure10 minutes.
- Do a quick release. Sprinkle with cayenne pepper, thyme and grated Gorgonzola cheese. Serve hot.

## Chickpea Bell Pepper Soup

Ready in about: **25 minutes** | Serves: **4** | Per serving: Calories 289; Carbs 49g; Fat 10g; Protein 15g

INGREDIENTS
2 Red Bell Peppers, divined and chopped
6 ounces Chickpeas, soaked overnight
4 ½ cups Vegetable Stock
2 Shallots, thinly sliced
1 cup fresh Chives, thinly sliced
1 cup Sweet Potatoes, peeled and diced
3 tsp Olive Oil
½ tsp White Pepper
2 tbsp Tamari Sauce
2 tbsp Cider vinegar

DIRECTIONS
- Heat oil on SAUTÉ at High and cook the shallots until translucent, for 2-3 minutes. Add the rest of the ingredients, except for the fresh chives.
- Seal the lid, press SOUP and cook for 20 minutes at High. Once the cooking is complete, do a quick pressure release. Serve topped with freshly chopped chives.

## Potato & Leek Patties

Ready in about: **15 minutes** | Serves: **3** | Per serving: Calories 265; Carbs 33g; Fat 11g; Protein 10g

INGREDIENTS
1 tbsp Olive Oil
4 ounces Leek, sliced
9 ounces Potatoes, boiled and mashed
½ cup Flour
¼ tsp Onion Powder
¼ tsp Paprika
¼ tsp Garlic Powder
A pinch of Pepper

DIRECTIONS
- Place all ingredients, except the oil, in a bowl. Mix with your hands until well combined and shape the mixture into 6 small patties. Add olive oil to the pressure cooker and set to SAUTÉ at High.
- When hot, add the patties and cook them for about 3 minutes on each side. Serve as desired.

## Lime & Mint Zoodles

Ready in about: **10 minutes** | Serves: **2** | Per serving: Calories 139; Carbs 73g; Fat 15g; Protein 4g

INGREDIENTS
2 Zucchini, spiralized
1 tsp Lime Zest
2 tbsp Lime Juice
2 tbsp Mint, chopped
2 tbsp Olive Oil
1 tsp Garlic, minced
¼ tsp Black Pepper

DIRECTIONS
- Heat olive oil on SAUTÉ at High. When hot and sizzling, add garlic and lime zest, and cook for about 30 seconds.
- Add the rest of the ingredients, stir well to combine, and cook for only 2 minutes. Divide the mixture among two serving bowls. Enjoy!

## Cabbage, Beet & Apple Stew

Ready in about: **30 minutes** | Serves: **4** | Per serving: Calories 156; Carbs 33g; Fat 2g; Protein 7g

INGREDIENTS
2 Carrots, chopped
½ Cabbage, chopped
1 Apple, diced
1 Onion, diced
1 tbsp grated Ginger
2 Beets, chopped
4 cups Veggie Broth
2 tbsp Parsley, chopped
½ tsp Garlic Salt
¼ tsp Pepper

DIRECTIONS
- Place all ingredients in your pressure cooker. Stir well to combine everything and seal the lid. Hit the BEANS/CHILI, and set the cooking time to 20 minutes at High pressure.
- When it goes off, do a quick pressure release. Pour into serving bowls and serve immediately.

## Blueberry Oatmeal with Walnuts

Ready in about: **20 minutes** | Serves: **2** | Per serving: Calories 340; Carbs 49g; Fat 12g; Protein 13g

INGREDIENTS
1 cup blueberries
1 ¼ cups Steel-cut oats
½ cup Walnut Milk
3 tbsp Walnuts, toasted and roughly chopped
1 cup Apricots, pitted and diced
1 tsp Vanilla Extract
½ tsp ground Cinnamon
1 ½ cups Water

DIRECTIONS
- Place all ingredients, except for blueberries and walnuts, in your pressure cooker. Select BEANS/CHILI and seal the lid. Cook for 10 minutes at High Pressure. Release the pressure quickly.
- Ladle the oatmeal between two serving bowls and top with blueberries and chopped walnuts.

## Quick Coconut Moong Dhal

Ready in about: **20 minutes** | Serves: **4** | Per serving: Calories 155; Carbs 27g; Fat 3g; Protein 12g

INGREDIENTS

1 cup Moong Dal
3 tsp Olive Oil
½ tsp Salt
1 tsp ground Turmeric
1 tbsp Cumin Seeds
½ tsp Cayenne Pepper
½ tsp ground Bay Leaves
¼ tsp Black Pepper, ground
3 cups Water
Fresh Cilantro leaves, yogurt, jalapeño slices, to garnish
DIRECTIONS
- Put all ingredients in the cooker and seal the lid. Cook for 10 minutes on BEANS/CHILI at High. Do a quick pressure release.
- Serve garnished with fresh cilantro, jalapeño slices and coconut yogurt.

## Squash in Cheesy Cream

Mild taste from your Slow Cooker!

**Prep time: 15 minutes Cooking time: 1 hour Servings: 10**

INGREDIENTS:
Small onion
3 tbsp butter
Large yellow summer squash
Processed cheese food
DIRECTIONS:
- Finely grease Slow Cooker with melted butter or coat with nonstick spray.
- Peel and seed the squash. Place into a large pot. Pour over with water to cover.
- Add onion and bring to boil. Simmer the vegetables for about 10 minutes to get tender. Do not stir. Drain both onion and squash. Transfer to Slow Cooker.
- Add processed cheese food and butter to Slow Cooker.
- Set your Slow Cooker to LOW temperature setting and cook just until the squash gets really tender (approximately for 1 hour).
- Serve in small serving bowls with white or French crispy bread.

**Nutrition: Calories: 189 Fat: 12g Carbohydrates: 12g Protein: 7g**

## Veggie Cassoulet with navy beans

Easy vegetarian meal!

**Prep time: 5 minutes Cooking time: 9 hours Servings: 7**

INGREDIENTS:
One onion
2 tbsp olive oil
4 cups mushroom broth
1 sprig lemon thyme
1 bay leaf
1 sprig rosemary
Navy beans
1 large potato
1 cube vegetable bouillon
1 sprig fresh savory
DIRECTIONS:
- Soak navy beans in cold water overnight.
- Preheat a skillet with a small amount of oil. Add chopped carrots and onion. Stir until tender. Grease Slow Cooker and transfer the skillet mixture into it.
- Add beans, bouillon, potato and bay leaf. Add water to cover the ingredients.
- Tie together herbal sprigs and place inside the cooking dish. Cook for 9 hours over LOW temperature mode.
- To serve, transfer to a large dish and garnish with lime wedges.

**Nutrition: Calories: 279 Fat: 5g Carbohydrates: 47g Protein: 15g**

## Marinated Mushrooms in Slow Cooker

Fast and delicious with vegetables!

**Prep time: 5 minutes Cooking time: 10 hours Servings: 20**

INGREDIENTS:
2 cups water
2 cups white sugar
4 packs fresh mushrooms
2 cups soy sauce
1 cup butter
DIRECTIONS:
- Take a medium saucepan and place it over medium heat. Pour in water. Add soy sauce and butter.
- Cook, stirring, just until butter has melted.
- Mix in sugar and continue to stir until the crystals are completely dissolved. Remove stems from the mushrooms. Place mushrooms to Slow Cooker.
- Pour in the saucepan mixture.
- Cook on LOW temperature setting for 10 hours.
- When ready, drain mushrooms and let to cool. You can even place it in the refrigerator for a couple of hours.
- Serve in a bowl along with chopped green onions and olive oil.

**Nutrition: Calories: 228 Fat: 11g Carbohydrates: 29g Protein: 4g**

## Vegan Corn Chowder in Slow Cooker

Wonderfully easy and tasty!

**Prep time: 9 minutes Cooking time: 1 hour Servings: 7**

INGREDIENTS:
3 cans kernel corns
3 diced potatoes
Clove garlic
Salt
Large onion
3 cups vegetable broth
1 tbsp. Chili powder
2 red chili peppers
Parsley flakes
Soy sauce
Black pepper
Juiced lime
Margarine
DIRECTIONS:

- 🌿 Grease your Slow Cooker with cooking spray or simple butter at room temperature.
- 🌿 Fill a large bowl with chopped potatoes, red chile peppers, minced garlic, chili powder and salt/pepper.
- 🌿 Pour in vegetable broth.
- 🌿 Place the mixture into kitchen blender and mix well until puree consistency. Transfer puree mixture to your Slow Cooker.
- 🌿 Pour in soy milk with slightly melted margarine.
- 🌿 Set Slow Cooker to LOW mode and cook for one hour.

**Nutrition: Calories: 320 Fat: 10g Carbohydrates: 53g Protein: 9g**

## Green Collard Beans in Slow Cooker

Tender beans for any occasion!

⏱ **Prep time: 12 minutes Cooking time: 8 hours**
**Servings: 8**

INGREDIENTS:
3 slices bacon
Bunch collard greens
2 sliced jalapenos
Chicken stock
Salt
Black pepper
DIRECTIONS:
- 🌿 Generously grease your Slow Cooker with some melted butter or coat with special cooking spray. In a large pot, combine collard beans and salted water. Slowly bring to boil and simmer for 10 minutes.
- 🌿 In a large skillet, cook bacon until it is evenly browned on all sides (for around 10 minutes). Drain the beans and transfer to prepared Slow Cooker.
- 🌿 Add bacon and jalapenos. Pour in chicken stock. Season with salt and black pepper.
- 🌿 Set to LOW temperature, cook for 8 hours or even overnight.

**Nutrition: Calories: 124 Fat: 10g Carbohydrates: 4g Protein: 4g**

## Loaded Potato Soup in Slow Cooker

Everyone will love this creamy taste and amazing flavors!

⏱ **Prep time: 5 minutes Cooking time: 4 hours**
**Servings: 6**

INGREDIENTS:
4 cups milk
1 pack hash browns
4 green onions
Ground black pepper
Sour cream
1 pack cream cheese
8 slices cooked bacon
1 pack Cheddar cheese
DIRECTIONS:
- 🌿 Spray the dish of your Slow Cooker with a cooking spray or grease with melted butter. Right in Slow Cooker dish, combine cream cheese, pepper and sour cream.
- 🌿 Pour in milk and stir. Mix well until you are sure the mixture is smooth.
- 🌿 Add diced potatoes, bacon slices and shredded Cheddar cheese. Combine and close the lid. Cook on LOW temperature mode for 4 hours.
- 🌿 To serve, sprinkle with chopped green onions.

**Nutrition: Calories: 240 Fat: 14g Carbohydrates: 19g Protein: 10g**

## Hot Smashed Potato Soup

This will be your favorite recipe!

⏱ **Prep time: 5 minutes Cooking time: 10 hours**
**Servings: 6**

INGREDIENTS:
3 large potatoes
Ground black pepper
Small sweet yellow pepper
4 cups chicken broth
Roasted garlic
Cheddar cheese
Half cup whipping cream
Green onions
DIRECTIONS:
- 🌿 Slightly grease your Slow Cooker with melted butter.
- 🌿 Right in the cooking dish, combine chopped potatoes, sweet peppers, black pepper and garlic. Pour the broth over vegetables. Mix everything well until the consistency is smooth.
- 🌿 Cook covered for 10 hours using LOW setting. When ready, mash potatoes with potato masher.
- 🌿 Add shredded Cheddar, whipping cream and sliced green onions.
- 🌿 Serve in small bowls, garnished with green onions and white bread cubes.

**Nutrition: Calories: 289 Fat: 11g Carbohydrates: 37g Protein: 10g**

## Onion, Pepper and Sausage Mix

This is fast and Easy for busy days!

⏱ **Prep time: 5 minutes Cooking time: 8 hours**
**Servings: 12**

INGREDIENTS:
Sweet Italian sausage
1 pack elbow macaroni
2 green bell peppers
1 jar pasta sauce
Hot Italian sausages
1 red bell pepper
1 large sweet pepper
DIRECTIONS:
- 🌿 Grease your Slow Cooker with melted butter.
- 🌿 Chop onions, sweet sausage, green bell peppers, hot sausage, red bell pepper. Combine the ingredients along with pasta sauce in prepared Slow Cooker.
- 🌿 Add one cup water.
- 🌿 Set your Slow Cooker to LOW mode and cook for 8 hours.
- 🌿 When It is 30 minutes left before serving, cook elbow macaroni according to package directions. Serve Slow Cooker dish over cooked macaroni. Garnish with shredded cheese or chopped green onions.

**Nutrition: Calories: 573 Fat: 24g Carbohydrates: 61g Protein: 25g**

## Taco Chili in Slow Cooker

A flavored meal with low fat!

**Prep time: 5 minutes Cooking time: 8 hours Servings: 6**

INGREDIENTS:
Two cans tomatoes
Ground beef
Enchilada sauce
Canned chili beans
Can corn with peppers
1 pack seasoning mix
1 can homily
1 can kidney beans
One pack taco seasoning

DIRECTIONS:
- Preheat an oiled skillet over medium heat.
- Cook beef for around 5-7 minutes until golden brown. Add one packet taco seasoning to skillet. Set aside.
- Generously grease your Slow Cooker with olive oil or cooking spray.
- Place corn and peppers, tomatoes, hominy, kidney beans, enchilada sauce and chili beans into Slow Cooker.
- Add cooked beef. Stir to combine and close the lid. Cook for 8 hours on LOW temperature mode.
- Serve hot in small bowls.

**Nutrition: Calories: 504 Fat: 19g Carbohydrates: 56g Protein: 29g**

# POULTRY RECIPES

## Delicious BBQ Pulled Turkey

**Ready in about: 100 minutes | Serves: 6 | Per serving: Calories 456; Carbs 19g; Fat 26g; Protein 37g**

INGREDIENTS
2 pounds Turkey Breasts, boneless and skinless
1 cup Beer
1 ½ tbsp Oil

SAUCE:

2 tbsp Honey
½ cup Apple Cider Vinegar
1 tsp Liquid Smoke
2 tsp Sriracha
1 tsp Garlic Powder
1 tsp Onion Powder
½ cup Mustard
1 tbsp Worcestershire Sauce
2 tbsp Honey
1 tsp Mustard Powder
2 tbsp Olive Oil

DIRECTIONS
- Heat the oil on SAUTÉ mode at High. Add turkey and brown on all sides. Whisk together all the sauce ingredients in a small bowl. Add beef and sauce to the Pressure cooker. Stir to combine.
- Seal the lid and cook for 45 minutes on MEAT/STEW mode at High. When ready, release the pressure quickly. Remove the turkey to a plate and shred with two forks.
- Set to SAUTÉ, and cook until the sauce is reduced and thickened, lid off. Return the turkey and stir to coat well.

## Balsamic Chicken Thighs with Pears

**Ready in about: 30 minutes | Serves: 6 | Per serving: Calories 488; Carbs 11g; Fat 34g; Protein 33g**

INGREDIENTS
6 large Chicken Thighs
½ cup Sweet Onions, chopped
3 small Pears, peeled and sliced
2 tbsp Balsamic Vinegar
3 tsp Butter
1 cup Chicken Broth
1 tsp Cayenne Pepper
Salt and Pepper, to taste

DIRECTIONS
- Melt the butter on SAUTÉ mode at High. Add chicken and sprinkle with the spices. Brown on all sides. Stir in the remaining ingredients. Seal the lid and cook for 20 minutes on POULTRY at High.
- When ready, release the pressure naturally, for 10 minutes, and serve immediately.

## Cheesy Drumsticks in Marinara Sauce

**Ready in about: 35 minutes | Serves: 4 | Per serving: Calories 588; Carbs 15g; Fat 43g; Protein 36g**

INGREDIENTS
4 Chicken Drumsticks
1 cup Sour Cream
1 ¾ cups Marinara Sauce
1 cup grated Cheddar Cheese
½ Butter Stick
1 tsp Chipotle Powder
½ tsp Rosemary

Salt and Pepper, to taste

DIRECTIONS
- Melt the butter on SAUTÉ at High. Add marinara, chipotle, rosemary, and chicken. Season with salt and pepper.
- Seal the lid and cook for 20 minutes on POULTRY at High pressure. When ready, release the pressure naturally, for 10 minutes. Stir in the cheese and sour cream, and serve.

## Turkey Thighs with Fig Sauce

Ready in about: **35 minutes | Serves: 6 | Per serving: Calories 455; Carbs 62g; Fat 8g; Protein 34g**

INGREDIENTS
2 pounds Turkey Thighs, skinless
1 cup Carrots, sliced
1 Onion, chopped
4 Potatoes, cubed
¼ cup Balsamic Vinegar
12 dried Figs, halved
2 cups Chicken Broth
½ Celery Stalk, diced
Salt and Black Pepper, to taste

DIRECTIONS
- Place carrots, onion, potatoes, celery and turkey inside the pressure cooker. Whisk together the remaining ingredients, except the figs, in a bowl and pour the mixture over the turkey.
- Season with salt and pepper, and stir in the figs, and 1 cup of water. Seal the lid, and cook for 15 minutes on MEAT/STEW, at High. When done, do a natural release, for 10 minutes.
- Remove the figs, turkey, and veggies to serving plates. To serve, strain the sauce that's left in the cooker, and pour over the turkey and veggies.

## Creamy Chicken with Mushrooms and Carrots

Ready in about: **30 minutes | Serves: 6 | Per serving: Calories 603; Carbs 14g; Fat 31g; Protein 59g**

INGREDIENTS
6 Chicken Breasts, boneless and skinless
1 Sweet Onion, diced
1 cup Water
8 ounces Mushrooms, sliced
1 can Cream of Mushroom Soup
1 pound Baby Carrots
1 tbsp Butter
1 tbsp Olive Oil
2 tbsp Heavy Cream

DIRECTIONS
- Heat oil and butter on SAUTÉ mode at High, until melted. Add onions and mushrooms, and cook for 3 minutes, until soft. Stir in the carrots, add chicken, and pour mushroom soup, and water.
- Seal the lid and cook for 8 minutes on BEANS/CHILI mode at High. When ready, do a quick pressure release and remove the mushrooms, chicken, and carrots to a plate.
- In the pressure cooker, stir in the heavy cream and cook the sauce until it thickens, on SAUTÉ, for a few minutes. Serve the chicken and veggies drizzled with the sauce.

## Turkey with Tomatoes and Red Beans

Ready in about: **20 minutes | Serves: 6 | Per serving: Calories 212; Carbs 12g; Fat 8g; Protein 23g**

INGREDIENTS
1-pound Turkey Breast, cut into bite-sized cubes
1 (16 oz) can Stewed Tomatoes
1 (16 oz) can Red Kidney Beans, drained
2 cups Chicken Stock
½ cup Sour Cream
Salt and Black Pepper, to taste
2 tbsp Parsley, chopped

DIRECTIONS
- Place beans, tomatoes, turkey, stock, and sour cream in your pressure cooker. Season to taste. Seal the lid, set on SOUP, cook for 20 minutes at High.
- Release the pressure quickly. Sprinkle with freshly chopped parsley to serve.

## Orange and Cranberry Turkey Wings

Ready in about: **40 minutes | Serves: 4 | Per serving: Calories 525; Carbs 20g; Fat 38g; Protein 26g**

INGREDIENTS
1 pound Turkey Wings
¼ cup Orange Juice
1 stick Butter, softened
2 cups Cranberries
2 Onions, sliced
2 cups Vegetable Stock
½ tsp Cayenne Pepper
Salt and Pepper, to taste

DIRECTIONS
- Melt the butter on SAUTÉ. Add the turkey wings, season with salt, pepper, and cayenne pepper, and cook until browned, for a few minutes. Stir in the remaining ingredients. Seal the lid.
- Cook for 25 minutes on POULTRY at High. Release the pressure naturally, for 10 minutes, and serve.

## Chicken Drumettes in Creamy Tomato Sauce

Ready in about: **25 minutes | Serves: 2 | Per serving: Calories 525; Carbs 21g; Fat 41g; Protein 28g**

INGREDIENTS
2 Chicken Drumsticks, trimmed of **fat**
2 cups Tomato Sauce
1 cup Heavy Cream
1 cup sharp Parmesan cheese, grated
4 tbsp Butter
1 tsp Garlic paste
1 tsp Chipotle powder
1 tbsp fresh Basil leaves, chopped
Salt and ground Black Pepper, to taste
½ tsp fresh Rosemary, chopped

DIRECTIONS
- Melt butter on SAUTÉ at High. Add garlic paste, chipotle, tomato sauce, rosemary, and basil. Sprinkle the chicken

drumsticks with salt and ground black pepper. Place the chicken down into the sauce, so it resembles a nestle.
- Seal the lid, select POULTRY and cook at High pressure for 20 minutes. Once it goes off, release the pressure naturally, for 10 minutes. Stir in the cheese and sour cream and serve right away.

## Delicious Turkey Meatloaf

Ready in about: **30 minutes** | Serves: **4** | Per serving: Calories 317; Carbs 7g; Fat 16g; Protein 37g

INGREDIENTS
1 ½ pounds ground Turkey
1 Carrot, grated
1 Onion, diced
1 Celery Stalk, diced
½ cup Breadcrumbs
1 Egg, cracked in the bowl
1 tsp Garlic, minced
½ tsp Thyme
¼ tsp Oregano
¼ tsp Salt
¼ tsp Black Pepper
1 tsp Worcestershire Sauce
1 ½ cups Water
Cooking spray, to grease
DIRECTIONS
- Pour the water in your pressure cooker. Combine the remaining ingredients in a large bowl. Grease a baking pan with cooking spray and add in the mixture, pressing it tightly.
- Lay the trivet and lower the pan on top of the trivet, inside your Pressure cooker. Seal the lid and cook on POULTRY de for 15 minutes at High. Do a natural release, for 10 minutes.

## Spicy Rosemary Chicken

Ready in about: **55 minutes** | Serves: **4** | Per serving: Calories 294; Carbs 4g; Fat 7g; Protein 50g

INGREDIENTS
1 Whole Chicken
1 tbsp Cayenne Pepper
2 Rosemary Sprigs
2 Garlic Cloves, crushed
¼ Onion, halved, or sliced
1 tsp dried Rosemary
Salt and Pepper, to taste
1 ½ cups Chicken Broth
DIRECTIONS
- Wash and pat dry the chicken. Season with salt, pepper, rosemary, and cayenne pepper. Rub the spices onto the meat. Stir in onion, garlic, and rosemary sprig inside the chicken's cavity.
- Place the chicken in the cooker, and pour in broth around the chicken, not over. Seal the lid and cook for 30 minutes on MEAT/STEW, at High. When done, let pressure drop naturally, for about 10 minutes.

## Creamy Chicken in Beer Sauce

Ready in about: **40 minutes** | Serves: **4** | Per serving: Calories 534; Carbs 9g; Fat 33g; Protein 46g

INGREDIENTS
1 ½ pounds Chicken Breasts
10 ounces Beer
1 cup Green Onions, chopped
1 ¼ cups Greek Yogurt
¼ cup Arrowroot
½ tsp Sage
2 tsp dried Thyme
2 tsp dried Rosemary
2 tbsp Olive Oil
DIRECTIONS
- Heat the oil on SAUTÉ mode at High. Add onions and cook for 2 minutes. Coat the chicken with the arrowroot. Add the chicken to the cooker and cook until browned on all sides.
- Pour the beer over and bring the mixture to a boil. Stir in the herbs and cook on SOUP for 30 minutes at High pressure. Do a quick release, and stir in yogurt before serving.

## Barbecue Wings

Ready in about: **15 minutes** | Serves: **4** | Per serving: Calories 140; Carbs 2g; Fat 3g; Protein 19g

INGREDIENTS
12 Chicken Wings
¼ cup Barbecue Sauce
1 cup of Water
DIRECTIONS
- Place chicken wings and water in your pressure cooker. Seal the lid. Cook for 5 minutes on BEANS/CHILI at High. When ready, do a quick release.
- Rinse under cold water and pat wings dry. Remove the liquid from the pot. Return the wings to the pressure cooker and pour in barbecue sauce. Mix with hands to coat them well.
- Cook on SAUTÉ, lid off, on all sides, until sticky. Serve hot.

## Lemon-Garlic Chicken Thighs

Ready in about: **30 minutes** | Serves: **4** | Per serving: Calories 487; Carbs 8g; Fat 36g; Protein 28g

INGREDIENTS
4 Chicken Thighs
1 ½ tbsp Olive Oil
½ tsp Garlic Powder
Salt and Black Pepper to taste
½ tsp Red Pepper Flakes
½ tsp Smoked Paprika
1 small Onion, chopped
2 cloves Garlic, sliced
½ cup Chicken Broth
1 tsp Italian Seasoning
1 Lemon, zested and juiced
1 ½ tbsp Heavy Cream
Lemon slices to garnish
Chopped parsley to garnish
DIRECTIONS

- Warm the olive oil on SAUTÉ, and add the chicken thighs; cook to brown on each side for 3 minutes. Remove the browned chicken onto a plate. Add butter to the pot to melt, then, add garlic, onions, and lemon juice.
- Stir them with a spoon to deglaze the bottom of the pot and let them cook for 1 minute. Add Italian seasoning, chicken broth, lemon zest, and the chicken. Seal the lid, select MEAT/STEW at High pressure for 15 minutes.
- Once the timer has ended, let the pot sit closed for 2 minutes, then do a quick pressure release. Open the lid.
- Remove the chicken onto a plate and add the heavy cream to the pot. Select SAUTÉ and stir the cream into the sauce until it thickens.
- Turn off the cooker and return the chicken. Coat the chicken with sauce.
- Dish the sauce into a serving platter and serve with the steamed kale and spinach mix. Garnish with the lemon and parsley.

## Italian-Style Chicken Breasts with Kale Pesto

Ready in about: **30 minutes** | Serves: **4** | Per serving: Calories 372; Carbs 5g; Fat 19g; Protein 35g

INGREDIENTS
4 Chicken Breasts, skinless and boneless
½ cup Heavy Cream
½ cup Chicken Broth
¼ tsp minced Garlic
Salt and Black Pepper to taste
¼ tsp Italian Seasoning
¼ cup Roasted Red Peppers
1 tbsp Tuscan Kale Pesto
1 tbsp Cornstarch
DIRECTIONS
- Place the chicken at the bottom of the cooker. Pour the broth over, and add the Italian seasoning, garlic, salt, and pepper. Seal the lid, select MEAT/STEW mode at High pressure for 15 minutes.
- Once the timer has ended, do a natural pressure release for 5 minutes, then a quick pressure release to let the remaining steam out, and open the pot. Use a spoon to remove the chicken onto a plate and select SAUTÉ mode.
- Scoop out any **fat** or unwanted chunks from the sauce. In a bowl, add cream, cornstarch, red peppers, and pesto.
- Mix them with a spoon. Pour the creamy mixture into the pot and whisk it for 4 minutes until it is well mixed and thickened.
- Put the chicken back in the pot and let it simmer for 3 minutes.
- Turn the pot off and dish the sauce onto a serving platter. Serve the chicken with sauce over a bed of cooked quinoa.

## Jasmine Rice and Chicken Taco Bowls

Ready in about: **20 minutes** | Serves: **4** | Per serving: Calories 523; Carbs 41g; Fat 22g; Protein 44g

INGREDIENTS
4 Chicken Breasts
2 cups Chicken Broth
2 ¼ packets Taco Seasoning
1 cup Jasmine Rice
1 Green Bell Pepper, seeded and diced
1 Red Bell Pepper, seeded and diced
1 cup Salsa
Salt and Black Pepper to taste

**To Serve:**
Grated Cheese, of your choice
Chopped Cilantro
Sour Cream
Avocado Slices
DIRECTIONS
- Pour in the chicken broth, add the chicken, and pour the taco seasoning over it. Add the salsa and stir it lightly with a spoon. Seal the lid and select MEAT/STEW at High setting for 15 minutes. Do a quick pressure release.
- Add the rice and peppers, and use a spoon to push them into the sauce. Seal the lid, and select BEANS/CHILI mode on High pressure for 15 minutes. Once the timer has ended, do a quick pressure release, and open the lid.
- Gently stir the mixture, adjust the taste with salt and pepper and spoon the chicken dish into serving bowls. Top it with some sour cream, avocado slices, sprinkle with chopped cilantro and some cheese, to serve.

## Honey-Ginger Shredded Chicken

Ready in about: **35 minutes** | Serves: **4** | Per serving: Calories 462; Carbs 38g; Fat 16g; Protein 37g

INGREDIENTS
4 Chicken Breasts, skinless
¼ cup Sriracha Sauce
2 tbsp Butter
1 tsp grated Ginger
2 cloves Garlic, minced
½ tsp Cayenne Pepper
½ tsp Red Chili Flakes
½ cup Honey
½ cup Chicken Broth
Salt and Black Pepper to taste
Chopped Scallion to garnish
DIRECTIONS
- In a bowl, add chicken broth, honey, ginger, sriracha sauce, red pepper flakes, cayenne pepper, and garlic. Use a spoon to mix them well and set aside. Put the chicken on a plate and season them with salt and pepper.
- Set aside too. On the cooker, select SAUTÉ mode. Melt the butter, and add the chicken in 2 batches to brown on both sides for about 3 minutes. Add all the chicken back to the pot and pour the pepper sauce over it.
- Seal the lid, select MEAT/STEW at High pressure for 20 minutes. Once the timer has ended, do a natural pressure release for 5 minutes, then a quick pressure release to let the remaining steam out, and open the lid.
- Remove the chicken onto a cutting board and shred them using two forks. Plate the chicken in a serving bowl, pour the sauce over it, and garnish it with the scallions. Serve with a side of sautéed mushrooms.

## Coconut-Lime Chicken Curry

Ready in about: **35 minutes** | Serves: **4** | Per serving: Calories 643; Carbs 30g; Fat 44g; Protein 42g

## INGREDIENTS
- 4 Chicken Breasts
- 4 tbsp Red Curry Paste
- ½ cup Chicken Broth
- 2 cups Coconut Milk
- 4 tbsp Sugar
- Salt and Black Pepper to taste
- 2 Red Bell Pepper, seeded and cut in 2-inch sliced
- 2 Yellow Bell Pepper, seeded and cut in 2-inch slices
- 2 cup Green Beans, cut in half
- 2 tbsp Lime Juice

## DIRECTIONS
- Add the chicken, red curry paste, salt, pepper, coconut milk, broth and swerve sugar. Seal the lid, select MEAT/STEW at High pressure for 15 minutes. Once the timer has ended, do a quick pressure release.
- Remove the chicken onto a cutting board and select SAUTÉ. Add the bell peppers, green beans, and lime juice. Stir the sauce with a spoon and let it simmer for 4 minutes. Slice the chicken with a knife and return it to the pot.
- Stir and simmer for a minute. Dish the chicken with sauce and vegetable, and serve with coconut flatbread.

# Hungarian Chicken Thighs in Cherry Tomato Sauce

Ready in about: **30 minutes** | Serves: **4** | Per serving: **Calories 437; Carbs 8g; Fat 37g; Protein 24g**

## INGREDIENTS
- 4 Chicken Thighs, skinless but with bone
- 4 tbsp Olive Oil
- 1 cup Crushed Cherry Tomatoes
- 2 tbsp Hungarian Paprika
- 1 large Red Bell Pepper, seeded and diced
- 1 large Green Bell Pepper, seeded and diced
- 1 Red Onion, diced
- Salt and Black Pepper to taste
- 1 tbsp chopped Basil
- ½ cup Chicken Broth
- 1 bay Leaf
- ½ tsp dried Oregano

## DIRECTIONS
- Place the chicken on a clean flat surface and season with hungarian paprika, salt and pepper. Select SAUTÉ mode, on the pressure cooker. Pour the oil in, once heated add the chicken. Brown on both sides for 6 minutes.
- Then, add the onions and peppers. Cook until soft for 5 minutes. Add tomatoes, bay leaf, salt, broth, pepper, and oregano. Stir using a spoon. Seal the lid, select MEAT/STEW mode at High pressure for 20 minutes.
- Do a natural pressure release for 5 minutes, then a quick pressure release to let the remaining steam out.
- Discard the bay leaf. Dish the chicken with the sauce into a serving bowl and garnish it with the chopped basil. Serve over a bed of steamed squash spaghetti.

# Black Currant and Lemon Chicken

Ready in about: **20 minutes** | Serves: **6** | Per serving: **Calories 286; Carbs 8g; Fat 18g; Protein 25g**

## INGREDIENTS
- 1 ½ pound Chicken Breasts
- ¼ cup Red Currants
- 2 Garlic Cloves, minced
- 6 Lemon Slices
- 1 cup Scallions, chopped
- 1 cup Black Olives, pitted
- 2 tbsp Canola Oil
- ¼ tsp Pepper
- 1 tsp Coriander Seeds
- 1 tsp Cumin
- ¼ tsp Salt
- 2 ¼ cups Water

## DIRECTIONS
- Heat the oil on SAUTÉ at High. Add scallions, coriander, and garlic and cook for 30 seconds. Add the chicken and top with olives and red currants. Season with salt and pepper.
- Arrange the lemon slices on top, and pour the water over. Seal the lid and cook on POULTRY for 15 minutes at High pressure. When ready, release the pressure naturally, for 10 minutes.

# Buffalo Chicken Chili

Ready in about: **40 minutes** | Serves: **4** | Per serving: **Calories 487; Carbs 8g; Fat 34g; Protein 41g**

## INGREDIENTS
- 4 Chicken Breasts, boneless and skinless
- ½ cup Buffalo Sauce
- 2 large White Onion, finely chopped
- 2 cups finely chopped Celery
- 1 tbsp Olive Oil
- 1 tsp dried Thyme
- 3 cups Chicken Broth
- 1 tsp Garlic Powder
- ½ cup crumbled Blue Cheese + extra for serving
- 4 oz Cream Cheese, cubed in small pieces
- Salt and Pepper, to taste

## DIRECTIONS
- Put the chicken on a clean flat surface and season with pepper and salt. Set aside. Select SAUTÉ mode. Heat olive oil, add the onion and celery. Sauté constantly stirring, until they soft and fragrant, for about 5 minutes.
- Add the garlic powder and thyme. Stir and cook them for about a minute, and add the chicken, hot sauce, and chicken broth. Season with salt and pepper. Seal the lid, select MEAT/STEW at High pressure for 20 minutes.
- Meanwhile, add the blue cheese and cream cheese in a bowl, and use a fork to smash them together. Set the mixture aside. Once the timer has ended, do a natural pressure release for 5 minutes.
- Remove chicken onto a flat surface with a slotted spoon and use forks to shred it; then return it back the pot. Select SAUTÉ mode. Add the cheese to the pot and stir until is slightly incorporated into the sauce.
- Dish the buffalo chicken soup into bowls. Sprinkle the remaining cheese over and serve with sliced baguette.

# Tuscany-Style Sund-Dried Tomato Chicken

**Ready in about: 30 minutes | Serves: 4 | Per serving:**
Calories 576; Carbs 12g; Fat 44g; Protein 45g

### INGREDIENTS
4 Chicken Thighs, cut into 1-inch pieces
1 tbsp Olive Oil
1 ½ cups Chicken Broth
Salt to taste
1 cup chopped Sun-Dried Tomatoes with Herbs
2 tbsp Italian Seasoning
2 cups Baby Spinach
¼ tsp Red Pepper Flakes
6 oz softened Cream Cheese, cut into small cubes
1 cup shredded Pecorino Cheese

### DIRECTIONS
- Pour the chicken broth in the cooker, and add Italian seasoning, chicken, tomatoes, salt, and red pepper flakes. Stir with a spoon. Seal the lid, select MEAT/STEW mode at High pressure for 15 minutes.
- Once the timer has ended, do a quick pressure release, and open the lid. Add and stir in the spinach, parmesan cheese, and cream cheese until the cheese melts and is fully incorporated. Let it stay in the warm for 5 minutes.
- Dish the Tuscan chicken over a bed of zoodles or a side of steamed asparagus and serve.

# Gorgeous Chicken Fajitas with Guacamole

**Ready in about: 30 minutes | Serves: 4 | Per serving:**
Calories 423; Carbs 9g; Fat 22g; Protein 40g

### INGREDIENTS
2 lb Chicken Breasts, skinless and cut in 1-inch slices
½ cup Chicken Broth
1 Yellow Onion, sliced
1 Green Bell Pepper, seeded and sliced
1 Yellow Bell Pepper, seeded and sliced
1 Red Bell Pepper, seeded and sliced
2 tbsp Cumin Powder
2 tbsp Chili Powder
Salt to taste
Half a Lime
Cooking Spray
Fresh cilantro, to garnish

### Assembling:
Tacos, Guacamole, Sour Cream, Salsa, Cheese

### DIRECTIONS
- Grease the pot with cooking spray and line the bottom with the peppers and onion. Lay the chicken on the bed of peppers and sprinkle with salt, chili powder, and cumin powder. Squeeze some lime juice.
- Pour the chicken broth over, seal the lid and select MEAT/STEW at High for 20 minutes. Once the timer has ended, do a quick pressure release. Dish the chicken with the vegetables and juice onto a large serving platter. Add the sour cream, cheese, guacamole, salsa, and tacos in one layer on the side of the chicken.

# Mediterranean Chicken Meatballs

**Ready in about: 30 minutes | Serves: 4 | Per serving:**
Calories 378; Carbs 13g; Fat 19g; Protein 26g

### INGREDIENTS
1 lb Ground Chicken
1 Egg, cracked into a bowl
6 tsp Flour
Salt and Black Pepper to taste
2 tbsp chopped Basil + Extra to garnish
1 tbsp Olive Oil + ½ tbsp Olive Oil
1 ½ tsp Italian Seasoning
1 Red Bell Pepper, seeded and sliced
2 cups chopped Green Beans
½ lb chopped Asparagus
1 cup chopped Tomatoes
1 cup Chicken Broth

### DIRECTIONS
- In a mixing bowl, add chicken, egg, flour, salt, pepper, 2 tablespoons of basil, 1 tablespoon of olive oil, and Italian seasoning. Mix well with hands, and make 16 large balls out of the mixture. Set the meatballs aside.
- Select SAUTÉ mode. Heat half teaspoon of olive oil, add the peppers, green beans, and asparagus. Cook for 3 minutes while stirring frequently. After 3 minutes, use a spoon the veggies onto a plate and set aside.
- Heat the remaining oil, and then fry the meatballs in batches, for 2 minutes on each side to brown them lightly. Next, put all meatballs back to the pot along with the vegetables and chicken broth.
- Seal the lid.
- Select MEAT/STEW mode at High pressure for 15 minutes. Once it goes off, do a quick pressure release. Dish the meatballs with sauce into a serving bowl and garnish with basil. Serve with over cooked tagliatelle pasta.

# Sweet and Gingery Whole Chicken

**Ready in about: 60 minutes | Serves: 6 | Per serving:**
Calories 234; Carbs 5g; Fat 8g; Protein 33g

### INGREDIENTS
1 medium Whole Chicken
1 Green Onion, minced
2 tbsp Sugar
1 tbsp Ginger, grated
2 tsp Soy Sauce
¼ cup White Wine
½ cup Chicken Broth
1 ½ tbsp Olive Oil
1 tsp Salt
¼ tsp Pepper

### DIRECTIONS
- Heat oil on SAUTÉ mode at High. Season the chicken with sugar and half the salt and pepper, and brown on all sides, for a few minutes. Remove from the cooker and set aside.

- Whisk in together wine, broth, soy sauce, and salt. Add the chicken and seal the lid. Cook for 35 minutes on MEAT/STEW mode at High. When ready, release the pressure quickly.

## Feta and Spinach Stuffed Chicken Breasts

Ready in about: **30 minutes | Serves: 4 | Per serving: Calories 417; Carbs 3g; Fat 27g; Protein 33g**

INGREDIENTS
4 Chicken Breasts, skinless
Salt and Black Pepper to taste
1 cup Baby Spinach, frozen
½ cup crumbled Feta Cheese
½ tsp dried Oregano
½ tsp Garlic Powder
2 tbsp Olive Oil
2 tsp dried Parsley
1 cup Water

DIRECTIONS
- Cover the chicken in plastic wrap and place on a cutting board. Use a rolling pin to pound flat to a quarter inch thickness. Remove the plastic wrap.
- In a bowl, mix spinach, salt, feta cheese and scoop the mixture onto the chicken breasts. Wrap the chicken to secure the spinach filling in it. Use some toothpicks to secure the wrap firmly from opening.
- Carefully season the chicken pieces with the oregano, parsley, garlic powder, and pepper. Set on SAUTÉ mode. Heat the oil, add the chicken to sear, until golden brown on each side. Work in 2 batches.
- Remove the chicken onto a plate and set aside. Pour the water into the pot and use a spoon to scrape the bottom of the pot. Fit the steamer rack into the pot. Transfer the chicken onto the steamer rack.
- Seal the lid and select MEAT/STEW at High pressure for 15 minutes. Once the timer has ended, do a quick pressure release. Plate the chicken and serve with a side of sautéed asparagus, and slices of tomatoes (optional).

## Lemon-Garlic Chicken with Herby Stuffed

Ready in about: **50 minutes | Serves: 6 | Per serving: Calories 376; Carbs 5g; Fat 15g; Protein 48g**

INGREDIENTS
4 lb Whole Chicken
1 tbsp Herbes de Provence Seasoning
1 tbsp Olive Oil
Salt and Black Pepper to season
2 cloves Garlic, peeled
1 tsp Garlic Powder
1 Yellow Onion, peeled and quartered
1 Lemon, quartered
1 ¼ cups Chicken Broth

DIRECTIONS
- Put the chicken on a clean flat surface and pat it dry using paper towels. Sprinkle the top and cavity with salt, black pepper, and garlic powder. Stuff onion, lemon, Herbes de Provence, and garlic cloves into the cavity.
- Arrange the steamer rack inside. Pour in the broth and place the chicken on the rack. Seal the lid, select MEAT/STEW at High for 30 minutes. Do a natural pressure release for 15 minutes, then a quick pressure release to let the remaining steam out. Remove the chicken onto a prepared baking pan, and to a preheat oven to 350 F.
- Broil chicken for 5 minutes untol golden brown color on each side. Dish on a bed of steamed mixed veggies.

## Fennel Chicken Breast

Ready in about: **25 minutes | Serves: 8 | Per serving: Calories 422; Carbs 3g; Fat 22g; Protein 51g**

INGREDIENTS
2 pounds Chicken Breasts, boneless and skinless
1 cup Celery, chopped
1 cup Fennel, chopped
2 ¼ cups Chicken Stock
Salt and Pepper, to taste

DIRECTIONS
- Chop the chicken into small pieces and place in your pressure cooker. Add the remaining ingredients and stir well to combine. Seal the lid, and set to BEANS/CHILI for 15 minutes at High.
- When ready, release the pressure naturally, for 10 minutes. Season with salt and pepper, to taste.

## BBQ Sticky Drumettes

Ready in about: **30 minutes | Serves: 4 | Per serving: Calories 374; Carbs 3g; Fat 11g; Protein 38g**

INGREDIENTS
2 lb Chicken Drumettes, bone in and skin in
½ cup Chicken Broth
½ tsp Dry Mustard
½ tsp Sweet Paprika
½ tbsp. Cumin Powder
½ tsp Onion Powder
¼ tsp Cayenne Powder
Salt and Pepper, to taste
1 stick Butter, sliced in 5 to 7 pieces
BBQ Sauce to taste
Cooking Spray

DIRECTIONS
- Pour the chicken broth in and insert the trivet. In a zipper bag, pour in dry mustard, cumin powder, onion powder, cayenne powder, salt, and pepper. Add the chicken, then zip, close the bag and shake it to coat the chicken well with the spices. You can toss the chicken in the spices in batches too.
- After, remove the chicken from the bag and place on the steamer rack. Top with butter slices, seal the lid, select MEAT/STEW mode at High pressure for 20 minutes. Meanwhile, preheat an oven to 350 F.
- Once it goes off, do a quick pressure release, and open the lid. Remove the chicken onto a clean flat cutting board and brush with barbecue sauce. Grease a baking tray with cooking spray and arrange the chicken pieces on it.
- Tuck the tray into the oven and broil the chicken for 4 minutes while paying close attention to prevent burning.

# Herby Balsamic Chicken

**Ready in about: 50 minutes | Serves: 4 | Per serving:**
**Calories 412; Carbs 13g; Fat 16g; Protein 38g**

INGREDIENTS
2 lb Chicken Thighs, bone in and skin on
2 tbsp Olive Oil
Salt and Pepper, to taste
1 ½ cups diced Tomatoes
¾ cup Yellow Onion
2 tsp minced Garlic
½ cup Balsamic Vinegar
3 tsp chopped fresh Thyme
1 cup Chicken Broth
2 tbsp chopped Oregano

DIRECTIONS
- Using paper towels, pat dry the chicken and season with salt and pepper. Select SAUTÉ mode. Warm the olive and add the chicken with skin side down. Cook to golden brown on each side, for about 9 minutes. Set aside.
- Then, add the onions and tomatoes, and sauté them for 3 minutes while stirring occasionally. Top the onions with the garlic, and cook for 30 seconds, until fragrant Stir in chicken broth, salt, thyme, and balsamic vinegar.
- Add back the chicken, seal the lid, and set on MEAT/STEW at High pressure for 20 minutes. Meanwhile, preheat oven to 350 F. Do a quick pressure release. Remove the chicken to a baking tray and leave the sauce inside the pot to thicken for about 10 minutes, on SAUTÉ mode. Tuck the baking tray in the oven and let the chicken broil on each side until golden brown, for about 5 minutes. Remove and set aside to cool slightly.
- Adjust the seasoning of the sauce and cook the sauce until desired thickness. Place chicken in a serving bowl and drizzle the sauce all over. Garnish with parsley and serve with roasted tomatoes, carrots, and sweet potatoes.

# Effortless Coq Au Vin

**Ready in about: 60 minutes | Serves: 8 | Per serving:**
**Calories 538; Carbs 40g; Fat 30g; Protein 26g**

INGREDIENTS
2 pounds Chicken Thighs
4 ounces Bacon, chopped
14 ounces Red Wine
1 cup Parsley, chopped
2 Onions, chopped
4 small Potatoes, halved
7 ounces White Mushrooms, sliced
1 tsp Garlic Paste
2 tbsp Flour
¼ cup Olive Oil
2 tbsp Cognac
Salt and Black Pepper, to taste
Water, as needed

DIRECTIONS
- Heat oil on SAUTÉ mode at High, and brown the chicken on all sides. Then, set aside. Add in onion, garlic, and bacon and cook for 2 minutes, until soft. Whisk in the flour and cognac.
- Stir in the remaining ingredients, except for the mushrooms. Add enough water to cover everything. Seal the lid, press SOUP mode and cook for 20 minutes at High. When cooking is over, release the pressure quickly.
- Stir in the mushrooms, seal the lid and cook for 5 more minutes on STEAM at High. Do a quick pressure release

# Cajun Chicken and Green Beans

**Ready in about: 35 minutes | Serves: 4 | Per serving:**
**Calories 449; Carbs 13g; Fat 12g; Protein 68g**

INGREDIENTS
4 boneless and skinless Chicken Breasts, frozen
2 cups Green Beans, frozen
14 ounces Cornbread Stuffing
1 tsp Cajun Seasoning
1 cup Chicken Broth

DIRECTIONS
- Combine the chicken and broth in the cooker, seal the lid, and cook on POULTRY for 20 minutes at High. Do a quick pressure release. Add the green beans, seal the lid again, and cook for 2 more minutes on STEAM at High.
- Do a quick release, stir in the cornbread stuffing and Cajun seasoning and cook for another 5 minutes, on SAUTÉ, lid off. When ready, release the pressure quickly.

# Turkey Breasts in Maple and Habanero Sauce

**Ready in about: 30 minutes | Serves: 4 | Per serving:**
**Calories 446; Carbs 23g; Fat 16g; Protein 51g**

INGREDIENTS
2 pounds Turkey Breasts
6 tbsp Habanero Sauce
½ cup Tomato Puree
¼ cup Maple Syrup
1 ½ cups Water
½ tsp Cumin
1 tsp Smoked Paprika
Salt and Black Pepper, to taste

DIRECTIONS
- Pour the water in your pressure cooker and place the turkey inside. Season with salt and black pepper. Seal the lid, press POULTRY for 15 minutes at High pressure. Release the pressure naturally, for 10 minutes.
- Discard cooking liquid. Shred turkey inside the cooker and add the remaining ingredients. Cook on SAUTÉ at High, lid off, for a few minutes, until thickened.

# Greek-Style Chicken Legs with Herbs

**Ready in about: 35 minutes | Serves: 4 | Per serving:**
**Calories 317; Carbs 15g; Fat 16g; Protein 28g**

INGREDIENTS
4 Chicken Legs, skinless
1 cup Onions, thinly sliced
2 ripe Tomatoes, chopped
1 tsp Garlic, minced
2 tbsp corn Flour

1 ½ cups Chicken broth
3 tsp Olive Oil
1 tsp ground Cumin
2 tsp dried Rosemary
Salt and ground Black Pepper
½ cup Feta Cheese, cubes for garnish
10 Black Olives for garnish

DIRECTIONS
- Season the chicken with salt, black pepper, rosemary, and cumin. Heat oil on SAUTÉ mode at High. Brown the chicken legs, for 3 minutes per side. Stir in the onions and cook for another 4 minutes.
- Add the garlic and cook for another minute. In a measuring cup, stir the corn flour into the stock to make a slurry. When mixed, add the stock to the chicken. Add the tomatoes and give it a good stir.
- Seal the lid and switch the pressure release valve to close. Hit POULTRY and set to 20 minutes at High. Once it goes off, release the pressure quickly. Serve with a side of feta cheese and black olives.

## Chicken Stew with Shallots and Carrots

*Ready in about:* **25 minutes | Serves: 6 | Per serving: Calories 305; Carbs 15g; Fat 5g; Protein 39g**

INGREDIENTS
1 cup Chicken Stock 3 tsp Vegetable Oil
3 Carrots, peeled, cored, and sliced
6 Shallots, halved and thinly sliced
½ tsp ground Black Pepper
1 tsp Cayenne Pepper
1 tsp Salt
10 boneless, skinless Chicken Thighs, trimmed bone-in, skin-on
2 tbsp Balsamic Vinegar
1 tbsp chopped fresh Parsley, for garnish

DIRECTIONS
- Sprinkle the chicken with the salt, cayenne pepper, and black pepper. Select SAUTÉ at High and heat the oil. Add in the thighs and brown lightly on both sides, turning once or twice. Set it aside.
- Add the remaining ingredients. Dip the browned chicken in the mixture. Seal the lid and cook for 20 minutes on POULTRY at Hgh Pressure. Allow for a natural pressure release, for 10 minutes, sprinkle with parsley and serve.

## Thyme and Lemon Drumsticks with Red Sauce

*Ready in about:* **35 minutes | Serves: 4 | Per serving: Calories 268; Carbs 2g; Fat 16g; Protein 26g**

INGREDIENTS
4 Chicken Drumsticks, fresh
1 Onion, sliced
½ cup canned, diced, Tomatoes
2 tsp dried Thyme
1 tsp Lemon Zest
½ cup Water
2 tbsp Lemon Juice
1 tbsp Olive Oil
Salt and Black Pepper, to taste

DIRECTIONS
- Heat oil on SAUTÉ at High. Add drumsticks and cook them for a few minutes, until lightly browned. Stir in the remaining ingredients. Seal the lid and cook for 15 minutes on POULTRY at High.
- Once cooking is complete, release the pressure naturally, for 10 minutes. Serve immediately.

## Easy and Flavorful Chicken Legs

*Ready in about:* **30 minutes | Serves: 4 | Per serving: Calories 418; Carbs 7g; Fat 18g; Protein 53g**

INGREDIENTS
4 Chicken Legs about 8-ounce each
1 Onion, chopped
1 Tomato, chopped
½ cup Sour Cream
1 cup Chicken Broth
1 tbsp Olive Oil
2 tsp Smoked Paprika
½ tsp Garlic Powder
¼ tsp Salt
¼ tsp Black Pepper

DIRECTIONS
- Season the chicken with salt, black pepper, garlic powder, and smoked paprika, in a big bowl. Heat the oil on SAUTÉ at High, and add the seasoned chicken legs.
- Cook until browned on all sides. Stir in the remaining ingredients and seal the lid. Cook for 15 minutes on MEAT/STEW at High. When ready, release the pressure naturally, for 15 minutes.

## Creamy and Garlicky Chicken

*Ready in about:* **25 minutes | Serves: 4 | Per serving: Calories 455; Carbs 3g; Fat 26g; Protein 57g**

INGREDIENTS
1 cup Spinach, chopped
2 lbs Chicken Breasts, boneless and skinless, cut in half
¾ cup Chicken Broth
2 Garlic Cloves, minced
2 tbsp Olive Oil
¾ cup Heavy Cream
½ cup Sun-Dried Tomatoes
2 tsp Italian Seasoning
½ cup Parmesan Chicken
½ tsp Salt

DIRECTIONS
- In a small bowl, combine oil with garlic, salt, and seasonings. Rub the chicken on all sides with this mixture. Heat oil and brown the chicken on all sides, about 4-5 minutes, on SAUTÉ at High.
- Pour the broth in and seal the lid. Press MEAT/STEW and cook for 20 minutes at High pressure. After 9 minutes, hit CANCEL and do a quick pressure release. Open the lid and stir in cream.
- Let simmer for 5 minutes with the lid off, on SAUTÉ at High, and then stir in the cheese. Add in tomatoes and spinach and cook just until the spinach wilts. Serve and enjoy.

## Asian-style Sweet Chicken Drumsticks

⌀ **Ready in about: 25 minutes | Serves: 4 | Per serving:**
**Calories 384; Carbs 26g; Fat 19g; Protein 25g**

INGREDIENTS
4 Chicken Drumsticks
1 cup Pineapples, chopped
½ cup Coconut Milk
½ cup Tomato Sauce
2 tbsp Brown Sugar
2 tbsp Apple Cider Vinegar
1 tbsp Lime Juice
4 tbsp Water
Salt and Pepper, to taste
DIRECTIONS
- In a bowl, whisk together all ingredients, except for the chicken and pineapples. Place the chicken drumsticks and pineapples in the pressure cooker and pour the sauce over.
- Seal the lid, set to MEAT/STEW, and adjust the cooking time to 15 minutes at High. Once the cooking is complete, do a quick pressure release. Give it a good stir before serving hot!

## Mexican Cheesy Turkey Breasts

⌀ **Ready in about: 25 minutes | Serves: 4 | Per serving:**
**Calories 404; Carbs 20g; Fat 12g; Protein 50g**

INGREDIENTS
24 ounces Turkey Breasts, frozen
1 cup shredded Mozzarella Cheese
1 cup mild Salsa
½ cup Chicken Broth
1 cup Tomato Sauce
3 tbsp Lime Juice
Salt and Pepper, to taste
DIRECTIONS
- Place the tomato sauce, salsa, broth, lime juice, and turkey in your pressure cooker. Seal the lid, and cook on MEAT/STEW for 15 minutes at High.
- Do a natural pressure release, for 10 minutes. Shred the turkey inside the cooker, and stir in the cheese. Cook for 1 minute on SAUTÉ, to melt cheese.

## Sweet Potato & Chicken Curry

⌀ **Ready in about: 30 minutes | Serves: 4 | Per serving:**
**Calories 343; Carbs 19g; Fat 15g; Protein 26g**

INGREDIENTS
1 pound Boneless and Skinless Chicken Breast, cubed
2 cups cubed Sweet Potatoes
2 cups Green Beans
½ Onion, chopped
1 Bell Pepper, sliced
1 ½ tsp Garlic, minced
1 tsp Cumin
1 cup Milk
2 tsp Butter
3 tbsp Curry Powder
1 tsp Turmeric
½ cup Chicken Broth
Salt and Pepper, to taste
DIRECTIONS
- Melt butter on SAUTÉ mode at High. Add the onions and cook for about 3 minutes, until soft. Add the garlic and cook for 30 seconds more. Add the remaining ingredients, except the milk.
- Stir well to combine and seal the lid. Hit BEANS/CHILI, and set to 12 minutes at High. Do a quick pressure release. Stir in the milk and set to SAUTÉ at High. Cook for 3 minutes, lid off. Serve immediately.

## Chicken with Water Chestnuts

⌀ **Ready in about: 15 minutes | Serves: 4 | Per serving:**
**Calories 274; Carbs 11g; Fat 8g; Protein 32g**

INGREDIENTS
1 pound Ground Chicken
¼ cup Chicken Broth
2 tbsp Balsamic Vinegar
½ cup Water Chestnuts, sliced
¼ cup Soy Sauce
A pinch of Allspice
DIRECTIONS
- Place all ingredients in your pressure cooker. Give the mixture a good stir to combine. Seal the lid, and hit BEANS/CHILI mode.
- Set the cooking time to 10 minutes at High pressure. Quick-release the pressure.

## Chicken with Red Potatoes & Green Beans

⌀ **Ready in about: 30 minutes | Serves: 6 | Per serving:**
**Calories 467; Carbs 16g; Fat 33g; Protein 32g**

INGREDIENTS
2 pounds Chicken Thighs
1 tbsp Butter
¼ tsp dried Parsley
¼ tsp dried Oregano
½ tsp dried Thyme
Juice of 1 Lemon
½ cup Chicken Broth
2 tbsp Olive Oil
1 Garlic Clove, minced
1 pound Green Beans
1 pound Red Potatoes, halved
DIRECTIONS
- Heat oil and butter on SAUTÉ at High, and cook until they melt. Add the minced garlic and cook for a minute. Place the chicken thighs inside and cook them on both sides, until golden.
- Stir in the herbs and the lemon juice and cook for an additional minute, until fragrant. Add all remaining ingredients and stir well to combine. Seal the lid, and cook on BEANS/CHILI at High for 15 minutes.
- After you hear the beep, release the pressure quickly. Serve immediately.

## Creamy Southern Chicken

⌀ **Ready in about: 25 minutes | Serves: 4 | Per serving:**
**Calories 291; Carbs 32g; Fat 8g; Protein 31g**

INGREDIENTS
- 1 ½ pounds Boneless Chicken Thighs
- 2 tsp Paprika
- 2 Bell Peppers, sliced
- 1 cup Chicken Broth
- ½ cup Milk
- 1 tbsp Chili Powder
- ¼ cup Lime Juice
- 1 tsp Cumin
- ½ tsp Garlic Powder
- ½ tsp Onion Powder
- 1 tsp Ground Coriander
- ½ tsp Cayenne Pepper
- 1 tbsp Olive Oil
- 1 tbsp Cornstarch

DIRECTIONS
- Warm oil, and cook until hot and sizzling. Meanwhile, combine all spices in a small bowl and rub the mixture all over the chicken. Add the chicken, and cook until golden on both sides.
- Pour broth and lime juice over, and stir in the peppers. Seal the lid, set the timer to 7 minutes on BEANS/CHILI at High. Do a quick release. Stir in milk and cornstarch and press SAUTÉ at High. Cook until the sauce thickens.

## Easy Chicken Soup

Ready in about: **30 minutes** | Serves: **6** | Per serving: Calories 272; Carbs 9g; Fat 11g; Protein 33g

INGREDIENTS
- 1 ½ pounds Boneless and Skinless Chicken Breasts
- 1 tbsp Chili Powder
- 2 tsp Garlic, minced
- 2 cups Chicken Broth
- ½ cup Water
- 1 tbsp Cumin
- ½ tsp Smoked Paprika
- 1 tsp Oregano
- 14 ounces canned diced Tomatoes
- 1 Bell Pepper, sliced
- 1 Onion, sliced

DIRECTIONS
- Place all ingredients in your pressure cooker. Stir well to combine everything and seal the lid. Select BEANS/CHILI, set the timer to 20 minutes, at High.
- Do a natural pressure release, for about 10 minutes.

## Pear and Onion Goose

Ready in about: **35 minutes** | Serves: **6** | Per serving: Calories 313; Carbs 14g; Fat 8g; Protein 38g

INGREDIENTS
- 2 cups Chicken Broth
- 1 tbsp Butter
- ½ cup slice Onions
- 1 ½ pounds Goose, chopped into large pieces
- 2 tbsp Balsamic Vinegar
- 1 tsp Cayenne Pepper
- 3 Pears, peeled and sliced
- ¼ tsp Garlic Powder
- ½ tsp Pepper

DIRECTIONS
- Melt the butter on SAUTÉ. Add the goose and cook until it becomes golden on all sides. Transfer to a plate. Add the onions and cook for 2 minutes. Return the goose to the cooker.
- Add the rest of the ingredients, stir well to combine and seal the lid. Select BEANS/CHILI mode, and set the timer to 18 minutes at High pressure. Do a quick pressure release. Serve and enjoy!

## Chicken Piccata

Ready in about: **20 minutes** | Serves: **6** | Per serving: Calories 318; Carbs 15g; Fat 19g; Protein 19g

INGREDIENTS
- 6 Chicken Breast Halves
- ¼ cup Olive Oil
- ¼ cup Freshly Squeezed Lemon Juice
- 1 tbsp Sherry Wine
- ½ cup Flour
- 4 Shallots, chopped
- 3 Garlic Cloves, crushed
- ¾ cup Chicken Broth
- 1 tsp dried Basil
- 2 tsp Salt
- ¼ cup grated Parmesan Cheese
- 1 tbsp Flour
- ¼ cup Sour Cream
- 1 cup Pimento Olives, minced
- ¼ tsp White Pepper

DIRECTIONS
- In a small bowl combine flour with some salt and pepper. Dip the chicken into flour and shake off the excess. Warm olive oil and brown the chicken on all sides for 3-4 minutes, on SAUTÉ at High.
- Remove to a plate and set aside. Add shallots, and garlic and sauté for 2 minutes. Stir in sherry, broth, lemon juice, salt, olives, basil, and pepper. Return the chicken and any juices to the cooker.
- Seal the lid, set to POULTRY and cook for 20 minutes at High. Do a quick pressure release. Stir in sour cream and parmesan.

## Stewed Chicken with Kale

Ready in about: **30 minutes** | Serves: **6** | Per serving: Calories 280; Carbs 14g; Fat 15g; Protein 21g

INGREDIENTS
- 1 pound Ground Chicken
- 1 cup Tomatoes, chopped
- 1 cup diced Onions
- 1 cup Carrots, chopped
- 1 cup Kale, chopped
- ½ cup Celery, chopped
- 6 cups Chicken Broth
- 2 Thyme Sprigs
- 1 tbsp Olive Oil
- 1 tsp Red Pepper Flakes
- 10 ounces Potato Noodles

DIRECTIONS
- Warm oil on SAUTÉ mode at High. Add the chicken and cook until golden. Stir in the onions, carrots, and celery, and cook for

about 5 minutes. Stir in the remaining ingredients, except the noodles.
- Seal the lid, press BEANS/CHILI, and cook for 6 minutes at High. Do a quick pressure release. Stir in the potato noodles and seal the lid again. Cook at High pressure for 4 minutes. Do a quick pressure release, and serve hot.

## Turkey with Fennel and Celery

**Ready in about: 25 minutes | Serves: 6 | Per serving: Calories 272; Carbs 7g; Fat 4g; Protein 48g**

INGREDIENTS
2 pounds Boneless and Skinless Turkey Breast
1 cup Fennel Bulb, chopped
1 cup Celery with leaves, chopped
2 ¼ cups Chicken Stock
¼ tsp Pepper
¼ tsp Garlic Powder
DIRECTIONS
- Throw all ingredients in your pressure cooker. Give it a good stir and seal the lid. Press BEANS/CHILI, and cook for 15 minutes at High. Do a quick pressure release. Shred the turkey with two forks.

## Mexican Chicken

**Ready in about: 30 minutes | Serves: 6 | Per serving: Calories 342; Carbs 11g; Fat 14g; Protein 38g**

INGREDIENTS
1 Red Bell Pepper, diced
1 Green Bell Pepper, diced
1 Jalapeno, diced
2 pounds Chicken Breasts
10 ounces canned diced Tomatoes, undrained
1 Red Onion, diced
½ tsp Cumin
¾ tsp Chili Powder
¼ tsp Pepper
Juice of 1 Lime
½ cup Chicken Broth
1 tbsp Olive Oil
DIRECTIONS
- Heat oil on SAUTÉ mode at High. When sizzling, add the onion and bell peppers and cook for about 3-4 minutes, until soft.
- Add the remaining ingredients and give it a good stir to combine. Seal the lid, press POULTRY set for 15 minutes at High. After it beeps, release the pressure quickly.
- Shred the chicken inside the pot with two forks, then stir to combine it with the juices. Serve and enjoy!

## Chicken in Roasted Red Pepper Sauce

**Ready in about: 25 minutes | Serves: 6 | Per serving: Calories 207; Carbs 5g; Fat 7g; Protein 32g**

INGREDIENTS
1 ½ pounds Chicken Breasts, cubed
1 Onion, diced
4 Garlic Cloves
12 ounces Roasted Red Peppers
2 tsp Adobo Sauce
½ cup Beef Broth
1 tbsp Apple Cider Vinegar
1 tsp Cumin
Juice of ½ Lemon
3 tbsp chopped Cilantro
1 tbsp Olive Oil
Salt and Pepper, to taste
DIRECTIONS
- Place garlic, red pepper, adobo sauce, lemon juice, vinegar, cilantro, and some salt and pepper, in a food processor. Process until the mixture becomes smooth. Set your pressure cooker to SAUTÉ at High and heat the oil.
- Add the onion and cook for 2 minutes. Add the chicken cubes and cook until they are no longer pink. Pour sauce and broth over. Seal the lid, press BEANS/CHILI button, and set the timer to 8 minutes at High pressure.
- After you hear the beeping sound, do a quick pressure release. Serve and enjoy!

## Turkey and Potatoes with Buffalo Sauce

**Ready in about: 30 minutes | Serves: 4 | Per serving: Calories 377; Carbs 32g; Fat 9g; Protein 14g**

INGREDIENTS
3 tbsp Olive Oil
4 tbsp Buffalo Sauce
1 pound Sweet Potatoes, cut into cubes
1 ½ pounds Turkey Breast, cut into pieces
½ tsp Garlic Powder
1 Onion, diced
½ cup Water
DIRECTIONS
- Heat 1 tbsp of olive oil on SAUTÉ mode at High. Stir-fry onion in hot oil for about 3 minutes. Stir in the remaining ingredients.
- Seal the lid, set to MEAT/STEW mode for 20 minutes at High pressure. When cooking is over, do a quick pressure release, by turning the valve to "open" position.

## Fall-Off-Bone Chicken Drumsticks

**Ready in about: 45 minutes | Serves: 3 | Per serving: Calories 454; Carbs 7g; Fat 27g; Protein 43g**

INGREDIENTS
1 tbsp Olive Oil
6 Skinless Chicken Drumsticks
4 Garlic Cloves, smashed
½ Red Bell Pepper, diced
½ Onion, diced
2 tbsp Tomato Paste
2 cups Water
DIRECTIONS
- Warm olive oil, and sauté onion and bell pepper, for about 4 minutes, on SAUTÉ at High. Add garlic and cook until golden, for a minute.
- Combine the paste with water and pour into the cooker. Arrange the drumsticks inside. Seal the lid, set to POULTRY mode for 20 minutes at High pressure. When it beeps, do a quick pressure release. Serve immediately.

## Coconut Chicken with Tomatoes

Ready in about: **25 minutes** | Serves: **4** | Per serving: Calories **278**; Carbs **28g**; Fat **8g**; Protein **19g**

INGREDIENTS
1 ½ pounds Chicken Thighs
1 ½ cups chopped Tomatoes
1 Onion, chopped
1 ½ tbsp Butter
2 cups Coconut Milk
½ cup chopped Almonds
2 tsp Paprika
1 tsp Garam Masala
2 tbsp Cilantro, chopped
1 tsp Turmeric
1 tsp Cayenne Powder
1 tsp Ginger Powder
1 ¼ tsp Garlic Powder
Salt and Pepper, to taste

DIRECTIONS
- Melt butter on SAUTÉ at High. Add the onions and sauté until translucent, for about 3 minutes. Add all spices, and cook for an additional minute, until fragrant. Stir in the tomatoes and coconut milk.
- Place the chicken thighs inside and seal the lid. Cook on BEANS/CHILI on High pressure for 13 minutes. When it goes off, do a quick pressure release. Serve topped with chopped almonds and cilantro.

## Cherry Tomato and Basil Chicken Casserole

Ready in about: **30 minutes** | Serves: **4** | Per serving: Calories **337**; Carbs **12g**; Fat **21g**; Protein **27g**

INGREDIENTS
8 small Chicken Thighs
½ cup Green Olives
1 pound Cherry Tomatoes
1 cup Water
A handful of Fresh Basil Leaves
1 ½ tsp Garlic, minced
1 tsp dried Oregano
1 tbsp Olive Oil

DIRECTIONS
- Season chicken with salt and pepper. Melt butter on SAUTÉ at High, and brown the chicken for about 2 minutes per side. Place tomatoes in a plastic bag and smash with a meat pounder.
- Remove the chicken to a plate.
- Combine tomatoes, garlic, water, and oregano in the pressure cooker. Top with the chicken and seal the lid. Cook on POULTRY at High for 15 minutes. When ready, do a quick pressure release. Stir in the basil and olives.

## Sweet and Smoked Slow Cooked Turkey

Ready in about: **4 hours 15 minutes** | Serves: **4** | Per serving: Calories **513**; Carbs **15 g**; Fat **42g**; Protein **65g**

INGREDIENTS
1.5 pounds Turkey Breast
2 tsp Smoked Paprika
1 tsp Liquid Smoke
1 tbsp Mustard
3 tbsp Honey
2 Garlic Cloves, minced
4 tbsp Olive Oil
1 cup Chicken Broth

DIRECTIONS
- Brush the turkey breast with olive oil and brown it on all sides, for 3-4 minutes, on SAUTÉ at High. Pour the chicken broth and all remaining ingredients in a bowl. Stir to combine.
- Pour the mixture over the meat. Seal the lid, set on SLOW COOK mode for 4 hours. Do a quick pressure release.

## Chicken and Beans Casserole with Chorizo

Ready in about: **35 minutes** | Serves: **5** | Per serving: Calories **587**; Carbs **52g**; Fat **29g**; Protein **29g**

INGREDIENTS
1 tsp Garlic, minced
1 cup Onions, chopped
1 pound Chorizo Sausage, cut into pieces
4 Chicken Thighs, boneless, skinless
3 tbsp Olive Oil
2 cups Chicken Stock
11 ounces Asparagus, quartered
1 tsp Paprika
½ tsp ground Black Pepper
1 tsp Salt
2 Jalapeno Peppers, stemmed, cored, and chopped
26 oz canned whole Tomatoes, roughly chopped
1 ½ cups Kidney Beans

DIRECTIONS
- On SAUTÉ, heat the oil and brown the sausage, for about 5 minutes per side. Transfer to a large bowl. In the same oil, add the thighs and brown them for 5 minutes. Remove to the same bowl as the sausage.
- In the cooker, stir in onions and peppers. Cook for 3 minutes. Add in garlic and cook for 1 minute. Stir in the tomatoes, beans, stock, asparagus, paprika, salt, and black pepper.
- Return the reserved sausage and thighs to the cooker. Stir well. Seal the lid and cook for 10 minutes on BEANS/CHILI mode at High Pressure. When ready, do a quick release and serve hot.

## Creamy Turkey Breasts with Mushrooms

Ready in about: **35 minutes** | Serves: **4** | Per serving: Calories **192**; Carbs **5g**; Fat **12g**; Protein **15g**

INGREDIENTS
20 ounces Turkey Breasts, boneless and skinless
6 ounces White Button Mushrooms, sliced
3 tbsp Shallots, chopped
½ tsp dried Thyme
¼ cup dry White Wine
cup Chicken Stock
1 Garlic Clove, minced
2 tbsp Olive Oil
3 tbsp Heavy Cream
1 ½ tbsp Cornstarch
Salt and Pepper, to taste

DIRECTIONS
- Warm half of the olive oil on SAUTÉ mode at High. Meanwhile, tie turkey breast with a kitchen string horizontally, leaving approximately 2 inches apart. Season the meat with salt and pepper. Add the turkey to the pressure cooker and cook for about 3 minutes on each side. Transfer to a plate. Heat the remaining oil and cook shallots, thyme, garlic, and mushrooms until soft.
- Add white wine and scrape up the brown bits from the bottom. When the alcohol evaporates, return the turkey to the pressure cooker. Seal the lid, and cook on MEAT/STEW for 25 minutes at High.
- Meanwhile, combine heavy cream and cornstarch in a small bowl. Do a quick pressure release. Open the lid and stir in the mixture. Bring the sauce to a boil, then turn the cooker off. Slice the turkey in half and serve topped with the creamy mushroom sauce.

## Sweet Gingery and Garlicky Chicken Thighs

Ready in about: **25 minutes** | Serves: **4** | Per serving: Calories 561; Carbs 61g; Fat 21g; Protein 54g

INGREDIENTS
2 pounds Chicken Thighs
½ cup Honey
3 tsp grated Ginger
2 tbsp Garlic, minced
5 tbsp Brown Sugar
2 cups Chicken Broth
½ cup plus 2 tbsp Soy Sauce
½ cup plus 2 tbsp Hoisin Sauce
4 tbsp Sriracha
2 tbsp Sesame Oil

DIRECTIONS
- Lay the chicken at the bottom. Mix the remaining ingredients in a bowl. Pour the mixture over the chicken.
- Seal the lid, select POULTRY and set the time to 20 minutes at High. Do a quick pressure release.

## Simple Pressure Cooked Whole Chicken

Ready in about: **40 minutes** | Serves: **4** | Per serving: Calories 376; Carbs 0g; Fat 30g; Protein 25g

INGREDIENTS
1 2-pound Whole Chicken
2 tbsp Olive Oil
1 ½ cups Water
Salt and Pepper, to taste

DIRECTIONS
- Season chicken all over with salt and pepper. Heat the oil on SAUTÉ at High, and cook the chicken until browned on all sides. Set aside and wipe clean the cooker. Insert a rack in your pressure cooker and pour the water in.
- Lower the chicken onto the rack. Seal the lid. Choose POULTRY setting and adjust the time to 25 minutes at High pressure. Once the cooking is over, do a quick pressure release, by turning the valve to "open" position.

## Chicken Bites Snacks with Chili Sauce

Ready in about: **25 minutes** | Serves: **6** | Per serving: Calories 405; Carbs 18g; Fat 19g; Protein 31g

INGREDIENTS
1 ½ pounds Chicken, cut up, with bones
¼ cup Tomato Sauce
Kosher Salt and Black Pepper to taste
2 tsp dry Basil
¼ cup raw Honey
1 ½ cups Water

**FOR CHILI SAUCE:**

2 spicy Chili Peppers, halved
½ cup loosely packed Parsley, finely chopped
1 tsp Sugar
1 clove Garlic, chopped
2 tbsp Lime juice
¼ cup Olive Oil

DIRECTIONS
- Put a steamer basket in the cooker's pot and pour the water in. Place the meat in the basket, and press BEANS/CHILI button. Seal the lid and cook for 20 minutes at High Pressure.
- Meanwhile, prepare the sauce by mixing all the sauce ingredients in a food processor. Blend until the pepper is chopped and all the ingredients are mixed well. Release the pressure quickly. To serve, place the meat in serving bowl and top with the sauce.

## Hot and Buttery Chicken Wings

Ready in about: **20 minutes** | Serves: **16** | Per serving: Calories 50; Carbs 1g; Fat 2g; Protein 7g

INGREDIENTS
16 Chicken Wings
1 cup Hot Sauce
1 cup Water
2 tbsp Butter

DIRECTIONS
- Add in all ingredients, and seal the lid. Cook on MEAT/STEW for 15 minutes at High. When ready, press CANCEL and release the pressure naturally, for 10 minutes.

# Tasty Turkey with Campanelle and Tomato Sauce

⌚ Ready in about: **20 minutes** | Serves: **4** | Per serving: **Calories 588; Carbs 71g; Fat 11g; Protein 60g**

INGREDIENTS
3 cups Tomato Sauce
½ tsp Salt
½ tbsp Marjoram
1 tsp dried Thyme
½ tbsp fresh Basil, chopped
¼ tsp ground Black Pepper, or more to taste
1 ½ pounds Turkey Breasts, chopped
1 tsp Garlic, minced
1 ½ cup spring Onions, chopped
1 package dry Campanelle Pasta
2 tbsp Olive Oil
½ cup Grana Padano cheese, grated

DIRECTIONS
- Select SAUTÉ at High and heat the oil in the cooker. Place the turkey, spring onions and garlic. Cook until cooked, about 6-7 minutes. Add the remaining ingredients, except the cheese.
- Seal the lid and press BEANS/CHILI button. Cook for 5 minutes at High Pressure. Once cooking has completed, quick release the pressure. To serve, top with freshly grated Grana Padano cheese.

# Chicken with Mushrooms and Leeks

⌚ Ready in about: **25 minutes** | Serves: **6** | Per serving: **Calories 321; Carbs 31g; Fat 18g; Protein 39g**

INGREDIENTS
2 pounds Chicken Breasts, cubed
4 tbsp Butter
1 ¼ pounds Mushrooms, sliced
½ cup Chicken Broth
2 tbsp Cornstarch
½ cup Milk
¼ tsp Black Pepper
2 Leeks, sliced
¼ tsp Garlic Powder

DIRECTIONS
- Melt butter on SAUTÉ mode at High. Place chicken cubes inside and cook until they are no longer pink, and become slightly golden. Transfer the chicken pieces to a plate.
- Add the leeks and sliced mushrooms to the pot and cook for about 3 minutes. Return the chicken to the pressure cooker, season with pepper and garlic powder, and pour in broth.
- Give the mixture a good stir to combine everything well, then seal the lid. Set on BEANS/CHILI mode, for 8 minutes at High pressure. When it goes off, release the pressure quickly.
- In a bowl, whisk together the milk and cornstarch. Pour the mixture over the chicken and set the pressure cooker to SAUTÉ at High. Cook until the sauce thickens.

# Hearty and Hot Turkey Soup

⌚ Ready in about: **40 minutes** | Serves: **6** | Per serving: **Calories 398; Carbs 40g; Fat 11g; Protein 51g**

INGREDIENTS
1 ½ pounds Turkey thighs, boneless, skinless and diced
1 cup Carrots, trimmed and diced
2 (8 oz) cans White Beans
2 Tomatoes, chopped
1 potato, chopped
1 cup Green Onions, chopped
2 Cloves Garlic, minced
6 cups Vegetable Stock
¼ tsp ground Black Pepper
¼ tsp Salt
½ tsp Cayenne Pepper
½ cup Celery head, peeled and chopped

DIRECTIONS
- Place all ingredients, except the beans, into the pressure cooker, and select SOUP mode. Seal the lid and cook for 20 minutes at High Pressure. Release the pressure quickly.
- Remove the lid and stir in the beans. Cover the cooker and let it stand for 10 minutes before serving.

# Green BBQ Chicken Wings

⌚ Ready in about: **20 minutes** | Serves: **4** | Per serving: **Calories 311; Carbs 1g; Fat 10g; Protein 51g**

INGREDIENTS
2 pounds Chicken Wings
5 tbsp Butter
1 cup Barbeque Sauce
5 Green Onions, minced

DIRECTIONS
- Add the butter, ¾ parts of the sauce and chicken in the pressure cooker. Select POULTRY, seal the lid and cook for 15 minutes at High.
- Do a quick release. Garnish wings with onions and top with the remaining sauce.

# Hot and Spicy Shredded Chicken

⌚ Ready in about: **1 hour** | Serves: **4** | Per serving: **Calories 307; Carbs 12g; Fat 10g; Protein 38g**

INGREDIENTS
1 ½ pounds boneless and skinless Chicken Breasts
2 cups diced Tomatoes
½ tsp Oregano
2 Green Chilies, seeded and chopped
½ tsp Paprika
2 tbsp Coconut Sugar
½ cup Salsa
1 tsp Cumin
2 tbsp Olive Oil

DIRECTIONS
- In a small mixing dish, combine the oil with all spices. Rub the chicken breast with the spicy marinade. Lay the meat into your pressure cooker. Add the tomatoes. Seal the lid, and cook for 20 minutes on POULTRY at High.
- Once ready, do a quick pressure release. Remove chicken to a cutting board; shred it. Return the shredded chicken to the cooker. Set to SAUTÉ at High, and let simmer for about 15 minutes.

## Homemade Cajun Chicken Jambalaya

⌛ **Ready in about: 30 minutes | Serves: 6 | Per serving:**
Calories 299; Carbs 31g; Fat 8g; Protein 41g

INGREDIENTS
1 ½ pounds, Chicken Breast, skinless
3 cups Chicken Stock
1 tbsp Garlic, minced
1 tsp Cajun Seasoning
1 Celery stalk, diced
1 ½ cups chopped Leeks, white part
1 ½ cups dry White Rice
2 tbsp Tomato Paste

DIRECTIONS
- Select SAUTÉ at High and brown the chicken for 5 minutes. Add the garlic and celery, and fry for 2 minutes until fragrant. Deglaze with broth. Add the remaining ingredients to the cooker. Seal the lid.
- Select POULTRY, and cook for 15 minutes at High. Do a quick pressure release and serve

## Salsa and Lime Chicken with Rice

⌛ **Ready in about: 35 minutes | Serves: 4 | Per serving:**
Calories 403; Carbs 44g; Fat 16g; Protein 19g

INGREDIENTS
¼ cup Lime Juice
3 tbsp Olive Oil
½ cup Salsa
2 Frozen Chicken Breasts, boneless and skinless
½ tsp Garlic Powder
1 cup Rice
1 cup Water
½ tsp Pepper
½ cup Mexican Cheese Blend
½ cup Tomato Sauce

DIRECTIONS
- Lay the chicken into the pressure cooker. Pour lime juice, salt, garlic powder, olive oil, tomato sauce, and pepper, over the chicken. Seal the lid, and cook for 15 minutes on MEAT/STEW mode at High.
- When ready, do a quick pressure release. Remove the chicken to a plate. Add in rice, cooking juices and water the total liquid in the pressure cooker should be about 2 cups.
- Seal the lid and adjust the time to 10 minutes on BEANS/CHILI at High pressure. Do a quick pressure release and serve with cooked rice.

## Homemade Whole Chicken

⌛ **Ready in about: 40 minutes | Serves: 6 | Per serving:**
Calories 207; Carbs 1g; Fat 8g; Protein 29g

INGREDIENTS
3 - pound Whole Chicken
1 cup Chicken Broth
1 ½ tbsp Olive Oil
1 tsp Paprika
¾ tsp Garlic Powder
¼ tsp Onion Powder

DIRECTIONS
- Rinse chicken under cold water, remove the giblets, and pat it dry with some paper towels. In a small bowl, combine the oil and spices. Rub the chicken well with the mixture. Set your pressure cooker to SAUTÉ at High. Add the chicken and sear on all sides until golden.
- Pour the chicken broth around the chicken not over it), and seal the lid. Cook on BEANS/CHILI, for 25 minutes at High. Do a quick pressure release. Transfer the chicken to a platter and let sit for 10 minutes before carving.

## Herbed and Garlicky Chicken Wings

⌛ **Ready in about: 25 minutes | Serves: 4 | Per serving:**
Calories 177; Carbs 1g; Fat 10g; Protein 19g

INGREDIENTS
12 Chicken Wings
½ cup Chicken Broth
1 tbsp Basil
1 tbsp Oregano
½ tbsp Tarragon
1 tbsp Garlic, minced
2 tbsp Olive Oil
¼ tsp Pepper
1 cup Water

DIRECTIONS
- Pour the water in the pressure cooker and lower the rack. Place all ingredients in a bowl and mix with your hands to combine well. Cover the bowl and let the wings sit for 15 minutes.
- Arrange on the rack and seal the lid. Select BEANS/CHILI, and set the timer to 10 minutes at High pressure. When done, do a quick pressure release. Serve drizzled with the cooking liquid and enjoy!

## Duck and Green Pea Soup

⌛ **Ready in about: 30 minutes | Serves: 6 | Per serving:**
Calories 191; Carbs 14g; Fat 5g; Protein 21g

INGREDIENTS
1 cup Carrots, diced
4 cups Chicken Stock
1 pound Duck Breasts, chopped
20 ounces diced canned Tomatoes
1 cup Celery, chopped
18 ounces Green Peas
1 cup Onions, diced
2 Garlic Cloves, minced
1 tsp dried Marjoram
½ tsp Pepper
½ tsp Salt

DIRECTIONS
- Place all ingredients, except the peas, in your pressure cooker. Stir well to combine and seal the lid. Select SOUP mode and set the cooking time to 20 minutes at High.
- After the beep, do a quick pressure release. Stir in the peas. Seal the lid again but do NOT turn the pressure cooker on. Let blanch for about 7 minutes. Ladle into serving bowls.

## Teriyaki Chicken Under Pressure

⏱ **Ready in about: 25 minutes | Serves: 8 | Per serving:** Calories 352; Carbs 31g; Fat 11g; Protein 31g

INGREDIENTS
1 cup Chicken Broth
¾ cup Brown Sugar
2 tbsp ground Ginger
1 tsp Pepper
3 pounds Boneless and Skinless Chicken Thighs
¼ cup Apple Cider Vinegar
¾ cup low-sodium Soy Sauce
20 ounces canned Pineapple, crushed
2 tbsp Garlic Powder

DIRECTIONS
- Stir all of the ingredients, except for the chicken. Add the chicken meat and turn to coat. Seal the lid, press POULTRY and cook for 20 minutes at High. Do a quick pressure release, by turning the valve to "open" position.

## Young Goose for Slow Cooker

The mild taste of wild goose!

⏱ **Prep time: 21 minutes Cooking time: 6 hours Servings: 6**

INGREDIENTS:
3 tbsp fresh rosemary
Chopped celery
Cream of mushroom soup
Fresh sage
2 goose
Cream of celery soup
Fresh thyme
Cream of chicken soup
1 cup mushrooms
1 pack baby carrots

DIRECTIONS:
- Finely mince fresh thyme, rosemary, and sage leaves. Chop celery and baby carrots.
- In a wide bowl, mix cream of celery, carrots, cream of chicken soup. Celery, cream of mushroom soup, sage, thyme, mushrooms and rosemary.
- Cut goose into pieces and place into Slow Cooker. Pour the cream mixture over the meat.
- Set to HIGH and cook for 8 hours until tender.

**Nutrition: Calories: 998 Fat: 56g Carbohydrates: 17g Protein: 91g**

## Homemade Chicken with Dumplings

Try this freshly cooked chicken with your family!

⏱ **Prep time: 21 minutes Cooking time: 6 hours Servings: 6**

INGREDIENTS:
1 cup water
4 cans chicken broth
4 carrots
Salt
2 tbsp flour
4 baking potatoes
2 cups baking mix
2 cups chopped broccoli
Black pepper
4 tbsp milk

DIRECTIONS:
- Right in Slow Cooker, mix potatoes, chicken meat, broccoli and carrots.
- In a separate bowl, mix water and flour until it appears to be paste-like. Season with pepper and salt to taste.
- Pour in over the Slow Cooker ingredients and stir well. Cover and cook for 5 hours on LOW mode.
- In small bowl, combine baking mix and milk. Carefully add to Slow Cooker, using a teaspoon. Cook for another hour.

**Nutrition: Calories: 649 Fat: 22g Carbohydrates: 62g Protein: 47g**

## Mexican-styled Slow Cooker Chicken

Add this to your tacos and salads, or just serve with pasta or rice!

⏱ **Prep time: 11 minutes Cooking time: 4 hours Servings: 4**

INGREDIENTS:
Half cup tomato salsa
Half cup tomato preserves
Half cup chipotle salsa
One chicken

DIRECTIONS:
- In a bowl, mix pineapple preserves, chipotle salsa and tomato salsa. If needed, remove skin and bones from the chicken meat.
- Place chicken into Slow Cooker and pour over with the sauce. Toss meat to cover evenly. Cook for 3 hours on LOW mode.
- Remove chicken meat from Slow Cooker and finely shred with two forks. Return to Slow Cooker and prepare for 1 more hour.

**Nutrition: Calories: 238 Fat: 2g Carbohydrates: 31g Protein: 23g**

## Yellow Rice with Turkey wings

Quick and easy for working days!

⏱ **Prep time: 21 minutes Cooking time: 6 hours Servings: 6**

INGREDIENTS:
1 tsp seasoned salt
3 turkey wings
1 tsp garlic powder
Ground black pepper
Water to cover
Cream of mushroom soup
1 pack saffron rice

DIRECTIONS:
- Clean the turkey wings and transfer to Slow Cooker.
- In a bowl, mix garlic powder, salt, cream of mushroom soup, black pepper. Season the wings with this mixture.
- Pour in water into Slow Cooker – just enough to cover the wings. Stir everything well and cover. Cook for 8 hours on LOW mode.

- When it is time, stir the rice into Slow Cooker and prepare for 20 minutes more.

**Nutrition: Calories: 272 Fat: 5g Carbohydrates: 39g Protein: 17g**

## Slow Cooker Turkey Wings

You can try it with your favorite sauce and side dishes!

Prep time: 11 minutes Cooking time: 7 hours Servings: 12

INGREDIENTS:
Salt
Ground black pepper
6 turkey legs
3 tsp poultry seasoning
DIRECTIONS:
- Wash the turkey legs with running water and remove excess liquid.
- Rub each turkey leg with one teaspoon of poultry seasoning. Add salt and black pepper. Cut aluminum foil into leg-fitting parts and wrap each turkey leg with a foil.
- Place the wrapped legs into Slow Cooker. Add no water or other liquids. Cook on LOW for 8 hours. Check the tenderness before serving.

**Nutrition: Calories: 217 Fat: 7g Carbohydrates: 1g Protein: 36g**

## Chicken Alfredo in Slow Cooker

Easy with Alfredo sauce and Swiss cheese!

Prep time: 16 minutes Cooking time: 4 hours Servings: 6

INGREDIENTS:
Black pepper
3 tbsp grated Parmesan cheese
4 chicken breast halves
Salt
4 slices Swiss cheese
Garlic powder
DIRECTIONS:
- Wash your chicken breasts with running water. Remove the bones and skin. Cut chicken meat into small cubes.
- Right in Slow Cooker, combine chicken cubes and Alfredo sauce. Toss to cover. Cook under lid on LOW mode, approximately for two hours.
- Add both cheeses and cook for another 30 minutes.
- Just before serving, season with salt, garlic powder and black pepper to taste.

**Nutrition: Calories: 610 Fat: 50g Carbohydrates: 9g Protein: 31g**

## Quick-to-Cook Chicken

It will wait for you to come home!

Prep time: 16 minutes Cooking time: 8 hours Servings: 6

INGREDIENTS:
Half cup sour cream
4 chicken breast halves
Cream of celery
Cream of chicken soup
DIRECTIONS:
- Discard the skin and bones from the chicken. Wash and drain.
- Grease your Slow Cooker with melted butter or olive oil. If you prefer cooking spray, use it. Transfer cleared chicken into Slow Cooker.
- In a bowl, whisk both creams. Mix well until smooth. Pour the chicken meat with cream mixture.
- Cover with the lid and prepare for 8 hours on LOW mode. Just before serving, add the sour cream.
- To serve, transfer cooked chicken onto a large bowl. Garnish with chopped green onion or other vegetables or berries. Serve hot.

**Nutrition: Calories: 304 Fat: 16g Carbohydrates: 12g Protein: 27g**

## Slow Cooker Turkey with Dumplings

Creamy and hot, perfect choice for a cold day!

Prep time: 9 minutes Cooking time: 4 hours Servings: 4

INGREDIENTS:
3 medium carrots
1 cans cream of chicken soup
Garlic powder
1 can chicken broth
Half onion
Buttermilk biscuit dough
5 large potatoes
2 tbsp butter
Cooked turkey
Poultry seasoning
DIRECTIONS:
- Cook the turkey before start.
- Chop the potatoes, onion and carrots.
- In a bowl, mix butter, onion, potatoes, turkey, chicken broth and cream of chicken soup. Season with garlic powder.
- Transfer into Slow Cooker and pour in water to cover. Cook on HIGH mode for 3 hours, stirring occasionally. Place the biscuits over turkey and cook for 1 more hour

**Nutrition: Calories: 449 Fat: 22g Carbohydrates: 38g Protein: 23g**

## Flavored Chicken in Rustic Italian Style

Perfect with veggies and Italian seasoning!

Prep time: 22 minutes Cooking time: 5 hours Servings: 6

INGREDIENTS:
3 cups penne pasta
Red bell pepper
Chicken thighs
Canned tomatoes
Salt
Canned crushed tomatoes
Black pepper
Fresh mushrooms

2 carrots
4 garlic cloves
DIRECTIONS:
- Grease Slow Cooker with oil or spray with anti-stick cooking spray. Transfer chicken to Slow Cooker.
- Chop carrots into 1-inch slices, slice bell peppers and mushrooms. Mice garlic.
- Add the vegetables and add canned tomatoes, salt/pepper and season with two tablespoons of Italian seasoning.
- Cover and cook on LOW for 8 hours.
- To serve, use 3 cups penne pasta or fresh parsley.

**Nutrition: Calories: 441 Fat: 16g Carbohydrates: 41g Protein: 31g**

## Hot Turkey Meatballs

Perfectly to serve with vegetables!

⌛ Prep time: 17 minutes Cooking time: 3 hours
Servings: 4

INGREDIENTS:
Water
Dry onion soup mix (2 envelopes)
2 Chicken eggs
Beef flavored rice
Fresh turkey meat
DIRECTIONS:
- Fill your Slow Cooker with water and onion soup mix (there should be enough liquid to fill crockpot halfway).
- Turn on Slow Cooker to high and leave until the liquid boils.
- Meanwhile, make meatballs. In a bowl, combine rice with turkey and flavoring mix. Add beaten chicken eggs and mix together.
- Form 2-inch meatballs and fry them to brown on large skillet with oil.
- When soup is boiling. Transfer meatballs to Slow Cooker and prepare 9 hours on LOW temperature mode.

**Nutrition: Calories: 567 Fat: 22g Carbohydrates: 42g Protein: 47g**

## Shredded Turkey in Barbeque Sauce

Full of protein and healthy meal!

⌛ Prep time: 13 minutes Cooking time: 10 hours
Servings: 8

INGREDIENTS:
1 tsp ground cumin
8 potato rolls
2 cans baked beans
1 medium onion
1 tbsp yellow mustard
2 bone-in turkey thighs
salt
DIRECTIONS:
- Finely chop onion.
- Grease your Slow Cooker with melted plain butter.
- Right in Slow Cooker pot, combine onion, baked beans, barbeque sauce, cumin, yellow mustard and salt.
- Carefully place the turkey thighs into the mixture.
- Set Slow Cooker to LOW temperature and cook for 11 hours.
- Remove turkey and discard bones. Shred and place back to Slow Cooker. Serve the turkey placed over potato rolls.

**Nutrition: Calories: 385 Fat: 6g Carbohydrates: 59g Protein: 26g**

## Lemon-Fragrant Chicken

Easy and great to taste!

⌛ Prep time: 22 minutes Cooking time: 9 hours
Servings: 6

INGREDIENTS:
1 medium onion
1 cup hot water
Salt
One stalk celery
One whole chicken
One big apple
Half tsp dried rosemary
zest and juice of 1 lemon
ground black pepper
DIRECTIONS:
- Peel and core apple. Cut into quarters.
- Wash the chicken and dry with a paper towel.
- Rub the salt and pepper mix into chickens' skin and place apple and chopped celery into chicken. Place chicken into Slow Cooker and sprinkle with chopped onion, lemon zest and juice, rosemary. Pour in one cup water.
- Cover and cook on HIGH for 1 hour. Then, turn to LOW and cook for 7 hours.

**Nutrition: Calories: 309 Fat: 17g Carbohydrates: 7g Protein: 31g**

## Turkey with Indian Spice

Perfect with rice and fresh herbs!

⌛ Prep time: 17 minutes Cooking time: 6 hours
Servings: 4

INGREDIENTS:
Turkey thigh meat
Canned stewed tomatoes
3 tbsp dried onion flakes
Dried thyme leaves
4 tbsp white wine
Half tsp Italian seasoning
6 cubes chicken bouillon
Garlic powder
Lemon pepper seasoning
DIRECTIONS:
- In a bowl, whisk together wine and canned tomatoes.
- Pour in the tomato mixture into your Slow Cooker and add onion flakes, bouillon cubes and thyme. Season with garlic powder and Italian seasoning.
- Carefully place the turkey into Slow Cooker.
- Cover the lid and cook for 10 hours on LOW temperature mode.

**Nutrition: Calories: 317 Fat: 7g Carbohydrates: 9g Protein: 51g**

## Gluten-free Chicken Soup

Easy to cook on a busy day!

⌛ **Prep time: 13 minutes Cooking time: 8 hours**
**Servings: 9**

INGREDIENTS:
Medium onion
1/2 cup water
2 carrots
Gluten-free chicken broth
Salt
Frozen vegetables
4 tbsp. long-grain rice
2 celery stalks
Garlic
Black pepper
Dried basil
tomatoes
Red pepper flakes
DIRECTIONS:
- In a bowl, combine diced tomatoes, diced carrots, garlic, celery and onions.
- Transfer the vegetable mix into Slow Cooker and season with dried basil, red pepper flakes, salt and pepper.
- Carefully place chicken into the mixture. Stir everything well to cover the meat. Cook on LOW temperature mode for 7 hours.
- Add rice and frozen vegetable mix. Cook for 1 more hour on HIGH.

**Nutrition: Calories: 198 Fat: 6g Carbohydrates: 20g Protein: 16g**

## Hawaiian Spice Slow Cooker Chicken

Amazingly tastes with rice!

⌛ **Prep time: 5 minutes Cooking time: 4 hours**
**Servings: 9**

INGREDIENTS:
Chicken breasts
Canned sliced pineapples
1 tsp soy sauce
1 bottle honey bbq sauce
DIRECTIONS:
- Carefully grease the bottom and sides of your Slow Cooker with melted butter or spray with anti- stick spray.
- Wash and drain chicken breasts, place into Slow Cooker.
- In a bowl, mix pineapple slices and barbeque sauce, add soy sauce. Pour in this mixture over chicken breasts into Slow Cooker.
- Cover the lid and turn Slow Cooker to HIGH temperature mode. Cook for 5 hours. To serve, garnish chicken with chopped parsley and green onion. Serve while hot.

**Nutrition: Calories: 274 Fat: 3g Carbohydrates: 29g Protein: 30g**

## Chicken Soup with Rice

Your whole family will like this soup!

⌛ **Prep time: 5 minutes Cooking time: 8 hours**
**Servings: 6**

INGREDIENTS:
3 celery sticks
4 tbsp long-grain rice
2 cups frozen mixed vegetables
Half cup water
1 tbsp dried parsley
Lemon seasoning
3 cans chicken broth
Herb seasoning
DIRECTIONS:
- Remove bones from chicken breast halves. Cook and dice the meat. In a bowl, combine chopped celery, rice, mixed vegetables.
- Season the mixture with lemon and herbal seasoning. Add some salt to taste and transfer to Slow Cooker.
- Whisk water and chicken broth; pour over the vegetable and chicken mixture in Slow Cooker. Cover and cook for 8 hours, using LOW temperature mode.

**Nutrition: Calories: 277 Fat: 7g Carbohydrates: 27g Protein: 25g**

## Tunisian-Styled Turkey

Satisfying and tasty dish for any holiday!

⌛ **Prep time: 11 minutes Cooking time: 4 hours**
**Servings: 6**

INGREDIENTS:
2 tbsp flour
1 turkey breast half
Chipotle chili powder
1 tbsp olive oil
Half tsp garlic powder
1 acorn squash
Ground cinnamon
3 large carrots
Coriander
2 red onions
Salt
6 garlic cloves
Ground black pepper
DIRECTIONS:
- Mix chipotle and garlic powder, black pepper, cinnamon and salt.
- Rub turkey meat with spicy mix and brown in a large skillet (use medium heat). Grease your Slow Cooker with olive oil.
- Cover the bottom of Slow Cooker with diced carrots, acorn squash quarters, garlic cloves and red onions.
- Place the turkey atop the vegetables. Cook on HIGH mode for 8 hours.

**Nutrition: Calories: 455 Fat: 5g Carbohydrates: 19g Protein: 81g**

## Hot Buffalo Chicken Lettuce Envelopes

So much healthier than traditional Buffalo wings!

⌛ **Prep time: 11 minutes Cooking time: 6 hours**
**Servings: 10**

INGREDIENTS:
2 chicken breasts
1 pack ranch dressing mix
One head Boston lettuce leaves

Cayenne pepper sauce

DIRECTIONS:
- Remove skin and bones from the chicken and put the breasts into Slow Cooker.
- In a bowl, stir to smooth ranch dressing mix and cayenne pepper. Stir the mixture until it is smooth.
- Pour the chicken breasts with the sauce. Make sure that all the chicken surface is covered with the sayce.
- Cover and cook during 7 hours (use LOW temperature mode).
- Using spotted spoon, place chicken meat over the lettuce leaves and roll.

**Nutrition: Calories: 105 Fat: 2g Carbohydrates: 2g Protein: 18g**

# Chicken with Pear and Asparagus

Unusual seasoning for incredibly tasty dish!

⌚ **Prep time: 21 minutes Cooking time: 4 hours**
**Servings: 4**

INGREDIENTS:
4 cloves garlic
1 tbsp vegetable oil
2 tbsp balsamic vinegar
4 chicken breast halves
3 tbsp apple juice
One onion
Dried rosemary
Black pepper, salt
Grated fresh ginger
Two Bartlett pears
2 tbsp brown sugar
Fresh asparagus

DIRECTIONS:
- Core and slice Bartlett pears.
- Warm the olive on preheated skillet. Cook chicken meat until it is completely browned. Transfer to Slow Cooker.
- Dice the onion and spread it over the chicken. Season with salt and pepper.
- Place asparagus and pears into Slow Cooker.
- Separately mix balsamic vinegar, sugar, apple juice, sugar, ginger and garlic. Add to Slow Cooker. Cover and cook for 5 hours on LOW mode.

**Nutrition: Calories: 309 Fat: 7g Carbohydrates: 33g Protein: 29g**

# Sweet Chicken with Parmesan

This one will be your favorite!

⌚ **Prep time: 11 minutes Cooking time: 5 hours**
**Servings: 6**

INGREDIENTS:
Black pepper
6 tbsp butter
Salt to taste
Onion soup mix
Cream of mushroom soup
Grated Parmesan
1 cup milk
1 cup rice
6 chicken breasts

DIRECTIONS:
- Remove skin and bones off the chicken.
- Separately mix milk, onion soup mix, rice and cream of mushroom soup. Slightly grease Slow Cooker, lay chicken meat over the bottom.
- Pour the sauce mixture all over it.
- In addition, season with pepper/salt.
- Finally, cover with grated Parmesan cheese.
- Set Slow Cooker to LOW and prepare for 10 hours.

**Nutrition: Calories: 493 Fat: 21g Carbohydrates: 37g Protein: 35g**

# Cornish Hens with Olives

Perfect with wild rice or vegetables!

⌚ **Prep time: 21 minutes Cooking time: 4 hours**
**Servings: 2**

INGREDIENTS:
1 tsp garlic salt
2 Cornish game hens
One large zucchini
Golden mushroom soup
Pimento-stuffed green olives
Baby Portobello mushrooms

DIRECTIONS:
- To start, prepare the vegetables: chop zucchini, mushrooms and green olives. Slightly coat the hens with 3 tablespoons of golden mushroom soup.
- In a bowl, mix olives, remaining mushroom soup, garlic salt and zucchini. Stuff the hens with this mixture.
- Transfer hens into Slow Cooker and pour over with some more mushroom soup (all that remained).
- Set your Slow Cooker to HIGH mode and cook for 4 hours.

**Nutrition: Calories: 851 Fat: 57g Carbohydrates: 24g Protein: 59g**

# Slow Cooker Chicken in Thai Sauce

Slightly spiced, this is an awesome dish for any occasion!

⌚ **Prep time: 23 minutes Cooking time: 5 hours**
**Servings: 6**

INGREDIENTS:
Half cup roasted peanuts
6 chicken breast halves
Fresh cilantro
1 large bell pepper
3 green onions
Large onion
Chicken broth
Soy sauce
3 cloves garlic
2 tbsp cornstarch
Salt/pepper
6 tbsp creamy butter cream
1 tbsp ground cumin
Red pepper flakes

DIRECTIONS:
- Grease your Slow Cooker with melted butter.
- Right in a cooking pot, combine chopped bell pepper, onion and chopped to trips chicken. In a bowl, whisk together red pepper

- flakes, minced garlic, cumin, pepper/salt. Stir to blend. Cover Slow Cooker with the lid and cook for 5 hours on low mode.
- Drain 1 cup liquid from Slow Cooker to whisk lime juice, soy sauce, peanut butter and cornstarch in it. Pour in back to Slow Coker.
- Cook on HIGH for 30 minutes more.
- To serve, garnish with cilantro, green onions and chopped peanuts.

**Nutrition: Calories: 410 Fat: 26g Carbohydrates: 18g Protein: 35g**

## Leftovers Soup with Turkey Meat

A hearty soup with noodles and turkey for your family!

**Prep time: 23 minutes Cooking time: 10 hours**
**Servings: 8**

INGREDIENTS:
2 cups penne pasts
Chicken broth
Small onion
Cream of mushroom soup
One turkey carcass
2 bay leaves
3 cup cooked turkey
Chopped celery
3 celery steaks
One quartered onion
2 medium carrots

DIRECTIONS:
- Place the turkey carcass into your Slow Cooker.
- Place quartered onion, halved celery and carrots and bay leaves into Slow Cooker too. Cover and cook for approximately 4 hours. Carefully remove solids from Slow Cooker. Add chopped vegetables and cook for 3 hours on LOW regime.
- Add penne paste and leave to prepare for additional 2 hours.
- In the end of time, mix in mushroom cream and turkey meat. Cook for 30 minutes.

**Nutrition: Calories: 1876 Fat: 140g Carbohydrates: 54g Protein: 87g**

## Chicken Livers Mix

Perfect with noodles and rice!

**Prep time: 34 minutes Cooking time: 6-7 hours**
**Servings: 4**

INGREDIENTS:
3 green onions
1 tsp salt
Dry white wine
3 slices bacon
Black pepper
One cup chicken stock
Canned sliced mushrooms
1 pound chicken livers
Golden mushroom soup

DIRECTIONS:
- In a medium bowl, mix salt, flour and pepper. Place livers into this mixture and toss to cover. Cook bacon on a skillet, over the medium heat). Remove and drain with paper towels.
- Place the livers into the same skillet and cook until lightly browned. Place the livers and bacon into Slow Cooker. Pour in the chicken stock. Add golden mushroom soup and wine.
- Cook under the lid for 6 hours. Use LOW temperature mode.

**Nutrition: Calories: 352 Fat: 16g Carbohydrates: 21g Protein: 24g**

## Slow Cooker Chicken with Italian dressing

This melts in the mouth!

**Prep time: 19 minutes Cooking time: 6 hours**
**Servings: 7**

INGREDIENTS:
Sea salt
1 pack angel hair pasta
Pepper
Malt vinegar
1 tsp garlic powder
Ground cumin
Plain flour
Italian seasoning
Sour cream
Italian salad dressing
Parmesan cheese

DIRECTIONS:
- In a bowl, whisk pepper, garlic powder, paprika, salt, cumin, cumin and Italian seasoning. Add Italian dressing, Parmesan, cream of mushroom soup, vinegar, flour, sour cream.
- Set Slow Cooker to low. Cook for 6 hours using LOW temperature mode. Shred the chicken, continue cooking.
- Separately, cook angel hair.
- Serve chicken over the cooked pasta.

**Nutrition: Calories: 483 Fat: 25g Carbohydrates: 40g Protein: 24g**

## Barbeque Chicken Sliders

Creamy and delicious taste for your family!

**Prep time: 23 minutes Cooking time: 3 hours**
**Servings: 7**

INGREDIENTS:
16 mini rolls
4 breast halves
Sugar
1 tbsp olive oil
Red wine vinegar
1 pack coleslaw mix
3 tbsp mayonnaise
1 cup barbeque sauce
Half cup water
Salt/Black pepper

DIRECTIONS:
- Place skinless, boneless chicken breast on aluminum foil. Season with salt and pepper. Place wraps over dry skillet or grill for 3 minutes.
- Transfer chicken breasts into Slow Cooker and pour over with mixed bbq sauce and water. Cover and cook for 5 hours on LOW mode.

- Take out the chicken and shred it using two forks.
- Mix chicken meat with mayonnaise, coleslaw, sugar, vinegar and pepper/salt. Serve over sweet rolls.

**Nutrition: Calories: 396 Fat: 12g Carbohydrates: 340g Protein: 13g**

## Slow Cooker Turkey in Beer Marinade

Feel the traditional flavors of turkey with ranch seasoning!

**Prep time: 14 minutes Cooking time: 8 hours**
**Servings: 7**

INGREDIENTS:
6 slices bacon
Cooking spray
Light beer
Ranch dressing mix
Bone-in turkey breast
Butter

DIRECTIONS:
- Spray the inside of your Slow Cooker with cooking spray. In a bowl, combine half pack of ranch dressing with butter.
- Carefully place butter mixture under the turkey's skin. Transfer to Slow Cooker.
- Sprinkle turkey with remaining ranch dressing mix. Arrange the bacon pieces over turkey. Pour in lager beer.
- Cook on HIGH 1 hour. Then, turning to LOW, continue cooking for 8 hours.

**Nutrition: Calories: 194 Fat: 15g Carbohydrates: 3g Protein: 8g**

## French Onion and Chicken Soup

Super easy and delicious meal!

**Prep time: 16 minutes Cooking time: 5 hours**
**Servings: 9**

INGREDIENTS:
White sugar
6 tbsp. butter
Shredded Mozzarella
1 bay leaf
Shredded Parmesan
4 yellow onions
Emmental cheese
Gruyere cheese
Garlic
7 cups broth
Cooking sherry
Sea salt
Chicken breast half
Dried thyme
French bread slices

DIRECTIONS:
- Heat butter on a skillet and cook onions until translucent. Add sugar and cook for 30 minutes over medium heat. Add garlic and cook until fragrant.
- Pour in sherry into onion mixture, transfer to Slow Cooker. Add beef broth and cubed chicken meat.
- Season with species and place a bay leaf.
- Cook on HIGH for 6 hours or on LOW for 10 hours.

- Mix four shredded cheeses and top each bowl of soup with cheese. Warm bread slices. Serve with soup.

**Nutrition: Calories: 258 Fat: 14g Carbohydrates: 17g Protein: 11g**

## Turkey Bacon Cassoulet

Simple and delicious French receipt!

**Prep time: 32 minutes Cooking time: 4 hours**
**Servings: 6**

INGREDIENTS:
2 bay leaves
Fresh parsley
Olive oil
Dried thyme
Canned diced tomatoes
Ground black pepper
6 slices turkey bacon
3 cans Northern beans
One large onion
3 cloves garlic
Smoked sausage
3 tbsp. tomato paste
Black pepper

DIRECTIONS:
1. Cook the turkey bacon on a greased skillet until crispy. Dry with paper towel. Set aside. In the same skillet, fry onion until translucent.
- Add chicken meat, bay leaves, thyme, sausage, black pepper and garlic. Cook for around 7 minutes.
- Stir in tomato paste and transfer the mixture to Slow Cooker. Add northern beans, turkey bacon and diced tomatoes.
- Cook for 5 hours on LOW temperature setting.

**Nutrition: Calories: 522 Fat: 19g Carbohydrates: 53g Protein: 35g**

## Tagine Chicken in Slow Cooker

Moroccan chicken meal for your Slow Cooker

**Prep time: 24 minutes Cooking time: 5 hours**
**Servings: 12**

INGREDIENTS:
Olive oil
1 cup couscous
8 chicken thighs
1 cup water
1 eggplant
Black pepper
2 onions
Cinnamon
2 cups chicken broth
4 carrots
1 tsp ground ginger
Half cup dried cranberries
Cumin
2 tbsp lemon juice
2 tbsp tomato paste
Half cup dried apricots
Flour
Garlic salt

DIRECTIONS:
- Cut chicken and eggplant. Cook both on large greased skillet until the chicken is slightly browned. Place the skillet ingredients into Slow Cooker, cover with diced carrots, onion, garlic, apricots and cranberries.
- In a bowl, whisk tomato paste, chicken broth, flour, lemon juice and species. Pour the spicy mixture over the chicken.
- Cook under the lid for 8 hours on LOW mode. Serve with couscous.

**Nutrition: Calories: 380 Fat: 15g Carbohydrates: 38g Protein: 22g**

## Slow Cooker Turkey with Potatoes

Hearty and healthy for you and your friends!

Prep time: 21 minutes Cooking time: 6 hours
Servings: 6

INGREDIENTS:
Black pepper
6 cups water
Cream of chicken soup
2 cups rice
Cream of mushroom soup
Garlic powder
3 turkey legs
3 medium onions
Seasoned meat tenderizer
Green bell pepper
Salt
Red bell pepper

DIRECTIONS:
- Right in Slow Cooker, combine creams of chicken and mushroom soup. Add chopped onion and red and green bell peppers.
- Place the turkey legs over the bottom of your Slow Cooker and pour over with the sauce. Set your Cooker HIGH temp mode and cook for 3 hours, stirring time after time.
- Stir in garlic powder, salt/pepper, tenderizer and diced potatoes.
- Take out turkey and cut off meat off the bones. Return and cook for one more hour. Serve with separately cooked rice.

**Nutrition: Calories: 655 Fat: 17g Carbohydrates: 74g Protein: 45g**

## Chicken Breast with Bacon and Feta

Just five ingredients for tasty receipt!

Prep time: 17 minutes Cooking time: 3 hours
Servings: 8

INGREDIENTS:
Half cup crumbled feta
2 tbsp fresh basil
8 slices bacon
Diced tomatoes
8 chicken breast halves

DIRECTIONS:
- Preheat a large skillet over medium heat. Place the bacon into it. Cook about 10 minutes. Drain and dry with paper towels.
- Using a small bowl, mix feta cheese and crumbled bacon.
- Cut split lengthwise chicken meat to create some kind of pocket. Fill it with the sauce mixture. To secure, use toothpicks. Transfer chicken to Slow Cooker. Top with tomatoes and chopped basil. Cook on HIGH regime for about three hours.

**Nutrition: Calories: 246 Fat: 7g Carbohydrates: 7g Protein: 33g**

## Chicken with Quinoa and Mustard

Quickly and easy receipt for your weekend or holiday!

Prep time: 15 minutes Cooking time: 3 hours
Servings: 4

INGREDIENTS:
1 tbsp honey
1 cup quinoa
4 chicken breasts
Dill weed
Hot water
3 tbsp spicy brown mustard
1 tsp onion powder
1 tbsp chopped chives
1 tsp red wine vinegar
Sea salt
3 tbsp nutritional yeast flakes
1 tbsp butter
Ground turmeric

DIRECTIONS:
- In a small bowl, soak quinoa just for several minutes and drain.
- In a bowl, combine dill, yeast flakes, turmeric, sea salt, chives and onion powder. Stir in quinoa, one cup water, vinegar and butter.
- Add yeast flake mixture. Stir everything well and pour into Slow Cooker. Place chicken meat atop the mixture and season with salt or species you like. Spoon mixed honey and mustard over.
- Cook for 3 hour on HIGH mode.

**Nutrition: Calories: 344 Fat: 8g Carbohydrates: 34g Protein: 31g**

## Creamy Chicken with Pasta

Make your chicken absolutely tender with sour cream and mushrooms!

Prep time: 12 minutes Cooking time: 6 hours
Servings: 4

INGREDIENTS:
1 tsp Italian seasoning
Sour cream
1 pack cream cheese
2 chicken breast halves

DIRECTIONS:
- 2 hours before cooking take cream cheese out of refrigerator – it should be at room temperature. Wash the chicken breast under cold running water. Discard bones and skin, cut into 1-inch cubes. Grease your Slow Cooker and right in it mix cream of mushroom soup, cream cheese, Italian seasoning and sour cream.
- Carefully stir in chicken cubes until smooth. Cook for 6 hours, using LOW temperature mode.

**Nutrition: Calories: 357 Fat: 28g Carbohydrates: 7g Protein: 19g**

## Summer Burrito with Turkey

You can use Thanksgiving leftovers for these burritos!

⌛ **Prep time: 13 minutes Cooking time: 1 hour Servings: 10**

INGREDIENTS:
1 cup prepared stuffing
Salt to taste
3 cups cooked turkey
3 tbsp self-rising flour
3 tbsp jalapeno juice
1 tbsp dried parsley
Shredded Cheddar
1 large onion
Turkey broth
3 jalapeno peppers
1 cup mashed potatoes
1 cup gravy
Black pepper
10 flour tortillas

DIRECTIONS:
- Grease your Slow Cooker with olive oil or anti-stick spray.
- Right in a cooking pot, mix turkey, broth, stuffing, gravy, mashed potatoes, onion. Cook for 1 hour on HIGH temperature mode.
- Meanwhile, warm tortillas, using a dry frying pan or baking sheet.
- Spoon the Slow Cooker mixture over each tortilla, add cheese and roll into burrito. Garnish with chopped parsley and jalapeno slices.

**Nutrition: Calories: 516 Fat: 15g Carbohydrates: 54g Protein: 28g**

## Bloody Mary Chicken

Incredibly easy and tasty chicken receipt!

⌛ **Prep time: 18 minutes Cooking time: 4 hours Servings: 4**

INGREDIENTS:
2 chicken breasts
Blue cheese dressing
Brown sugar
Vegetable juice cocktail
Small lemon
Celery salt
Hot pepper sauce
1 tsp horseradish
Worcestershire sauce
4 stalks celery
Steak sauce

DIRECTIONS:
- Remove skin off chicken breasts, place them into Slow Cooker.
- Combine celery salt, lemon juice, sugar, Worcestershire sauce, hot pepper sauce and horseradish.
- Pour in the vegetable juice cocktail, stir until sugar is fully dissolved. Pour the mixture into Slow Cooker.
- Add blue cheese dressing into Slow Cooker and combine well. Set Slow Cooker to LOW and cook for 8 hours.

**Nutrition: Calories: 530 Fat: 34g Carbohydrates: 23g Protein: 27g**

## Super Easy Cornish Hens

Juicy hens with awesome flavor!

⌛ **Prep time: 18 minutes Cooking time: 4 hours Servings: 6**

INGREDIENTS:
Lemon juice
Salt
3 tbsp margarine
1\4 cup cubed margarine
Garlic powder
Red pepper flakes
Thyme
Ground cumin
Chicken broth
2 Cornish hens

DIRECTIONS:
- In a bowl, mix melted margarine, garlic powder, lemon juice, red pepper flakes and cumin. Rub the lemon mixture into two Cornish game hens.
- In a bowl, mix thyme, black pepper and salt and sprinkle the hens. Start preheating your Slow Cooker and fill in to half with chicken broth.
- Place one tablespoon of margarine onto each chick and carefully transfer hens into Slow Cooker. Cook on LOW for 8 hours.

**Nutrition: Calories: 516 Fat: 43g Carbohydrates: 4g Protein: 26g**

## Balsamic Chicken in Slow Cooker

You can cook this even with frozen chicken!

⌛ **Prep time: 17 minutes Cooking time: 4 hours Servings: 6**

INGREDIENTS:
Half cup vinegar
Olive oil
Dried rosemary
1 tsp oregano
4 chicken breast halves
Garlic
2 cans crushed tomatoes
Dried basil
Dried thyme
Dried oregano
One large onion
Black pepper/salt to taste

DIRECTIONS:
- Remove skin from chicken breasts.
- Drizzle some olive oil over the bottom of your Slow Cooker.
- Place the breasts into Slow Cooker, rub each one with pepper/salt to your taste. Dice onion and garlic, place atop the chicken breasts.
- Season with basil, oregano, thyme and rosemary. Pour tomatoes and balsamic vinegar.
- Cook for 4 hours using HIGH temperature mode.

**Nutrition: Calories: 200 Fat: 7g Carbohydrates: 18g Protein: 19g**

## Hot Turkey in Italian Style

Serve this with veggies or sandwiches!

Prep time: 27 minutes  Cooking time: 8 hours
Servings: 6

INGREDIENTS:
Worcestershire sauce
4 ouillon cubes
Dried oregano
1 medium onion
1 turkey breast half
Half cup water
White vinegar
Green bell pepper
Brown gravy mix
2 cloves garlic

DIRECTIONS:
- Pour one quart water into your Slow Cooker. Dissolve bouillon cubes in it. Remove skin from turkey and place meat into Slow Cooker.
- Cover and cook for 8 hours on LOW temperature regime.
- Two hours before the end, stir in Worcestershire sauce, vinegar, green bell pepper, oregano, onion and garlic.
- In the end, combine some water and gravy mix in a small bowl and add into Slow Cooker. Cook for additional 20 minutes.

**Nutrition: Calories: 117 Fat: 1g Carbohydrates: 6g Protein: 20g**

## Slow Cooker Baked Chicken with Paprika

Perfectly fits for busy days!

Prep time: 21 minutes  Cooking time: 10 hours
Servings: 6

INGREDIENTS:
Salt
1 tsp paprika
One whole chicken
Black pepper to taste

DIRECTIONS:
- Roll small balls out of aluminum foil and place them into your Slow Cooker.
- Rinse the chicken all over (inside and out), better under cold running water. Dry with paper towels. Mix black pepper, paprika and salt and rub the chicken with this mixture.
- Place seasoned chicken onto aluminum balls in Slow Cooker.
- Set HIGH mode and cook firstly for an hour, then turn to LOW and cook for approximately 9 hours.

**Nutrition: Calories: 408 Fat: 28g Carbohydrates: 1g Protein: 35g**

## Sour and Sweet Chicken

Quick and tasty weekend meal!

Prep time: 19 minutes  Cooking time: 8 hours
Servings: 4

INGREDIENTS:

2 chicken breast halves
Half tsp thyme leaves
3 tbsp lemon juice
Black pepper
Chicken broth
2 tbsp butter
Garlic
2 cups rice

DIRECTIONS:
- Remove skin and bones from your chicken breast halves. Transfer chicken breast to Slow Cooker.
- In separate dish, whisk chicken stock and lime juice. Pour into Slow Cooker. Add minced garlic, chopped pepper, butter and thyme.
- Cover with the lid. Cook until tender (on LOW mode for 10 hours). In the end, stir in rice and continue to prepare for 15 more minutes.
- To serve, take the chicken out of Slow Cooker and serve on a large dish.

**Nutrition: Calories: 395 Fat: 9g Carbohydrates: 40g Protein: 37g**

## Turkey breast with herbs

Try this one as a main dish for a family meeting!

Prep time: 11 minutes  Cooking time: 4 hours
Servings: 6

INGREDIENTS:
2 tbsp softened butter
1 turkey breast half
Fresh parsley
Ground black pepper
Dried basil
Dried thyme
Garlic powder
1 tbsp soy sauce
Dried sage
Whipped cream cheese

DIRECTIONS:
- Grease your Slow Cooker, using simple unsalted butter.
- Do not remove the bone from turkey and place it into Slow Cooker.
- In a small bowl, combine parsley, whipped cream cheese, garlic powder, soy sauce, black pepper, sage, melted butter, basil and thyme.
- Mix well and pour the herb mixture over turkey. Rub the meat with your hands. Cover the lid of your Slow Cooker. Cook on LOW mode to 8 or 10 hours.

**Nutrition: Calories: 324 Fat: 8g Carbohydrates: 1g Protein: 60g**

## Spicy Buffalo Wings in Slow Cooker

Serve this with your favorite dressing!

Prep time: 26 minutes  Cooking time: 4 hours
Servings: 8

INGREDIENTS:
Half cup butter
1 bottle hot sauce
2 tsp dried oregano

Chicken wing sections
2 tsp garlic powder
2 tsp onion powder
Worcestershire sauce

DIRECTIONS:
- In a saucepan, whisk butter, hot pepper sauce, oregano, Worcestershire sauce, onion, garlic. Place saucepan over medium heat and bring to boil. Reduce to low and simmer for 6 minutes. Put chicken wings in greased and preheated Slow Cooker. Pour over with sauce.
- Cook for 4 hours: first 2 hours on HIGH and the second 2 – on LOW.
- Before serving, spread the wings over the baking sheet and cook for 30 minutes.

**Nutrition: Calories: 385 Fat: 34g Carbohydrates: 3g Protein: 16g**

## Slow Cooker Jambalaya

Hot and flavored homemade meal!

Prep time: 21 minutes  Cooking time: 8 hours
Servings: 12

INGREDIENTS:
Andouille sausage
2 tsp parsley
Dried oregano
1 large onion
1 tsp cayenne pepper
Dried thyme
Celery
2 tsp Cajun seasoning
1 green bell pepper
Cooked shrimp without tails
Canned tomatoes
One cup chicken broth

DIRECTIONS:
- Cut chicken breast and sausage into small cubes. Finely chop onion, celery and green bell pepper.
- Right in your Slow Cooker dish, mix sausage, chicken, onion, tomatoes (along with the juice), celery, and pepper.
- Pour in chicken broth and stir everything finely.
- Season with Cajun seasoning, oregano, cayenne pepper, parsley and thyme. Cook under cover for 4 hours on HIGH mode.
- Add shrimp during last 30 minutes of cooking.

**Nutrition: Calories: 235 Fat: 14g Carbohydrates: 6g Protein: 21g**

## Italian-styled creamy chicken

This is amazing to serve with hot rice or pasta!

Prep time: 9 minutes  Cooking time: 4 hours
Servings: 4

INGREDIENTS:
Unsalted butter
Half cup white wine
Onion cream cheese
Italian salad dressing mix
Golden mushroom soup
4 chicken breast halves

DIRECTIONS:
- Remove the skin from chicken breasts. If needed, remove the bones too. In a saucepan, melt unsalted butter and turn medium heat.
- Add cream cheese, the salad dressing mix, wine and mushroom soup. Stir until smooth. Grease your Slow Cooker and place chicken meat over its' bottom.
- Pour the saucepan sauce over the chicken meat.
- Cover and cook about 4 hours on LOW, until the chicken is tender.

**Nutrition: Calories: 456 Fat: 28g Carbohydrates: 13g Protein: 27g**

## Tortilla Soup with Duck

It tastes better than in a restaurant!

Prep time: 31 minutes  Cooking time: 5 hours
Servings: 8

INGREDIENTS:
Cooked and shredded duck
Vegetable oil
Canned and peeled tomatoes
7 corn tortillas
Canned enchilada sauce
Chopped cilantro
1 medium onion
Bay leaf
Green chili peppers
1 pack frozen corn
2 cloves garlic
Black pepper
1 cups water
Salt
Canned chicken broth
1 tsp chili powder
1 tsp cumin

DIRECTIONS:
- Combine duck meat, enchilada sauce, peeled tomatoes, garlic, chiles and green onions in your Slow Cooker.
- Pour in mixed water and broth.
- Add seasoning of mixed cumin, salt, chili powder, black pepper. Add bay leaf. In the end, add corn and cilantro.
- Turn on your Slow Cooker on LOW setting and prepare for 8 hours. Using an oven, slightly fry the tortillas and cut them into strips.
- Serve soup with tortillas.

**Nutrition:  Calories: 262 Fat: 11g Carbohydrates: 25g Protein: 18g**

## Chicken Fajitas in Slow Cooker

Perfect on cold days!

Prep time: 5 minutes  Cooking time: 7 hours
Servings: 16

INGREDIENTS:
2 chicken breasts
3 tbsp chunky salsa
1 medium onion
Chopped tomatoes
1 large green bell pepper
Guacamole

Shredded cheese
Sour cream
16 inch flour tortillas
Fajita seasoning mix
Cayenne pepper

DIRECTIONS:
- Grease your Slow Cooker with melted butter and place the chicken into it.
- Dice green bell pepper and onion and place the vegetables onto chicken in Slow Cooker.
- In separate bowl, mix sauce: combine fajita seasoning, salsa and cayenne pepper. Pour over the chicken.
- Place the lid on Slow Cooker and set to LOW mode. Cook for 7 hours.
- To serve, spoon the chicken mixture over each tortilla with a slotted spoon. Serve while hot.

**Nutrition: Calories: 332 Fat: 9g Carbohydrates: 43g Protein: 19g**

## Spice Chicken legs

This is so tasty and simple!

Prep time: 6 minutes Cooking time: 3 hours
Servings: 6

INGREDIENTS:
12 chicken drumsticks
Salt to taste
Half tsp onion powder
Black pepper
3 tbsp butter
Hot red pepper sauce
1-2 cups blue cheese salad dressing
Half tsp garlic powder

DIRECTIONS:
- Grease your Slow Cooker with some olive oil or melted unsalted butter.
- Put the chicken drumsticks into Slow Cooker and sprinkle with cubed unsalted butter. Pour in the red hot pepper sauce.
- Mix onion and garlic powders and salt/pepper. Season the chicken with spicy mixture. Cover the lid and cook for 3 hours on HIGH mode.
- Serve with blue cheese salad dressing.

**Nutrition: Calories: 685 Fat: 55g Carbohydrates: 6g Protein: 41g**

## Latin Chicken in Slow Cooker

The spicy mix gives this amazing taste and flavor!

Prep time: 27 minutes Cooking time: 4 hours
Servings: 6

INGREDIENTS:
Lime wedges
Olive oil
3 cloves garlic
Skinless chicken thighs
Ground cumin
Cilantro leaves
2 sweet potatoes
Hot salsa
Red bell pepper

Half cup chicken broth
2 cans black beans
Half tsp allspice

DIRECTIONS:
- Preheat the olive oil in the large skillet over the medium heat.
- Rub the chicken thighs with salt and pepper. Additionally, sprinkle with cilantro. Brown the chicken for 5 minutes on each side.
- Transfer the thighs to the Slow Cooker and arrange them all over its' bottom. Cover with chopped potatoes, black beans and red bell peppers.
- In a separate bowl, mix together cilantro leaves, chicken broth, cumin, salsa, garlic and allspice. Add to Slow Cooker.
- Cook on LOW mode for 4 hours. Serve with lime wedges.

**Nutrition: Calories: 591 Fat: 18g Carbohydrates: 57g Protein: 50g**

## Turkey for Thanksgiving

You can place ingredients into Slow Cooker in the morning, so the night will smell like Thanksgiving!

Prep time: 16 minutes Cooking time: 8 hours
Servings: 12

INGREDIENTS:
1 tsp dried sage
5 slices bacon
1 tbsp Worcestershire sauce
Canned turkey gravy
1 bone-in turkey breast
2 tbsp all-purpose flour
Half tsp garlic pepper

DIRECTIONS:
- Cook the bacon on medium heat until it is evenly brown. Cool, then drain and crumble. Spray your Slow Cooker with enough cooking spray.
- Transfer turkey to Slow Cooker.
- Mix garlic with pepper and season the turkey.
- In a small bowl, mix gravy, bacon, Worcestershire sauce, flour, sage. Pour over the meat in Slow Cooker.
- Cover the lid. Cook for 8 hours using LOW temperature mode.

**Nutrition: Calories: 382 Fat: 15g Carbohydrates: 3g Protein: 54g**

## Whole Baked Chicken

Amazing the people, who owned a large Slow Cooker!

Prep time: 22 minutes Cooking time: 10 hours
Servings: 11

INGREDIENTS:
Whole chicken
1 tsp paprika
Salt
Aluminum foil
Black pepper

DIRECTIONS:
- Make three balls out of foil. Place the balls into Slow Cooker.
- Rinse the chicken under cold running water. Drain and dry chicken, use the paper towels. Sprinkle the chicken with salt, paprika and freshly ground black pepper.

- Carefully arrange the chicken over the aluminum balls in Slow Cooker.
- Set your Slow Cooker to HIGH mode and cook the first hour, then turn on low temperature for 10 hours.

**Nutrition: Calories: 411 Fat: 29g Carbohydrates: 1g Protein: 35g**

## Boneless Turkey with Garlic and Herbs

Amazing for both Thanksgiving and simple family dinner!

**Prep time: 12 minutes Cooking time: 8 hours**
**Servings: 11**

INGREDIENTS:
1 tbsp dried oregano
garlic powder
Boneless turkey breast
Water
1 tbsp dried basil
Dry onion soup mix
Seasoned salt
Onion powder

DIRECTIONS:
- Grease your Slow Cooker and transfer the turkey into it. Whisk water with onion soup and pour carefully over turkey.
- In a bowl, stir onion powder and garlic powder, basil, seasoned salt, parsley, oregano. Sprinkle over the meat.
- Set your Slow Cooker to LOW regime and cook for 9 hours. You can serve it with mashed potatoes, pasta or rice.

**Nutrition: Calories: 468 Fat: 3g Carbohydrates: 6g Protein: 99g**

## Chicken Corn with Chili

These Great for a cold winter dinners!

**Prep time: 16 minutes Cooking time: 12 hours**
**Servings: 6**

INGREDIENTS:
2 chicken breasts
Canned pinto beans
Canned salsa
Mexican-style corn
2 tsp garlic powder
1 tsp ground cumin
Salt
1 tsp chili powder
Black pepper

DIRECTIONS:
- Remove skin and bones out of the chicken breasts. Grease your Slow Cooker with enough amount of olive oil. Rub the chicken with salsa and transfer to Slow Cooker.
- Season to your taste with chili powder, black pepper, cumin, salt, garlic powder. Turn on Slow Cooker and set to LOW. Cook for 7 hours.
- In 4 hours, shred the meat with two forks and add pinto beans and corn. Cook the remaining time.

**Nutrition: Calories: 188 Fat: 3g Carbohydrates: 23g Protein: 21g**

## Barbeque Goose for Sandwich

Easy and fast goose receipt!

**Prep time: 7 minutes Cooking time: 6 hours**
**Servings: 3**

INGREDIENTS:
2 tbsp butter
1 goose breast
2 cups chicken broth
1 clove garlic
2 tbsp Worcestershire sauce
1 yellow onion

DIRECTIONS:
- Finely mince 1 clove garlic. Slice one small yellow onion.
- In a large saucepan, melt unsalted butter (use medium heat). Cook onion and garlic just for 5 minutes.
- Place goose breast into saucepan and cook until evenly browned. Transfer goose to Slow Cooker and sprinkle with Worcestershire sauce. Pour in chicken broth (just to cover).
- Cook on HIGH temperature setting for 7 hours. Shred to serve.

**Nutrition: Calories: 200 Fat: 16g Carbohydrates: 5g Protein: 10g**

## Turkey Soup with Split Peas

Smoked turkey for those who do not like pork!

**Prep time: 21 minutes Cooking time: 4 hours**
**Servings: 8**

INGREDIENTS:
One onion
Dried split peas
3 small carrots
Dried oregano
Celery
Half tsp garlic powder
3 cups chicken broth
Smoked turkey legs
2 bay leaves
Water
2 potatoes

DIRECTIONS:
- Finely chop onion, celery and carrot. Place smoked turkey legs to Slow Cooker.
- In a large bowl, combine peas, carrots, potatoes, celery and onion. Top the turkey with vegetable mix.
- Pour in water and chicken broth.
- Season with oregano and garlic powder. Add bay leaves. Cook on HIGH mode for 5 hours.

**Nutrition: Calories: 613 Fat: 18g Carbohydrates: 50g Protein: 63g**

## Classic Pheasants for Slow Cooker

Very simple and fast receipt for tender meat!

**Prep time: 21 minutes Cooking time: 5 hours**
**Servings: 16**

INGREDIENTS:
One small onion

4 small pheasants
Canned sliced mushrooms
Sliced bacon
Salt
One cup water
Black pepper
Dry onion soup mix
One cup sour cream
Cream of mushroom soup

DIRECTIONS:
- Slice bacon and finely chop small onion.
- Grease your Slow Cooker with melted and unsalted butter. Clean and rinse peasants. Place birds into Slow Cooker.
- Cover the pheasants with sliced bacon. Try to cover the birds as much as you can.
- In a bowl, whisk sour cream, condensed soup, water, finely chopped onion, mushrooms and onion soup mix. Add some salt and pepper and pour over pheasants.
- Cook for 9 hours on LOW temperature mode.

**Nutrition: Calories: 256 Fat: 18g Carbohydrates: 4g Protein: 20g**

## Cornish Hens in Plum Glazing

Try this as a holiday meal!

Prep time: 11 minutes Cooking time: 8 hours
Servings: 6

INGREDIENTS:
Half tsp crushed red pepper flakes
3 Cornish game hens
Dry onion soup mix
Plum jam
2 kiwi fruits

DIRECTIONS:
- Slightly grease your Slow Cooker.
- Place the game hens into cooking dish and sprinkle over with red pepper flakes. In a bowl, mix onion soup mix and plum jam. Brush the mixture over the hens.
- Turn on Slow Cooker and set to LOW temperature regime. Cook for 8 hours. Serve the hens garnished with kiwi slices.

**Nutrition: Calories: 437 Fat: 22g Carbohydrates: 35g Protein: 26g**

## Shredded Chicken in Barbeque Sauce

You can eat this as a main dish or as a sandwich ingredient!

Prep time: 11 minutes Cooking time: 8 hours
Servings: 5

INGREDIENTS:
Cup barbeque sauce
1 chicken breast
1 sweet onion

DIRECTIONS:
- Wash the chicken under cold running water. Remove skin and bones. Finely chop sweet onion.
- Grease your Slow Cooker with unsalted butter.
- Place chicken into Slow Cooker and set on HIGH. Prepare for 4 hours. Shred your chicken with two forks. Continue to cook for 2 more hours.

**Nutrition: Calories: 203 Fat: 2g Carbohydrates: 21g Protein: 22g**

## Whole Lemon Chicken in Slow Cooker

Simple dish for the lazy weekends!

Prep time: 17 minutes Cooking time: 8 hours
Servings: 6

INGREDIENTS:
1 tsp Worcestershire sauce
olive oil
Whole chicken
1 tsp sesame oil
lemon juice
4 tbsp honey
2 cloves garlic
5 tbsp soy sauce

DIRECTIONS:
- First of all, wash the chicken and remove the skin. If needed, empty inner cavity. Remove excess liquid with paper towel.
- Grease Slow Cooker with olive oil. Place the chicken into Slow Cooker.
- In a bowl, whisk together soy sauce, chicken broth, honey, Soy sauce, Worcestershire sauce, lemon juice, balsamic vinegar, garlic and sesame oil.
- Pour the sauce mixture over chicken.
- Cover the lid and cook for 8 hours on LOW mode.

**Nutrition: Calories: 393 Fat: 28g Carbohydrates: 15g Protein: 22g**

## Buffalo Soup with Chicken Wings

A true Buffalo dish just matching for Slow Cooker!

Prep time: 19 minutes Cooking time: 7 hours
Servings: 9

INGREDIENTS:
6 cups sour cream
4 carrots
3 cans cream of chicken soup
3 celery stalks
2 chicken breast halves
3 potatoes
Blue cheese
Hot pepper sauce

DIRECTIONS:
- In a saucepan filled with water, cook chicken breasts. Shred and drain. Dice carrots and celery stalks. Peel and cube the potatoes.
- In a bowl, combine sour cream, cream of chicken soup, hot pepper sauce, chicken meat, celery, carrots and potatoes.
- Stir well and transfer to Slow Cooker.
- Cover and set to LOW. Cook for 6 hours. Stir time after time. When it is one hour left, stir in blue cheese.

**Nutrition: Calories: 634 Fat: 42g Carbohydrates: 36g Protein: 28g**

# BEANS & GRAINS RECIPES

## Prawns in Moong Dal

*Ready in about:* **25 minutes | Serves: 6 | Per Serving: Calories 255; Carbs 41g; Fat 3g; Protein 32g**

INGREDIENTS
2 ½ cups Moong Dal
1 pound Tiger Prawns, frozen
1 cup Leeks, chopped
½ tbsp Miso paste
2 Bell Peppers, stemmed, cored, and chopped
3 ½ cups Vegetable Stock
2 tbsp Grapeseed Oil
2 ripe Plum Tomatoes, chopped
1 tsp Molasses
1 tsp Sea Salt
¼ tsp ground Black Pepper
½ tsp Cumin powder

DIRECTIONS
- Heat oil on SAUTÉ at High, and stir-fry the prawns, leeks and peppers for 4 minutes. Place prawns aside. Add the rest of the
- Ingredients, seal the lid, and cook on BEANS/CHILI for 15 minutes at High. Once the cooking is over, do a quick pressure release. Add in the prawns and serve immediately.

## Herby White Bean and Corn Dip

*Ready in about:* **30 minutes | Serves: 12 | Per serving: Calories 150; Carbs 19g; Fat 5g; Protein 8g**

INGREDIENTS
1 cup fresh Corn Kernels
5 cups Water
1 pound White Beans, rinsed and drained
1 cup Onion, finely chopped
½ tsp Celery seeds
4 Garlic Cloves, minced
2 tbsp Vegetable Oil
½ tsp Sea Salt
¼ tsp ground Black Pepper
½ tsp Cumin Seeds
1 cup mild Picante sauce
1 Garlic Clove, crushed

DIRECTIONS
- Place the beans and pour water into the pressure cooker. Seal the lid, select BEANS/CHILI and cook for 25 minutes at High. Meanwhile, in a saucepan, cook the remaining ingredients for about 5 minutes.
- Once the cooking is complete, do a quick pressure release. Add in the sautéed mixture. Give it a good stir and blend the mixture in a blender or a food processor, in batches.

## Delicious Yellow Split Lentil Beef Stew

*Ready in about:* **30 minutes | Serves: 4 | Per serving: Calories 343; Carbs 45g; Fat 5g; Protein 21g**

INGREDIENTS
1 ½ cups Yellow Split Lentils, rinsed
½ pound Beef Stew Meat, cubed
1 cup Scallions, chopped
2 Garlic Cloves, minced
4 Potatoes, peeled and diced
1 cup Carrots, chopped
3 tsp Vegetable Oil
1 cup Celery, chopped
5 cups Chicken Stock
Sea Salt and Black Pepper, to taste
1 tsp Saffron

DIRECTIONS
- Heat oil on SAUTÉ at High, and cook scallions and garlic for 2 minutes. Add meat and cook for another 5 minutes, until slightly browned.
- Add the remaining ingredients, seal the lid and set on BEANS/CHILI. Cook for 20 minutes at High pressure. When ready, do a quick pressure release. Serve immediately.

## Celery and Cheese Chickpea Stew

*Ready in about:* **30 minutes | Serves: 4 | Per serving: Calories 355; Carbs 48g; Fat 9g; Protein 18g**

INGREDIENTS
2 cups Chickpeas, soaked 1 fennel bulb, chopped
½ cup Parmesan cheese, finely grated
½ cup Scallions, chopped
3 tsp Olive Oil
3 Cloves Garlic, minced
Salt and ground Black Pepper
4 cups Water

DIRECTIONS
- Select SAUTÉ at High and heat the oil. Add in the garlic, fennel, scallions and sauté until tender. Then, add in the remaining ingredients, except for the cheese.
- Seal the lid, press BEANS/CHILI and cook for 20 minutes at High pressure. Once the cooking is done, do a quick pressure release. Serve topped with grated Parmesan cheese.

## Meatless Lasagna

*Ready in about:* **1 hour | Serves: 6 | Per serving: Calories 325; Carbs 29g; Fat 19g; Protein 11g**

INGREDIENTS
1 ¼ cups Mushrooms, thinly sliced

1 ½ jars Pasta Sauce
1 tsp Cayenne Pepper
2 tsp dried Basil
1 tsp dried Rosemary
1 tsp Red Pepper flakes
½ tsp dried Oregano
½ tsp Sea Salt
1 ½ cups Cream Cheese
½ tsp ground Black Pepper
1 ½ packages pre-baked Lasagne Noodles

DIRECTIONS

- Place two lasagne shells at the bottom of a baking dish. Spread the pasta sauce. Add a layer of cream cheese on top. Arrange sliced fresh mushrooms over the cheese layer.
- Sprinkle with spices and herbs. Repeat the layering until you have used all ingredients.
- Place a trivet and pour 1 cup of water. Lower the dish onto the trivet. Seal the lid and cook for 45 minutes at High pressure on MEAT/STEW. Do a quick pressure release, and serve immediately.

## Banana and Fig Millet

**Ready in about:** 20 minutes | **Serves:** 6 | **Per serving:** Calories 363; Carbs 53g; Fat 8g; Protein 9g

INGREDIENTS

2 cups Millet
1 cup Milk
2 Bananas, sliced
¼ cup dried Figs, chopped
½ tsp Vanilla
½ tsp Cinnamon
2 tbsp Coconut Oil
2 cups Water
A pinch of Salt

DIRECTIONS

- Combine all ingredients, except the bananas, in your pressure cooker.
- Seal the lid, and cook for 10 minutes on BEANS/CHILI mode at High pressure. When ready, let the pressure drop naturally, for about 10 minutes. Serve topped with banana slices.

## Parsley Pureed Navy Beans

**Ready in about:** 35 minutes | **Serves:** 6 | **Per serving:** Calories 302; Carbs 45g; Fat 2g; Protein 18g

INGREDIENTS

1 ½ cups Water
1 ½ tsp Garlic powder
1 cup Red Onions, peeled and chopped
2 ¼ cups dry Pinto Beans, soaked
3 tsp Vegetable Oil
¼ tsp Black Pepper
1 tsp Chipotle powder
¼ tsp Red Pepper
½ tsp Sea Salt
½ cup fresh Cilantro, roughly chopped

DIRECTIONS

- Heat the oil on SAUTÉ at High. Cook the onions, cilantro, garlic, and chipotle powders, for about 2-3 minutes. Add in the beans and the water. Season with salt, black and red pepper.
- Seal the lid, select BEANS/CHILI mode and cook for 25 minutes at High pressure.
- Do a quick release. Puree the beans using a potato masher. Season with black pepper and salt.

## Mexican-Style Black Bean and Avocado Salad

**Ready in about:** 35 minutes | **Serves:** 4 | **Per serving:** Calories 485; Carbs 62g; Fat 29g; Protein 19g

INGREDIENTS

1 tsp Garlic, smashed
2 Avocados, diced
½ tsp freshly cracked Black Pepper
1 tsp Salt
2 tbsp Wine Vinegar
½ cup fresh Cilantro, chopped
1 tsp dried Dill Weed
¼ tsp hot Pepper Sauce
¼ tsp Chili powder
1 tbsp ground Cumin
½ cup Olive Oil
2 cups Black Beans, soaked overnight
1 ½ cups Water
1 Lime, juiced
1 cup Red Onions, peeled and coarsely chopped

DIRECTIONS

- Pour water and add black beans in the pressure cooker. Select BEANS/CHILI mode and cook for 25 minutes at High Pressure. Do a quick pressure release, and drain the beans.
- Add in the remaining ingredients. Serve chilled with diced avocado.

## Rosemary Goat Cheese Barley

**Ready in about:** 30 minutes | **Serves:** 6 | **Per serving:** Calories 570; Carbs 53g; Fat 31g; Protein 21g

INGREDIENTS

2 cups Barley
6 cups Stock
1 Butter Stick, melted
1 cup Spring Onions, chopped
½ cup Goat Cheese
¼ tsp Black Pepper
½ tsp Salt
2 tsp Rosemary

DIRECTIONS

- Melt butter on SAUTÉ at High. Add onions and cook until soft, for about 3 minutes. Stir in the remaining ingredients, except the cheese. Seal the lid and cook for 15 minutes on BEANS/CHILI at High pressure.
- When ready, do a quick pressure release. Stir in the goat cheese and serve.

## African Lentil Dip

**Ready in about: 15 minutes | Serves: 12 | Per serving:**
**Calories 185; Carbs 19g; Fat 7g; Protein 12g**

INGREDIENTS
2 cups dry Green Lentils, rinsed
½ tsp Dukkah
3 Garlic Cloves, minced
¼ cup Tomato Paste
2 tbsp tahini
2 tbsp Vegetable Oil
1 tsp Maple Syrup
½ tsp ground Black Pepper
1 tsp Salt
1 tsp dry Thyme, minced
¼ tsp Cardamom
4 cups Water

DIRECTIONS
- Pour 4 cups water, and add lentils to the pressure cooker. Cook on BEANS/CHILI for 5 minutes at High.
- When ready, allow for a natural pressure release, for 10 minutes. Stir in the remaining ingredients, and serve.

## Quinoa Pilaf with Cherries

**Ready in about: 20 minutes | Serves: 4 | Per serving:**
**Calories 281; Carbs 44g; Fat 7g; Protein 11g**

INGREDIENTS
1 ½ cups Quinoa
½ cup Almonds, sliced
¼ cup Cherries, chopped 1 Celery Stalk, chopped
½ Onion, chopped
14 ounces Chicken Broth
¼ cup Water
1 tbsp Butter

DIRECTIONS
- Melt butter on SAUTÉ at High, and cook the onions for 2 minutes, until translucent. Add celery and cook for 2 more, until soft. Stir in the remaining ingredients. Seal the lid and cook for 8 minutes on RICE/RISOTTO at High.
- Release the pressure quickly and serve.

## Bean and Bacon Dip

**Ready in about: 30 minutes | Serves: 12 | Per serving: Calories 105; Carbs 12g; Fat 4g; Protein 5g**

INGREDIENTS
20 ounces frozen Lima Beans
4 Bacon slices, cooked and crumbled
3 tsp Butter, melted
½ tsp Cayenne Pepper
Salt and Black Pepper, to taste
Water, as needed

DIRECTIONS
- Place the beans in the pressure cooker and cover with water. Seal the lid and cook on BEANS/CHILI for 25 minutes at High. Do a quick pressure release. Transfer to a food processor along with the remaining ingredients.
- Process until smooth.

## Cinnamon Bulgur with Pecans

**Ready in about: 20 minutes | Serves: 8 | Per serving:**
**Calories 105; Carbs 21g; Fat 2g; Protein 2g**

INGREDIENTS
2 cups Bulgur Wheat
¼ cup Pecans, chopped
½ tsp Cloves
1 tsp Cinnamon
¼ tsp Nutmeg
½ cup Honey
6 cups Water

DIRECTIONS
- Place all ingredients in your pressure cooker. Stir to combine well. Seal the lid and cook on BEANS/CHILI mode for 15 minutes at High. When ready, do a quick pressure release.

## Peach Quinoa Pudding

**Ready in about: 20 minutes | Serves: 4 | Per serving:**
**Calories 456; Carbs 76g; Fat 10g; Protein 16g**

INGREDIENTS
2 cups Quinoa
2 Peaches, diced
2 tbsp Raisins
2 cups Milk
2 tsp Peanut Oil
½ tsp Cardamom
2 cups Water
A pinch of Nutmeg
A pinch of Ground Star Anise
2 tbsp Honey

DIRECTIONS
- Combine all ingredients, except peaches and honey, in the pressure cooker. Seal the lid and cook on RICE/RISOTTO for 13 minutes, at High. Quick-release the pressure, and stir in the peaches.
- Drizzled with honey.

## Mushroom and Farro Beans

**Ready in about: 25 minutes | Serves: 4 | Per serving:**
**Calories 408; Carbs 75g; Fat 3g; Protein 23g**

INGREDIENTS
1 ¼ cups Navy Beans
¾ cup Farro
2 ½ cups Mushrooms, sliced
4 Green Onions, chopped
1 tsp Garlic, minced
½ Jalapeno, minced
1 cup Tomatoes, diced
3 cups Chicken Broth

DIRECTIONS
- Combine all ingredients in your pressure cooker. Seal the lid and cook on BEANS/CHILI mode for 25 minutes at High pressure. When ready, do a quick pressure release.

## Pear and Almond Oatmeal

**Ready in about: 15 minutes | Serves: 4 | Per serving: Calories 180; Carbs 42g; Fat 5g; Protein 8g**

INGREDIENTS
½ cup Almonds, chopped
1 ½ cups Oats
½ cup Milk
2 ½ cups Water
2 Pears, sliced
1 tbsp Maple Syrup
2 tsp Butter
½ tsp Vanilla
A pinch of Sea Salt

DIRECTIONS
- Place all ingredients, except the pears, in the pressure cooker. Seal the lid and cook for 8 minutes on RICE/RISOTTO mode at High.
- Do a quick pressure release. Top with pears, to serve.

## Kidney Beans with Bacon and Tomatoes

**Ready in about: 35 minutes | Serves: 4 | Per serving: Calories 173; Carbs 6g; Fat 14g; Protein 6g**

INGREDIENTS
2 cups Kidney Beans, soaked overnight
1 ½ cups Tomatoes, chopped
4 Bacon slices, diced
4 cups Water
½ cup Cumin
1 tsp Rosemary
Salt and Black Pepper, to taste

DIRECTIONS
- Cook bacon on SAUTÉ at High until crispy, for about 3 minutes. Set aside. Add tomatoes, cumin, and rosemary, and cook for 2 minutes. Stir in the remaining ingredients and seal the lid.
- Cook for 25 minutes on BEANS/CHILI mode at High. When ready, do a quick pressure release. Transfer to a bowl and stir in the bacon. Serve and enjoy!

## Navy Beans with Ground Beef

**Ready in about: 25 minutes | Serves: 8 | Per serving: Calories 196; Carbs 6g; Fat 11g; Protein 18g**

INGREDIENTS
2 pounds canned Navy Beans
1 pound mixed Ground Beef
½ cup Cheddar Cheese, shredded
1 tsp Garlic, minced
2 tbsp Onion, chopped
1 tbsp Olive Oil
3 cups Water
Salt and Black Pepper, to taste

DIRECTIONS
- Heat oil on SAUTÉ mode at High, add onion and garlic and cook for 2 minutes, until soft and fragrant. Add meat and cook until browned, for a few minutes.
- Stir the remaining ingredients. Seal the lid, and cook for 10 minutes on BEANS/CHILI at High. Do a quick release.

## Curried Chickpeas

**Ready in about: 40 minutes | Serves: 8 | Per serving: Calories 341; Carbs 53g; Fat 8g; Protein 16g**

INGREDIENTS
3 cups Chickpeas, soaked and rinsed
2 Tomatoes, chopped
2 Onions, chopped
2 tbsp Curry Powder
2 tbsp Oil
2 tsp Garlic, minced
½ tsp Cumin
2 tsp Chipotle Powder
Salt and Black Pepper, to taste
Water, as needed

DIRECTIONS
- Place the chickpeas, salt, pepper, and 1 tbsp oil in the pressure cooker. Cover with water and seal the lid. Cook for 30 minutes on BEANS/CHILI mode at High pressure.
- When ready, do a quick pressure release. Stir in the remaining ingredients. Cook for 5 more minutes, on SAUTÉ mode at High, with the lid off. Serve and enjoy!

## Mixed Bean Italian Sausage Chili

**Ready in about: 35 minutes | Serves: 8 | Per serving: Calories 335; Carbs 47g; Fat 10g; Protein 18g**

INGREDIENTS
4 Italian Sausages, sliced
1 ½ cups Black Beans, soaked, drained and rinsed
1 ½ cups Pinto Beans, soaked, drained and rinsed
2 Red Bell Peppers, deveined and thinly sliced
4 cups Chicken Broth
2 Tomatoes, chopped
2 tbsp Ketchup
3 tsp Vegetable Oil
2 Carrots, chopped into sticks
1 tsp Chili Pepper, minced
½ tsp ground Black Pepper
½ tsp Sea Salt, to taste
1 cup Green Onions, chopped
3 Cloves Garlic, minced
1 Bay Leaf

DIRECTIONS
- Heat oil on SAUTÉ at High. Add in sausage and brown for 3-5 minutes. Stir in the onions and garlic and keep stirring for another 2-3 minutes, until tender.
- Add in the remaining ingredients, and cook for 20 minutes BEANS/CHILI at High pressure. Do a quick pressure release.

## Navy Bean Dip

**Ready in about: 35 minutes | Serves: 12 | Per serving: Calories 103; Carbs 11g; Fat 2g; Protein 3g**

INGREDIENTS
¼ cup Jalapenos, seeded and chopped

3 cups navy Beans, soaked and rinsed
2 Red Onions, peeled and chopped
2 ripe Tomatoes, chopped
2 tbsp Cilantro, chopped
2 tbsp Olive Oil
2 tbsp lime juice
Salt and Black Pepper, to taste
6 cups Water
Pita crackers, to serve

DIRECTIONS
- Add beans with 6 cups of water in your pressure cooker. Seal the lid and select BEANS/CHILI mode for 30 minutes at High Pressure. Once the cooking is complete, do a quick pressure release.
- Transfer to a bowl and add the rest of the ingredients. Puree cooled mixture with an immersion blender until smooth, working in batches and serve with pita crackers.

## Cannellini Beans Chili

Ready in about: **25 minutes** | Serves: **4** | Per serving: Calories 261; Carbs 41g; Fat 9g; Protein 6g

INGREDIENTS
2 cups Cannellini Beans, soaked overnight
1 cup Red Onions, chopped
4 ½ cups Water
1 cup canned Corn, drained
½ cup Cilantro, chopped
1 tsp Cumin
1 tsp Chili Powder
1 tsp Garlic, minced
Salt and Pepper, to taste
2 tbsp Olive Oil
2 Tomatoes, chopped

DIRECTIONS
- On SAUTÉ, heat oil and cook onion, garlic, cumin, and chili powder for 3 minutes, stirring frequently. Pour in water, and add tomatoes and beans. Seal the lid, and set to BEANS/CHILI for 30 minutes at High.
- Do a quick release. Adjust the seasoning. Ladle into bowls and serve garnished with corn.

## Ham and Parmesan Grits

Ready in about: **30 minutes** | Serves: **6** | Per serving: Calories 296; Carbs 9g; Fat 21g; Protein 17g

INGREDIENTS
1 cup Quick-Cooking Grits
1 cup grated Parmesan Cheese
10 ounces cooked Ham, diced
2 Eggs, whisked
½ Butter Stick
1 Shallot, chopped
1 tsp Paprika
Salt and Pepper, to taste
3 cups Water

DIRECTIONS
- Melt the butter, and brown the ham on SAUTÉ mode at High. Stir in the shallots and spices and cook for 2 minutes. Add the grits and pour the water.
- Seal the lid, and cook for 13 minutes on RICE/RISOTTO mode, at High. Do a quick pressure release, and stir in the parmesan and eggs. Seal again, and cook for 3 minutes at High. Do a quick release and serve.

## Black Bean and Mushroom Spread

Ready in about: **25 minutes** | Serves: **6** | Per serving: Calories 256; Carbs 43g; Fat 3g; Protein 16g

INGREDIENTS
2 cups Black Beans, soaked and rinsed
1 cup Porcini Mushrooms, sliced
1 cup Red Onions, chopped
2 ½ cups Water
2 cups Beef Broth
1 ½ tsp Paprika
1 tbsp Butter
1 tsp Rosemary
½ tsp Cumin
Salt and Black Pepper

DIRECTIONS
- Melt butter and sauté the onions for a few minutes, until soft, on SAUTÉ mode at High. Add mushrooms and cook for 3 more minutes, until tender. Stir in the remaining ingredients and seal the lid.
- Cook on BEANS/CHILI for 25 minutes at High. When ready, do a quick pressure release. Drain and transfer to a food processor. Pulse until smooth.

## Farmer's Meal

Ready in about: **25 minutes** | Serves: **4** | Per serving: Calories 215; Carbs 3g; Fat 7g; Protein 16g

INGREDIENTS
½ cup Barley
½ pound cooked Ham, chopped
1 cup Mushrooms, sliced
1 cup Bell Peppers, chopped
2 tbsp Butter
2 Green Onions, chopped
2 cups Veggie Stock
1 tsp Ginger, minced
¼ cup Celery, chopped
Salt and Pepper, to taste

DIRECTIONS
- Melt the butter on SAUTÉ mode at High, add the onions and cook for 3 minutes, until soft. Stir in mushrooms, celery, and bell peppers, and cook for 3 more minutes, until tender.
- Add ham and ginger and cook for 1 minute. Stir in the remaining ingredients. Seal the lid and cook on RICE/RISOTTO for 13 minutes at High. When cooking is over, release the pressure quickly.

## Butter Bean and Kale Stew

Ready in about: **30 minutes** | Serves: **6** | Per serving: Calories 394; Carbs 57g; Fat 8g; Protein 18g

INGREDIENTS
2 cups Butter Beans, soaked overnight

1 cup Spinach
2 cups Vegetable Stock
2 Cloves Garlic, peeled and smashed
2 tbsp Olive Oil
2 Shallots, chopped
1 can Tomatoes, crushed
¼ tsp ground Black Pepper
2 sprigs fresh Rosemary, finely chopped
1 tsp Salt
4 cups Water
DIRECTIONS
- Place butter beans in the pressure cooker and pour the water. Seal the lid, select BEANS/CHILI, at High Pressure for 15 minutes. Do a quick pressure release. Drain and rinse beans under cold water.
- Discard cooking liquid, and set aside. Warm the oil on SAUTÉ mode at High and cook shallots and garlic for 3 minutes. Add in the tomatoes, stock, and rinsed beans; season to taste. Seal the lid and set to High.
- Cook for 10 minutes. Quick release the pressure. Stir in kale and rosemary, and cook until kale wilts.

## Mushroom and Parmesan Barley

Ready in about: **45 minutes** | Serves: **4** | Per serving: Calories 385; Carbs 48g; Fat 16g; Protein 16g

INGREDIENTS
3 cups Chicken Broth
1 cup Barley
½ cup Parmesan Cheese, grated
1 pound Mushrooms, sliced
1 Onion, chopped
3 tbsp Olive Oil
2 tbsp Thyme
1 tsp Garlic, minced
DIRECTIONS
- Heat oil in on SAUTÉ at High. Stir in the onions and cook for 2 minutes, until soft. Add garlic and cook for 1 more, until fragrant. Stir in the mushrooms and cook for 4 more minutes, until soft.
- Stir in the remaining ingredients, except the cheese. Seal the lid, and cook for 8 minutes on RICE/RISOTTO at High pressure. Do a natural release, for 10 minutes. Stir in the parmesan, and serve immediately.

## Tasty Three-Bean Stew

Ready in about: **30 minutes** | Serves: **6** | Per serving: Calories 455; Carbs 73g; Fat 13g; Protein 19g

INGREDIENTS
½ cup Pinto Beans, soaked overnight
½ cup Black Beans, soaked overnight
½ cup Cannellini Beans, soaked overnight
2 Bell Peppers, deveined and chopped
2 tbsp Olive Oil
2 Onions, chopped
1 (14 oz) can Tomatoes, crushed
1 tbsp Garlic paste
Sea Salt and freshly ground Black Pepper, to taste
4 cups Water

1 Avocado, sliced, to serve
DIRECTIONS
- Add the water, beans, oil, bell peppers, tomatoes, garlic paste, and onions to the pressure cooker. Season to taste. Seal the lid. Select BEANS/CHILI mode and cook for 25 minutes at High pressure.
- Once the cooking is over, do a quick pressure release. Serve topped with avocado slices.

## Simple Cornbread

Ready in about: **40 minutes** | Serves: **4** | Per serving: Calories 423; Carbs 41g; Fat 21g; Protein 12g

INGREDIENTS
1 ¼ cup Cornmeal
1 cup Buttermilk
½ Butter Stick, melted
2 Eggs, beaten
½ cup Water
½ tsp Salt
1 tsp Baking Powder
DIRECTIONS
- Combine the dry ingredients in one bowl. Whisk the wet ones in another bowl. Gently stir in the wet ingredients into the dry ingredients. Transfer the mixture into a greased baking dish.
- Pour water in your pressure cooker and lower the trivet. Place the dish on top of the trivet, and seal the lid. Cook on SOUP for 30 minutes at High pressure. Do a quick release.

## Lemony Oats with Chia Seeds

Ready in about: **15 minutes** | Serves: **4** | Per serving: Calories 360; Carbs 59g; Fat 16g; Protein 13g

INGREDIENTS
1 ½ cups Lemon Juice
1 ½ cups Oats
½ cup Chia Seeds
3 tbsp Brown Sugar
1 tbsp Honey
A pinch of Salt
1 tbsp Butter
¼ tsp Lemon Zest
DIRECTIONS
- Melt the butter on SAUTÉ mode at High for 3 minutes. Stir in the remaining ingredients and seal the lid.
- Cook for 8 minutes on RICE/RISOTTO mode, at High. When ready, do a quick pressure release.

## Cheesy Chicken Quinoa

Ready in about: **20 minutes** | Serves: **4** | Per serving: Calories 484; Carbs 47g; Fat 20g; Protein 29g

INGREDIENTS
1 ½ cups Quinoa
2 ½ cups Chicken Broth
½ cup Cheddar Cheese, shredded
1 cup Chicken Breasts, cooked and shredded
1 cup Sour Cream
¼ cup Parmesan Cheese, grated

Salt and Black Pepper, to taste

DIRECTIONS
- Combine quinoa and broth in pressure cooker. Seal the lid and cook on RICE/RISOTTO for 8 minutes, at High. Do a quick pressure release.
- Stir in the remaining ingredients. Cook for 3 minutes, on SAUTÉ, lid off.

## Mouth-Watering Lima Beans

Ready in about: **20 minutes | Serves: 6 | Per serving: Calories 95; Carbs 9g; Fat; 2g Protein 3g**

INGREDIENTS
2 tsp Olive Oil
2 cups Lima Beans, soaked and rinsed
2 Cloves Garlic, finely minced
½ tsp ground Black Pepper
½ tsp ground Bay Leaf
½ tsp Salt
4 cups Water

DIRECTIONS
- Put all ingredients in the pressure cooker. Select BEANS/CHILI mode, and cook for 15 minutes at High pressure. Once done, do a quick pressure release. Discard bay leaf and serve hot.

## Pearl Barley with Mushrooms

Ready in about: **25 minutes | Serves: 4 | Per serving: Calories 265; Carbs 41g; Fat 1g; Protein 19g**

INGREDIENTS
½ tbsp Shallot powder
1 tsp Jalapeno Pepper, finely minced
1 tbsp Garlic, smashed
¾ cup Pearl Barley
1 ¼ cups dried navy Beans
4 Green Onions, chopped
1 cup Tomatoes, diced
2 cups Mushrooms, thinly sliced
2 cups Vegetable Broth

DIRECTIONS
- In the pressure cooker, add all ingredients, except for the tomatoes. Select BEANS/CHILI mode and cook for 25 minutes at High pressure.
- Do a quick pressure release. Stir in the diced tomatoes, and serve.

## Cheesy Sausage and Egg Bundt Cake

Ready in about: **25 minutes | Serves: 6 | Per serving: Calories 381; Carbs 14g; Fat 26g; Protein 25g**

INGREDIENTS
8 Eggs, cracked into a bowl
8 oz Breakfast Sausage, chopped
3 Bacon Slices, chopped
1 large Green Bell Pepper, chopped
1 large Red Bell Pepper, chopped
1 cup chopped Green Onion
1 cup grated Cheddar Cheese
1 tsp Red Chili Flakes
Salt and Black Pepper to taste
½ cup Milk
4 slices Bread, cut into ½ -inch cubes
2 cups Water

DIRECTIONS
- Whisk the eggs, sausage, bacon slices, green bell pepper, red bell pepper, green onion, chili flakes, cheddar cheese, salt, pepper, and milk in a bowl. Grease the bundt pan with cooking spray and pour in the egg mixture.
- After, drop the bread slices in the egg mixture all around while using a spoon to push them into the mixture.Pour water in the cooker, and fit the trivet at the center of the pot. Place bundt pan on the trivet and seal the lid.
- Select STEAM at High for 8 minutes. Once the timer goes off, do a quick pressure release. Use a napkin to gently remove the bundt pan onto a flat surface.
- Run a knife around the egg in the bundt pan, place a serving plate on the bundt pan, and then, turn the egg bundt over. Cut into slices, and serve with sauce of your choice.

# SOUPS AND STEWS

## Irish Lamb Stew

Ready in about: **25 minutes | Serves: 4 | Per serving: Calories 321; Carbs 29g; Fat 11g; Protein 25g**

INGREDIENTS
1 pound Lamb, cut into pieces
1 Onion, sliced
2 tbsp Cornstarch or Arrowroot
1 ½ tbsp Olive Oil
2 Sweet Potatoes, cut into cubes
3 Carrots, chopped
2 ½ cups Veggie Broth
½ tsp dried Thyme

DIRECTIONS
- Season lamb with salt and pepper. On SAUTÉ mode at High, heat olive oil and sear the lamb until browned on all sides, about 4-5 minute. Add all remaining ingredients, except for the cornstarch, and stir well to combine. Close the lid, turn the steaming vent clockwise to seal.
- Cook on BEANS/CHILI at High for 18 minutes. When ready, do a quick pressure release. Whisk the cornstarch with a little bit of

water and stir it into the stew. Cook on SAUTÉ at High for 3 more minutes, lid off. Serve hot.

## Spicy Beef and Potato Soup

⌀ Ready in about: **25 minutes** | Serves: **8** | Per serving: Calories 242; Carbs 27g; Fat 9g; Protein 14g

INGREDIENTS
1 pound Ground Beef
4 cups Water
24 ounces Tomato Sauce
2 cups Fresh Corn
1 tsp Salt
4 cups cubed Potatoes
1 Onion, chopped
½ tsp Hot Pepper Sauce
1 ½ tsp Black Pepper
3 tbsp Vegetable Oil
DIRECTIONS
- Heat the oil on SAUTÉ mode at High, and brown the beef for about 3-4 minutes. Add onions and cook for 2 more minutes. Stir in the remaining ingredients, and seal the lid.
- Cook on BEANS/CHILI mode, at High pressure for 12 minutes. Once the cooking is over, press CANCEL and do a quick pressure release, by turning the valve to "open" position.

## Creamy Curried Cauliflower Soup

⌀ Ready in about: **35 minutes** | Serves: **4** | Per serving: Calories 115; Carbs 20g; Fat 3g; Protein 3g

INGREDIENTS
1 Cauliflower Head, chopped
1 tbsp Curry Powder
½ tsp Turmeric Powder
1 Sweet Potato, diced
1 Onion, diced
1 Carrot, diced
1 cup Coconut Milk
2 cups Veggie Broth
½ tbsp Coconut Oil
DIRECTIONS
- Melt coconut oil on SAUTÉ at High, and cook onion and carrot until tender, 3-4 minutes. Season with salt and pepper. Add the rest of the ingredients, except milk, and stir to combine well.
- Seal the lid, set to BEANS/CHILI mode for 20 minutes at High pressure. When ready, do a quick pressure release. Blend the soup with immersion blender until smooth, and garnish with coconut milk to serve.

## Pressure Cooked Chili

⌀ Ready in about: **45 minutes** | Serves: **4** | Per serving: Calories 388; Carbs 15g; Fat 27g; Protein 22g

INGREDIENTS
1 pound Ground Beef
½ cup Beef Broth
1 Onion, diced
1 tbsp Olive Oil
28 ounces canned Tomatoes, undrained
½ tbsp Cumin
1 ½ tbsp Chili Powder
1 tsp Garlic Powder
2 tbsp Tomato Paste
DIRECTIONS
- On SAUTÉ at High, heat the oil and sauté the beef until browned, for about 4-5 minutes. Add onion, cumin, chili, garlic, tomato paste, and cook for 3-4 more minutes. Stir in tomatoes and beef broth.
- Seal the lid, set to BEANS/CHILI at High, and cook for 30 minutes. Do a quick pressure release, and serve hot.

## Pumpkin, Corn, and Chicken Chowder

⌀ Ready in about: **15 minutes** | Serves: **4** | Per serving: Calories 314; Carbs 17g; Fat 21g; Protein 15g

INGREDIENTS
2 Chicken Breasts
2 cups Corn, canned or frozen
1 Onion, diced
¼ tsp Pepper
½ cup Half & Half
15 ounces Pumpkin Puree
2 cups Chicken Broth
½ tsp dried Oregano
1 Garlic Clove, minced
A pinch of Nutmeg
A pinch of Red Pepper Flakes
2 Potatoes, cubed
2 tbsp Butter
DIRECTIONS
- Melt butter on SAUTÉ at High, and stir-fry onion, for 2-3 minutes. Stir in garlic and cook for an additional minute. Add in pumpkin puree, broth, potatoes, chicken, and all the seasonings.
- Close the lid, turn the steaming vent clockwise to seal. Cook for 10 minutes on BEANS/CHILI at High pressure. When it beeps, do a quick pressure release. Stir in the half & half and corn, and serve.

## Cheesy Swiss Chard Relish

⌀ Ready in about: **10 minutes** | Serves: **4** | Per serving: Calories 324; Carbs 4g; Fat 24g; Protein 22g

INGREDIENTS
½ pound Cheddar cheese, diced
3 cups Swiss chard, chopped
2 ½ cups stock
½ cup Onions, chopped
2 Cloves Garlic, crushed
1 tbsp dry Thyme
Sea Salt and ground Black Pepper, to taste
DIRECTIONS
- Cook onions and garlic for about 2 minutes, on SAUTÉ at High. Add the rest of the ingredients and seal the lid.
- Select BEANS/CHILI and cook for 5 minutes at High. Do a quick release the pressure, and serve.

## Spanish-Style Chorizo and Broccoli Soup

Ready in about: **15 minutes** | Serves: **6** | Per serving: Calories 205; Carbs 6g; Fat 10g; Protein 13g

INGREDIENTS
3 Spanish Chorizo, chopped
2 cups Broccoli, torn into pieces
½ lb. Zucchini, sliced
½ tsp Sugar
1 Red Onion, chopped
½ tsp dry Basil
1 tsp Red Pepper flakes, crushed
½ tsp dried Oregano
3 tsp Olive Oil
¼ cup sour cream
2 Cloves Garlic, peeled and minced
6 ½ cups Vegetable Broth
Salt and ground Black Pepper, to taste

DIRECTIONS
- Select SAUTÉ at High and heat the oil for a few minutes, then sauté the chorizo, garlic and onion. Cook the chorizo until brown. Add the remaining ingredients, except the sour cream.
- Seal the lid and cook for 5 minutes on BEANS/CHILI at High Pressure. Once cooking is complete, release the pressure quickly. Remove the lid and add the sour cream, stir and serve.

## Chicken Enchilada Soup

Ready in about: **40 minutes** | Serves: **8** | Per serving: Calories 397; Carbs 46g; Fat 5g; Protein 45g

INGREDIENTS
8 cups Butternut Squash, cubed
1 pound Chicken Breasts, boneless and skinless
8 ounces canned Tomato Soup
2 tsp Cumin
1 Onion, chopped
3 ½ ounces canned Chillies, chopped
2 tsp Taco Seasoning
2 tsp Salt
3 Russet Potatoes, quartered
3 Garlic Cloves, minced
4 cups Chicken Broth
30 ounces canned Cannellini Beans
1 Red Bell Pepper, chopped

DIRECTIONS
- Add all ingredients and stir to combine well. Select MEAT/STEW mode; and the time to 25 minutes. Lock the lid; turn the presed" position. When it beeps, press CANCEL and do a quick pressure release.
- Remove the chicken from the cooker to a bowl. With a hand blender, puree the soup until smooth. Shred the chicken with two forks and return to the soup. Adjust the seasoning and serve.

## Spicy Beef Chili with Worcestershire Sauce

Ready in about: **40 minutes** | Serves: **4** | Per serving: Calories 437; Carbs 15g; Fat 19g; Protein 38g

INGREDIENTS
2 lb Ground Beef
2 tbsp Olive Oil
1 large Red Bell Pepper, seeded and chopped
1 large Yellow Bell Pepper, seeded and chopped
1 White Onion, Chopped
2 cups Chopped Tomatoes
2 cups Beef Broth
2 Carrots, cut in little bits
2 tsp Onion Powder
2 tsp Garlic Powder
5 tsp Chili Powder
2 tbsp Worcestershire Sauce
2 tsp Paprika
½ tsp Cumin Powder
2 tbsp chopped Parsley
Salt and Black Pepper to taste

DIRECTIONS
- Select SAUTÉ mode at High, heat oil and add ground beef. Cook until browned, stirring occasionally, for about 8 minutes. Mix in the remaining ingredients.
- Seal the lid and cook on BEANS/CHILI at High for 20 minutes.
- Do a quick pressure release. Dish it into serving bowls. Serve with some crackers.

## Cream of Broccoli Soup

Ready in about: **25 minutes** | Serves: **6** | Per serving: Calories 523; Carbs 12g; Fat 39g; Protein 17g

INGREDIENTS
3 cups Heavy Cream
3 cups Vegetable Broth
4 tbsp Butter
4 tbsp All-purpose Flour
4 cups chopped Broccoli Florets, only the bushy tops
1 medium Red Onion, chopped
3 cloves Garlic, minced
1 tsp Italian Seasoning
Salt and Black Pepper to taste
1 ½ oz Cream Cheese
1 ½ cups grated Yellow and White Cheddar Cheese + extra for topping

DIRECTIONS
- Select SAUTÉ mode at High, and melt the butter. Add flour and use a spoon to stir until it clumps up. Gradually stir in the heavy cream until white sauce forms. Fetch out the butter sauce into a bowl and set aside.
- Press Cancel, and stir in onions, garlic, broth, broccoli, Italian seasoning, and cream cheese. Seal the lid and select BEANS/CHILI at High pressure for 15 minutes. Once the timer has ended, do a quick pressure release.
- Keep the pot in Warm mode and stir in butter sauce and cheddar cheese, salt, and pepper, until the cheese melts. Dish the soup into serving bowls, top it with extra cheese, and serve.

## Chicken & Pancetta Noodle Soup

**Ready in about: 35 minutes | Serves: 8 | Per serving:**
**Calories 419; Carbs 15g; Fat 19g; Protein 34g**

INGREDIENTS

5 oz dry Egg Noodles
4 Chicken Breasts, skinless and boneless
1 large White Onion, chopped
8 Pancetta Slices, chopped
4 cloves Garlic, minced
Salt and Black Pepper to taste
2 medium Carrots, sliced
2 cups sliced Celery
½ cup chopped Parsley
1 ½ tsp Dried Thyme
8 cups Chicken Broth

DIRECTIONS

- Select SAUTÉ mode at High. Cook the pancetta for 5 minutes until brown and crispy. Add the onion and garlic, and cook for 3 more minutes. Then, transfer the pancetta mixture with a slotted spoon to a plate and set aside.
- Remove the grease from the pot. Pour the pancetta mixture back into the pot and add chicken breasts, noodles, carrots, celery, chicken broth, thyme, salt, and pepper. Seal the lid, select BEANS/CHILI at High for 5 minutes.
- Once the timer has ended, do a quick pressure release. Remove the chicken onto a plate. Shred it with two forks and add it back to the soup. Stir well with a wooden spoon. Adjust the seasoning, and dish the soup into serving bowls. Sprinkle with cheddar cheese and serve with a side of bread.

## Fall Pumplin and Cauliflower Soup

**Ready in about: 35 minutes | Serves: 4 | Per serving:**
**Calories 183; Carbs 25g; Fat 5g; Protein 10g**

INGREDIENTS

2 tsp Olive Oil
1 large White Onion, chopped
4 cloves Garlic, minced
1 (2 pounds) Pumpkin, peeled, seeded, and cubed
2 heads Cauliflower, cut in florets
3 cups Chicken Broth
3 tsp Paprika
Salt and Black Pepper to taste
1 cup Milk, full **fat**

### Topping:

Grated Cheddar Cheese, Crumbled Bacon, Chopped Chives, Pumpkin Seeds

DIRECTIONS

- Select SAUTÉ at High. Heat olive oil, add the onion and sauté it for about 3 minutes, until soft. Then, add the garlic and cook until fragrant, for about 2 minutes. Stir in pumpkin, cauliflower, broth, paprika, pepper, and salt.
- Seal the lid, select BEANS/CHILI mode at High pressure for 10 minutes. Once the timer has ended, do a quick pressure release. Top the ingredients with the milk and use a stick blender to puree them.
- Adjust the seasoning, stir, and dish the soup into serving bowls. Add the toppings on the soup and serve warm.

## Pork Roast Green Chili

**Ready in about: 70 minutes | Serves: 6 | Per serving:**
**Calories 410; Carbs 16g; Fat 18g; Protein 38g**

INGREDIENTS

1 ½ lb Pork Roast, cut into 1-inch cubes
1 lb Tomatillos, husks removed
2 tbsp Olive Oil, divided into 2
1 bulb Garlic, tail sliced off
2 Green Chilies
3 cups Chicken Broth
1 Green Bell Pepper, seeded and roughly chopped
Salt and Pepper, to taste
½ tsp Cumin Powder
1 tsp dried Oregano
1 Bay Leaf
1 bunch Cilantro, chopped and divided into 2
2 Potatoes, peeled and cut into ½-inch cubes

DIRECTIONS

- Preheat an oven to 450 F. Put the garlic bulb on a baking tray and drizzle with olive oil. Add bell peppers, onion, green chilies, and tomatillos on the baking tray in a single layer. Tuck the tray in the oven and roast the veggies and spices for 25 minutes. Then, remove them from the oven to let cool.
- Peel the garlic with a knife and place it in a blender. Add the green bell pepper, tomatillos, onion, and green chilies to the blender. Pulse for a few minutes not to be smooth but slightly chunky.
- On the pressure cooker, select SAUTÉ mode. Heat the remaining oil. Season the pork with salt and pepper. Brown the pork in the oil, for about 5 minutes. Stir in oregano, cumin, bay leaf, green sauce, potatoes, and broth.
- Seal the lid, and select MEAT/STEW on High pressure for 35 minutes. Do a natural pressure release for 10 minutes. Remove and discard bay leaf, stir half of the cilantro, adjust with salt and pepper.
- Dish the chili into serving bowls and garnish with the remaining cilantro. Serve topped with a side of chips or crusted bread.

## Pepperoni and Vegetable Stew

**Ready in about: 35 minutes | Serves: 4 | Per serving:**
**Calories 435; Carbs 34g; Fat 31g; Protein 15g**

INGREDIENTS

3 tbsp Olive Oil
2 large White Onions, chopped
8 oz Pepperoni, sliced
2 Eggplants, cut in half moons
2 cups Vegetable Broth
2 cloves Garlic, minced
¾ lb Brussels Sprouts, halved
Salt and Black Pepper to taste
1 ½ lb Tomatoes, chopped
3 Zucchinis, quartered
¾ lb Green Beans

DIRECTIONS

- Select SAUTÉ mode at High. Warm 1 tbsp of oil, stir in onions, garlic, and pepperoni. Cook for 8 minutes. Sit in the remaining oil, eggplants, Brussel sprouts, tomatoes, zucchinis, beans, broth, salt, and pepper. Seal the lid.

- Select BEANS/CHILI mode at High pressure for 15 minutes. Once the timer has stopped, do a quick pressure release. Dish the stew into a serving bowl and serve with a side of braised bamboo shoots.

## Smoked Sausage and Seafood Stew

Ready in about: **40 minutes** | Serves: **8** | Per serving: Calories 465; Carbs 39g; Fat 21g; Protein 35g

INGREDIENTS
1 lb Halibut, skinless and cut into 1-inch pieces
1 lb medium Shrimp, peeled and deveined
2 lb Mussels, debearded and scrubbed
2 (16 oz) Clam Juice
6 cups Water
2 (8 oz) Smoked Sausage, sliced
1 cup White Wine
Salt and Black Pepper to taste
4 tbsp Olive Oil
4 cloves Garlic, minced
2 small Fennel Bulb, chopped
4 small Leeks, sliced
A little pinch Saffron
2 Bay Leaves
2 (28 oz) can Diced Tomatoes
4 tbsp chopped Parsley

DIRECTIONS
- Select SAUTÉ at High. Warm the oil, and cook sausages, fennel, and leeks, for 5 minutes stirring occasionally. Stir in garlic, saffron, and bay leaf, and wine, and cook for 2 minutes. Add tomatoes, clam juice, water, mussels, halibut, and shrimp. se the spoon to cover them with the sauce but don't stir. Seal the lid.
- Select BEANS/CHILI at High pressure for 15 minutes. Once the timer has ended, do a quick pressure release. Remove and discard the bay leaf. Add parsley, adjust the seasoning, and stir. Serve with a side of garlic bread.

## White Wine Red Peppers

Ready in about: **15 minutes** | Serves: **6** | Per serving: Calories 97; Carbs 7g; Fat 8g; Protein 2g

INGREDIENTS
1 ½ pounds Red Bell Peppers, deveined and sliced
1 cup Tomato Puree
½ cup Vegetable Broth
½ tbsp miso paste
1 tbsp Garlic, crushed
½ cup Green Onions, chopped
3 tbsp Butter, melted
Sea Salt and freshly ground Black Pepper
2 tbsp White Wine

DIRECTIONS
- Melt butter on SAUTÉ at High and sauté onions, until soft, for about 3 minutes. Add garlic and stir for about a minute, until fragrant. Pour broth, tomato and pesto sauce, salt, and pepper.
- Seal the lid, press BEANS/CHILI and cook for 10 minutes at High pressure. When ready, do a quick release. Season with salt, and black pepper. Serve drizzled with white wine.

## Ham and Pea Soup

Ready in about: **40 minutes** | Serves: **6** | Per serving: Calories 276; Carbs 46g; Fat 1g; Protein 19g

INGREDIENTS
1 Onion, diced
1 pound Split Peas, dried
2 Carrots, diced
8 cups Water
2 Celery Stalks, diced
1 pound Ham Chunks
1 ½ tsp dried Thyme

DIRECTIONS
- Put all ingredients in the pressure cooker. Seal the lid, and select SOUP at High. Cook for 20 minutes. Do a quick pressure release.
- Taste and adjust the seasoning. If you don't like the density, cook for an additional 10 minutes.

## Pomodoro Soup

Ready in about: **25 minutes** | Serves: **8** | Per serving: Calories 314; Carbs 16g; Fat 23g; Protein 11g

INGREDIENTS
3 pounds Tomatoes, peeled and quartered
1 Carrot, diced
1 Onion, diced
¼ cup Fresh Basil
1 cup Half & Half
1 tbsp Tomato Paste
3 tbsp Butter
½ tsp Salt
½ tsp Pepper
4 cups Chicken Broth
½ cup Parmesan Cheese, grated
1 tsp Garlic, minced

DIRECTIONS
- Melt the butter on SAUTÉ mode at High, and cook the onions, celery, garlic, and carrots until soft, for about 4 minutes. Stir in the remaining ingredients, except the cream and cheese.
- Seal the lid, select SOUP mode, and cook for 25 minutes at High pressure. When it goes off, do a quick pressure release. Stir in half & half and freshly grated Parmesan cheese.

## Skim and Fast Miso and Tofu Soup

Ready in about: **12 minutes** | Serves: **4** | Per serving: Calories 94; Carbs 4g; Fat 2g; Protein 4g

INGREDIENTS
4 cups Water
½ cup Corn
2 tbsp Miso Paste
1 Onion, sliced
1 tsp Wakame Flakes
1 cup Silken Tofu, cubed
2 Celery Stalks, chopped
2 Carrots, chopped
Soy Sauce, to taste

DIRECTIONS

- Add all ingredients, except for miso paste and soy sauce. Seal the lid, select BEANS/CHILI for 7 minutes at High pressure.
- Do a quick pressure release. Mix the miso paste with one cup of broth. Stir it into the soup. Add some soy sauce and stir. Ladle to serving bowls and serve.

## Navy Bean and Ham Shank Soup

Ready in about: **8 hours 30 minutes** | Serves: **12** | Per serving: **Calories 427, Carbs 49g, Fat 34g, Protein 36g**

INGREDIENTS
½ cup Vegetable Oil
4 cups dried Navy Beans
3 pounds Ham Shank
2 Onions, chopped
4 Carrots, sliced
½ cup minced Green Pepper
3 Quarts Water
2 cups Tomato Sauce
4 Celery Stalks, chopped
2 Garlic Cloves, minced
Salt and Pepper, to taste

DIRECTIONS
- Soak the beans in water overnight. Drain and discard water. Heat oil on SAUTÉ at High and cook onion, garlic, carrots, celery, salt, and pepper for 4-5 minutes, until tender. Stir in the remaining ingredients.
- Seal the lid and cook on BEANS/CHILI for 25 minutes at High. Do a quick pressure release, and serve.

## Lentil Soup

Ready in about: **30 minutes** | Serves: **4** | Per serving: **Calories 259; Carbs 35g; Fat 8g; Protein 13g**

INGREDIENTS
4 Garlic Cloves, minced
1 tsp Cumin
4 cups Veggie Broth
½ Onion, chopped
2 Celery Stalks, chopped
2 Carrots, chopped
1 cup dry Lentils
2 Bay Leaves
2 tbsp Olive Oil
Salt and Pepper, to taste

DIRECTIONS
- Heat the olive oil and sweat onions, garlic, and carrots for 3-4 minutes, on SAUTÉ mode at High. Add celery and sauté for one more minute. Stir in the remaining ingredients. Seal the lid.
- Set to BEANS/CHILI mode and adjust the timer to 25 minutes. When it beeps, press CANCEL and do a natural release, for 10 minutes. Season with salt and pepper, and serve warm.

## Beef Soup with Tacos Topping

Ready in about: **30 minutes** | Serves: **8** | Per serving: **Calories 498; Carbs 21g; Fat 26g; Protein 47g**

INGREDIENTS
2 tbsp Olive Oil
6 Green Bell pepper, diced
2 medium Yellow Onion, chopped
3 lb Ground Beef, grass fed
Salt and Black Pepper to taste
3 tbsp Chili Powder
2 tbsp Cumin Powder
2 tsp Paprika
1 tsp Garlic Powder
1 tsp Cinnamon
1 tsp Onion Powder
6 cups chopped Tomatoes
½ cup chopped Green Chilies
3 cups Bone Broth
3 cups Milk

**Topping:**

Chopped Jalapenos, Sliced Avocados, Chopped Cilantro, Chopped Green Onions, Lime Juice

DIRECTIONS
- Select SAUTÉ mode at High, heat the oil. Add the yellow onion and green peppers. Sauté them until soft, for about 5 minutes. Add the ground beef, stir the ingredients, and cook for about 8 minutes until the beef browns.
- Next, sitr in chili powder, cumin powder, black pepper, paprika, cinnamon, garlic powder, onion powder, and jalapenos. Top with tomatoes, milk, broth, and stir. Seal the lid and select SOUP at High for 20 minutes.
- Once the timer has ended, do a quick pressure release. Keep in Warm mode. Season with salt and pepper.
- Dish the taco soup into serving bowls and add the toppings. Serve warm with a side of tortillas.

## Creamy Chicken Stew with Mushrooms & Spinach

Ready in about: **55 minutes** | Serves: **4** | Per serving: **Calories 456; Carbs 22g; Fat 26g; Protein 42g**

INGREDIENTS
4 Chicken Breasts, diced
1 ¼ lb White Button Mushrooms, halved
3 tbsp Olive Oil
1 large Onion, sliced
5 cloves Garlic, minced
Salt and Black Pepper to taste
1 ¼ tsp Cornstarch
½ cup Spinach, chopped
1 Bay Leaf
1 ½ cups Chicken Stock
1 tsp Dijon Mustard
1 ½ cup Sour Cream
3 tbsp Chopped Parsley

DIRECTIONS
- Select SAUTÉ mode at High. Heat the olive oil, and sauté onion for 3 minutes. Stir in mushrooms, chicken, garlic, bay leaf, salt, pepper, mustard, and broth. Seal the lid, select POULTRY at High pressure for 15 minutes.
- Once the timer has ended, do a natural release for 5 minutes, then a quick pressure release to let the remaining steam out. Select SAUTÉ again. Stir the stew, remove the bay leaf, and scoop some of the liquid into a bowl.

- Add the cornstarch and mix until completely lump free. Pour the liquid into the sauce, stir, and thicken the sauce to your desired consistency.
- Top with sour cream, stir the sauce, and hit Warm mode.
- After 4 minutes, dish the sauce into serving bowls and garnish with chopped parsley. Serve with steamed green peas.

## White Beans and Easy Chicken Chili

*Ready in about:* **40 minutes** | Serves: **4** | Per serving: Calories 535; Carbs 15g; Fat 33g; Protein 48g

INGREDIENTS
3 Chicken Breasts, cubed
3 cups Chicken Broth
1 tbsp Butter
1 White Onion, chopped
Salt and Black Pepper
2 (14.5 ounce) cans White beans, drained and rinsed
1 tsp Cumin Powder
1 tsp dried Oregano
½ cup heavy Whipping Cream
1 cup Sour Cream

DIRECTIONS
- Select SAUTÉ mode at High. Melt the butter, and stir in the onion and chicken. Cook for 6 minutes, until lightly browned. Stir in the cannellini beans, cumin powder, oregano, salt, and pepper. Stir in the broth, and sel the lid.
- Select BEANS/CHILI mode at High pressure for 10 minutes. Once the timer has ended, do a quick pressure release, after 10 minutes. Stir in the whipping and sour creams. Dish the sauce into serving bowls.

## Mushroom and Beef Stew

*Ready in about:* **25 minutes** | Serves: **4** | Per serving: Calories 527; Carbs 50g; Fat 18g; Protein 45g

INGREDIENTS
2 tbsp Canola Oil
1 tsp dried Parsley
1 Onion, chopped
1 ½ pound Beef, cut into pieces
4 Red Potatoes, cut into chunks
4 Carrots, cut into chunks
8 Button Mushrooms, sliced
10 ounces Golden Mushroom Soup
12 ounces Water

DIRECTIONS
- Set to SAUTÉ at High and heat oil. Cook the meat in until browned, 5-6 minutes per side. Stir in the remaining ingredients.
- Lock the lid, turn the pressure valve to "closed" position and set on BEANS/CHILI at High for 20 minutes. When it beeps, do a quick pressure release. Serve warm and enjoy.

## Tortellini Minestrone Soup

*Ready in about:* **20 minutes** | Serves: **6** | Per serving: Calories 245; Carbs 34g; Fat 9g; Protein 7g

INGREDIENTS
1 Onion, diced
2 Carrots, diced
1 tbsp Garlic, minced
2 tbsp Olive Oil
4 cups Veggie Broth
24 ounces Jarred Spaghetti Sauce
1 tsp Sugar
2 Celery Stalks, sliced
¼ tsp Black Pepper
1 ½ tsp Italian Seasoning
14 ounces canned diced Tomatoes
8 ounces dry Cheese Tortellini

DIRECTIONS
- Heat oil on SAUTÉ at High. Add onions, garlic, celery, and carrots, and cook until soft, about 3 minutes.
- Stir in the rest of the ingredients. Seal the lid, and set to BEANS/CHILI for 15 minutes at High pressure.
- When ready, do a quick pressure release. Adjust the seasoning and serve hot.

## Chipotle Chile sin Carne

*Ready in about:* **30 minutes** | Serves: **4** | Per serving: Calories 387; Carbs 42g; Fat 26g; Protein 18g

INGREDIENTS
4 Celery Stalks, chopped
2 (15 oz) cans Diced Tomatoes
1 tbsp Olive Oil
3 Carrots, chopped
2 cloves Garlic, minced
2 tsp Smoked Paprika
2 Green Bell Pepper, diced
½ cup Water
1 tbsp Cumin Powder
1 Sweet Onion, chopped
2 cups Tomato Sauce
1.5 oz Dark Chocolate, chopped
1 small Chipotle, minced
1 ½ cups raw Walnuts, chopped + extra to garnish
Salt and Pepper, to taste
Chopped Cilantro to garnish

DIRECTIONS
- Heat oil, and add onion, celery, and carrots. Sauté for 4 minutes on SAUTÉ. Add garlic, cumin, and paprika. Stir and cook the sauce for 2 minutes. Stir in peppers, tomatoes, tomato sauce, chipotle, water, and walnuts.
- Seal the lid, select BEANS/CHILI mode at High pressure for 15 minutes. Once the timer has ended, do a quick pressure release, and open the lid. Stir in chocolate until it melts. Season with salt and pepper.
- Dish the chili into a serving bowl, garnish with the remaining walnuts and cilantro. Serve with noodles.

## Fresh Tagliatelle Pasta Bolognese

*Ready in about:* **20 minutes** | Serves: **6** | Per serving: Calories 523; Carbs 56g; Fat 23g; Protein 31g

INGREDIENTS
2 tsp Butter
20 ounces Tagliatelle

1 ½ pounds mixed Ground Meat
1 ½ pounds Tomato Pasta Sauce
1 tsp Oregano
1 cup Onions, chopped
2 tsp Garlic, minced
6 ounces Bacon, diced
½ cup White Wine
1 cup Heavy Cream
1 cup Parmesan cheese grated
Water, as needed
Salt and Pepper, to taste

DIRECTIONS
- Melt the butter on SAUTÉ mode at High, and cook the onions and garlic for 3 minutes, until soft and fragrant. Add meat and cook until browned, for a few minutes.
- Stir in the remaining ingredients, except for the heavy cream and Parmesan cheese. Pour in water to cover entirely.
- Seal the lid and cook for 10 minutes on BEANS/CHILI at High pressure. When ready, do a quick release. Stir in heavy cream and serve with grated parmesan cheese.

## Spicy Sweet Potato Cubes

Ready in about: **15 minutes** | Serves: **6** | Per serving: Calories 191; Carbs 38g; Fat 3g; Protein 4g

INGREDIENTS
6 Large Sweet Potatoes, cubed
2 tbsp Butter, melted
1 tsp Chili Powder
¼ tsp Black Pepper
½ tsp Salt
¼ tsp Cayenne Pepper
¼ tsp Turmeric Powder
1 tbsp freshly Parmesan Cheese, grated
1 ½ cups Water

DIRECTIONS
- Pour the water in your pressure cooker. Place the potatoes in the steamer basket. Seal the lid and cook on BEANS/CHILI for 10 minutes at High.
- When ready, do a quick release. Sprinkle the potatoes with spices, drizzle with butter, and top with grated parmesan.

## Noodles with Tuna

Ready in about: **20 minutes** | Serves: **2** | Per serving: Calories 461; Carbs 17g; Fat 29g; Protein 37g

INGREDIENTS
8 ounces Egg Noodles, uncooked
1 can diced Tomatoes
1 can Tuna Flakes, drained
½ cup Red Onion, chopped
1 ¼ cups Water
1 jar Artichoke, marinated and chopped
1 tbsp Olive Oil
1 tsp Parsley
½ cup Feta Cheese, crumbled

DIRECTIONS
- Heat oil on SAUTÉ at High, and cook the onions for a few minutes, until translucent. Stir in the remaining ingredients, except cheese. Seal the lid and cook for 5 minutes BEANS/CHILI at High pressure.
- When ready, release the pressure quickly. Stir in the feta cheese and serve and enjoy.

## Cabbage-Onion Side with Pears

Ready in about: **35 minutes** | Serves: **4** | Per serving: Calories 163; Carbs 24g; Fat 5g; Protein 3g

INGREDIENTS
1 pound Cabbage, shredded
1 cup diced Onions
1 cup Pears, peeled and chopped
1 tbsp Cornstarch
2 tbsp Water
1 ½ cups Veggie Stock
1 tbsp Olive Oil
½ tsp Sea Salt
¼ tsp Pepper
¼ tsp Cumin

DIRECTIONS
- Heat the oil on SAUTÉ mode at High, add the onions and pears, and cook for about 6-7 minutes. When softened, add the rest of the ingredients, except the cornstarch and water. Seal the lid, and select BEANS/CHILI mode.
- Set the timer to 15 minutes at High. Do a quick pressure release. Whisk together the cornstarch and water, and stir in the mixture in the pot. Cook on SAUTÉ at High, until the sauce thickens, for about 3 minutes.

## Classic Mashed Potatoes

Ready in about: **20 minutes** | Serves: **4** | Per serving: Calories 211; Carbs 34g; Fat 7g; Protein 4g

INGREDIENTS
4 Medium Potatoes
2 tbsp Olive Oil
¼ cup Milk
A pinch of Nutmeg
Sea Salt and Black Pepper
Water, as needed

DIRECTIONS
- Wash and peel the potatoes. Place them inside the pressure cooker. Add water, just enough to cover. Seal the lid, press BEANS/CHILI, and set the timer to 8 minutes High pressure.
- Once it goes off, release the pressure quickly. Transfer the potatoes to a bowl. Grab a potato masher and mash the cooked potatoes well until there are no more lumps left.
- Stir in the remaining ingredients until the mixture is thoroughly combined and smooth.

## Creamy Potato and Scallion Salad

Ready in about: **25 minutes** | Serves: **6** | Per serving: Calories 225; Carbs 39g; Fat 8g; Protein 7g

INGREDIENTS
½ cup chopped Scallions
3 Celery Stalks, chopped
1 Carrot, peeled and chopped

½ Red Onion, sliced
4 Hardboiled Eggs, sliced, optional
1 ½ pounds Potatoes
½ cup Mayonnaise
½ tbsp Vinegar
½ tsp Sea Salt
½ tsp Cayenne Pepper
¼ tsp Black Pepper
2 cups Water

DIRECTIONS
- Wash the potatoes thoroughly, scrub them, and place inside the pressure cooker. Pour in water and seal the lid. Select BEANS/CHILI mode, and set the timer to 10 minutes at High.
- When it goes off, do a quick pressure release. Transfer the potatoes to a bowl and let them cool slightly. When safe to handle, peel the potatoes and chop them. Season with salt, cayenne, and black pepper.
- Place the potatoes in a bowl along with carrot, celery, onion, and scallions. In a small bowl, whisk together mayo and vinegar, and sprinkle over salad. If using eggs, slice them thinly and arrange on top.

## Chili and Cheesy Beef Pasta

**Ready in about: 15 minutes | Serves: 6 | Per serving: Calories 346; Carbs 29g; Fat 14g; Protein 26g**

INGREDIENTS
1 pound Ground Beef
2 Scallions, chopped
3 cups Fusilli Pasta, cooked
1 tbsp Butter
½ cup Cheddar Cheese, grated
1 tsp Garlic, minced
2 cups Mild Salsa
½ cup Tomato Puree
1 tbsp Chili Powder
Water, as needed

DIRECTIONS
- Melt the butter on SAUTÉ mode at High, and cook scallions for 3 minutes, until soft. Stir in the garlic and cook for one minute, until fragrant. Add beef and cook until browned, for a few minutes.
- Stir in salsa, tomato paste, and spices. Seal the lid and cook for 8 minutes on RICE/RISOTTO at High. Do a quick pressure release, and stir in cheese and pasta. Cook uncovered for 2 minutes, until well incorporated.

## Garlic & Herb Potatoes

**Ready in about: 15 minutes | Serves: 2 | Per serving: Calories 322; Carbs 43g; Fat 15g; Protein 6g**

INGREDIENTS
1 pound Potatoes, peeled and quartered
1 tbsp Cilantro, chopped
1 tbsp Parsley, chopped 1 tbsp Basil, chopped
3 tsp Garlic, minced
3 tbsp Olive Oil
1 cup Water

DIRECTIONS
- Pour the water into the pressure cooker and lower the trivet. Place the potatoes in a baking dish that fits into the cooker. Sprinkle herbs and garlic over, and drizzle with olive oil.
- Place the baking dish on top of the trivet and seal t the lid. Select BEANS/CHILI mode, and set the timer to 6 minutes High pressure. When ready, do a quick pressure release.

## Potatoes and Green Beans

**Ready in about: 20 minutes | Serves: 6 | Per serving: Calories 123; Carbs 14g; Fat 7g; Protein 3g**

INGREDIENTS
½ pound Green Beans, chopped
1 ½ pound Potatoes, peeled and chopped
1 tsp Garlic, minced
1 Onion, diced
½ tsp Turmeric Powder
¼ tsp Hot Paprika
1 tbsp Olive Oil
Salt and Pepper, to taste
Water, as needed

DIRECTIONS
- Heat olive oil on SAUTÉ at High. Add the onions and cook them for about 3 minutes. Once softened, add the garlic and saute for a minute. Add the potatoes and cover them with water. Seal the lid.
- Select BEANS/CHILI mode and set to 5 minutes at High pressure. Do a quick pressure release. Stir in the green beans, and seal the lid again.
- Cook for 3 more minutes on STEAM mode at High. Do a quick release. Season with turmeric, paprika, salt, and pepper.

## Paprika Hash Browns

**Ready in about: 20 minutes | Serves: 4 | Per serving: Calories 168; Carbs 21g; Fat 8g; Protein 3g**

INGREDIENTS
1 pound Potatoes, grated
1 tsp Smoked Paprika
1 ½ tbsp Butter
1 ½ tbsp Corn Oil
½ tsp Pepper
1 tsp Salt
½ small Onion, sliced
1 cup Water

DIRECTIONS
- Rinse grated potatoes in cold water to dissolve excess starch, then drain, and pat dry with paper towels. Melt the butter along with the oil on SAUTÉ mode at High.
- Cook onion and potatoes for 6 minutes, until soft, lid off. Season with salt, pepper, and smoked paprika and transfer to a baking dish. Press the potatoes with a metal spatula.
- Place a trivet in the pressure cooker and pour water inside. Lower the dish onto the trivet and close the lid. Cook at High on BEANS/CHILI for 15 minutes. Release the pressure immediately, for 5 minutes.

### Cauliflower and Pea Bowl

⏱ **Ready in about: 30 minutes | Serves: 6 | Per serving:**
Calories 134; Carbs 18g; Fat 4g; Protein 7g

INGREDIENTS
6 cups Cauliflower Florets
2 Sweet Potatoes, peeled and cubed
2 Tomatoes, diced
2 cups Peas
1 tsp Garlic, minced
1 cup Scallions, chopped
1 tbsp Olive Oil
4 cups Vegetable Stock
Salt and Pepper, to taste

DIRECTIONS
- Heat oil on SAUTÉ at High, add the scallions and cook for about 3-4 minutes, until soft. Add the cauliflower, tomatoes, and pour the stock. Seal the lid and cook at High pressure for 6 minutes. Do a quick pressure release.
- Stir in the remaining ingredients. Seal the lid, hit BEANS/CHILI for 10 minutes at High. Do a quick release.

# DESSERTS RECIPES

### Pressure Cooked Cherry Pie

⏱ **Ready in about: 45 minutes | Serves: 6 | Per serving:**
Calories 393; Carbs 69g; Fat 12g; Protein 2g

INGREDIENTS
1 9-inch double Pie Crust
2 cups Water
½ tsp Vanilla Extract
4 cups Cherries, pitted
¼ tsp Almond Extract
4 tbsp Quick Tapioca
1 cup Sugar
A pinch of Salt

DIRECTIONS
- Pour water inside your cooker and add the trivet. Combine the cherries with tapioca, sugar, extracts, and salt, in a bowl. Place one pie crust at the bottom of a lined springform pan.
- Spread the cherries mixture and top with the other crust. Lower the pan onto the trivet. Seal the lid, set to BEANS/CHILI mode for 18 minutes at High pressure. Once cooking is completed, do a quick pressure release. Let cool the pie on a cooling rack. Slice to serve.

### Impossible Oatmeal Chocolate Cookies

⏱ **Ready in about: 30 minutes | Serves: 2 | Per serving:**
Calories 412; Carbs 59g; Fat 20g; Protein 6g

INGREDIENTS
¼ cup Whole Wheat Flour
¼ cup Oats
1 tbsp Butter
2 tbsp Sugar
½ tsp Vanilla Extract
1 tbsp Honey
2 tbsp Milk
2 tsp Coconut Oil
¾ tsp Sea Salt
3 tbsp Chocolate Chips

DIRECTIONS
- Mix all ingredients, in a bowl. Line a baking pan with parchment paper. Shape lemon-sized cookies out of the mixture, and flatten onto the lined pan. Pour 1 cup water, and add a trivet. Lower the baking pan onto the rack.
- Seal the lid, set on MEAT/STEW mode for 15 minutes at High pressure. When cooking is over, do a quick pressure. Cool for 15 minutes to serve.

### Honeyed Butternut Squash Pie

⏱ **Ready in about: 30 minutes | Serves: 4 | Per serving:**
Calories 172; Carbs 39g; Fat 2g; Protein 3g

INGREDIENTS
1 pound Butternut Squash, diced
1 Egg
¼ cup Honey
½ cup Milk
½ tsp Cinnamon
½ tbsp Cornstarch
1 cup Water
A pinch of Sea Salt

DIRECTIONS
- Pour the water inside your pressure cooker and add a trivet. Lower the butternut squash onto the trivet. Seal the lid, and cook on BEANS/CHILI mode for 5 minutes at High pressure.
- Meanwhile, whisk all remaining ingredients in a bowl. Do a quick pressure. Drain the squash and add it to the milk mixture. Pour the batter into a greased baking dish. Place in the cooker, and seal the lid.
- Cook for 10 minutes BEANS/CHILI at High. Do a quick pressure release. Transfer pie to wire rack to cool.

### Homemade Chocolate Pudding

⏱ **Ready in about: 20 minutes | Serves: 4 | Per serving:**
Calories 388; Carbs 33g; Fat 29g; Protein 11g

INGREDIENTS

Zest and Juice from ½ Lime
2 oz chocolate, coarsely chopped
¼ cup Sugar
2 tbsp Butter, softened
3 Eggs, separated into whites and yolks
¼ cup Cornstarch
1 cup Almond Milk
A pinch of Salt
½ tsp Ginger, caramelized
1 ½ cups of Water

DIRECTIONS
- Combine together the sugar, cornstarch, salt, and softened butter, in a bowl. Mix in lime juice and grated lime zest. Add in the egg yolks, ginger, almond milk, and whisk to mix well.
- Mix in egg whites. Pour this mixture into custard cups and cover with aluminium foil. Add 1 ½ cups of water to the pressure cooker. Place a trivet into the pressure cooker, and lower the cups onto the rack.
- Select BEANS/CHILI mode and cook for 25 minutes at High Pressure. Once the cooking is complete, do a quick pressure release. Carefully open the lid, and stir in the chocolate. Serve chilled.

## Almond Pear Wedges

**Ready in about: 15 minutes | Serves: 3 | Per serving: Calories 240; Carbs 22g; Fat 17g; Protein 1g**

INGREDIENTS
2 Large Pears, peeled and cut into wedges
3 tbsp Almond Butter
2 tbsp Olive Oil

DIRECTIONS
- Pour 1 cup of water in the ´pressure cooker. Place the pear wedges in a steamer basket and then lower the basket at the bottom. Seal the lid, and cook for 2 minutes on STEAM at High pressure.
- When the timer goes off, do a quick pressure release. Remove the basket, discard the water and wipe clean the cooker. Press the SAUTÉ at High and heat the oil.
- Add the pears and cook until browned. Top them with almond butter, to serve.

## Vanilla and Yogurt Light Cheesecake

**Ready in: 70 minutes + chilling time | Serves: 8 | Per serving: Calories 280; Carbs 26g, Fat 9g, Protein 6g**

INGREDIENTS
2 Eggs
¼ cup Sugar
1 ½ cups Yogurt
1 tsp Vanilla
4 ounces Cream Cheese, softened
1 ½ cups ground Graham Cracker Crumbs
4 tbsp Butter, melted
1 cup Water

DIRECTIONS
- Mix the butter and cracker crumbs, and press the mixture onto the bottom of a springform pan. In a bowl, beat cream cheese with yogurt, vanilla, and sugar. Beat in the eggs one at a time. Spread the filling on top of the crust. Pour water in your cooker and add the trivet.
- Lower the pan onto the trivet. Lock the lid, press MEAT/STEW for 35 minutes at High. Once cooking is completed, do a quick pressure release. Let cool and refrigerate for 6 hours.

## Chocolate Molten Lava Cake

**Ready in about: 20 minutes | Serves: 4 | Per serving: Calories 413; Carbs 48g; Fat 23g; Protein 8g**

INGREDIENTS
2 tbsp Butter, melted
1 cup Dark Chocolate, melted
6 tbsp Almond Flour
1 cup Water
1 tsp Vanilla
3 Eggs plus
1 Yolk, beaten
¾ cup Coconut Sugar

DIRECTIONS
- Combine all ingredients, except the water, in a bowl. Grease four ramekins with cooking spray. Divide the filling between the ramekins. Pour the water in your Pressure cooker.
- Place the ramekins on the trivet. Seal the lid and cook for 10 minutes BEANS/CHILI at High pressure. When ready, do a quick pressure release. Serve immediately and enjoy.

## Peaches with Chocolate Biscuits

**Ready in about: 20 minutes | Serves: 4 | Per serving: Calories 302; Carbs 39g; Fat 16g; Protein 7g**

INGREDIENTS
4 small Peaches, halved lengthwise and pitted
8 dried Dates, chopped
4 tbsp Walnuts, chopped
1 cup Coarsely Crumbled Cookies
1 tsp Cinnamon Powder
¼ tsp grated nutmeg
¼ tsp ground Cloves

DIRECTIONS
- Pour 2 cups of water into the pressure cooker and add a trivet. Arrange the peaches on a greased baking dish cut-side-up. To prepare the filling, mix all of the remaining ingredients.
- Stuff the peaches with the mixture. Cover with aluminium foil and lower it onto the trivet. Seal the lid, press BEANS/CHILI and cook for 15 minutes at High. Do a quick pressure release.

## Peanut Butter Bars

**Ready in about: 55 minutes | Serves: 6 | Per serving: Calories 561; Carbs 61g; Fat 18g; Protein 8g**

INGREDIENTS
1 cup Flour
1 ½ cups Water
1 Egg
½ cup Peanut Butter, softened
½ cup Butter, softened
1 cup Oats
½ cup Sugar

½ tsp Baking Soda
½ tsp Salt
½ cup Brown Sugar

DIRECTIONS
- Grease a springform pan and line it with parchment paper. Set aside. Beat together the eggs, peanut butter, butter, salt, white sugar, and brown sugar. Fold in the oats, flour, and baking soda.
- Press the batter into the pan. Cover the pan with a paper towel and with a piece of foil. Pour the water into the pressure cooker and add a trivet. Lower the springform pan onto the trivet. Seal the lid.
- Press MEAT/STEW mode, and cook for 35 minutes at High pressure. When ready, do a quick release. Wait for 15 minutes before inverting onto a plate and cutting into bars.

## Apricots with Blueberry Sauce

Ready in about: **15 minutes** | Serves: **4** | Per serving: Calories 205; Carbs 45g; Fat 2g; Protein 2g

INGREDIENTS
8 Apricots, pitted and halved
2 cups Blueberries
¼ cup Honey
1 ½ tbsp Cornstarch
½ Vanilla Bean, sliced lengthwise
¼ tsp ground Cardamom
½ Cinnamon stick
1 ¼ cups Water

DIRECTIONS
- Add all ingredients, except for the honey and the cornstarch, to your pressure cooker. Seal the lid, select RICE/RISOTTO mode and cook for 8 minutes at High pressure. Do a quick pressure release and open the lid.
- Remove the apricots with a slotted spoon. Choose SAUTÉ at High, add the honey and cornstarch, then let simmer until the sauce thickens, for about 5 minutes.
- Split up the apricots among serving plates and top with the blueberry sauce, to serve.

## Cinnamon and Lemon Apples

Ready in about: **13 minutes** | Serves: **2** | Per serving: Calories 144; Carbs 25g; Fat 5g; Protein 2g

INGREDIENTS
2 Apples, peeled and cut into wedges
½ cup Lemon Juice
½ tsp Cinnamon
1 tbsp Butter
1 cup Water

DIRECTIONS
- Combine lemon juice and water in the pressure cooker. Place the apple wedges in the steaming basket and lower the basket into the cooker. Seal the lid, select the STEAM for 3 minutes at High.
- Release the pressure quickly. Open the lid and remove the steaming basket. Transfer the apple wedges to a bowl. Drizzle with almond butter and sprinkle with cinnamon.

## Milk Dumplings in Sweet Cardamom Sauce

Ready in about: **30 minutes** | Serves: **20** | Per serving: Calories 134; Carbs 29g; Fat 2g; Protein 2g

INGREDIENTS
6 cups Water
2 ½ cups Sugar
3 tbsp Lime Juice
6 cups Milk
1 tsp ground Cardamom

DIRECTIONS
- Bring to a boil the milk, on SAUTÉ at High, and stir in the lime juice. The solids should start to separate. Pour milk through a cheesecloth-lined colander. Drain as much liquid as you can. Place the paneer on a smooth surface. Form a ball and divide into 20 equal pieces.
- Pour water and bring to a boil. Add sugar and cardamom and cook until dissolved. Shape the dumplings into balls, and place them in the syrup. Seal the lid and cook for 5 minutes on STEAM at High.
- Once done, do a quick pressure release. Let cool and refrigerate for at least 2 hours.

## Delicious Stuffed Apples

Ready in about: **20 minutes** | Serves: **6** | Per serving: Calories 152; 3g Fat; 21g Carbs; 2g Protein

INGREDIENTS
3 ½ pounds Apples, cored
½ cup dried Apricots, chopped
¼ cup Sugar
¼ cup Pecans, chopped
¼ cup Graham Cracker Crumbs
¼ tsp Cardamom
½ tsp grated Nutmeg
½ tsp ground Cinnamon
1 ¼ cups Red Wine

DIRECTIONS
- Lay the apples at the bottom of your cooker, and pour in the red wine. Combine the other ingredients, except the crumbs. Seal the lid, and cook BEANS/CHILI at High pressure for 15 minutes.
- Once ready, do a quick pressure release. Top with graham cracker crumbs and serve!

## Coconut Crème Caramel

Ready in about: **20 minutes** | Serves: **4** | Per serving: Calories 121; Carbs 17g; Fat 3g; Protein 3g

INGREDIENTS
2 Eggs
7 ounces Condensed Coconut Milk
½ cup Coconut Milk
1 ½ cups Water
½ tsp Vanilla
4 tbsp Caramel Syrup

DIRECTIONS

- Divide the caramel syrup between 4 small ramekins. Pour water in the pressure cooker and add the trivet.
- In a bowl, beat the rest of the ingredients. Divide them between the ramekins. Cover them with aluminum foil and lower onto the trivet. Seal the lid, and set on RICE/RISOTTO for 13 minutes at High pressure.
- Do a quick pressure release. Let cool completely. To unmold the flan, insert a spatula along the ramekin' sides and flip onto a dish.

## Juicy Apricots with Walnuts and Goat Cheese

Ready in about: **10 minutes | Serves: 4 | Per serving: Calories 302; Carbs 31g; Fat 17g; Protein 11g**

INGREDIENTS
1 pound Apricots, pitted and halved
½ cup Orange Juice
4 tbsp Honey
¾ cup Goat Cheese
½ cup Walnuts, chopped
¼ tsp grated Nutmeg
½ tsp ground Cinnamon
½ tsp Vanilla Extract
½ cup Water
DIRECTIONS
- Add all ingredients, except for cheese and walnuts, to your pressure cooker. Select BEANS/CHILI mode and cook for 5 minutes at High pressure. Do a quick pressure release.
- Remove apricots to serving plates and top with cheese and walnuts, to enjoy.

## Almond Butter Bananas

Ready in about: **8 minutes | Serve: 1 | Per serving: Calories 310; Carbs 28g; Fat 23g; Protein 2g**

INGREDIENTS
1 Banana, sliced
1 tbsp Coconut oil
2 tbsp Almond Butter
½ tsp Cinnamon
DIRECTIONS
- Melt oil on SAUTÉ mode at High. Add banana slices and fry them for a couple of minutes, or until golden on both sides.
- Top the fried bananas with almond butter and sprinkle with cinnamon.

## Crema Catalana

Ready in about: **20 minutes + 2h chilled | Serves: 4 | Per serving: Calories 420; Carbs 57g; Fat 13g; Protein 4g**

INGREDIENTS
1 ¼ cups Water
½ tsp Vanilla Paste
1 ½ cups warm Heavy Cream
3 large-sized Egg yolks,
1 cup Sugar
DIRECTIONS

- In a bowl, mix the vanilla, heavy cream, sugar and egg yolks. Fill 4 ramekins with this mixture and wrap with foil. Pour the water into the Pressure Cooker. Add the trivet and lay the ramekins on top. Seal the lid, press BEANS/CHILI and cook for 10 minutes at High.
- Once the cooking is complete, do a quick pressure release. Refrigerate Crema Catalana for at least 2 hours.

## Tutty Fruity Sauce

Ready in about: **15 minutes | Serves: 2 | Per serving: Calories 125; Carbs 16g; Fat 4g; Protein 1g**

INGREDIENTS
1 cup Pineapple Chunks
1 cup Berry Mix
2 Apples, peeled and diced
¼ cup Almonds, chopped
¼ cup Fresh Orange Juice
1 tbsp Olive Oil
DIRECTIONS
- Pour ½ cup of water, orange juice, and fruits, in the pressure cooker. Give it a good stir and seal the lid. Press BEANS/CHILI and set the timer to 5 minutes at High pressure.
- When it goes off, release the pressure quickly. Blend the mixture with a hand blender and immediately stir in the coconut oil. Serve sprinkled with chopped almonds. Enjoy!

## Homemade Egg Custard

Ready in about: **20 minutes | Serves: 4 | Per serving: Calories 425; Carbs 48g; Fat 25g; Protein 11g**

INGREDIENTS
1 Egg plus 2 Egg yolks
½ cup Sugar
½ cups Milk
2 cups Heavy Cream
½ tsp pure rum extract
2 cups Water
DIRECTIONS
- Beat the egg and the egg yolks in a bowl. Gently add pure rum extract. Mix in the milk and heavy cream. Give it a good, and add the sugar. Pour this mixture into 4 ramekins.
- Add 2 cups of water, insert the trivet, and lay the ramekins on the trivet. Select BEANS/CHILI and cook for 10 minutes at High. Do a quick pressure release. Wait a bit before removing from ramekins.

## Hazelnut Chocolate Spread

Ready in about: **25 minutes | Serves: 16 | Per serving: Calories 166; Carbs 23g; Fat 10g; Protein 1g**

INGREDIENTS
1 ¼ pounds Hazelnuts, halved
½ cup Cocoa Powder
½ cups icing Sugar, sifted
1 tsp Vanilla Extract
¼ tsp Cardamom, grated
¼ tsp Cinnamon powder
½ tsp grated Nutmeg

10 ounces Water

DIRECTIONS

- Place the hazelnut in a blender and blend until you obtain a paste. Place in the cooker along with the remaining ingredients. Seal the lid, select RICE/RISOTTO and cook for 13 minutes at High pressure.
- Once the cooking is over, allow for a natural pressure release, for 10 minutes.

## Tiramisu Cheesecake

*Ready in: 1 hour + chilling time | Serves: 12 | Per serving: Calories 426, Carbs 47g, Fat 23g, Protein 8g*

INGREDIENTS

1 tbsp Kahlua Liquor
1 ½ cups Ladyfingers, crushed
1 tbsp Granulated Espresso
1 tbsp Butter, melted
16 ounces Cream Cheese, softened
8 ounces Mascarpone Cheese, softened
2 Eggs
2 tbsp Powdered Sugar
½ cup White Sugar
1 tbsp Cocoa Powder
1 tsp Vanilla Extract

DIRECTIONS

- In a bowl beat the cream cheese, mascarpone, and white sugar. Gradually beat in the eggs, the powdered sugar and vanilla. Combine the first 4 ingredients, in another bowl.
- Spray a springform pan with cooking spray. Press the ladyfinger crust at the bottom. Pour the filling over. Cover the pan with a paper towel and then close it with aluminum foil.
- Pour 1 cup of water in your pressure cooker and lower the trivet. Place the pan inside and seal the lid. Select MEAT/STEW mode and set to 35 minutes at High pressure.
- Wait for about 10 minutes before pressing Cancel and releasing the pressure quickly. Allow to cool completely before refrigerating the cheesecake for 4 hours.

## Citrus Cheesecake

*Ready in about: 55 minutes | Serves: 8 | Per serving: Calories 353; Carbs 21g; Fat 27g; Protein 7g*

INGREDIENTS

4 oz Graham Crackers
1 tsp ground Cinnamon
3 tbsp Butter, melted
1 cup Water

**FOR THE FILLING:**

1 lb Cream Cheese, room temperature
¾ cup granulated Sugar
¼ cup Sour Cream, room temperature
2 Eggs
1 tsp Vanilla Extract
1 tsp Lemon Zest
1 tbsp Lemon Juice
1 pinch Salt
1 cup Water

DIRECTIONS

- Mix graham crackers and cinnamon in a blender and blitz until the mixture resembles wet sand. Add the butter and blend a few more times. Pour crumbs into the bottom of a baking dish in a single layer.
- For the fillisng, beat sour cream, sugar, and cream cheese with an electric mixer until creamy and fluffy, for about 2-3 minutes. Add eggs, vanilla extract, lemon zest, lemon juice, and salt.
- Beat the mixture until the color is solid, for about 1-2 minutes more. Stir in filling over crust in the baking dish. Pour the water into your pressure cooker and lower the trivet.
- Place the baking dish on the trivet. Seal the lid, and set to MEAT/STEW mode for 40 minutes at High. Once ready, do a quick pressure release. Refrigerate for at least 2 hours or until set. Once the cake has set, carefully remove from the dish and transfer to a serving plate.

## Chocolate and Banana Squares

*Ready in about: 25 minutes | Serves: 6 | Per serving: Calories 140; Carbs 14g; Fat 10g; Protein 3g*

INGREDIENTS

½ cup Butter
3 Bananas
2 tbsp Cocoa Powder
1 ½ cups Water
Cooking spray, to grease

DIRECTIONS

- Place the bananas and almond butter in a bowl and mash finely with a fork. Add the cocoa powder and stir until well combined. Grease a baking dish that fits into the pressure cooker.
- Pour the banana and almond batter into the dish. Pour the water in the pressure cooker and lower the trivet. Place the baking dish on top of the trivet and seal the lid.
- Select BEANS/CHILI mode, for 15 minutes at High pressure. When it goes off, do a quick release. Let cool for a few minutes before cutting into squares

## Compote with Blueberries and Lemon

*Ready in about: 10 minutes + chilling time | Serves: 4 | Per serving: Calories 220; Carbs 61g; Fat 0g; Protein 1g*

INGREDIENTS

2 cups Frozen Blueberries
2 tbsp Arrowroot or Cornstarch
¾ cups Coconut Sugar
Juice of ½ Lemon
½ cup Water + 2 tbsp

DIRECTIONS

- Place blueberries, lemon juice, 1/2 cup water, and coconut sugar in your cooker. Seal the lid, cook on STEAM mode for 3 minutes at High pressure. Once done, do a quick pressure.
- Meanwhile, combine the arrowroot and water, in a bowl. Stir in the mixture into the blueberries and cook until the mixture thickens, lid off, on SAUTÉ at High. Transfer the compote to a bowl and let cool completely before refrigerating for 2 hours.

## Full Coconut Cake

⌛ **Ready in about: 55 minutes | Serves: 4 | Per serving: Calories 350; Carbs 47g; Fat 14g; Protein 8g**

INGREDIENTS

3 Eggs, Yolks and Whites separated
¾ cup Coconut Flour
½ tsp Coconut Extract
1 ½ cups warm Coconut Milk
½ cup Coconut Sugar
2 tbsp Coconut Oil, melted
1 cup Water

DIRECTIONS

- In a bowl, beat in the egg yolks along with the coconut sugar. In a separate bowl, beat the whites until soft form peaks. Stir in coconut extract and coconut oil. Gently fold in the coconut flour. Line a baking dish and pour the batter inside. Cover with aluminum foil.
- Pour the water in your pressure cooker and add a wire rack. Lower the dish onto the rack. Seal the lid, set on MEAT/STEW cook for 40 minutes at High pressure. Do a quick pressure release, and serve.

## Restaurant-Style Crème Brulee

⌛ **Ready in: 30 minutes + 6h for cooling | Serves: 4 | Per serving: Calories 487; Carbs 23g; Fat 41g; Protein 5g**

INGREDIENTS

3 cups Heavy Whipping Cream
6 tbsp Sugar
7 large Egg Yolks
2 tbsp Vanilla Extract
2 cups Water

DIRECTIONS

- In a mixing bowl, whisk the yolks, vanilla, whipping cream, and half of the swerve sugar, until well combined.
- Pour the mixture into the ramekins and cover them with aluminium foil. Fit the trivet in the pot, and pour in the water. Lay 3 ramekins on the trivet and place the remaining ramekins to sit on the edges of the ramekins below.
- Seal the lid and select BEANS/CHILI mode at High pressure for 8 minutes. Do a natural pressure release for 15 minutes, then a quick pressure release. With a napkin in hand, remove the ramekins onto a flat surface.
- Then refrigerate for at least 6 hours. After refrigeration, remove the ramekins and remove the aluminium foil. Sprinkle the remaining sugar over and use a hand torch to brown the top of the crème brulee.

## Bonfire Lava Cake

⌛ **Ready in about: 40 minutes | Serves: 8 | Per serving: Calories 461; Carbs 28g; Fat 24g; Protein 10g**

INGREDIENTS

1 cup Butter
4 tbsp Milk
4 tsp Vanilla Extract
1 ½ cups Chocolate Chips
1 ½ cups Sugar
Powdered sugar to garnish
7 tbsp All-purpose Flour
5 Eggs
1 cup Water

DIRECTIONS

- Grease the cake pan with cooking spray and set aside. Fit the trivet at the bottom of the pot, and pour in water.
- In a heatproof bowl, add the butter and chocolate and melt them in the microwave for about 2 minutes. Stir in sugar. Add eggs, milk, and vanilla extract and stir again. Finally, add the flour and stir it until even and smooth.
- Pour the batter into the greased cake pan and use spatula to level it. Place the pan on the trivet, inside the pot, seal the lid, and select BEANS/CHILI mode at High for 15 minutes.
- Do a natural pressure release for 12 minutes, then a quick pressure release. Remove the trivet with the pan on it and place the pan on a flat surface. Put a plate over the pan and flip the cake over onto the plate.
- Pour the powdered sugar in a fine sieve and sift over the cake. Cut the cake into 8 slices and serve immediately.

## Buttery Banana Bread

⌛ **Ready in about: 45 minutes | Serves: 12 | Per serving: Calories 295; Carbs 48g; Fat 14g; Protein 5g**

INGREDIENTS

3 ripe Bananas, mashed
1 ¼ cups Sugar
1 cup Milk
2 cups all-purpose Flour
1 tsp Baking Soda
1 tsp Baking Powder
1 tbsp Orange Juice
1 stick Butter, room temperature
A pinch of Salt
¼ tsp Cinnamon
½ tsp Pure Vanilla Extract

DIRECTIONS

- In a bowl, mix together the flour, baking powder, baking soda, sugar, vanilla, and salt. Add in the bananas, cinnamon, and orange juice. Slowly stir in the butter and milk.
- Give it a good stir until everything is well combined. Pour the batter into a medium-sized round pan.
- Place the trivet at the bottom of the pressure cooker and fill with 2 cups of water. Place the pan on the trivet. Select MEAT/STEW and cook for 40 minutes at High. Do a quick pressure release.

## Strawberry Cottage Cheesecake

⌛ **Ready in about: 35 minutes | Serves: 6 | Per serving: Calories 241; Carbs 8g; Fat 20g; Protein 9g**

INGREDIENTS

10 oz Cream Cheese
¼ cup Sugar
½ cup Cottage Cheese
One Lemon, zested and juiced
2 Eggs, cracked into a bowl
1 tsp Lemon Extract
3 tbsp Sour Cream

1 ½ cups Water
10 Strawberries, halved to decorate
DIRECTIONS
- Blend with electric mixer, the cream cheese, quarter cup of sugar, cottage cheese, lemon zest, lemon juice, and lemon extract, until smooth consistency is formed. Adjust the sweet taste to liking with more sugar.
- Reduce the speed of the mixer and add the eggs. Fold in at low speed until fully incorporated. Make sure not to fold the eggs in high speed to prevent a cracked crust. Grease the spring form pan with cooking spray.
- Spoon the mixture into the pan. Level the top with spatula and cover with foil. Fit the trivet in the pot, and pour the water in. Place the cake pan on the trivet, seal the lid and select BEANS/CHILI at High for 15 minutes.
- Meanwhile, mix the sour cream and one tablespoon of sugar. Set aside. Once the timer has gone off, do a natural pressure release for 10 minutes, then a quick pressure release to let out any extra steam, and open the lid.
- Remove the trivet, place the spring form pan on a flat surface, and open. Use a spatula to spread the sour cream mixture on the warm cake. Refrigerate for 8 hours. Top with strawberries; slice into 6 pieces and serve firm.

## Berry-Vanilla Pudding Temptation

**Ready in: 35 minutes + 6h for cooling | Serves: 4 | Per serving: Calories 183; Carbs 12g; Fat 14g; Protein 3g**

INGREDIENTS
1 cup Heavy Cream
4 Egg Yolks
4 tbsp Water + 1 ½ cups Water
½ cup Milk
1 tsp Vanilla
½ cup Sugar
4 Raspberries
4 Blueberries
DIRECTIONS
- Fit the trivet at the bottom of the pot, and pour one and a half cups of water. In a small pan set over low heat on a stove top, add 4 tablespoons for water and the sugar. Stir constantly until it dissolves. Turn off the heat.
- Add milk, heavy cream, and vanilla. Stir it with a whisk until evenly combined. Crack the eggs into a bowl and add a tablespoon of the cream mixture. Whisk, and then very slowly, whisk in the remaining cream mixture.
- Pour the mixture into the ramekins and place them on the trivet. Seal the lid and select STEAM at High Pressure for 4 minutes. Once the timer has gone off, do a quick pressure release. With a napkin in hand, carefully remove the ramekins onto a flat surface. Let them cool for about 15 minutes and then refrigerate for 6 hours.
- After 6 hours, remove from the fridge and garnish with raspberries and blueberries.

## Fruity Cheesecake

**Ready in about: 30 minutes | Serves: 6 | Per serving: Calories 498; Carbs 48g; Fat 28g; Protein 9g**

INGREDIENTS

1 ½ cups Graham Cracker Crust
1 cup Raspberries
3 cups Cream Cheese
1 tbsp fresh Orange Juice
3 Eggs
½ stick Butter, melted
¾ cup Sugar
1 tsp Vanilla Paste
1 tsp finely grated Orange Zest
1 ½ cups Water
DIRECTIONS
- Insert the tray into the pressure cooker, and add 1 ½ cups of water. Grease a spring form. Mix in graham cracker crust with sugar and butter, in a bowl. Press the mixture to form a crust at the bottom.
- Blend the raspberries and cream cheese with an electric mixer. Crack in the eggs and keep mixing until well combined. Mix in the remaining ingredients, and give it a good stir.
- Pour this mixture into the pan, and cover the pan with aluminium foil. Lay the spring form on the tray.
- Select BEANS/CHILI mode and cook for 20 minutes at High pressure. Once the cooking is complete, do a quick pressure release. Refrigerate the cheesecake for at least 2 hours.

## Black Currant Poached Peaches

**Ready in about: 15 minutes | Serves: 4 | Per serving: Calories 140; Carbs 15g; Fat 1g; Protein 1g**

INGREDIENTS
½ cup Black Currants
4 Peaches, peeled, pits removed
1 cup Freshly Squeezed Orange Juice
1 Cinnamon Stick
DIRECTIONS
- Place black currants and orange juice in a blender. Blend until the mixture becomes smooth. Pour the mixture in your pressure cooker, and add the cinnamon stick.
- Add the peaches to the steamer basket and then insert the basket into the pot. Seal the lid, select BEANS/CHILI, and set to 5 minutes at High. Do a quick pressure release. Serve the peaches drizzled with sauce, to enjoy!

## Easiest Pressure Cooked Raspberry Curd

**Ready in: 10 minutes + chilling time | Serves: 5 | Per serving: Calories 249; Carbs 48g; Fat 7g; Protein 2g**

INGREDIENTS
12 ounces Raspberries
2 tbsp Butter
Juice of ½ Lemon
1 cup Sugar
2 Egg Yolks
DIRECTIONS
Add the raspberries, sugar, and lemon juice in your pressure cooker. Seal the lid and cook for 2 minutes on STEAM at High. Once ready, do a quick pressure release.
- With a hand mixer, puree the raspberries and discard the seeds. Whisk the yolks in a bowl. Combine the yolks with the hot raspberry puree. Pour the mixture in your pressure cooker.

- On SAUTÉ at High, cook for a minute, lid off. Stir in the butter and cook for a couple more minutes, until thick. Transfer to a container with a lid. Refrigerate for at least an hour before serving.

## Apple and Peach Compote

Ready in about: **2 hours 10 minutes | Serves: 4 | Per serving: Calories 120; Carbs 23g; Fat 1g; Protein 1g**

INGREDIENTS
2 ½ cups Peach, chopped
2 cups Apples, diced
Juice of 1 Orange
2 tbsp Cornstarch
½ cup Water
¼ tsp Cinnamon
DIRECTIONS
- Place the peaches, apples, water, and orange juice, in the pressure cooker.
- Stir to combine and seal the lid, Select STEAM and set the timer to 3 minutes at High.
- Do a quick release. Press SAUTÉ at High and whisk in the cornstarch. Cook until the compote thickens, for about 5 minutes. When thickened, transfer to an airtight container, and refrigerate for at least 2 hours.

## Very Berry Cream

Ready in about: **4 hours 10 minutes | Serves: 2 | Per serving: Calories 90; Carbs 11g; Fat 3g; Protein 1g**

INGREDIENTS
½ cup Blueberries
½ cup Strawberries, chopped
½ cup Raspberries
1 cup Milk
¼ tsp Vanilla Extract
DIRECTIONS
- Place all ingredients, except the vanilla extract, inside your pressure cooker. Seal the lid, select STEAM mode and set the timer to 2 minutes at High pressure.
- When it goes off, do a quick pressure release. Remove to a blender. Add vanilla extract and pulse until smooth. Divide between two serving glasses and cool for 4 hours before serving.

## Creamy Almond and Apple Delight

Ready in about: **14 minutes | Serves: 4 | Per serving: Calories 60; Carbs 10g; Fat 1g; Protein 0**

INGREDIENTS
3 Apples, peeled and diced
½ cup Almonds, chopped or slivered
½ cup Milk
¼ tsp Cinnamon
DIRECTIONS
- Place all ingredients in the pressure cooker. Stir well to combine and seal the lid. Cook on BEANS/CHILI for 5 minutes at High.
- Release the pressure quickly. Divide the mixture among 4 serving bowls.

## Coconut Pear Delight

Ready in about: **15 minutes | Serves: 2 | Per serving: Calories 140; Carbs 18g; Fat 8g; Protein 2g**

INGREDIENTS
¼ cup Flour
1 cup Coconut Milk
2 Large Pears, peeled and diced
¼ cup Shredded Coconut, unsweetened
DIRECTIONS
- Combine all ingredients in the pressure cooker. Seal the lid, select BEANS/CHILI and set the timer to 5 minutes at High pressure.
- When ready, do a quick pressure release. Divide the mixture between two bowls.

## Hot Milk Chocolate Fondue

Ready in about: **5 minutes | Serves: 12 | Per serving: Calories 198; Carbs 12g; Fat 16g; Protein 3g**

INGREDIENTS
10 ounces Milk Chocolate, chopped into small pieces
2 tsp Coconut Liqueur
8 ounces Heavy Whipping Cream
¼ tsp Cinnamon Powder
1 ½ cups Lukewarm Water
A pinch of Salt
DIRECTIONS
- Melt the chocolate in a heat-proof recipient. Add the remaining ingredients, except for the liqueur. Transfer this recipient to the metal trivet. Pour 1 ½ cups of water into the cooker, and place a trivet inside.
- Seal the lid, select BEANS/CHILI and cook for 5 minutes at High. Do a quick pressure release. Pull out the container with tongs. Mix in the coconut liqueur and serve right now with fresh fruits. Enjoy!

## Poached Pears with Orange and Cinnamon

Ready in about: **20 minutes | Serves: 4 | Per serving: Calories 170; Carbs 43g; Fat 1g; Protein 1g**

INGREDIENTS
4 Pears cut in half
1 tsp powdered Ginger
1 tsp Nutmeg
1 cup Orange Juice
2 tsp Cinnamon
¼ cup Coconut Sugar
DIRECTIONS
- Place the trivet at the bottom of the pressure cooker. Stir in the juice and spices. Lay the pears on the trivet. Seal the lid, cook on BEANS/CHILI for 7 minutes, at High pressure.
- When ready, do a quick release. Remove pears onto a serving plate. Pour juice over to serve.

## Crispy and Sweet Holiday Treats

Small sweets for your weekend or party!

⌛ **Prep time: 30 minutes Cooking time: 3 hours**
**Servings: 36**

INGREDIENTS:
Tiny marshmallows
Pistachios
Cup dried cranberries
Butter
Crisp rice cereal

DIRECTIONS:
- Cover the inside of your Slow Cooker with melted butter.
- In a large bowl, combine butter and several cups of tiny marshmallows. Set your Slow Cooker on LOW heat regime.
- Cover the lid and cook for next 2 hours. Open lid every 30 minutes to check the dish and stir it. Add dried cranberries, cereal, and pistachios. Stir to coat evenly.
- Turn off and let stand to cool.
- Form 36 small balls out of Slow Cooker mixture. Arrange bowls over a large plate and leave them until thick and non-sticky.
- Serve along with hot tea or other drinks.

**Nutrition: Calories: 328 Fat: 9g Carbohydrates: 5g Protein: 20g**

## Caramel-Pear Pudding Cake

You should definitely try this!

⌛ **Prep time: 32 minutes Cooking time: 3 hours**
**Servings: 19**

INGREDIENTS:
Greek yogurt
Flour
Flax seed
Sugar
Butter
Canola oil
Fat-free milk
Dried apples
Hot water
Baking powder
Pure pear nectar
Brown sugar

DIRECTIONS:
- Coat your Slow Cooker with a cooking spray.
- In a medium bowl, combine flour, flax seed meal, baking powder, grounded cinnamon, granulated sugar.
- Stir in milk and add some olive oil. Stir until the mixture is evenly smooth. Add dried pears. Mix for again.
- Pour the batter into Slow Cooker. Using a large spoon, arrange evenly over the bottom.
- In a saucepan, whisk the water, brown sugar, pear nectar. Stir in the butter. Simmer until the sugar dissolves. Pour into Slow Cooker.
- Cook on LOW setting for 3 hours.

**Nutrition: Calories: 132 Fat: 4g Carbohydrates: 51g Protein: 33g**

## Double-Berry Cobbler

Fresh berries and delicious topping!

⌛ **Prep time: 29 minutes Cooking time: 3 hours**
**Servings: 7**

INGREDIENTS:
Fresh blueberries
Fresh blackberries
Sugar
Water
Tapioca
Cup flour
Cornmeal
Sugar
Baking powder
Salt
1 chicken egg
Cup milk
Butter, melted
Lemon zest
Vanilla ice cream

DIRECTIONS:
- Grease your Slow Cooker with a small amount of melted butter.
- Right in your Slow Cooker, combine one egg, tapioca, sugar, milk, water, half cup flour and baking powder.
- Combine all the ingredients well and cover the lid of your Slow Cooker. Cook on HIGH temperature mode for 1 hour.
- Meanwhile, make a topping out of fresh berries, lemon zest, melted butter. When the cobbler is ready, serve it with berry topping.

**Nutrition: Calories: 354 Fat: 12g Carbohydrates: 24g Protein: 23g**

## Dark Chocolate Fondue with Fruit Kabobs

Unusual recipe with sweet ingredients!

⌛ **Prep time: 23 minutes Cooking time: 1 hour**
**Servings: 16**

INGREDIENTS:
Whipped dessert topping
Dark chocolate pieces
Hot strong coffee
Strawberry halves
Pineapple
Apple
Kiwifruit chunks
Raspberries

DIRECTIONS:
- Grease your Slow Cooker with butter or cooking spray.
- In a bowl, combine fresh whipped topping with chocolate pieces. Stir the mixture until smooth, the transfer to Slow Cooker.]
- Cover the lid. Set you Slow Cooker to LOW temperature mode and cook for 45 minutes (just until the chocolate melts).
- Whisk in coffee - use the spoon and continue adding coffee until pourable.

- Make fruit kabobs - dice fruits and place it on large and long toothpicks along with berries. Serve warm with fruit kabobs.

**Nutrition: Calories: 198 Fat: 2g Carbohydrates: 5g Protein: 7g**

## Raspberry Fudge Brownies

So delicious with fresh berries and gooey chocolate!

Prep time: 32 minutes Cooking time: 2 hours
Servings: 18

INGREDIENTS:
Half cup margarine
Unsweetened chocolate
Two chicken eggs
3 tbsp sugar
Red raspberry jam
Vanilla
Flour
Baking powder
Vanilla ice cream (optional)
DIRECTIONS:
- Generously grease two cooking jars and sprinkle them with the flour. In a large saucepan, melt margarine with chocolate (set low heat).
- When ready, remove from heat and stir in jam, eggs, vanilla and sugar. Slightly beat and combine with flour mixture.
- Pour the mixture into jars, and place the jars into Slow Cooker. Cook on HIGH temperature mode for 2 hours.
- Serve with fresh berries or vanilla jam. You can add your favorite topping – chocolate or fruit.

**Nutrition: Calories: 263 Fat: 23g Carbohydrates: 32g Protein: 53g**

## Walnut Apple Crisp

Amazing and fast one for busy days!

Prep time: 11 minutes Cooking time: 4 hours
Servings: 8

INGREDIENTS:
Granulated sugar
2 tsps lemon juice
Teaspoons cornstarch
Ground ginger
Ground cinnamon
6 tart apples
Half cup flour
Light brown sugar
Ground nutmeg
Salt
Unsalted butter
Chopped walnuts
Vanilla ice cream (optional)
DIRECTIONS:
- Coat the inside surface of your Slow Cooker with cooking spray.
- In a large bowl mix three tablespoons of granulated sugar, add lemon juice, cornstarch and cinnamon.
- Carefully stir in the spice mixture chopped apples. Transfer apple butter to your Slow Cooker.

- Meanwhile, make the topping. In a small bowl whisk flour with granulated sugar, light brown sugar, and mixed cinnamon, salt and nutmeg. Stir in walnuts.
- Add the topping over the main butter in Slow Cooker.
- Cover the lid tightly. Leave the meal preparing for 4 hours. Use LOW heat mode. Serve with preferred ice cream.

**Nutrition: Calories: 128 Fat: 3g Carbohydrates: 8g Protein: 2g**

## Peppermint Pretzel Candies

Unusual recipe with white chocolate and nuts!

Prep time: 25 minutes Cooking time: 2 hours
Servings: 24

INGREDIENTS:
Vanilla-flavor candy coating
White baking chocolate
Butter-flavor shortening
Peppermint extract
1 pack pretzel twists
Round peppermint candies
Dark chocolate
DIRECTIONS:
- Grease your Slow Cooker with olive oil or butter. You can also use the cooking spray if you want. Right in Slow Cooker, gather white chocolate, candy coating, shortening. Carefully stir until smooth.
- Cover your Slow Cooker with a lid. Cook on LOW temperature setting for 1 hour. When the mixture is melted and became smooth, start to stir every 30 minutes.
- Add peppermint extract, pretzels. Stir in peppermint candies.
- When ready, transfer the mixture to two baking sheets and drizzle with melted dark chocolate. Cook for 5 or 7 minutes.
- To serve, sprinkle with peppermint candies.

**Nutrition: Calories: 311 Fat: 8g Carbohydrates: 17g Protein: 20g**

## Pumpkin Spiced and Pomegranate Cheesecake

The perfect duo of two different kinds of fruits!

Prep time: 23 minutes Cooking time: 3 hours
Servings: 11

INGREDIENTS:
Cream cheese
Granulated sugar
All-purpose flour
Pumpkin pie spice
Vanilla
Canned pumpkin
Frozen egg product
Shredded orange peel
Warm water
Pomegranate juice
Sugar
Cornstarch
Pomegranate seeds
DIRECTIONS:

- Lightly coat your Slow Cooker with a cooking spray or melted butter. In a large bowl beat cream cheese (use an electric mixer).
- Add sugar, sifted flour, pumpkin pie spice and vanilla. Beat until combined. Add pumpkin and egg product until smooth.
- Sprinkle with orange peel.
- Pour the dough into Slow Cooker.
- Cover with the lid. Prepare on HIGH mode for 2 hours.

**Nutrition: Calories: 342 Fat: 23g Carbohydrates: 47g Protein: 33g**

## Coconut-Mocha Poached Pears

Tropical taste from your Slow Cooker!

Prep time: 23 minutes Cooking time: 4 hours
Servings: 8

INGREDIENTS:
6 ripe pears
Sugar
Cocoa powder
Light coconut milk
Strong coffee
2 tbsp coffee liqueur
Whipped dessert topping
Toasted coconut
Grated chocolate
DIRECTIONS:
- Wash and eel pears. Quarter the pears lengthwise, carefully remove the cores. Put pears into greased with melted butter Slow Cooker.
- In a bowl, combine sugar with cocoa powder. Add coconut milk, coffee, liqueur.
- Pour the coffee mixture over the pears in your Slow Cooker. Cover under cover during 4 hours. Use LOW temperature setting
- With a slotted spoon, place the pears in dessert dishes. Add cooking liquid. To serve, use dessert topping, coconut or chocolate.

**Nutrition: Calories: 523 Fat: 34g Carbohydrates: 35g Protein: 32g**

## Ginger-Orange Cheesecake

You can forget about baking with this one!

Prep time: 24 minutes Cooking time: 3 hours
Servings: 11

INGREDIENTS:
Cream cheese
Half cup sugar
1 tsp orange peel
Orange juice
1tbsp flour
Vanilla
Half cup sour cream
Frozen egg product
Water
2 blood oranges
DIRECTIONS:
- Cover your Slow Cooker dish with thin layer of melted butter. In a bowl, mix sugar, cream cheese and vanilla.
- Pour in orange juice and beat everything with a kitchen mixer. Add sour cream and beat again until it is all smooth.
- Add orange peel and pour the batter with some water into greased Slow Cooker. Cook on HIGH temperature mode for around 3 hours.
- To serve, garnish pie with sliced orange or crystallized ginger.

**Nutrition: Calories: 243 Fat: 23g Carbohydrates: 21g Protein: 45g**

## Candy Bar Fondue

The easy and delicious dessert you will not forget!

Prep time: 12 minutes Cooking time: 3 hours
Servings: 12

INGREDIENTS:
4 bar nougat with almonds
Milk chocolate
Jar marshmallow crème
Whipping cream
Finely chopped almonds
Raspberry liqueur (optional)
Assorted dippers
DIRECTIONS:
- In a large bowl, combine chopped nougat bars, milk chocolate bars and cream. Grease your Slow Cooker. You can use plain melted butter or olive oil.
- Mix well and transfer nougat mixture into Slow Cooker. Cover the lid tightly.
- Set your Slow Cooker to LOW temperature mode and prepare for 2 hours. When ready, add almonds and your favorite liquor (if desired).
- Once it is ready, serve with fruit dippers or cookies.

**Nutrition: Calories: 182 Fat: 2g Carbohydrates: 1g Protein: 12g**

## Dutch Apple Sweet Pudding Cake

Homespun and healthy recipe!

Prep time: 23 minutes Cooking time: 3 hours
Servings: 6

INGREDIENTS:
Apple pie filling
Dried cherries
Flour
Sugar
Baking powder
Salt
Half milk
Butter
Chopped walnuts
Apple juice
Brown sugar
Melted butter
Whipped cream
Walnuts
DIRECTIONS:
- Slightly grease your Slow Cooker with cooking spray or melted butter.

- In a small saucepan, bring apple pie filling to boil. Stir in cherries and simmer for several minutes. Transfer the cherry-apple mixture greased Slow Cooker.
- In a medium bowl, mix flour with baking powder and granulated sugar. Add a pinch of salt. Pour in milk and add melted butter. Stir well just to combine the ingredients.
- Transfer the mixture to your Slow Cooker and spread evenly over the bottom. Cook for 2 hours. Use a HIGH temp setting.

**Nutrition: Calories: 242 Fat: 21g Carbohydrates: 65g Protein: 72g**

## Chocolate Fondue

Just three ingredients for the delicious recipe!

Prep time: 11 minutes Cooking time: 2 hours
Servings: 16

INGREDIENTS:
Milk chocolate bar
Large marshmallows
Half-and-half
Assorted dippers
DIRECTIONS:
- Grease your Slow Cooker with unsalted and melted butter.
- In a large bowl, gather chocolate, half-and-half and large marshmallows. Stir well. Cover your Slow Cooker with a lid.
- Set LOW temperature setting and cook for two hours. Once during the cooking process, open the lid and stir the ingredients.
- Serve just after it is ready.

**Nutrition: Calories: 352 Fat: 32g Carbohydrates: 24g Protein: 61g**

## Crustless Lemony Cheesecake

Try this one with your friends!

Prep time: 21 minutes Cooking time: 3 hours
Servings: 8

INGREDIENTS:
Cream cheese
Sugar
Lemon juice
Flour
Vanilla
Sour cream
3 chicken eggs
Shredded lemon peel
Warm water
Fresh raspberries
Mint
DIRECTIONS:
- Cover the bottom of your Slow Cooker with a layer of melted butter or just a spray.
- In a bowl, whisk cream cheese, lemon juice, plain sugar, vanilla and flour. Beat with a kitchen mixer.
- Add eggs and stir in lemon peel. Beat until smooth.
- Transfer the mixture into prepared Slow Cooker. Cover with the lid.
- Start cooking on HIGH temperature. Turn your Slow Cooker off in 2 hours. To serve, you can garnish the dish with mint leaves or fresh raspberries.

**Nutrition: Calories: 352 Fat: 32g Carbohydrates: 62g Protein: 26g**

## Gingerbread Pudding Cake

An awesome taste for the cold autumn season!

Prep time: 14 minutes Cooking time: 2 hours
Servings: 8

INGREDIENTS:
Pack gingerbread mix
Milk
Cup raisins
Water
Brown sugar
Butter
Ice cream (optional)
DIRECTIONS:
- Grease your Slow Cooker with a cooking spray. If you do not have one, simply use melted butter. In a bowl, combine milk and gingerbread mix. Stir until it is evenly wet.
- Add raisins and mix again until the batter is thick.
- Transfer the mixture into Slow Cooker and spread evenly all over its' bottom.
- In a saucepan, mix brown sugar, butter, water. Stir until sugar dissolves. Pour into Slow Cooker. Cook under the lid for 2 hours. Apply HIGH temperature mode.
- Serve in small dessert bowls with your favorite ice cream.

**Nutrition: Calories: 132 Fat: 32g Carbohydrates: 44g Protein: 21g**

## Chocolate Bread Pudding with Mocha

Amazing for those who are fans of chocolate!

Prep time: 21 minutes Cooking time: 3 hours
Servings: 8

INGREDIENTS:
Fat-free milk
Semisweet chocolate pieces
Cocoa powder
Frozen egg substitute
Chia seeds
Bread cubes
Mocha sauce
DIRECTIONS:
- Grease your Slow Cooker - use melted butter or cooking spray. Heat the milk in a saucepan until warm, but not boiling.
- Add cocoa powder and chocolate pieces. Don't stir! Let stand for several minutes, then slightly whisk.
- In a bowl, combine chia seeds, egg substitute. Pour in the chocolate mixture. Add bread cubes. Transfer the mixture to Slow Cooker and cover the lid.
- Choose a LOW temperature mode and cook for 2 hours. Serve with Mocha sauce.

**Nutrition: Calories: 264 Fat: 13g Carbohydrates: 41g Protein: 21g**

## Orange-Caramel Pudding Cake

Sweet and a little spicy dessert for your family!

⏱ **Prep time: 23 minutes Cooking time: 5 hours**
**Servings: 6**

INGREDIENTS:
1cup flour
Granulated sugar
Baking powder
Ground cinnamon
Salt
Half cup milk
2tbsp butter
Half cup pecans
Raisins
Cup water
Finely shredded orange peel
Orange juice
Brown sugar
Tablespoon butter
Caramel ice cream topping
Pecans
Whipped cream

DIRECTIONS:
- Lightly grease the inside of your Slow Cooker with melted butter or cooking spray. Set crockpot aside.
- In a bowl, combine and whisk flour, baking powder, sugar, cinnamon. Add a little salt Add milk and some melte butter. Slightly mix just until combined.
- Add pecans and fresh currants.
- Spread the mixture in the prepared cooker and spread it evenly.
- In a preheated saucepan, mix the water with orange peel, juice, dark brown sugar, and melted butter. Bring to boil.
- Carefully pour the saucepan mixture in cooker. Cover the lid. Prepare with LOW mode on for 5 hours.
- Let stand, without the lid, for 45 minutes.

**Nutrition: Calories: 186 Fat: 1g Carbohydrates: 8g Protein: 5g**

## Fruit Compote with Spicy Ginger

Use as many fruits as you like!

⏱ **Prep time: 16 minutes Cooking time: 8 hours**
**Servings: 11**

INGREDIENTS:
3 medium pears
Can pineapple chunks
Dried apricots, quartered
Frozen orange juice
Brown sugar
Tapioca
Grated fresh ginger
Frozen unsweetened cherries
Flaked coconut
Macadamia nuts

DIRECTIONS:
- In a large bowl, combine undrained pineapple, pear and dried apricots. Add brown sugar, ginger and tapioca.
- Pour in the orange juice. Stir everything well to dissolve sugar.
- Grease your Slow Cooker with melted butter or olive oil. If can, use special cooking spray. Transfer the mixture to Slow Cooker and cover tightly with the lid.
- Prepare during 8 hours on LOW mode.
- Cool a little to serve. Serve warm in a little dessert dishes.

**Nutrition: Calories: 218 Fat: 9g Carbohydrates: 2g Protein: 10g**

## Old-Fashioned Rice Pudding

This is awesome and easy to prepare!

⏱ **Prep time: 16 minutes Cooking time: 3 hours**
**Servings: 11**

INGREDIENTS:
4 cups rice
Evaporated milk
Cup milk
Cup sugar
Cold water
Raisins
Dried cherries
Softened butter
Tablespoon vanilla
Teaspoon ground cinnamon

DIRECTIONS:
- Cover the bottom and sides of your Slow Cooker with melted butter or cooking spray with anti-stick effect.
- Take a large bowl and gather cooked rice and sugar. Combine until mixed well. Add butter, raisins, cinnamon and vanilla. Transfer to Slow Cooker.
- Pour over with plain milk, water and evaporated milk. Mix until sugar dissolved. Cover the lid of your Slow Cooker. Prepare during 3 hours on LOW setting.
- To serve, stir for one more time.

**Nutrition: Calories: 342 Fat: 14g Carbohydrates: 21g Protein: 34g**

## White Chocolate with Apricot Bread Pudding

Delicious and simple summertime dessert!

⏱ **Prep time: 32 minutes Cooking time: 4 hours**
**Servings: 8**

INGREDIENTS:
1 cup half-and-half
White chocolate squares Snipped dried apricots
2 chicken eggs
Cup sugar
Ground cardamom
Dried bread cubes
Sliced almonds
Cup warm water
Fresh raspberries

DIRECTIONS:
- In a small saucepan preheat half-and-half using a medium heat. When it is warm enough, but not boiling yet, set aside.
- Add finely chopped white baking squares along with apricots. Blend until chocolate squares are completely melted.
- In another bowl, beat chicken eggs with a fork. Add and whisk cardamon and sugar. Blend egg mixture with a hot chocolate mixture. Stir in almonds.
- Transfer the mixture into Slow Cooker. Leave to prepare hours on LOW temperature setting. Serve warm in small dessert dishes. Garnish with chocolate or fresh berries.

Nutrition: Calories: 422 Fat: 24g Carbohydrates: 23g Protein: 56g

## Strawberry Mojito Shortcakes

Sweet and easy receipt for summer!

Prep time: 34 minutes Cooking time: 2 hours
Servings: 6

INGREDIENTS:
Sugar
1 cup flour
Butter
Baking powder
2 tbsp rum
1 chicken egg
Half cup whipping cream
Lime zest
Fresh mint
2 cup strawberries
1 cup sour milk

DIRECTIONS:
- In a wide bowl, combine baking soda, flour, butter, and sour milk. In addition, blend everything with a blender.
- In a separate bowl, beat one egg and whisk it with buttermilk. Combine two mixtures and stir, until the smooth consistency.
- Prepare small cake cooking jars and cover each jar with a small piece of foil. Place into Slow Cooker and leave for 2 covers under HIGH heat mode.
- Make a topping out of crushed strawberries, zest, mint, sugar and rum.
- Cool the topping for several hours. To serve, top cakes with strawberry mixture and garnish with whole strawberries and mint leaves.

Nutrition: Calories: 159 Fat: 3g Carbohydrates: 10g Protein: 22g

## Peach Graham Cracker Summer Cake

This will make your life so much simpler!

Prep time: 23 minutes Cooking time: 3 hours
Servings: 8

INGREDIENTS:
Butter
White sugar
3 peaches
Baking soda
Cup milk
Ginger
Salt
Graham cracker
Grated nutmeg
2 cups flour
Vanilla ice cream

DIRECTIONS:
- Grease your Slow Cooker with olive oil or just spread cooking over its bottom and sides. Slice the peaches and add them to Slow Cooker.
- In a saucepan, sugar, softened butter and one cup sugar. Cook on high heat until the sugar is dissolved.
- Pour the peaches into sugar mixture from the saucepan.
- In a bowl, combine graham crackers (previously crashed) and milk.
- Add chicken eggs, ginger, nutmeg, baking soda, sifted flour. Mix the ingredients and add to Slow Cooker.
- Cook on HIGH mode for approximately 2 hours. Serve with white vanilla ice cream or fruit topping.

Nutrition: Calories: 371 Fat: 22g Carbohydrates: 31g Protein: 32g

## Slow Cooker Berry Crisp

Fast and delicious dessert for summertime!

Prep time: 5 minutes Cooking time: 3 hours
Servings: 8

INGREDIENTS:
2 cups blueberries
1 cup blackberries
Old fashioned oats
Flour
1 cup raspberries
Brown sugar
2 cups strawberries
Cinnamon
1/2 cup butter

DIRECTIONS:
- Before you start cooking, chop the berries into halves and set aside for a little while.
- Finely grease your Slow Cooker with melted butter. If you prefer, use for greasing special anti-stick spray.
- In a bowl, combine brown sugar, oats and flour. Add room temperature butter and stir until crumbly.
- Place the berries into prepared Slow Cooker. Sprinkle fruits with sugar and oats mixture.
- Put the lid on and start cooking on HIGH temperature mode for 2 hours.

Nutrition: Calories: 211 Fat: 1g Carbohydrates: 2g Protein: 7g

## Ginger Chicken in Lettuce Cups

The spicy chicken will light your day!

Prep time: 16 minutes Cooking time: 7 hours
Servings: 4

INGREDIENTS:
2clove garlic
3tbsp. brown sugar
1 tbsp. soy sauce
Half teaspoon red pepper (crushed)
1 tbsp. fresh ginger (grated)
2-4chicken thighs (boneless)
¾ cup white rice (long grain)
2 scallions
1 large orange
1 small Boston lettuce)
Balsamic vinegar

DIRECTIONS:
- Butter your Slow Cooker and mix in it the sugar, soy sauce, balsamic vinegar, garlic, ginger and red pepper.
- Add chicken and toss to coat with balsamic mixture.

- Cook under the lid for 6-7 hours on LOW temperature mode or for 3-4 hour on HIGH. When it is about thirty minutes left before serving, cook the rice according to the package instruction.
- Meanwhile, cut and peel the orange, remove the peel and white parts. Fold in the scallions. When the chicken is ready, shared it with two forks and mix with the cooking liquid.
- To serve, fill the lettuce with the rice, chicken and orange slices.

**Nutrition: Calories: 746 Fat: 55g Carbohydrates: 76g Protein: 88g**

## Peach Upside Down Cake

Amazing choice for a summer dessert!

Prep time: 5 minutes Cooking time: 3 hours
Servings: 8

INGREDIENTS:
Three cans peaches
2 cups flour
Salt
5 tbsp melted butter
Baking powder
Almond extract
5 tbsp brown sugar
Cinnamon
Nutmeg
1 cup whole milk

DIRECTIONS:
- Drain the peaches, but reserve liquid from the cans.
- Melt the butter, pour it into Slow Cooker. Spread evenly over its surface to coat.
- Combine brown sugar, ground nutmeg and cinnamon. Sprinkle the sweet mixture over butter in Slow Cooker.
- Place peaches in one layer over the butter and sugar mix.
- Using an electric mixer, combine white sugar with softened butter. Add eggs and almond extract. Separately, mix flour, salt and baking powder. Working in batches, combine all the ingredients and make a batter.
- Place into Slow Cooker and fit the batter over the bottom. Cook for 2 hours using HIGH temperature mode.

**Nutrition: Calories: 654 Fat: 27g Carbohydrates: 97g Protein: 6g**

## Apple-Cherry Cobbler

Warm and Autumn-Spiced Dessert!

Prep time: 5 minutes Cooking time: 3 hours
Servings: 6

INGREDIENTS:
Half cup sugar
Quick-cooking tapioca
Light cream
Cooking apples
Half cup dried cherries
Apple pie spice
Ice cream,
Refrigerated crescent rolls
Melted butter
Pitted tart cherries

DIRECTIONS:
- Line the bottom of your Slow Cooker with a parchment paper.
- Right in a cooking dish, combine sugar, apple pie spice, tapioca. Slightly stir to combine. Chop apples into small slices and place into Slow Cooker.
- Add canned cherries (along with liquids), and dried cherries. Stir for one more time. Cover the lid of your Cooker. Turn it on LOW temp and prepare for 7 hours.
- Serve cherry-and-apple mixture over your favorite buns or with apple chips.

**Nutrition: Calories: 414 Fat: 12g Carbohydrates: 71g Protein: 5g**

## Chocolate Cherry Slow Cooker Cake

The great dessert for any holiday!

Prep time: 5 minutes Cooking time: 4 hours
Servings: 8

INGREDIENTS:
Half cup water
Chocolate chips
Red velvet cake mix
Half cup sour cream
2 chicken eggs
Chocolate fudge mix
Canned cherry filling

DIRECTIONS:
- Grease your Slow Cooker with preferred oil or simply with unsalted melted butter.
- In a bowl, combine beaten chicken eggs, chocolate pudding mix, sour cream and water. You can also do in with a kitchen mixer.
- Add cake mix and mix for one more time.
- In a bowl, combine chocolate chips with canned cherry filling. When it is all smooth, stir into the main batter.
- Transfer the mixture into Slow Cooker and stir for one more time. Cover the lid. Cook, using a LOW temperature regime, for at least 4 hours.

**Nutrition: Calories: 558 Fat: 17g Carbohydrates: 97g Protein: 7g**

## Slow Cooker Apple Crisp

It tastes delicious with ice cream!

Prep time: 38 minutes Cooking time: 3 hours
Servings: 6

INGREDIENTS:
Light brown sugar
Ground cinnamon
Cup flour
Nutmeg
Salt
Half cup butter
Cornstarch
Chopped walnuts
Ground ginger
Lemon juice
3 apples

DIRECTIONS:
- In a large bowl, combine brown and white sugars with cinnamon, salt and grounded nutmeg. Stir together until smooth.

- Stir the butter into flour mixture until it is crumbled. You can use a fork for it or simply combine the ingredients with your fingers.
- In another bowl, combine cornstarch, sugar, cinnamon and ginger.
- Arrange chopped apples over the Slow Cookers' bottom add lemon juice and cornstarch mixture. Stir everything well.
- Sprinkle with walnut sprinkles.
- Cook under the lid for 2 hours using HIGH temperature mode.

**Nutrition: Calories: 593 Fat: 29g Carbohydrates: 83g Protein: 5g**

## Rice Pudding in a Slow Cooker

Perfect with baked apples!

- Prep time: 14 minutes Cooking time: 2 hours
- Servings: 19

INGREDIENTS:
White sugar
Vanilla extract
Ground nutmeg
2 cans evaporated milk
1 cup white rice
Cinnamon stick

DIRECTIONS:
- In a bowl, combine uncooked rice, vanilla, sugar, nutmeg.
- Pour the rice mixture over with evaporated milk. Whisk the ingredients to distribute evenly with milk.
- Grease Slow Cooker with melted butter, just in case. Start preheating it. Pour the rice mixture into prepared Slow Cooker.
- Place the cinnamon stick into the mixture.
- Cover the lid of your Slow Cooker. Start to cook on LOW mode for around 2 hours. Remember to stir the content time after time.
- To serve, remove cinnamon stick. Stick while the pie is still warm.

**Nutrition: Calories: 321 Fat: 7g Carbohydrates: 56g Protein: 8g**

## Caramel Apples in Sweet Dip

Amazing Autumn Flavors in Your House

- Prep time: 5 minutes Cooking time: 2 hours
- Servings: 18

INGREDIENTS:
3 medium onions
Salt
One cup milk
Cinnamon
2 tbsp sugar
Pinch nutmeg
1 can caramel sauce
Refrigerated pie dough

DIRECTIONS:
- Grease your Slow Cooker or simply cover it with cooking spray.
- Right in your Slow Cooker, bring together cored and chopped apples, nutmeg and cinnamon. Stir in caramel and add one pinch of salt. Stir well to combine all ingredients well.
- Cook for 2 hours on HIGH temperature regime. When ready, transfer pie crust onto baking sheet.
- In a separate bowl mix cinnamon with sugar and sprinkle the pie. Cook in oven for several minutes. Serve.

**Nutrition: Calories: 341 Fat: 16g Carbohydrates: 66g Protein: 34g**

## Autumn Pumpkin Sweet Pie

Crusty and flavored for the season!

- Prep time: 5 minutes Cooking time: 4
- Servings: 20

INGREDIENTS:
2 cans evaporated milk
Half tsp baking powder
4 tbsp brown sugar
2 tbsp melted butter
Half cup flour
2 tsp pumpkin spice
Salt
2 chicken eggs
1 large pumpkin

DIRECTIONS:
- Grease your Slow Cooker with olive oil or melted butter, just what you like better. Peel pumpkin and remove all the seeds. Cut into small bite-sized pieces.
- In a bowl, whisk chicken eggs, evaporated milk, remaining melted butter, brown sugar, salt, pumpkin spice and baking powder.
- When all the other ingredients are well combined, stir in sliced pumpkin. Cover the lid of your Slow Cooker and turn it on.
- Cook the pie for 4 hours, use LOW temperature mode.

**Nutrition: Calories: 380 Fat: 12g Carbohydrates: 32g Protein: 9g**

## Sweet Scones with Chocolate Drops

Hot and delicious for tea and coffee!

- Prep time: 5 minutes Cooking time: 2 hours
- Servings: 14

INGREDIENTS:
Pinch salt
Self-raising flour
Half cup chocolate chips
Half cup milk
Cubed butter
1 tbsp sugar

DIRECTIONS:
- In a bowl, combine the flour with sugar and some salt to your taste. Slightly melt the butter cubes and carefully stir them into the flour mixture. Add milk and whisk until the mixture transforms into a soft dough.
- Add chocolate chips or any other filling you may like.
- Form into long and cut into small bite-sized pieces. You may also form small triangles out of this dough if you like.
- Place into greased Slow Cooker for approximately 2 hours. Cook on HIGH temperature mode.

**Nutrition: Calories: 235 Fat: 7g Carbohydrates: 21g Protein: 3g**

## Pumpkin and Coffee Sweet Cake

Amazing duo of two tastes!

⌀ Prep time: 8 minutes Cooking time: 2 hours
Servings: 10

INGREDIENTS:
Baking soda
Salt
2 cups pastry flour
Chicken egg
Vanilla extract
Unsalted butter
Maple syrup
1 cup pumpkin puree
Ginger
Lemon juice
Nutmeg
Baking powder
Cinnamon
DIRECTIONS:
- Cover the bottom of Slow Cooker with a foil and spray with anti-sticking cooking spray. In a bowl, whisk flour and oats. Add cinnamon, as you usually like.
- Pour in melted and unsalted butter and maple syrup. Stir well to make a homogenous mass without any dry bits.
- In a bowl, combine flour along with the other cake ingredients. In a third bowl, mix egg white with vanilla and melted butter.
- Add maple syrup along with lemon juice. Mix in pumpkin.
- Place the batter all over the Slow Cooker bottom. Prepare on LOW for 2 hours.

Nutrition: Calories: 385 Fat: 4g Carbohydrates: 33g Protein: 12g

## Peach Cobbler in Slow Cooker

Try this with ice cream in summer!

⌀ Prep time: 17 minutes Cooking time: 4 hours
Servings: 11

INGREDIENTS:
Cinnamon
Three peaches
3 tbsp sugar
Bisquick mix
Half cup milk
Nutmeg
Vanilla extract
DIRECTIONS:
- Cover the bottom and sides of Slow Cooker with your favorite cooking spray. You can also line the bottom with a parchment.
- In a bowl of medium size, combine peaches with sugar and ground cinnamon. Place the spiced peaches all over the bottom of your cooking pot.
- Take a bowl one more time and place the Bisquick mix, cinnamon, brown or white sugar, nutmeg and extract of vanilla in it. Pour in milk and stir to get a smooth mass.
- Pour and spread the milk mixture all over the peaches in your Slow Cooker. Set your Slow Cooker to LOW temperature setting and leave for 4 hours.
- Serve with vanilla ice cream and mint leaves.

Nutrition: Calories: 229 Fat: 1g Carbohydrates: 33g Protein: 9g

## Cinnamon Roll for Slow Cooker

Easy and fast sweet dessert!

⌀ Prep time: 8 minutes Cooking time: 2 hours
Servings: 12

INGREDIENTS:
1 tsp cinnamon
Half cup unsalted butter
Granulated sugar
Canned cinnamon rolls
Half cup brown sugar
DIRECTIONS:
- Open the cans of cinnamon rolls and cut each roll into six slices. Sprinkle sliced rolls with granulated sugar and set aside.
- In a medium bowl, combine brown sugar with previously melted plain butter.
- Spray the sides and bottom of your Slow Cooker with cooking spray or simply coat with a thin layer of melted butter.
- Place cinnamon slices into Cooker and evenly arrange all over the bottom. Pour in with the butter mixture.
- Cover the lid tightly. Prepare the dessert for 2 hours on HIGH temperature regime.

Nutrition: Calories: 311 Fat: 9g Carbohydrates: 14g Protein: 24g

## Pineapple and Coconut Cake

Exotic conclusion for any dinner!

⌀ Prep time: 14 minutes Cooking time: 2 hours
Servings: 11

INGREDIENTS:
Yellow cake mix
Melted butter
Cup crashed pineapples
3 chicken eggs
Cup water
Coconut
Chopped pecans
DIRECTIONS:
- Spray your Slow Cooker with special cooking spray or simply grease with olive oil.
- Slice coconut into small pieces and mix it with melted butter, one cup water and three beaten eggs.
- Carefully stir in crashed pineapples and chopped pecans. Season with yellow cake mix. Transfer the batter into Slow Cooker and make it spread evenly, use the spatula or large spoon. Cover the lid and do not remove it until the cake is ready. Cook for 2 hours using a HIGH temperature mode.
- To serve, add some whipped cream on the serving plate.

Nutrition: Calories: 288 Fat: 6g Carbohydrates: 24g Protein: 55g

## Chocolate Chip Slow Cooker Cookie

Amazing with chocolate ice cream!

⌀ Prep time: 5 minutes Cooking time: 3 hours
Servings: 24

INGREDIENTS:
Room temperature butter
Half cup sugar
Baking powder
2 cups flour
Half cup dark chocolate
Raisins
Muscovado sugar
Half cup choco-chips
Vanilla extract
Salt to taste

DIRECTIONS:
- In a bowl, beat to fluffy chicken eggs, slightly melted butter, vanilla extract and both sugars. In a large bowl, finely combine the flour with salt to your taste and baking powder.
- Working in small batches, combine the flour with butter mixture.
- Add the chocolate chips and mix to smooth mass. The chips should be completely distributed in the dough.
- Grease your Slow Cooker and start preheating it.
- Pour the dough into Slow Cooker and cook for 3 hours with the lid on. Use a LOW temperature regime.

**Nutrition: Calories: 299 Fat: 12g Carbohydrates: 14g Protein: 61g**

# Pumpkin and Bread Pecan Pudding

Healthy and delicious choice!

Prep time: 5 minutes Cooking time: 4 hours
Servings: 8

INGREDIENTS:
2- day-old bread loaf
Ground ginger
Cinnamon
Ground cloves
Half cup toasted pecans
1 cup cream
Canned pumpkin
Half cup sugar
Caramel topping
Ice cream

DIRECTIONS:
- Cut the yesterday bread into small cubes. Slice enough cubes to fill eight full cups. Grease your Slow Cooker with melted and unsalted butter.
- Place bread cubes into Slow Cooker and spread evenly. Slightly sprinkle with cinnamon and chopped pecans.
- In a bowl, whisk chicken eggs with cream and melted butter.
- Add nutmeg, vanilla, pumpkin, melted butter cloves and ground ginger. Mix and pour the liquid mixture over the bread in Slow Cooker.
- Cover with the lid and cook for 4 hours on LOW mode.

**Nutrition: Calories: 431 Fat: 23g Carbohydrates: 4g Protein: 24g**

# Carrot Cake with Creamy Topping

Sweet root vegetables for your tea!

Prep time: 5 minutes Cooking time: 3 hours
Servings: 18

INGREDIENTS:
Unsweetened applesauce
3 chicken eggs
Baking powder
Soda
2 cups sugar
Shredded coconut
Vanilla extract
2 cups flour
3 grated carrots
1 cup nuts
Canned pineapple

DIRECTIONS:
- Cover the bottom of your Slow Cooker with foil or parchment paper.
- In a bowl, beat chicken eggs and whisk them with sugar and applesauce. Add baking soda, flour, salt, baking soda and cinnamon.
- Mix well and combine with chopped carrots, vanilla extract, chopped nuts, pineapple and coconut. Make sure that all ingredients are combined and smooth. Pour the batter mixture into Slow Cooker.
- Cook on LOW temperature mode for 3 hours. Check the readiness with a wooden toothpick. If needed, cook for one more hour.

**Nutrition: Calories: 412 Fat: 8g Carbohydrates: 33g Protein: 8g**

# Dump Cake with Chocolate

This is amazing for all chocolate fans!

Prep time: 5 minutes Cooking time: 4 hours
Servings: 12

INGREDIENTS:
One cup Nutella
Devils cake mix
Chocolate pudding mix
One stick butter
One cup milk

DIRECTIONS:
- Cover the bottom of your Slow Cooker with parchment paper or special cooking spray. Arrange dry cake mix all over the bottom of your Slow Cooker.
- Place the second layer with chocolate pudding mix and pour it over with melted butter. Pour in milk and slightly stir.
- Finally, top everything with the content of one Nutella can. Press the mixture with a spoon or just your hands so all dry ingredients can be wet.
- Set your Slow Cooker to LOW temperature mode and leave to cook for 4 hours. You may serve it right from Slow Cooker or transfer into small bowls.

**Nutrition: Calories: 155 Fat: 8g Carbohydrates: 1g Protein: 7g**

# Fudged Brownies in Slow Cooker

Full of chocolate and flavors!

Prep time: 15 minutes Cooking time: 3 hours
Servings: 12

INGREDIENTS:

2 chicken eggs
1 box brownie mix
Water
Mini chocolate chips
Packed caramel bits
Hot fudge sauce
3 tbsp applesauce
Heavy cream
3 tbsp chopped pecans

DIRECTIONS:
- Generously spray your Slow Cooker with cooking spray.
- In a separate bowl, bring together chocolate chips, brownie mix, water, applesauce (or oil), chicken eggs and hot water. Mix to combine all ingredients well.
- Carefully transfer your brownie batter in prepared Slow Cooker.
- Separately, cook the caramel and heavy cream. Combine ingredients into a bowl and place into microwave. Cook for several minutes, stopping each 30 seconds and stirring, until caramel is completely dissolved.
- Stir in pecans and pour the caramel sauce over the brownie mixture. With a knife, swirl the caramel in.
- Whisk hot fudge sauce with water until smooth and add to Slow Cooker. Cook on HIGH temperature mode for 3 hours.

**Nutrition: Calories: 386 Fat: 32g Carbohydrates: 32g Protein: 19g**

## Dump Cherry Cake

Sweet and melt-in-your-mouth!

Prep time: 5 minutes Cooking time: 4 hours
Servings: 8

INGREDIENTS:
Boxed yellow cake mix
Canned cherry pie filling (you need 2 cans)
Half cup melted butter

DIRECTIONS:
- In a separated bowl. Combine cake mix with melted butter. Stir until the mix is well distributed with melted butter.
- Reserve some melted butter and spend it to grease your Slow Cooker. You can also use special spray with anti-stick effect.
- Open the cans with cherry filling and pour the filling inside the Slow Cooker. Spread evenly. Carefully transfer the butter mixture over the cherries. Arrange it over cherry filling so you do not mix them.
- Cover the lid of your Slow Cooker. Leave the dish cooking for 4 hours on LOW temperature mode.

**Nutrition: Calories: 324 Fat: 21g Carbohydrates: 44g Protein: 36g**

## Fudgy Brownies with Strawberries

A perfect dessert for a breakfast!

Prep time: 17 minutes Cooking time: 3 hours
Servings: 10

INGREDIENTS:
Butter
1 tsp vanilla
1 cup strawberry jam
3 tbsp flour
Whipped dessert topping
Raspberries or strawberries
Salt
Refrigerated egg product
Unsweetened chocolate

DIRECTIONS:
- Slightly coat the bottom and sides of your Slow Cooker with cooking spray.
- Take a medium saucepan and slowly melt the butter in it. Add chocolate and continue melting over low heat.
- When the chocolate is liquid, remove saucepan from heat and beat in eggs. Stirring, add vanilla, jam and sugar.
- Stir in flour, salt and baking powder.
- Pour the batter into Slow Cooker and leave under the lid on HIGH mode for 3 hours. To serve, use chocolate topping and fresh berries.

**Nutrition: Calories: 198 Fat: 12g Carbohydrates: 5g Protein: 3g**

## Butterscotch Fondue

The next level of fondue!

Prep time: 5 minutes Cooking time: 5 hours
Servings: 12

INGREDIENTS:
Sweetened condensed milk
Melted butter
Vanilla
Apples
Cubed sponge cake
Rum or milk
Whole strawberries
Cubed brownies
Light corn syrup

DIRECTIONS:
- Grease your Slow Cooker with olive oil or use remaining butter.
- In a large cooing bowl, combine brown sugar, corn syrup and melted butter. Pour in the milk and stir to the dough mixture.
- Pour the dough into preheated Slow Cooker and spread evenly over the bottom with a spoon or kitchen spatula.
- Set Slow Cooker for 3 hours and cook on low heat setting. Time after time, open the lid to stir pie slightly.
- Add rum and turn Slow Cooker to LOW. Cook for another 2 hours. Serve with brownie slices and fresh slices of your favorite fruits.

**Nutrition: Calories: 279 Fat: 17g Carbohydrates: 33g Protein: 38g**

## Chocolate and Peanut Butter Cake

This perfectly matches with chocolate syrup!

Prep time: 18 minutes Cooking time: 2 hours
Servings: 12

INGREDIENTS:
Cooking spray
Brown sugar
Almond pure extract
Plain flour
Baking powder
Creamy peanut butter
Baking soda

Sour cream
3 tablespoons butter
Cocoa powder
White sugar
Boiling water
Chocolate syrup

DIRECTIONS:
- Coat the inside parts and bottom of Slow Cooker with a special cooking spray. In a bowl, whisk flour, add baking powder, brown sugar and baking soda.
- In a separate bowl, add peanut butter, melted butter, sour cream, almond extract, and 2 tablespoons boiling water. Mix until smooth.
- Combine the mixtures to make a thick batter. Transfer butter to Slow Cooker.
- In another bowl, whisk sugar, water and cocoa powder. Pour chocolate mix over batter. Cook on HIGH temperature, about 1 hour.
- To serve, cool and sprinkle with chocolate syrup.

**Nutrition: Calories: 329 Fat: 17g Carbohydrates: 38g Protein: 8g**

## Triple-Berry Cobbler

You can cook this both with fresh or frozen berries!

Prep time: 23 minutes Cooking time: 2 hours
Servings: 6

INGREDIENTS:
One cup flour
2 chicken eggs
2 tbsp milk
Cup water
Half-and-half
6 cups frozen berries
Cinnamon
Ground nutmeg
Sugar
Quick-cooking tapioca
Baking powder

DIRECTIONS:
- Take a medium bowl. Combine sugar, salt, baking powder, sifted flour, nutmeg and cinnamon. In a smaller bowl, whisk eggs with milk and oil.
- Pour the egg mixture into the flour and combine until moistened.
- In a large skillet, bring to boil frozen berries with tapioca, sugar and water. Meanwhile, grease your Slow Cooker with melted butter.
- Once the berry mixture boils, spoon it into Slow Cooker.
- Top berries with batter and cover the lid of your Slow Cooker. Cook on HIGH mode of temperature for 2 hours.
- Serve in dessert dishes with half-and-half or ice cream.

**Nutrition: Calories: 285 Fat: 12g Carbohydrates: 7g Protein: 23g**

## Chocolate Pudding Cake

Simple and fast enough for Slow Cooker!

Prep time: 9 minutes Cooking time: 1 hour Servings: 16

INGREDIENTS:
Chocolate pudding mix
Sour cream
4 chicken eggs
Water
1 pack chocolate cake mix
Vegetable oil
Chocolate chips

DIRECTIONS:
- In a bowl, combine cake mix with pudding mix.
- Pour in some sour cream, beaten chicken eggs, water, oil. Whisk until all ingredients are smoothly blended.
- Stir in fresh semisweet chocolate chips. Blend to stir chips into the mixture. Coat Slow Cooker with cooking spray, pour batter into it.
- Cover and prepare on LOW temp for around 6 hours.

**Nutrition: Calories: 384 Fat: 25g Carbohydrates: 37g Protein: 5g**

## Vanilla Tapioca Pudding

You can serve this warm or cool!

Prep time: 5 minutes Cooking time: 6 hours
Servings: 14

INGREDIENTS:
Half cup whole milk
1cup white sugar
small pearl tapioca
4 chicken eggs
vanilla extract

DIRECTIONS:
- Grease your Slow Cooker with olive oil or simply cover with cooking spray to avoid sticking. In a bowl, combine half cup milk, tapioca, white sugar and eggs.
- Mix everything until perfectly smooth and transfer to Slow Cooker crock.
- Set your Slow Cooker to LOW temperature mode and cook, stirring once per hour. Prepare for 6 hours.
- Just before the serving. Stir the vanilla extract into the pudding.
- To serve, pour in cooked pudding into a small bowl and garnish with fresh mint, lime wedges or fresh berries to your taste.

**Nutrition: Calories: 218 Fat: 6g Carbohydrates: 35g Protein: 6g**

## Apples with Cinnamon and Dark Brown Sugar

Easy preparations and minimal cleanup!

Prep time: 26 minutes Cooking time: 3 hours
Servings: 4

INGREDIENTS:
4 tart baking apples
Raisins
Half cup regular oats
2 tbsp brown sugar
Cinnamon
1 tbsp butter
Apple juice

DIRECTIONS:

- To start, cover the bottom of Slow Cooker with parchment paper or grease with butter. Pell and carefully core the apples. Layer them over the bottom of Slow Cooker.
- In a small bowl, combine one by one cinnamon, oats, brown sugar, raisins and butter. Stir everything well, spoon the mixture into cored apples just to fill them.
- Transfer stuffed apples into Slow Cooker and sprinkle with the remaining oat mixture. Cover the lid and cook for 3 hours. Use LOW temperature mode for cooking.
- To serve, place the apples in a small portion bowls and pour over with the cooking mixture.

**Nutrition: Calories: 211 Fat: 8g Carbohydrates: 1g Protein: 2g**

## Bananas Foster in Slow Cooker

Perfect with tea and ice-cream!

⌛ **Prep time: 11 minutes Cooking time: 2 hours**
**Servings: 5**

INGREDIENTS:
4 bananas
4 tablespoons butter
1 cup brown sugar
4 tbsp rum
Vanilla extract
5 tbsp walnuts
Cinnamon
Shredded coconut
DIRECTIONS:
- To start the cooking process, peel the bananas and slice them into 1-inch pieces.
- Cover the bottom and sides of your Slow Cooker with melted butter or anti-stick cooking spray. Comfortably layer banana slices over the bottom of your Slow Cooker.
- In a separate bowl, combine rum, butter, vanilla, sugar and cinnamon and stir well to combine. Pour the rum mixture into Slow Cooker. Toss to cover all the banana slices evenly.
- Cover the lid. Using a LOW temperature mode, prepare for 2 hours.
- When it is about thirty minutes before the end of cooking time, add walnuts with coconut atop the bananas.

**Nutrition: Calories: 539 Fat: 20g Carbohydrates: 83g Protein: 3g**

## Slow Cooker Reindeer Poop

Little sweet candies for any occasion!

⌛ **Prep time: 15 minutes Cooking time: 2 hours**
**Servings: 50**

INGREDIENTS:
White candy coating
German sweet chocolate
Semi-sweet chocolate chips
2 cans roasted peanuts
DIRECTIONS:
- Slightly grease your Slow Cooker with vegetable or olive oil.
- In a bowl, whisk together white candy coating, chocolate chips, German sweet chocolate and peanuts. Stir well to make a smooth batter-like mixture.
- Transfer the chocolate batter into Slow Cooker.
- Set your Slow Cooker to LOW temperature mode and cover the lid. Cook for 2 hours, and then gently stir the mixture.
- Leave to cook for another 45 to 60 minutes.
- When the time is over, line the baking sheet with the parchment and place small drops of the mixture over it. Wait for sweets to cook and became thick. Serve.

**Nutrition: Calories: 174 Fat: 12g Carbohydrates: 13g Protein: 4g**

## Warm Berry Slow Cooker Compote

Serve as a dessert or with ice cream!

⌛ **Prep time: 19 minutes Cooking time: 2 hours**
**Servings: 7**

INGREDIENTS:
6 cups mixed berries
Half cup sugar
Orange zest (grated)
4 tbsp orange juice
Cornstarch
2 tbsp water
DIRECTIONS:
- In a bowl, combine together frozen berries, grated zest of the orange and white sugar. Pour in the juice from one orange. Mix all ingredients to combine well.
- Transfer to Slow Cooker and prepare on HIGH mode for about 1 or 2 hours. In a cup (or bowl), dissolve 2 tablespoons cornstarch in water.
- Pour your cornstarch mixture into Slow Cooker and combine with other ingredients. Cook covered with the lid for additional ten minutes (or until the mixture become thick). Serve while the dessert is still warm or at least at room temperature.

**Nutrition: Calories: 149 Fat: 1g Carbohydrates: 37g Protein: 1g**

## Triple Coconut Cake

Super delicious and unusual for your table!

⌛ **Prep time: 7 minutes Cooking time: 3 hours**
**Servings: 10**

INGREDIENTS:
Coconut oil
Cup sugar
3 chicken eggs
Baking powder
Unsalted butter
Half cup coconut milk
Cream cheese
Vanilla
Coconut flakes
2 cups flour
Salt
DIRECTIONS:
- In a bowl, beat with a mixer sugar, butter and coconut oil. One by one, add chicken eggs and beat for one more time. In a bowl, whisk flour, salt and baking powder.
- Carefully stir flour mixture into the butter mixture. Add coconut milk. Stir well until everything is combined.
- Cover the inside of your Slow Cooker with a cooking spray. Transfer the batter into crockpot and spread evenly.

- Use HIGH temperature for cooking. Cook for 2 hours.
- To serve, cool and make a frosting out of cream cheese with butter.

**Nutrition: Calories: 761 Fat: 47g Carbohydrates: 73g Protein: 8g**

## Slow Cooker Black Forest Cake

Amazing berry mix!

Prep time: 5 minutes Cooking time: 3 hours
Servings: 12

INGREDIENTS:
Butter
Canned pineapples
Chocolate cake mix
Cooking spray
Canned cherry pie filling

DIRECTIONS:
- Take a large saucepan and melt the butter in it.
- Pour in the pineapple liquid and chocolate mix. Simmer for several minutes and remove from fire. Coat the inside surface of your Slow Cooker with a cooking spray.
- Layer the bottom with pineapple chunks.
- Top the chunks with cherry pie filling. Arrange the filling into the even layer. Stir the saucepan-butter mixture and pour it into your Slow Cooker.
- Prepare on LOW mode for about 3 hours. Cool before serving. Serve with milk or tea.

**Nutrition: Calories: 385 Fat: 17g Carbohydrates: 57g Protein: 3g**

## Apple Bread Pudding with Cinnamon

Perfect for cold autumn and winter nights!

Prep time: 17 minutes Cooking time: 4 hours
Servings: 9

INGREDIENTS:
4 large apples
1- inch bread cubes
4 chicken eggs
2 cans milk
Brown sugar
Cinnamon to taste

DIRECTIONS:
- Prepare the apples: peel them and remove the core. Cut apples into small cubes. Gather chopped apples in a bowl.
- Grease crock-pot of your Slow Cooker with butter or oil to your choice. You need to do this to avoid sticking of batter during the cooking process.
- Transfer chopped apples into Slow Cooker. Add cubed bread and mix the ingredients. In a bowl, beat chicken eggs with milk.
- Stir in white sugar. Add nutmeg and cinnamon.
- Pour in the egg and cinnamon mixture over bread and apples.
- Turn your Slow Cooker on and set to HIGH. Prepare on HIGH regime for 4 hours.

**Nutrition: Calories: 266 Fat: 7g Carbohydrates: 48g Protein: 11g**

## Peanut Butter Cake in Slow Cooker

Amuse your friends with this happy recipe!

Prep time: 12 minutes Cooking time: 2 hours
Servings: 11

INGREDIENTS:
Cup peanut butter
Baking soda
1 cup flour
Vanilla extract
4 tbsp warm milk
Baking powder
Salt
Cocoa powder
Sour cream
White sugar

DIRECTIONS:
- In a bowl, carefully combine flour, salt, baking soda, brown sugar and baking powder. In another bowl, combine sour cream, peanut butter, boiling water and simple butter.
- Generously spray the inside of your Slow Cooker with a cooking spray. Carefully check there is no missed space without spray bits.
- Spread the batter mixture all over the bottom of Slow Cooker. Set Slow Cooker to HIGH and cook for approximately 2 hours.
- To serve, let the cake to cool and place each portion in a bowl, or arrange it with tea or preferred ice-cream.

**Nutrition: Calories: 610 Fat: 32g Carbohydrates: 74g Protein: 13g**

## Bread Pudding in the Slow Cooker

Simple ingredients and healthy recipe!

Prep time: 12 minutes Cooking time: 3 hours
Servings: 12

INGREDIENTS:
One cup raisins
8 cups cubed bread
4 chicken eggs
3 tbsp white sugar
2 cups milk
Melted butter
2 tsp nutmeg
Vanilla

DIRECTIONS:
- Slightly grease your Slow Cooker with melted butter.
- Combine cubed bread with raisins and transfer to Slow Cooker. Arrange evenly over the bottom. In a bowl, beat chicken eggs and whisk them with butter, milk, nutmeg and vanilla extract.
- Pour the egg mixture into Slow Cooker and toss to cover the bread with the mixture.
- Set Sow Cooker to LOW mode and cook for 3 hours. Check the readiness with a knife or wooden toothpick.
- When ready, serve bread pudding with tea or coffee to your taste.

**Nutrition: Calories: 396 Fat: 14g Carbohydrates: 57g Protein: 11g**

## Stuffed Apples

You can choose the stuffing by yourself!

 Prep time: 17 minutes Cooking time: 5 hours
Servings: 4

INGREDIENTS:
4 medium apples
1 tbsp butter
Apple juice
Raisins
4 figs
Half tsp apple spice
Cinnamon
2 tbsp brown sugar

DIRECTIONS:
- Wash and carefully core the apples: you need to remove the core without slicing fruits. Cut a strip of peel from the top of each fruit.
- Coat the bottom of your Slow Cooker with a cooking spray or just a little bit of slightly melted butter.
- In a bowl, whisk apple pie spice, cinnamon and brown sugar. Add figs and raisins. Using a spoon, fill the apples with fig mixture.
- Pour the apple juice into Slow Cooker. Place a small piece of butter atop each apple. Cook for 5 hours on LOW heat. Cover the lid to get better flavors.
- Serve, while warm, in small dessert bowls.

**Nutrition: Calories: 311 Fat: 9g Carbohydrates: 18g Protein: 7g**

## Hazelnut Pudding Cake

A sweet dessert that all your guests will love!

 Prep time: 16 minutes Cooking time: 3 hours
Servings: 11

INGREDIENTS:
Half cup butter
Water
Fudge brownie mix
1 cup water
Chocolate-hazelnut spread
Cocoa powder
Sugar
Hazelnut liqueur (optional)
Half cup hazelnuts
2 chicken eggs

DIRECTIONS:
- Before you start cooking, coat the bottom and sides of your Slow Cooker with melted butter or cooking spray.
- In a bowl, make a base dough: mix water, melted butter, eggs and sugar. Add hazelnuts and combine until smooth.
- Pour the mixture into greased Slow Cooker and spread the batter evenly over the bottom.
- Using a spoon, drop chocolate-hazelnut spread over the batter and make a little swirl with a knife. In a bowl, mix liquor with water and add to Slow Cooker. Mix in cocoa powder with sugar/ Pour into Slow Cooker.
- Cook covered for 2 hours. Use HIGH temperature mode.

**Nutrition: Calories: 299 Fat: 10g Carbohydrates: 7g Protein: 20g**

## Cherry-Chocolate Cluster Bits with Salted Almonds

Small and tasty, this is very simple to cook!

 Prep time: 23 minutes Cooking time: 32
 Servings: 2 hours

Ingredients:
Sweet baking chocolate
Sea salt
Three cups almonds
Semisweet chocolate pieces
Half pack vanilla coating
Dried sweet cherries

DIRECTIONS:
- Slightly coat your Slow Cooker with melted unsalted butter.
- Finely chop the almonds and sprinkle them around the bottom of your Slow Cooker. Top the almonds with baking chocolate and semisweet chocolate pieces.
- Add dry cherries and, finally, top with candy coating.
- Place with the lid. Turn your Slow Cooker to LOW temperature setting and cook for around 2 hours (wait until the chocolate is melted).
- To serve, spoon the chocolate mixture into small paper bowls. Sprinkle with sea salt. Serve.

**Nutrition: Calories: 335 Fat: 6g Carbohydrates: 15g Protein: 28g**

## Nutty Pumpkin-Pie Pudding

The perfect one for the autumn season!

 Prep time: 5 minutes Cooking time: 2 hour Servings: 6

INGREDIENTS:
Canned pumpkin
Evaporated milk
Cup sugar
Pumpkin pie spice
Yellow cake mix
Cup walnuts
Butter, melted
Dessert topping

DIRECTIONS:
- Lightly cover the inside of your Slow Cooker with cooking spray or simply line with parchment paper.
- Right in greased Slow Cooker, stir evaporated milk, pumpkin, sugar, and pumpkin pie spice. Spread the batter evenly in the cooking dish of Slow Cooker.
- Separately, combine cake mix, pumpkin spice, preferred nuts, Sprinkle over pumpkin in Slow Cooker. Carefully sprinkle with melted butter.
- Cover the lid. Cook on HIGH setting. Turn Slow Cooker off in around 2 hours. Remove the lid. Let cool for 30 minutes.
- Serve in dessert dishes with your favorite dessert topping.

**Nutrition: Calories: 324 Fat: 7g Carbohydrates: 32g Protein: 45g**

# Main Dishes Recipes

## Summer Cabbage Rolls for Slow Cooker

Perfect choice for a summer party!

⌀ Prep time: 32 minutes  Cooking time: 9 hours
Servings: 6

INGREDIENTS:
Cabbage leaves
5 tbsp. milk
Chicken egg
Cup white rice
Worcestershire sauce
Salt
Brown sugar
1 can tomato sauce
lemon juice
Ground beef
Ground pepper

DIRECTIONS:
- Place the cabbage leaves in a large pot with water. Boil for 2 minutes. Drain.
- In a separate bowl, mix the cooked rice, beef, minced onion, milk and one chicken egg. Season the rice with salt\pepper.
- Place the meat mixture in the middle of cabbage leaf. Make a long roll. Repeat this with other products. Transfer into Slow Cooker.
- In a bowl, get together sugar, tomato and Worcestershire sauce with lemon juice. Add to the rolls. Cook for 9 hours with LOW temperature settings.

Nutrition: Calories: 248 Fat: 9g Carbohydrates: 18g Protein: 19g

## Risotto with Bacon and Mushroom

Try this with your family!

⌀ Prep time: 23 minutes  Cooking time: 2,5 hours
Servings: 4

INGREDIENTS:
6 slices bacon
Whipping cream
Broth of chicken
1\2 cup shallots
White wine
Salt
Parmesan
2 cups rice
Mushrooms

DIRECTIONS:
- Cover the cooking dish with cooking spray.
- Heat the skillet and cook bacon just for 10 minutes (to get crispy). Transfer to Slow Cooker. Cook the mushrooms with shallots until browned.
- Add rice and wine. Prepare for 3 minutes. Place to Slow Cooker. Pour in the broth.
- Prepare on HIGH for 2 hours. Stir occasionally. To serve, stir in Parmesan with sour cream.

Nutrition: Calories: 411 Fat: 8g Carbohydrates: 31g Protein: 9g

## Tangy Roast in Slow Cooker

Delicious meat dish for a special occasion!

⌀ Prep time: 11 minutes  Cooking time: 6,5 hours
Servings: 8

INGREDIENTS:
Boneless pork roast
Hot water
Large onion
2 tbsp. soy sauce
Sugar and salt
hot pepper sauce
Half tsp black pepper
Ketchup
Garlic powder
White wine vinegar

DIRECTIONS:
- Slice the onion into small pieces.
- Cover the bottom of a cooking dish with some butter. Place the onion over the bottom of your cooking dish. Place the boneless pork roast over the onion.
- In a separate bowl, combine water, vinegar, ketchup. Add some soy sauce and sugar. Season with black pepper, garlic powder, salt, hot sauce.
- Pour in the spicy mixture over the meat into Slow Cooker. Cover and leave to cook on LOW temp for 8 hours.

Nutrition: Calories: 210 Fat: 7g Carbohydrates: 9g Protein: 24g

## Chicken Stroganoff for Slow Cooker

You will be amazed how tasty chicken could be!

⌀ Prep time: 10 minutes  Cooking time: 5 hours
Servings: 4

INGREDIENTS:
Four chicken breasts
1 tbsp. margarine
One can cream chicken soup
1 pack Italian dressing mix
1 pack cream cheese

DIRECTIONS:
- Grease your Slow Cooker with olive oil or plain unsalted butter.

- Remove the skin and bones out of chicken breasts and place them into Slow Cooker dish.
- In a separate bowl, combine all the dressing mixes. Pour them into Slow Cooker and carefully rub into the breasts.
- Mix the ingredients one more time and leave to cook for 5 hours on LOW mode. Add the cream of chicken soup and cream cheese to the cooking bowl.
- Cook for another 30 minutes.

**Nutrition: Calories: 456 Fat: 31g Carbohydrates: 9g Protein: 33g**

## Zesty Chicken Barbeque

A chicken meal with a spicy lemon accent!

**Prep time: 11 minutes Cooking time: 4 hours**
**Servings: 6**

INGREDIENTS:
Chicken breast halves
Italian salad dressing
2 tbsp. Worcestershire sauce
1 bottle barbeque sauce
Brown sugar

DIRECTIONS:
- Grease your Slow Cooker with special cooking spray. Remove the bones and skin of chicken.
- Place the chicken into your Slow Cooker.
- In a bowl, combine Italian salad dressing, barbeque sauce, Worcestershire sauce, brown sugar. Pour the sauce mix over the chicken.
- Cover and prepare on HIGH mode for 3-4 hour, or on LOW mode – for 8 hours.

**Nutrition: Calories: 300 Fat: 8g Carbohydrates: 32g Protein: 23g**

## Chicken with Dumplings in Slow Cooker

Just try these dumplings!

**Prep time: 13 minutes Cooking time: 6 hours**
**Servings: 9**

INGREDIENTS:
chicken breast halves
One onion
2 cans condensed cream of chicken soup
Butter
2 packs biscuit dough

DIRECTIONS:
- Remove the skin from chicken. Finely dice the onion.
- Grease your Slow Cooker with some butter.
- Place the chicken into Slow Cooker. Cover with diced onion, cream of chicken soup, butter. Pour in some water.
- Prepare during 5 hours on HIGH mode. When it is 30 minutes before serving, place the torned biscuit into the dish.

**Nutrition: Calories: 387 Fat: 10g Carbohydrates: 38g Protein: 12g**

## Beef Roast for Slow Cooker

Try this with fresh vegetables or salad leaves!

**Prep time: 19 minutes Cooking time: 6 hours**
**Servings: 9**

INGREDIENTS:
Bone-in beef roast
Medium onion
Sliced mushrooms
Vegetable oil
Salt/pepper
Chicken broth
1 tbsp. tomato paste
2 sprigs thyme
3 medium carrots
2 cloves garlic
Simple flour
Celery
1 sprig rosemary (fresh)
1 tbsp. butter

DIRECTIONS:
- Season the roast from all sides with salt and pepper. Sprinkle a little with flour just to cover. Heat the vegetable oil in a large frying pan and brown the meat evenly.
- Add butter and mushrooms, cook for 5 minutes. Then, stir in garlic, onion, 1-tablespoon flour and tomato paste.
- Slowly stir in chicken stock and let to simmer.
- Cut the carrots and celery. Then place to Slow Cooker along with roast and other vegetables, thyme and rosemary.
- Pour the mushroom mixture. Cook on LOW for 5-6 hours.

**Nutrition: Calories: 777 Fat: 57g Carbohydrates: 7g Protein: 754g**

## Seasoned Beef with cream

The seasoning of this dish is just incredible!

**Prep time: 16 minutes Cooking time: 5 hours**
**Servings: 8**

INGREDIENTS:
Lean ground beef
5 tbsp. milk
Half cup water
1 pack dry au jus mix
2 tbsp. vegetable oil
3 tbsp. flour
Half cup Italian seasoned bread crumbs
Dry onion soup mix
2 cans condensed cream of chicken soup

DIRECTIONS:
- In a separate and large bowl combine the beef, bread crumbs, onion soup mix, milk. Stir with hands.
- Separate the mixture into 8 parts and form the patties out of them.
- Heat the vegetable oil in a large frying pan and quickly cook the patties until brown. Transfer the patties into greased Slow Cooker dish.
- In a separate bowl, combine au jus mix, cream of chicken soup, water. Pour into Slow Cooker. Cook on LOW temperature for 4-5 hours.

**Nutrition: Calories: 388 Fat: 24g Carbohydrates: 18g Protein: 23g**

## Slow Cooker Kalua Pig

Try this tasty receipt!

**Prep time: 10 minutes  Cooking time: 20 hours
Servings: 12**

INGREDIENTS:
1 tbsp. liquid smoke flavoring
One pork butt roast
1-2 tbsp. sea salt

DIRECTIONS:
- Using a carving fork, pierce the pork roast all over.
- Rub some salt into the meat and sprinkle with liquid smoke. Place the roast into prepared (buttered or oiled) Slow Cooker.
- Cover the Slow Cooker with lid and leave to cook for around 16-20 hours on LOW mode. When it is half of time passed, torn the pork once.
- To serve, remove the meat out of Slow Cooker and shred with two forks.

**Nutrition: Calories: 243 Fat: 14g Carbohydrates: 1g Protein: 25g**

## Slow Cooker Spicy Pulled Pork

Easy to make spicy pork with seasoning!

**Prep time: 19 minutes  Cooking time: 6 hours
Servings: 11**

INGREDIENTS:
Chili powder
Cayenne pepper
1 tsp cumin
Half cup flour (all-purpose)
1 tsp paprika
Pork loin roast
2 onions
3 tbsp. hot pepper sauce
Brown sugar
2 cloves garlic
3 tbsp. barbeque sauce
Can diced tomatoes

DIRECTIONS:
- Take a bowl and mix chili powder, plain flour, cumin, cayenne, paprika. Cut the pork into pieces and place them into the spicy mixture.
- Meanwhile, in a pan melt the butter. Fry the pork until it is browned on all the sides. Transfer to Slow Cooker.
- Using the same skillet, cook garlic with onion until fragrant. Add barbeque sauce, tomatoes, sugar, hot sauce. Then pour over the pork.
- Set Slow Cooker on LOW and prepare for 5-6 hours.

**Nutrition: Calories: 248 Fat: 8g Carbohydrates: 19g Protein: 22g**

## Soup with Italian sausage

Try this hot receipt!

**Prep time: 23 minutes  Cooking time: 6 hours
Servings: 8**

INGREDIENTS:
Sweet Italian sausage
2 zucchini
Half tsp dried oregano
Beef broth
2 cans peeled tomatoes
2 cloves garlic
Dried basil
3 tbsp. chopped parsley
1 pack spinach pasts
Green bell pepper
Dry red wine

DIRECTIONS:
- Take a large pot and cook sausage till it is evenly brown. Remove from pan and drain (you can use paper towels).
- Reserve the fat and cook chopped onion and garlic in it. Add tomatoes, pour in broth and wine, oregano and basil.
- Transfer the pan mixture into greased Slow Cooker. Add bell pepper, zucchini, parsley and sausage.
- Cook, covered, for 4-6 hours (use a LOW temperature mode).
- Meanwhile, cook the pasta until al dente (for 6-7 minutes). Serve along with sausages.

**Nutrition: Calories: 436 Fat: 17g Carbohydrates: 43g Protein: 21g**

## Chicken with Lemon Juice and Oregano

Species make this meal just amazing!

**Prep time: 34 minutes  Cooking time: 3 hours
Servings: 6**

INGREDIENTS:
Chicken breast halves
1tsp dried oregano
5 tbsp. water
Half tsp salt
2 tbsp. butter
Black pepper
3 tbsp. lemon juice
1 tsp chicken lemon granules
2 cloves minced garlic
parsley

DIRECTIONS:
- In a separate bowl, combine salt, oregano, pepper. Rub the species into the chicken. Take a medium skillet, then melt the butter. Then brown chicken for about 5 minutes. Grease your Slow Cooker and place the chicken breasts into it.
- Use the same skillet to mix lemon juice, water, bouillon and minced garlic. Heat until boil and pour over the chicken.
- Cook, covered, for 3 hours on HIGH or 6 hours on LOW temperature regime. Before the serving, add some chopped parsley.

**Nutrition: Calories: 191 Fat: 9g Carbohydrates: 1g Protein: 29g**

## Lasagna with Beef for Slow Cooker

Try this one in your Slow Cooker!

**Prep time: 30 minutes  Cooking time: 4,5 hours
Servings: 10**

INGREDIENTS:
1 tap dried oregano
1 chopped onion
Beef
Minced garlic
One can tomato paste
1 tsp salt
Tomato sauce
Half cup parmesan cheese
Pack lasagna noodles
Shredded mozzarella cheese

DIRECTIONS:
- In a large skillet over a medium heat, fry some beef with onion and garlic until slightly brown. Add tomato paste and sauce. Cook for 14 minutes, add oregano and some salt.
- In a separate bowl, combine the cheeses and mix well.
- Grease your Slow Cooker and place all the ingredients, in even layers, into it. When all the layers are done, top the meal with cheese mix.
- Cover on LOW temperature mode for 4,5 hours.

**Nutrition: Calories: 446 Fat: 20g Carbohydrates: 35g Protein: 31g**

## Mexican Meat in Slow Cooker

Delicious receipt for flavored meat!

⌀ **Prep time: 30-40 minutes Cooking time: 8 hours Servings: 12**

INGREDIENTS:
One chuck roast
1 tsp ground pepper
chili powder
one onion
Salt to taste
olive oil
Hot pepper sauce
cayenne pepper
garlic powder

DIRECTIONS:
- Delete all the excess fat from the roast and season meat with pepper and salt. Using a large skillet with olive oil, brown the roast from all the sides.
- Cover the bottom of cooking dish some butter and place the roast into it. Add chopped onion, pepper sauce, powders and peppers.
- Pour in the water (slightly cover the roast) and cover the lid.
- Set your Slow Cooker on HIGH mode (for 6 hours). Then reduce to LOW and carry on cooking for another 2-4 hours (when meat easily fall apart).
- To serve, shred the roast with two forks and serve in tacos or burritos.

**Nutrition: Calories: 260 Fat: 19g Carbohydrates: 3g Protein: 18g**

## Summer Pot Roast for Slow Cooker

Just a perfect meal for a hot summer!

⌀ **Prep time: 17 minutes Cooking time: 7,5 hours Servings: 8**

INGREDIENTS:

4-5tbsp flour
Pack beef mix
1 sliced onion
One pack ranch dressing mix
Half cup water
1 pack Italian dressing mix
Salt pepper
One beef chuck roast (remove the bones)
5 whole and peeled carrots

DIRECTIONS:
- Cover the bottom of your cooking dish with butter or a little cooking spray. Place the sliced onion in an even layer onto the Slow Cooker bottom.
- Sprinkle the beef meat with species and rub into its surface. Roll meat in the flour just to cover from all sides. Place the meat into Slow Cooker.
- In a large bowl, combine Italian dressing mix, ranch dressing mix and beef gravy mix. Whisk and pour over the meat.
- Place the carrots around the chuck roast.
- Set your Slow Cooker on LOW mode and cook for around 8 hours (until tender).

**Nutrition: Calories: 385 Fat: 22g Carbohydrates: 20g Protein: 23g**

## Pork Chops in Sour Cream

Usual pork with amazing dressing!

⌀ **Prep time: 15 minutes Cooking time: 8 hours Servings: 10**

INGREDIENTS:
Six pork chops
Garlic powder (to taste)
Half cup flour
Salt
2 cups water
Black pepper
Container sour cream
chicken bouillon
Large onion

DIRECTIONS:
- Cover the chops with a spice mixture of pepper, garlic powder and some salt. Lightly brown chops in a large frying pan.
- Cover the bottom of your cooking dish with some cooking spray and place the chops over it. Cover with onion.
- Dissolve the cubes of bouillon in boiling water, and then pour the chops with this mixture. Cook, covered, for 7-8 hours using a LOW temperature mode.
- To serve, mix the sauce out of sour cream and 2 tablespoons flour.

**Nutrition: Calories: 257 Fat: 14g Carbohydrates: 14g Protein: 16g**

## Corned Beef with Cabbage

Try this receipt of the beef with cabbage!

⌀ **Prep time 17 minutes Cooking time: 9 hours Servings: 8**

INGREDIENTS:
Four large carrots
1 onion

Beer
One beef brisket
4 cups water
10 red potatoes
Half head cabbage
DIRECTIONS:
- Prepare vegetables: peel carrots, cut into matchstick pieces. Quarter the potatoes and slice onion to bite-size pieces. Coarsely chop the cabbage.
- Grease your cooking dish and place the vegetables over its bottom. Place the beef on top of the vegetables.
- Pour in beer to cover ingredients and season with spices.
- Set Slow Cooker to HIGH regime and leave to cook for 8 hours.
- When the beef is almost ready, add the cabbage and cook for another hour.

**Nutrition: Calories: 472 Fat: 19g Carbohydrates: 49g Protein: 23g**

## Beef Stroganoff in Slow Cooker

Try this with your family – and you will love it forever!

⌛ **Prep time: 11 minutes Cooking time: 8 hours Servings: 4**

INGREDIENTS:
Beef stew meat
Small onion
5 tbsp. water
Worcestershire sauce
Cream cheese
1 can mushroom soup
DIRECTIONS:
- Grease Slow Cooker with some butter.
- Cut the beef into cubes, place evenly over bottom of a cooking bowl. Chop the onion, cover the meat with it.
- Add some mushroom soup and some Worcestershire sauce. Add the water. Cover with the lid. Cook for 5 hours using a HIGH mode (or for 8 hours on LOW). When the meal is ready, add and stir in cream cheese.

**Nutrition: Calories: 377 Fat: 26g Carbohydrates: 11g Protein: 25g**

## Carnitas in Slow Cooker

Soft pork meat – what else do you need for beautiful dinner?

⌛ **Prep time: 12 minutes Cooking time: 9-10 hours Servings: 12**

INGREDIENTS:
One boneless pork shoulder
Salt
Cumin
Dried oregano
Garlic powder
Ground cinnamon
Bay leaves
Chicken broth
DIRECTIONS:
- In a small bowl, combine some garlic powder, some salt, dried oregano, cumin, coriander and some cinnamon.
- Grease your Slow Cooker. Place two bay leaves on the bottom. Place the pork meat to your Slow Cooker. Pour in the broth.
- Cook under the lid for about 10 hours on LOW, wait until the meat begins to fall off. Shred with forks before serving.

**Nutrition: Calories: 223 Fat: 13g Carbohydrates: 1g Protein: 22g**

## Hot Potatoes with Pork

Tasty and satisfying – what else do you need?

⌛ **Prep time: 13 minutes Cooking time: 9 hours Servings: 8**

INGREDIENTS:
3 carrots
Chuck roast
1 pack dry onion soup mix
Stalk celery
3 large potatoes
Onion
1 cup water
Species to taste
DIRECTIONS:
- Cube the potatoes. Chop carrots, celery, onion.
- Rub the roast with pepper and salt. Take a large skillet and brown the meat on other sides. Grease your Slow Cooker with butter or cooking spray, as you like.
- Place the roast into it and cover with water, soup mix, onion, carrots, celery and potatoes. Cover the lid and leave, cooking, for 8-10 hours with LOW temperature setting.

**Nutrition: Calories: 540 Fat: 30g Carbohydrates: 18g Protein: 45g**

## Pizza for Slow Cooker

Try pizza right from Slow Cooker!

⌛ **Prep time: 24 minutes Cooking time: 4 hours Servings: 6**

INGREDIENTS:
Ground beef
Classic pizza sauce
Shredded mozzarella cheese
1 pack rigatoni pasts
Pepperoni sausage
Cream of tomato soup
DIRECTIONS:
- Pour cold water into a pot. Add a little salt.
- Bring liquid to boil and add some pasta. Cook for 10 minutes (try if it is al dente). Place the skillet over medium fire and prepare the beef until it is brown.
- Grease your Slow Cooker and place the ingredients in layers: noodles, beef, Mozzarella, pepperoni, sauce and soup.
- Turn Slow Cooker and set on LOW. Prepare for 5 hours.

**Nutrition: Calories: 682 Fat: 47g Carbohydrates: 50g Protein: 53g**

## Autumn Mushroom and Beef Delight

Perfect choice for your autumn dinner!

⌛ **Prep time: 19 minutes Cooking time: 5-6 hours Servings: 4**

INGREDIENTS:

1 can cream of mushroom soup (with garlic)
One yellow onion
2tsp vegetable oil
2 cans cream of mushroom soup
One cup water
1 peck dry onion soup mix
4 beef cube steaks
Half pack egg noodles
DIRECTIONS:
- Take a deep bowl and whisk water, onion soup and cream of mushroom soup.
- Place a large skillet over small heat and cook the onion. Rise heat to medium and stir until onion gets brown.
- Add the cube sticks in the skillet about 7 minutes on every side. Place all the ingredients in Slow Cooker. Pour in mushroom mixture. Turn on the LOW mode and cook until the beef steaks are tender.
- Meanwhile, cook the noodles following package directions.

**Nutrition: Calories: 562 Fat: 21g Carbohydrates: 66g Protein: 26g**

## Sausages with Sauce

Simple, but delicious!

⌀ **Prep time: 5 minutes Cooking time: 6 hours Servings: 6**

INGREDIENTS:
8 links Italian sausage
6 hoagie rolls
One onion
One green bell pepper
One jar spaghetti sauce
DIRECTIONS:
- Peel green bell pepper and remove the seeds. Slice, along with onion, into small cuts. Grease your Slow Cooker with some butter or anti-sticking spray.
- Transfer the Italian sausage links, green pepper, spaghetti sauce and onion into Slow Cooker. Stir well to be sure that everything is covered with sauce.
- Cover the lid and turn on Slow Cooker on LOW mode. Leave to cook for 6 hours.

**Nutrition: Calories: 1024 Fat: 57g Carbohydrates: 88g Protein: 35g**

## Beef and Broccoli in Slow Cooker

A perfect couple of beef and broccoli

⌀ **Prep time: 11 minutes Cooking time: 7 hours Servings: 8**

INGREDIENTS:
Warm water
Beef bouillon cube
2 cloves garlic
Half cup soy sauce
Sesame oil
Brown sugar
2 tbsp. cornstarch
2 cups cooked jasmine rice
Beef sirloin
1 tbsp. sesame seeds
Broccoli florets
DIRECTIONS:
- Dissolve bouillon cube in warm water. Add sugar, soy sauce, oil and garlic. Place the beef strips into a cooking dish. Pour the sauce mixture over.
- Set on Slow Cooker on LOW mode and cook for 7 hours.
- Take 3 tablespoons out of Slow Cooker mixture and whisk cornstarch into it. Pour it back into Slow Cooker.
- In a separate saucepan, cook broccoli.
- To serve, separate broccoli into portions and top with beef.

**Nutrition: Calories: 814 Fat: 16g Carbohydrates: 98g Protein: 46g**

## Chicken with Pineapples in Slow Cooker

Try this one with pineapples or peaches!

⌀ **Prep time: 17 minutes Cooking time: 4 hours Servings: 4**

INGREDIENTS:
1 cup flour
1 cup pineapple chunks
1 clove garlic
Half cup soy sauce
2 tbsp. ketchup
4 tbsp. brown sugar
4 chicken thighs
Half cup pineapple juice
DIRECTIONS:
- In a shallow bowl, sprinkle the flour and dredge chicken thighs to coat. Tap slightly to remove excess flour.
- Grease the Slow Cooker with olive oil or cooking spray.
- Place chicken thighs evenly over the Slow Cooker bottom and top with pineapples. In a small bowl, whisk soy sauce, pineapple juice, ketchup, brown sugar and garlic.
- Place the lid on the cooking dish and prepare for 4 hours on LOW temperature mode.

**Nutrition: Calories: 448 Fat: 11g Carbohydrates: 62g Protein: 23g**

## Western Omelette in Slow Cooker

Perfect for morning time!

⌀ **Prep time: 23 minutes Cooking time: 12 hours Servings: 10**

INGREDIENTS:
Onion
Diced cooked ham
12 chicken eggs
Salt/pepper to taste
Shredded cheddar cheese
1 cup milk
Green bell pepper
1 pack hash brown potatoes
DIRECTIONS:
- Grease the inside of your Slow Cooker.
- Transfer the 1/3 part of hash browns into Slow Cooker and evenly spread them over the bottom. Cover potatoes with 1/3 of onion, ham, bell pepper, Cheddar. Repeat two times.

- In another bowl, whisk milk with chicken eggs. Whisk in species. Pour into Slow Cooker. Place the lid and set your Slow Cooker on LOW mode for 11 hours.

**Nutrition: Calories: 310 Fat: 22g Carbohydrates: 16g Protein: 19g**

## Western Omelette in Slow Cooker

Perfect for morning time!

Prep time: 23 minutes Cooking time: 12 hours
Servings: 10

INGREDIENTS:
Onion
Diced cooked ham
12 chicken eggs
Salt/pepper to taste
Shredded cheddar cheese
1 cup milk
Green bell pepper
1pack hash brown potatoes
DIRECTIONS:
- Grease the inside of your Slow Cooker.
- Transfer the 1/3 part of hash browns into Slow Cooker and evenly spread them over the bottom. Cover potatoes with 1/3 of onion, ham, bell pepper, Cheddar. Repeat two times.
- In another bowl, whisk milk with chicken eggs. Whisk in species. Pour into Slow Cooker. Place the lid and set your Slow Cooker on LOW mode for 11 hours.

**Nutrition: Calories: 310 Fat: 22g Carbohydrates: 16g Protein: 19g**

## Cheesy Macaroni for Slow Cooker

Can easily fit as a supper!

Prep time: 17 minutes Cooking time: 4 hours
Servings: 8 servings

INGREDIENTS:
One cup milk
2cups pasta or macaroni
Cubed cream cheese
3tsp butter
Dijon mustard
1can evaporated milk
Whipping cream
Can diced tomatoes
Cubed American cheese
DIRECTIONS:
- Start with greasing of your Slow Cooker. You can cover the bottom with butter. Place two cups of macaroni pasta into Slow Cooker. Spread evenly over the bottom.
- One by one, place the other ingredients over the pasta (except tomatoes). Stir everything until combined well.
- Turn on your Slow Cooker and prepare on LOW temperature mode for about 4 hours. To serve, stir in tomatoes.

**Nutrition: Calories: 437 Fat: 29g Carbohydrates: 27g Protein: 16g**

**Nutrition: Calories: 544 Fat: 23g Carbohydrates: 52g Protein: 29g**

## Stuffed Cabbage with Meat and Tomatoes

Satisfying and delicious one!

Prep time: 31 minutes Cooking time: 2 hours
Servings: 8

INGREDIENTS:
One large Savoy
4 garlic cloves
White rice
Olive oil
1 carrot
Yellow onion
Fresh Parmesan cheese
Grated lemon rind
Ground black pepper
Salt to taste1 large chicken egg
Lean ground beef
3 cups tomatoes
DIRECTIONS:
- Preheat the large pan with one tablespoon olive oil.
- Mix in onion, carrot, 2 cups chopped cabbage, garlic. Cook for 4-5 minutes, then remove, slightly cool.
- In a bowl, grate Parmesan cheese.
- Add rice, lemon rind, chopped dill, salt, beef, pepper, egg. Add cabbage and stir finely. Make the logs out of this mixture and cabbage leaves.
- Mix tomato paste with remaining oil. Pour one cup mixture over Sow Cooker bottom, place the cabbage logs. Top with remaining tomatoes.
- Cook on LOW for 6 hours.

**Nutrition: Calories: 327 Fat: 16g Carbohydrates: 28g Protein: 19g**

## Chicken Thighs with Peaches

Just simple, sweet and healthy!

Prep time: 11 minutes Cooking time: 2 hours
Servings: 8

INGREDIENTS:
Ground cumin
Olive oil
Chopped basil
Sugar
6 garlic cloves
2 tbsp. red onion
2 tsp lime juice
Chicken thighs on bone
Fresh mint
2 peaches
6 lime wedges (to serve)
Salt to taste
1 jalapeno pepper
Ground pepper
DIRECTIONS:
- In a bowl, whisk 3 tablespoons oil with minced garlic. Add cumin. Add chicken and toss in the garlic mixture to coat.

- For salsa, combine fresh mint, basil, chopped onion, lime juice, sugar, jalapeno and diced peaches. Add salt.
- Grease your Slow Cooker with olive oil. Then, place the chicken into it. Pour a little marinade over it.
- Cook on LOW for 3 hours.
- To serve, add salsa and cut the lime into wedges.

**Nutrition: Calories: 196 Fat: 11g Carbohydrates: 5g Protein: 20g**

## Potato Casserole with Cheddar

Classical casserole now in your Slow Cooker!

Prep time: 21 minutes Cooking time: 6 hours
Servings: 10

INGREDIENTS:
1 pack hash brown potatoes
1 pack maple-flavored sausage
1 cup milk
12 chicken eggs
1 tbsp. ground mustard
1 pack shredded Cheddar

DIRECTIONS:
- Spray the bottom of your cooking dish with cooking spray.
- Divide hash browns into halves and spread them over Slow Cooker bottom. In a bowl, whisk milk, mustard, salt, chicken eggs, black pepper.
- In a skillet, cook sausage until crumbly. Place over hash browns in Slow Cooker. Cover the lid and prepare on LOW for 6 hours.

**Nutrition: Calories: 641 Fat: 54g Carbohydrates: 21g Protein: 35g**

## Baked Potatoes Stuffed with Ham

Baked and stuffed – two in one!

Prep time: 11 minutes Cooking time: 2 hours
Servings: 6

INGREDIENTS:
2 tbsp. water
5 potatoes
Greek yogurt (fat-free)
Salt to taste
3 small green onions
Black pepper
Bag baby spinach
Lower-sodium ham
Shredded Cheddar cheese

DIRECTIONS:
- Grease Slow Cooker with unsalted butter.
- Cut potatoes into halves, place into Slow Cooker. Prepare on LOW for 2 hours. When ready, try with a fork if they are tender.
- In a skillet, cook spinach with water until wilted. Then, use a paper towel and remove all excess liquid.
- Take out the potatoes and remove pulp.
- In a bowl, mix yogurt, potato pulp, pepper, ham, salt, spinach and cheese. Fill the potato shells with this mixture.
- To serve, sprinkle with diced green onions.

**Nutrition: Calories: 273 Fat: 5g Carbohydrates: 46g Protein: 12g**

## Spaghetti Squash in Slow Cooker

Develop your spaghetti skills!

Prep time: 23 minutes Cooking time: 4 hours
Servings: 4

INGREDIENTS:
1 spaghetti squash
Salt
Butter to grease
2 cups water

DIRECTIONS:
- Grease your Slow Cooker dish with some butter.
- Take a long knife and prink the whole squash with it for several (up to 10-15) times. Put the squash into a cooking crock and pour in water to cover the squash.
- Turn on Slow Cooker and set to LOW temperature mode. Cook for 4-6 hours. Take the squash out and drain. Wait to cool.
- Cut and remove the seeds. To serve, shred with a fork (make strands) and remove the skin.

**Nutrition: Calories: 54 Fat: 1g Carbohydrates: 12g Protein: 1g**

## Hash Brown Casserole with Cheese

Your family will love this one!

Prep time: 27 minutes Cooking time: 9 hours
Servings: 9

INGREDIENTS:
Salt to taste
1-2 cups onion
6 chicken eggs
Half cup sour cream
Canada oil
Black pepper
1 pack hash browns
Chopped pancetta
Red bell pepper (chopped)
1 cup milk
Green onions (to garnish)

DIRECTIONS:
- Mix half cheese, 2 tbsp sour cream, half cup onion, 1 egg in a large bowl. Add salt/pepper to taste. Add hash brown potatoes.
- Take a skillet and preheat 4 tablespoons into it. Prepare hash browns for 7 minutes. When evenly browned, place to Slow Cooker.
- In the same skillet, add remaining vegetables and cook for 3 minutes.
- Whisk half cup cheese, 5 eggs, milk and salt/pepper. Pour into Slow Cooker. Cook on LOW for 4 hours.

**Nutrition: Calories: 136 Fat: 9g Carbohydrates: 36g Protein: 12g**

## Chicken Chili Recipe

Hot recipe for those who loves chili!

Prep time: 26 minutes Cooking time: 4 hours
Servings: 11

INGREDIENTS:

Large onion
Boneless chicken meat
Green bell pepper
1 bay leaf
Mango salsa
Kidney beans
Canned tomato paste
Black pepper
Rice vinegar
Smoked paprika
Chili powder
Salt to taste
1can stewed tomatoes
Canned black beans

DIRECTIONS:
- Remove the skin and bones from chicken meat.
- Place chicken, all beans, green pepper, onion, tomato paste, mango salsa, stewed tomatoes, bay leaf into Slow Cooker.
- Sprinkle with rice vinegar, season with chili, salt, paprika, black pepper. Turn on the Slow Cooker and set the HIGH.
- Cook for one hour, then turn to LOW and leave for 3 hours.

**Nutrition: Calories: 212 Fat: 5g Carbohydrates: 26g Protein: 16g**

## Steak with Beans and Crumbs

Just simple and healthy for you and your family!

 Prep time: 19 minutes Cooking time: 5 hours
Servings: 9

INGREDIENTS:
Vegetable oil
Milk
Lean ground beef
Half cup bread crumbs
6 tbsp. water
Condensed cream of chicken soup
Onion soup mix
Flour
Au jus

DIRECTIONS:
- Take a bowl, combine onion soup mix with milk and breadcrumbs.
- Add ground beef. Combine 8 even patties and dredge each one in flour. In a skillet, cook patties real quick.
- Place into your Slow Cooker, trying to form the pyramid.
- In a bowl, combine chicken soup, water and au jus. Pour into Slow Cooker. Set LOW and prepare for 5 hours.

**Nutrition: Calories: 387 Fat: 24g Carbohydrates: 18g Protein: 23g**

## Turkey and Summer Vegetables in Slow Cooker

Perfect choice for summer!

 Prep time: 5 minutes Cooking time:
 Servings:

INGREDIENTS:
Skinless turkey thighs
3 parsnips
2cubes chicken bouillon
4 cups chicken broth
1 yellow squash
1 can garbanzo beans
7-8 baby carrots
1 jar artichoke hearts
1 can diced tomatoes
Salt and black pepper to taste
1 green bell pepper
1 tsp chopped dill

DIRECTIONS:
- Cut turkey into even cubes and rub in the salt with pepper to your taste. Place the meat into greased Slow Cooker.
- Pour in the diced tomatoes mixture over turkey. Then, add a layer of artichoke hearts. Place all the other INGREDIENTS: baby carrots, parsnips, green pepper and yellow squash.
- Pour the chicken broth over the ingredients in Slow Cooker, just to cover them evenly. Add whole bouillon cubes.
- Cook, covered, on LOW temperature mode for 8-10 hours. To serve, garnish with some fresh chopped dill.

**Nutrition: Calories: 339 Fat: 6g Carbohydrates: 34g Protein: 36g**

## Chicken Spaghetti in Slow Cooker

If you love spaghetti, you should try this!

 Prep time: 9 minutes Cooking time: 2 hours
Servings: 6

INGREDIENTS:
Can condensed cream of chicken soup
Spaghetti
Processed cheese food
1 can cream of mushroom soup
canned diced tomatoes
Chicken breast halves

DIRECTIONS:
- Bring cold water to boil and add some salt. Put spaghetti, cook until al dente. Grease your Slow Cooker with some olive oil.
- Place tomatoes with green peppers, mushroom soup and chicken soup into Slow Cooker. Turn on the MEDIUM temperature heat and cook until the cheese is melted.
- In the end, stir in spaghetti and prepare for 40-50 minutes.

**Nutrition: Calories: 653 Fat: 24g Carbohydrates: 65g Protein: 40g**

## Slow Cooker Chicken with Carrots

Healthy and satisfying!

 Prep time: 29 minutes Cooking time: 8 hours
Servings: 8

INGREDIENTS:
Boneless and skinless chicken breasts
5 tbsp. water
Greek style seasoning
4 cubes chicken bouillon
Water
1 head cabbage (medium)
1 tsp poultry seasoning
Cornstarch
3carrots

DIRECTIONS:
- Grease your Slow Cooker with cooking spray.
- Place the rinsed chicken breasts into the cooking dish along with one-inch carrot slices. Add enough water to cover the meat.
- Place the bouillon cubes and season with poultry seasoning and Greek seasoning to taste. Cover the Slow Cooker lid and leave to cook on high temperature on LOW for 8 hours.

**Nutrition: Calories: 315 Fat: 3g Carbohydrates: 14g Protein: 54g**

## Summer Risotto in Slow Cooker

Delicious and satisfying summer meal!

Prep time: 27 minutes Cooking time: 2 hours Servings: 6

INGREDIENTS:
Arborio rice
Parmesan cheese
Salt
Dried onion flakes
4 cloves garlic
Olive oil
Black pepper
4tbsp. white wine

DIRECTIONS:
- Cover the bottom of your Cooker with olive oil or melted unsalted butter. Right in a cooking pot, mix rice, garlic, salt, oil, onion flakes and black pepper. Add the chicken broth and stir the ingredients until even.
- Turn on the Slow Cooker and choose HIGH mode. Cook for 1-2 hours.
- When it is time, stir in shredded parmesan. Cook for 15 minutes, uncovered, until cheese is melted.

**Nutrition: Calories: 325 Fat: 12g Carbohydrates: 43g Protein: 7g**

## Tropical Chicken with Pineapple

Exotic chicken for all family!

Prep time: 24 minutes Cooking time: 6 hours Servings: 6

INGREDIENTS:
2 chicken breasts
1 onion
Dried thyme
1 tbsp. lemon zest
4 sweet potatoes
Jamaican jerk seasoning
Canned pineapple chunks
Dried cumin
1 tsp ginger
Half cup raisins

DIRECTIONS:
- Cut all the vegetables, grease the Slow Cooker.
- Place the potatoes, chicken and onion to the cooking dish.
- In a separate bowl, combine the pineapples (along with juice), jerk seasoning, raisins, Worcestershire sauce, cumin, ginger and lime zest.
- Pour this mixture over the chicken in your Slow Cooker and sprinkle with dried thyme. Cover the lid and set your Slow Cooker to LOW temp. Cook until tender (for about 6 hours).

**Nutrition: Calories: 361 Fat: 2g Carbohydrates: 68g Protein: 19g**

## Sauerkraut with Sausage in Slow Cooker

Try this one with sauerkraut!

Prep time: 19 minutes Cooking time: 4 hours Servings: 5

INGREDIENTS:
One medium onion
One can sauerkraut
Ground pork sausage
5 tbsp. brown sugar

DIRECTIONS:
- Grease your Slow Cooker with some melted butter.
- In a separate bowl of medium size, combine the sugar with sauerkraut and mix well. Place the sauerkraut into Slow Cooker. Then, cover with diced onion and pork sausage.
- Turn on the Slow Cooker. Top with the lid. Cook for 2-3 hours on HIGH temperature mode. You can also add some water during the process, if needed.
- Reduce the settings to LOW temperature mode and cook for another 2 hours.

**Nutrition: Calories: 640 Fat: 55g Carbohydrates: 18g Protein: 16g**

## Slow Cooker Vegetarian Mash

Both vegetarian and meat-eater will love this!

Prep time: 7 minutes Cooking time: 5 hours Servings: 6

INGREDIENTS:
1 container vegetable broth
1 cup cremini mushrooms
1 pack cream cheese
1 pack fresh spinach
1pack cheese-filled tortellini (frozen)

DIRECTIONS:
- Spray your Slow Cooker with anti-stick cooking spray.
- Right in a cooking pot, stir together cream cheese, tortellini, mushrooms and spinach. Mix until even consistency.
- Pour in one container of vegetable broth.
- Stir all the ingredients one more time, place the dish into Slow Cooker and turn it on. Set the LOW temperature mode and prepare for 5 or 6 hours.

**Nutrition: Calories: 398 Fat: 20g Carbohydrates: 40g Protein: 15g**

## Simple Slow Cooker Enchiladas

Perfect dish for busy mornings!

Prep time: 28 minutes Cooking time: 5 hours Servings: 7

INGREDIENTS:

One cup onion
Cheddar
Salt to taste
2cloves garlic
Ground turkey
Ground pepper
Canned black beans
Water
6 corn tortillas
Monterey Jack cheese
Ground cumin
1-2 tsp chili powder
1 can diced tomatoes (with green chili peppers)
1 can kidney beans
Chopped green bell pepper

DIRECTIONS:
- Place turkey into large frying pan; add bell pepper, garlic and onion. Cook until the meat is completely browned.
- Stir in kidney beans, water, diced tomatoes, chili powder, salt, black beans, cumin and salt with pepper. Simmer for 10 minutes.
- Mix Monterey Jack cheese and Cheddar cheese in separate bowl.
- Divide the pan mixture and cheeses into 3-4 parts and place in layers over the greased Slow Cooker bottom.
- Set up the LOW cooking mode and leave to cook for 5-7 hours.

**Nutrition: Calories: 614 Fat: 31g Carbohydrates: 41g**

**Protein: 44g**

## Stuffed Peppers for Slow Cooker

Amazing choice for summertime!

Prep time: 17 minutes Cooking time: 5 hours
Servings: 4

INGREDIENTS:
Ground pork
4 green bell peppers
1 cup peas
Water
Cup processed cheese (cubed)
Half cup barbeque sauce
White rice

DIRECTIONS:
- Peel peppers, remove the seeds and set hollow peppers aside.
- In a separate bowl, combine rice, peas, meat, half cup water and barbeque sauce. Mix until blended.
- Fill the pepper shells with the rice mixture.
- Right in your Slow Cooker cooking pot, combine remaining barbeque sauce and water. Place stuffed peppers into Slow Cooker and cover the lid.
- Cook on LOW mode for 5-7 hours.

**Nutrition: Calories: 383 Fat: 14g Carbohydrates: 42g Protein: 19g**

## Slow Cooker Chicken with Vegetables

A satisfying meal for great dinner!

Prep time: 17 minutes Cooking time: 3 hours
Servings: 8

INGREDIENTS:
4 chicken breasts
Red potatoes
2 carrots
Olive oil
Green bell pepper
Lemon
Garlic
Soy sauce
2 tomatoes
Yellow bell pepper
Red bell pepper
Green peas
Black pepper

DIRECTIONS:
- Cut the tomatoes and potatoes into cubes, slice the peppers, onion, chop the carrots. Grease your Cooker with some butter.
- Place cubed chicken breasts, lemon juice, soy sauce, garlic, lemon juice and black pepper into Slow Cooker dish.
- Add red potatoes, peppers, carrots, peas, onion to Slow Cooker. Set LOW temperature mode and cook for 8 hours.

**Nutrition: Calories: 331 Fat: 20g Carbohydrates: 19g Protein: 19g**

## Baby Carrots Roast in Slow Cooker

Healthy and tasty dish!

Prep time: 17 minutes Cooking time: 6 hours
Servings: 11

INGREDIENTS:
Salt to taste
Beef chuck roast (boneless)
Soy sauce
Cream of mushroom soup
Half cup brown sugar
1pack onion soup mix
Ground pepper
White vinegar (distilled)
1 can beef gravy
2tbsp. flour
1 tbsp. Worcestershire sauce
Half cup brown sugar

DIRECTIONS:
- Grease your Slow Cooker crock and place the boneless beef roast into it.
- In a separate bowl, mix together beef gravy, vinegar, cream of mushroom soup, soy sauce, salt, Worcestershire sauce and pepper. Stir well.
- Pour the mixture over the meat into Slow Cooker.
- Cover the Slow Cooker lid and cook for 6-7 hours on HIGH temperature mode. If you have time – use a LOW mode and cook for 12-14 hours.
- Ladle the liquid from Slow Cooker to saucepan and bring to boil. Add some flour and stir until thick gravy.
- Serve the roast with hot gravy.

**Nutrition: Calories: 663 Fat: 44g Carbohydrates: 24g Protein: 36g**

## Slow Cooker Creamy Oatmeal

Just tasty and creamy one!

⌀ **Prep time: 7 minutes Cooking time: 8 hours**
**Servings: 4**

INGREDIENTS:
1 cup half-and-half or any regular cream
3 cups water
1 cup oats
4 tbsp. brown sugar
1 pinch salt or to taste

DIRECTIONS:
- Place the oats into a medium bowl and cover with cold water. Let stand for 1-2 hours. Wash and drain oats and place them into Slow Cooker.
- Pour in fresh water to cover the beans.
- Turn on your Slow Cooker, set on LOW temperature mode, and cook for 7-8 hours. As a variant, you can leave it cooking overnight.
- In the morning, add half-and-half and salt into cooked oats. Serve in small bowls, sprinkled with brown sugar.

**Nutrition: Calories: 208 Fat: 8g Carbohydrates: 29g Protein: 4g**

## Mac in Cheese for Slow Cooker

Try this with your friends!

⌀ **Prep time: 23 minutes Cooking time: 3 hours**
**Servings: 11**

INGREDIENTS:
2 cups milk
2 eggs
Half cup butter
1 pack macaroni
1 can evaporated milk
Condensed cheese soup
Paprika
Pepper and salt

DIRECTIONS:
- Fill a pot with enough water and cook macaroni in salted water, according to package directions. Place to buttered Slow Cooker.
- Add half cup butter to the pasta. Combine until melted. Season the macaroni with salt, paprika and pepper.
- Add ½ of Cheddar and stir.
- In a separate bowl, whisk beaten eggs and evaporated milk to get smooth consistency. Add into Slow Cooker.
- Top the ingredients with remaining Cheddar cheese and sprinkle with milk and paprika. Mix one more time.
- Cook on LOW temperature for 3 hours.

**Nutrition: Calories: 430 Fat: 21g Carbohydrates: 33g Protein: 17g**

## Spicy Pasta with Mushrooms and Chicken

Cook this pasta for great dinner!

⌀ **Prep time: 12 minutes Cooking time: 6 hours**
**Servings: 6**

INGREDIENTS:
Boneless chicken breasts
Basil
Small yellow onion
Half green bell pepper
Jar spaghetti sauce
Dried oregano
3 tbsp. minced garlic
Canned tomato sauce
Sliced mushrooms
Red pepper flakes
Black pepper to taste

DIRECTIONS:
- Cut the chicken breasts into halves. Place to greased Slow Cooker. Add tomato paste and spaghetti sauce.
- Mince the onion, garlic, peel and seed pepper. Add the veggies into Slow Cooker. Season the chicken with pepper, flakes, basil.
- Cover and prepare for 6 to 8 hours on LOW temperature mode.

**Nutrition: Calories: 364 Fat: 8g Carbohydrates: 42g Protein: 30g**

## Pepperoni Pizza in Slow Cooker

For pepperoni lovers!

⌀ **Prep time: 21 minutes Cooking time: 2 hours**
**Servings: 6**

INGREDIENTS:
Marinara sauce
1 pack klushki noodles
2 cans sliced mushrooms
Grong beef
2 cups Cheddar cheese
Canned pizza sauce
2 cups Mozzarella
1 pack sliced pepperoni

DIRECTIONS:
- Boil water in a large pot, slightly salt. Cook noodles for 5 minutes, then drain.
- Heat a large frying pan with some oil. Place the beef into frying pan and wait until slightly brown and a little crumbly (around 5-7 minutes). Add marinara and pizza sauce.
- Grease the bottom of your Slow Cooker with some butter or olive oil and cover with a half of noodles.
- Add ½ ground beef mixture, ½ mushrooms, ½ cheese and pepperoni. Repeat one more time. Place the lid on Slow Cooker and prepare on LOW mode for 1-2 hours.

**Nutrition: Calories: 677 Fat: 31g Carbohydrates: 56g Protein: 40g**

## Venison Stew in Slow Cooker

Easy-to-make one!

⌀ **Prep time: 23 minutes Cooking time: 9 hours**
**Servings: 8**

INGREDIENTS:
8 medium potatoes
Venison stew meat
3 stalks celery
3 cubes beef bouillon
Pepper/salt to taste
3 medium onions
8 large carrots
3 cans beef broth
2 cups fresh mushrooms

Half cup cornstarch
2 cups green peas
1 cup water
2 tbsp. seasoning and browning sauce

DIRECTIONS:
- Grease the Slow Cooker pot with some butter or cover with special cooking spray.
- Place diced potatoes, carrots, celery, seasoning sauce, celery and venison in Slow Cooker. Pour in the broth and bouillon; add some water just to cover ingredients.
- Turn Slow Cooker on high mode and wait until the liquid starts to boil. Reduce to LOW and leave for 8-10 hours.
- Add diced mushrooms, pepper, salt and peas.
- Whisk in some cornstarch and cook on high until the peas are warmed through.

**Nutrition: Calories: 407 Fat: 3g Carbohydrates: 61g Protein: 32g**

## Chile Verde in Slow Cooker

Cook this, if you love spicy food!

**Prep time: 17 minutes Cooking time: 8 hours**
**Servings: 8**

INGREDIENTS:
1 small onion
Boneless pork shoulder
1 can diced tomatoes
5 cans green salsa
2 cloves garlic
3 tbsp. olive oil
1 can jalapeno peppers (diced)

DIRECTIONS:
- In a large skillet, preheat the olive oil over medium heat.
- Add diced onion and minced garlic. Cook, stirring, until fragrant.
- Cut the pork into cubes and transfer it into skillet. Cook until it is browned on all sides. Place all the skillet ingredients to Slow Cooker.
- Stir in the jalapeno peppers, green salsa and diced tomatoes.
- Cook under the lid for 3 hours (on HIGH mode), then reduce to LOW and leave for 4-5 hours.

**Nutrition: Calories: 265 Fat: 12g Carbohydrates: 12g Protein: 22g**

## Slow Cooker Chicken with Pasta and Cream

Great satisfying meal for big company!

**Prep time: 11 minutes Cooking time: 6 hours**
**Servings: 4**

INGREDIENTS:
One can cream of mushroom soup
1 pack cream cheese (room temperature)
1 tbsp. Italian seasoning
3 tbsp. sour cream
One chicken breast

DIRECTIONS:
- Remove the skin and bones from chicken breast. Divide it into small cubes.
- Cover the bottom of your Slow Cooker with some olive oil or melted unsalted butter.
- Right in the cooking dish, combine cream of mushroom soup, cream cheese, Italian seasoning and sour cream and stir well.
- Place the chicken cubes into Slow Cooker.
- Turn on and set your Slow Cooker to LOW temperature. Cook for 6 hours.

**Nutrition: Calories: 357 Fat: 27g Carbohydrates: 7g Protein: 19g**

## Mussaman Potato Curry in Slow Cooker

Amazing and exotic one!

**Prep time: 33 minutes Cooking time: 6 hours**
**Servings: 9**

INGREDIENTS:
Small onion
2 potatoes
3 tbsp. curry powder
3 cloves garlic
2tbsp. butter
Coconut milk
3tbsp. Thai sauce
Beef broth
3 tbsp. brown sugar
Peanut butter
Half cup peanuts (unsalted)

DIRECTIONS:
- Dice the potatoes and onions. Place into buttered Cooker.
- In a skillet, melt the butter and cook beef, along with minced garlic. When the beef is evenly browned, place into Slow Cooker.
- In the same skillet, heat peanut butter, coconut milk, curry powder. Pour over the beef. Add brown sugar, then fish sauce with beef broth.
- Turn on the LOW mode and prepare the beef until tender, for 6 hours.

**Nutrition: Calories: 545 Fat: 40g Carbohydrates: 29g Protein: 21g**

## Mexican Roast in Slow Cooker

Mexican and spicy dish for the perfect evening!

**Prep time: 32 minutes Cooking time: 10 hours**
**Servings: 7 servings**

INGREDIENTS:
Beef broth
Avocado oil
1 tsp ground cumin
2 onions
Beef roast
Some salt
3 bell peppers
Red wine vinegar
Chopped cilantro
1 can tomato paste
2 tbsp. minced garlic

DIRECTIONS:

- Preheat a large skillet with avocado oil. Cook the beef roast.
- When it is brown, transfer to Slow Cooker and add tomato paste, bell peppers, beef broth and minced onion.
- In a bowl, mix vinegar, olive oil, cumin, garlic, tomato paste and salt. Pour over the peppers. Cook on HIGH mode for 1 hour, then reduce to LOW and continue for 8 hours.
- When almost ready, shred the beef and add cilantro. Leave for another 1 hour.

**Nutrition: Calories: 329 Fat: 11g Carbohydrates: 20g Protein: 30g**

## Chili Chicken with Beans

Amuse your friends with chili meal!

Prep time: 23 minutes Cooking time: 4 hours
Servings: 6

INGREDIENTS:
Bay leaf
Green bell pepper
Any chicken meat without bones
Large onion
Chili powder
Tomato paste
Canned kidney beans
Black pepper
Stewed tomatoes
Canned black beans
2 tbsp. rice vinegar
Half cup mango salsa
Salt
Smoked paprika

DIRECTIONS:
- Peel and seed peppers, cut all the vegetables into small slices. Drain the beans. Grease your Slow Cooker and place bite-sized chicken over its bottom.
- Add green pepper, black and kidney beans, mango salsa, tomatoes and tomato paste.
- Mix the beans liquid, rice vinegar, salt, bay leaf, pepper, paprika and chili powder. Pour into Slow Cooker.
- Set on HIGH temperature mode and leave for 1 hour. Add chili and reduce to LOW. Prepare for 4 hours.

**Nutrition: Calories: 213 Fat: 5g Carbohydrates: 26g Protein: 16g**

## Chicken with Bread Cubes

Just simple and healthy!

Prep time: 13 minutes Cooking time: 8 hours
Servings: 6

INGREDIENTS:
3 medium onions
Poultry seasoning
Salt
Celery
Half tsp ground pepper
Cup butter
4 chicken breast halves
12 cups dry bread cubes
Dried sage
Condensed cream of mushroom soup
Chicken liquid

DIRECTIONS:
- Finely chop onions and celery.
- In a pot, boil chicken meat in salted water.
- Slightly grease your Cooker with some oil, place the boiled chicken breasts over its bottom.
- In separate bowl, mix butter, onion, poultry seasoning, bread cubes, mushroom soup, reserved cooking liquid with celery.
- Add pepper, sage, salt and stir everything well. Pour the dressing into Slow Cooker. Turn on Slow Cooker and set the LOW mode. Prepare for 6 hours.

**Nutrition: Calories: 158 Fat: 8g Carbohydrates: 1g Protein: 7g**

## Broccoli Beef in Slow Cooker

A healthy meal for every member of your family!

Prep time: 19 minutes Cooking time: 7 hours
Servings: 4

INGREDIENTS:
1 cup water
2 cloves garlic
Half cup soy sauce
Broccoli florets
Cornstarch
Beef sirloin
2 cups jasmine rice
Sesame oil
Beef bouillon cube
Brown sugar
Sesame seeds (to garnish)

DIRECTIONS:
- Cut beef into strips and place to Slow Cooker.
- Into a bowl with warm water, dissolve bouillon cube, sugar, add garlic, sesame oil and soy sauce. Pour over the beef.
- Turn on LOW mode and cook for 6 hours.
- Take 3 tablespoons liquid from Slow Cooker and dissolve cornstarch. Place back to the cooking dish and cook for about 30 minutes.
- In a separate pan cook broccoli and jasmine rice.
- To serve, place the meat on top of broccoli and rice. Garnish with sesame seeds.

**Nutrition: Calories: 814 Fat: 16g Carbohydrates: 91g Protein: 46**

## Slow Cooker Pizza with Ravioli

Try this one with cold juice!

Prep time: 5 minutes Cooking time: 4 hours
Servings: 8

INGREDIENTS:
1 clove garlic
Ground beef
1 tsp dried basil
2 cups shredded Mozzarella cheese
Half tsp ground black pepper
1 tsp garlic powder
Salt to taste
1 pack frozen ravioli
1 tsp dried oregano

1 tsp Italian seasoning
DIRECTIONS:
- Cook the beef in a large skillet along with garlic powder, pepper, and garlic, salt. Cook until gets brown and aromatic.
- Add basil, Italian seasoning, and oregano and pasta sauce. Grease your Slow Cooker with olive oil or plain butter, as you like. Ladle, in several layers, meat, ravioli and tomato mixture.
- Turn on LOW and cook for 3-5 hours.
- In the end, sprinkle with Mozzarella and leave until it melts, for another hour,

# PASTA & SIDE DISHES

## Turmeric Carrot Mash

Ready in about: **15 minutes** | Serves: **4** | Per serving: Calories 77; Carbs 16g; Fat 2g; Protein 2g

INGREDIENTS
1 tsp Turmeric Powder
¼ tsp Black Pepper
¼ tsp Sea Salt
1 ½ pounds Carrots, chopped
1 tbsp Heavy Cream
1 ½ cups Water
DIRECTIONS
- Pour water into the cooker, and place carrots to the steaming basket, and lower the basket into the pot.
- Seal the lid, cook on STEAM mode for 4 minutes at High. Do a quick release. Remove steaming basket and transfer the carrots to a food processor. Add the rest of the ingredients. Process until smooth.

## Kale and Carrots Side

Ready in about: **15 minutes** | Serves: **6** | Per serving: Calories 54; Carbs 6g; Fat 3g; Protein 3g

INGREDIENTS
10 ounces chopped Kale
3 Carrots, sliced
½ Onion, chopped
½ cup Broth
1 tbsp Olive Oil
4 Garlic Cloves, minced
1 tbsp Lemon Juice
Salt and Black Pepper, to taste
DIRECTIONS
- Heat oil on SAUTÉ at High, add garlic and cook for a minute, until fragrant. Stir in the remaining ingredients. Seal the lid and cook for 10 minutes on BEANS/CHILI at High. Release the pressure quickly, drain and serve.

## Balsamic Capers Beets

Ready in about: **45 minutes** | Serves: **4** | Per serving: Calories 78; Carbs 11g; Fat 4g; Protein 2g

INGREDIENTS
4 Beets
1 tbsp Olive Oil
2 tbsp Capers
1 tsp Garlic, minced
1 tbsp chopped Parsley
2 tbsp Balsamic Vinegar
Salt and Pepper, to taste
Water, as needed
DIRECTIONS
- Place the beets in the pressure cooker and cover with water. Seal the lid and cook on MEAT/STEW mode for 25 minutes, at High. Release the pressure quickly.
- Let the beets cool. Whisk together the remaining ingredients, in a bowl. Slice beets and combine with dressing, to serve.

## Mushroom and Zucchini Platter

Ready in about: **25 minutes** | Serves: **8** | Per serving: Calories 44; Carbs 5g; Fat 2g; Protein 2g

INGREDIENTS
12 ounces Mushrooms, sliced
4 medium Zucchinis, sliced
15 ounces canned Tomatoes, undrained
1 cup chopped Onion
1 Garlic Clove, minced
1 tbsp chopped Parsley
¼ tsp Red Pepper Flakes
2 tbsp Butter
DIRECTIONS
- Melt butter on SAUTÉ mode at High. Add onion and garlic and cook for 2 minutes, until soft and crispy. Add mushrooms and cook for 5 minutes, until soft.
- Add zucchini and top with tomatoes. Seal the lid. Cook for 2 minutes on STEAM at High. Quick release the pressure. Stir in parsley and flakes and season to taste.

## Frascati and Sage Broccoli

Ready in about: **15 minutes** | Serves: **6** | Per serving: Calories 73; Carbs 9g; Fat 3g; Protein 4g

INGREDIENTS
1 ½ pounds Broccoli, broken into florets
1 large Sweet Onion, sliced
1 cup Frascati, Italian White Wine
½ cup Water

2 tsp Sage
3 tsp Olive Oil
1 tsp Garlic Paste
Salt and Pepper, to taste
DIRECTIONS
- Heat the oil on SAUTÉ at High and cook the onions until soft, for about 3 minutes. Add garlic paste and cook for 1 minute until fragrant. Stir in the remaining ingredients.
- Seal the lid and cook for 4 minutes on STEAM at High pressure. Do a quick release and serve.

## Cabbage and Pepper Side

Ready in about: **20 minutes** | Serves: **8** | Per serving: Calories **60**; Carbs **10g**; Fat **2g**; Protein **2g**

INGREDIENTS
2 pounds Cabbage, shredded
1 cup Bell Peppers, diced sliced
¼ cup White Wine
½ cup Veggie Stock
1 cup Scallions, chopped
¼ cup Parsley, chopped
1 tbsp Oil
½ tsp Salt
¼ tsp Pepper
DIRECTIONS
- Heat oil on SAUTÉ mode at High. Add scallions and cook until soft, for about 3 minutes. Stir in the remaining ingredients. Seal the lid and cook for 10 minutes on STEAM mode at High.
- Once done, release the pressure quickly. Serve topped with freshly chopped parsley.

## Lemony Buckwheat Salad

Ready in: **15 minutes + chilling time** | Serves: **6** | Per serving: Calories **286**; Carbs **51g**; Fat **9g**; Protein **12g**

INGREDIENTS
¼ cup Extra-Virgin Olive Oil
¼ cup fresh Basil, minced
½ tsp Sea Salt
1 tsp Cayenne Pepper
5 cups Water
3 tsp Vegetable Oil
¼ cup fresh Lemon Juice
2 cups Buckwheat, rinsed and drained
½ cup Green Bell Pepper, seeded and chopped
1 cup Red Onions, minced
1 ½ cups Zucchini, diced
Sea Salt and freshly cracked Black Pepper
DIRECTIONS
- Add water, buckwheat, salt, oil, and cayenne pepper into your pressure cooker. Seal the lid, set on BEANS/CHILI, and cook for 8 minutes at High. Once cooking is over, allow for a natural pressure release, for about 10 minutes. Carefully open the lid, and stir in the remaining ingredients.
- Refrigerate and serve chilled.

## Sweet and Mustardy Carrots

Ready in about: **20 minutes** | Serves: **4** | Per serving: Calories **122**; Carbs **21g**; Fat **4g**; Protein **2g**

INGREDIENTS
1 pound Carrots
2 tbsp Mustard
2 tbsp Butter
2 tbsp Honey
2 tsp Garlic, minced
1 tsp Paprika
Salt and Black Pepper, to taste
DIRECTIONS
- Place the carrots and a cup of water in the pressure cooker. Seal the lid, and cook on BEANS/CHILI mode for 10 minutes at High pressure. When ready, release the pressure quickly.
- Whisk together the remaining ingredients, in a bowl. Brush over the carrots, and serve.

## Pizza Pasta

Ready in about: **30 minutes** | Serves: **6** | Per serving: Calories **491**; Carbs **38g**; Fat **23g**; Protein **35g**

INGREDIENTS
1 pound Pasta
16 ounces Pasta Sauce
8 ounces Pizza Sauce
1 pound Italian Sausage
4 ounces Pepperoni
8 ounces Mozzarella Cheese, shredded
3 ½ cups Water
1 tbsp Butter
1 tsp Garlic, minced
DIRECTIONS
- Heat oil on SAUTÉ mode at High. Cook the sausage and garlic for a few minutes, until lightly browned. Stir in the remaining ingredients, except the cheese and half of the pepperoni.
- Seal the lid and cook for 8 minutes on RICE/RISOTTO mode at High pressure. When it goes off, do a quick pressure release. Stir in the cheese and pepperoni. Serve immediately.

## Stewed Yams with Zucchini

Ready in about: **25 minutes** | Serves: **4** | Per serving: Calories **210**; Carbs **39g**; Fat **4g**; Protein **5g**

INGREDIENTS
1 pound Yams, peeled and diced
2 Zucchinis, peeled and chopped
2 Large Tomatoes, chopped
1 tsp Garlic, minced
1 Onion, diced
1 cup Chicken Stock
¼ tsp Cayenne Pepper
1 tsp Italian Seasoning
Salt and Pepper, to taste
1 tbsp Olive Oil
DIRECTIONS
- Heat the oil, on SAUTÉ mode at High. Add the onions and cook for about 4 minutes. When soft, add the garlic and cook for

another minute. Stir in the remaining ingredients and seal the lid.
- Select BEANS/CHILI mode, and set to 10 minutes at High pressure. Do a quick pressure release.

## Lemony Rutabaga and Onion Salad

Ready in about: **20 minutes** | Serves: **4** | Per serving: Calories 185; Carbs 18g; Fat 13g; Protein 3g

INGREDIENTS
1 cup Green Onions, sliced
2 Rutabagas, peeled and cubed
4 tbsp Olive Oil
2 tbsp Lemon Juice
Salt and Pepper, to taste
1 cup Water

DIRECTIONS
- Heat 1 tbsp of oil on SAUTÉ at High. Add the green onions, and cook them for about 2-3 minutes. Add the rutabaga and pour the water. Seal the lid, and cook at High pressure for 5 minutes.
- When it goes off, quick release the pressure. Drain rutabaga and green onions, and transfer them to a bowl. Mix the remaining ingredients, in another bowl, and pour over the rutabagas.

## Creamy Goat Cheese Cauliflower

Ready in about: **30 minutes** | Serves: **4** | Per serving: Calories 352; Carbs 7g; Fat 29g; Protein 16g

INGREDIENTS
1 Cauliflower Head, cut into florets
2 tbsp Lemon Juice
2 tbsp Olive Oil
1 cup Vegetable Broth
2 tsp Red Pepper Flakes
Water, as needed

SAUCE:
6 ounces Goat Cheese
1 tsp Nutmeg
½ cup Heavy Cream
1 tbsp Olive Oil
Salt and Black Pepper, to taste

DIRECTIONS
- Combine the lemon juice and cauliflower in your pressure cooker and cover with water. Seal the lid, and cook for 4 minutes on STEAM mode, at High pressure. Release the pressure quickly and transfer to a plate.
- Discard the liquid and clean the cooker. Heat the oil on SAUTÉ mode at High. Add red pepper flakes and cook until fragrant, for about a minute. Add cauliflower and cook for 1 minute uncovered; then return to the bowl.
- In a food processor, pulse all sauce ingredients and pour over cauliflower. Serve and enjoy!

## Garlicky Sweet Potato Mash

Ready in about: **20 minutes** | Serves: **6** | Per serving: Calories 263; Carbs 43g; Fat 9g; Protein 4g

INGREDIENTS
4 Garlic Cloves, minced
¾ cup Milk
2 tbsp Oil
2 pounds Sweet Potatoes, peeled and chopped
½ tsp Sea Salt
¼ tsp Pepper
A pinch of Nutmeg
A pinch of dried Thyme
Water, as needed

DIRECTIONS
- Place the sweet potato chunks inside the pressure cooker. Add enough water to cover the potatoes.
- Seal the lid, press BEANS/CHILI and cook for 10 minutes at High. Release the pressure quickly. Drain the potatoes and place in a bowl. Add the remaining ingredients and mash with a potato masher until smooth and creamy.

## Lime Cabbage with Coconut

Ready in about: **20 minutes** | Serves: **4** | Per serving: Calories 191; Carbs 21g; Fat 11g; Protein 5g

INGREDIENTS
1 tbsp Coconut Oil
½ cup desiccated Coconut
½ cup Lime Juice
1 Cabbage, shredded
1 Onion, sliced
1 Carrot, sliced
1 tsp Garlic, minced
½ tsp Curry Powder
¼ tsp Turmeric Powder

DIRECTIONS
- Melt coconut oil on SAUTÉ mode at High, add the onion slices and cook for about 3-4 minutes. When softened, add the garlic and saute for another minute. Stir in the remaining ingredients. Seal the lid.
- Press BEANS/CHILI, and set to 5 minutes at High pressure. Do a quick pressure release, and serve.

## Gnocchi with Butternut Squash and Tomatoes

Ready in about: **20 minutes** | Serves: **4** | Per serving: Calories 485; Carbs 67g; Fat 12g; Protein 21g

INGREDIENTS
1 lb Potato Gnocchi
10 oz Butternut squash, peeled, deseeded and diced
1 cup Green Onions, white parts only
1 cup Bell Peppers, stemmed, cored, and chopped
1 ½ cups Water
1 sprig dry Rosemary, crushed
¼ tsp ground Black Pepper
¼ tsp Salt
½ tsp Garlic powder
3 tsp Olive Oil
20 ounces canned diced Tomatoes

DIRECTIONS

- Heat oil on SAUTÉ at High and add in the leeks. Cook for 3-4 minutes, stirring constantly. Stir in squash and bell peppers, and continue to cook for 2 more minutes. Add in tomatoes, rosemary, water, garlic powder, salt, black pepper, and wine vinegar. Press CANCEL.
- Throw in the gnocchi and stir with a wooden spoon until it is well coated. Seal the lid, switch the pressure release valve to close and set to BEANS/CHILI mode, for 8 minutes, for al dente taste.
- Once done, do a quick pressure release. Serve topped with fresh chives and grated parmesan.

## Ricotta Cheese Lasagna with Mushrooms

Ready in about: **40 minutes** | **Serves: 6** | **Per serving: Calories 613; Carbs 86g; Fat 11g; Protein 28g**

INGREDIENTS
2 Cloves Garlic, minced
2 pounds dry lasagna Noodles
2 cups Pasta Sauce
2 cups Ricotta Cheese
1 tsp Red Pepper flakes, crushed
½ tsp Sea Salt
½ tsp dried Oregano
½ tsp ground Black Pepper
2 cups Mushrooms, thinly sliced
¼ cup chopped fresh Basil, plus more for garnish
Non-stick Cooking Spray, for greasing
2 cups Water

DIRECTIONS
- Grease spring-form pan with cooking spray. Place the lasagna noodles at the bottom and spread the pasta sauce evenly on top. Then place a layer of ricotta cheese and sprinkle roughly with mushrooms.
- Season with garlic, herbs, and spices and repeat the process until you run out of products. Cover with aluminum foil. Place the trivet at the bottom of your cooker, and pour 2 cups water.
- Place down the spring-form pan on the trivet and seal the lid. Cook for 25 minutes on BEANS/CHILI at High pressure. Do a quick pressure release. Garnish with basil to serve.

## Basil Eggplant Delight

Ready in about: **40 minutes** | **Serves: 4** | **Per serving: Calories 183; Carbs 6g; Fat 18g; Protein 1g**

INGREDIENTS
2 cups Eggplants, cubed
¼ cup Olive Oil
½ cup freshly Basil, chopped
2 tsp Garlic, minced
1 cup Red Onion, sliced
2 tbsp Red Wine
½ cup Water
1 tbsp Salt

DIRECTIONS
- Sprinkle the eggplants with the salt and place them in a colander for 20 minutes. Rinse and squeeze them, reserving the liquid. Heat oil on SAUTÉ mode at High.
- Cook the eggplants, garlic, and onion for a few minutes, until soft and lightly browned. Pour in the wine, water, and reserved liquid. Seal the lid and cook for 7 minutes on STEAM at High.
- When ready, release the pressure quickly. Serve topped with freshly chopped basil.

## Orange Potatoes with Walnuts

Ready in about: **20 minutes** | **Serves: 6** | **Per serving: Calories 313; Carbs 45g; Fat 22g; Protein 6g**

INGREDIENTS
12 Small Potatoes, peeled and chopped
¾ cup Walnuts, chopped
1 cup Mayonnaise
Juice of 1 Lemon
2 tbsp Olive Oil
¼ tsp Ginger Powder
Salt and Pepper, to taste
2 Oranges, peeled and chopped
Water, as needed

DIRECTIONS
- Place the potato chunks inside your pressure cooker and add enough water to cover them. Seal the lid, select BEANS/CHILI mode and cook at High pressure for 10 minutes.
- Quick release the pressure, and drain the potatoes. Add oranges and walnuts. Whisk the remaining ingredients, in a bowl, and pour over the potatoes.

## Red Cabbage with Apple

Ready in about: **30 minutes** | **Serves: 4** | **Per serving: Calories 183; Carbs 18g; Fat 5g; Protein 5g**

INGREDIENTS
1 small head Red Cabbage, shredded and stems removed
1 ½ cups Vegetable Stock
½ cup dry Red wine
1 Onion, diced
¼ tsp Allspice
½ tsp ground Black Pepper
1 tsp Salt
2 tbsp Olive Oil
2 apples, peeled, cored and diced
½ tbsp Cornstarch dissolved in 6 tsp dry Red Wine

DIRECTIONS
- Warm the oil on SAUTÉ at High. Stir in the apples, and onions and sauté until soft, for about 5 minutes.
- Add in the remaining ingredients, except for cornstarch slurry. Select BEANS/CHILI mode and cook for 15 minutes at High. Do a quick pressure release. Stir in the already prepared cornstarch slurry.
- Boil for another 5 minutes, lid off, on SAUTÉ. It has to thicken before it is ready to be served. Serve hot.

## Cheese Tortellini with Broccoli and Turkey

Ready in about: **30 minutes** | **Serves: 6** | **Per serving: Calories 395; Carbs 9g; Fat 23g; Protein 35g**

INGREDIENTS

3 Bacon Slices, chopped
1 ½ pounds Turkey Breasts, diced
3 cups Broccoli Florets
8 ounces Cheese Tortellini
¼ cup Heavy Cream
¼ cup Half and Half
2 cups Chicken Stock
1 Onion, chopped
1 Carrot, chopped
1 tbsp chopped Parsley
Salt and Pepper, to taste

DIRECTIONS
- Cook the bacon on SAUTÉ mode at High until crispy. Add onions and garlic and cook for 2 minutes, until sweaty Add turkey and cook until no longer pink, for a few minutes.
- Stir in the remaining ingredients, except heavy cream. Seal the lid, and cook for 8 minutes on RICE/RISOTTO mode at High pressure. When ready, release the pressure quickly. Stir in the heavy cream and serve.

## Spinach and Tomato Side

**Ready in about: 25 minutes | Serves: 6 | Per serving: Calories 45; Carbs 8g; Fat 1g; Protein 3g**

INGREDIENTS
10 cups Spinach
1 cup Tomatoes, chopped
1 tbsp Garlic, minced
1 Onion, diced
1 ¼ cups Veggie Broth
1 tbsp Lemon Juice
½ cup Tomato Puree
Salt and Black Pepper, to taste
Cooking Spray, to grease

DIRECTIONS
- Coat the pressure cooker with cooking spray and cook the onion for a few minutes, until soft. Add garlic and cook for one more minute. Stir in the remaining ingredients and seal the lid.
- Cook for 3 minutes on STEAM mode at High. When ready, do a natural release, for about 8 minutes.

## Smoky Asian-Style Tomato Chutney

**Ready in: 20 minutes + chilling time | Serves: 12 | Per serving: Calories 155; Carbs 32g; Fat 1g; Protein 2g**

INGREDIENTS
½ tbsp Curry Paste
½ tsp ground Ginger
1 clove Garlic, peeled and minced
2 cups Dark Brown Sugar
1 cup Onions, peeled and diced
3 pounds Cherry Tomatoes, blanched, chopped and pureed
1 tbsp Paprika
2 tbsp Golden Sultanas
½ Pomegranate, seeded, to garnish
½ cup Water

DIRECTIONS
- Add all ingredients in your pressure cooker. Give it a good stir and select BEANS/CHILI. Seal the lid and cook for 15 minutes at High.
- When done, do a quick pressure release. Refrigerate before serving.

## Vegetable Soup

**Ready in about: 20 minutes | Serves: 8 | Per serving: Calories 115; Carbs 16g; Fat 4g; Protein 4g**

INGREDIENTS
2 cups canned diced Tomatoes
1 cup Fennel Bulb, trimmed and chopped
1 pound Green Beans, trimmed, cut into bite-sized pieces
5 cups Vegetable Broth
2 tbsp Butter
1 tbsp Olive Oil
½ tsp ground Black Pepper
½ tsp Salt
1 cup Onions, cut into rings
1 ½ cups fresh corn kernels

DIRECTIONS
- Heat oil and butter on SAUTÉ at High. Stir-fry the onion for about 3-4 minutes. Add in broth, tomatoes, fennel, and dill. Season to taste, and seal the lid. Cook on BEANS/CHILI for 10 minutes at High.
- Once the cooking is complete, perform a quick pressure release. Add in the corn and green beans. Cook for another 5 more minutes without the lid on SAUTÉ mode at High. Serve immediately.

## Savoy Cabbage and Beetroot Borscht Soup

**Ready in about: 15 minutes | Serves: 5 | Per serving: Calories 202; Fat 10g; Carbs 18g; Protein 11g**

INGREDIENTS
1 ½ cups Savoy Cabbage, shredded
1 cup Red Onions, sliced
1 ½ cups Beetroot, trimmed and chopped
2 Potatoes, chopped
½ cup Sour Cream
1 tsp Cayenne Pepper
3 tsp Olive Oil
Salt and Black Pepper, to taste
1 Garlic clove, minced
5 cups Vegetable Broth

DIRECTIONS
- Heat oil on SAUTÉ at High. Add in the onions and garlic; stir-fry for about 3-4 minutes, or until soft. Add cabbage, beetroots, potatoes, broth, bay leaf, and cayenne pepper.
- Seal the lid, press BEANS/CHILI and cook for 10 minutes at High pressure. Once the cooking is complete, do a quick pressure release.
- Stir in yogurt and the shredded cheese. Season to taste. Top with a scoop of sour cream and serve.

## Hearty Artichokes and Garlic Green Beans

**Ready in about: 25 minutes | Serves: 8 | Per serving: Calories 163; Carbs 21g; Fat 6g; Protein 8g**

INGREDIENTS
- 2 pounds Artichoke, cut into small florets
- 2 ¼ cups fresh Green Beans
- 2 Tomatoes, diced
- 2 tbsp Green Garlic, finely minced
- ½ tsp Salt
- ½ tsp Red Pepper flakes, crushed
- ½ tsp ground Black Pepper
- 1 cup Scallions, white parts only, sliced
- 2 tsp Butter
- ½ tbsp Olive Oil
- 8 cups Vegetable Stock

DIRECTIONS
- Melt the butter and oil on SAUTÉ mode at High. Stir-fry the scallions, for about 3 minutes, until softened. Add in the tomatoes, artichokes, garlic, and stock. Season with salt, black and red pepper, and seal the lid.
- Select BEANS/CHILI and cook for 8 minutes at High. Once ready, do a quick pressure release. Stir in green beans and continue to cook for another 10 minutes, lid off on SAUTÉ. Serve immediately.

## Silky Cheese and Cauli Soup

Ready in about: **40 minutes** | Serves: **4** | Per serving: Calories 155; Carbs 12g; Fat 6g; Protein 8g

INGREDIENTS
- ¾ cups Vegetable Broth
- ½ cup Onions, chopped
- ½ cup Parsnip, finely chopped
- 1 cup Carrots, sliced
- ¼ cup ground Black Pepper, to taste
- 1 tsp Salt
- 1 cup Bell Pepper, seeded and chopped
- 1 cup Celery stalks, finely chopped
- 2 cups Cauliflower, broken into small florets
- ½ cup Colby cheese, grated

DIRECTIONS
- Place all ingredients, except for the Colby cheese, in your pressure cooker. Seal the lid. Select SOUP mode, and cook for 3 minutes at High Preesure. Do a quick pressure release.
- Purée soup with an electric mixer or hand blender. Serve soup topped with freshly grated Colby cheese.

## Easy Mushroom Pâté

Ready in about: **30 minutes** | Serves: **8** | Per serving: Calories 55; Carbs 4g; Fat 4g; Protein 1g;

INGREDIENTS
- ½ cup White Wine
- 2 Onions, peeled and sliced
- 1 ½ pounds Button Mushrooms, thinly sliced
- 1 ½ cups boiling Water
- ½ tsp Salt
- ¼ tsp Black Pepper, freshly cracked
- 1 cup dried Porcini Mushrooms, washed
- 3 tbsps Butter

DIRECTIONS
- Combine the mushrooms and boiling water in a heatproof cup. Cover and set aside. The mushrooms will soak up the water. Melt butter on SAUTÉ at High. Add in onions and cook for 3 minutes, until soft.
- Stir in mushrooms and sauté them until golden brown, for about 4 minutes. Pour in wine and let it fully evaporate. Stir in the soaked mushrooms and adjust the seasoning. Seal the lid.
- Select BEANS/CHILI and cook for 10 minutes at High. Do a quick release. To prepare the paté, blend the ingredients with an immersion blender, for about 5 minutes. Refrigerate and serve chilled.

## Cheesy Soup with Tortillas

Ready in about: **30 minutes** | Serves: **4** | Per serving: Calories 388; Carbs 51g; Fat 19g; Protein 13g

INGREDIENTS
- 1 cup Water
- 2 tbsp Butter
- 3 cups Vegetable Stock
- 1 cup Shallots, chopped
- ¼ cup fresh Lime Juice
- 6 ounces frozen Green peas
- 1 ½ cups canned Pumpkin Puree
- ½ habanero Pepper, seeded and diced 2 Green Bell Peppers, seeded and diced
- 1 cup Summer Squash, cut into bite-size pieces
- 3 Garlic Cloves, minced
- Non-stick Cooking Spray
- 6 corn Tortillas, cut into wide strips
- 2 ripe Tomatoes, chopped
- ¼ tsp ground Black Pepper
- ½ tsp ground Cumin
- ½ tsp dry Basil
- 1 tsp Sea Salt
- ½ tsp Chili powder
- ½ tsp dried Oregano
- Gruyere cheese, grated, for serving

DIRECTIONS
- Preheat oven to 400 degrees F. Line a baking sheet with parchment paper.
- Lightly spray both sides of each tortilla with a nonstick cooking spray. Spread the tortilla strips onto the baking sheet.
- Bake until they are crisp, turning once halfway through baking. It will take about 9 minutes.
- Melt butter on SAUTÉ at High. Cook the shallots for about 3 minutes. Add squash, peppers, garlic, and lime juice.
- Bring to a boil and let the liquid reduce by half. Add tomatoes, pumpkin puree, herbs, spices, water, and vegetable stock. Seal the lid, press BEANS/CHILI and cook for 10 minutes at High. Stir in the peas. Let it simmer, uncovered, for approximately 3 minutes.
- To serve, ladle the soup into bowls; top with crushed tortilla chips and Gruyere cheese.

## Power Kale and Chickpea Soup

Ready in about: **20 minutes** | Serves: **6** | Per serving: Calories 315; Carbs 41g; Fat 9g; Protein 11g

INGREDIENTS
- 1 (15.5 oz) can Chickpeas, rinsed, drained
- 2 cups Kale, torn into large pieces

3 tbsp dry White Wine
½ cup White Rice
3 tbsp Olive Oil
2 serrano Peppers, seeded and chopped
½ tsp Kosher Salt
½ tsp ground Black Pepper
1 Tomato, finely chopped
1 ½ cups Red Onions, white part only, sliced
1 cup Greek yogurt, room temperature
½ cup Celery with leaves, chopped
7 cups Vegetable Stock

DIRECTIONS
- Heat oil on SAUTÉ at High, and fry onions, peppers, and celery, for about 4 minutes. Add in the rice and cook for 3 minutes. Pour in stock, and stir in salt, black pepper, wine, chickpeas, chopped tomatoes, and kale.
- Seal the lid, select BEANS/CHILI mode and cook for 8 minutes at High Pressure. Once ready, do a quick pressure release. Divide soup among bowls.
- Add a dollop of yogurt and serve hot.

## Sour Cream Veggies

Ready in about: **20 minutes** | Serves: **4** | Per serving: Calories 399; Carbs 42g; Fat 21g; Protein 12g

INGREDIENTS
4 Bacon slices, chopped
2 Carrots, chopped
½ Onion, chopped
1 Garlic Clove, minced
2 Potatoes, chopped
1 cup Broccoli Florets
1 cup Cauliflower Florets
1 tbsp Lemon Juice
1 tbsp Olive Oil
1 cup Sour Cream
1 ½ cups Chicken Stock
Salt and Pepper, to taste

DIRECTIONS
- Cook the bacon until crispy on SAUTÉ mode at High. Remove to a plate. Add the onion and garlic and cook for 2 minutes, until soft. Add the potatoes and carrots and cook for 2 more minutes.
- Pour the stock and seal the lid. Cook for 5 minutes on BEANS/CHILI at High pressure. Do a quick release. Stir in sour cream and lemon juice. Adjust the seasoning. Serve topped with crispy bacon slices.

## Cajun Potatoes with Brussel Sprouts

Ready in about: **20 minutes** | Serves: **6** | Per serving: Calories 131; Carbs 27g; Fat 1g; Protein 5g

INGREDIENTS
1 ½ pounds Potatoes, chopped
½ pound Brussel Sprouts, halved
1 tsp Cajun Seasoning
½ Onion, chopped
1 Garlic Clove, minced
1 ½ cups Chicken Stock
1 tbsp Oil

DIRECTIONS
- Heat oil on SAUTÉ at High, and cook the onions and garlic for 2 minutes, until soft and fragrant. Pour the stock and add potatoes. Seal the lid and cook for 6 minutes on BEANS/CHILI at High pressure.
- When ready, release the pressure, add the Brussel sprouts, and continue cooking for 4 more minutes, lid off, on SAUTÉ at High. Drain and transfer to a plate. Season with Cajun, and serve.

## Turmeric Kale with Shallots

Ready in about: **20 minutes** | Serves: **3** | Per serving: Calories 102; Carbs 14g; Fat 4g; Protein 5g

INGREDIENTS
10 ounces Kale, chopped
5 Shallots, chopped
1 tsp Turmeric Powder
2 tsp Olive Oil
½ tsp Coriander Seeds
½ tsp Cumin
Salt and Black Pepper, to taste
1 cup Water

DIRECTIONS
- Pour 1 cup of water and place the kale in the steaming basket. Seal the lid and cook on STEAM for 3 minutes at High pressure. When ready, do a quick pressure release.
- Transfer to a plate. Discard the water and heat the oil on SAUTÉ at High. Add the spices and shallots and cook until soft, for about 5-6 minutes. Stir in the kale, serve and enjoy!

## Miso Sweet Potato Mash

Ready in about: **20 minutes** | Serves: **6** | Per serving: Calories 264; Carbs 43g; Fat 9g; Protein 4g;

INGREDIENTS
3 tbsp cold Butter, cut into pieces
½ tsp Miso Paste
¾ cup Milk
2 pounds Sweet Potatoes, peeled and cut into chunks
1 sprig dried Thyme, crushed
¾ tsp Red Pepper flakes, crushed
¼ tsp ground Black Pepper
2 sprigs dried Rosemary, crushed
½ tsp Salt
2 tbsp Pumpkin Seeds, toasted

DIRECTIONS
- Place the potatoes in your pressure cooker and fill with the water to cover them. Sprinkle with the salt and lock the lid. Select BEANS/CHILI mode and cook for 10 minutes at High Pressure. Do a quick release.
- Drain the potatoes in a colander. Mash with a potato masher, and season with red and black pepper, rosemary, thyme, and miso paste. Add butter and milk, and stir softly until smooth. Spoon the mash into a serving bowl, top with the toasted seeds and serve.

## Spaghetti with Meatballs

Ready in about: **30 minutes** | Serves: **6** | Per serving: Calories 306; Carbs 16g; Fat 13g; Protein 27g

INGREDIENTS
- 10 ounces Noodles
- 2 Eggs
- 1 pound Ground Beef
- ¼ cup Breadcrumbs
- ½ small Red Onion, grated
- 1 Egg
- 1 jar Spaghetti Sauce
- ½ tsp Garlic, minced
- Water as needed

DIRECTIONS
- Combine the beef, crumbs, garlic, onion, and egg, in a bowl. Mix with hands. Shape the mixture into about 6 meatballs. Add the sauce and spaghetti in your pressure cooker.
- Pour enough water to cover. Add the meatballs and seal the lid. Cook BEANS/CHILI at High pressure for 15 minutes. When ready, release the pressure naturally, for 10 minutes.

## Creamy Tomato and Basil Soup

Ready in about: **15 minutes** | Serves: **6** | Per serving: Calories 123; Carbs 14g; Fat 5g; Protein 7g

INGREDIENTS
- 1 pound fresh Cherry Tomatoes, finely chopped
- 1 cup Heavy Cream
- 2 cups Tomato Puree
- 1 tsp Garlic, minced
- 6 cups Vegetable Broth
- 1 Onion, chopped
- 1 ½ tbsp Olive Oil
- 1 tsp Oregano
- Salt and Black Pepper, to taste
- 1 tbsp fresh chopped Basil

DIRECTIONS
- Warm oil on SAUTÉ at High. Stir in onions and cook for about 3 minutes, until soft. Add the rest of the ingredients, except for the heavy cream. Seal the lid, select SOUP and cook for 15 minutes at High.
- Once the cooking process has completed, quick release the pressure. Blend soup inside the cooker with an immersion blender until smooth; add in the cream. Give it a gentle stir and serve right away.

## Sicilian Eggplant Delight

Ready in about: **60 minutes** | Serves: **4** | Per serving: Calories 184; Carbs 7g; Fat 15g; Protein 1g

INGREDIENTS
- 1 cup Red Onion, sliced
- 3 tbsp Red wine
- ½ cup Olive Oil
- ½ cup Water
- 2 cups Eggplant, unpeeled and cubed, Salted
- 1 tbsp Salt
- 2 Garlic Cloves, chopped
- ½ cup fresh Basil, chopped

DIRECTIONS
- Place cubed and salted eggplant in kitchen sieve and let them stand for 35 minutes. Then, rinse, squeeze and set aside. Heat oil on SAUTÉ at High. Stir-fry garlic, onion, and eggplant, for about 2-3 minutes.
- Pour in red wine and water. Seal the lid and cook for 8 minutes on BEANS/CHILI at High Pressure. Once the cooking is over, do a quick pressure release. Sprinkle with fresh basil to serve.

## Creamy Coconut Squash Soup

Ready in about: **25 minutes** | Serves: **6** | Per serving: Calories 210; Carbs 21g; Fat 17g; Protein 6g

INGREDIENTS
- 1 ½ pounds Butternut squash, cut into small pieces
- 5 cups Vegetable Broth
- 2 Shallots, diced
- 1 cup Coconut Milk
- 4 tsp Olive Oil
- 2 Garlic Cloves, finely minced
- A pinch of Black Pepper
- A pinch of Salt
- ½ tsp Smoked Cayenne Pepper
- Fresh Cilantro to garnish

DIRECTIONS
- Press the SAUTÉ at High and warm the oil. Cook the shallots until tender and translucent, about 3 minutes. Add the squash, garlic, salt, black pepper, and cayenne pepper; sauté for 4 minutes.
- Pour in the broth. Seal the lid, select BEANS/CHILI mode and cook for 10 minutes at High Pressure.
- Do a quick release. Add ¾ cup coconut milk and purée the soup using an immersion blender. Divide soup between six bowls. Add a drizzle of the remaining coconut milk, and top with fresh cilantro.

## Sicilian Eggplant Delight

Ready in about: **60 minutes** | Serves: **4** | Per serving: Calories 184; Carbs 7g; Fat 15g; Protein 1g

INGREDIENTS
- 1 cup Red Onion, sliced
- 3 tbsp Red wine
- ½ cup Olive Oil
- ½ cup Water
- 2 cups Eggplant, unpeeled and cubed, Salted
- 1 tbsp Salt
- 2 Garlic Cloves, chopped
- ½ cup fresh Basil, chopped

DIRECTIONS
- Place cubed and salted eggplant in kitchen sieve and let them stand for 35 minutes. Then, rinse, squeeze and set aside. Heat oil on SAUTÉ at High. Stir-fry garlic, onion, and eggplant, for about 2-3 minutes.
- Pour in red wine and water. Seal the lid and cook for 8 minutes on BEANS/CHILI at High Pressure. Once the cooking is over, do a quick pressure release. Sprinkle with fresh basil to serve.

## Creamy Coconut Squash Soup

Ready in about: **25 minutes** | Serves: **6** | Per serving: Calories 210; Carbs 21g; Fat 17g; Protein 6g

INGREDIENTS
1 ½ pounds Butternut squash, cut into small pieces
5 cups Vegetable Broth
2 Shallots, diced
1 cup Coconut Milk
4 tsp Olive Oil
2 Garlic Cloves, finely minced
A pinch of Black Pepper
A pinch of Salt
½ tsp Smoked Cayenne Pepper
Fresh Cilantro to garnish
DIRECTIONS
- Press the SAUTÉ at High and warm the oil. Cook the shallots until tender and translucent, about 3 minutes. Add the squash, garlic, salt, black pepper, and cayenne pepper; sauté for 4 minutes.
- Pour in the broth. Seal the lid, select BEANS/CHILI mode and cook for 10 minutes at High Pressure.
- Do a quick release. Add ¾ cup coconut milk and purée the soup using an immersion blender. Divide soup between six bowls. Add a drizzle of the remaining coconut milk, and top with fresh cilantro.

## Vegetable and Cannellini Beans Pottage

Ready in about: **28 minutes** | Serves: **4** | Per serving: **Calories 386; Carbs 49g; Fat 21g; Protein 14g**

INGREDIENTS
¼ cup Butter
1 cup Cannellini Beans, soaked overnight
1 cup Scallions, chopped
1 tbsp fresh Ginger, minced
½ pound Potatoes, peeled and cubed
1 ½ cups Tomato Puree
2 cups Vegetable Broth
2 tsp Sesame Oil
2 Red Bell Peppers, chopped
Salt and Black Pepper, to taste
1 tsp Garlic, finely minced
2 cups Water
DIRECTIONS
- Melt the butter and sauté the scallions, garlic, and peppers for 3-4 minutes, on SAUTÉ at High. Add the rest of the ingredients. Seal the lid, select SOUP mode cook for 15 minutes at High Pressure.
- Once the cooking is complete, perform a quick pressure release. Carefully open the lid and serve hot!

## Garlicky Zucchini and Carrot Noodles

Ready in about: **15 minutes** | Serves: **2** | Per serving: **Calories 198; Carbs 29g; Fat 7g; Protein 4g**

INGREDIENTS
4 Carrots, spiralized
2 Zucchinis, spiralized
2 tsp Garlic, minced
1 tbsp Olive Oil
¼ tsp Onion Powder
¼ tsp Black Pepper
¼ tsp Sea Salt
½ cup Tomato Sauce
DIRECTIONS
- Heat the olive on SAUTÉ at High, add the garlic and cook for a minute, until fragrant. Add the noodles and season with salt, pepper, and onion powder. Cook for about 3 minutes.
- Stir in the tomato sauce and cook for another 4 to 6 minutes. Serve as a side and enjoy!

## Rosemary and Garlic Potatoes

Ready in about: **30 minutes** | Serves: **4** | Per serving: **Calories 231; Carbs 41g; Fat 5g; Protein 6g**

INGREDIENTS
2 pounds Baby Potatoes
4 tsp Olive Oil
1 cup Vegetable Stock
2 tsp Garlic, minced
1 ½ tsp dried Rosemary
Salt and Black Pepper, to taste
DIRECTIONS
- Heat oil on SAUTÉ mode at High, and add the potatoes, garlic, and rosemary. Sprinkle with salt and pepper, and cook for 5 - 7 minutes, stirring occasionally, until nice and soft. Stir in the stock and seal the lid.
- Cook for 8 minutes on BEANS/CHILI mode at High. Release the pressure naturally for 10 minutes.

## Simple Mediterranean Asparagus

Ready in about: **5 minutes** | Serves: **4** | Per serving: **Calories 101; Carbs 5g; Fat 9g; Protein 3g**

INGREDIENTS
1 pound Asparagus Spears, rough ends trimmed
1 Garlic Clove, minced
1 tbsp Shallot, minced
2 ½ tbsp Olive Oil
1 tbsp Lemon Juice
1 cup Water
DIRECTIONS
- Place the asparagus and pour water in your pressure cooker. Seal the lid, and cook for 3 minutes on STEAM, at High. Once done, release the pressure quickly.
- Toss the asparagus with the remaining ingredients to combine thoroughly, and serve.

## Warm Chili Soup

Ready in about: **45 minutes** | Serves: **4** | Per serving: **Calories 135; Carbs 15g; Fat 7g; Protein 6g**

INGREDIENTS
4 cups Vegetable Stock
2 pickled Chili Peppers, chopped
2 Onions, finely chopped
½ tsp ground cumin
½ tsp dried Thyme
1 cup Parsnips, chopped
2 tbsp Olive Oil
1 ½ cups Carrots, chopped

½ cup Celery stalk, chopped
1 cup Croutons, for garnish

DIRECTIONS
- Heat oil on SAUTÉ mode at High. Add in celery, parsnips, carrots, onion and chili peppers, and sauté the vegetables for about 5 minutes. Add the remaining ingredients. Seal the lid, press SOUP and cook for 30 minutes at High.
- Once the cooking is complete, perform a quick pressure release. Serve with croutons.

## Spicy Cauliflower with Peas

Ready in about: 25 minutes | Serves: 8 | Per serving: Calories 173; Carbs 24g; Fat 4g; Protein 10g

INGREDIENTS
2 Tomatoes, diced
2 ¼ cups Green Peas
2 pounds Cauliflower, broken into florets
2 tbsp Garlic, minced
7 cups Stock
2 Yams, cubed
2 tbsp Butter
½ tsp Salt
¼ tsp Pepper
½ tsp Paprika
½ tsp Chili Powder
¼ tsp Red Pepper Flakes
¼ tsp Cayenne Pepper
½ tsp Onion Powder

DIRECTIONS
- Melt butter on SAUTÉ at High, and cook the garlic and spices for 1 minute. Stir in the remaining ingredients. Seal the lid and set for 10 minutes on BEANS/CHILI at High. Do a quick release, drain and serve the veggies.

## Flavorful Bell Peppers

Ready in about: 15 minutes | Serves: 4 | Per serving: Calories 214; Carbs 22g; Fat 13g; Protein 6g

INGREDIENTS
1 ½ pounds Red Bell Peppers
½ cup Stock
¾ cup Tomato Soup
½ cup chopped Scallions
½ tbsp Miso Paste
½ Butter Stick
1 tsp Garlic, minced
2 tbsp Champagne Vinegar
Salt and Pepper, to taste

DIRECTIONS
- Melt the butter on SAUTÉ mode at High, and cook the scallions for 3 minutes, until soft. Add garlic and cook for a minute, until fragrant. Stir in the remaining ingredients.
- Seal the lid and cook for 3 minutes on STEAM mode at High pressure. Release the pressure quickly.

## Spinach with Cottage Cheese

Ready in about: 25 minutes | Serves: 4 | Per serving: Calories 152; Carbs 15g; Fat 6g; Protein 13g

INGREDIENTS
18 ounces Spinach, chopped
10 ounces Cottage Cheese
1 Onion, chopped
8 Garlic Cloves, minced
1 tbsp Butter
2 tbsp Corn Flour
1 tsp Cumin
½ cup Water
½ tsp Coriander
1 tsp grated Ginger

DIRECTIONS
- Melt the butter on SAUTÉ mode at High, and cook the onions, ginger, and garlic for 2 minutes, until soft. Stir in the spices and spinach and cook for 2 minutes, until tender.
- Pour in the water and stir in flour. Seal the lid, and cook for 3 minutes on STEAM at High. When ready, do a quick pressure release, and stir in the cottage cheese.

## Sausage Penne

Ready in about: 20 minutes | Serves: 6 | Per serving: Calories 413; Carbs 48g; Fat 18g; Protein 21g

INGREDIENTS
18 ounces Penne Pasta
16 ounces Sausage
2 cups Tomato Paste
1 tbsp Olive Oil
2 tsp Garlic, minced
1 tsp Oregano
¼ cup Parmesan Cheese, grated
Water, as needed

DIRECTIONS
- Heat oil on SAUTÉ mode at High. Add sausage, cook until browned while crumbling. Add garlic and cook for 1 minute. Stir in the remaining ingredients, except Parmesan and oregano.
- Cover with water, seal the lid, and cook for 10 minutes on BEANS/CHILI at High. Release the pressure quickly. To serve, top with freshly grated Parmesan cheese and sprinkle with dry oregano.

## Zucchini and Cherry Tomato Delight

Ready in about: 20 minutes | Serves: 8 | Per serving: Calories 60; Carbs 11g; Fat 2g; Protein 1g

INGREDIENTS
1 pound Cherry Tomatoes
2 small Onion, chopped
6 medium Zucchinis, chopped
1 ½ tsp Garlic, minced
1 tbsp Olive Oil
1 cup Water
2 tbsp Basil, chopped
Salt and Pepper, to taste

DIRECTIONS
- Heat oil on SAUTÉ mode at High. Stir onions and cook for 3 minutes, until soft and translucent. Add garlic and cook for 1 minute, until fragrant. Stir in tomatoes and zucchini.
- Cook for 2 minutes, until soft, and pour in the water. Seal the lid and cook for 5 minutes on BEANS/CHILI at High. Do a quick

pressure release, stir in the basil and season with salt and pepper, to serve.

## Cauliflower Side with Pomegranate and Walnuts

Ready in about: **20 minutes** | Serves: **8** | Per serving: **Calories 158; Carbs 20g; Fat 9g; Protein 4g**

INGREDIENTS
2 cups Pomegranate Seeds
3 medium Cauliflower Heads, broken into florets
¼ cup Hazelnuts, toasted
1 tbsp Capers
3 tbsp Olive Oil
3 tbsp Orange Juice
1 cup Water

DIRECTIONS
- Add 1 cup of water and place cauliflower in the steaming basket. Seal the lid and cook for 3 minutes on STEAM mode at High. Do a quick release, transfer to a bowl, and stir in the remaining ingredients to serve.

## Simple Steamed Potatoes

Ready in about: **15 minutes** | Serves: **8** | Per serving: **Calories 132; Carbs 30g; Fat 1g; Protein 3g**

INGREDIENTS
3 pounds Potatoes, peeled and quartered
1 tsp Cayenne Pepper
1 tsp Sea Salt
½ tsp Black Pepper
Water, as needed

DIRECTIONS
- Place the potatoes inside the pressure cooker. Add enough water to cover them. Seal the lid, choose BEANS/CHILI mode and set the cooking time to 8 minutes at High pressure.
- When the timer goes off, do a quick pressure release. Drain the potatoes and place them in a bowl. Cut them if you want, and sprinkle with the seasonings to serve.

## Pea and Sweet Potato Bowl

Ready in about: **20 minutes** | Serves: **6** | Per serving: **Calories 155; Carbs 29g; Fat 3g; Protein 4g**

INGREDIENTS
1 pound Sweet Potatoes, peeled and cubed
¾ pound Frozen Peas
1 tsp Ginger, minced
1 tsp Garlic, minced
¼ tsp dried Thyme
¼ tsp dried Basil
1 ½ cups Chicken Stock
1 tbsp Olive Oil

DIRECTIONS
- Heat oil on SAUTÉ, add the garlic and ginger and cook just for a minute. Add potatoes and pour in the stock. Seal the lid, select BEANS/CHILI, and set to 10 minutes at High. After the beep, do a quick pressure release.
- Stir in the peas and seal the lid again. Cook on STEAM mode for 4 more minutes at High. Do a quick pressure release again. Drain the potatoes and peas and transfer to a bowl. Stir in the basil and thyme. Enjoy!

## Orange Broccoli Parmesan

Ready in about: **5 minutes** | Serves: **4** | Per serving: **Calories 60; Carbs 3g; Fat 4g; Protein 3g**

INGREDIENTS
2 cups Broccoli Florets
¼ cup freshly grated Parmesan Cheese
1 tbsp Orange Juice
¾ cup Water
2 tbsp Butter, melted
A pinch of Salt

DIRECTIONS
- Pour the water and add the broccoli. Seal the lid and cook at High pressure mode on STEAM mode, for 3 minutes.
- fWhen ready, release the pressure quickly and transfer florets to a bowl. Add the remaining ingredients and toss to combine. Serve and enjoy!

# SNACKS & APPETIZERS RECIPES

## Christmas Egg Custard

Ready in about: **20 minutes** | Serves: **4** | Per serving: **Calories 314; Carbs 17g; Fat 25g; Protein 6g**

INGREDIENTS
1 Egg plus 2 Yolks
1 ½ cups Milk
2 cups Heavy Cream
½ tsp Rum Extract
¾ cup Sugar
1 tsp Anise Seeds
1 ½ cups Water

DIRECTIONS
- Beat eggs and yolks in a bowl. Beat in the milk, rum, and heavy cream. Whisk in star anise and sugar. Divide the mixture between 4 ramekins. Pour 1 ½ cups of water in the cooker.
- Place the ramekins inside onto an inserted trivet. Seal the lid and cook for 10 minutes on BEANS/CHILI at High pressure. Once cooking is complete, release the pressure naturally, for 5 minutes, and serve.

## Chicken Enchilada Pasta

⌀ Ready in about: **20 minutes** | Serves: **6** | Per serving:
Calories 567; Carbs 49g; Fat 25g; Protein 31g

INGREDIENTS
2 Chicken Breasts, diced
3 cups dry Pasta
10 ounces canned Tomatoes
20 ounces canned Enchilada Sauce
1 ¼ cups Water
1 cup diced Onion
1 tsp Garlic, minced
1 tsp Taco Seasoning
1 tbsp Olive Oil
2 cups Cheddar Cheese, shredded

DIRECTIONS
- Heat oil on SAUTÉ at High, and cook the onions until soft, for about 3 minutes. Stir in the remaining ingredients, except the cheese.
- Seal the lid and cook for 8 minutes BEANS/CHILI at High pressure. Quick-release the pressure. Stir in cheese and cook for 2 minutes, lid off, on SAUTÉ, until melted.

## Paprika Potato Slices

⌀ Ready in about: **20 minutes** | Serves: **4** | Per serving:
Calories 183; Carbs 29g; Fat 7g; Protein 3g

INGREDIENTS
4 Potatoes, peeled and sliced
½ tsp Smoked Paprika
Salt and Pepper, to taste
1 tbsp Olive Oil
Water, as needed

DIRECTIONS
- Place the potato slices in the pressure cooker and pour enough water to cover them. Seal the lid, select STEAM and set the timer to 10 minutes at High pressure. Release the pressure quickly.
- Drain the potatoes and discard the water. Transfer the potatoes to a bowl. Wipe clean the cooker. Press SAUTÉ, set on High, and add heat oil. Sprinkle the potatoes with paprika, salt, and pepper, and toss to combine.
- Be careful not to break them. When the oil is hot, add the potatoes and cook for about a minute per side.

## Cheesy Fingerling Potato Rounds

⌀ Ready in about: **20 minutes** | Serves: **4** | Per serving:
Calories 331; Carbs 30g; Fat 18g; Protein 13g

INGREDIENTS
1 ½ pounds Fingerling Potatoes, sliced
1 cup Gorgonzola Cheese, crumbled
4 tbsp Butter
½ cup Vegetable Broth
½ tsp Cayenne Pepper
½ tsp Salt

DIRECTIONS
- Melt butter on SAUTÉ at High, and add the potato slices, beef broth, salt, and pepper. Seal the lid and cook for 10 minutes on BEANS/CHILI at High pressure. Do a quick pressure release.
- Serve the potatoes immediately, topped with crumbled blue cheese.

## Tahini, Carrot, and Spinach "Hummus"

⌀ Ready in about: **15 minutes** | Serves: **6** | Per serving:
Calories 173; Carbs 17g; Fat 6g; Protein 4g

INGREDIENTS
3 cups chopped Carrots
3 tbsp Tahini
2 cups chopped Spinach
1 Garlic Clove, crushed
2 tbsp Lemon Juice
2 tbsp Olive Oil
2 cups Water
Salt and Pepper, to taste

DIRECTIONS
- Combine carrots and water in the cooker. Seal the lid, select BEANS/CHILI, and set the timer to 5 minutes at High pressure. When it goes off, release the pressure quickly, and drain the carrots.
- Transfer to a food processor. Add the remaining ingredients, and pulse until smooth and creamy.

## Balsamic Carrots

⌀ Ready in about: **15 minutes** | Serves: **4** | Per serving:
Calories 185; Carbs 12g; Fat 11g; Protein 2g

INGREDIENTS
1 pound Baby Carrots
3 tbsp Balsamic Vinegar
½ tsp Pepper
3 tbsp Thyme, chopped
½ tsp Sea Salt
¼ cup Olive Oil
1 tbsp Sunflower Seeds, chopped
Water, as needed

DIRECTIONS
- Place the carrots inside the pressure cooker, and add water to cover them. Seal the lid, select BEANS/CHILI, and set the timer to 8 minutes at High pressure. When ready, release the pressure quickly.
- Drain the carrots, and place in a bowl. Discard water from the cooker, and wipe clean. Set on SAUTÉ at High and add in the carrots. Add the rest of the ingredients and toss to coat well. Cook for about 3 minutes.

## Colby Cheese and Pancetta Frittata

⌀ Ready in about: **30 minutes** | Serves: **4** | Per serving:
Calories 325; Carbs 4g; Fat 24g; Protein 22g

INGREDIENTS
6 Eggs, beaten
½ cup grated Colby Cheese
6 Pancetta Slices, cooked and crumbled

3 tbsp Sour Cream
½ tsp Onion Powder
2 tsp Butter, melted
¼ tsp Pepper
1 ½ cups Water

DIRECTIONS
- Pour the water in your pressure cooker and lower the trivet. Whisk the remaining ingredients in a baking dish.
- Place the dish on top of the trivet. Seal the lid and cook on BEANS/CHILI for 20 minutes at High. Release the pressure quickly, and serve.

## Eggs de Provence

Ready in about: **20 minutes | Serves: 8 | Per serving: Calories 331; Carbs 3g; Fat 29g; Protein 10g**

INGREDIENTS
8 Eggs
1 cup Heavy Cream
2 Shallots, chopped
1 cup Bacon de Provence, cooked and crumbled
1 ½ cups chopped Kale
1 tbsp Herbs de Provence
Salt and Black Pepper, to taste
1 ½ cups + 4 tbsp Water

DIRECTIONS
- Whisk the eggs with water and cream in a baking dish. Stir in shallots, bacon, kale, and herbs. Season with salt and pepper.
- Cover with a piece of foil. Pour 1 ½ cups of water in the pressure cooker. Lower the trivet, and place the dish on top. Seal the lid and cook on BEANS/CHILI for 15 minutes at High. When ready, do a quick release.

## Kale Hummus

Ready in about: **25 minutes | Serves: 10 | Per serving: Calories 206; Carbs 27g; Fat 8g; Protein 10g**

INGREDIENTS
2 cups Chickpeas
2 cups Kale, chopped
3 tbsp Tahini
1 cup Green Onions, minced
4 ½ cups Water
½ tsp Salt
¼ tsp Pepper
2 tbsp Olive Oil

DIRECTIONS
- Combine the chickpeas and water in your pressure cooker. Seal the lid and cook on BEANS/CHILI mode for 25 minutes at High pressure. When ready, release the pressure quickly.
- Drain the chickpeas and place in a food processor. Add the remaining ingredients. Blend until smooth.

## Pea and Avocado Dip

Ready in about: **25 minutes | Serves: 4 | Per serving: Calories 123; Carbs 15g; Fat 8g; Protein 5g**

INGREDIENTS
1 ½ cups dried Green Peas
1 tbsp Lime Juice
1 Avocado, peeled and deseeded
¼ tsp Pepper
1 Garlic Clove, peeled
2 cups Water

DIRECTIONS
- Combine the water and peas in the pressure cooker. Seal the lid and turn clockwise to seal. Select the BEANS/CHILI mode, set the timer to 16 minutes at High pressure.
- When the timer goes off, release the pressure quickly. Drain the peas and transfer them to a food processor. Add the remaining ingredients, and pulse until smooth and creamy.

## Pressure Cooked Eggplant Dip

Ready in about: **20 minutes | Serves: 8 | Per serving: Calories 84; Carbs 9g; Fat 5g; Protein 2g**

INGREDIENTS
2 Eggplants, diced
1 cup Water
¼ cup chopped Cilantro
2 Garlic Cloves
1 ½ tbsp Sesame Paste
2 tbsp Olive Oil
½ tsp Pepper
½ tsp Salt

DIRECTIONS
- Add water and eggplants in your cooker. Seal the lid, set on STEAM for 10 minutes at High.
- Release the pressure quickly. Drain and transfer the drained eggplants to a food processor. Add the remaining ingredients, and process until smooth.

## Garlicky Pepper and Tomato Appetizer

Ready in about: **15 minutes | Serves: 4 | Per serving: Calories 123; Carbs 12g; Fat 7g; Protein 3g**

INGREDIENTS
1 pounds Bell Peppers, cut into strips
2 Large Tomatoes, chopped
1 cup Tomato Sauce
½ cup Chicken Broth
1 tbsp Garlic, minced
2 tbsp chopped Parsley
1 tbsp Olive Oil
Salt and Pepper

DIRECTIONS
- Heat oil on SAUTÉ at High, add the peppers and cook for 2-3 minutes. Add garlic and sauté for 1 minute.
- Stir in the remaining ingredients, and seal the lid. Cook on BEANS/CHILI at High pressure for 6 minutes. When ready, do a quick release.

## Turnip and Sultana Dip with Pecans

Ready in about: **10 minutes | Serves: 4 | Per serving: Calories 273; Carbs 45g; Fat 10g; Protein 5g**

INGREDIENTS

1 cup Water
2 pounds Turnips, peeled and chopped
½ cup Sultanas
1 tbsp Vinegar
1 tbsp Olive Oil
¼ tsp Sea Salt
¼ tsp Black Pepper

DIRECTIONS
- Heat oil on SAUTÉ at High, and cook turnips, until softened, for about 3 minutes.
- Stir in sultanas and water. Seal the lid, select the STEAM for 2 minutes at High pressure. Do a quick release.
- Drain turnips and sultanas, and place in a food processor.
- Add some of the cooking water in, to make it creamier. Add vinegar, salt, and pepper, and pulse until smooth. Serve topped with chopped pecans.

## Spicy Homemade Peanuts

Ready in about: **50 minutes** | Serves: **16** | Per serving: **Calories 211; Carbs 15g; Fat 13g; Protein 11g**

INGREDIENTS
2 ¼ cups Peanuts, raw
1 tsp Chili Powder
¼ cup Sea Salt
½ tsp Garlic Powder
4 quarts Water

DIRECTIONS
- Place peanuts in your pressure cooker, and pour in water. Seal the lid and cook on MEAT/STEW for 40 minutes at High.
- Do a quick release. Sprinkle with spices and discard any remaining liquid, to serve.

## Lemony Cippolini Onions

Ready in about: **15 minutes** | Serves: **6** | Per serving: **Calories 130; Carbs 21g; Fat 1g; Protein 3g**

INGREDIENTS
1 ½ pounds Cipppolini Onions, peeled
2 tbsp Lemon Juice
3 tbsp Olive Oil
½ tsp Rosemary, chopped
2 Bay Leaves
1 cup Water
1 tsp Lemon Zest
Salt and Pepper, to taste

DIRECTIONS
- Combine water, onions, and bay leaves in your pressure cooker. Seal the lid, press BEANS/CHILI, and cook for 6 minutes at High. When it goes off, do a quick release. Drain the onions and transfer them a cutting board.
- Cut into quarters. Whisk together the remaining ingredients and pour over the onions.

## Party Duck Bites

Ready in about: **30 minutes** | Serves: **6** | Per serving: **Calories 400; Carbs 5g; Fat 23g; Protein 31g**

INGREDIENTS
1 ½ pounds Duck Legs
½ cup Maple Syrup
½ cup Tomato Puree
1 ½ cups Water
2 tsp Basil
Salt and Pepper, to taste

SAUCE:
½ cup Sour Cream
½ cup chopped Parsley
¼ cup Olive Oil
2 tbsp Lemon Juice
2 Jalapeños, chopped
1 Garlic Clove

DIRECTIONS
- Pour the water in the pressure cooker and place the duck a baking pan. In a bowl combine all of the duck ingredients and pour over the meat.
- Put the baking pan on the inserted rack. Seal the lid. Cook on MEAT/STEW for 20 minutes at High. Release the pressure naturally, for 10 minutes.
- Pulse all sauce ingredients in a food processor and transfer to a serving bowl. Serve duck bites with the sauce.

## Ziti Pork Meatballs

Ready in about: **25 minutes** | Serves: **4** | Per serving: **Calories 421; Carbs 25g; Fat 23g; Protein 28g**

INGREDIENTS
¾ pound Ground Pork
1 box Ziti Pasta
2 Tomatoes, chopped
1 cup Veggie Stock
3 tsp Oil
2 cups Cauliflower Florets
2 Bell Peppers, chopped
½ cup Cider
1 cup Water
1 Red Onion, chopped
½ tbsp Basil

DIRECTIONS
- Combine pork and basil and shape the mixture into 4-5 meatballs. Heat the oil on SAUTÉ at High. Cook meatballs until browned. Set aside. Cook onions, cauliflowers, and peppers for a few minutes, until soft.
- Stir in the remaining ingredients, including the meatballs. Seal the lid and cook for 20 minutes on BEANS/CHILI at High. When done, quick release the pressure.

## Chili Hash Browns

Ready in about: **20 minutes** | Serves: **4** | Per serving: **Calories 161; Carbs 18g; Fat 8g; Protein 2g**

INGREDIENTS
1 pound Potatoes, peeled and grated
1 tsp Chili Powder
¼ tsp Smoked Paprika
¼ tsp Black Pepper
½ tsp Sea Salt

1 ½ tbsp Olive Oil
DIRECTIONS
- Heat oil on SAUTÉ at High, and add the potatoes. Season with spices and stir to combine. Press them with a spatula and cook for about 10 minutes. Flip over once. Divide the hash browns between 4 plates, to serve.

## Cheese and Prosciutto Eggs

Ready in about: **10 minutes** | Serves: **4** | Per serving: Calories 457; Carbs 5g; Fat 34g; Protein 31g

INGREDIENTS
8 Eggs
8 Prosciutto Slices
4 Swiss Cheese Slices
4 tbsp Spring Onions, chopped
2 tbsp Parsley, chopped
2 tbsp Butter
1 ½ cups Water
DIRECTIONS
- Pour 1 ½ cups water in the pressure cooker and lower the trivet. Coat 4 ramekins with butter. Break 2 eggs into each ramekin and top with the spring onions.
- Place 2 prosciutto slices over the onions and top with ½ slice of cheese. Sprinkle with parsley. Cover the ramekins with foil and place them in the cooker.
- Seal the lid and cook for 8 minutes on RICE/RISOTTO at High. Use a natural release, for 10 minutes, and serve.

## Porcini and Sesame Dip

Ready in about: **15 minutes** | Serves: **8** | Per serving: Calories 195; Carbs 19g; Fat 8g; Protein 5g

INGREDIENTS
2 pounds Porcini Mushrooms, sliced
2 tbsp Sesame Paste
3 tbsp Sesame Seeds
1 tbsp Lemon Juice
2 tsp Garlic, minced
2 tbsp Olive Oil
1 cup Water
DIRECTIONS
- Heat the oil on SAUTÉ at High. Add the garlic and mushrooms and cook for a minute. Pour in the water and seal the lid. Set on STEAM mode for 4 minutes at High. Do a quick pressure release.
- Drain the mushrooms and garlic. Transfer to a food processor. Add the lemon juice, olive oil, salt, pepper, and sesame paste. Process until smooth, and stir in the sesame seeds. Serve and enjoy!

## Pico de Gallo with Carrots

Ready in about: **70 minutes** | Serves: **4** | Per serving: Calories 85; Carbs 12g; Fat 4g; Protein 2g

INGREDIENTS
1 cup Onions, chopped
1 cup Carrots, chopped
2 cups Tomatoes, chopped
½ cup Bell Peppers, chopped
2 tbsp Cilantro, chopped
1 tsp Garlic, minced
¼ cup Lime Juice
½ cup Water
1 Jalapeño, deseed and minced
1 tbsp Olive Oil
½ tsp Sea Salt
¼ tsp Black Pepper
DIRECTIONS
- Heat oil on SAUTÉ at High, add onions, peppers, and carrots, and cook for 4 minutes. Add the tomatoes and cook for 3 minutes. Stir in the garlic and sauté for another minute.
- Transfer to a bowl and let cool for about 15 minutes. Stir in the remaining ingredients. Cover the bowl with a plastic wrap and refrigerate for about 45 minutes before serving.

## Buttery Beets

Ready in about: **30 minutes** | Serves: **4** | Per serving: Calories 185; Carbs 19g; Fat 11g; Protein 3g

INGREDIENTS
1 tbsp Olive Oil
1 pound Beets, peeled and sliced
½ tsp Garlic Salt
4 tbsp Butter, melted
1 tsp dried Basil
1 cup Chicken Broth
DIRECTIONS
- Add the beets and pour broth in your pressure cooker. Seal the lid and cook on BEANS/CHILI mode for 25 minutes at High. When ready, do a quick pressure release.
- Drain the liquid and drizzle the beets with olive oil. Cook for 5 minutes, on SAUTÉ, lid off. Stir in garlic salt and basil, and cook for 2 more minutes. Serve drizzled with the melted butter.

## Ricotta and Cheddar Veggie Appetizer

Ready in about: **30 minutes** | Serves: **6** | Per serving: Calories 259; Carbs 22g; Fat 15g; Protein 10g

INGREDIENTS
1 cup Cheddar Cheese, grated
½ cup Ricotta Cheese
1 ½ pounds Potatoes, diced
1 cup Broccoli Florets
½ cup Carrots, chopped
¾ tsp Paprika
½ tsp Cumin Powder
2 cups Water
2 tbsp Oil
1 tsp Salt
DIRECTIONS
- Combine the water, potatoes, carrots, and broccoli, in your pressure cooker. Seal the lid and cook on BEANS/CHILI for 20 minutes at High. Release the pressure quickly. Drain the veggies and place in a food processor.
- Add the remaining ingredients and process until smooth. Chill until ready to serve.

## Southern Chicken Dip

**Ready in about: 30 minutes | Serves: 12 | Per serving: Calories 188; Carbs 5g; Fat 13g; Protein 12g**

INGREDIENTS

1 pound Chicken Breasts, cut into cubes
3 Bacon Slices, chopped
1 cup Cheddar Cheese, shredded
½ cup Sour Cream
½ cup Salsa
1 Onion, diced
¼ cup Ketchup
½ cup Cilantro, minced
2 tbsp Olive Oil
½ cup Chicken Broth
3 Garlic Cloves
½ tsp Onion Powder
1 tbsp Flour
½ tsp Cumin
½ tsp Cayenne Pepper
1 tsp Chili Powder

DIRECTIONS

- Heat oil and brown the bacon in your cooker on SAUTÉ at High. Add onions, cilantro, and garlic. Cook for 3 minutes, until translucent and fragrant. Stir in the chicken, salsa, broth, and spices.
- Seal the lid and cook for 20 minutes on BEANS/CHILI at High. When ready, quick release the pressure. Whisk in flour and cook for a few more minutes, until thickened, lid off, on SAUTÉ. Transfer to a food processor, and add cheddar and sour cream. Pulse until smooth. Serve with crackers.

## Appetizer Meatballs

**Ready in about: 25 minutes | Serves: 8 | Per serving: Calories 202; Carbs 10g; Fat 15g; Protein 11g**

INGREDIENTS

½ pound Ground Pork
½ pound Ground Beef
½ cup Grape Jelly
1 tbsp Mustard
1 cup diced Onions
2/3 cup Breadcrumbs
1 ½ tbsp Cornstarch
¼ cup Sugar
¼ cup Chili Sauce
Salt and Pepper, to taste
1 ½ cups Water

DIRECTIONS

- Mix in meat, breadcrumbs, and onion in a large bowl. Season with salt and pepper. Form small meatballs out of the mixture. Coat the cooker with cooking spray and cook the meatballs on SAUTÉ at High, until lightly browned.
- Transfer to a plate. Whisk together the remaining ingredients in the pressure cooker. Seal the lid and cook on BEANS/CHILI, at High, for 17 minutes. Release the pressure naturally, for 10 minutes.

## Potato and Bacon Snack

**Ready in about: 25 minutes | Serves: 4 | Per serving: Calories 214; Carbs 21g; Fat 12g; Protein 7g**

INGREDIENTS

1 pound Potatoes
4 Bacon Slices, chopped
1 tsp Garlic Salt
¼ tsp Pepper
4 tbsp Sour Cream
¼ cup Chicken Broth
1 ½ cups Water

DIRECTIONS

- Combine the water and potatoes in the pressure cooker. Seal the lid and cook on MEAT/STEW mode for 15 minutes at High. When ready, do a quick pressure release and drain the potatoes.
- Dice the potatoes and transfer them to a bowl. In the pressure cooker, add the bacon slices and cook until crisp on SAUTÉ, lid off. Remove bacon to the potatoes bowl and stir to combine.
- In a separate bowl, whisk together cream, broth, and spices. Drizzle the potatoes to serve.

## Chili Sriracha Eggs

**Ready in about: 20 minutes | Serves: 6 | Per serving: Calories 156; Carbs 3g; Fat 11g; Protein 10g**

INGREDIENTS

6 Eggs
½ tsp Chili Powder
1 ½ tbsp Sour Cream
1 tbsp Mayonnaise
A pinch of Black Pepper
1 tsp Sriracha
1 tbsp grated Parmesan Cheese
2 cups Water, enough to cover the Eggs

DIRECTIONS

- Combine the eggs and water in the pressure cooker. Seal the lid and cook on BEANS/CHILI for 8 minutes at High. Do a quick pressure release, and remove eggs to cold water, let cool for a few minutes, and peel.
- Meanwhile, in a bowl, whisk together the sour cream, mayonnaise, black pepper, chili powder, and sriracha. Cut the eggs in half and top with the mixture. To serve, sprinkle with Parmesan cheese.

## Bacon and Cheese Pasta

**Ready in about: 10 minutes | Serves: 6 | Per serving: Calories 437; Carbs 72g; Fat 12g; Protein 13g**

INGREDIENTS

16 ounces Dry Rigatoni Pasta
1 cup chopped Onions
1 cup diced Bacon
2 ½ cups Tomato Puree
1 tsp Sage
1 tsp Thyme
½ cup Cheddar Cheese, grated
Water, as needed

Salt to taste
Freshly chopped basil, to garnish
DIRECTIONS
- Fry the bacon on SAUTÉ at High, until brown and crispy, for about 3 minutes. Add the onions and cook for a few minutes, until soft. Stir in rigatoni pasta, tomato puree, sage, thyme, and salt. Add enough water to cover them.
- Seal the lid and cook for 6 minutes BEANS/CHILI at High pressure. When ready, release the pressure quickly. Stir in the freshly grated Cheddar cheese and serve topped with fresh basil.

## Mini Beefy Cabbage Rolls

Ready in about: **35 minutes | Serves: 15 | Per serving: Calories 185; Carbs 17g; Fat 8g; Protein 11g**

INGREDIENTS
1 Cabbage, leaves separated
1 pound Ground Beef
1 Red Bell Pepper, chopped
1 cup Rice
1 cup Beef Broth
3 cups Water
2 tbsp Lemon Juice
1 Onion, diced
½ cup Olive Oil
1 tsp Fennel Seeds
Salt and Pepper, to taste
DIRECTIONS
- Pour 1 cup of water and place the cabbage leaves in the pressure cooker. Seal the lid and cook on STEAM mode for 3 minutes, at High. When ready, release the pressure quickly. Remove the leaves to an ice bath, to cool.
- In a bowl, combine the remaining ingredients, except water and broth. Divide this mixture between the cabbage leaves. Roll them up and return them to the pressure cooker. Pour in water and broth.
- Seal the lid and cook for 15 minutes on BEANS/CHILI at High. Do a quick release. Serve with yogurt if desired.

## Salmon Bites

Ready in about: **15 minutes | Serves: 4 | Per serving: Calories 327; Carbs 12g; Fat 18g; Protein 25g**

INGREDIENTS
1 can Salmon, flaked
1 Spring Onion, minced
1 cup Breadcrumbs
½ cup Cream Cheese
1 tbsp Parsley, chopped
¼ tsp Salt
¼ tsp Black Pepper
1 tbsp Butter
½ cup Tomato Sauce
1 cup Water
DIRECTIONS
- Combine the first 7 ingredients in a bowl. Mix well with hands and make 4 balls out of the mixture. Melt butter in the cooker on SAUTÉ at High. Add the balls and cook until golden on all sides, for about 5 minutes, lid off.
- Remove to a baking dish, that fits in your pressure cooker, and pour the tomato sauce over. Pour the water in and lower the trivet. Place baking dish on top of the trivet, inside the cooker.
- Seal the lid, and cook for 5 minutes on BEANS/CHILI at High. Use a naturally pressure release, for 10 minutes.

## Salty and Peppery Potato Snack

Ready in about: **20 minutes | Serves: 6 | Per serving: Calories 213; Carbs 43g; Fat 5g; Protein 3g**

INGREDIENTS
2 pounds Potatoes
1 tsp Sea Salt
1 tsp Pepper
2 tbsp Olive Oil
1 ½ cups Water
DIRECTIONS
- Pour water in the cooker and lower the trivet. Wash and peel the potatoes, and place each of them on a piece of aluminum foil. Season with salt and pepper, and drizzle with olive oil.
- Wrap them in foil and place the wraps on top of the trivet. Seal the lid, select BEANS/CHILI mode and set the timer to 11 minutes at High pressure. After the beep, do a quick pressure release.
- Place the potatoes on your kitchen counter. Unwrap gently, chop or slice them to your liking, and enjoy.

## Blue Cheese and Bacon Polenta Squares

Ready in about: **80 minutes | Serves: 6 | Per serving: Calories 271; Carbs 19g; Fat 17g; Protein 11g**

INGREDIENTS
2 cups Polenta
6 Bacon Slices, cooked and crumbles
1 Onion, chopped
2 ounces Blue Cheese, crumbled
2 tsp Rosemary
1 tsp Thyme
4 cups Beef Stock
1 tbsp Oil
½ tsp Garlic, minced
Salt and Black Pepper, to taste
DIRECTIONS
- Heat oil and cook the onions until soft, on SAUTÉ mode at High. Add garlic and cook for another minute, until fragrant. Stir in thyme, rosemary, stock, polenta. Season with salt and pepper.
- Seal the lid and cook for 10 minutes on BEANS/CHILI at High pressure. Release the pressure quickly. Stir in the cheese and bacon. Place in a lined baking pan and refrigerate for 1 hour. Cut into squares to serve.

## Turmeric Potato Sticks

Ready in about: **15 minutes | Serve: 1 | Per serving: Calories 140; Carbs 16g; Fat 4g; Protein 1g**

INGREDIENTS
1 Potato, peeled and cut into sticks
1 tbsp Olive Oil

¼ tsp Pepper
¼ tsp Sea Salt
1 tsp Turmeric
1 ½ cups Water

DIRECTIONS
- Combine water and potato sticks in the pressure cooker. Seal the lid, press BEANS/CHILI and set the timer to 5 minutes at High pressure. When ready, do a quick pressure release. Drain the potatoes.
- Discard the water, and wipe the cooker clean. Set to SAUTÉ at High and heat the oil. When hot, add potato sticks and sprinkle with turmeric, salt, and pepper. Sauté for 5 minutes, flipping once. Serve and enjoy!

## Jalapeno and Pineapple Salsa

Ready in about: **65 minutes** | Serves: **6** | Per serving: Calories 41; Carbs 8g; Fat 1g; Protein 0

INGREDIENTS
1 cup Red Onions, diced
2 cups Pineapple, diced
¼ cup Cilantro, chopped
3 Jalapenos, minced
¼ tsp Garlic Powder
2 tbsp Lime Juice
¼ tsp Sea Salt
1 tbsp Olive Oil

DIRECTIONS
- Heat oil on SAUTÉ at High, add the onions and cook until softened, for about 3 minutes. Then, stir in jalapenos, pineapple, and garlic powder, and cook just for 1-2 minutes. Transfer to a bowl.
- In a small bowl, whisk together lime juice, pepper, and salt. Pour over the pineapples and coat to combine. Stir in the cilantro. Let sit at room temperature for about 15 minutes.
- Cover the bowl with a plastic wrap. Refrigerate for 45 minutes before serving.

## Three-Cheese Small Macaroni Cups

Ready in about: **15 minutes** | Serves: **8** | Per serving: Calories 224; Carbs 25g; Fat 9g; Protein 11g

INGREDIENTS
½ pound Elbow Macaroni
2 cups Water
4 ounces Cheddar Cheese, shredded
4 ounces Monterey Jack Cheese, shredded
¼ cup Parmesan Cheese, shredded
2 tbsp Butter
½ can Evaporated Milk
Salt and Black Pepper, to taste

DIRECTIONS
- Add the water, butter, macaroni, salt, and pepper, in the cooker. Seal the lid and cook for 8 minutes on BEANS/CHILI mode at High. When ready, do a quick pressure release and stir in milk and cheeses.
- Seal the lid again, and cook for a minute at High. When done, do a quick pressure release. Divide between 8 cups.

## Agave Carrot Sticks

Ready in about: **10 minutes** | Serves: **4** | Per serving: Calories 145; Carbs 16g; Fat 8g; Protein 2g

INGREDIENTS
1 pound Carrots, sliced into sticks
½ Stick Butter, melted
2 tbsp Agave Nectar
2 cups Water
½ tsp Cinnamon
A pinch of Salt

DIRECTIONS
- Place the carrot sticks in your cooker. Pour in the water. Seal the lid and cook on STEAM for 5 minutes at High. Release the pressure quickly. Whisk together the remaining ingredients and coat the carrots with this mixture.

## Nutty Carrot Sticks

Ready in about: **15 minutes** | Serves: **8** | Per serving: Calories 163; Carbs 17g; Fat 10g; Protein 2g

INGREDIENTS
¼ cup Olive Oil
3 ½ cups Water
3 pounds Carrots, peeled and cut into matchsticks
¼ cup chopped Nuts by choice
2 tbsp Balsamic Vinegar
1 tbsp Orange Juice
2 tsp Lemon Juice
½ tsp Onion Powder

DIRECTIONS
- Combine the water and carrots in your pressure cooker. Seal the lid, select BEANS/CHILI, and set the timer to 5 minutes at High. When it goes off, do a quick pressure release. Drain the carrots and place in a bowl.
- Whisk together vinegar, orange juice, lemon juice, onion powder, and olive oil. Pour mixture over the carrots and toss to coat well. Sprinkle over the nuts, to serve.

## Buttery Potato Sticks

Ready in about: **20 minutes** | Serves: **6** | Per serving: Calories 130; Carbs 27g; Fat 1g; Protein 3g

INGREDIENTS
2 pounds Potatoes, cut into sticks
1 tsp Salt
½ tsp Paprika
¼ tsp Pepper
1 ½ cups Water
1 tbsp Butter, melted

DIRECTIONS
- Place all ingredients, except butter, in your ´pressure cooker. Seal the lid and cook for 10 minutes on BEANS/CHILI at High.
- Release the pressure quickly. Drain the liquid and drizzle with butter.

## Chicken Dip with Black Beans

Another simple dip!

⏱ **Prep time: 7 minutes Cooking time: 1-2 hours**
**Servings: 12**

INGREDIENTS:
2 medium onions
1 can diced tomatoes with green chili peppers
3 tbsp. sour cream
3 jalapeno peppers
1 cup black beans
1-2 tbsp. taco seasoning mix
1 loaf processed cheese
2 chicken breast halves

DIRECTIONS:
- Mince the onions and jalapeno peppers. Rinse and drain black beans.
- Grease the Slow Cooker dish and fill it with sour cream, processed cheese, diced tomatoes and chicken meat.
- Add jalapeno peppers and taco seasoning.
- Turn on Slow Cooker and set on HIGH. Cook until hot melted cheese (for around 1-2 hours). In the end, stir in black beans and continue cooking for 17 minutes.

**Nutrition: Calories: 232 Fat: 13g Carbohydrates: 8g Protein: 19g**

## Taco Bean for Tortilla or Chips

Tacos with bacon and beans!

⏱ **Prep time: 5 minutes Cooking time: 1 hour Servings: 12**

INGREDIENTS:
Sour cream
Cheddar cheese
3 tbsp. salsa
1 pack taco seasoning mix
2 cans condensed beans with bacon soup

DIRECTIONS:
- Shred Cheddar cheese to get half cup or one cup of it.
- Take a medium bowl and combine the seasoning mix, condensed soup and salsa. Mix well. Transfer the salsa mixture into the greased Slow Cooker.
- Top with shredded Cheddar cheese and cook on LOW for about 1 hour (or just until the cheese melts).
- Serve with tacos or any king of cheese.

**Nutrition: Calories: 132 Fat: 6g Carbohydrates: 12g Protein: 5g**

## Little Smokie Sausages

Glazed sausages are small and easy to make!

⏱ **Prep time: 11 minutes Cooking time: 2 hours**
**Servings: 16**

INGREDIENTS:
1 cup brown sugar
1 tbsp. Worcestershire sauce
2 packs little wieners
Half cup ketchup
1 bottle barbeque sauce
1 medium onion

DIRECTIONS:
- Cover the bottom of your Slow Cooker with olive oil or plain unsalted butter.
- In separate bowl, mix together brown sugar, Worcestershire sauce, barbeque sauce and ketchup. Finely mince the onion and add it to the ketchup mixture.
- Place little wieners into Slow Cooker dish and pour in over with the ketchup mixture. Turn on Slow Cooker and set on LOW temperature mode. Cook for 1-2 hours.

**Nutrition: Calories: 285 Fat: 16g Carbohydrates: 28g Protein: 6g**

## Mushrooms in Marinade

Love mushrooms? Here is another way to make them delicious!

⏱ **Prep time: 9 minutes Cooking time: 8 hours**
**Servings: 16**

INGREDIENTS:
2 cups white sugar
2 cups soy sauce
1 cup butter
2 cups water
4 packs fresh mushrooms

DIRECTIONS:
- Take a medium saucepan and combine water, butter and soy sauce. Mix until the butter has melted.
- Add the sugar and continue to stir, until it is dissolved.
- Grease your Slow Cooker with butter or oil, or spay with a cooking spray.
- Remove stems and place mushrooms into Slow Cooker dish. Cover with soy sauce mixture. Set up to LOW temperature setting for around 8-10 hours.

**Nutrition: Calories: 228 Fat: 11g Carbohydrates: 29g Protein: 3g**

## Seafood Dip with Cheese

An amazing dish for any case!

⏱ **Prep time: 5 minutes Cooking time: 1 hour Servings: 10**

INGREDIENTS:
1-2 cups sour cream
Half cup cooked lobster
Half cup small shrimp
2 tbsp. cream cheese (reduced fat)
1 tsp Worcestershire sauce
2 tsp seafood seasoning
Half cup crab meat
1 loaf bread
1 pack processed cheese food

DIRECTIONS:
- Flake crabmeat and lobster, cook half-cup small shrimp.
- In a medium bowl, combine cream cheese, sour cream, processed cheese food, crabmeat, shrimp and lobster.
- Grease your Slow Cooker with some melted and unsalted butter.
- Place the cream and lobster mixture into your Slow Cooker and set the LOW cooking mode. Wait for around 1 hour to get cheese melted.

- Add Worcestershire sauce and seafood seasoning. To serve, cut French white bread.

**Nutrition: Calories: 308 Fat: 14g Carbohydrates: 29g Protein: 15g**

## Jalapeno Peppers with Chicken

Hot peppers for hot snack!

Prep time: 22 minutes Cooking time: 4 hours
Servings: 4

INGREDIENTS:
Cream cheese
1 tsp cumin
4 chicken breasts
1-2 cups shredded cheese
1 tsp salt
Half cup jalapenos
1 tsp garlic powder
16 taco tortillas
DIRECTIONS:
- Place chicken, jalapenos, cream cheese, salt, garlic powder, cumin and salt into Slow Cooker. Cover the lid and leave to cook for 6-8 hours on LOW mode.
- Heat the tortillas in microwave and shred chicken meat with forks. Place the chicken onto tortillas and top with cheese.
- Transfer the tortillas to large baking sheet and cook for 10-13 minutes.

**Nutrition: Calories: 321 Fat: 18g Carbohydrates: 61g Protein: 23g**

## Pumpkin Granola with Nutella

Perfectly fits for autumn!

Prep time: 11 minutes Cooking time: 2-3 hours
Servings: 10

INGREDIENTS:
Pumpkin puree
Nutella
Half cup raisins
Honey or maple syrup
Old-fashioned oats
Vegetable oil
Pure vanilla extract
Sunflower or pumpkin seeds
Ground cloves
1 cup cereal
Ground ginger and cinnamon
Salt to taste
DIRECTIONS:
- Grease Slow Cooker to avoid sticking.
- In a mixing bowl, combine pumpkin puree, maple syrup, Nutella, oil and vanilla. In another bowl, mix rice cereal, oats, cinnamon, seeds, cloves and ginger.
- Add the wet ingredients into cereal and combine well to coat.
- Place the mixture into your Slow Cooker and set to HIGH temperature. Cook for 2 hours, stirring every 30 minutes.

**Nutrition: Calories: 344 Fat: 17g Carbohydrates: 35g Protein: 2g**

## Slow Cooker Sauerkraut Dip

Unusual ingredients for tasty dip!

Prep time: 5 minutes Cooking time: 1-2 hours
Servings: 12

INGREDIENTS:
Thousand island dressing
1 jar sauerkraut
2 cups shredded Swiss cheese
1 pack cream cheese
2 cups corned beef (cooked and shredded)
DIRECTIONS:
- Slightly cover your Slow Cooker with unsalted butter.
- Right in a cooking dish, mix cream cheese, sauerkraut, Swiss cheese, Thousand Island dressing and corned beef.
- Cover the lid and cook for 1-2 hours on HIGH temperature mode. Stir occasionally during the cooking process.
- Serve with crackers or cocktail rye.

**Nutrition: Calories: 298 Fat: 22g Carbohydrates: 5g Protein: 17g**

## Meatballs Appetizer

Funny meatballs are easy and fast to make!

Prep time: 17 minutes Cooking time: 2 hours
Servings: 6

INGREDIENTS:
2 tbsp. lemon juice
1 can pineapple chunks in juice
2 tbsp. cornstarch
1 green bell pepper
1 bag frozen meatballs
Half cup brown sugar
2 tbsp. soy sauce
DIRECTIONS:
- Place pineapple chunks (along with the juice) into large saucepan.
- Add brown sugar, green bell pepper, soy sauce, and cornstarch and lemon juice. Stir to dissolve cornstarch.
- Bring the cornstarch mixture to boil and wait, stirring, until thick (about 10 minutes). Put the meatball into Slow Cooker and pour in (to cover) the pineapple juice.
- Cook on MEDIUM temperature regime for 2 hours, stir each 30 minutes.

**Nutrition: Calories: 611 Fat: 29g Carbohydrates: 46g Protein: 38g**

## Barbeque Kielbasa in Slow Cooker

Love barbeque! Try to cook this one!

Prep time: 11 minutes Cooking time: 2 hours
Servings: 20

INGREDIENTS:
2 bottles barbeque sauce
Polish kielbasa sausage
Butter to grease
1 jar grape jelly
DIRECTIONS:

- Cover the bottom of your Slow Cooker with a thin layer of butter. Cut the sausage inti small (1-2 inch size) pieces.
- Place kielbasa slices into Slow Cooker.
- In separate bowl, whisk together jelly and barbeque sauce. Pour the mixture over the sausage pieces.
- Turn on Slow Cooker and set on MEDIUM or HIGH temperature mode for 2 hours.

**Nutrition: Calories: 262 Fat: 15g Carbohydrates: 23g Protein: 6g**

# Cheese and Beef Carne

Tasty meat snack for any company!

Prep time: 27 minutes Cooking time: 1 hour Servings: 16

INGREDIENTS:
1 pack taco seasoning
Ground beef
1 loaf processed cheese
4 cans diced tomatoes (with green chili peppers)
Half cup milk
DIRECTIONS:
- Place the cheese into greased Slow Cooker, sprinkle with milk.
- Take a large skillet and it over the medium heat. Prepare beef until it is well crumbled and evenly browned.
- Add taco seasoning and diced tomatoes. Stir everything well and bring to simmer.
- Transfer the beef and tomato mixture into Slow Cooker and mix in processed cheese with milk. Set Slow Cooker on HIGH mode and cook about 1 hour, or until the cheese is melted.

**Nutrition: Calories: 227 Fat: 15g Carbohydrates: 6g Protein: 14g**

# Superheated Peanuts in Syrup

Simple and fast sweet appetizer!

Prep time: 23 minutes Cooking time: 1 hour Servings: 8

INGREDIENTS:
Half cup salt
1 tbsp. garlic powder
Raw peanuts in shells
Half cup jalapeno peppers
Half cup red pepper flakes
1 pack dry crab boil
Half cup salt
DIRECTIONS:
- Place crab boil, peanuts, and jalapeno peppers (minced) into your Slow Cooker dish. Season with garlic powder, Cajun seasoning, salt and red pepper flakes.
- Pour in enough water to cover peanuts and stir well to combine everything.
- Cover the lid of Slow Cooker and prepare at least for 24 hours om LOW mode, until the peanuts are soft.
- Stir time after time and add additional water, if needed. Drain to serve.

**Nutrition: Calories: 360 Fat: 29g Carbohydrates: 16g Protein: 16g**

# Spicy Beef Balls

Spicy meatballs for those, who loves hot!

Prep time: 5 minutes Cooking time: 1 hour Servings: 10

INGREDIENTS:
1 small onion
Half cup water
2 cloves garlic
Ground beef
1 jigger whiskey
Half cup soy sauce
Half cup seasoned bread crumbs
DIRECTIONS:
- Into wide bowl, mix ground beef, minced onion and bread crumbs with seasoning. Make small bite-sized balls out of bread and beef mixture.
- In a large frying pan with oil slightly brown meatballs from every side.
- In separate bowl, mix soy sauce, whiskey, minced garlic and water. Put the balls into this mixture and place into refrigerator for 1-2 hours.
- Place the balls into buttered Slow Cooker and sat it on LOW mode. Cook for 30 minutes or, if needed, for 1 hour.

**Nutrition: Calories: 185 Fat: 12g Carbohydrates: 5g Protein: 9g**

# Buffalo Chicken Dip

Perfect and fast chicken dip!

Prep time: 5 minutes Cooking time: 3 hours Servings: 30

INGREDIENTS:
Cream cheese
Chicken meat
Half cup ranch dressing
Shredded Mozzarella cheese
Half cup hot wing sauce
Half cup crumbled blue cheese
2 tbsp unsalted butter
Half cup ranch dressing
DIRECTIONS:
- Spray the cooking dish with non-stick spray or grease with melted butter.
- In a bowl, combine chopped chicken, Mozzarella, cream cheese blue cheese, wing sauce, ranch dressing, butter, Stir well to combine.
- Transfer the chicken mixture to Slow Cooker.
- Cook under the lid on HIGH temperature mode for around 2-3 hours. Do not forget to stir every 40 minutes.
- To serve, turn on LOW mode.

**Nutrition: Calories: 158 Fat: 8g Carbohydrates: 31g Protein: 23g**

# Meatballs with Bacon in Slow Cooker

Tasty meatballs, upgraded with bacon strips!

Prep time: 5 minutes Cooking time: 2 hours Servings: 22

INGREDIENTS:
3 tbsp maple syrup
1 pack frozen meatballs
Cooked bacon
Pinch dried chili peppers
2 tbsp bourbon
1 cup barbeque sauce
DIRECTIONS:
- In a separate bowl, mix maple syrup, barbeque sauce, chili peppers and bourbon. Line your Slow Cooker with parchment and place frozen meatball over it.
- Pour the bourbon sauce over it and set Slow Cooker on HIGH. Cook for 2 hours and stir time after time.
- To serve, place the meatballs on long toothpick along with bacon strips.

**Nutrition: Calories: 237 Fat: 16g Carbohydrates: 36g Protein: 28g**

## Chutney and Spiced Chips

Another delicious chutney for your evening!

⌛ Prep time: 5 minutes Cooking time: 2 hours
Servings: 20

INGREDIENTS:
2 large apples
1 sweet onion
4 tbsp balsamic vinegar
2 large pears
Ground cinnamon
1 cup cranberries
3 tbsp brown sugar
1 tsp fround ginger
Salt
Spiced chips
1 tbsp cornstarch
Goat cheese
2 tbsp cold water
DIRECTIONS:
- Grease your Slow Cooker with plain butter or olive oil.
- In the cooking dish, combine pears, onion, apples, brown sugar, cranberries, cinnamon, vinegar, salt and ginger.
- Cover Slow Cooker with lid and cook for 1 hour on HIGH mode.
- In a small plate combine water and cornstarch and pour into Slow Cooker. Cook for another hour. Serve warm with spicy chips.

**Nutrition: Calories: 102 Fat: 2g Carbohydrates: 18g Protein: 11g**

## Broccoli Dip with Cheese

Just amazing for kids and grown-ups!

⌛ Prep time: 5 minutes Cooking time: 4 hours
Servings: 22

INGREDIENTS:
Reduced-fat cream cheese
1 cup broccoli
Reduced-fat cheese product
Fat-free milk
3 tbsp salsa
Potato dippers (to serve)
4 tsp vegetable protein bits
DIRECTIONS:
- Grease your Slow Cooker with anti-stick spray.
- Right in a cooking dish, combine cheese product, cream cheese, salsa, broccoli and bacon-flavor bits.
- Cover the Slow Cooker lid and set to LOW. Cook for 4 hours. Stir in the end, just before serving.
- Serve along with Potato Dippers.

**Nutrition: Calories: 147 Fat: 12g Carbohydrates: 22g Protein: 9g**

## Cocktail Sausages in Glaze

Just try this amazing glaze!

⌛ Prep time: 5 minutes Cooking time: 4 hours
Servings: 34

INGREDIENTS:
3 tbsp maple syrup
Cocked and smoked Polish sausage
1 tbsp bourbon
Apricot preserves (low-sugar)
1 tsp quick-cooking tapioca
DIRECTIONS:
- Cover the bottom and sides of your Slow Cooker with melted butter.
- In a cooking dish, combine the sausage slices, maple syrup, apricot preserves. Sprinkle with bourbon and tapioca.
- Cover the lid and leave for 4 hours on LOW-heat mode. Serve while hot with wooden toothpicks.

**Nutrition: Calories: 211 Fat: 13g Carbohydrates: 31g Protein: 6g**

## Slow Cooker Snacks with Lemon Zest

The taste of lemon zest in it is everything!

⌛ Prep time: 5 minutes Cooking time: 2 hours
Servings: 35

INGREDIENTS:
Half cup chopped walnuts
Multigrain cereal
3 tbsp pumpkin seeds
2 cups pita chips
1 tsp dried rosemary
Ranch salad dressing mix (dry)
2 tbsp olive oil
2 tbsp dried dill mix
1 tbsp lemon zest (finely shredded)
DIRECTIONS:
- Grease Slow Cooker with cooking spray or line with the foil.
- Right in Slow Cooker dish, mix pita chips, cereal, pumpkin seeds, walnuts. Add dill weed, salad dressing mix and dried rosemary.
- Cook, covered, for 2 hours, using LOW temperature settings. Stir every 20 minutes. Sprinkle with lemon zest and slightly toss to combine.
- Cool to serve.

**Nutrition: Calories: 186 Fat: 22g Carbohydrates: 32g Protein: 7g**

## Pork Wraps in Slow Cooker

Amazing wraps for your dinner!

Prep time: 5 minutes Cooking time: 8-24 hours
Servings: 10-20

INGREDIENTS:
5 tbsp water
Half cup lemon juice
1 cup sliced onion
1 tsp dried oregano
Half tsp ground cumin
3 cloves garlic
6 tbsp grapefruit juice
Ground black pepper
Boneless pork roast
Bottled salsa
Flour tortillas

DIRECTIONS:
- To make marinade, mix lime juice, garlic, water, oregano, salt, grapefruit juice, cumin and pepper. Place the meat into marinade and leave in refrigerator for 8-24 hours.
- Grease your Slow Cooker and arrange the minced onion over its bottom. Top with meat and marinade.
- Cover and cook for 10-12 hours on LOW temperature mode. Shred meat and serve in tortillas with green onions.

Nutrition: Calories: 301 Fat: 23g Carbohydrates: 30g Protein: 9g

## Italian Mix in Slow Cooker

Try this one for your family dinner!

Prep time: 5 minutes Cooking time: 6 hours
Servings: 30

INGREDIENTS:
2 medium onions
2 tbsp red wine vinegar
1 cup sliced celery
Zucchini
Roma tomatoes
Eggplant
Half cup Italian parsley
3 tbsp tomato paste
Raisins
Salt to taste
1 tbsp sugar

DIRECTIONS:
- Cut tomatoes, eggplant and zucchini into 2 inch-size slices. Chop onion and celery.
- Grease your Slow Cooker with some melted butter or just with olive oil.
- In Slow Cooker dish, mix tomatoes, celery, eggplant, zucchini, raisins, parsley, onion, vinegar, tomato paste pepper, sugar and salt.
- Cover the lid and cook for 5-6 hours on LOW settings.

Nutrition: Calories: 224 Fat: 5g Carbohydrates: 14g Protein: 7g

## Hoisin mushrooms with garlic

Another mushroom receipt for your kitchen!

Prep time: 5 minutes Cooking time: 6 hours
Servings: 20

INGREDIENTS:
4 tbsp water
Half cup hoisin sauce (bottled)
1 tsp crushed red pepper
2tbsp minced garlic
Fresh button mushrooms

DIRECTIONS:
- Wash and trim the mushrooms.
- In a large bowl, combine water, hoisin sauce, red pepper and garlic.
- Add trimmed mushrooms and stir well to coat them evenly with sauce mixture. Cover the lid of your Slow Cooker and set LOW temperature mode.
- Cook for 5-6 hours.
- To serve, discard the liquid and place the decorative toothpicks.

Nutrition: Calories: 228 Fat: 21g Carbohydrates: 34g Protein: 22g

## Chicken with Peanut Sauce

Try this chicken in amazing sauce!

Prep time: 5 minutes Cooking time: 6 hours
Servings: 20

INGREDIENTS:
3tbsp water
24 chicken wing drummettes
1 tbsp lime juice
Peanut sauce
Half tsp ground ginger

DIRECTIONS:
- Place chicken wings into your Slow Cooker. Add lime juice and ginger, pour in a little water.
- Cover your Slow Cooker with a lid and set LOW heat regime. Cook for 5-6 hours. Remove the liquid from chicken and toss the meat with ½ peanut sauce.
- Serve warm with peanut sauce.

Nutrition: Calories: 312 Fat: 17g Carbohydrates: 15g Protein: 7g

## Asian Tacos with Cabbage

Everything Asian is definitely tasty!

Prep time: 5 minutes Cooking time: 8 hours
Servings: 25

INGREDIENTS:
2 cloves garlic
1 large orange
1 pork shoulder
1 pork shoulder
2 tbsp soy sauce
Balsamic vinegar
Dark sugar
Salt\pepper to taste

Red pepper flakes
1 medium carrot
1 small onion
8 small tortillas
Fresh ginger
Olive oil

DIRECTIONS:
- Right in the Slow Cooker, mix vinegar, soy sauce, sugar, ginger, red pepper, garlic and orange zest.
- Place the pork into Slow Cooker and toss to cover evenly. Cover the lid and cook on LOW for 7-8 hours.
- In 30 minutes before serving, make the slaw and sprinkle it with orange juice, oil, pepper and salt. Warm tortillas in oven or microwave.
- To serve, shred the meat and place it over tortillas, along with cabbage mix.

**Nutrition: Calories: 198 Fat: 17g Carbohydrates: 33g Protein: 6g**

## Crab Dip in Slow Cooker

Seafood dip for crabmeat lovers!

Prep time: 5 minutes Cooking time: 2 hours
Servings: 20

INGREDIENTS:
Cream cheese
Juice of 1 lemon
Half cup parmesan
2 cloves garlic
1 tbsp Worcestershire sauce
1 tsp Old Bay seasoning
Half cup mayonnaise
Green onions
Canned crab meat
Cracker for serving

DIRECTIONS:
- In a wide dish, mix cream cheese, mayonnaise, garlic, minced green onions. Season with old Bay and Worcestershire sauce. Sprinkle with lemon juice.
- Finely grate the Parmesan cheese and carefully stir in to other ingredients. Add canned crabmeat and stir it well to combine.
- Cook on LOW temperature mode for 2 hours.
- Serve with crackers and green onions and Parmesan garnish.

**Nutrition: Calories: 177 Fat: 8g Carbohydrates: 25g Protein: 15g**

## Greek Meatballs with Cheese Stuffing

Amazing cheese stuffing makes this dish creamy!

Prep time: 5 minutes Cooking time: 3 hours
Servings: 20

INGREDIENTS:
4 cloves garlic
2 chicken eggs
Ground lamb
Chopped green olives
1 cup bread crumbs (seasoned)
1 tsp salt
Chopped black olives
Lean ground beef

Greek Tomato Sauce
3 tbsp chopped parsley
Cubed feta cheese

DIRECTIONS:
- In separate bowl, beat chicken eggs with fork and mix in green olives, breadcrumbs, garlic, parsley, black olives. Add salt/pepper.
- Chop the cheese into small cubes and, using a meat mixture, form a ball around each one. Place the meatball into wide saucepan and bake in preheated oven for 35 minutes.
- Transfer ball into Slow Cooker and pour over with Greek Tomato sauce, Toss. Cook, covered, for 3-4 hours on HIGH mode.

**Nutrition: Calories: 341 Fat: 12g Carbohydrates: 41g Protein: 22g**

## Crabmeat Dip Recipe

You can cook this for white wine serving!

Prep time: 5 minutes Cooking time: 2 hours
Servings: 15

INGREDIENTS:
Juice 1 lemon
2 medium onions
Cream cheese
2 cloves garlic
Half cup mayonnaise
1 tsp Old Bay seasoning
Crackers to serve
Canned crab meat
1tbsp Worcestershire sauce

DIRECTIONS:
- Finely mince green onions and garlic cloves.
- In separate bowl, combine Parmesan cheese, garlic, Old Bay seasoning, mayonnaise, lemon juice, green onions, Worcestershire and stir to combine.
- Transfer this mixture into greased Slow Cooker. Fold the crabmeat into the mixture.
- Cover the lid and cook for around 2 hours, use a LOW temperature mode. To serve, add crackers and garnish with green onions and Parmesan.

**Nutrition: Calories: 201 Fat: 14g Carbohydrates: 33g Protein: 9g**

## Queso Dip for Slow Cooker

Enjoy this dip with your family!

Prep time: 5 minutes Cooking time: 2 hours
Servings: 20

INGREDIENTS:
2tsp paprika
1cup milk
Velveeta
2cloves garlic
1 tsp cayenne pepper
2 jalapeno peppers
Kosher salt
Half cup cotija
Cilantro as a garnish
Tortilla chips (to serve)

DIRECTIONS:
- Take a medium bowl and combine Cotija, minced jalapenos, Velveeta in it. Season with garlic, cayenne pepper, salt and paprika.
- Grease your Slow Cooker with olive oil or simply spray with cooking spray. Transfer the Cotija mixture into Slow Cooker and cover its lid.
- Turn on Slow Cooker and set on HIGH. Cook for 1-2 hours until bubbly.
- To serve, garnish with remaining jalapenos, cilantro and Cotija. Serve with tortillas.

**Nutrition: Calories: 211 Fat: 21g Carbohydrates: 44g Protein: 7g**

## Tamale Dish with Chips

Hot dip for chili-lovers!

Prep time: 5 minutes Cooking time: 2 hours
Servings: 3

INGREDIENTS:
Cubed cream cheese
Monterey Jack
1 tbsp chili powder
1 jalapeno
Salt
Cheddar cheese
2 cloves garlic
1 can enchilada sauce
Ground black pepper
1 cup rotisserie chicken
Canned corn
Tortilla chips for garnish.

DIRECTIONS:
- Finely mince jalapeno and garlic, shred Monterey Jack and Cheddar cheese.
- In a deep bowl, mix cheeses, jalapeno, shredded rotisserie chicken, garlic, enchilada sauce, chili powder. Add black pepper and salt to taste.
- Grease your Slow Cooker and start preheating it.
- Transfer the cheese mixture into Slow Cooker and set to LOW mode. Cook for 2 hours. Serve along with tortilla chips and cilantro garnishing.

**Nutrition: Calories: 136 Fat: 12g Carbohydrates: 2g Protein: 9g**

## Asian Spicy Wings

Asian-style wings for family dinner!

Prep time: 5 minutes Cooking time: 4 hours
Servings: 3

INGREDIENTS:
3 tbsp honey
32 chicken wings
Half tsp chicken wings
2tbsp grated fresh ginger
1 cup teriyaki sauce
3tbsp lime juice
3 cloves garlic

DIRECTIONS:
- Grate the fresh ginger (about 2 tablespoons). Cut the garlic cloves into small slices. Place the chicken wings onto slightly greased broiler pan.
- Cook until it just browned, then transfer to Slow Cooker.
- In separate bowl, stir together the remaining ingredients. Pour this mixture into your Slow Cooker. Cook under the lid for 4 hours on LOW settings.

**Nutrition: Calories: 159 Fat: 8g Carbohydrates: 12g Protein: 22g**

## Lettuce Cups with Chicken

Healthy and interesting to make!

Prep time: 5 minutes Cooking time: 6 hours
Servings: 15

INGREDIENTS:
Half tbsp. apple cider vinegar
1 yellow onion
Mayonnaise
Salt/pepper
4bacon slices
1 whole chicken
Ground red pepper
Green onion slices
6 garlic cloves
1 apple
Lettuce leaves

DIRECTIONS:
- Combine wedged onion and apple with garlic and bacon in your Slow Cooker. Add half vinegar and half-cup water. Place the whole chicken into mixture.
- Season with pepper and salt and cook for six hours on LOW mode. Remove the skin and bones from chicken, shred it and let to cool.
- To make sauce, whisk the remaining chicken liquid with mayonnaise, vinegar and red pepper. Place chicken in lettuce leaves and serve while hot.

**Nutrition: Calories: 147 Fat: 33g Carbohydrates: 14g Protein: 7g**

## Chocolate oatmeal bars

For those, who loves sweet snacks!

Prep time: 11 minutes Cooking time: 8 hours
Servings: 8

INGREDIENTS:
Half teaspoon vanilla
2 chicken eggs
Half cup ground flaxseed
1 large banana
2cups rolled oats
Chocolate topping
1 cup milk
1 tsp vanilla stevia
Salt to taste
1 tsp baking powder
Ground cinnamon

DIRECTIONS:
- In a large bowl, mix eggs, banana, milk, vanilla stevia and vanilla extract.

- In separate bowl, mix all the other ingredients, except the chocolate topping. Combine the mixtures from both bowls and blend well until fully incorporated.
- Place the parchment paper over the bottom of Slow Cooker and spread the batter over it. Turn on Slow Cooker and prepare on LOW temperature mode for 7-8 hours.
- To serve, cut into small portions and cover with chocolate topping.

**Nutrition:** Calories: 168 Fat: 4g Carbohydrates: 25g Protein: 7g

## Chocolate Fudge for Slow Cooker

Just another chocolate appetizer, but so delicious!

⌀ **Prep time: 7 minutes Cooking time: 2 hours Servings: 10**

INGREDIENTS:
1 tsp vanilla extract
Chocolate chips
1 tbsp. salted butter
1 can condensed milk (sweetened)
Butter

DIRECTIONS:
- Spray your Cooker with cooking spray or melted butter.
- Place all ingredients into Slow Cooker and leave to cook for 2 hours (LOW0 mode) or for 1 hour (for HIGH mode).
- Stir the mixture in your Slow Cooker every 20 or 30 minutes.
- When ready, spread the chocolate mixture over the deep baking pan. Place into refrigerator for at least 4 hours, but better overnight.
- To serve, cut into bite-size cubes.

**Nutrition:** Calories: 238 Fat: 8g Carbohydrates: 32g Protein: 9g

## Balsamic Pork with Honey

Sweet pork for any case!

⌀ **Prep time: 13 minutes Cooking time: 9 hours Servings: 6**

INGREDIENTS:
Half cup chicken broth
Half cup honey
Hoisin sauce
3 cloves garlic
Half cup balsamic vinegar
12 buns
2 small onions
1 tbsp. cornstarch
Blackberry notes
Half cup chicken broth

DIRECTIONS:
- Remove the excess fat from pork and place trimmed meat into greased Slow Cooker.
- Take a medium bowl and mix balsamic vinegar, chicken broth, jam, honey, garlic, hoisin and onion.
- Turn on Slow Cooker and set on LOW mode. Cook for 8-9 hours.
- When ready, shred the pork with two forks (you can do it right in Slow Cooker).
- Pour the liquid from Slow Cooker into large saucepan and add cornstarch. Simmer until slurry. Serve the pork on buns with slurry sauce.

**Nutrition:** Calories: 411 Fat: 9g Carbohydrates: 36g Protein: 12g

## Jalapeno Peppers stuffed with Sausage

Hot sausages with spicy peppers!

⌀ **Prep time: 19 minutes Cooking time: 2 hours Servings: 12**

INGREDIENTS:
Ground pork sausage
1 bottle Ranch dressing
1 pack cream cheese
Large jalapeno peppers
1 cup Parmesan cheese (shredded)

DIRECTIONS:
- Grease your Slow Cooker with some butter or olive oil.
- Take a medium skillet and preheat it with oil. Cook sausage until it is all-sides brown. Drain. Take a large bowl and combine the sausage, Parmesan and cream cheese.
- Seed and divide jalapeno peppers into halves and stuff each half with sausage mixture. Arrange peppers over the bottom of your Slow Cooker and turn it on. Cook for 2 hours on LOW mode.

**Nutrition:** Calories: 362 Fat: 34g Carbohydrates: 4g Protein: 9g

## Spinach Dip with Artichokes

Healthy dip with spinach!

⌀ **Prep time: 5 minutes Cooking time: 3 minutes Servings: 3**

INGREDIENTS:
Garlic salt
1 package cream cheese
Dried basil
Shredded Mozzarella cheese
Salt/pepper to taste
Grated Romano cheese
1 clove garlic
Half cup chopped spinach
1 can artichoke hearts
3 tbsp. mayonnaise

DIRECTIONS:
- Lightly grease with olive oil or unsalted butter your cooking dish.
- In a medium bowl, stir mayonnaise, Romano cheese, cream cheese and Parmesan cheese. Add minced garlic, salt, basil, black pepper and garlic salt.
- Stir into this mixture chopped spinach and artichoke hearts. Transfer to Slow Cooker and top with shredded Mozzarella. Cook for 3-4 hours on LOW temperature mode.

**Nutrition:** Calories: 134 Fat: 11g Carbohydrates: 3g Protein: 4g

# Stuffed Potato Skins

Simple dish with unusual serving!

⏱ **Prep time: 29 minutes Cooking time: 1-2 hours Servings: 6**

INGREDIENTS:
1 container sour cream
6 large potatoes
Shredded Cheddar cheese
1 cup vegetable oil
Sliced bacon

DIRECTIONS:
- Grease your Slow Cooker with unsalted and melted butter.
- Do not peel the potatoes; just pierce them with a fork or knife and place into microwave to get soft for 11-12 minutes.
- Halve the potatoes and remove the inside part.
- Put the potato shells into Slow Cooker and set on LOW. Cook for 2 hours. When ready, drain with paper towels.
- Fill the shells with bacon and place back to Slow Cooker for 30 minutes.

**Nutrition: Calories: 519 Fat: 32g Carbohydrates: 40g Protein: 17g**

# Jalapeno Taquitos in Slow Cooker

Hot taquitos for any kind of party!

⏱ **Prep time: 32 minutes Cooking time: 3 hours Servings: 4**

INGREDIENTS:
16 flour tortillas
8 chicken thighs
Green enchilada sauce
2 cups pepper jack cheese
Salt/pepper to taste
1 can diced jalapenos
2 tbsp. vegetable oil
1 pack cream cheese (softened)

DIRECTIONS:
- Grease your Slow Cooker and fill in with skinless chicken thighs, green enchilada sauce, cream cheese, salt, jalapenos with juice and black pepper.
- Set on HIGH and cook, covered, for 3 or 4 hours.
- Shred chicken with two forks and stir well with Slow Cooker sauce. Heat tortillas in oven or microwave.
- Fill it with meat mixture, roll and place back to oven and wait, until cheese melts.

**Nutrition: Calories: 975 Fat: 67g Carbohydrates: 71g Protein: 74g**

# Barbeque Bites in Slow Cooker

Small barbeque appetizers for any occasion!

⏱ **Prep time: 27 minutes Cooking time: 12 hours Servings: 30**

INGREDIENTS:
Beef broth
3 cloves garlic
1 bison brisket
Sour cream
Chili powder
Cider vinegar
Worcestershire sauce
Fresh cilantro (chopped)
2 packs baked phyllo shells
Half cup barbeque sauce
Cayenne pepper
Cheddar cheese

DIRECTIONS:
- Divide bison brisket into small, bite-sized pieces and transfer to the buttered Slow Cooker.
- In medium bowl, combine Worcestershire sauce, chili powder, broth, garlic, cayenne pepper and vinegar. Pour the sauce mixture over the meat.
- Cover the lid and leave cooking on LOW mode for 12 hours.
- Meanwhile, preheat oven to 200 degrees and place the phyllo dough shells over baking sheet. Fill each shell with shredded bison and cook for 10 minutes.
- To serve, top with cilantro, cheese or sour cream.

**Nutrition: Calories: 119 Fat: 3g Carbohydrates: 6g Protein: 13g**

# Chicken Bites in Moroccan Style

Just try this exotic recipe!

⏱ **Prep time: 5 minutes Cooking time: 7 hours Servings: 20**

INGREDIENTS:
One large onion
Boneless chicken thighs
Hummus
2 tbsp. cumin
2 tbsp. lemon juice
1 tbsp. paprika
1 tbsp. minced garlic
5-6 slices bread
Minced garlic
Cinnamon
3 tbsp. oil
Salt
Parsley (to garnish)
1-2 cups chicken stock
Green olives

DIRECTIONS:
- Take a large skillet and cook the minced onion with some oil and peppers. Add ginger and garlic and cook until fragrant, just a minute.
- Mix in cinnamon and cumin, cook for another 2 minutes.
- Place the thighs over the bottom of your Slow Cooker and pour in the pepper mixture. Add olives, lemon juice, salt and pepper. Fill with 2 cups chicken stock.
- Cover and set your Slow Cooker on LOW mode. Cook for 7 hours. To serve, arrange meat with sauce on small bread slices.

**Nutrition: Calories: 322 Fat: 8g Carbohydrates: 37g Protein: 22g**

# Jalapeno Bites with Cheese and Bacon

Hot bacon dips!

**Prep time: 9 minutes Cooking time: 2-4 hours Servings: 32**

INGREDIENTS:
1 tbsp. bacon bits
1 cup dried bread crumbs
Softened cream cheese
Jalapeno peppers
1 cup flour
Olive oil
1 pack shredded Cheddar
One cup milk

DIRECTIONS:
- Take a medium bowl and combine bacon bits, Cheddar cheese and cream cheese. Fill the jalapeno peppers halves with this mixture.
- In two separated bowls, prepare milk and flour. Dip stuffed jalapenos firstly in milk, secondly in flour.
- Roll jalapenos into breadcrumbs and let dry.
- Place the parchment onto the bottom of your Slow Cooker and arrange jalapenos over it. Set on HIGH and let cook for 3 hours.

**Nutrition: Calories: 149 Fat: 12g Carbohydrates: 6g Protein: 3g**

# Spicy Cajun Pecans

Just pecans, but so tasty in Slow Cooker!

**Prep time: 9 minutes Cooking time: 2 hours Servings: 20**

INGREDIENTS:
1 tsp salt
Pecan halves
1 tsp dried thyme
3 tbsp. melted butter
1 tsp dried oregano
Half tsp onion powder
Ground cayenne pepper
Garlic powder
1 tbsp. chili powder

DIRECTIONS:
- In a separate bowl, combine all the ingredients and stir carefully. Slightly grease your Slow Cooker with cooking spray.
- Transfer pecan and spices mixture into your Slow Cooker. Cover the lid and prepare for 10-17 minutes on high temperature mode.
- Turn to LOW and remove the lid. Continue to cook for 2 more hours.
- Before serve, place the nuts onto baking sheet or plain paper towel and cool.

**Nutrition: Calories: 156 Fat: 18g Carbohydrates: 1g Protein: 8g**

# Seafood Dip Appetizer

Love seafood? This one is for you!

**Prep time: 11 minutes Cooking time: 2 hours Servings: 25**

INGREDIENTS:
1 cup Cheddar cheese (shredded)
2 cans condensed cream of shrimp
1 cup lobster (cooked and diced)
Dash cayenne pepper
1 cup American cheese
Half cup cooked shrimp
Dash nutmeg
1 cup crabmeat
1 loaf crusty bread

DIRECTIONS:
- Cover with melted butter the side parts and bottom of your Slow Cooker. Right in Slow Cooker dish, combine all ingredients (except bread).
- Stir everything well.
- Cook under the lid for 2 hours on HIGH mode (check if the cheese is melted). Cut the bread into cubes and serve along with seafood dip.

**Nutrition: Calories: 178 Fat: 8g Carbohydrates: 22g Protein: 9g**

# Wrapped Bacon Hot Dogs

Just hot dogs, but in Slow Cooker!

**Prep time: 15 minutes Cooking time: 1 hour Servings: 20**

INGREDIENTS:
1 pack little smokies or mini cocktail franks
Half cup brown sugar
4 tbsp. maple syrup
1 tsp chili paste
Bacon (about 15 strips)
Ground black pepper
1 tsp Dijon mustard

DIRECTIONS:
- Wrap each smokie sausage with thin strip of bacon. If needed, pin it with toothpick to avoid falling apart.
- Preheat the oven to 200 degrees and arrange wrapped smokies over it. Bake around 30 minutes, just until slightly brown.
- Make a sauce: in saucepan, mix maple syrup, sugar, chili paste, mustard and black pepper. Transfer sausages to Slow Cooker and pour over with sauce. Set on LOW and cook for 1 hour. Serve along with sauce.

**Nutrition: Calories: 322 Fat: 12g Carbohydrates: 15g Protein: 9g**

# Swiss Fondue in Slow Cooker

Amazing fondue that everyone will love!

**Prep time: 9 minutes Cooking time: 1 hour Servings: 10**

INGREDIENTS:
1 loaf crusty bread
3 tbsp. flour
Ground pepper
Shredded Swiss cheese
2 cups dry white wine

3 tbsp. Kirsch
Paprika
Freshly ground nutmeg
Cheddar cheese
1 clove garlic

DIRECTIONS:
- Rub the pan with garlic halves. Pour in dry white wine and heat until bubble (use a medium heat). Add lemon juice.
- In a medium bowl, mix the four with cheeses. Stir the mixture into wine. Cook until the cheese is blended.
- Cover the inner surface of your Slow Cooker with cooking spray.
- Pour in the cheese mixture into Slow Cooker and add Kirsch. In addition, sprinkle with pepper, nutmeg and paprika.
- Cook under cover, firstly on high for 25 minutes, then on LOW for 1-3 hours.

**Nutrition: Calories: 212 Fat: 12g Carbohydrates: 7g Protein: 1g**

## Bean Queso with Cheese

Try this beans with cheese!

⌀ **Prep time: 15 minutes Cooking time: 2 hours**
**Servings: 16**

INGREDIENTS:
1 cup beer
1 cup salsa
Half tsp garlic powder
2 cans cheesy sauce
Ground cumin
1 can green chiles (chopped)
2 cans refried beans
Half cup chopped cilantro

DIRECTIONS:
- In a large bowl, combine chiles, refried beans. Also, you can do it right in a Slow Cooker dish. Season with oregano, garlic powder, salsa and cumin.
- Add cheese sauce and one cup of beer.
- Turn on the LOW temperature mode and cook for 2 hours.
- At the end, add cilantro and cook well to combine the ingredients. To serve, use bread cubes or tortilla chips.

**Nutrition: Calories: 158 Fat: 9g Carbohydrates: 12g Protein: 6g**

## Spicy Champignons

If you love mushrooms, try this spicy ones!

⌀ **Prep time: 13 minutes Cooking time: 3 hours**
**Servings: 8**

INGREDIENTS:
4 tbsp. water
Half cup hoisin sauce (bottled)
Crushed red pepper
2 tbsp. minced garlic
Cleaned fresh mushrooms

DIRECTIONS:
- In a small bowl, mix together water, hoisin sauce, crushed red pepper and garlic. Slightly grease your Slow Cooker and pour in the spicy mixture.
- Place the mushrooms into Slow Cooker and toss to cover with the sauce. Cover the lid and leave to cook for 2-3 hours on LOW temperature mode. Serve with toothpicks and any garnish you like.

**Nutrition: Calories: 36 Fat: 1g Carbohydrates: 4g Protein: 1g**

## Sugared and Spicy Nuts

Unusual taste of your future favorite snack!

⌀ **Prep time: 5 minutes Cooking time: 3 hours**
**Servings: 12**

INGREDIENTS:
Half cup powdered sugar
Pecan or walnuts halves
Ground cloves
Ground ginger
Half cup melted and unsalted butter
Ground cinnamon

DIRECTIONS:
- Preheat your Slow Cooker before start.
- When Slow Cooker is hot, stir nuts and melted butter in it. Add the sugar powder and stir until evenly coat.
- Place the lid and cook for 15 minutes on high. Reduce to LOW and cook without cover for 2-3 hours.
- Meanwhile, in small bowl combine the spices and stir into nuts. Cool spice nuts to serve.

**Nutrition: Calories: 200 Fat: 8g Carbohydrates: 19g Protein: 17g**

## Small Beef Nachos

Try these homemade nachos!

⌀ **Prep time: 7 minutes Cooking time: 8 hours**
**Servings: 30**

INGREDIENTS:
1 can beef broth
Boneless beef roast
Tortilla chips
Salt/pepper to taste
Chopped tomatoes
1 jar banana pepper rings
1 tbsp. vegetable oil
Shredded Monterey jack cheese
3 garlic cloves
1 can beef broth
Minced onion
1 can black beans
Sour cream, cilantro and avocado to serve

DIRECTIONS:
- Use salt and pepper to season the beef. Then, brown the meat from all sides in a large frying pan. When ready, transfer beef into your Slow Cooker.
- Mix in beef broth, garlic and banana pepper rings.
- Cover the lid and cook for 8 hours using a LOW mode. Shred the beef with two forks, when it is cooked.
- Top tortillas with shredded meat and place in preheated oven for 10 minutes. To serve, use an avocado, cilantro and sour cream.

**Nutrition: Calories: 233 Fat: 15g Carbohydrates: 34g Protein: 7g**

## Cereal Mix for Slow Cooker

Sweet and perfect for kids!

**Prep time: 11 minutes  Cooking time: 3 hours
Servings: 16**

INGREDIENTS:
8 cups cereal
1 cup peanuts
2 cups pretzels
1 tsp garlic powder
1 cup Cheerios
3 tbsp. Worcestershire sauce
Seasoned salt

DIRECTIONS:
- Right in the bowl of your Slow Cooker, combine pretzels, cereal, peanuts and cheerios. In another bowl, whisk salt, butter and Worcestershire sauce.
- Sprinkle this sauce over the cereal mixture and toss to combine ingredients evenly. Cover the Slow cooker with lid and set to LOW.
- Cook for 3 hours, stirring occasionally.

**Nutrition: Calories: 159 Fat: 31g Carbohydrates: 1g Protein: 6g**

## Baked Tater Tots

Tater tot appetizer – choose this receipt!

**Prep time: 11 minutes  Cooking time: 3 hours
Servings: 30**

INGREDIENTS:
1 can Rotel
Browned ground beef
Small onion
Cream of chicken soup
1 pack frozen Tater Tots
Cheddar (shredded)

DIRECTIONS:
- In a large frying pan, brown the beef with some oil and add Rotel and diced onion. Grease your Slow Cooker and pour beef and onion mix into the cooking dish.
- Add cream of chicken soup and mix everything well. Across top, place the tater tots.
- Turn on your Slow Cooker and set to LOW. Cook for 2-3 hours. When it is 30 minutes left, sprinkle with shredded cheese.

**Nutrition: Calories: 188 Fat: 8g Carbohydrates: 19g Protein: 27g**

## Spice Nachos with Chicken

Chicken and nachos – unforgettable taste!

**Prep time: 5 minutes  Cooking time: 2 hours
Servings: 26**

INGREDIENTS:
1 container sour cream
3 green onions
Chicken breast strips
1 red bell pepper
1 can black beans
3 tsp salsa
1 loaf cheese product

DIRECTIONS:
- Grease your Slow Cooker – use a special cooking spray for it.
- Right in a cooking dish, combine chicken with salsa, cheese and beans.
- Set your Slow Cooker on LOW temperature regime and cook for 2 hours, stirring.
- Add cream, onions and bell pepper. Increase temperature to HIGH and cook for another 45 minutes.
- To serve, place over tortilla chips.

**Nutrition: Calories: 268 Fat: 19g Carbohydrates: 11g Protein: 33g**

## Fajitas with Chicken and Beef

Cook and try it with your family!

**Prep time: 5 minutes  Cooking time: 4 hours
Servings: 30**

INGREDIENTS:
Boneless and skinless chicken breast
Half cup beer
2 tbsp tomato paste
Lime juice
2 cloves garlic
2 bell peppers
1 tbsp chili powder
1 yellow onion
1 tsp ground cumin
Avocado
Greek yogurt

DIRECTIONS:
- Grease your Slow Cooker with oil or simply cover with cooking spray. Place chicken with pepper and onions into greased bowl.
- In separate bowl, whisk tomato paste, lime juice, beer, cumin and chili powder. Pour over chicken meat.
- Set Slow Cooker on HIGH and cook for 4 hours.
- Serve with dressing, made of avocado and Greek yogurt.

**Nutrition: Calories: 288 Fat: 22g Carbohydrates: 38g Protein: 2g**

## Marsala Mushrooms in Slow Cooker

Try this mushroom receipt with Marsala sauce!

**Prep time: 5 minutes  Cooking time: 8 hours
Servings: 3**

INGREDIENTS:
1 small shallot
Cremini mushrooms
2 cloves garlic
1 tsp cornstarch
3 tbsp sweet Marsala
Half cup heavy whipping cream
3 tbsp chicken stock
2 tbsp parsley
Salt pepper to taste

DIRECTIONS:
- Lightly grease your slow cooker and cover its bottom with mushrooms. Sprinkle with minced parsley, shallot and garlic.

- In separate bowl, combine chicken stock with Marsala. Pour over mushrooms with this mixture. Add some pepper and salt.
- Cover the Slow Cooker lid and prepare mushrooms on LOW settings for 8 hours. In the end, dissolve cornstarch with heavy cream and add into Slow Cooker.
- To serve, sprinkle with Parmesan and parsley.

**Nutrition: Calories: 322 Fat: 16g Carbohydrates: 31g Protein: 12g**

## Hot Dogs with Chili and Cheese

Really spiced hotdogs!

⌀ **Prep time: 11 minutes Cooking time: 3 hours Servings: 30**

INGREDIENTS:
Worcestershire sauce
Tomato sauce
3 medium onions
1 tsp mustard
Half cup celery
Butter
Ground beef meat
Salt
Lemon juice
Brown sugar
Chili seasoning hot dog buns
1 pack sausages
Colby Jack cheese

DIRECTIONS:
- In a medium skillet, melt butter and add chopped onion and celery. Cook for several minutes until tender.
- In another pan, cook beef until lightly brown. Drain with paper towels. Grease your Slow Cooker and place the beef inti it.
- Add the mixture from the first pan and all other ingredients. Cover with the lid and simmer on HIGH for 3-4 hours.
- Place hot dogs into buns, along with chili and cheese.

**Nutrition: Calories: 188 Fat: 18g Carbohydrates: 28g Protein: 41g**

## Beer chicken buns

Chicken with beer – why not?

⌀ **Prep time: 5 minutes Cooking time: 8 hours Servings: 28**

INGREDIENTS:
Chicken breasts
Salt and pepper to taste
2 tbsp flour
Beer
2 tbsp chopped chives
2 tbsp butter
Half cup milk
Grated Cheddar
2 cloves garlic

DIRECTIONS:
- Put chicken in the Slow Cooker, season with salt, garlic and pour in the beer. Turn on the Slow Cooker and choose the LOW mode. Cook for 8 hours.
- When ready, shred the chicken with fork and knife or two forks.
- Make a cheese sauce out of melted butter, milk and a little beer (just heat the ingredients in saucepan until thickened).
- Turn heat to low and add chives and cheese. Serve on heated buns.

**Nutrition: Calories: 276 Fat: 18g Carbohydrates: 21g Protein: 8g**

## Sandwiches with Pulled Beef

Satisfying sandwiches for you and your friends!

⌀ **Prep time: 5 minutes Cooking time: 8 hours Servings: 25**

INGREDIENTS:
3 large bell peppers
1 cup beef broth
1 beef chuck roast
Salt
American cheese
Black pepper
2 medium onions
Half cup jalapenos
8 long sandwich buns

DIRECTIONS:
- Slightly rub the beef with black pepper and salt.
- Along with broth, add the beef chuck roast to Slow Cooker. Sprinkle with jalapenos and green peppers.
- Place the lid and cook on LOW mode for 8 hours.
- Shred the meat and divide it, along with vegetables, over the hot dog buns. Cover with the cheese and place into preheated oven until it melts.

**Nutrition: Calories: 344 Fat: 27g Carbohydrates: 34g Protein: 12g**

## Sweet Bacon Pigs

Simple, but very delicious!

⌀ **Prep time: 17 minutes Cooking time: 5 hours Servings: 10**

INGREDIENTS:
Half tsp Chinese spicy powder
1 pack little smokey sausages
Hot pepper sauce (1 dash)
Bacon in slices
1-2 cups brown sugar
Cola-flavored beverage

DIRECTIONS:
- Wrap each sausage with thin slice of bacon. To secure, pin each one with toothpick. Place all the appetizers over baking sheet and sprinkle with brown sugar.
- Bake on 165 degrees for 40 minutes (20 minutes for each side).
- Transfer bacon pigs from baking sheet to Slow Cooker. Sprinkle with sugar and Chinese powder. Drizzle with hot sauce and cola.
- Set to HIGH mode and cook for 4 hours.

**Nutrition: Calories: 291 Fat: 17g Carbohydrates: 24g Protein: 10g**

## Cheese and Beer Dip

The secret ingredient makes the dish better!

⌀ Prep time: 5 minutes Cooking time: 1 hour Servings: 16

INGREDIENTS:
Half cup salsa
Processed cheese food
1 tsp chili powder
Cayenne pepper (optional)
Half teaspoon onion powder
2 tbsp. Worcestershire sauce
1 cup Irish beer
DIRECTIONS:
- Grease your Slow Cooker with unsalted butter. Place processed cheese food into Slow Cooker.
- Turn on and set on HIGH temperature mode and cook until melted, for about 20 minutes.
- In separate bowl, combine salsa, chili powder, Worcestershire sauce, cayenne pepper and onion powder.
- Stir the spicy mix with cheese and wait for 10 more minutes.

Nutrition: Calories: 224 Fat: 17g Carbohydrates: 2g Protein: 12g

## Buffalo Wings for Slow Cooker

The perfect choice for those, who loves wings!

⌀ Prep time: 33 minutes Cooking time: 4 hours Servings: 8

INGREDIENTS:
Half cup butter
2tsp garlic powder
1 bottle hot sauce
2 tsp onion powder
2 tsp dried oregano
Chicken wing sections
DIRECTIONS:
- In a pot, mix together hot pepper sauce, Worcestershire sauce, half-cup butter. Add onion powder, dried oregano, garlic powder. Simmer for about 5 minutes.
- Put the chicken wings in Slow Cooker and pour the spicy mixture over it.
- Cook on HIGH mode and prepare for 2 hours. Then reduce to LOW and leave for another 2 hours. Place the wings over buttered baking sheet and bake in oven until browned and crisp.
- Melt hot sauce with butter and simmer to get thick. Serve the wings with the sauce.

Nutrition: Calories: 385 Fat: 34g Carbohydrates: 3g Protein: 16g

# MEAT RECIPES

## Pork Meatballs with Apple Sauce

⌀ Ready in about: **30 minutes** | Serves: **8** | Per serving: Calories 454; Carbs 7g; Fat 30g; Protein 38g

INGREDIENTS
2 ½ pounds Ground Pork
¼ cup Tamari Sauce
3 Garlic Cloves, minced
½ tbsp dried Thyme
½ cup diced Onions
2 tsp Honey
¼ cup Apple Juice
1 ½ cups Water
1 cup Breadcrumbs
Salt and Pepper, to taste
DIRECTIONS
- Whisk in honey, tamari, apple juice, water, and thyme in the pressure cooker. Season with salt and pepper. Set on SAUTÉ at High and cook for 15 minutes, lid off. Meanwhile, combine all the remaining ingredients in a bowl.
- Shape meatballs out of the mixture. Drop the meatballs into the sauce, and press CANCEL. Seal the lid, and set on BEANS/CHILI for 15 minutes at High. When done, release the pressure naturally, for 10 minutes. Serve hot.

## Pork Steaks with Apple and Prunes

⌀ Ready in about: **30 minutes** | Serves: **4** | Per serving: Calories 587; Carbs 24g; Fat 31g; Protein 43g

INGREDIENTS
4 Pork Steaks
¼ cup Milk
8 Prunes, pitted
½ cup White Wine
2 Apples, peeled and sliced
¼ cup Heavy Cream
1 tbsp Fruit Jelly
½ tsp ground Ginger
Salt and Pepper, to taste
DIRECTIONS
- Place all ingredients, except the jelly, in your pressure cooker. Stir to combine well, and season with salt and pepper. Seal the lid and cook on BEANS/CHILI at High pressure for 15 minutes.
- Once done, wait 5 minutes and do a quick pressure release. Stir in the jelly, serve, and enjoy.

## Pork Sausage with Bell Peppers and Sweet Onions

*Ready in about:* **20 minutes** | Serves: 8 | Per serving: Calories 278; Carbs 11g; Fat 19g; Protein 14g

INGREDIENTS
- 8 Pork Sausages
- 2 large Sweet Onions, sliced
- 4 Red Bell Peppers, cut into strips
- 1 tbsp Olive Oil
- ½ cup Beef Broth
- ¼ cup White Wine
- 1 tsp Garlic, minced

DIRECTIONS
- On SAUTÉ, add the sausages, and brown them for a few minutes. Remove to a plate and discard the liquid. Press CANCEL. Wipe clean the cooker and heat the oil on SAUTÉ at High mode.
- Stir in onions and peppers. Stir-fry them for 5 minutes, until soft. Add garlic and cook for a minute. Add the sausages and pour in broth and wine. Seal the lid and cook for 5 minutes on BEANS/CHILI at High pressure. Once done, do a quick pressure release.

## Pork with Rutabaga and Granny Smith Apples

*Ready in about:* **40 minutes** | Serves: 4 | Per serving: Calories 418; Carbs 33g; Fat 17g; Protein 33g

INGREDIENTS
- 1 pound Pork Loin, cut into cubes
- 1 Onion, diced
- 2 Rutabagas, peeled and diced
- 1 cup Chicken Broth
- ½ cup White Wine
- 2 Granny Smith apples, peeled and diced
- ½ cup sliced Leeks
- 1 tbsp Vegetable Oil
- 1 Celery Stalk, diced
- 2 tbsp dried Parsley
- ¼ tsp Thyme
- ½ tsp Cumin
- ¼ tsp Lemon Zest
- Salt and Black Pepper, to taste

DIRECTIONS
- Season the pork with salt and pepper. Heat oil on SAUTÉ at High. Add pork and cook for a few minutes, until browned. Add onions and cook for 2 more minutes, until soft.
- Stir in the remaining ingredients, except for the apples. Seal the lid and cook for 15 minutes on BEANS/CHILI mode at High. When ready, release the pressure quickly. Stir in apples, seal the lid again, and cook at High for another 5 minutes. Do a quick release.

## Gourmet Bacon, Potato, and Endive Casserole

*Ready in about:* **30 minutes** | Serves: 4 | Per serving: Calories 489; Carbs 74g; Fat 17g; Protein 17g

INGREDIENTS
- ½ pound Smoked Bacon, chopped
- ½ cup Carrots, sliced
- 2 cups Water
- 1 cup Chicken Stock
- ¾ cup Half and Half
- 4 Golden Potatoes, peeled and chopped
- 4 Endives, halved lengthwise
- Salt and Pepper, to taste

DIRECTIONS
- Set on SAUTÉ mode at High and add the bacon. Cook for 2 minutes until slightly crispy. Add the potatoes, carrots, and chicken stock. Seal the lid and cook for 10 minutes on BEANS/CHILI at High.
- Press CANCEL and release the pressure quickly. Add the endives and cook for 5 more minutes on BEANS/CHILI at High pressure. Press CANCEL again and quick-release the pressure.
- Strain the bacon and veggies and return them to the pressure cooker. Add the half and half and season with salt and pepper. Cook on SAUTÉ mode at High, for 3 more minutes, lid off.

## Pork Chops in Merlot

*Ready in about:* **30 minutes** | Serves: 4 | Per serving: Calories 455; Carbs 13g; Fat 24g; Protein 43g

INGREDIENTS
- 4 Pork Chops
- 3 Carrots, chopped
- 1 Tomato, chopped
- 1 Onion, chopped
- 2 Garlic Cloves, minced
- ¼ cup Merlot Red Wine
- ½ cup Beef Broth
- 1 tsp dried Oregano
- 2 tbsp Olive Oil
- 2 tbsp Flour
- 2 tbsp Water
- 2 tbsp Tomato Paste
- 1 Beef Bouillon Cube
- ¼ tsp Black Pepper
- ¼ tsp Salt

DIRECTIONS
- Heat the oil on SAUTÉ mode at High. In a bowl, mix in flour, pepper, and salt. Coat the pork chops. Place them in the pressure cooker and cook for a few minutes, until browned on all sides.
- Add the carrots, onion, garlic, and oregano. Cook for 2 more minutes. Stir in the remaining ingredients and seal the lid. Cook on SOUP mode and cook for 25 minutes at High. When ready, do a natural pressure release, for 10 minutes, and serve immediately.

## Braised Red Cabbage and Bacon

Ready in about: **20 minutes** | Serves: **8** | Per serving: **Calories 149; Carbs 5g; Fat 12g; Protein 5g**

INGREDIENTS
1 pound Red Cabbage, chopped
8 Bacon Slices, chopped
1 ½ cups Beef Broth
2 tbsp Butter
1 tsp Salt
½ tsp Black Pepper

DIRECTIONS
- Add bacon slices in your pressure cooker, and cook for 5 minutes, until crispy, on SAUTÉ. Stir in cabbage, salt, pepper, and butter.
- Seal the lid, hit STEAM for 10 minutes at High. Release the pressure naturally, for 10 minutes.

## Orange & Cinnamon Pork

Ready in about: **60 minutes** | Serves: **10** | Per serving: **Calories 635; Carbs 14g; Fat 47g; Protein 61g**

INGREDIENTS
2 tbsp Olive Oil
5 pounds Pork Shoulder
1 Cinnamon Stick
2 cups Fresh Orange Juice
1 tbsp Cumin
½ tsp Garlic Powder
¼ tsp Onion Powder
1 Onion, chopped
1 Jalapeno Pepper, diced
2 tsp Thyme
½ tsp Oregano
½ tsp Pepper

DIRECTIONS
- Place half of the oil in a small bowl. Add all of the spices and stir well to combine the mixture. Rub it all over the meat, making sure that the pork is well-coated.
- Heat the remaining oil on SAUTÉ at High. Add the pork and sear it on all sides until browned. Transfer to a plate. Pour the orange juice into the pan and deglaze the bottom with a spatula.
- Add the rest of the ingredients and stir to combine well. Return the pork to the pot. Seal the lid, select the MEAT/STEW cooking mode for 40 minutes, at High pressure.
- When ready, allow for a natural pressure release, for about 10 minutes. Grab two forks and shred the pork inside the pot. Stir to combine with the juices, and serve.

## Pork Roast with Mushrooms in Beer Sauce

Ready in about: **50 minutes** | Serves: **8** | Per serving: **Calories 379; Carbs 10g; Fat 16g; Protein 47g**

INGREDIENTS
3 pounds Pork Roast
8 ounces Mushrooms, sliced
12 ounces Root Beer
10 ounces Cream of Mushroom Soup
1 package Dry Onion Soup

DIRECTIONS
- In the pressure cooker, whisk together soup, dry onion soup mix, and root beer. Add the mushrooms and pork. Seal the lid, and set to MEAT/STEW for 40 minutes at High. Let sit for 5 minutes before doing a quick release.

## BBQ Pork Butt

Ready in about: **55 minutes** | Serves: **6** | Per serving: **Calories 488; Carbs 20g; Fat 26g; Protein 38g**

INGREDIENTS
2 pounds Pork Butt
¼ tsp Garlic Powder
¼ tsp Salt
¼ tsp Pepper
1 cup Barbecue Sauce
¼ tsp Cumin Powder
½ tsp Onion Powder
1 ½ cups Beef Broth
Cooking oil, to grease

DIRECTIONS
- In a bowl, combine the barbecue sauce and all of the spices. Brush the pork with the mixture. On SAUTÉ, coat with cooking oil. Add the pork, and sear on all sides, for a few minutes. Pour the beef broth around the meat.
- Seal the lid and cook for 40 minutes on MEAT/STEW at High. Wait 5 minutes before quick- releasing the pressure.

## Apple and Cherry Pork Tenderloin

Ready in about: **55 minutes** | Serves: **4** | Per serving: **Calories 349; Carbs 18g; Fat 12g; Protein 40g**

INGREDIENTS
1 ¼ pounds Pork Tenderloin
1 chopped Celery Stalk
2 cups Apples, peeled and chopped
1 cup Cherries, pitted
½ cup Apple Juice
½ cup Water
¼ cup Onions, chopped
Salt and Pepper, to taste
2 tbsp Olive Oil

DIRECTIONS
- Heat oil on SAUTÉ mode at High, and cook the onion and celery for 5 minutes until softened. Season the pork with salt and pepper, and add to the cooker. Brown for 2-3 minutes per side.
- Then, top with apples and cherries, and pour the water and apple juice. Seal the lid and cook on MEAT/STEW mode for 40 minutes, at High pressure. Do a quick pressure release.
- Slice the pork tenderloin and arrange on a platter. Spoon the apple-cheery sauce over the pork slices, to serve.

## Pork Chops with Brussel Sprouts

Ready in about: **35 minutes** | Serves: **4** | Per serving: **Calories 406; Carbs 7g; Fat 22g; Protein 44g**

INGREDIENTS
4 Pork Chops
½ pound Brussel Sprouts
¼ cup Sparkling Wine
1 ½ cups Beef Stock
2 Shallots, chopped
1 tbsp Olive Oil
1 cup Celery Stalk, chopped
1 tbsp Coriander
¼ tsp Salt
¼ tsp Black Pepper

DIRECTIONS
- Heat olive oil on SAUTÉ. Add the pork chops and cook until browned on all sides. Stir in the remaining ingredients.
- Seal the lid and cook for 25 minutes on MEAT/STEW at High. Release the pressure quickly.

## Spicy Ground Pork

⏲ Ready in about: **55 minutes | Serves: 6 | Per serving:** **Calories 510; Carbs 4g; Fat 34g; Protein 41g**

INGREDIENTS
2 pounds Ground Pork
1 Onion, diced
1 can diced Tomatoes
1 can Peas
5 Garlic Cloves, crushed
3 tbsp Butter
1 Serrano Pepper, chopped
1 cup Beef Broth
1 tsp ground Ginger
2 tsp ground Coriander
1 tsp Salt
¾ tsp Cumin
¼ tsp Cayenne Pepper
½ tsp Turmeric
½ tsp Black Pepper

DIRECTIONS
- Melt butter on SAUTÉ at High. Add onions and cook for 3 minutes, until soft. Stir in the spices and garlic and cook for 2 more minutes.
- Add pork and cook until browned. ADD broth, serrano pepper, peas, and tomatoes. Seal the lid and cook for 30 minutes on MEAT/STEW at High. Release the pressure naturally for 10 minutes.

## Beans and Pancetta Kale and Chickpeas

⏲ Ready in about: **30 minutes | Serves: 8 | Per serving:** **Calories 486; Carbs 49g; Fat 21g; Protein 31g**

INGREDIENTS
5 cups Water, divided
1 pack (2 oz) Onion soup mix
¼ cup Olive Oil
1 tbsp Garlic, minced
1 ½ pounds canned Chickpeas, soaked overnight
2 tsp Mustard
½ pound Pancetta slices, chopped
1 Onion, chopped
1 cup Kale, chopped

DIRECTIONS
- Heat the oil and cook the onions, garlic, and pancetta for 5 minutes on SAUTÉ mode at High. Add 1 cup of water and the soup mix, and cook for 5 more minutes. Then, add the chickpeas and 4 cups of water.
- Add in the kale and mustard. Seal the lid and cook for 15 minutes on BEANS/CHILI at High Pressure. Once cooking is completed, perform a quick pressure release and serve immediately.

## Rutabaga & Apple Pork

⏲ Ready in about: **40 minutes | Serves: 4 | Per serving:** **Calories 421; Carbs 2g; Fat 23g; Protein 44g**

INGREDIENTS
1 tbsp Olive Oil
1 pound Pork Loin, cut into cubes
2 Apples, peeled and chopped
2 Rutabaga, peeled and chopped
1 Onion, diced
1 Celery Stalk, diced
1 tbsp Parsley, chopped
½ cup Leeks, sliced
1 ½ cups Beef Broth
½ tsp Cumin
½ tsp Thyme

DIRECTIONS
- Heat half of the olive oil on SAUTÉ at High. Add the beef and cook until it browned on all sides. Remove to a plate. Add leeks, onions, celery, and drizzle with the remaining oil.
- Stir to combine and cook for 3 minutes. Add the beef back to the cooker, pour the broth over, and stir in all of the herbs and spices. Seal the lid, and cook on BEANS/CHILI at High pressure for 10 minutes.
- After the beep, do a quick pressure release. Stir in the rutabaga and apples. Seal the lid again and cook for 5 minutes on BEANS/CHILI at High. Do a quick pressure release, and serve right away.

## Brussel Sprout Pork Chops with Onions

⏲ Ready in about: **40 minutes | Serves: 4 | Per serving:** **Calories 434; Carbs 13g; Fat 29g; Protein 31g**

INGREDIENTS
1 pound Pork Chops
1 cup Onions, sliced
1 cup Carrots, sliced
1 tbsp Butter
2 cups Brussel Sprouts
1 tbsp Arrowroot
1 tsp Garlic, minced
1 cup Chicken Stock
½ tsp dried Thyme

DIRECTIONS
- Melt butter on SAUTÉ mode at High. Add the pork chops, and cook on all sides until golden in color. Transfer to a plate. Add the onions, and cook for 3 minutes, then add the garlic.

- Saute for one more minute. Return the pork chops to the pot and pour the broth over. Seal the lid and cook on BEANS/CHILI at High pressure for 15 minutes.
- When the timer goes off, do a quick pressure release. Stir in carrots and brussel sprouts. Seal the lid again, and cook for 3 minutes on STEAM at High pressure. Do a quick pressure release.
- Transfer the chops and veggies to a serving platter. Whisk the arrowroot into the pot and cook on SAUTÉ at High until it thickens. Pour the sauce over the chops and veggies. Serve immediately.

## Sunday Night Pork Meatloaf

**Ready in about: 30 minutes | Serves: 4 | Per serving: Calories 290; Carbs 29g; Fat 11g; Protein 21g**

### INGREDIENTS

**FOR THE MEATLOAF:**

2 pounds Ground Pork
2 Garlic Cloves, minced
1 cup Breadcrumbs
1 large-sized Egg
1 cup Milk
2 small Onions, finely chopped
Salt and cracked Black Pepper, to taste
½ tsp Turmeric powder
½ tsp dried Oregano
Nonstick Cooking Spray, for greasing

**FOR THE TOPPING:**

1 cup Ketchup
2 tbsp Brown Sugar
¼ cup Tomato Paste
1 tsp Garlic powder
½ tsp Onion powder
½ tsp Cayenne Pepper

### DIRECTIONS

- Place the trivet at the bottom of your pressure cooker and pour 1 cup of water. Lightly grease a round sheet pan, that fits in your pressure cooker.
- Mix ground pork, bread crumbs, milk, onion, egg, salt, black pepper, oregano, and thyme in a mixing bowl. Use your hands to combine thoroughly. Shape into a loaf and place onto the prepared sheet pan.
- In another bowl, mix the ingredients for the topping. Spread the topping over the meatloaf and lower the sheet pan onto the trivet. Seal the lid, select BEANS/CHILI and cook for 25 minutes at High.
- Once ready, do a quick pressure release. Remove to a cutting board and slice before serving.

## Holiday Sweet Spare Ribs

**Ready in about: 35 minutes | Serves: 6 | Per serving: Calories 634; Carbs 43g; Fat 41g; Protein 47g**

### INGREDIENTS

3 pounds Spare Ribs, cut into 3-inch pieces
18 ounces canned Pineapple, undrained
1 cup Onions, sliced
½ tsp Garlic Salt
¼ cup Tamari Sauce
2 tbsp Apple Cider Vinegar
½ cup Tomato Paste
3 tsp Olive Oil
¼ tsp Ginger Powder
¼ tsp Pepper

### DIRECTIONS

- Heat oil and brown spare ribs on all sides, 4-5 minutes per side on SAUTÉ mode at High. Remove to a plate. Sauté onion in hot oil for 3-4 minutes until translucent.
- Add the remaining ingredients, return the spareribs to the cooker, and seal the lid. Cook for 25 minutes on MEAT/STEW at High. Use a natural release, for 10 minutes and serve.

## Shredded Pork in Sweet BBQ Sauce

**Ready in about: 70 minutes | Serves: 8 | Per serving: Calories 420; Carbs 47g; Fat 12g; Protein 33g**

### INGREDIENTS

4 pounds Pork Shoulder
1 tbsp Onion Powder
1 tbsp Garlic Powder
1 tbsp Pepper
1 tbsp Chili Powder
2 cups Chicken Stock

**For BBQ Sauce:**

6 Dates, soaked
¼ cup Tomato Paste
½ cup Coconut Aminos

### DIRECTIONS

- In a small bowl combine onion powder, garlic powder, pepper, and chili powder. Rub the mixture onto the pork. Place the pork inside your pressure cooker. Pour the broth around the meat, not over it, and then seal the lid. Select MEAT/STEW and set the timer to 60 minutes, at High.
- Meanwhile, place all sauce ingredients in a food processor and pulse until smooth. Release the pressure quickly. Grab two forks and shred the meat inside the pot. Pour the sauce over and stir to combine.

## Pork & Cabbage Soup with Veggies

**Ready in about: 25 minutes | Serves: 6 | Per serving: Calories 351; Carbs 20g; Fat 18g; Protein 26g**

### INGREDIENTS

1 pound Ground Pork
1 Onion, diced
2 pounds Napa Cabbage, chopped
1 Potato, diced
6 Button Mushrooms, sliced
3 Scallions, sliced
2 Carrots, chopped
1 tbsp Butter
4 cups Chicken Broth
Salt and Pepper, to taste

### DIRECTIONS

- Melt butter on SAUTÉ at High, and add the pork. Cook until it browned, breaking it with a spatula. Once browned, add onions and mushrooms, and cook for another 4-5 minutes.
- Season with salt and pepper. Pour in chicken broth and stir in the remaining ingredients. Seal the lid, cook on BEANS/CHILI for 6 minutes at High. Do a quick release. Ladle into serving bowls and serve.

## Pineapple Pork Loin

Ready in about: **35 minutes** | Serves: **6** | Per serving: Calories 546; Carbs 42g; Fat 21g; Protein 41g

INGREDIENTS
2 pounds Pork Loin, cut into 6 equal pieces
16 ounces canned Pineapple
1 cup Vegetable Broth
1 tbsp Brown Sugar
3 tbsp Olive Oil
½ cup Tomato Paste
1 cup sliced Onions
½ tsp Ginger, grated
½ tsp Garlic Salt
½ tsp Pepper
¼ cup Tamari
¼ cup Rice Wine Vinegar
½ tbsp. Cornstarch
1 tbsp. Water
DIRECTIONS
- Heat the 2 tbsp oil on SAUTÉ at High. Cook the onions a few minutes, until translucent. Add the pork and stir in the rest of the ingredients, except for water and cornstarch.
- Seal the lid and cook for 20 minutes on SOUP mode at High. Release the pressure quickly.
- In a bowl, mix cornstarch and water, with a fork, until slurry. Stir in the cornstarch slurry in the pressure cooker, and cook for 2 more minutes, or until thickened, on SAUTÉ at High. Serve hot to enjoy!

## Pork Cutlets with Baby Carrots

Ready in about: **35 minutes** | Serves: **4** | Per serving: Calories 213; Carbs 13g; Fat 9g; Protein 22g

INGREDIENTS
1 pound Pork Cutlets
1 pound Baby Carrots
1 Onion, sliced
1 tbsp Butter
1 cup Vegetable Broth
1 tsp Garlic Powder
Salt and Black Pepper, to taste
DIRECTIONS
- Season the pork with salt and pepper. Melt butter on SAUTÉ at High, and brown the pork on all sides. Stir in carrots and onions and cook for 2 more minutes, until soft. Pour in the broth, and add garlic powder.
- Season to taste. Seal the lid and cook for 25 minutes on MEAT/STEW at High. Release the pressure quickly.

## Ground Pork and Sauerkraut

Ready in about: **35 minutes** | Serves: **4** | Per serving: Calories 415; Carbs 16g; Fat 9g; Protein 33g

INGREDIENTS
1 pound Ground Pork
4 cups Sauerkraut, shredded
1 cup Tomato Puree
1 cup Chicken Stock
1 Red Onion, chopped
2 Garlic Cloves, minced
2 Bay Leaves
Salt and Pepper, to taste
DIRECTIONS
- Add onions, garlic, and cook until soft and fragrant, on SAUTÉ at High. Add the pork and cook it until lightly browned. Stir in the remaining ingredients, and season with salt, and black pepper.
- fSeal the lid and cook for 25 minutes on MEAT/STEW mode at High. When done, press CANCEL and release the pressure quickly. Discard the bay leaves, serve and enjoy.

## Chili Pork Meatloaf

Ready in about: **70 minutes** | Serves: **6** | Per serving: Calories 529; Carbs 29g; Fat 29g; Protein 42g

INGREDIENTS
1 pound ground Sausage
1 pound Ground Pork
1 cup cooked Rice
1 cup Milk
½ tsp Cayenne Powder
½ tsp Marjoram
2 Eggs, beaten
2 Garlic Cloves, minced
1 Onion, diced
Cooking spray, to grease

TOPPING:

2 tbsp Brown Sugar
1 cup Ketchup
DIRECTIONS
- In a bowl, crack the eggs and whisk them with milk. Stir in the meat, cayenne, marjoram, rice, onion and garlic. With hands, mix in the ingredients to combine and form meatloaf mixture.
- Grease a baking dish with cooking spray. Add and shape the meatloaf mixture inside. Whisk together the ketchup and sugar and pour over the meatloaf.
- Place the trivet inside the pressure cooker, and pour 1 cup of water. Lay the dish on top, seal the lid and cook on on MEAT/STEW for 50 minutes at High. When ready, do a quick release.

## Pork and Green Onion Frittata

Ready in about: **30 minutes** | Serves: **5** | Per serving: Calories 275; Carbs 3g; Fat 19g; Protein 15g

INGREDIENTS
1 tbsp Butter, melted
1 cup Green Onions, chopped

1 pound Ground Pork, chopped
6 Eggs
Salt and ground Black Pepper, to taste
1 cup Water

DIRECTIONS
- In a deep bowl, break the eggs and whisk until frothy. Mix in the onions and ground meat, and season with the salt and pepper. Grease a casserole dish with 1 tablespoon of melted butter. Pour the egg mixture into the dish.
- Place a metal trivet in the pressure cooker and add 1 cup of water. Select BEANS/CHILI mode and cook for 25 minutes at High. Do a quick pressure release and serve immediately.

## Herby Pork Butt and Yams

**Ready in about:** 20 minutes | **Serves:** 4 | **Per serving:** Calories 488; Carbs 41g; Fat 22g; Protein 31g

INGREDIENTS
1 pound Pork Butt, cut into 4 equal pieces
1 pound Yams, diced
2 tsp Butter
¼ tsp Thyme
¼ tsp Oregano
1 ½ tsp Sage
1 ½ cups Beef Broth
Salt and Black Pepper, to taste

DIRECTIONS
- Season the pork with thyme, sage, oregano, salt, and pepper. Melt butter on SAUTÉ mode at High.
- Add pork and cook until brown, for a few minutes. Add the yams and pour the broth. Seal the lid and cook for 20 minutes on BEANS/CHILI at High. Do a quick release and serve hot.

## Tangy Pork in Tomato Sour Cream Sauce

**Ready in about:** 45 minutes | **Serves:** 6 | **Per serving:** Calories 416; Carbs 12g; Fat 26g; Protein 32g

INGREDIENTS
1 ½ pounds Pork Shoulder, cut into pieces
2 Onions, chopped
1 ½ cups Sour Cream
1 cup Tomato Puree
½ tbsp Coriander
¼ tsp Cumin
¼ tsp Cayenne Pepper
1 tsp Garlic, minced
Salt and Pepper, to taste
Cooking spray, to grease

DIRECTIONS
- Coat with cooking spray and add the pork. Cook for a few minutes on SAUTÉ mode at High, until lightly browned. Add onions and garlic and cook for 1 minute, until fragrant.
- Stir in the remaining ingredients and turn the vent clockwise to seal. Set to 30 minutes on SOUP at High. When it beeps, let sit for 5 minutes before quick release the pressure.

## Ground Pork with Cabbage and Veggies

**Ready in about:** 25 minutes | **Serves:** 6 | **Per serving:** Calories 352; Carbs 13g; Fat 21g; Protein 27g

INGREDIENTS
1 ¼ pounds Ground Pork
1 cup Cabbage, shredded
½ cup chopped Celery
2 Red Onions, chopped
2 large Tomatoes, chopped
1 Carrot, shredded
2 cups Water
1 Red Bell Pepper, chopped
1 Green Bell Pepper, chopped
1 Yellow Bell Pepper, chopped
¼ tsp Cumin
1 tsp Red Pepper Flakes
Salt and Black Pepper, to taste
Cooking spray, to grease
Freshly chopped Coriander leaves, for garnish

DIRECTIONS
- Coat with cooking spray. Add the pork and cook them until browned on SAUTÉ at High. Stir in the remaining ingredients, and pour the water.
- Seal the lid and set to BEANS/CHILI for 15 minutes at High. Do a quick pressure release. Sprinkle with freshly chopped coriander, to serve.

## Dinner Pork Roast

**Ready in about:** 45 minutes | **Serves:** 6 | **Per serving:** Calories 290; Carbs 4g; Fat 6g; Protein 52g

INGREDIENTS
3 pounds Sirloin Pork Roast
1 tbsp Honey
1 tsp Chili Powder
1 tbsp Rosemary
1 tbsp Olive Oil
1 ¼ cups Water
2 tbsp Lemon Juice

DIRECTIONS
- Combine the spices, in a bowl, and rub them onto the pork. Heat oil on SAUTÉ mode at High and sear the pork on all sides. Stir in the remaining ingredients and seal the lid.
- Cook for 30 minutes, on MEAT/STEW at High. Do a natural pressure release, for 15 minutes.

## Short Ribs with Mango Sauce

**Ready in about:** 35 minutes | **Serves:** 6 | **Per serving:** Calories 625; Carbs 41g; Fat 31g; Protein 62g

INGREDIENTS
1 lb Short Ribs, cut into 3-inch pieces
18 ounces canned Mango, undrained
½ tsp Black Pepper, to taste
½ tsp ground Parsley
1 tsp Salt

1 cup Onions, sliced
1-inch piece Ginger, finely chopped
½ tsp Garlic, minced
½ cup Tomato Paste
3 tsp Olive Oil
½ cup Soy sauce
2 tbsp Vinegar
¼ cup prepared Arrowroot slurry

DIRECTIONS
- On SAUTÉ, heat oil and cook the onions until tender, about 4 minutes. Stir in the remaining ingredients, except the arrowroot.
- Seal the lid, hit BEANS/CHILI, and cook for 20 minutes at High. Once ready, do a quick release. Stir in the arrowroot slurry and cook on SAUTÉ at High until the sauce thickens.

## Pork Sausage with Cauliflower and Tater Tots

Ready in about: **20 minutes** | Serves: **6** | Per serving: Calories 431; Carbs 66g; Fat 12g; Protein 23g

INGREDIENTS
1 pound Pork Sausage, sliced
1 pound Tater Tots
1 pound Cauliflower Florets, frozen and thawed
10 ounces canned Mushroom Soup
10 ounces canned Cauliflower Soup
10 ounces Evaporated Milk
Salt and Pepper, to taste

DIRECTIONS
- Place roughly ¼ of the sausage slices in your pressure cooker. In a bowl, whisk together the soups and milk. Pour some of the mixtures over the sausages.
- Top the sausage slices with ¼ of the cauliflower florets followed by ¼ of the tater tots. Pour some of the soup mixtures again. Repeat the layers until you use up all ingredients.
- Seal the lid, and cook on BEANS/CHILI for 10 minutes, at High. When ready, do a quick release.

## Tamari Sauce Pork Belly with Garlic

Ready in about: **40 minutes** | Serves: **6** | Per serving: Calories 520; Carbs 5g; Fat 28g; Protein 49g

INGREDIENTS
4 Garlic Cloves, sliced
½ tsp ground Cloves
1 tsp grated fresh Ginger
1 ½ pounds Pork Belly, sliced
2 ¼ cups Water
¼ cup White Wine
½ cup Yellow Onions, peeled and chopped
¼ cup Tamari Sauce
1 tsp Sugar Maple Syrup
4 cups short-grain White Rice, cooked, warm

DIRECTIONS
- Brown pork belly, for about 6 minutes per side, on SAUTÉ at High. Add the remaining ingredients. Seal the lid and cook for 25 minutes on BEANS/CHILI at High Pressure. Cook until the meat is tender.
- Once ready, switch the pressure release valve to open, and do a quick pressure release. Serve with rice.

## Pork Fillets with Worcestershire Sauce

Ready in about: **30 minutes** | Serves: **6** | Per serving: Calories 587; Carbs 39g; Fat 29g; Protein 48g

INGREDIENTS
1 lb Pork Loin Filets
16 ounces canned peach
½ tsp Black Pepper
½ tsp Cilantro, ground
½ tsp Ginger, finely chopped
½ cup Worcestershire sauce
¼ cup Apple Cider Vinegar
½ tsp Garlic, minced
1 tsp Salt
1 cup Onions, sliced
1 tbsp Brown Sugar
2 tbsp Olive Oil
1 cup Tomato Sauce
1 tbsp Arrowroot slurry

DIRECTIONS
- On SAUTÉ at High, heat oil. Cook onions until tender, for about 4 minutes. Stir in the remaining ingredients, except for the arrowroot.
- Seal the lid, Select on BEANS/CHILI and cook for 20 minutes at High. Do a quick release. Stir in the arrowroot slurry and cook on SAUTÉ, until the sauce thickens.

## Italian Sausage over Muffins

Ready in about: **20 minutes** | Serves: **8** | Per serving: Calories 478; Carbs 29g; Fat 31g; Protein 28g

INGREDIENTS
8 toasted English Muffins, split
1 ½ pounds Italian Sausage
1 ¼ cups Milk
¼ cup Flour
1 cup Eggplants, sliced
1 cup Bone Broth
1 tsp Salt
½ tsp Black Pepper, freshly cracked
2 sprigs dry Thyme
2 sprigs dry Rosemary

DIRECTIONS
- Select SAUTÉ at High and add in the eggplants and sausage. Cook for 5 minutes. Sprinkle with rosemary and thyme, and pour in the broth. Seal the lid, select on BEANS/CHILI and cook for 5 minutes at High. Do quick pressure release.
- In a measuring cup, whisk flour and milk, and season with salt and pepper. Add the mixture to the pressure cooker. Select SAUTÉ, and let simmer for 3 minutes, lid off. Spoon gravy over the toasted split muffins and enjoy.

## Rosemary Dijon-Apple Pork

**Ready in about: 60 minutes | Serves: 6 | Per serving:**
**Calories 513; Carbs 14g; Fat 23g; Protein 61g**

INGREDIENTS
3 pounds Pork Roast
2 Apples, peeled and slices
3 tbsp Dijon Mustard
1 tbsp dried Rosemary
½ cup White Wine
1 cup Water
1 tbsp Garlic, minced
1 tbsp Olive Oil
Salt and Pepper, to taste

DIRECTIONS
- Brush the pork with mustard. Heat oil on SAUTÉ at High, and sear the pork on all sides, for a few minutes. Add apples and stir in the remaining ingredients. Seal the lid and cook for 40 minutes on MEAT/STEW at High.
- When ready, release the pressure naturally, for 10 minutes. The internal temperature should be at least 160 F.

## Short Ribs with Red Wine Gravy

**Ready in about: 70 minutes | Serves: 4 | Per serving:**
**Calories 479; Carbs 4g; Fat 31g; Protein 46**

INGREDIENTS
2 pounds boneless Beef Short Ribs, cut into 3-inch pieces
1 tsp Kosher Salt
½ tsp ground Black Pepper
½ Onion, chopped
½ cup Red Wine
3 tbsp Oil
½ tbsp Tomato paste
2 Carrots, sliced

DIRECTIONS
- Rub the ribs on all sides with salt, and black pepper. Heat the oil on SAUTÉ at High, and brown short ribs on all sides, 3-5 minutes per side, working in batches. Remove ribs to a plate.
- Add onions and cook for 3-5 minutes, until tender. Pour in wine and tomato paste to deglaze by scraping any browned bits from the bottom of the cooker. Cook for 2 minutes until wine has reduced slightly.
- Return ribs to pot and cover with carrots, garlic, parsley, rosemary, and oregano. Pour beef broth over ribs and vegetables. Hit Cancel to stop SAUTÉ mode at High. Seal the lid, and select MEAT/STEW at High Pressure for 35 minutes. When ready, let pressure release naturally for 10 minutes. Transfer ribs to a plate.
- Remove and discard vegetables and herbs. Stir in mushrooms. Press SAUTÉ at High and cook until mushrooms are soft, 2-4 minutes. In a bowl, add water and cornstarch and mix until smooth.
- Pour this slurry into broth, stirring constantly, until it thickens slightly, 2 minutes. Season gravy with salt and pepper to taste. Pour over the ribs and garnish with minced parsley to serve.

## Fast Onion-Flavoured Pork Ribs

**Ready in about: 35 minutes | Serves: 4 | Per serving:**
**Calories 355; Carbs 8g; Fat 19g; Protein 28g**

INGREDIENTS
1 ½ cups Tomato Puree
1 tbsp Garlic, minced
1 ½ cups Water
½ tsp Black Pepper
1 tsp Salt
½ tsp dried Sage
1 ¼ cups Sweet Onions
½ cup Carrots, thinly sliced
1 lb cut Pork Spare Ribs

DIRECTIONS
- Brown the ribs on SAUTÉ. Pour in water and tomato puree. Add the remaining ingredients. Seal the lid and cook for 30 minutes on BEANS/CHILI at High. Once ready, do a quick pressure release and serve.

## Apple Pork Ribs

**Ready in about: 40 minutes | Serves: 4 | Per serving:**
**Calories 432; Carbs 28g; Fat 3g; Protein 47g**

INGREDIENTS
½ cup Apple Cider Vinegar
2 pounds Pork Ribs
3 ½ cups Apple Juice

DIRECTIONS
- Pour apple juice and apple cider vinegar into the pressure cooker and lower the trivet. Place the pork ribs on top of the trivet and seal the lid. Cook on BEANS/CHILI at High pressure for 30 minutes.
- Once it goes off, let the valve drop on its own for a natural release, for about 10 minutes.

## BBQ Pork Rib Chops with Root Vegetables

**Ready in about: 30 minutes | Serves: 4 | Per serving:**
**Calories 332; Carbs 42g; Fat 7g; Protein 29g**

INGREDIENTS
4 Pork Rib Chops
1 cup Carrots, thinly sliced
1 cup Turnips, thinly sliced
1 cup Onions, slice into rings
1 ½ cups BBQ sauce
2 cups Water

DIRECTIONS
- Add the pork cutlets in your cooker. Pour in half cup of BBQ sauce and 2 cups of water. Select on BEANS/CHILI mode. Stir in the onions, turnip, and carrots. Lock the lid and cook for 20 minutes at High.
- Once ready, release the pressure quickly. Open the lid, drizzle with the remaining BBQ sauce and serve.

## Pork Chops with Apple Cider

⏱ Ready in about: **35 minutes** | Serves: **4** | Per serving: Calories 402; Carbs 20g; Fat 21g; Protein 28g

INGREDIENTS
1 lb Pork Fillets
½ lb Granny Smith apples, peeled, cored and cut into wedges
2 Leeks, white part only, cut into rings
2 tbsp Olive Oil
1 ¼ cups Cider
1 tsp Chilli Pepper
Kosher Salt and ground Black Pepper, to taste
1 tsp dry Rosemary
1 tsp dry Thyme

DIRECTIONS
- On SAUTÉ mode at High, heat 1 tbsp of olive oil. Season the pork with salt, black and cayenne pepper. Brown the fillets for about 4 minutes per side. Set aside. Heat the remaining oil in the pressure cooker.
- Add in leeks and sauté until soft, for about 4 minutes. Add in apples, rosemary, thyme and pour in cider. Place the pork loin among the apples and leeks. Seal the lid and cook for 25 minutes on MEAT/STEW at High.
- Once cooking is complete, perform a quick pressure release and remove the lid. To serve, arrange the pork on a plate and pour the apple leeks mixture over the pork tenderloins.

## Savory Fettuccine with Beef Sausage

⏱ Ready in about: **40 minutes** | Serves: **6** | Per serving: Calories 512; Carbs 58g; Fat 10g; Protein 23g

INGREDIENTS
1 pound Beef Sausage, chopped
1 pound dried Fettuccine Pasta
½ cup dry White Wine
1 clove Garlic, minced
½ cups Green Peas, frozen
½ Chipotle Pepper, seeded and chopped
1 cup Black Beans, soaked overnight
2 Yellow Bell Peppers, seeded and chopped
2 tsp Olive Oil
2 cups Water
1 cup Scallions, chopped
1 (28 ounce) can whole plum Tomatoes
¼ tsp crushed Red Pepper flakes
1 cup Parmesan cheese, shredded
½ tsp dried Basil
½ tsp dried Oregano
1 tsp Salt
¼ tsp ground Black Pepper
Fresh Parsley, for garnish

DIRECTIONS
- Heat the oil, and sauté the scallions, peppers, and garlic for 3 minutes on SAUTÉ mode at High. Stir in the beef sausage. Sear until lightly browned, for about 3-4 minutes.
- Add the remaining ingredients, except for the parsley and parmesan cheese.
- Add more water if needed. Seal the lid, Select BEANS/CHILI mode and cook for 10 more minutes at High Pressure.
- Once ready, do a quick release. Stir in parmesan cheese until melted. Serve sprinkled with parsley.

## Sloppy Joes and Coleslaw

⏱ Ready in about: **30 minutes** | Serves: **6** | Per serving: Calories 313; Carbs 18g; Fat 22g; Protein 24g

INGREDIENTS
1 cup Tomatoes, chopped
1 Onion, chopped
1 Carrot, chopped
1 pound Ground Beef
1 Bell Pepper, chopped
½ cup Rolled Oats
4 tbsp Apple Cider Vinegar
1 tbsp Olive Oil
4 tbsp Tomato Paste
1 cup Water
2 tsp Garlic Powder
1 tbsp Worcestershire Sauce
1 ½ tsp Salt

**COLESLAW:**
½ Red Onion, chopped
1 tbsp Honey
½ head Cabbage, sliced
2 Carrots, grated
2 tbsp Apple Cider Vinegar
1 tbsp Dijon Mustard

DIRECTIONS
- Warm olive oil on SAUTÉ at High, and brown the meat for 3-4 minutes.
- Sauté onions, carrots, pepper, garlic, and salt, until soft. Stir in tomatoes, vinegar, Worcestershire sauce, water, and paste.
- When starting to boil, stir in the oats. Seal the lid, select BEANS/CHILI for 25 minutes at High. Do a quick pressure release. Mix all slaw ingredients in a large bowl. Serve the sloppy joes with the slaw.

## Tomato Meatballs

⏱ Ready in about: **30 minutes** | Serves: **4** | Per serving: Calories 329; Carbs 12g; Fat 16g; Protein 34g

INGREDIENTS
1 pound Ground Beef
½ cup Breadcrumbs
½ Onion, diced
1 tsp Garlic, minced
1 Egg
1 tsp dried Parsley
1 tsp dried Thyme
¼ tsp Salt
¼ tsp Black Pepper
1 ½ cups Tomato Juice
1 cup canned Diced Tomatoes
1 tbsp Brown Sugar
¼ tsp Garlic Powder
¼ tsp Oregano
Cooking Spray, to grease

DIRECTIONS

- Combine the first 9 ingredients in a bowl. Mix well with hands. Shape the mixture into meatballs, about 4. Coat the Pressure cooker with cooking spray.
- Place meatballs in the cooker and brown them for a few minutes, on SAUTÉ mode at High. Stir in the remaining ingredients. Seal the lid and cook for 20 minutes on MEAT/STEW at High.
- When ready, release the pressure quickly and serve hot.

## Mexican Brisket

**Ready in about: 55 minutes | Serves: 6 | Per serving: Calories 407; Carbs 3g; Fat 30g; Protein 30g**

INGREDIENTS
2 ½ pounds Beef Brisket
1 tbsp Chili Powder
1 tbsp Tomato Paste
½ cup Salsa
1 cup Beef Broth
1 tbsp Butter
1 Spanish Onion, sliced
2 Garlic Cloves, minced

DIRECTIONS
- Season the beef with chili powder. Coat the pressure cooker with cooking spray and cook the beef until browned on all sides, for about 4 – 6 minutes.
- Add onion and cook for 2 more minutes, until soft. Stir in the remaining ingredients. Seal the lid and cook for 35 minutes on MEAT/STEW at High. Do a natural release, for 10 minutes.

## Beef Stew with Quinoa

**Ready in about: 50 minutes | Serves: 8 | Per serving: Calories 285; Carbs 49g; Fat 8g; Protein 31g**

INGREDIENTS
2 pounds Lean Beef Stew Meat, cut into cubes
2 tbsp Cayenne Pepper
2 tsp Fish Sauce
2 (14.5 oz) cans Tomatoes
2 cups Quinoa, rinsed
½ tsp Red Pepper flakes, crushed
Salt and freshly ground Black Pepper, to taste
4 cups Water

DIRECTIONS
- Select SAUTÉ mode at High and add the beef; brown it for 5 minutes, stirring occasionally. Add the rest of the ingredients. Seal the lid, press MEAT/STEW button and cook for 30 minutes at High Pressure.
- When ready, do a quick release. Taste and adjust the seasoning. Fluff quinoa with a fork and serve.

## Mustard Rump Roast with Potatoes

**Ready in about: 65 minutes | Serves: 6 | Per serving: Calories 559; Carbs 63g; Fat 11g; Protein 51g**

INGREDIENTS
3-pound Rump Roast
6 medium Red Potatoes, quartered
1 Onion, diced
1 Celery Stalk, chopped
1 ½ tbsp Dijon Mustard
2 cups Beef Broth
1 tbsp Butter
2 Garlic Cloves, minced
Salt and Pepper, to taste

DIRECTIONS
- Heat the oil on SAUTÉ mode at High. Add onion and celery, and cook for a few minutes, until soft. Brush the mustard over the beef and season with salt and pepper.
- Place in the cooker and sear on all sides, for a few minutes. Stir in the remaining ingredients and seal the lid. Cook for 45 minutes on MEAT/STEW at High. Do a natural release, for 10 minutes.

## Traditional Beef Ragu

**Ready in about: 60 minutes | Serves: 6 | Per serving: Calories 276; Carbs 18g; Fat 11g; Protein 31g**

INGREDIENTS
18 ounces Beef Stew Meat, cubed
2 Bay Leaves
5 Garlic Cloves, crushed
7 ounces jarred Roasted Red Peppers, chopped
28 ounces canned crushed Tomatoes, undrained
1 tbsp Parsley, chopped
½ cup Beef Broth
½ tbsp Olive Oil
1 tsp Sea Salt
½ tsp Black Pepper

DIRECTIONS
- Season the beef with salt and pepper. Heat the oil on SAUTÉ at High, and place the beef inside. Cook until the meat is browned on all sides. Add the rest of the ingredients and stir to combine.
- Seal the lid, select MEAT/STEW mode for 45 minutes at High pressure. When ready, wait for the valve to drop on its own for a natural pressure release, for about 10 minutes.

## Spicy Shredded Beef

**Ready in about: 55 minutes | Serves: 8 | Per serving: Calories 346; Carbs 7g; Fat 15g; Protein 46g**

INGREDIENTS
3 pounds Beef Roast
½ cup Ketchup
½ cup Red Wine
1 cup Water
2 tsp Soy Sauce
1 tbsp Brown Sugar
1 tbsp Balsamic Vinegar
2 tbsp Onions, minced
2 tsp Mustard Powder
1 tsp Chili Powder
1 tsp Garlic, minced
¼ tsp Nutmeg
½ tsp Cinnamon ground
1 tsp Black Pepper
¼ tsp Salt
¼ tsp Ginger powder

DIRECTIONS

- Place the beef in your pressure cooker. Whisk together the remaining ingredients in a bowl. Pour this mixture over the beef. Seal the lid and cook for 40 minutes on MEAT/STEW mode at High.
- When ready, release the pressure naturally, for 10 minutes.

## Bourbon and Apricot Meatloaf

Ready in about: **30 minutes** | Serves: **4** | Per serving: **Calories 523; Carbs 58g; Fat 13g; Protein 34g**

INGREDIENTS

1 ½ cups Water

**MEATLOAF:**

1 pound Ground Beef
1 Egg White
cup Breadcrumbs
2 tbsp Ketchup
cup Onion, diced
½ tsp Basil
1 tsp Garlic, minced

**GLAZE:**

1 cup Apricot Jam
½ cup Bourbon
½ cup Barbecue Sauce
¼ cup Honey
1 tbsp Hot Sauce

DIRECTIONS

- Combine all of the meatloaf ingredients in a bowl. Mix well with hands and shape into a meatloaf. Place on a greased pan that can fit in your pressure cooker. Whisk the glaze ingredients in another bowl.
- Brush this mixture over the meatloaf. Place a trivet and pour in the water. Place the baking dish on top of the trivet, and seal the lid. Cook for 50 minutes on MEAT/STEW mode at High. When ready, do a quick pressure release.

## Beef Hot Pot

Ready in about: **40 minutes** | Serves: **4** | Per serving: **Calories 542; Carbs 78g; Fat 19g; Protein 11g**

INGREDIENTS

1 ½ pounds Beef Stew Meat, cubed
2 Carrots, chopped
2 Celery Stalks, chopped
4 Potatoes, diced
1 Onion, chopped
2 cups Water
2 tbsp Red Wine
2 tbsp Olive Oil
4 tbsp Flour
1 tsp Thyme
Salt and Pepper, to taste

DIRECTIONS

- In a bowl, mix in flour, salt, and pepper. Toss the beef. Heat oil on SAUTÉ mode at High. Add the beef and cook until browned, for a few minutes. Add onion and cook until soft, for 2 minutes.
- Stir in the remaining ingredients. Seal the lid and cook for 25 minutes on MEAT/STEW mode at High pressure. When ready, release the pressure naturally, for 10 minutes.

## Beef Sausage and Spinach Stew

Ready in about: **25 minutes** | Serves: **4** | Per serving: **Calories 388; Carbs 49g; Fat 13g; Protein 15g**

INGREDIENTS

1 pound Spinach, shredded
1 pound Beef Sausage, crumbled
2 Cloves Garlic, minced
1 ½ cups Tomatoes, chopped
1 cup Brown rice, cooked
1 cup Onion, chopped
1 tsp Salt
¼ tsp ground Black Pepper
½ cup fresh Parsley, chopped
1 cup Beef Broth

DIRECTIONS

- In a mixing bowl, stir in spinach and fennel seeds. Take half of this mixture to make a bed at the bottom of the cooker. In another bowl, mix in rice, sausage, fresh cilantro, scallions, garlic, salt, and pepper.
- Ladle half of this mixture over the spinach mixture and then, top with another layer of the remaining spinach mixture. Finally, top with the remaining part of the meat mixture.
- In a large-sized mixing bowl, whisk the tomato puree, cider vinegar, and water. Pour over the mixture.
- Select on BEANS/CHILI seal the lid and cook for 15 minutes at High Pressure. Once the cooking is complete, do a quick pressure release. Serve immediately in individual serving bowls.

## Simple Cheesy Meatballs

Ready in about: **30 minutes** | Serves: **4** | Per serving: **Calories 460; Carbs 9g; Fat 28g; Protein 40g**

INGREDIENTS

1 pound Ground Beef
⅓ cup Onion, diced
1 Egg
½ tsp Garlic Powder
½ cup Feta Cheese, crumbled
1 tbsp mixed dried Herbs
½ cup Breadcrumbs
¼ tsp Black Pepper
1 cup canned Cream of Mushroom Soup
½ cup Water
½ cup Cheddar Cheese, grated
Cooking Spray, to grease

DIRECTIONS

- In a bowl, combine the first 8 ingredients. Mix well with hands, and shape into meatballs, about 4. Coat the pressure cooker with spray. Add the meatballs and brown on all sides, for a few minutes, on SAUTÉ at High. Pour in water and soup, seal the lid, and cook for 20 minutes on MEAT/STEW mode at High.
- Do a quick pressure release. Stir in the freshly grated cheddar cheese. Cook for an additional 3 minutes, until the cheese melts, lid off, on SAUTÉ mode at High. Serve immediately.

## No-Fuss Beef Chuck Roast

⌛ **Ready in about: 1 hour | Serves: 6 | Per serving:**
**Calories 485; Carbs 29g; Fat 15g; Protein 48g**

INGREDIENTS
2 pounds boneless Beef Chuck Roast, trimmed
½ pound Carrots, peeled and chopped
2 pounds Yukon Gold Potatoes, chopped
1 (14.5 ounce) can Beef Broth
4 Cloves Garlic, minced
3 tsp Olive Oil
½ pound Celery, chopped
2 Bell Peppers, sliced
1 cup Tomato Paste
2 Yellow Onions, chopped
¼ cup dry White Wine
1 ½ cups Water
3 tsp Flour
½ tsp dried Basil
2 sprigs dried Thyme
Kosher Salt and ground Black Pepper, to taste

DIRECTIONS
- Heat the oil on SAUTÉ mode at High. Brown the beef for 3-4 minutes. Dissolve the cooker with a little bit of beef broth. Stir in the onions and garlic, and sauté for another 3 minutes.
- Stir in the rest of the ingredients, except the flour. Seal the lid and switch the pressure release valve to close. Select MEAT/STEW mode and cook for 50 minutes at High Pressure.
- Once the cooking is complete, do a quick pressure release. Make the slurry by whisking the flour with 1 tbsp. of water. Add to the cooker and place the lid on. Let simmer for about 5 minutes before serving.

## Chuck Roast with Root Vegetables and Herbs

⌛ **Ready in about: 50 minutes | Serves: 8 | Per serving:**
**Calories 403; Carbs 13g; Fat 11g; Protein 52g**

INGREDIENTS
1 pound Sweet Potatoes
½ cup White Wine
1 tbsp Garlic, minced
½ cup Celery Root, peeled and thinly sliced
1 tsp Salt
¼ tsp ground Black Pepper, to taste
2 ½ pounds Chuck Roast
4 tbsp Tomato Puree
1 ½ cups Vegetable Broth
2 sprigs Thyme
1 tsp Rosemary
3 tsp oil
1 cup Onions, thinly sliced
2 Carrots, peeled and thinly sliced

DIRECTIONS
- Season the roast with salt, and black pepper. Heat the oil on SAUTÉ mode at High and brown the beef on all sides. Set aside. Add the veggies to the cooker and cook for about 6 minutes, until lightly browned.
- Return the beef to the cooker, along with the remaining ingredients. Lock the lid and, select MEAT/STEW and cook for 40 minutes at High Pressure. Once ready, do a quick pressure release and serve.

## Beef Coconut Curry

⌛ **Ready in about: 45 minutes | Serves: 4 | Per serving:**
**Calories 541; Carbs 47g; Fat 21g; Protein 41g**

INGREDIENTS
1 Onion, diced
1 cup Milk
4 Carrots, sliced
4 Potatoes, peeled and chopped
1 cup Beef Broth
1 pound Beef, cubed
2 tsp Garlic, minced
2 tbsp Curry Powder
½ tsp Black Pepper
½ tsp Paprika
½ tsp Sea Salt
½ tsp dried Parsley
2 tbsp Olive Oil

DIRECTIONS
- Heat olive oil on SAUTÉ at High. Add garlic and onions, and cook for 2 minutes. Stir in beef and cook until the browned, for a few minutes. Add the remaining ingredients and stir to combine.
- Seal the lid, press BEANS/CHILI, and set the timer to 30 minutes at High pressure. When it goes off, do a quick pressure release. Ladle into serving bowls immediately.

## Sweet Balsamic Beef

⌛ **Ready in about: 55 minutes | Serves: 8 | Per serving:**
**Calories 401; Carbs 30g; Fat 15g; Protein 37g**

INGREDIENTS
3 pounds Chuck Steak, sliced
1 cup Maple Syrup
½ cup Balsamic Vinegar
2 cups Bone Broth
1 tsp Garlic, minced
1 tsp Salt
2 tbsp Olive Oil
1 tsp ground Ginger

DIRECTIONS
- Heat oil on SAUTÉ at High. Season the beef with salt and ginger. Brown on all sides for a few minutes. Stir in the remaining ingredients. Seal the lid and cook for 45 minutes on MEAT/STEW at High. Do a quick release.

## Beef & Russet Potatoes Soup

⌛ **Ready in about: 35 minutes | Serves: 6 | Per serving:**
**Calories 273; Carbs 18g; Fat 8g; Protein 29g**

INGREDIENTS
1 pound Beef Stew Meat, cut into cubes
1 ½ Russet Potatoes, diced
2 Tomatoes, chopped
1 cup stalk Celery, chopped

1 cup Carrots, diced
1 cup Spring Onion, chopped
5 cups Beef Broth
Sea Salt and ground Black Pepper, to taste
½ cup fresh Cilantro, chopped
DIRECTIONS
- In your pressure cooker mix in all ingredients, except for the fresh cilantro. Select SOUP mode and adjust the cooking time for to 30 minutes at High pressure.
- Seal the lid and switch the pressure release valve to close. Once the cooking is complete, allow for natural pressure release, for 10 minutes. Open the lid and stir in fresh cilantro. Serve warm and enjoy!

## Spicy Beef and Pinto Bean Chili

Ready in about: **25 minutes** | Serves: **6** | Per serving: Calories 255; Carbs 12g; Fat 11g; Protein 35g

INGREDIENTS
1 ½ pounds Ground Beef
1 tbsp Chili powder
2 Green Bell Peppers, stemmed, seeded, and chopped
1 tsp Garlic, minced
2 Tomatoes, chopped
2 (14 oz) cans Pinto Beans, drained and rinsed
1 cup Red Onion, chopped
1 cup Beef Broth
2 tsp Grapeseed Oil
½ tsp dried Oregano
½ tsp dried Basil
DIRECTIONS
- Heat oil on SAUTÉ at High, and add onions and green peppers. Stir-fry for about 3-4 minutes, until translucent. Add in garlic and cook for about 30 seconds. Add the rest of the ingredients.
- Seal and switch the pressure release valve to close. Select BEANS/CHILI, and cook for 15 minutes at High pressure. Once the cooking is complete, perform a quick pressure release. Serve immediately.

## Russet Potatoes Flank Steak

Ready in about: **50 minutes** | Serves: **8** | Per serving: Calories 402; Carbs 38g; Fat 9g; Protein 41g

INGREDIENTS
1 pound Beef Flank Steak, cut into serving portions
2 Red Onions, peeled and sliced
1 pound Russet Potatoes, peeled and diced
½ Jalapeño Pepper, deveined and thinly sliced
2 Bell Peppers, deveined and thinly sliced
1 cup Celery with leaves, chopped
3 Cloves Garlic, peeled and minced
2 cups Water
2 Carrots, diced
1 6-ounce can Tomato Paste
Salt and ground Black Pepper, to taste
DIRECTIONS
- Place the meat in the cooker. Set on SAUTÉ at High and brown the meat on all sides, for about 7- 8 minutes. Set aside.
- Lay the vegetables at the bottom of your pressure cooker and place on top of the steak. In a deep bowl, mix in the remaining ingredients; give it a good stir, and pour over the meat.
- Seal the lid, select MEAT/STEW and cook for 30 minutes at High. Do a quick pressure release, and serve.

## Beef and Cabbage with Tomato Sauce

Ready in about: **50 minutes** | Serves: **5** | Per serving: Calories 293; Carbs 10g; Fat 11g; Protein 32g

INGREDIENTS
1 ½ pound Ground Beef
3 cups Cabbage, shredded and stems removed
1 cup Leeks, chopped
1 (10.75 oz) can Tomato Soup
1 tbsp Garlic, pressed
1 tbsp Olive Oil
1 tsp Mustard powder
1 Bay Leaf
Sea Salt and ground Black Pepper, to taste
DIRECTIONS
- Heat olive oil on SAUTÉ mode at High. Cook leeks and garlic in hot oil for about 5 minutes. Stir in ground beef, mustard, cabbage, tomato soup, and bay leaf and cook for about 10 minutes, stirring frequently.
- Season with salt and pepper. Seal the lid, select BEANS/CHILI mode and cook for 30 minutes at High pressure. Once the cooking is complete, do a quick pressure release, and serve.

## Sticky Baby Back Ribs

Ready in about: **55 minutes** | Serves: **4** | Per serving: Calories 228; Carbs 36g; Fat 7g; Protein 8g

INGREDIENTS
3 pounds Baby Beef Racks, cut into individual bones
2 tsp Olive Oil
1 cup Beer
Salt and Black Pepper to taste
12 ounces Barbecue Sauce
½ tsp Onion Powder
¼ tsp Paprika
¼ tsp Garlic Powder
DIRECTIONS
- Mix all spices in a small bowl. Pour the mixture over meat; turn ribs to coat. Heat oil on SAUTÉ at High, and sear the meat for 3 minutes per side, until browned. Insert the rack, arrange the ribs on top, and pour the beer over. Seal the lid, set to MEAT/STEW for 35 minutes, at High.
- Do a quick release. Pour barbecue sauce over the ribs. Simmer for 5 minutes until sticky, on SAUTÉ.

## Saucy Beef and Rice

Ready in about: **30 minutes** | Serves: **4** | Per serving: Calories 358; Carbs 64g; Fat 7g; Protein 8g

INGREDIENTS
2 tsp Salt
2 pounds Sirloin Steaks, cut into pieces
2 tbsp Vegetable Oil

2 Onions, chopped
½ tsp Paprika
¼ tsp Mustard Powder
½ tsp Black Pepper
3 tbsp Flour
2 Garlic Cloves, minced
4 cups cooked Rice
10 ½ ounces Beef Consommé

DIRECTIONS
- In a plastic bag, mix flour, mustard powder, salt, pepper, and paprika. Add beef and shake the bag to coat well. Heat oil and sear the meat on all sides, until browned, about 5-6 minutes, on SAUTÉ at High.
- Add the onions and garlic and cook until translucent. Stir in the beef consommé. Seal the lid press MEAT/STEW and adjust the time to 25 minutes at High. Do a quick pressure release. Let simmer, lid off, for a few minutes until desired consistency.

## Beef & Tomato Soup

Ready in about: **20 minutes** | Serves: **4** | Per serving: Calories 295; Carbs 12g; Fat 23g; Protein 18g

INGREDIENTS
1 cup diced Onions
1 cup Chicken Broth
1 cup Milk
1 ½ cups Ground Beef
30 ounces Tomatoes, diced
3 tsp Garlic, minced
¼ cup chopped Basil
1 tbsp Olive Oil

DIRECTIONS
- Heat oil on SAUTÉ at High, add the beef, and cook until browned on all sides. Add onions and garlic, and saute for 2 minutes, until soft. Meanwhile, blend tomatoes and milk in the blender. When the mixture becomes smooth, pour over the beef. Add the rest of the ingredients and stir to combine well.
- Seal the lid, select BEANS/CHILI mode for 5 minutes, High pressure. When the timer goes off, let the valve to drop on its own for a natural pressure release, for about 10 minutes.

## Ginger-Flavored and Sweet Pork Belly

Ready in about: **1 hour** | Serves: **4** | Per serving: Calories 525; Carbs 11g; Fat 55g; Protein 64g

INGREDIENTS
2 pounds Pork Belly, cut into pieces
1 tbsp Blackstrap Molasses
2 tbsp Coconut Aminos
3 tbsp Sherry
3 cups Water
2 tbsp Maple Syrup
1-inch Piece of Ginger, smashed
A pinch of Sea Salt

DIRECTIONS
- Bring 2 cups of water to a boil, on SAUTÉ. Add the pork belly and let boil for 3 minutes. Drain and rinse with cold water. Return the pork to the cooker, and stir in the maple syrup.
- Stir in the remaining ingredients, and 1 cup of water. Seal the lid, select the MEAT/STEW mode, and set the timer to 30 minutes at High. When ready, do a quick pressure release.

## Shredded Beef the Caribbean Way

Ready in about: **1 hour** | Serves: **4** | Per serving: Calories 562; Carbs 3g; Fat 57g; Protein 57g

INGREDIENTS
2 pounds Beef Roast
½ tsp Turmeric
1 tsp grated Ginger
1 cup Water
4 Whole Cloves
1 tsp dried Thyme
1 tsp Garlic Powder
1 tbsp Olive Oil

DIRECTIONS
- Rub olive oil onto the roast to coat. Mix the turmeric, garlic, thyme, and ginger in a small bowl, and rub the mixture into the meat. Stick the cloves into the beef roast. Place the beef inside your pressure cooker and pour the water around it.
- Seal the lid, and set to 50 minutes on MEAT/STEW mode, at High pressure. When cooking is over, do a quick pressure release. Shred the meat to serve.

## Port Wine Garlicky Lamb

Ready in about: **30 minutes** | Serves: **4** | Per serving: Calories 587; Carbs 9g; Fat 35g; Protein 60g

INGREDIENTS
2 pounds Lamb Shanks
1 tbsp Olive Oil
½ cup Port Wine
1 tbsp Tomato Paste
10 Whole Garlic Cloves, peeled
½ cup Chicken Broth
1 tsp Balsamic Vinegar
½ tsp dried Rosemary
1 tbsp Butter

DIRECTIONS
- Season lamb shanks with salt and pepper. Warm the oil and brown the lamb shanks on all sides, about 2-3 minutes, on SAUTÉ at High. Add the garlic and cook until fragrant. Stir in the rest of the ingredients, except for the butter and vinegar.
- Lock and seal the lid, set on MEAT/STEW and adjust the timer to 35 minutes at High pressure. Do a quick pressure release. Remove lamb shanks and let the sauce boil for 5 minutes. lid off on SAUTÉ mode at High. Stir in vinegar and butter. Serve the gravy poured over the shanks.

## Pork Loin Chops with Sauerkraut

Ready in about: **35 minutes** | Serves: **4** | Per serving: Calories 383; Carbs 11g; Fat 18g; Protein 22g

INGREDIENTS
4 Pork Loin Chops, boneless
4 cups Sauerkraut, shredded
1 cup dry White Wine

cloves Garlic, peeled and crushed
1 cup Carrots, coarsely chopped
½ cup Celery, coarsely chopped
2 Onions, sliced
2 cups Vegetable Stock
2 tsp Mustard
1 tsp Salt
½ tsp Chili powder
½ cup Tomato Paste
½ tsp ground Black Pepper

DIRECTIONS
- Place the pork on the bottom of the pressure cooker. Add the shredded cabbage on top of the pork.
- Add in the remaining ingredients and seal the lid. Select BEANS/CHILI and cook for 30 minutes at High Pressure. Once cooking is done, do a quick pressure release. Serve immediately.

## Pork with Tangy Tomato Sauce

**Ready in about: 35 minutes | Serves: 6 | Per serving: Calories 503; Carbs 11g; Fat 41g; Protein 32g**

INGREDIENTS
1 ½ pounds Pork Shoulder, cubed
1 cup Tomato Sauce
½ cups Buttermilk
1 cup Green Onions, chopped
2 tsp Butter, melted
¼ tsp Chili Pepper
3 Garlic Cloves, minced
½ tbsp Cilantro
Salt and Black Pepper, to taste

DIRECTIONS
- Select SAUTÉ at High and melt butter. Cook onions and minced garlic until soft, 2-3 minutes. Add the remaining ingredients, except for the buttermilk. Sea the lid and cook for 25 minutes on MEAT/STEW at High.
- Once cooking is complete, do a quick pressure release. Stir in the sour cream until well incorporated.

## Cheesy Rigatoni with Pancetta

**Ready in about: 30 minutes | Serves: 6 | Per serving: Calories 481; Carbs 2g; Fat 32g; Protein 19g**

INGREDIENTS
1 ½ box Penne Pasta
6 slices Pancetta, fried and crumbled
½ cup Grana Padano cheese, grated
1 cup Cottage cheese
3 tsp Olive Oil
1 cup Yellow Onions, finely chopped
3 Garlic Cloves, finely minced
3 ½ cups Vegetable Broth
1 ½ cups Water
2 sprigs dry Rosemary
Salt and freshly ground Black Pepper, to taste

DIRECTIONS
- Add rigatoni, broth, water, salt, black pepper, and rosemary to your pressure cooker. Seal the lid, select BEANS/CHILI for 12 minutes at High Pressure. Once ready, do a quick pressure release. Set aside.
- Select SAUTÉ at High and melt the butter. Cook onions and garlic, until fragrant, about 2-3 minutes. Add pancetta, cottage cheese, and rigatoni mixture back to the cooker, and toss until everything is well mixed.
- Serve immediately topped with freshly grated Grana Padano cheese.

## Delicious Pork Shoulder with White Cabbage

**Ready in about: 25 minutes | Serves: 6 | Per serving: Calories 203; Carbs 13g; Fat 2g; Protein 25g**

INGREDIENTS
1 head Cabbage, shredded
½ cup Vegetable Stock
4 Cloves Garlic, finely minced
2 Red Onions, chopped
1 cup Tomato Puree
3 Tomatoes, chopped
1 ¼ pounds Pork Shoulder, boneless, cut into cubes
1 Bay Leaf
½ tsp Paprika, crushed
Salt and Black Pepper, to taste

DIRECTIONS
- Select SAUTÉ at High and add the pork, onions and garlic. Cook the pork until lightly browned. Remove any **fat**. Add in the remaining ingredients.
- Seal the lid, press on BEANS/CHILI and cook for 15 minutes at High. Once cooking is complete, do a quick pressure release. Discard the bay leaf and serve.

## Braised Chili Pork Chops

**Ready in about: 30 minutes | Serves: 4 | Per serving: Calories 437; Carbs 11g; Fat 24g; Protein 44g**

INGREDIENTS
4 Pork Chops
1 Onion, chopped
2 tbsp Chili Powder
14 ounces canned Tomatoes with Green Chilies
1 Garlic Clove, minced
½ cup Beer
½ cup Vegetable Stock
1 tsp Olive Oil
Salt and Pepper, to taste

DIRECTIONS
- Heat oil on SAUTÉ mode at High. Add onion, garlic, and chili powder and cook for 2 minutes. Add the pork chops and cook until browned on all sides. Stir in the tomatoes, broth, and beer. Season with salt and pepper.
- Seal the lid and cook for 20 minutes on BEANS/CHILI at High. Quick release the pressure and serve hot.

## Pork Butt with Mushrooms and Celery

Ready in about: **354 minutes** | Serves: **8** | Per serving: **Calories 318; Carbs 2g; Fat 20g; Protein 29g**

INGREDIENTS
1 pound Pork Butt, sliced
2 cups Mushrooms, sliced
1 ½ cups Celery Stalk, chopped
½ cup White Wine
1 tsp Garlic, minced
½ cup Chicken Broth
½ tsp Salt
¼ tsp Black Pepper
Cooking spray, to grease

DIRECTIONS
- Grease with cooking spray and heat on SAUTÉ mode at High. Brown the pork slices and for a few minutes.
- Stir in the remaining ingredients. Season with salt and pepper. Seal the lid and cook for 25 minutes on MEAT/STEW at High. When done, do a quick release.

## Pork Ribs in Walnut Sauce

Ready in about: **30 minutes** | Serves: **4** | Per serving: **Calories 273; Carbs 4g; Fat 16g; Protein 27g**

INGREDIENTS
1 pound Pork Ribs
¼ cup Roasted Walnuts, chopped
4 Garlic Cloves, minced
1 ½ cups Beef Broth
2 tbsp Apple Cider Vinegar
3 3 tbsp Butter
½ tsp Red Pepper Flakes
1 tsp Sage
Salt and Black Pepper, to taste

DIRECTIONS
- Melt butter on SAUTÉ at High. Season the ribs with salt, pepper, sage, and pepper flakes. Place them in the pressure cooker and brown, for about 5 minutes. Stir in the remaining ingredients.
- Seal the lid.
- Cook for 20 minutes on BEANS/CHILI at High. Release the pressure quickly. Serve drizzled with the sauce.

## Pork Chops and Mushrooms in Tomato Sauce

Ready in about: **35 minutes** | Serves: **4** | Per serving: **Calories 446; Carbs 18g; Fat 21g; Protein 42g**

INGREDIENTS
4 large Bone-In Pork Chops
1 cup Tomato Sauce
1 ½ cups White Button Mushrooms, sliced
1 Onion, chopped
1 tsp Garlic, minced
½ cup Water
1 tbsp Oil
Salt and Black Pepper, to taste

DIRECTIONS
- Heat oil on SAUTÉ. Add garlic, onion and cook for 2 minutes, until soft and fragrant. Add pork and cook until browned on all sides. Stir in the remaining ingredients and seal the lid.
- Cook for 25 minutes on MEAT/STEW mode at High. When ready, do a quick pressure release.

## Citrusy Beef

Ready in about: **90 minutes** | Serves: **6** | Per serving: **Calories 477; Carbs 8g; Fat 36g; Protein 35g**

INGREDIENTS
Juice of 1 Lemon
Juice of 2 Oranges
2 pounds Beef, cut into chunks
1 tbsp Butter
1 tbsp Italian Seasoning
½ tsp Sea Salt

DIRECTIONS
- Place the beef in the pressure cooker and sprinkle with salt, pepper, and seasoning. Massage the meat with hands to season it well. Pour the lemon and orange juice over and seal the lid.
- Select MEAT/STEW for 50 minutes, at High pressure. When the timer goes off, do a quick pressure release. Shred the meat inside the pot with two forks. Set to SAUTÉ mode at High, lid off.
- Stir to combine well and cook for about 20 minutes, or until the liquid is absorbed. Add butter, give it a good stir, and cook for an additional 5 minutes.

## Chuck Roast with Potatoes

Ready in about: **50 minutes** | Serves: **6** | Per serving: **Calories 441; Carbs 20g; Fat 17g; Protein 53g**

INGREDIENTS
2 ½ pounds Chuck Roast
1 pound Red Potatoes, chopped
2 Carrots, chopped
½ cup Parsnip, chopped
1 cup Onions, sliced
½ cup Red Wine
½ Celery Stalk, sliced
1 tbsp Rosemary
1 tsp Thyme
½ tsp Pepper
½ tsp Salt
2 tbsp Tomato Paste
1 tbsp Garlic, minced
1 cup Beef Broth

DIRECTIONS
- Coat the cooker with cooking spray. In a bowl, combine the thyme, rosemary, salt, and pepper and rub the mixture onto the meat. Place the meat inside the cooker and sear on all sides.
- Add the remaining ingredients and seal the lid. Set to MEAT/STEW for 40 minutes at High. Once the cooking is over, do a quick pressure release. Serve and enjoy!

## Beef Medley with Blue Cheese

⌛ **Ready in about: 50 minutes | Serves: 6 | Per serving: Calories 267; Carbs 6g; Fat 13g; Protein 30**

INGREDIENTS
1 pound Sirloin Steak, cut into cubes
6 ounces Blue Cheese, crumbled
½ Cabbage, diced
1 cup Parsnip, chopped
2 Red Bell Peppers, chopped
1 cup Beef Broth
2 cups canned Tomatoes, undrained
1 Onion, diced
1 tsp Garlic, minced
Salt and Black Pepper, to taste
Cooking spray, for greasing

DIRECTIONS
- Coat the cooker with cooking spray and add the sirloin steak. On SAUTÉ at High, brown the steak on all sides, for a few minutes. Then, add the remaining ingredients, except for the cheese.
- Seal the lid and cook for 40 minutes on MEAT/STEW mode at High. Once cooking is complete, release the pressure quickly. Top with blue cheese, to serve.

## Steak and Veggies with Ale Sauce

⌛ **Ready in about: 50 minutes | Serves: 6 | Per serving: Calories 370; Carbs 32g; Fat 11g; Protein 36g**

INGREDIENTS
2 pounds Beef Steak, cut into 6 or 8 equal pieces
1 Sweet Onion, chopped
1 cup Celery, chopped
1 pound Sweet Potatoes, diced
2 Carrots, chopped
3 Garlic Cloves, minced
2 Bell Peppers, chopped
1 ½ cups Tomato Puree
1 cup Ale
1 Chicken Bouillon Cube
Salt and Pepper, to taste
1 tbsp Olive Oil

DIRECTIONS
- Heat oil on SAUTÉ at High and sear the steaks, for a few minutes. Then, set aside. Press CANCEL. Arrange the veggies in the pressure cooker and top with the steak.
- In a bowl, whisk together bouillon cube, ale, and tomato puree. Pour over the steaks. Season with salt and pepper, and seal the lid. Cook for 30 minutes on MEAT/STEW at High. Quick-release the pressure.

## Beef Cabbage Rolls

⌛ **Ready in about: 25 minutes | Serves: 10 | Per serving: Calories 467; Carbs 36g; Fat 17g; Protein 36g**

INGREDIENTS
10 Cabbage Leaves, blanched
1 ½ pounds Ground Beef
2 cups Rice
22 ounces canned, diced, Tomatoes
1 tbsp Garlic, minced
15 ounces Tomato Sauce
½ Cup Water
1 Onion, chopped
½ tsp Cayenne Pepper
Salt and Pepper, to taste

DIRECTIONS
- In a bowl, combine the beef, rice, cayenne pepper, garlic, diced tomatoes, and onions. Spoon mixture between the cabbage rolls and roll them up.
- Arrange the rolls in the cooker. Pour the tomato sauce on top, and add the water. Seal the lid, select SOUP and adjust to 20 minutes at High. Wait 5 minutes before doing a release.

## Beer-Dijon Braised Steak

⌛ **Ready in about: 40 minutes | Serves: 4 | Per serving: Calories 525; Carbs 12g; Fat 21g; Protein 69g**

INGREDIENTS
4 Beef Steaks
12 ounces Dark Beer
2 tbsp Dijon Mustard
2 Carrots, chopped
1 tbsp Tomato Paste
1 Onion, chopped
1 tsp Paprika
2 tbsp Flour
1 cup Beef Broth
Salt and Pepper, to taste
Olive oil, to grease

DIRECTIONS
- Brush the meat with the mustard and season with paprika, salt, and pepper. Coat the pressure cooker with cooking spray and sear the steak on SAUTÉ mode at High. Remove steaks to a plate.
- Press CANCEL. Pour ¼ cup water and scrape the bottom of the cooker. Wipe clean. Whisk in the tomato paste and flour. Gradually stir in the remaining ingredients, except for the beer.
- Return the steak to the cooker, pour in beer and seal the lid. Cook for 25 minutes on MEAT/STEW mode at High. When ready, release the pressure quickly and serve hot.

## Beef with Creamy Sour Sauce

⌛ **Ready in about: 35 minutes | Serves: 6 | Per serving: Calories 340; Carbs 10g; Fat 19g; Protein 33g**

INGREDIENTS
1 ½ pounds Beef Roast, cubed
1 cup Onion, diced
1 can Cream of Mushroom Soup
1 ½ cups Sour Cream
½ cups Water
½ tbsp Cumin
½ tbsp Coriander
1 tbsp Garlic, minced
1 tbsp Butter
½ tsp Chili Powder
Salt and Pepper, to taste

DIRECTIONS
- Melt butter on SAUTÉ at High and stir in the onion. Stir-fry until soft, for about 3 minutes. Add garlic and cook for one more minute. Add beef and cook until browned, for about 3 – 5 minutes.
- Combine the remaining ingredients in a bowl and pour this mixture over the beef. Seal the lid and cook for 25 minutes on MEAT/STEW mode at High. Once done, do a quick release.

## Smothered Cinnamon BBQ Ribs

Ready in about: **75 minutes** | Serves: **6** | Per serving: **Calories 422; Carbs 25g; Fat 13g; Protein 47g**

INGREDIENTS
3 pounds Pork Ribs
½ cup Apple Jelly
1 cup Barbecue Sauce
1 Onion, diced
2 tbsp ground Cloves
½ cup Water
1 tbsp Brown Sugar
1 tsp Worcestershire Sauce
1 tsp ground Cinnamon

DIRECTIONS
- Whisk together all ingredients in your pressure cooker, except the ribs. Place the ribs inside and seal the lid.
- Set the cooker to MEAT/STEW and cook for 45 minutes at High. Release the pressure naturally, for 10 minutes.

## Onion Steaks in Gravy

Ready in about: **30 minutes** | Serves: **4** | Per serving: **Calories 445; Carbs 6g; Fat 21g; Protein 53g**

INGREDIENTS
4 Round Steaks
2 Onions, sliced
1 ½ cups Beef Broth
1 tsp Garlic, minced
1 tbsp dried Parsley
½ tsp Rosemary
1 tbsp Oil
½ tsp Red Pepper Flakes
¼ cup Half and Half
2 tbsp Flour
¼ tsp Salt
¼ tsp Black Pepper

DIRECTIONS
- Heat the oil on SAUTÉ mode at High. Add the beef and brown the steaks on all sides. Remove to a plate. Sauté the onions and garlic for 2 minutes, until translucent and fragrant.
- Return the steaks to the pressure cooker. Stir in the salt, pepper, pepper flakes, rosemary, parsley, and pour in broth. Seal the lid and cook for 25 minutes on MEAT/STEW at High.
- When ready, do a quick pressure release, and stir in the flour and half and half. Cook for 3 more minutes, until thickened, with the lid off, on SAUTÉ mode at High. Serve immediately.

## Ground Beef and Sauerkraut

Ready in about: **25 minutes** | Serves: **6** | Per serving: **Calories 337; Carbs 8g; Fat 20g; Protein 30g**

INGREDIENTS
1 ½ pounds Ground Beef
10 ounces canned Tomato Soup
½ cup Beef Broth
3 cups Sauerkraut
1 cup sliced Leeks
1 tbsp Butter
1 tsp Mustard Powder
Salt and Pepper, to taste

DIRECTIONS
- Melt butter on SAUTÉ at High. Add leeks and cook for a few minutes, until soft. Add beef and brown, for a few minutes. Stir in the sauerkraut, broth and mustard powder and season with salt and pepper.
- Seal the lid and cook for 20 minutes on SOUP mode at High. When ready, do a quick pressure release.

## Beef Ribs with Button Mushrooms

Ready in about: **30 minutes** | Serves: **6** | Per serving: **Calories 509; Carbs 9g; Fat 43g; Protein 22g**

INGREDIENTS
1 ½ pounds Beef Ribs
2 cups White Button Mushrooms, quartered
1 Onion, chopped
¼ cup Ketchup
2 cups Veggie Stock
1 cup chopped Carrots
¼ cup Olive Oil
1 tsp Garlic, minced
Salt and Pepper, to taste

DIRECTIONS
- Heat the oil on SAUTÉ mode at High. Season the ribs with salt and pepper, and brown them on all sides. Then, set aside. Add the onion, garlic, carrots, and mushrooms and cook for 5 minutes.
- Add the ribs back to the cooker and stir in the remaining ingredients. Seal the lid and cook for 35 minutes on MEAT/STEW at High pressure. When cooking is over, do a quick release.

## Veal Shoulder and Mushrooms

Ready in about: **45 minutes** | Serves: **4** | Per serving: **Calories 521; Carbs 42g; Fat 17g; Protein 53g**

INGREDIENTS
2 pounds Veal Shoulder, cut into chunks
16 ounces Shallots, chopped
16 ounces Potatoes, chopped
10 ounces Beef Stock
8 ounces Mushrooms, sliced
3 ½ tbsp Olive Oil
2 tbsp Chives, chopped
2 ounces White Wine
1 tsp Garlic, minced

1 tbsp Flour
1 tsp Sage
DIRECTIONS
- Heat 1 ½ tbsp oil on SAUTÉ at High, add veal and coat with flour. Cook until browned. Stir 2 tbsp of the oil and cook the mushrooms for 3 minutes. Add onions and garlic, and cook for 2 minutes, until soft and translucent.
- Pour in the wine, stock, and sage, and stir. Seal the lid and cook on SOUP mode for 20 minutes at High pressure. When cooking is over, release the pressure quickly. Serve and enjoy!

## Potted Rump Steak

Ready in about: **35 minutes** | Serves: **15** | Per serving: Calories 616; Carbs 11g; Fat 34g; Protein 59g

INGREDIENTS
3 tbsp Olive Oil
3 Bay Leaves
9 pounds Rump Steak
2 cups Celery, diced
1 tsp Salt
3 Onions, chopped
2 cups Mushrooms, sliced
18 ounces canned Tomato Paste
10 ½ ounces Beef Broth
1 ½ cups Dry Red Wine
DIRECTIONS
- Warm the oil on SAUTÉ at High, and brown the steak on all sides. Add the vegetables and stir in all of the seasonings. Combine the paste with the wine and broth.
- Add this mixture to the cooker. Seal the lid, set on MEAT/STEW for 35 minutes at High. When ready, do a quick release.

## Pot Roast in Gravy

Ready in about: **1 hour 10 minutes** | Serves: **8** | Per serving: Calories 324; Carbs 21g; Fat 10g; Protein 37g

INGREDIENTS
3-4 pounds Beef Roast
1 Onion, peeled and quartered
3 ½ tbsp Cornstarch
1 ½ quarts Peach Juice
1 cup Beef Broth
3 ounces Cold Water
2 Garlic Cloves, minced
2 tbsp Olive Oil
Salt and Pepper, to taste
DIRECTIONS
- Generously season the beef with salt and pepper. Warm olive oil and add the pot roast; brown on all sides, for about 5-6 minutes per side, on SAUTÉ at High. Remove to a plate. Add onions and garlic and cook for 2 minutes.
- Pour beef broth to deglaze the bottom of your cooker's pot. Return the beef, seal the lid, select MEAT/STEW for 50 minutes at High. Do a quick pressure release, remove the roast to a plate and leave to rest.
- Whisk the water and cornstarch together and stir into the juice in the cooker. Simmer, lid off, until the gravy thickens. Slice the meat and pour the gravy over.

## Herbed Lamb Roast with Potatoes

Ready in about: **60 minutes** | Serves: **4** | Per serving: Calories 562; Carbs 2g; Fat 51g; Protein 56g

INGREDIENTS
6 pounds Leg of Lamb
1 tsp dried Sage
1 tsp dried Marjoram
1 Bay Leaf, crushed
1 tsp dried Thyme
3 Garlic Cloves, minced
3 pounds Potatoes, cut into pieces
2 tbsp Olive Oil
3 tbsp Arrowroot Powder
½ cup Water
2 cups Chicken Broth
Salt and Pepper, to taste
DIRECTIONS
- Combine the herbs with salt and pepper and rub the mixture onto the meat. Melt the butter and brown the lamb on all sides, about 3-4 minutes, on SAUTÉ at High. Pour the broth around the meat, seal the lid, and cook for 45 minutes on MEAT/STEW mode at High pressure.
- When cooking is over, release the pressure quickly, and add the potatoes. Seal the lid and turn the pressure valve to close. Set on BEANS/CHILI mode at High for 10 minutes.
- Once cooking is complete wait 5 minutes before releasing the pressure quickly. Transfer the meat and potatoes to a plate. Combine the water and arrowroot and stir the mixture into the pot sauce. Pour the gravy over the meat and potatoes and enjoy.

## Lamb Habanero Chili

Ready in about: **50 minutes** | Serves: **4** | Per serving: Calories 332; Carbs 21g; Fat 13g; Protein 41g

INGREDIENTS
1 pound Ground Beef
3 Carrots, chopped
3 Celery Stalks, chopped
1 Bell Pepper, chopped
1 Onion, diced
1 Habanero, minced
1 tsp Garlic, minced
14 ounces canned diced Tomatoes
1 tbsp Chili Powder
1 tsp Cumin
2 cups Chicken Broth
½ tsp Paprika
½ tsp Sea Salt
½ tsp Pepper
1 tbsp Olive Oil
DIRECTIONS
- Add the onions and cook for 3 minutes, on SAUTÉ mode at High. Add garlic and cook for 1 minute. Stir in the ground beef and cook until lightly browned, for a few minutes.

- Add the remaining ingredients, and give it a good stir. Seal the lid, select the MEAT/STEW mode, and set the timer to 35 minutes at High pressure. Do a natural pressure release, for about 10 minutes.

## Lamb Stew with Apricots

**Ready in about: 40 minutes | Serves: 4 | Per serving: Calories 422; Carbs 14g; Fat 19g; Protein 43g**

INGREDIENTS

1 pound Lamb, cubed
4 dried Apricots, diced
1 tsp Garlic, minced
1 Onion, diced
2 Potatoes, peeled and chopped
2 Carrots, peeled and chopped
2 ½ cups Chicken Broth
3 cups chopped Kale
28 ounces diced canned Tomatoes
½ tsp Cinnamon
1 tsp Cumin
½ tsp Ginger Powder
¼ tsp Allspice
¼ tsp Pepper
½ tsp Sea Salt
1 tbsp Olive Oil

DIRECTIONS
- Heat oil on SAUTÉ at High, add the lamb and cook until browned on all sides. Add onions and cook for 3 more minutes. When softened a bit, stir in the garlic, and sauté only for a minute.
- Stir in all remaining ingredients, and seal the lid. Press the BEANS/CHILI, and set the timer to 20 minutes at High pressure. When it goes off, do a quick pressure release.

## Marinated Flank Steak

**Ready in about: 80 minutes | Serves: 4 | Per serving: Calories 589; Carbs 43g; Fat 21g; Protein 55g**

INGREDIENTS

2 pounds Flank Steak
1 cup Beef Broth
1 Onion, diced
2 tbsp Potato Starch
1 Carrot, chopped
Cooking Spray, to grease

**MARINADE:**

2 tbsp Fish Sauce
½ tsp Cajun Seasoning
2 tsp Garlic, minced
½ cup Soy Sauce
1 tbsp Sesame Oil

DIRECTIONS
- Combine marinade ingredients in a bowl. Add in the beef and let marinate for 30 minutes. Coat the pressure cooker with cooking spray. Add onions and carrots and cook until soft on SAUTÉ at High. A

- dd the beef along with the marinade. Whisk in the broth and starch. Seal the lid and cook for 40 minutes on MEAT/STEW at High. Do a quick release and serve.

## Corned Beef with Celery Sauce

**Ready in about: 50 minutes | Serves: 6 | Per serving: Calories 287; Carbs 8g; Fat 20g; Protein 18g**

INGREDIENTS

1 ½ pounds Corned Beef Brisket
2 cups Cream of Celery Soup
1 tsp Garlic, minced
1 Onion, diced
1 cup Water
2 Tomatoes, diced
2 tsp Olive Oil
Salt and Black Pepper, to taste

DIRECTIONS
- Season the beef with salt, and black pepper. Heat oil on SAUTÉ, and stir onions. Cook for 2 minutes, until translucent. Add garlic and cook for 1 minute. Add beef and sear on all sides, for a few minutes.
- Pour in soup and water. Seal the lid, cook for 40 minutes on MEAT/STEW at High. Do a quick pressure release.

## Tender Onion Beef Roast

**Ready in about: 55 minutes | Serves: 8 | Per serving: Calories 369; Carbs 9g; Fat 16g; Protein 47g**

INGREDIENTS

3 pounds Beef Roast
2 Large Sweet Onions, sliced
1 envelope Onion Mix
1 cup Beef Broth
1 cup Tomato Juice
1 tsp Garlic, minced
2 tbsp Worcestershire Sauce
1 tbsp Olive Oil
Salt and Pepper, to taste

DIRECTIONS
- Warm the oil on SAUTÉ mode at High. Season the beef with salt and pepper, and sear on all sides. Transfer to a plate. Add onions, and cook for 3 minutes. Stir in garlic and cook for 1 minute.
- Add the beef and stir in the remaining ingredients. Seal the lid and cook for 40 minutes on MEAT/STEW at High. Release the pressure naturally, for 10 minutes.

## Herbed Beef & Yams

**Ready in about: 50 minutes | Serves: 6 | Per serving: Calories 391; Carbs 22g; Fat 27g; Protein 43g**

INGREDIENTS

1 Onion, diced
2 Yams, peeled and cubed
1 tbsp Basil, chopped
1 tbsp Parsley, chopped
1 tbsp Coriander, chopped
2 pounds Beef, cubed

1 tsp Garlic, minced
1 ½ cups Bone Broth
3 tbsp Tomato Paste
1 Bell Pepper, chopped
1 tbsp Olive Oil
DIRECTIONS
- Heat oil on SAUTÉ at High. Add the peppers and onions and cook for about 3 minutes. Stir in the garlic and sauté for another minute. Add the beef and cook until browned on all sides. Add the rest of the ingredients.
- Stir to combine. Seal the lid and cook on BEANS/CHILI mode, at High pressure for 30 minutes. When it goes off, do a quick pressure release. Meat Recipes

## London Broil in Slow Cooker

Easy and creamy taste for any occasion!

⌛ **Prep time: 11 minutes Cooking time: 10 hours**
**Servings: 8**

INGREDIENTS:
1 pack dry onion soup
2 pounds flank steak
Condensed tomato soup
Condensed mushroom soup
DIRECTIONS:
- Grease your Slow Cooker with olive oil or melted unsalted butter.
- Place the meat into Slow Cooker and arrange evenly over the bottom. If needed, cut it into smaller pieces to fit.
- In a separate bowl, combine tomato and mushroom soups. Mix until smooth and pour over the meat.
- Add the dry onion soup mixture sprinkles.
- Cook under the cover for 10 hours, use LOW temperature mode.
- To serve, arrange the Slow Cooker meal over a nice serving plate. You can also serve it with favorite side dish.

**Nutrition: Calories: 198 Fat: 11g Carbohydrates: 9g Protein: 15g**

## Three Packs roast mix

Just three spice mixes for amazing taste!

⌛ **Prep time: 12 minutes Cooking time: 6 hours**
**Servings: 6**

INGREDIENTS:
Beef chuck roast
1 pack ranch dressing mix
2 pack dry Italian salad dressing
One cup water
Dry brown gravy mix
DIRECTIONS:
- If needed, discard the bones from chuck roast. Remove the skin and fat, and all the other excess parts.
- In a bowl, mix ranch dressing mix, Italian dressing mix and brown gravy mix. Combine until smooth.
- Pour one cup water into a bowl and whisk well.
- Transfer the beef roast into Slow Cooker and pour over with the spicy sauce. Turn on Slow Cooker and cook on LOW mode for 6 to 8 hours.

- To serve, prepare fresh leaves of salad or tortillas and place the hot roast mix on them.

**Nutrition: Calories: 610 Fat: 46g Carbohydrates: 6g Protein: 39g**

## Mongolian Beef in Slow Cooker

Your kids and friends will love this!

⌛ **Prep time: 28 minutes Cooking time: 4 hours**
**Servings: 4**

INGREDIENTS:
1 flank steak
Half cup hoisin sauce
Cornstarch
Half tsp minced ginger
2 tsp olive oil
Half cup brown sugar
1 onion
3 green onions
Half cup soy sauce
1 tbsp minced garlic
DIRECTIONS:
- Coat the flank steak with a cornstarch. Rub to coat evenly. Preheat the large skillet with olive oil over medium heat.
- Place the steak over the skillet and brown until it is evenly brown – just for 4 minutes. Set aside to cool a little bit.
- Add sliced diagonally green onions, water, garlic, steak, onion, ginger, sugar and hoisin sauce to Slow Cooker.
- Carefully place cooled pork into Slow Cooker mixture.
- Set Slow Cooker to LOW temperature setting and cook for 4 hours.

**Nutrition: Calories: 450 Fat: 13g Carbohydrates: 55g Protein: 28g**

## Sweet Pork in Slow Cooker

Serve this with vegetables and make a healthy dinner for your family!

⌛ **Prep time: 12 minutes Cooking time: 8 hours**
**Servings: 6**

INGREDIENTS:
Dry spaghetti
Soy sauce
Canned water chestnuts
3 cloves garlic
1 cup snow peas
2 tbsp brown sugar
2 stalks celery
Pork shoulder
1 tsp sesame oil
2 carrots
1 tbsp oyster sauce
3 cups broccoli florets
1 tbsp chile paste
DIRECTIONS:
- Grease your Slow Cooker or line it with parchment paper.
- In a separate bowl, whisk chili paste, soy sauce, brown sugar, minced ginger and garlic, oil. Place the pork shoulder into Slow Cooker and pour it over with whisked sauce.

- Cover the lid and cook on a LOW temperature for 8 hours. Separately cook spaghetti according to package instructions. Serve immediately, meat atop the pasta.

**Nutrition: Calories: 506 Fat: 8g Carbohydrates: 72g Protein: 32g**

## Shoyu Pork Recipe for Slow Cooker

Cook it to infuse the delicate taste and flavors!

**Prep time: 11 minutes Cooking time: 8 hours**
**Servings: 9**

INGREDIENTS:
One cup sake
1 pork butt roast
3 cloves garlic
1 cup white sugar
Canned tomato sauce
Soy sauce

DIRECTIONS:
- Grease your Slow Cooker using some olive oil or spray with anti-sticking-effect cooking spray. Transfer pork roast into Slow Cooker.
- In a bowl, mix sugar, tomato paste, sake, minced garlic and soy sauce. Whisk everything until smooth.
- Pour the sauce mixture into Slow Cooker. Cover your Slow Cooker with the lid. Set Slow Cooker to LOW temperature regime and prepare for 10 hours.
- In an hour before the pork is ready, prepare your favorite side dish or just serve the meat with vegetables.
- Serve the meal while it is still hot.

**Nutrition: Calories: 427 Fat: 17g Carbohydrates: 30g Protein: 27g**

## Ham and Pineapple in Slow Cooker

Amazing holiday dish for all your family!

**Prep time: 11 minutes Cooking time: 7 hours**
**Servings: 14**

INGREDIENTS:
Cola-flavored carbonated beverage
1 picnic ham
Canned pineapple rings
Water (additional)

DIRECTIONS:
- Start with preheating your Slow Cooker. Cut ham into thick slices.
- Drain the pineapple rings and attach the ham slice to each ring (you can use toothpicks). Place pineapples with ham into Slow Cooker and pour in remaining pineapple juice.
- Pour cola into Slow Cooker. If needed, add water to cover the ingredients.
- Cook on LOW mode for 8 or 10 hours. Check occasionally the readiness of the meal. Stir time after time.
- To serve, use a large cooking plate garnished with vegetables.

**Nutrition: Calories: 382 Fat: 23g Carbohydrates: 9g Protein: 30g**

## Pork Spare Ribs in Slow Cooker

Tender and delicious for your friends or family!

**Prep time: 14 minutes Cooking time: 8 hours**
**Servings: 5**

INGREDIENTS:
2 tbsp soy sauce
Cold water (optional)
Condensed tomato soup
Worcestershire sauce
1 tsp cornstarch
Medium onion
Brown sugar
Pork spareribs
3 cloves garlic

DIRECTIONS:
- In a large pot, bring the ribs to boil and simmer for 13 minutes.
- In a bowl, combine onion, brown sugar, Worcestershire sauce, onion, soy sauce and soup. Drain ribs and place them in Slow Cooker. Carefully arrange the ribs on the bottom of the crockpot, so they will be cooked through.
- Pour the ribs over with the sauce mixture.
- Cook under the lid for 8 hours, using a LOW temperature mode.
- To cook sauce, drain some liquid from Slow Cooker and combine with cornstarch.

**Nutrition: Calories: 483 Fat: 31g Carbohydrates: 18g Protein: 31g**

## Puerto Rican styled Pork

So much tender and flavors!

**Prep time: 19 minutes Cooking time: 6 hours**
**Servings: 6**

INGREDIENTS:
One lime
4 cloves garlic
Pork loin roast
Large onion
White wine vinegar
Chopped fresh oregano
Olive oil
Ground cumin
Black pepper
Ground ancho chili pepper
Salt to taste

DIRECTIONS:
- Combine quartered onion, cumin, garlic, chili pepper, black pepper, oregano and salt.
- To grease your Slow Cooker, use slightly melted and unsalted butter, or just coat with cooking spray.
- Pour in vinegar and olive oil. Blend until smooth.
- Carefully place pork loin into Slow Cooker and cover it with blended mixture. Set your Slow Cooker to LOW mode and cook for 8 hours.
- To serve, cut the meat into chunks and garnish with lime wedges or preferred vegetables.

**Nutrition: Calories: 367 Fat: 21g Carbohydrates: 5g Protein: 37g**

## Juicy Turkey Breast in Slow Cooker

Quick and delicious dish!

⏱ **Prep time: 17 minutes Cooking time: 8 hours**
**Servings: 12**

INGREDIENTS:
Dry onion soup mix
Salt
Olive oil
Black pepper
1 turkey breast with bone in

DIRECTIONS:
- Wash turkey breast under running water. Discard the excess skin, if needed, except breast skin. Leave the bones in the breast.
- Grease your Slow Cooker with butter or oil. If you like, you may also use a cooking spray. Mix species and rub the turkey with the mix, along with the breast parts under the skin.
- Transfer turkey to Slow Cooker. Stir the mixture and spread it evenly over the bottom. Cook on HIGH for 1 hour. Then, cook for 7 hours on LOW mode.
- When the meal is ready, serve it on a beautiful plate. Garnish with chopped vegetables and salad leaves.

**Nutrition: Calories: 273 Fat: 1g Carbohydrates: 1g Protein: 58g**

## Black Beans with Pork Tenderloin

Healthy and satisfying recipe!

⏱ **Prep time: 18 minutes Cooking time: 10 hours**
**Servings: 12**

INGREDIENTS:
Pork tenderloin
pinch chili powder
small onion
ground cumin
1 can salsa
oregano
Half cup chicken broth
Small red bell pepper
3 cans black beans

DIRECTIONS:
- In a bowl, combine salsa, black beans, red pepper, onion, cumin, chili powder and oregano. Rub pork tenderloin with pork mixture and place into Slow Cooker.
- Carefully, trying not to wash species off, pour in chicken broth.
- Set Slow Cooker to LOW temperature mode and cook for 9 to 10 hours. Break up pork pieces before serving, so you can get a thickened chili.
- Serve over cooked rice or any other side dish you prefer.

**Nutrition: Calories: 248 Fat: 31g Carbohydrates: 31g Protein: 24g**

## Slow Cooker Chuck and Potato Roast

Juicy and delicious pork with vegetables!

⏱ **Prep time: 15 minutes Cooking time: 9 hours**
**Servings: 8**

INGREDIENTS:
Chuck roast
1 stalk celery
Salt
3 carrots
Black pepper
Onion soup mix
1 onion
water
3 great potatoes

DIRECTIONS:
- Peel and cube potatoes. Dice potatoes into quarters. Chop the other vegetables. Season the meat with salt and pepper to your taste.
- Use a large skillet with olive oil to brown meat from all sides (approximately 4 minutes per one size).
- Put the roast into Slow Cooker.
- Arrange chopped vegetables around it and season with soup mix. Pour in one cup water. Stir all ingredients to combine well.
- Set slow cooker to LOW and cover the lid. Cook for 9 hours or more, if needed.

**Nutrition: Calories: 540 Fat: 30g Carbohydrates: 18g Protein: 45g**

## Beef Barbacoa with Tomato Sauce

It could be served over tortillas or simply with vegetables!

⏱ **Prep time: 17minutes Cooking time: 6 hours**
**Servings: 7**

INGREDIENTS:
1 onion
Salt
Beef chuck roast
Garlic powder
Chili powder
Black pepper
3 tbsp white vinegar
Canned tomato sauce

DIRECTIONS:
- Grease your Slow Cooker and place the roast in it.
- Cover with chopped onion, black pepper, bay leaves, vinegar, garlic powder. Toss the cooking dish just to be sure that everything is well combined.
- Pour in the water to cover completely. Set Slow Cooker to HIGH temperature.
- Remove meat from Slow Cooker and drain any excess liquids.
- To serve, shred meat and mix in tomato sauce, salt and chili powder. Place back to Slow Cooker for another 2 hours.

**Nutrition: Calories: 292 Fat: 19g Carbohydrates: 9g Protein: 22g**

## Cranberry Pork in Slow Cooker

Tangy and sweet recipe for your family!

⏱ **Prep time: 11 minutes Cooking time: 4 hours**
**Servings: 6**

INGREDIENTS:
Pork loin roast
Canned cranberry sauce
Large onion
5 tbsp French salad dressing

DIRECTIONS:
- Wash pork meat under running water and drain with paper towels.

- In a separate bowl, combine cranberry sauce, chopped onion and French salad dressing. Stir well. Grease your Slow Cooker with plain unsalted butter before you start using it.
- Transfer pork to Slow Cooker and cover with the sauce.
- Cover the lid and leave to cook for 8 hours (use a LOW temperature mode). Serve with chopped vegetables or simply make sandwiches.

**Nutrition: Calories: 374 Fat: 15g Carbohydrates: 32g Protein: 26g**

## Slow Cooker Beef Lasagna

Easy and delicious meal for the weekend!

⏲ **Prep time: 24 minutes Cooking time: 4 hours**
**Servings: 10**

INGREDIENTS:
Shredded Mozzarella cheese
Lean ground beef
Parmesan cheese
Salt
One onion
Cottage cheese
Canned tomato paste
One pack lasagna noodles
Canned tomato sauce
Dried oregano
4 cloves garlic
DIRECTIONS:
- Take a large skillet and preheat it with olive oil. Fry ground beef with onion and garlic until brown.
- Add tomato paste and sauce, season with oregano and salt. When heated through, set aside. In a bowl, combine shredded cheeses and toss well.
- Pour one spoon of meat mixture into Slow Cooker, top with noodles and cheese. Repeat layers until the end.
- Cook under the lid for 6 hours on LOW mode.

**Nutrition: Calories: 446 Fat: 20g Carbohydrates: 35g Protein: 31g**

## Pork Chops for Slow Cooker

Easy and delicious creamy recipe!

⏲ **Prep time: 32 minutes Cooking time: 2 hours**
**Servings: 12**

INGREDIENTS:
Large onion
Salt
Water
Dry onion soup
Pepper
Canned mushroom soup
Trimmed pork chops
Ranch dressing mix
DIRECTIONS:
- Grease your Slow Cooker with melted butter and start to preheat it on low temperature mode. Meanwhile, cut the onion and spread a half of it over the bottom of Slow Cooker.
- Place the chops over onion and cover with remaining onion. If needed, arrange pork chops in layers.

- Mix cream of onion soup and cream of mushroom soup over pork chops. Season with onion soup mix, salt, ranch dressing and black pepper.
- Cover. Cook on HIGH for 3 hours.
- Serve the chops while hot, with mashes or vegetable dishes.

**Nutrition: Calories: 273 Fat: 10g Carbohydrates: 9g Protein: 25g**

## Slow Cooker Beef Chops

Perfect and tender for all members of your family!

⏲ **Prep time: 14 minutes Cooking time: 8 hours**
**Servings: 6**

INGREDIENTS:
1 tbsp butter
1 beef tongue
Water
2 cloves garlic
Ground pepper and salt
1 bay leaf
Small onion
DIRECTIONS:
- Gather chopped onion, beef tongue, bay leaf and garlic in your Slow Cooker. Combine the ingredients well.
- Season with salt and black pepper to your taste. Pour in enough water to cover the ingredients.
- Turn on your Slow Cooker and set to LOW temperature. Cook during 8 hours.
- Take out the tongue and remove all excess skin and rough end. Cut into small bite-sized slices. Preheat butter in a large skillet and cook chopped tongue for 10 minutes.
- Serve the beef chops along with mashed potatoes or fresh vegetables.

**Nutrition: Calories: 492 Fat: 38g Carbohydrates: 1g Protein: 32g**

## Leg of Lamb with Herbs

Super easy and delicious for any taste!

⏲ **Prep time: 23 minutes Cooking time: 7 hours**
**Servings: 6**

INGREDIENTS:
Fresh cracked pepper
1 lamb leg
Dried thyme
Sea salt
1 juiced lemon
Half cup red wine
Dried rosemary
3 cloves garlic
2 tbsp Dijon mustard
1 tbsp apple cider vinegar
2 tbsp raw honey
DIRECTIONS:
- Grease your Slow Cooker with melted butter or oil.
- Take a lamb leg of room temperature, if using frozen – leave it on the table for several hours. Pour the wine into your Slow Cooker.
- In a bowl, combine sea salt, thyme, black pepper, rosemary, garlic, mustard, honey and lemon juice.

- When the sauce is thick, massage it into lamb leg. Cook for 5 hours on LOW temperature level.
- You can serve lamb as a main dish along with mashers or hot rice.

**Nutrition: Calories: 285 Fat: 14g Carbohydrates: 10g Protein: 25g**

## Apple-Cider Marinated Pork

You will get not only pork, but flavored sauce for it!

*Prep time: 5 minutes  Cooking time: 7 hours*
*Servings: 8*

INGREDIENTS:
1 bay leaf
2 cups apple cider
2 tbsp cold butter
Salt
2 shallots
4 cloves garlic
1 tbsp chopped herbs
Half cup apple cider vinegar
1 tbsp vegetable oil
Cayenne pepper
1 tsp Dijon mustard
1 rib celery
Ground black pepper

DIRECTIONS:
- Season pork with salt and pepper and bring to brown on a large skillet. Transfer to Slow Cooker. In the same skillet, cook celery, shallots and cider vinegar. Pour into Slow Cooker.
- Add garlic cloves, apple cider and bay leaf.
- Cook on LOW for 6 hours. Turn pork time after time.
- When ready, preheat the Slow Cooker mixture in a saucepan; add cayenne pepper and Dijon mustard. Set aside and mix in cold butter and fresh herbs.
- Serve the meat along with the sauce.

**Nutrition: Calories: 388 Fat: 25g Carbohydrates: 13g Protein: 23g**

## Pepperoncini Beef in Slow Cooker

Super easy filling for any sandwiches!

*Prep time: 22 minutes  Cooking time: 8 hours*
*Servings: 8*

INGREDIENTS:
16 slices provolone cheese
1 beef chuck roast
8 hoagie rolls
1 jar pepperoncini
4 cloves garlic

DIRECTIONS:
- First of all, grease your Slow Cooker as you like, using plain unsalted butter or preferred olive oil. Cut the beef into small cuts.
- Finely chop garlic and place each slice into cuts in chuck roast.
- Place your chuck roast into Slow Cooker and cover with canned pepperoncini along with its liquid. Cover the lid and cook on LOW mode for 8 hours. Do not forget to open the lid time after time and stir the contents of Slow Cooker.
- Serve as a stuffing for sandwiches along with cheese, fresh salad leaves, and vegetables.

**Nutrition: Calories: 998 Fat: 52g Carbohydrates: 71g Protein: 55g**

## Chili Beef Soup

Easy and very quick receipt!

*Prep time: 22 minutes  Cooking time: 6 hours*
*Servings: 6*

INGREDIENTS:
Lean ground beef
Half cup red wine
Salt
Dash Worcestershire sauce
3 cans dark kidney beans
Dried parsley
3 cans stewed tomatoes
2 tbsp chili powder
Cumin
Red wine vinegar
2 stalks celery
1 red bell pepper

DIRECTIONS:
- Take a large skillet and fry beef until it is evenly browned. Drain and season with pepper and salt just a little.
- Right in Slow Cooker, combine kidney beans, chopped celery and red bell pepper, tomatoes and red wine vinegar. Stir all the ingredients until smooth consistence.
- Place the cooked beef into Slow Cooker. Stir one more time. Cook on LOW mode for 8 hours.
- During the last 2 hours of cooking, pour in red wine.

**Nutrition: Calories: 414 Fat: 11g Carbohydrates: 49g Protein: 28g**

## Juicy Kalua Pig in Slow Cooker

Try this traditional Hawaiian meal right in your Slow Cooker!

*Prep time: 11 minutes  Cooking time: 20 hours*
*Servings: 11*

INGREDIENTS:
1-2 tbsp Hawaiian sea salt
1 pork butt roast
1 tbsp liquid smoke flavoring

DIRECTIONS:
- To start, wash pork meat with running water and pierce it with carving fork.
- Grease your Slow Cooker with melted butter or spray with anti-stick spray for cooking. Season meat with sea salt and liquid smoke. Rub species into the meat.
- Transfer pork to Slow Cooker and cook on LOW mode from 16 to 20 hours. Remember to stir kalua pig for several times during cooking.
- Remove meat from cooking pot and finely shred.
- Serve along with mashed potatoes, pasta or simply on sandwiches with fresh salad leaves.

**Nutrition: Calories: 243 Fat: 14g Carbohydrates: 1g Protein: 25g**

## Slow Cooker Braciole in Slow Cooker

Cook classical Italian dish in your Slow Cooker!

⏱ Prep time: 28 minutes  Cooking time: 6 hours
Servings: 6

INGREDIENTS:
2 tbsp vegetable oil
2 jars marinara sauce
5 slices bacon
2 chicken eggs
1 cup Italian cheese blend
Half cup bread crumbs
Black pepper
1 flank steak
1 tsp salt

DIRECTIONS:
- Preheat the marinara sauce into Slow Cooker on high mode.
- Meanwhile, combine breadcrumbs and chicken eggs in a separated bowl. Sprinkle meat with salt and pepper from all sides.
- Place breadcrumbs, bacon slices and shredded cheese mix over one side of meat. Carefully roll and secure with toothpicks or string.
- Brown stuffed flank over preheated skillet and transfer to Slow Cooker. Cook in Slow Cooker for 8 hours using LOW temperature mode.

Nutrition: Calories: 614 Fat: 36g Carbohydrates: 41g Protein: 28g

## Greek Pulled Pork in Slow Cooker

You can serve it with pasta or simply with chips and dip.

⏱ Prep time: 12 minutes  Cooking time: 4 hours
Servings: 8

INGREDIENTS:
1 pork tenderloin
Canned pepperoncini peppers
Tbsp. Greek seasoning

DIRECTIONS:
- Wash pork tenderloin and carefully place it into Slow Cooker. Drain and dry with paper towels. Sprinkle the meat with Greek seasoning to cover evenly.
- Pour over with canned pepperoncini peppers (sliced ones) along with the liquids. Cover Slow Cooker with the lid and cook for 4 hours on HIGH temperature mode.
- In 15 minutes before serving shred the meat and cook for 10-15 minutes. When it is ready, set aside and let to cool just for several minutes.
- Serve hot with your favorite side dish or simply fresh vegetables.

Nutrition: Calories: 146 Fat: 4g Carbohydrates: 3g Protein: 21g

## Pork with Sauerkraut in Slow Cooker

Easy and delicious dish for your Slow Cooker!

⏱ Prep time: 11 minutes  Cooking time: 8 hours
Servings: 4

INGREDIENTS:
One cup water
Whole pork tenderloin
4 tbsp butter
1 bag baby potatoes
Salt
Canned sauerkraut
Black pepper to taste

DIRECTIONS:
- Grease your Slow Cooker with plain unsalted butter. You can also spray the crockpot with cooking spray, if you like this method more.
- Wash whole pork tenderloin and place it into your Slow Cooker.
- Place unpeeled baby potatoes all around the pork. Arrange the ingredients evenly in layers.
- Cut cooled butter into small cubes and arrange them, along with black pepper and salt, into Slow Cooker.
- Cook until the pork is tender, on LOW mode for 9 hours. Add more water if needed.

Nutrition: Calories: 358 Fat: 14g Carbohydrates: 35g Protein: 22g

## Texas-styled pulled pork

Serve this over buttered or toasted roll!

⏱ Prep time: 14 minutes  Cooking time: 5 hours
Servings: 8

INGREDIENTS:
1 tsp vegetable oil
2 tbsp butter
1 pork shoulder
8 hamburger buns
1 cup barbeque sauce
Dried thyme
Half cup cider vinegar
2 cloves garlic
Half cup chicken broth
1 large onion
3 tbsp light brown sugar
1 tbsp chili powder
1 tbsp yellow mustard
1 tbsp Worcestershire sauce

DIRECTIONS:
- Pour one tablespoon over the bottom of Slow Cooker and place pork roast into it. Combine barbeque sauce, chicken broth and apple cider vinegar over the pork.
- Add yellow mustard, sugar, chili powder, Worcestershire sauce, garlic, thyme and onion. Cook under the lid for 6 hours on HIGH.
- To serve, shred the meat and arrange over the buns.

Nutrition: Calories: 527 Fat: 23g Carbohydrates: 45g Protein: 31g

## Barbacoa Beef in Slow Cooker

Flavored and delicious meat meal from Slow Cooker!

⏱ Prep time: 5 minutes  Cooking time: 8 hours
Servings: 11

INGREDIENTS:
4 canned chipotle peppers

1 head garlic
Half cup apple cider vinegar
Kosher salt
5 bay leaves
4 cups beef stock
4 limes (juiced)
Beef brisket
Ground cloves
Medium red onion
Fresh cilantro

DIRECTIONS:
- Grease your Slow Cooker with melted butter or just coat with cooking spray.
- Right in Slow Cooker dish, combine chipotle peppers, red onion, cilantro, clove, garlic, salt, lime juice and cider vinegar.
- Transfer beef brisket to Slow Cooker and place atop the vegetables. Place the lid on and cook on LOW temperature node for 8 hours.
- To serve, shred beef with two forks and arrange over warmed tortillas, chopped onion or salsa.

**Nutrition: Calories: 452 Fat: 21g Carbohydrates: 62g Protein: 36g**

## Brisket with Yellow Onions

Try this one at a family meeting!

⌀ **Prep time: 17 minutes Cooking time: 8 hours**
**Servings: 12**

INGREDIENTS:
3 yellow onions
Coarse salt
Beef brisket
Worcestershire sauce
2 cups beef broth
Soy sauce
Black pepper

DIRECTIONS:
- On a large and preheated skillet, warm oil and caramelize chopped onions (cook for 20 minutes). Pat beef with paper towels and rub it with salt and pepper. Place beef in skillet and cook until brown.
- Sprinkle minced garlic over beef brisket.
- Add Worcestershire sauce, beef broth and soy sauce.
- Grease your Slow Cooker with melted butter or spray with nonstick cooking spray. Transfer beef to Slow Cooker.
- Cook on LOW temperature mode for 8 hours.
- To serve, arrange beef over the large serving plate and garnish with chopped parsley.

**Nutrition: Calories: 535 Fat: 17g Carbohydrates: 85g Protein: 44g**

## Slow-Cooker Shredded Orange Pork

Awesome dish for family dinner!

⌀ **Prep time: 9 minutes Cooking time: 8 hours**
**Servings: 16**

INGREDIENTS:
Pork butt
Ground cumin
Garlic, smashed
4 chipotle peppers
Cayenne pepper, or to taste
Dried oregano
Orange juice
Ground black pepper

DIRECTIONS:
- Trim all the excess fat from the pork and discard the bones and skin. Transfer all ingredients from the list to Slow Cooker.
- Set your Slow Cooker to LOW temperature mode and leave to cook for 8 hours. You can also leave your dish cooking overnight. When the meat is ready, it will fall off the bone.
- Cool for 25 minutes so you can remove the meat from Slow Cooker. Transfer pork to a large wide bowl and shred with two fork or knives.
- To serve, add the meat into tacos or serve with warm tortillas. You can also serve this with radishes, salad leaves, chopped onions or even lime wedges.

**Nutrition: Calories: 391 Fat: 23g Carbohydrates: 29g Protein: 44g**

## Tater Tot and Beef Casserole

Easy, but tasty and satisfying dish!

⌀ **Prep time: 5 minutes Cooking time: 7 hours**
**Servings: 12**

INGREDIENTS:
2 cans cream soup
1 bag Tater Tots
Browned hamburger
1 bag frozen vegetables
Melted butter

DIRECTIONS:
- Cook the beef in a large skillet. Use medium heat and cook for several minutes until there is no more pink.
- Grease the dish of your Slow Cooker with melted butter. If desired, use special cooking spray. Transfer half bag of Tater Tots into Slow Cooker. Add cream soup and cooked vegetables.
- Top with remaining Tater Tots. Cover the lid.
- Turn on your Slow Cooker and set to LOW temperature mode for 7 hours.
- To serve, arrange meal over a large and wide serving dish. Garnish with fresh herbs and vegetables.

**Nutrition: Calories: 531 Fat: 19g Carbohydrates: 42g Protein: 51g**

## Whole Meat Loaf in Slow Cooker

Slow Cooker will make it mild and flavored!

⌀ **Prep time: 32 minutes Cooking time: 5 hours**
**Servings: 6**

INGREDIENTS:
2 chicken eggs
2 tbsp ketchup
Salt
5 tbsp milk
Ground mustard
Half tsp Worcestershire sauce
Ground beef
Dried minced onion
2 tbsp brown sugar

Half cup seasoned breadcrumbs
Half cup mushrooms
Half tsp sage

DIRECTIONS:
- In a bowl, combine eggs, onion, breadcrumbs, salt, mushrooms and sage. Place ground beef into mixture and crumble well to combine.
- Shape a large meat loaf of this mixture.
- Grease your Slow Cooker with simple or olive oil.
- Transfer loaf into Slow Cooker. Cook for 6 hours on LOW mode.
- In a bowl, combine brown sugar, ketchup, Worcestershire sauce and mustard. Spoon over loaf and cook for 10 minutes.

**Nutrition: Calories: 328 Fat: 17g Carbohydrates: 18g Protein: 24g**

## Bulgari Beef in Slow Cooker

Could be a lazy main dish for your dinner!

⏱ **Prep time: 28 minutes Cooking time: 6 hours Servings: 4**

INGREDIENTS:
1 green onion
Half cup soy sauce
Beef
4 tbsp sesame oil
White sugar
1 tsp ground pepper
2 cloves garlic
Half tsp sesame seeds

DIRECTIONS:
- To start, cut the beef into slices and marinate overnight. To make the meat marinated well, hide it to the refrigerator.
- To make the marinade, whish 1 tablespoon soy sauce, sesame oil and sugar. Add minced garlic and black pepper.
- Leave the beef slices in the refrigerator until the next day.
- In the morning, toast sesame seeds in a skillet. When they become light brown, set aside. Transfer marinated beef along with liquid into Slow Cooker.
- Add green onions and sesame seeds. Cook on LOW mode during 8 hours.

**Nutrition: Calories: 365 Fat: 19g Carbohydrates: 16g Protein: 30g**

## Squirrel and Liver Dish

The perfect meal for the winter season!

⏱ **Prep time: 23 minutes Cooking time: 6 hours Servings: 8**

INGREDIENTS:
Olive oil
Bay leaf
2 cups tomato juice
2 squirrels
Black pepper
1 green bell pepper
6 cloves garlic
Salt
4 carrots
2 sweet onions
Dried thyme

Beef liver
Dried oregano

DIRECTIONS:
- Skin and gut squirrels, slice beef liver into thin strips. Preheat a skillet with olive oil over medium heat.
- Cook liver and squirrels until they are evenly brown on all sides. Place into Slow Cooker. Add chopped vegetables: bell pepper, carrots, garlic and onion.
- Pour in tomato juice. Stir the contents of your Slow Cooker well to combine the ingredients. Season with species, add bay leaf.
- Cook for 6 hours on HIGH temperature mode.

**Nutrition: Calories: 267 Fat: 7g Carbohydrates: 15g Protein: 33g**

## Slow Cooker Burrito Beef Pie

This will fit for any kind of side dishes!

⏱ **Prep time: 14 minutes Cooking time: 5 hours Servings: 16**

INGREDIENTS:
Colby cheese
Ground beef
Canned taco sauce
1 onion
12 flour tortillas
Minced garlic
2 cans refried beans
Canned green chili peppers
Canned tomatoes

DIRECTIONS:
- Start with greasing with olive oil and preheating your Slow Cooker.
- Place ground beef in the large skillet with olive oil. Sauté meat for 5 minutes. Add chopped onion and garlic, cook for another 5 minutes.
- Add olives, tomatoes, peppers, refried beans and taco sauce. Simmer for 15 minutes.
- Grease your Slow Cooker and place several tortillas. Top with a little meat and shredded cheese. Continue layers until it is no ingredients.
- Cook on LOW for 4 to 5 hours.

**Nutrition: Calories: 432 Fat: 23g Carbohydrates: 33g Protein: 20g**

## Small Meatloaves in Slow Cooker

Easy to make and fast to eat!

⏱ **Prep time: 5 minutes Cooking time: 6 hours Servings: 8**

INGREDIENTS:
1 tsp prepared mustard
One chicken egg
5 tbsp ketchup
3 tbsp ground beef
3 tbsp brown sugar
1 cup shredded Cheddar
1 tsp salt
Half cup quick cooking oats

DIRECTIONS:

- Grease and start to preheat your Slow Cooker on high mode. In a bowl, combine milk, chicken egg, oats and cheese.
- Stir in ground beef and combine well until smooth.
- Form eight small meatloaves and carefully place them into Slow Cooker, one by one.
- In a separate bowl, whisk brown sugar, mustard and ketchup. Pour the sauce mixture into Slow Cooker.
- Set to LOW mode and cook for 6 hours.
- To serve, slice meatloaves into portion slices and serve with any of your favorite side dishes.

**Nutrition: Calories: 255 Fat: 14g Carbohydrates: 16g Protein: 15g**

## Island Spiced Kielbasa

Easy and fast meal for lazy days!

**Prep time: 9 minutes Cooking time: 5 hours Servings: 6**

INGREDIENTS:
Canned pineapple chunks
Kielbasa sausage
2 cups brown sugar
2 cups ketchup
Olive oil to grease

DIRECTIONS:
- Grease your Slow Cooker with enough olive oil to cover bottom and sides. Set aside for a little while.
- Slice kielbasa sausage into small pieces – half-inch-sized will be enough.
- Combine kielbasa slices and pineapple chunks and transfer the mix into Slow Cooker.
- In a bowl, mix ketchup and sugar. Pour into Slow Cooker. Make sure that the sauce covered all other ingredients well. Toss to be sure/
- Cover the lid and set your Slow Cooker to LOW mode. Cook for 6 hours. Serve with your favorite side dish or with slices of fresh bread.

**Nutrition: Calories: 866 Fat: 41g Carbohydrates: 98g Protein: 20g**

## Stout Stew for your Slow Cooker

Flavored and hot – the perfect choice for wintertime!

**Prep time: 23 minutes Cooking time: 8 hours Servings: 8**

INGREDIENTS:
Chopped fresh parsley
3 tbsp flour
2 tbsp vegetable oil
Salt
2 cups Irish beer
Beef stew meat
2 yellow onions
2 large potatoes
1 sprig thyme
2 carrots

DIRECTIONS:
- Sprinkle the beef with flour. Toss and rub evenly, just to coat all sides.
- In a large skillet, preheat olive oil and cook beef until even brown color. Drain with paper towels. In Slow Cooker dish, combine diced potatoes, carrots, onions and thyme.
- Add beef and combine.
- Pour the beer all over ingredients.
- Cook on LOW temperature mode for 8 hours.

**Nutrition: Calories: 463 Fat: 22g Carbohydrates: 32g Protein: 27g**

## Philippine Sandwich Meat

Fast, easy and delicious for all your family!

**Prep time: 21 minutes Cooking time: 8 hours Servings: 4**

INGREDIENTS:
2 cubes beef bouillon
Dried thyme
1 can beer
Large onion
Half tsp sauce
3 cloves garlic
1 tsp mustard
Beef sirloin
1 tsp Worcestershire sauce
2 tbsp bourbon whiskey
Ground cumin
Soy sauce
Paprika
Dried basil
Half tsp garlic powder
Black pepper

DIRECTIONS:
- Wash beef sirloin and cut in into two or more strips. Grease your Slow Cooker or just spray with cooking spray.
- Cover the bottom of your Slow Cooker with diced onion and garlic. Layer beef strips atop the vegetables.
- Season with onion powder, black pepper, paprika, cumin and other species. Pour in mixed bourbon, mustard, hot sauce, beer and Worcestershire sauce. Cook on LOW for around 8 hours.

**Nutrition: Calories: 251 Fat: 10g Carbohydrates: 7g Protein: 20g**

## Stuffed Peppers in Slow Cooker

Prepare in the morning – you'll have an awesome dish by the dinner!

**Prep time: 16 minutes Cooking time: 5 hours Servings: 6**

INGREDIENTS:
White rice
Velveeta cheese
Half cup or more water
4 green bell peppers
Half cup barbeque sauce
Frozen peas
Ground pork

DIRECTIONS:
- Remove pepper tops and discard seeds.
- In a bowl, combine peas, ground meat, rice, barbeque sauce and water. Stir well before the mixture is smooth.

- Spoon the pea mixture into hollow pepper shells.
- Pour some water (you can also blend it with some barbeque sauce) into your Slow Cooker. Place the peppers over the Slow Cooker's bottom.
- Cook on LOW for around 7 hours, covered with the lid.

**Nutrition: Calories: 383 Fat: 14g Carbohydrates: 42g Protein: 19g**

## Slow Cooker Brats in Wisconsin Style

Easy and delicious!

Prep time: 17 minutes Cooking time: 4 hours
Servings: 8

INGREDIENTS:
Half cup ketchup
8 bratwurst
One large onion
1 bottles beer

DIRECTIONS:
- Finely slice the onion.
- Cover the bottom and sides of your Slow Cooker with an olive oil, just in case that nothing is going to stick.
- Place sliced onion, ketchup, bratwurst and beer into Slow Cooker. Pour in some water until everything is evenly covered.
- Cook on HIGH temperature for 4 hours.

**Nutrition: Calories: 377 Fat: 27g Carbohydrates: 12g Protein: 13g**

## Shepherd's Homemade Pie

A tasty casserole that even your kids will love!

Prep time: 12 minutes Cooking time: 2 hours
Servings: 7

INGREDIENTS:
One onion
4 large potatoes
Butter
2 tbsp flour
Half cup beef broth
5 carrots
Shredded Cheddar
Ketchup
Ground beef
Vegetable oil

DIRECTIONS:
- In a pot, cook the potatoes until soft. Darin and mash with butter. Mix in chopped onion and three tablespoons shredded cheese.
- In a pot, boil carrots for just 4 minutes, then add to mashed potatoes.
- On a large skillet, cook ground beef with remaining onion until it is slightly brown. Stir in ketchup and simmer for 5 minutes.
- Grease Slow Cooker and spread mashed potatoes over its bottom. Add beef and mashed carrots. Top with cheese.
- Cook on HIGH mode for 2 hours.

**Nutrition: Calories: 452 Fat: 17g Carbohydrates: 52g Protein: 23g**

# FISH & SEAFOOD RECIPES

## Lobster and Gruyere Pasta

Ready in about: **25 minutes | Serves: 4 | Per serving: Calories 441; Carbs 44g; Fat 15g; Protein 28g**

INGREDIENTS
6 cups Water
1 tbsp Flour
8 ounces dried Ziti
1 cup Half & Half
1 tbsp Tarragon, chopped
¾ cup Gruyere Cheese, shredded
3 Lobster Tails, about 6 oz each
½ cup White Wine
½ tsp Pepper
1 tbsp Worcestershire Sauce

DIRECTIONS
- Pour in water and add the lobster tails and ziti. Seal the lid, set to STEAM for 10 minutes at High. Once the cooking is over, do a quick pressure release. Drain the pasta and set aside.
- Remove the meat from the tails, chop it, and stir into the bowl with pasta. Mix in the rest of the ingredients, set on SAUTÉ at High, and cook until the sauce thickens, then stir in pasta and lobster.

## Prawns and Fish Kabobs

Ready in about: **15 minutes | Serves: 4 | Per serving: Calories 369; Carbs 22g; Fat 15g; Protein 40g**

INGREDIENTS
1 lb Tuna Fillets, cubed
1 lb King Prawns, peeled and deveined
1 tbsp Salt
½ Onion, diced
1 Red Bell Pepper, diced1 tsp lemon zest
1 packet dry Ranch dressing mix

1 cup Water
DIRECTIONS
- In a large bowl, and mix the fish and shrimp. Sprinkle with some salt. Toss to spread the salt over the ingredients and leave aside for 5 minutes for decent flavoring.
- Use wooden skewers to prick the fish and the shrimp by separating with bell pepper and slices of onion. Take the steel pot of your pressure cooker to mix water with the dressing.
- Wait for the dressing mix to dissolve. Then, insert the trivet in the same pot. Lay the sewers over the pot crosswise. Seal the lid, set on STEAM for about 4 minutes at High.
- When ready, do a quick release. Remove the lid so the skewers can rest and cool down.

## Glazed Orange Salmon

Ready in about: **25 minutes** | Serves: **4** | Per serving: Calories **449**; Carbs **4g**; Fat **17g**; Protein **65g**

INGREDIENTS
4 Salmon Filets
2 tsp Orange Zest
3 tbsp Orange Juice
1 tbsp Olive Oil
1 tsp Ginger, minced
1 cup White Wine
Salt and Pepper, to taste
DIRECTIONS
- Whisk in everything, except the salmon, in the pressure cooker. Then, add salmon and seal the lid. Cook on STEAM and cook for 7 minutes at High pressure. When ready, release the pressure quickly.

## Clams in White Wine

Ready in about: **17 minutes** | Serves: **4** | Per serving: Calories **224**; Carbs **6g**; Fat **14g**; Protein **16g**

INGREDIENTS
¼ cup White Wine
2 cups Veggie Broth
¼ cup Basil, chopped
¼ cup Olive Oil
2 ½ pounds Clams
2 tbsp Lemon Juice
2 Garlic Cloves, minced
DIRECTIONS
- Heat the olive oil, add garlic and cook for one minute, until fragrant, on SAUTÉ mode at High. Pour wine, broth, and add basil, lemon juice. Bring the mixture to a boil and let cook for one minute.
- Add your steaming basket, and place the clams inside. Seal the lid, and set to STEAM mode and adjust the time to 6 minutes at High. Wait 5 minutes before releasing the pressure quickly.
- Remove the clams to a bowl, discard any that did not open. Drizzle with the cooking juices to serve.

## Almond-Crusted Tilapia

Ready in about: **10 minutes** | Serves: **4** | Per serving: Calories **327**; Carbs **4g**; Fat **15g**; Protein **46g**

INGREDIENTS
4 Tilapia Fillets
cup sliced Almonds
1 cup Water
2 tbsp Dijon Mustard
1 tsp Olive Oil
¼ tsp Black Pepper
DIRECTIONS
- Pour water into inner pot of pressure cooker and place a trivet in water. Mix olive oil, pepper, and mustard in a small bowl. Brush the fish fillets with the mustard mixture on all sides.
- Coat the fish in almonds slices. Arrange the fish fillets on top of the trivet. Seal the lid, select STEAM and adjust the time to 10 minutes at High. When done, do a quick pressure release.

## Wrapped Fish and Potatoes

Ready in about: **15 minutes** | Serves: **4** | Per serving: Calories **310**; Carbs **9g**; Fat **14g**; Protein **30g**

INGREDIENTS
4 Cod Fillets
4 Thyme Sprigs
2 Medium Potatoes, sliced
1 Lemon, sliced thinly
1 Onion, sliced
A Handful of Fresh Parsley
2 cups Water
2 tbsp Olive Oil
DIRECTIONS
- Place each cod fillet onto a parchment paper. Divide the potatoes, thyme, parsley, onion, and lemon between the 4 parchment papers. Drizzle each of them with ½ tbsp of olive oil and mix with your hands to coat everything.
- Wrap the fish with the parchment paper. Wrap each of the 'packets' in aluminum foil.
- Pour the water in your pressure cooker and insert a steam rack. Place the packets inside. Seal the lid and cook for about 5 minutes on STEAM at High. When ready, do a quick release and serve.

## Fancy Shrimp Scampi with Soy Sauce

Ready in about: **45 minutes** | Serves: **4** | Per serving: Calories **183**; Carbs **4g**; Fat **8g**; Protein **24g**

INGREDIENTS
2 tbsp Butter
1 tbsp Parmesan Cheese, grated
2 Shallots, chopped
¼ cup White Wine
1 tsp Garlic, minced
2 tbsp Lemon Juice
1 pound Shrimp, peeled and deveined

**For the dip Sauce:**

2 TBSP SOY SAUCE
1 tbsp chopped chives
½ tbsp Olive Oil
DIRECTIONS
- Melt butter on SAUTÉ at High, and cook the shallots until soft. Add garlic and cook for 1 more minute. Stir in wine and cook for

another minute. Add the remaining ingredients and stir to combine.
- Seal the lid and cook for 2 minutes on STEAM, at High pressure. When ready, release the pressure quickly. Serve on a platter with dipping sauce on the side.

## Tuna and Pea Cheesy Noodles

Ready in about: **17 minutes** | Serves: **4** | Per serving: Calories 430; Carbs 42g; Fat 22g; Protein 18g

INGREDIENTS
1 can Tuna, drained
3 cups Water
4 ounces Cheddar Cheese, grated
16 ounces Egg Noodles
¼ cup Breadcrumbs
1 cup Frozen Peas
28 ounces canned Mushroom Soup
DIRECTIONS
- Place the water and noodles in your pressure cooker. Stir in soup, tuna, and frozen peas.
- Seal the lid, and cook for 5 minutes on STEAM at High pressure. When ready, do a quick pressure release. Stir in the cheese. Transfer to a baking dish; sprinkle with breadcrumbs on top.
- Insert a baking dish in your cooker, seal the lid, and cook 3 minutes on STEAM VEGETABLES mode at High.

## Lemon Sauce Salmon

Ready in about: **10 minutes** | Serves: **4** | Per serving: Calories 493; Carbs 6g; Fat 31g; Protein 41g

INGREDIENTS
4 Salmon Fillets
1 tbsp Honey
½ tsp Cumin
1 tbsp Hot Water
1 tbsp Olive Oil
1 tsp Smoked Paprika
1 tbsp chopped Fresh Parsley
¼ cup Lemon Juice
1 cup of Water
DIRECTIONS
- Pour the water inside your Pressure cooker. Place the salmon fillets on the rack. Seal the lid and cook for 3 minutes on STEAM at High pressure. Whisk together the remaining ingredients, to form a sauce.
- Once cooking is over, release the pressure quickly, and drizzle the sauce over the salmon. Seal the lid again, and cook for 3 more minutes on STEAM at High. Do a quick release and serve hot.

## Creamy Crabmeat

Ready in about: **12 minutes** | Serves: **4** | Per serving: Calories 450; Carbs 13g; Fat 10g; Protein 40g

INGREDIENTS
¼ cup Butter
1 small Red Onion, chopped
1 pound Lump Crabmeat
½ Celery Stalk, chopped
½ cup Heavy Cream
½ cup Chicken Broth
Salt and Pepper, to taste
DIRECTIONS
- Season the crabmeat with some salt and pepper to taste. Melt the butter and cook the celery for a minute, on SAUTÉ mode at High. Add onions and cook for another 3 minutes, or until soft.
- Place the crabmeat and stir in the broth. Seal the lid, set to STEAM for 10 minutes at High pressure. Once the cooking is over, do a quick pressure release. Season with salt and pepper, if needed.

## Mediterranean Salmon

Ready in about: **15 minutes** | Serves: **4** | Per serving: Calories 431 Carbs 6g; Fat 31g; Protein 42g

INGREDIENTS
4 Salmon Fillets
2 tbsp Olive Oil
1 Rosemary Sprig
1 cup Cherry Tomatoes
15 ounces Asparagus
1 cup Water
DIRECTIONS
- Pour in water and insert the rack. Place the salmon on top, sprinkle with rosemary, and arrange the asparagus on top. Seal the lid and cook on STEAM mode for 3 minutes at High.
- Do a quick release, add cherry tomatoes, and cook for 2 minutes, on SAUTÉ. Drizzled with oil, to serve.

## Scallops and Mussels Cauliflower Paella

Ready in about: **17 minutes** | Serves: **4** | Per serving: Calories 155; Carbs 11g; Fat 4g; Protein 7g

INGREDIENTS
2 Bell Peppers, diced
1 tbsp Coconut Oil
1 cup Scallops
2 cups Mussels
1 Onion, diced
2 cups ground Cauliflower
2 cups Fish Stock
A pinch of Saffron
DIRECTIONS
- Melt the coconut oil, add onions and bell peppers and cook for about 4 minutes, on SAUTÉ mode at High. Stir in scallops and saffron and cook for another 2 minutes. Add in the remaining ingredients.
- Seal the lid, and set to BEANS/CHILI mode for 12 minutes at High. When ready, do a quick release.

## Buttery and Lemony Dill Clams

Ready in about: **10 minutes** | Serves: **4** | Per serving: Calories 123; Carbs 12g; Fat 2g; Protein 15g

INGREDIENTS
28 Scrubbed Clams

1 tbsp minced Dill
1 ¼ cups Water
½ cup White Wine
3 tbsp Lemon Juice
2 tbsp Brown Sugar
1 tsp Garlic, minced

DIRECTIONS
- Combine all ingredients in the pressure cooker and add the clams inside. Seal the lid and cook on BEANS/CHILI at High pressure for 5 minutes. When ready, release the pressure quickly.

## Shrimp and Egg Risotto

Ready in about: **30 minutes** | Serves: **6** | Per serving: Calories **221**; Carbs **22g**; Fat **10g**; Protein **13g**

INGREDIENTS
4 cups Water
4 Garlic Cloves, minced
2 Eggs, beaten
½ tsp Ginger, grated
3 tbsp Sesame Oil
1 tbsp Butter
¼ tsp Cayenne Pepper
1 ½ cups frozen Peas
2 cups Brown Rice Arborio
¼ cup White Wine
1 cup chopped Onion
12 ounces peeled and pre-cooked Shrimp, thawed
3 tbsp Half & Half
¼ cup Parmesan cheese, grated

DIRECTIONS
- Warm oil and scramble the eggs, stirring constantly, about 4-5 minutes, on SAUTÉ at High. Transfer to a plate. Melt butter and cook the onions, garlic, and rice for 4 minutes, until translucent.
- Stir in the ginger, cayenne pepper, wine, peas, water, salt, and black pepper. Seal the lid, set to BEANS/CHILI mode and adjust the time to 15 minutes at High.
- Once the cooking is over, do a quick pressure release. Stir in the shrimp, parmesan cheese, cream, and eggs and let them heat for a couple of seconds with the lid off, on SAUTÉ mode at High.

## Garlicky Mackerel and Vegetables Parcels

Ready in: **25 minutes + 2h marinating** | Serves: **6** | Per serving: Calories **291**; Carbs **15g**; Fat **16g**; Protein **15**

INGREDIENTS
3 large Whole Mackerel, cut into 2 pieces
1 pound Asparagus, trimmed
1 Carrot, cut into sticks
1 Celery stalk, cut into sticks
½ cup Butter, at room temperature
6 medium Tomatoes, quartered
1 large Brown Onion, sliced thinly
1 Orange Bell Pepper, seeded and cut into sticks
Salt and Black Pepper to taste
2 ½ tbsp Pernod
3 cloves Garlic, minced
2 Lemons, cut into wedges
1 ½ cups Water

DIRECTIONS
- Cut 6 pieces of parchment paper a little longer and wider than a piece of fish. Cut 6 pieces of foil slightly longer than the parchment papers. Lay the foil wraps on a flat surface and place each parchment paper on each foil.
- In a bowl, mix tomatoes, onions, garlic, bell pepper, pernod, butter, asparagus, carrot, celery, salt, and pepper.
- Place each fish piece on the layer of parchment and foil wraps. Spoon the vegetable mixture on each fish. Then, wrap the fish and refrigerate these fish packets, to marinate, for 2 hours. Remove the fish onto a flat surface.
- Pour the water in the cooker, and fit the trivet at the bottom of the pot. Put the packets on the trivet. Seal the lid and select STEAM at High pressure for 5 minutes. Once the timer has ended, do a quick pressure release.
- Remove the trivet with the fish packets onto a flat surface. Carefully open the foil and using a spatula, transfer the fish with vegetables to serving plates. Serve with a side of the lemon wedges.

## Salmon with Broccoli and Potatoes

Ready in about: **8 minutes** | Serve: **1** | Per serving: Calories **432**; Carbs **19g**; Fat **15g**; Protein **35g**

INGREDIENTS
4-ounce Salmon Fillet
4 New Potatoes
4 ounces Broccoli Florets
2 tsp Olive Oil
Salt and Pepper, to taste
1 ½ cups Water

DIRECTIONS
- Pour water and lower the rack. Season the potatoes with salt and pepper, and place them on top of the rack. Drizzle half of the oil over. Seal the lid, select the FISH/STEWM mode for 2 minutes at High pressure.
- When the timer goes off, release the pressure quickly. Season the broccoli and salmon with salt and pepper. Arrange the broccoli on top of the potatoes and top with the salmon fillet.
- Drizzle them with the remaining olive oil. Seal the lid and cook on STEAM mode for 3 more minutes at High. Do a quick pressure release, and serve hot.

## Veggie Noodle Salmon

Ready in about: **15 minutes** | Serves: **4** | Per serving: Calories **313**; Carbs **12g**; Fat **13g**; Protein **40g**

INGREDIENTS
4 Trut Fillets
2 tsp Olive Oil
1 large Carrot, peeled and spiralized
2 Large Potatoes, peeled and spiralized
1 Zucchini, peeled and spiralized
1 cup Water
1 Thyme Sprig
¼ tsp Pepper
¼ tsp Salt

DIRECTIONS

- Pour the water and add thyme sprig. Arrange the noodles inside the steaming basket and top with the salmon. Season with salt and pepper, and drizzle with oil.
- Place the basket inside the cooker. Seal the lid, press STEAM, and set to 7 minutes at High. When the timer goes off, do a quick pressure release. Serve immediately and enjoy.

## Crab Cakes

Ready in about: **14 minutes** | Serves: **2** | Per serving: **Calories 321; Carbs 11g; Fat 8g; Protein 19g**

INGREDIENTS
1 cup Crab Meat
¼ cup Black Olives, chopped
1 Carrot, shredded
½ cup Potatoes, boiled and mashed
¼ cup Flour
¼ cup Onion, grated
1 ½ cup canned Tomatoes, diced
1 tbsp Olive Oil
½ cup Chicken Broth

DIRECTIONS
- Place crab meat, carrots, olives, flour, potatoes, and onion, in a bowl. Mix with hands until fully incorporated. Shape the mixture into two patties. Heat olive oil on SAUTÉ mode at High.
- When hot and sizzling, add the crab cakes and cook for a minute. Flip them over and cook for another minute. Pour tomatoes and broth over and seal the lid.
- Select STEAM mode and set the cooking time to 2 minutes at High pressure. When the timer goes off, do a quick pressure release and serve immediately.

## Steamed Salmon Filets with Paprika-Lemon Sauce

Ready in about: **10 minutes** | Serves: **4** | Per serving: **Calories 542; Carbs 7g; Fat 31g; Protein 62g**

INGREDIENTS
4 (5 oz) Salmon Filets
1 cup Water
Salt and Black Pepper to taste
2 tsp Cumin Powder
1 ½ tsp Paprika
2 tbsp chopped Parsley
2 tbsp Olive Oil
2 tbsp Hot Water
1 tbsp Maple Syrup
2 cloves Garlic, minced
1 Lime, juiced

DIRECTIONS
- In a bowl, mix cumin, paprika, parsley, olive oil, hot water, maple syrup, garlic, and lime juice. Pour the water in the pressure cooker, and fit the steamer rack in it. Season the salmon with pepper and salt; place on the steamer rack in the pot. Seal the lid, and select STEAM mode on High pressure for 5 minutes.
- Once the timer has ended, do a quick pressure release. Use a set of tongs to transfer the salmon to a serving plate and drizzle the lime sauce all over it. Serve with steamed swiss chard.

## Deliciously Sweet and Spicy Mahi Mahi

Ready in about: **10 minutes** | Serves: **4** | Per serving: **Calories 291; Carbs 20g; Fat 12g; Protein 23g**

INGREDIENTS
4 Mahi Mahi Fillets, fresh
4 cloves Garlic, minced
1 ¼-inch Ginger, grated
Salt and Black Pepper
2 tbsp Chili Powder
1 tbsp Sriracha Sauce
1 ½ tbsp Maple Syrup
1 Lime, juiced
1 cup Water

DIRECTIONS
- Place mahi mahi on a plate and season with salt and pepper on both sides. In a bowl, mix in garlic, ginger, chili powder, sriracha sauce, maple syrup, and lime juice. With a brush, apply the hot sauce mixture on the fillet.
- Then, pour the water in the cooker, and fit the trivet at the bottom. Put the fillets on the trivet. Seal the lid, select STEAM mode at High pressure for 5 minutes. Once the timer has ended, do a quick pressure release.
- Use a set of tongs to remove the mahi mahi onto serving plates. Serve with steamed or braised asparagus.

## Power Greens with Lemony Monf Fish

Ready in about: **25 minutes** | Serves: **4** | Per serving: **Calories 271; Carbs 20g; Fat 11g; Protein 12g**

INGREDIENTS:
2 tbsp Olive Oil
4 (8 oz) Monk Fish Fillets, cut in 2 pieces each
½ cup chopped Green Beans
2 cloves Garlic, sliced
1 cup Kale Leaves
½ lb Baby Bok Choy, stems removed and chopped largely
1 Lemon, zested and juiced
Lemon Wedges to serve
Salt and White Pepper to taste

DIRECTIONS
- Select SAUTÉ mode at High. Pour in the coconut oil, garlic, red chili, and green beans. Stir fry for 5 minutes. Add the kale leaves, and cook them to wilt, for about 3 minutes. Meanwhile, place the fish on a plate and season with salt, white pepper, and lemon zest. After, remove the green beans and kale to a plate and set aside.
- Back to the pot, add the olive oil and fish. Brown the fish on each side, for about 2 minutes, and add the bok choy.
- Pour the lemon juice over the fish and gently stir. Cook for 2 minutes and then turn off the pressure cooker. Spoon the fish with bok choy over the green beans and kale. Serve with a side of lemon wedges.

## Alaskan Cod with Fennel and Beans

**Ready in about: 25 minutes | Serves: 4 | Per serving:**
**Calories 294; Carbs 26g; Fat 14g; Protein 15g**

INGREDIENTS
2 (18 oz) Alaskan Cod, cut into 4 pieces each
4 tbsp Olive Oil
2 cloves Garlic, minced
2 small Onions, chopped
½ cup Olive Brine
3 cups Chicken Broth
Salt and Black Pepper to taste
½ cup Tomato Puree
1 head Fennel, quartered
1 cup Pinto Beans, soaked, drained and rinsed
1 cup Green Olives, pitted and crushed
½ cup Basil Leaves
Lemon Slices to garnish

DIRECTIONS
- Select SAUTÉ mode at High. Warm the olive oil and stir-fy the garlic and onion, until soft and fragrant. Pour in the broth and tomato puree. Let simmer for about 3 minutes. Add the fennel, olives, beans, salt, and pepper.
- Seal the lid and select BEANS/CHILI mode at High pressure for 20 minutes. Once the timer has stopped, do a quick pressure release. Transfer the beans to a plate with a slotted spoon. Season the broth with salt and pepper.
- Add the cod pieces to the cooker. Seal the lid again, and select STEAM mode at High for 3 minutes. Do a quick pressure release. Remove the cod to soup bowls, top with beans and basil leaves, and pour the broth over.

## Sea Bass Stew

**Ready in about: 25 minutes | Serves: 4 | Per serving:**
**Calories 390; Carbs 17g; Fat 18g; Protein 37g**

INGREDIENTS
1 Red Onion, diced
4 tbsp Olive Oil
½ cup Chicken Broth
1 cup Clam Juice
½ pound Potatoes, peeled and cubed
2 ½ cups Water
14 ounces canned diced Tomatoes
1 ½ pounds Sea Bass Fillets, chopped
1 tsp, minced, Garlic
2 tbsp chopped Dill
2 tbsp Lemon Juice
Salt and Pepper, to taste

DIRECTIONS
- Heat half of the oil on SAUTÉ mode at High. Add the onions and cook for 3 minutes. Add the garlic and sauté for a minute. Pour the broth over and deglaze the bottom of the pot.
- Stir in the tomatoes, potatoes, water, and clam juice. Seal the lid, select BEANS/CHILI mode, and set the cooking time to 5 minutes at High pressure.
- When the timer goes off, do a quick pressure release. Add the sea bass pieces. Seal the lid again and cook on BEANS/CHILI for another 5 minutes, at High.
- When ready, do a quick pressure release, and open the lid. Press the SAUTÉ at High. Stir in the remaining ingredients along with the rest of the oil, and cook for 3 more minutes, lid off.
- Ladle into serving bowls immediately, and enjoy!

## Tilapia Chowder

**Ready in about: 25 minutes | Serves: 4 | Per serving:**
**Calories 320; Carbs 14g; Fat 16g; Protein 25g**

INGREDIENTS
1 ½ cups Water
1 cup Milk
1 cup Potatoes, peeled and chopped
½ pounds Tilapia, chopped
½ cups chopped Celery
½ cup Chicken Stock
¾ cup diced Onion
¼ tsp Salt
¼ tsp Pepper
¼ tsp Onion Powder
1 tbsp Cornstarch mixed with 1 ½ tbsp Water

DIRECTIONS
- Combine everything, except for the cornstarch mixture, in your pressure cooker. Seal the lid, select STEAM and set the timer to 10 minutes at High pressure.
- When the timer goes off, do a quick pressure release. Set to SAUTÉ mode at High. Stir in the cornstarch mixture and cook for about 5 minutes, or until the chowder is thickened. Serve immediately!

## White Wine Steamed Mussels

**Ready in about: 15 minutes | Serves: 4 | Per serving:**
**Calories 211; Carbs 12g; Fat 5g; Protein 28g**

INGREDIENTS
1 Onion, chopped
2 pounds Mussels, cleaned
1 cup White Wine
1 Garlic Clove, crushed
½ cup Water

DIRECTIONS
- Heat oil on SAUTÉ mode at High, and cook the onion and garlic for 3 minutes, until soft and fragrant. Pour wine and cook for 1 more minute, constantly stirring.
- Tumble the mussels into the steaming basket. Insert trivet in the cooker and lower the basket onto the trivet, and seal the lid. Cook for 3 minutes on STEAM mode at High.
- When ready, let the pressure drop naturally, for about 10 minutes. Arrange the mussels on a serving platter. Spoon the cooking juices over and serve.

## Cod in a Tomato Sauce

**Ready in about: 15 minutes | Serves: 4 | Per serving:**
**Calories 251; Carbs 3g; Fat 5g; Protein 45g**

INGREDIENTS
4 Cod Fillets about 7-ounce each
2 cups Tomatoes, chopped
1 cup Water

1 tbsp Olive Oil
Salt and Pepper, to taste
¼ tsp Garlic Powder

DIRECTIONS
- Place the tomatoes in a baking dish and crush them with a fork. Sprinkle with salt, pepper, and garlic powder. Season the cod with salt and pepper and place it over the tomatoes.
- Drizzle the olive oil over the fish and tomatoes. Place the dish in your Pressure cooker. Seal the lid and set on STEAM for 5 minutes at High pressure. When ready, release naturally, for 5 minutes.

## Party Crab Legs

**Ready in about: 20 minutes | Serves: 4 | Per serving: Calories 263; Carbs 37g; Fat 10g; Protein 7g**

INGREDIENTS
1 ½ pounds Crab Legs
2 tbsp Butter, melted
1 cup Veggie Broth
½ cup White Wine

DIRECTIONS
- Pour broth and wine into the pressure cooker. Place crab legs in the steaming basket. Seal the lid and cook for 5 minutes on BEANS/CHILI at High. When ready, do a quick release, and serve drizzled with butter.

## Squid and Peas

**Ready in about: 30 minutes | Serves: 4 | Per serving: Calories 177; Carbs 18g; Fat 2g; Protein 22g**

INGREDIENTS
1 pound Squid, cleaned and chopped
1 pound Green Peas
1 Onion, chopped
½ pound canned Tomatoes
1 tbsp White Wine
Salt and Black Pepper, to taste
Cooking Spray, to grease
Water, as needed

DIRECTIONS
- Coat the pressure cooker with cooking spray and cook the onions for 3 minutes, until soft.
- Add squid and cook for another 3 minutes, stirring occasionally. Add in the remaining ingredients, and give it a good stir. Add water, enough to cover everything, and seal the lid.
- Cook on BEANS/CHILI at High pressure for 20 minutes. Once ready, do a natural pressure release, for 10 minute

## Sweet and Sour Slow Cooker Shrimp

The amazing taste for any party!

**Prep time: 5 minutes Cooking time:
Servings:**

INGREDIENTS:
2 tsp soy sauce
Fluffy rice
2 tbsp cornstarch
1 chicken bouillon cube
3 tbsp sugar
1 can pineapples
2 cans shrimp
1 pack Chinese pea pods
1 cup water
Ground ginger
2 tbsps cider vinegar

DIRECTIONS:
- Spray your Slow Cooker with cooking spray.
- Combine drained pineapple and pea pods into your Slow Cooker. In a separated saucepan, mix granulated sugar with cornstarch.
- Bring the water to boil and dissolve one bouillon cube. Add juice, ginger and soy sauce, bring to boil, and then blend with pods and pineapples.
- Cover the Slow Cooker's lid and cook on LOW mode for 5 hours. When it is almost time, add shrimp and vinegar.
- Serve hot over the rice.

**Nutrition: Calories: 134 Fat: 12g Carbohydrates: 9g Protein: 16g**

## Crawfish and Shrimp Duo

Amazing choice for any occasion!

**Prep time: 5 minutes Cooking time: 4 hours
Servings: 8**

INGREDIENTS:
Simple butter
Fresh shrimp
2 celery stalks
4 green onions
Minced garlic
Canned and diced tomatoes
Minced garlic
Water
Tomato paste
Crawfish tails
Ground black pepper
Hot cooked rice
Spices: basil, oregano, thyme, red pepper
Salt
Fresh parsley

DIRECTIONS:
- Peel shrimp and devein well. Then set aside.
- Finely chop red pepper, green onions, simple onion and two celery stalks.
- In a deep saucepan, melt butter and add chopped garlic and other vegetables. Stir in flour and cook for 1 minute till smooth.
- Add tomatoes, tomato paste and water. Season with thyme, basil and oregano and stir to combine.
- Transfer the mixture to preheated Slow Cooker and prepare on LOW for 4 hours. Add seafood and cook for another hour.

**Nutrition: Calories: 187 Fat: 12g Carbohydrates: 37g Protein: 23g**

## Shrimp Marinara for Slow Cooker

Unusual taste of Spicy Shrimp

**Prep time: 11 minutes Cooking time: 7 hours
Servings: 14**

**INGREDIENTS:**
Canned peeled tomatoes
Dried oregano
2 tsp minced parsley
Grated Parmesan cheese
Canned tomato paste
Cooked shrimp
Cooked spaghetti or pasta
Dried basal
2 clove garlic

**DIRECTIONS:**
- Cook the shrimp and remove the shells and tails. Finely grate Parmesan cheese.
- Grease your Slow Cooker with melted and unsalted butter or simply with olive oil.
- Right in your Slow Cooker pot, combine tomatoes, salt, oregano, basil, parsley. Add tomato paste. Cover the lid and cook on LOW regime for 7 hours.
- Then stir in shrimp and turn to high for 13-15 minutes. Serve with pasta and shredded parmesan.

**Nutrition: Calories: 210 Fat: 14g Carbohydrates: 31g Protein: 33g**

# Asian-styled salmon with diced vegetables

Healthy and delicious fish in Asian sauce

⌛ **Prep time: 16 minutes Cooking time: 3 hours Servings: 2**

**INGREDIENTS:**
Fresh salmon fillets
Salt
soy sauce
Pepper
1 pack Asian vegetable blend
2 tbsp lemon juice
1 tbsp honey
1 sesame seeds

**DIRECTIONS:**
- Coat your Slow Cooker with vegetable or olive oil. Place the vegetable mix into Slow Cooker.
- Rub salmon meat with salt and pepper to your taste and place on vegetables.
- In a small bowl, whisk together lemon juice, honey and soy sauce. Sprinkle the salmon with this sauce.
- Drizzle with sesame seeds.
- Cook with the lid on for 3 hours (use LOW temperature mode).
- Serve on a large serving dish along with fresh vegetables or preferred side dish.

**Nutrition: Calories: 235 Fat: 6g Carbohydrates: 26g Protein: 53g**

# Creamy spaghetti with shrimp and cheese

An unusual mix of corn, shrimp, and cheese – the perfect choice for a cold day!

⌛ **Prep time: 5 minutes Cooking time: 7 hours Servings: 4**

**INGREDIENTS:**
One spaghetti squash
1 tbsp butter
Salt
Half cup Parmesan cheese
Pepper to taste
1 tsp Italian seasoning
Jarred minced garlic
Fresh medium shrimp
One cup pasta sauce
Olive oil

**DIRECTIONS:**
- Cut the squash to remove the seeds.
- Slightly drizzle the squash halves with oil and sprinkle with enough of seasoning.
- Place the halves into Slow Cooker and ass 2 cups of water. Cook for 6 hours on LOW mode until it is easy to shred.
- Mix in sauce and top with shredded cheese and cook for 30 minutes.
- Using a skillet with oil, cook shrimp and garlic just for 4 minutes. Salt and pepper. Serve right in halves.

**Nutrition: Calories: 121 Fat: 21g Carbohydrates: 39g Protein: 32g**

# Poached Salmon in Slow Cooker

The amazing choice for a family!

⌛ **Prep time: 5 minutes Cooking time: 5 hours Servings: 6**

**INGREDIENTS:**
2 cups water
1 bay leaf
1 cup dry wine
6 salmon fillets (with skin)
Ground black pepper
One shallot
6 sprigs fresh herbs
Salt
Black peppercorns
Lemon wedges to serve

**DIRECTIONS:**
- Slightly coat your Slow Cooker with a melted unsalted butter.
- Take a wide bowl and combine lemon, herbs, shallots, peppercorns. Mix and transfer to Slow Cooker.
- Pour over with wine and water. Add one bay leaf.
- Place the salmon fillets into Slow Cooker (skin side down). Season with pepper and salt. Cover the lid and do not open often until the dish is not ready.
- Cook under cover on LOW mode until salmon is easy to flake with a fork. To serve, drizzle with olive oil and decorate with thin lemon wedges.

**Nutrition: Calories: 155 Fat: 8g Carbohydrates: 1g Protein: 7g**

# Clam Casserole with Green Peppers

Delicious and super-easy to cook!

⌛ **Prep time: 5 minutes Cooking time: 6 hours Servings: 4**

**INGREDIENTS:**

4 chicken eggs
Canned minced clams
4 tbsp milk
Butter
3 medium onions
Crackers
Green pepper
Salt to taste
DIRECTIONS:
- Prepare the vegetables: peel and mince the onions and green peppers. Also, mince the clams. Melt butter and whisk it with milk and chicken eggs. Beat until the ingredients just combined, about for 2 minutes.
- Crush the crackers and add to the milk mixture.
- Mix everything in one bowl and transfer to Slow Cooker.
- Cover the lid and prepare the casserole for 6 hours on LOW temperature mode. Do not open the lid until it is the time.
- Serve with freshly diced green peppers and sesame seed sprinkles.

**Nutrition: Calories: 123 Fat: 4g Carbohydrates: 18g Protein: 54g**

## Tuna and Celery Meat Casserole

Fresh and hot dish for your breakfast!

Prep time: 19 minutes Cooking time: 8 hours
Servings: 7

INGREDIENTS:
Tuna meat (can be tinned)
1 cup potato chips
3 chicken eggs
Celery
Cream of celery soup
Half cup salad dressing
Black pepper
DIRECTIONS:
- Put chicken eggs into saucepan and boil until hard-cooked. Finely chop. Grease your Slow Cooker with melted butter or vegetable oil.
- In a deep bowl, combine tuna, black pepper, diced celery, chopped eggs. Mix well until the mixture is smooth enough.
- Add salad dressing and condensed cream of tuna soup. Transfer the mixture into Slow Cooker and top with potato chips. Cook, covered, for 8 hours on LOW temperature mode.
- To serve, garnish pie with sesame seeds or leaves of fresh salad leaves.

**Nutrition: Calories: 125 Fat: 7g Carbohydrates: 1g Protein: 23g**

## Halibut with Lemon and Dill

This meal will make a holiday out of any occasion!

Prep time: 29 minutes Cooking time: 1 hour
Servings: 2

INGREDIENTS:
Halibut fillet (fresh or frozen)
1 tbsp fresh lemon juice
Salt to taste
1 tsp dried or 1 tbsp fresh dill
1 tbsp olive oil
Black pepper
DIRECTIONS:
- Take a large piece of aluminum non-stick foil and place your halibut fillet in the middle of it. Pepper and salt.
- Grease your Slow Cooker or simply coat with cooking spray. In a bowl, whisk lemon juice, dill and olive oil.
- Crimp the foil edges together, but leave some space inside so fish can steam. Place the foil into Slow Cooker and set on HIGH for 2 hours.
- When it is the time – carefully open the foil and check if the fish is flaky. Serve with the spinach and fresh dill.

**Nutrition: Calories: 143 Fat: 32g Carbohydrates: 4g Protein: 43g**

## Slow Cooker Chowder with Shrimp and Bacon

This will be a big heat for your dinner!

Prep time: 5 minutes Cooking time: 4 hours
Servings: 6

INGREDIENTS:
4 medium onions
Half tsp paprika
2 cups water
4 slices bacon
Chives
Red potatoes
Black pepper
Small shrimp
Evaporated milk
2 packs frozen corn
1 tsp Worcestershire sauce
DIRECTIONS:
- Finely chop the onion and chives.
- Dice the red potatoes (if you want, you can replace them with frozen hash-browns).
- Fry the bacon to get crispy. Add chopped onion and cook until soften. Transfer onions with bacon to Slow Cooker.
- One by one, ass Potatoes, Worcestershire sauce, corn, salt, water and pepper. Cook under the lid for 4 hours on LOW just until the potatoes are softened.
- Add evaporated milk and shrimp and cook for 30 minutes. When it is time to serve, add chives.

**Nutrition: Calories: 362 Fat: 23g Carbohydrates: 73g Protein: 45g**

## Crabmeat dip in Slow Cooker

Super tasty and easy appetizer with crabmeat!

Prep time: 5 minutes Cooking time: 2 hours
Servings: 5

INGREDIENTS:
Half cup mayonnaise
2 cans crab meat
1 tsp hot sauce
1 tsp parsley
Red bell pepper
lemon juice
Worcestershire sauce

Green bell pepper
Half tsp mustard powder
2 tbsp horseradish sauce
1 tsp dry parsley
Cream cheese

DIRECTIONS:
- Dice red bell pepper and green bell pepper. Grease your Slow Cooker with extra virgin olive oil.
- Start preheating your Slow Cooker while combining all the ingredients in a separated bowl. Transfer the bowl mixture to Slow Cooker and cook on LOW mode for 2 hours. Stir occasionally every 20 or 35 minutes.
- To serve, stir well and serve with bread slices or crackers.

**Nutrition: Calories: 245 Fat: 32g Carbohydrates: 13g Protein: 53g**

## Salmon with Lemon and Dijon sauce

Lovely meal for your dinner!

⏲ **Prep time: 7 minutes Cooking time: 2 hours Servings: 9**

INGREDIENTS:
Salt
Fresh salmon fillets
2 cups water
Minced garlic
1 cup barley
Dried dill weed
2 tsp oil
Black pepper
Water
1 tsp chicken bouillon
Half cup diced onion
Half cup Dijon mustard
Sour cream
2 tbsp olive oil
Lemon juice

DIRECTIONS:
- Chop the onion and garlic and transfer to a bowl. Place into the microwave for 5 minutes, then transfer to Slow Cooker.
- Add bouillon, barley, dill weed and pour in with water. Finely stir everything.
- Rub salt and pepper into salmon meat and arrange in over the mixture in Slow Cooker. Cover the lid and prepare, using a LOW temperature mode, for 2 hours.
- In a small bowl, make a sauce: combine Dijon mustard, lemon juice, olive oil. Sour cream and minced garlic.
- Serve as a main dish with bread or vegetables.

**Nutrition: Calories: 412 Fat: 23g Carbohydrates: 20g Protein: 55g**

## New England Clam Dip in Slow Cooker

The perfect choice for cold winter days!

⏲ **Prep time: 5 minutes Cooking time: 1 hour Servings: 14**

INGREDIENTS:
3 cans chopped clams
5 tbsp beer
1/3 cup cooked bacon
2 medium onions
3 packs cream cheese
1 tbsp Worcestershire sauce
Crushed oyster crackers
Melted butter

DIRECTIONS:
- Slice green onions.
- In a bowl, mix cream cheese, clams, bacon slices, green onions (reserve small part for topping), Worcestershire sauce and beer.
- Transfer the clam mixture to your greased Slow Cooker.
- In a small bowl, mix butter, remaining green onions and crushed crackers. Spread the topping over the clam mix.
- Cover the lid and cook for 1 hour on HIGH setting. To serve, use crackers or chips.

**Nutrition: Calories: 354 Fat: 32g Carbohydrates: 34g Protein: 62g**

## Tuna and Noodle casserole

Easy and tasty, just like in the childhood!

⏲ **Prep time: 5 minutes Cooking time: 4 hours Servings: 6**

INGREDIENTS:
Dried pasta
2 cups soy milk
Cup frozen peas
1 can of tuna
Shredded parmesan
Cream of mushroom soup
Half cup crushed tortilla

DIRECTIONS:
- Spray the inside of your Slow Cooker with cooking spray. If you do not have one, use a melted butter for greasing.
- Right in Slow Cooker pot, mix soup, noodles, cheese, milk and drained tuna. Stir with a spoon until smooth mass.
- Cook under the lid on LOW temperature mode for 4 hours.
- Forty minutes before serving, add frozen peas and stir everything one more time. Cook for 30 minutes or more, just until the peas are ready.
- Serve while the casserole is hot, along with chips, fresh vegetables or salted cookies.

**Nutrition: Calories: 235 Fat: 9g Carbohydrates: 19g Protein: 34g**

## Shrimp casserole with white

Satisfying and delicious family dish!

⏲ **Prep time: 14 minutes Cooking time: 8 hours Servings: 7**

INGREDIENTS:
red bell pepper
dried parsley
1 yellow onion
ground pepper
Cream of celery soup
Fresh garlic powder
salt
yellow bell pepper
cup chicken broth
Cream of chicken soup

white rice
Frozen shrimp
DIRECTIONS:
- Grease your Slow Cooker with some olive oil and start preheating it on low temperature. Devein and peel shrimp, remove the tails.
- Chop yellow onion, red and yellow bell peppers. Combine into one mixture. Combine all the ingredients in the Slow Cooker, finely stir to combine.
- Cook on LOW temperature during 8 hours.
- Serve while hot, maybe with your favorite vegetables or even bread slices.

**Nutrition: Calories: 218 Fat: 12g Carbohydrates: 12g Protein: 38g**

## Pineapple Milkfish in Slow Cooker

The sweet and delicious fish meal!

**Prep time: 11 minutes Cooking time: 4 hours Servings: 4**

INGREDIENTS:
Canned pineapple (with juice)
Milkfish fillet
3 tbsp white vinegar
3 jalapeno peppers
Ginger root
6 cloves garlic
Half tbsp. black peppercorns
DIRECTIONS:
- Grease your Slow Cooker dish with olive or even vegetable oil. Carefully peel and thinly slice the ginger.
- Cut jalapeno peppers into a medium (can be 1-inch sized) pieces. Season milkfish with salt, rub well.
- Combine fish with the other ingredients and transfer to Slow Cooker.
- Turn on your Slow Cooker and cover the lid. Cook for 4 hours on LOW mode. When the fish is ready, carefully transfer it from Slow Cooker to large serving plate. Serve along with lime or small lemon wedges.

**Nutrition: Calories: 125 Fat: 2g Carbohydrates: 7g Protein: 45g**

## Lobster Bisque in Slow Cooked

Quick and easy way to get your dinner to the new level!

**Prep time: 5 minutes Cooking time: 8 hours Servings: 12**

INGREDIENTS:
3 cups chicken broth
1 onion
Sliced mushrooms
1 tsp dried parsley
1 large leek
2 lobster tails
2 tsp Old Bay
Lemon wedges (to garnish)
1 tsp dill
1 cup heavy cream
DIRECTIONS:
- In a large Slow Cooker, combine tomatoes, clam juice, onions, leek, mushrooms, parsley, Old Bay seasoning and dill.
- Pour in 3 cups of chicken broth.
- Set your Slow Cooker to LOW mode and cook for 8 hours.
- With an immersible blender, make a chowdery soup out of ingredients. Add lobster tails and stir in heavy cream.
- Cook until the bisque is slightly thick.
- Serve with bread slices and freshly diced vegetables.

**Nutrition: Calories: 324 Fat: 18g Carbohydrates: 53g Protein: 36g**

## Clam and Vegetable Soup

Satisfying and healthy, this dish is perfect for any season!

**Prep time: 5 minutes Cooking time: 3 hours Servings: 6**

INGREDIENTS:
2 large potatoes
6 slices bacon
Salt
3 small carrots
2 cans minced clams
1 onion
3 tsp flour
2 cans evaporated milk
1 tsp Worcestershire sauce
Clam juice
Water
DIRECTIONS:
- In a medium dish, combine clam liquid and add enough water so you can get half cup in total. Add the mixture to Slow Cooker.
- Place minced onion, diced potatoes and carrots and bacon into Slow Cooker. Add salt and pour in one more cup of water.
- Cook covered for 3 hours on LOW temperature mode. In a separate bowl, whisk flour with evaporated milk. Add to Slow Cooker, along with clams and milk.
- Cook, stirring, for another 30 minutes.

**Nutrition: Calories: 213 Fat: 6g Carbohydrates: 1g Protein: 44g**

## Quick and easy Tuna Casserole

Super fast, delicious and easy!

**Prep time: 5 minutes Cooking time: 3 hours Servings: 12**

INGREDIENTS:
1 can cream of mushroom
3 cans tuna
Canned evaporated milk
2 cups water
Fresh mushrooms
1 can cheese soup
Noodles
Frozen peas and carrots
Shredded cheese
Salt/pepper
DIRECTIONS:

- Slightly spray the dish of your Slow Cooker with a cooking spray. Place tuna and reserved tuna juice from 2 cans into your Slow Cooker.
- Add noodles, water, cream of mushroom and cheese soup. Stir together. Mix in vegetables and milk.
- Salt and pepper. You can also add another species to your taste. Cook under the lid for 3 hours on HIGH temperature.
- To serve, transfer tuna casserole to a wide serving dish and sprinkle with shredded cheese.

**Nutrition: Calories: 138 Fat: 42g Carbohydrates: 32g Protein: 9g**

## Classical Clam Soup in Slow Cooker

Quick and easy, perfect for cold weather!

**Prep time: 13 minutes Cooking time: 16 hours**
**Servings: 6**

INGREDIENTS:
2 cups whipping cream
Canned clam chowder
Instant mash
Cream of chicken soup
Tinned baby clams
Cream of celery soup
5 cups single cream
DIRECTIONS:
- In a separate bowl, combine claims, single cream, instant mash and cream. Stir well to combine. Slightly grease Slow Cooker with melted and unsalted butter.
- Transfer the clam mixture to Slow Cooker.
- Pour in the cream of chicken and celery soup and clam chowder. Stir one more time. Cover the lid tightly. Cook on LOW temperature mode for around 6 or 8 hours.

**Nutrition: Calories: 211 Fat: 9g Carbohydrates: 13g Protein: 27g**

## Maple Syrup Salmon in Slow Cooker

Try this classic fish for Slow Cooker!

**Prep time: 22minutes Cooking time: 1 hour**
**Servings: 12**

INGREDIENTS:
lime juice
3 cloves garlic
Ginger root
5 tbsp soy sauce
maple syrup
6 salmon fillets
DIRECTIONS:
- Cover the bottom and sides of your Slow Cooker with a small amount of melted butter. Put the salmon fillets into Slow Cooker. You can use fresh or frozen if you like.
- In a bowl, mix lime juice, maple syrup, soy sauce.
- Add crushed garlic and grated ginger root and mix well. Pour in the sauce over the salmon pieces. Turn on your Slow Cooker. Set to HIGH temperature mode. Cover the lid. Cook for 1 hour.
- To serve, transfer the fish to serving plate. Garnish with lime slices.

**Nutrition: Calories: 356 Fat: 13g Carbohydrates: 28g Protein: 30g**

## Tilapia seasoned with Citrus

Tasty fish dinner will be ready just in few hours!

**Prep time: 8 minutes Cooking time: 2 hours**
**Servings: 6**

INGREDIENTS:
4 tilapia fillets
Salt
2 tbsp garlic butter
Canned mandarin oranges
Black pepper to taste
Aluminum foil
DIRECTIONS:
- Cut the aluminum foil into pieces big enough to wrap tilapia fillets. Spray the bottom of your Slow Cooker with cooking spray.
- Place the fish on the foil and drizzle with butter evenly.
- Put a handful of oranges over each fish piece and season with remaining species. Wrap the foil. Place fish wraps into your Slow Cooker and cover the lid. Cook on HIGH mode for 2 hours.
- To serve, arrange tilapia pieces over the large serving plate. You can garnish it with orange or tangerine slices.

**Nutrition: Calories: 238 Fat: 8g Carbohydrates: 11g Protein: 9g**

## Seafood with rice soup

Classical Asian meal is now available for your Slow Cooker

**Prep time:12 minutes Cooking time: 5 hours**
**Servings: 6**

INGREDIENTS:
One medium onion
1 tbsp olive oil
Canned chopped tomatoes
Thawed seafood mix
Half tsp paprika
2 cloves garlic
One bay leaf
1 cup short grain rice
3 cups fish stock
Water
3 tbsp white wine
DIRECTIONS:
- Using a deep pan, sauté onion and crushed garlic. Add some paprika and cook a little to get the flavor.
- Add chopped tomatoes to the pan. Leave to simmer for about 10 minutes. When it is almost ready, add white wine and prepare for 1 minute.
- Transfer the pan mixture to your Slow Cooker. Add bay leaf and pour in with stock.
- Turn on the Slow Cooker and cook for 5 hours on LOW mode. Add rice and cook for an half hour.

**Nutrition: Calories: 312 Fat: 7g Carbohydrates: 34g Protein: 26g**

## Classical Asian Miso Soup

Try this one in an unusual way – into your Slow Cooker

⏱ **Prep time: 14 minutes Cooking time: 2 hours**
**Servings: 4**

INGREDIENTS:
3 cloves garlic
Spring onion
2 tbsp Miso paste
fish stock powder
Dried wakame seaweed
leafy greens

DIRECTIONS:
- Slightly coat your Slow Cooker with anti-stick-cooking spray. Finely mince garlic and dice spring onion.
- In a separate bowl, combine garlic and onion with leafy greens, fish stock powder, dried wakame seaweed and miso paste.
- Spray your Slow Cooker with cooking spray.
- Transfer the ingredients to Slow Cooker and pour in one cup water. Blend everything and cook for 2 hours using HIGH temperature mode.
- To serve, pour the soup over small serving bowls. Serve while hot, garnish with sesame seeds and fresh herbs.

**Nutrition: Calories: 157 Fat: 4g Carbohydrates: 16g Protein: 10g**

## Summer Soup with Lemon Salmon

Perfectly tastes both hot and cold!

⏱ **Prep time: 5 minutes Cooking time: 5 hours**
**Servings: 5**

INGREDIENTS:
2 cups milk
Salmon fillets
2 tbsp butter
Potatoes
Salt
One pinch basil
Dried oregano
Black pepper
1 tbsp lemon zest
Dried thyme
Additional water (to cover)

DIRECTIONS:
- Grease your Slow Cooker well (you can use olive oil or simple butter).
- Cut potatoes into medium cubes and layer them over your Slow Cooker's bottom. Pour in water to cover the potatoes.
- Add lemon zest, remaining butter basil, salt, thyme, pepper and oregano. Turn your Slow Cooker to LOW and cook for 5 hours, loosely covered.
- Stir in milk and prepare for 2 more hours.
- To serve, pour soup into small serving bowls. Use lemon wedges as a garnish.

**Nutrition: Calories: 324 Fat: 8g Carbohydrates: 12g Protein: 17g**

## Easy Seafood Pie

Try this tasty and easy to cook one!

⏱ **Prep time: 5 minutes Cooking time: 2 hours**
**Servings: 8**

INGREDIENTS:
Half tsp salt
1 pack crabmeat
1 pack cream cheese
1 cup Bisquick mix
Ground nutmeg
1 cup milk
2 chicken eggs
1 cup Mozzarella
1 can diced pimientos

DIRECTIONS:
- Grease your Slow Cooker and start preheating it. Dice onions and finely shred Mozzarella cheese.
- Carefully combine crabmeat, onions and pimientos in a big bowl.
- Add all the remaining ingredients into Mozzarella mixture and blend well. Pour the fish pie dough into your Slow Cooker.
- Prepare for 2 hours using HIGH temperature mode. Check the readiness of your pie with a long wooden toothpick.
- Serve seafood pie while it is hot, with your favorite sauce or fresh vegetables.

**Nutrition: Calories: 311 Fat: 4g Carbohydrates: 27g Protein: 25g**

## Jambalaya in Slow Cooker

The French and Spanish inspiration!

⏱ **Prep time: 17 minutes Cooking time: 8 hours**
**Servings: 8**

INGREDIENTS:
Large onion
1 tsp parsley flakes
2 cups rice
Canned diced tomatoes
¼ tsp red pepper sauce
3 garlic cloves
green bell pepper
2 celery stalks
Cooked smoked sausage
Pepper/salt
Uncooked medium shrimp

DIRECTIONS:
- Cover the bottom and sides of your Slow Cooker with melted butter or anti-stick spray.
- Mix all ingredients (except shrimp and rice) in a separate bowl. Blend well and transfer to Slow Cooker.
- Turn to LOW mode and cook for 7 or 8 hours.
- In the end of time, stir in shrimp and cook for one more hour. Cook rice according to package directions.
- Serve jambalaya meal over a large serving plate with cooked rice.

**Nutrition: Calories: 356 Fat: 12g Carbohydrates: 30g Protein: 21g**

## Summer Seafood Casserole

Pasta and seafood due with Alfredo sauce

⏱ **Prep time: 5 minutes Cooking time: 2 hours**
**Servings: 12**

INGREDIENTS:

Half cup milk
4 cups uncooked pasta
One can Alfredo sauce
Parmesan cheese
Pepper to taste
Canned crabmeat
Cooked medium shrimp
¼ cup breadcrumbs

DIRECTIONS:
- Cook pasta separated, following the package directions. When it is 2 minutes of cooking pasta is remaining, add some broccoli. Drain and set aside.
- In a large bowl, whisk together milk, pepper and Alfredo sauce.
- Add shrimp, parsley, crabmeat and 2 tablespoons of shredded Parmesan cheese. Place all ingredients into Slow Cooker, toss to combine.
- Cover the lid, and cook for 2 hours on HIGH mode.
- To serve, transfer the casserole to a large plate and garnish with fresh herbs and lime wedges.

**Nutrition: Calories: 355 Fat: 15g Carbohydrates: 21g Protein: 36g**

## Hearty fish soup with corn

Perfect for a busy daytime!

Prep time: 21 minutes Cooking time: 6 hours
Servings: 7

INGREDIENTS:
2 cloves garlic
Half cup chicken broth
Medium onion
Nonfat milk powder
Whitefish fillets
Cream of celery soup
Kernel corn
Pack lima beans
Canned stewed tomatoes
Lemon-pepper seasoning

DIRECTIONS:
- Cover your Slow Cooker's bottom with thick parchment paper. You need to cover the bottom and sides of the cooking dish.
- Cut and combine potatoes, garlic and onion. Add cream of celery soup and lima beans, along with corn and lemon-pepper seasoning. Pour in the broth. Add white wine.
- Transfer the mixture to Slow Cooker, cook for 7 hours using a LOW-heat settings. Meanwhile, wash and rinse fish.
- Place it into Slow Cooker. Cook for an additional hour.

**Nutrition: Calories: 315 Fat: 7g Carbohydrates: 46g Protein: 23g**

## Asian Seafood mix

Incredible soup with homemade broth!

Prep time: 21 minutes Cooking time: 2 hours
Servings: 12

INGREDIENTS:
1 can diced abalone
Barley
2 tbsp dried scallops
3 Oyster sauce
Fish maw
6 Chinese mushrooms
One dried cuttlefish
Chicken bones

DIRECTIONS:
- To make the broth, boil cleaned chicken bones and dried cuttlefish in enough amount of water. Soak mushrooms in cold water and fish maw in hot water, both for 30 minutes.
- When the fish and mushrooms are ready, remove them from water and cut into small pieces. Add all the other ingredients to chicken soup. Add oyster sauce just to your taste.
- Stir everything and cook in your Slow Cooker for 2 hours (HIGH temperature mode). If you want a thicker broth, add some corn flour before serving.

**Nutrition: Calories: 289 Fat: 10g Carbohydrates: 29g Protein: 33g**

## Coconut Rice with Mango Shrimp

Perfect for lunchtime on busy days!

Prep time: 317 minutes Cooking time: 1 hour
Servings: 9

INGREDIENTS:
One cup rice
Half tsp Caribbean jerk seasoning
One cup coconut milk
One cup shrimp
diced mango (with juice)

DIRECTIONS:
- Peel the shrimp. Remove tails. Cook shrimp in slightly salted water. Grease your Slow Cooker with a cooking spray.
- Combine rice, Caribbean jerk seasoning, mango along with its' juice and cooked shrimp to the Slow Cooker pot.
- Pour in one cup of coconut milk and stir well.
- Cover your Slow Cooker with the lid and cook on HIGH for 1 hour. Try if the rice is tender, cook for 1 hour more.
- Serve immediately as soon as ready with French bread slices or cubed bread crisps.

**Nutrition: Calories: 251 Fat: 5g Carbohydrates: 12g Protein: 18g**

## Jamaican Spicy Salmon

Spicy, but tasty and healthy receipt for your family!

Prep time: 18 minutes Cooking time: 2 hours
Servings: 2

INGREDIENTS:
1 tsp salt
1 tsp mixed cloves, ginger, cayenne pepper, nutmeg and thyme
Chipotle chili powder
Half tsp cinnamon
Black pepper
Fresh salmon fillets
1 tsp onion powder
2 tsps white sugar

DIRECTIONS:
- In a separate small bowl, combine all the spice ingredients and mix well.

- 🌿 Spread the spicy mixture all over the foil length and put the fish slices over it. Fold the foil. Slightly spray your Slow Cooker with cooking spray to avoid sticking of foil.
- 🌿 Place the foil wraps over the bottom of your Slow Cooker. Cover the lid and leave for 2 hours on LOW regime.
- 🌿 You can also cook some rice or pasta as a garnish or just serve with fresh vegetables.

**Nutrition: Calories: 301 Fat: 10g Carbohydrates: 12g Protein: 27g**

## Crab Soup with Dry Sherry

Try this spicy and tasty one!

⏱ **Prep time: 5 minutes Cooking time: 3 hours Servings: 11**

INGREDIENTS:
Crab meat
6 tbsp butter
2 cans mushroom soup
Half tsp Worcestershire sauce
3 tbsp dry sherry
3 green onions
Half cup light cream
2 chicken eggs
Salt/pepper

DIRECTIONS:
- 🌿 To start, pick over and carefully flake crabmeat. Finely chop green onions.
- 🌿 Combine all the ingredients from the list (except chicken eggs) and mix them into Slow Cooker. Cover with the lid and cook for 1 hour, using a high temperature mode.
- 🌿 Reduce heat to LOW and prepare for 2-3 hours. When it is the last hour, stir in eggs.
- 🌿 To serve, let crab soup stand for 5 minutes. Then, serve in small deep bowls. You can also garnish it with fresh herbs if you want.

**Nutrition: Calories: 124 Fat: 32g Carbohydrates: 10g Protein: 23g**

## Crabmeat and Cream Corn Soup

An unusual combination, but delicious meal!

⏱ **Prep time: 7 minutes Cooking time: 8 hours Servings: 6**

INGREDIENTS:
4 cups chicken broth
1 sliced avocado
Half tsp cayenne pepper
1 tsp salt
1 tbsp butter
2 garlic cloves
Frozen corn
1 can lump crabmeat
Heavy cream

DIRECTIONS:
- 🌿 To start, pour in the broth into your Slow Cooker, add butter and diced onion. Stir in garlic, frozen corn, cayenne pepper, crabmeat and butter.
- 🌿 Cover with the lid and cook on LOW mode for 8 hours.
- 🌿 If you want to get a thicker broth, you can also pulse the mixture with immersible blender for several times.
- 🌿 In the end, add cream.
- 🌿 Serve in small bowls while hot and serve with French bread slices and cream.

**Nutrition: Calories: 323 Fat: 23g Carbohydrates: 15g Protein: 43g**

## Spice Chowder with Seafood

Delicious and easy to prepare!

⏱ **Prep time: 9 minutes Cooking time: 6 hours Servings: 7**

INGREDIENTS:
One cup onion
Red bell pepper
Chicken broth
Chopped celery
Sweet white corn
2 tsp cajun seasoning
2 cups small shrimp
Half cup potato flakes
White fish fillets

DIRECTIONS:
- 🌿 Right in your Slow Cooker, combine chopped celery, onions, corn and chopped red bell pepper. Add Cajun seasoning.
- 🌿 Pour in 4 cups of chicken broth. Stir everything well.
- 🌿 Cover and cook on LOW for around 6 hours, or until the vegetables are tender. When it is ready, make a puree with immersion blender. Mix for 5 minutes.
- 🌿 Add and stir in instant potato flakes, milk, fish, and shrimp. Prepare for another 30 minutes. Serve hot in small bowls with cubed bread or fresh vegetables.

**Nutrition: Calories: 199 Fat: 12g Carbohydrates: 5g Protein: 44g**

Thank you for reading my book, I hope you enjoyed it as much as I enjoyed writing it. Won't you please consider leaving a review? Even just a few works would help others decide if the book is right for them.

Printed in Great Britain
by Amazon